Introduction to Business Analysis & Valuation

Krishna G. Palepu, PhD

Thomas D. Casserly Jr. Professor of Business Administration
Harvard University

Victor L. Bernard, PhD, CPA

Price Waterhouse Professor of Accounting
University of Michigan

Paul M. Healy, PhD, ACA

Nanyang Technological University Chair in Management
Massachusetts Institute of Technology

SOUTH-WESTERN College Publishing

An International Thomson Publishing Company

Sponsoring Editor: David L. Shaut
Senior Development Editor: Ken Martin
Production Editor: Marci Dechter
Production Supplier: Julia Chitwood
Cover Design: Bruce Design
Cover Photograph: Reza Estakhrian/Tony Stone Images
Internal Design: Michael Stratton
Marketing Manager: Sharon Oblinger

Copyright © 1997
by South-Western Publishing Co.
Cincinnati, Ohio

I(T)P
International Thomson Publishing
South-Western Publishing Co. is an ITP Company. The ITP trademark is used under license.

Portions of this work have been reprinted by permission of the President and Fellows of Harvard College. Permission requests to use individual Harvard copyrighted cases should be directed to the Permission Manager, Harvard Business School Publishing Division, Boston, MA 02163.

Case material of the Harvard Graduate School of Business Administration is made possible by the cooperation of business firms and other organizations which may wish to remain anonymous by having names, quantities, and other identifying details disguised while maintaining basic relationships. Cases are prepared as the basis for class discussion rather than to illustrate either effective or ineffective handling of an administrative situation.

ISBN: 0-538-84331-4

2 3 4 5 6 7 8 9 0 D 3 2 1 0 9 8 7

Printed in the United States of America

Library of Congress Cataloging-in-Publication Data

Palepu, Krishna G., date.
    Introduction to business analysis and valuation : text and
cases / Krishna G. Palepu, Paul M. Healy
       p. cm.
   ISBN 0-538-84331-4
    1. Business enterprises—Valuation. 2. Financial statements.
3. Business enterprises—Valuation—Case studies. I. Healy, Paul M.
II. Title.
HF5681.V3P32 1996
658.1'6—dc20   96-25961
                                       CIP

This book is dedicated to the memory and spirit of

Vic Bernard

Scholar, colleague, friend

Krishna Palepu joined the Harvard Business School faculty in 1983 after receiving Bachelors and Masters degrees in physics from Andhra University, an MBA from the Indian Institute of Management, and a PhD from MIT. He has taught courses in finance and control, financial statement analysis, and competitive strategy in the Harvard MBA and Executive Educations programs, and he is currently co-leading a Harvard senior executive program on India and China, "Managing Global Opportunities in the Emerging Markets of Asia." Professor Palepu's research focuses on analyzing corporate finance and investment strategies and the process through which firms communicate these strategies to the capital markets. He has published numerous research papers and teaching cases on corporate disclosure, financing and dividend policies, and mergers and restructurings. He is also Associate Editor of several leading research journals, including the *Journal of Accounting and Economics, Accounting Review*, the *Journal of Financial Economics,* and the *Journal of Corporate Finance.* In addition to extensive consulting work, Professor Palepu serves on the International Board of the Academy of Management Excellence in India and of the EuroMBA Program of the Helsinki University of Technology in Finland.

Vic Bernard, who passed away November 14, 1995, was a CPA and held a PhD from the University of Illinois. He was Director of the Paton Accounting Center at the University of Michigan and Director of Research for the American Accounting Association. His research examined issues in financial reporting, financial statement analysis, and financial economics. He was one of ten persons in the last 30 years to have received the AAA/AICPA Notable Contributions to Accounting Literature Award more than once (in 1991 and 1993).

Paul Healy joined the MIT Sloan School of Management faculty in 1983, where he teaches financial accounting and financial statement analysis. He received his BCA Honors (1st class) in Accounting and Finance from Victoria University, New Zealand, and his MS in Economics and PhD in Business from the University of Rochester. Prior to coming to the U.S., he worked for Arthur Young and ICI Ltd. in New Zealand. Professor Healy received Sloan School awards for Teaching Excellence in 1991 and 1992. In 1993–94, he served as Deputy Dean at the Sloan School, and in 1994–95, he visited London Business School and Harvard Business School. Professor Healy's research, which has been published in *Accounting Review,* the *Journal of Accounting and Economics,* the *Journal of Accounting Research,* and the *Journal of Financial Economics,* includes studies of how firms' disclosure strategies affect their costs of capital, how investors interpret firms' dividend policy and capital structure decisions, the performance of merging firms after mergers, and the effect of managerial compensation and lending contracts on financial reporting. In 1990, he was awarded the AAA/AICPA Notable Contributions to Accounting Literature Award for his article, "The Effect of Bonus Schemes on Accounting Decisions."

preface

Financial statements are the basis for a wide range of business analysis. Managers use them to monitor and judge their firm's performance relative to its competitors, to communicate with external investors, to help judge what financial policies they should pursue, and to evaluate potential new businesses to acquire as part of their investment strategy. Securities analysts use financial statements to rate and value companies they recommend to clients. Bankers use them in deciding whether to extend a loan to a client and to determine the loan's terms. Investment bankers use them as a basis for valuing and analyzing prospective buyouts, mergers, and acquisitions. And consultants use them as a basis for competitive analysis for their clients. Not surprisingly, therefore, we find that there is a strong demand among business students for a course that provides a framework for using financial statement data in a variety of business analysis and valuation contexts. The purpose of this book is to provide such a framework for business students and practitioners.

KEY FEATURES

This book differs from other texts in business and financial analysis in a number of important ways. In the first two parts of the book, we introduce and develop a framework for business analysis and valuation using financial statement data. In Part 3, we show how this framework can be applied to a variety of decision contexts. We use Compaq Computer Corporation, whose annual report data are provided in Part 5, to illustrate both the framework and the applications. Part 4 provides a variety of cases that can be used to develop the concepts discussed in the text.

Framework for Analysis

In the framework section, we identify four key analysis components:

- Business Strategy Analysis
- Accounting Analysis
- Financial Analysis
- Prospective Analysis

The first of the components, business strategy analysis, involves developing an understanding of the business and competitive strategy of the firm being analyzed.

Accounting analysis implies examining how accounting rules and conventions represent the firm's business economics and strategy in its financial statements and, if necessary, developing adjusted accounting measures of performance. To analyze performance, financial analysis utilizes financial ratio and cash flow measures of operating, financing, and investing performance of a company, relative either to key competitors or historical data. Finally, under prospective analysis we show how to develop forecasted financial statements and how to use these to make estimates of firm value. Our discussion of valuation includes traditional cash flow methods as well as methods linked more directly to accounting numbers.

While we cover all four components of business analysis and valuation in the book, we recognize that the extent of their use depends on the user's decision context. For example, bankers are likely to use business strategy analysis, accounting analysis, financial analysis, and the forecasting portion of prospective analysis; they are less likely to be interested in formally valuing a prospective client.

Application of Framework to Decision Contexts

The decision contexts that we include in the third part of the book are:

- Securities Analysis
- Credit Analysis
- Merger and Acquisition Analysis
- Corporate Financing Policies Analysis
- Management Communications Analysis

For each of these topics we present an overview chapter to provide a foundation for class discussions. Where possible we discuss relevant institutional details and results of academic research that are useful in applying the analysis concepts developed in the first section of the book. For example, the chapter on credit analysis shows how banks and rating agencies analyze financial statement data to develop lending decisions and to rate public debt issues. This chapter also discusses academic research on how to analyze whether a company is financially distressed.

Case Approach

We have found that a course in business analysis and valuation is significantly enhanced, both for teachers and students, by using cases as a pedagogical tool. Students want to develop "hands-on" experience in applying the concepts of business analysis and valuation in decision contexts similar to those they will encounter in the business world. Cases achieve this objective in a natural way by presenting practical issues that might otherwise be ignored in a traditional classroom exercise. Our cases all present business analysis and valuation issues in a specific decision context, and we find that this makes the material more interesting and exciting.

To supplement the cases, we provide summary questions at the end of each chapter.

These questions may be used for class discussion or for assignment material.

USING THE TEXT

The text is most effectively used in an undergraduate course in financial statement analysis or in an MBA course.

Prerequisites

To get the most out of the text, students should have completed basic courses in financial accounting, finance, and either business strategy or business economics. The text provides a concise overview of some of these topics, primarily as background for preparing the cases. But it would probably be difficult for students with no prior knowledge in these fields to use the chapters as stand-alone coverage of them. We have integrated only a small amount of business strategy material into each case.

The extent of accounting knowledge required for the cases varies considerably. Some cases require only a basic understanding of accounting issues, whereas others require a more detailed knowledge at the level of a typical intermediate financial accounting course. However, we have found it possible to teach even these more complex cases to students without a strong accounting background by providing additional reading on the topic. For some cases, the Teaching Manual includes a primer on the relevant accounting issue, which instructors can hand out to help students prepare the case.

How to Use the Text and Case Materials

The materials can be used in a variety of ways. We teach the course using almost a pure case approach, adding relevant lecture sections as needed. However, a lecture class could be presented first, followed by an appropriate case. It is also possible to use the text material primarily for a lecture course and include some of the discussion questions and cases as in-class illustrations of the concepts discussed in the text. Alternatively, lectures could be used as a follow-up to the cases to more clearly lay out the conceptual issues raised in the discussion of the cases.

We have designed the cases so that they can be taught at a variety of levels. For students who need more structure to work through a case, the Teaching Manual includes a set of detailed questions which the instructor can hand out before class. For students who need less structure, the Teaching Manual includes a set of recommended questions.

The cases may be enriched with current information by encouraging students to visit the Internet sites of the companies discussed in the cases or mentioned in the text. In addition, we encourage instructors and students to visit South-Western's Palepu/Bernard/Healy Internet pages (www.swcollege.com/swcp/acct/palepu/palepu.html) for links to selected companies.

ACKNOWLEDGMENTS

We gratefully acknowledge the help of Jeff Abarbanell (University of Michigan) and G. Peter Wilson (MIT) for valuable discussions on pedagogical issues. We also thank the Harvard Business School for permission to include a number of their cases.

We appreciate the help of Paul Asquith (MIT), Edouard De Vitry D'Avaucourt, Raguvir Gurumurthy, and Charles Lee (University of Michigan) in developing the case materials. Research assistant help was provided by Marlene Plumlee and Rory Stace. We also wish to thank our colleagues who gave us feedback on our materials, particularly Tom Frecka (Notre Dame), Jeff Abarbanell, and Amy Sweeney (Harvard University). We also thank Brian Belt (University of Missouri-Kansas City), Marlin R. H. Jensen (Auburn University), Ron King (Washington University), James M. Wahlen (University of North Carolina), and David A. Ziebart (University of Illinois) for reviewing the initial outline of this project.

We are also very grateful to Ken Martin, Marci Dechter, and Julia Chitwood for their patient editorial and production help. We thank Bianca Baggio for providing excellent help in putting the manuscript together.

contents

ix

Part 3   BUSINESS ANALYSIS APPLICATIONS

8   Equity Security Analysis   8-1

9   Credit Analysis and Distress Prediction   9-1

10   Mergers and Acquisitions   10-1

Part 4   CASES IN FINANCIAL STATEMENT ANALYSIS

Part 5   COMPAQ COMPUTER CORPORATION

p a r t

Introduction

Chapter 1 A Framework for Doing Business Analysis Using Financial Statements

chapter 1

A Framework for Doing Business Analysis Using Financial Statements

The purpose of this chapter is to outline a comprehensive framework for financial statement analysis. Because financial statements provide the most widely available data on public corporations' economic activities, investors and other stakeholders rely on financial reports to assess the plans and performance of firms and corporate managers.

A variety of questions can be addressed by doing business analysis using financial statements, as shown in the following examples:

- A security analyst may be interested in asking: "How well is the firm I am following performing? Did the firm meet my performance expectations? If not, why not? What is the value of the firm's stock given my assessment of the firm's current and future performance?"
- A loan officer may need to ask: "What is the credit risk involved in lending a certain amount of money to this firm? How well is the firm managing its liquidity and solvency? What is the firm's business risk? What is the additional risk created by the firm's financing and dividend policies?"
- A management consultant might ask: "What is the structure of the industry in which the firm is operating? What are the strategies pursued by various players in the industry? What is the relative performance of different firms in the industry?"
- A corporate manager may ask: "Is my firm properly valued by investors? Is our investor communication program adequate to facilitate this process?"
- A corporate manager could ask: "Is this firm a potential takeover target? How much value can be added if we acquire this firm? How can we finance the acquisition?"
- An independent auditor would want to ask: "Are these financial statements consistent with my understanding of this business and its recent performance? Do these

financial reports communicate the current status and significant risks of the business?"

Financial statement analysis is a valuable activity when managers have complete information on a firm's strategies and a variety of institutional factors make it unlikely that they fully disclose this information. In this setting, outside analysts attempt to create "inside information" from analyzing financial statement data, thereby gaining valuable insights about the firm's current performance and future prospects.

To understand the contribution that financial statements analysis can make, it is important to understand the institutional forces that shape financial statements. Therefore, we present first a brief description of these forces; then we discuss the steps that an analyst must perform to extract information from financial statements and to provide valuable forecasts.

FROM BUSINESS ACTIVITIES TO FINANCIAL STATEMENTS

Corporate managers are responsible for acquiring physical and financial resources from the firm's environment and using them to create value for the firm's investors. Value is created when the firm earns a return on its investment in excess of the cost of capital. Managers formulate business strategies to achieve this goal, and they implement them through business activities. A firm's business activities are influenced by its economic environment and its own business strategy. The economic environment includes the firm's industry, its input and output markets, and the regulations under which the firm operates. The firm's business strategy determines how the firm positions itself in its environment to achieve a competitive advantage.

As shown in Figure 1-1, a firm's financial statements summarize the economic consequences of its business activities. The firm's business activities in any time period are too numerous to be reported individually to outsiders. Further, some of the activities undertaken by the firm are proprietary in nature, and disclosing these activities in detail could be a detriment to the firm's competitive position. The firm's accounting system provides a mechanism through which business activities are selected, measured, and aggregated into financial statement data.

An analyst using financial statement data to do business analysis has to be aware that financial reports are influenced both by the firm's business activities and by its accounting system. A key aspect of financial statement analysis, therefore, involves understanding the influence of the accounting system on the quality of the financial statement data being used in the analysis. The institutional features of accounting systems discussed below determine the extent of that influence.

Accounting System Feature 1: Accrual Accounting

One of the fundamental features of corporate financial reports is that they are prepared using accrual rather than cash accounting. Unlike cash accounting, accrual accounting

Figure 1-1 From Business Activities to Financial Statements

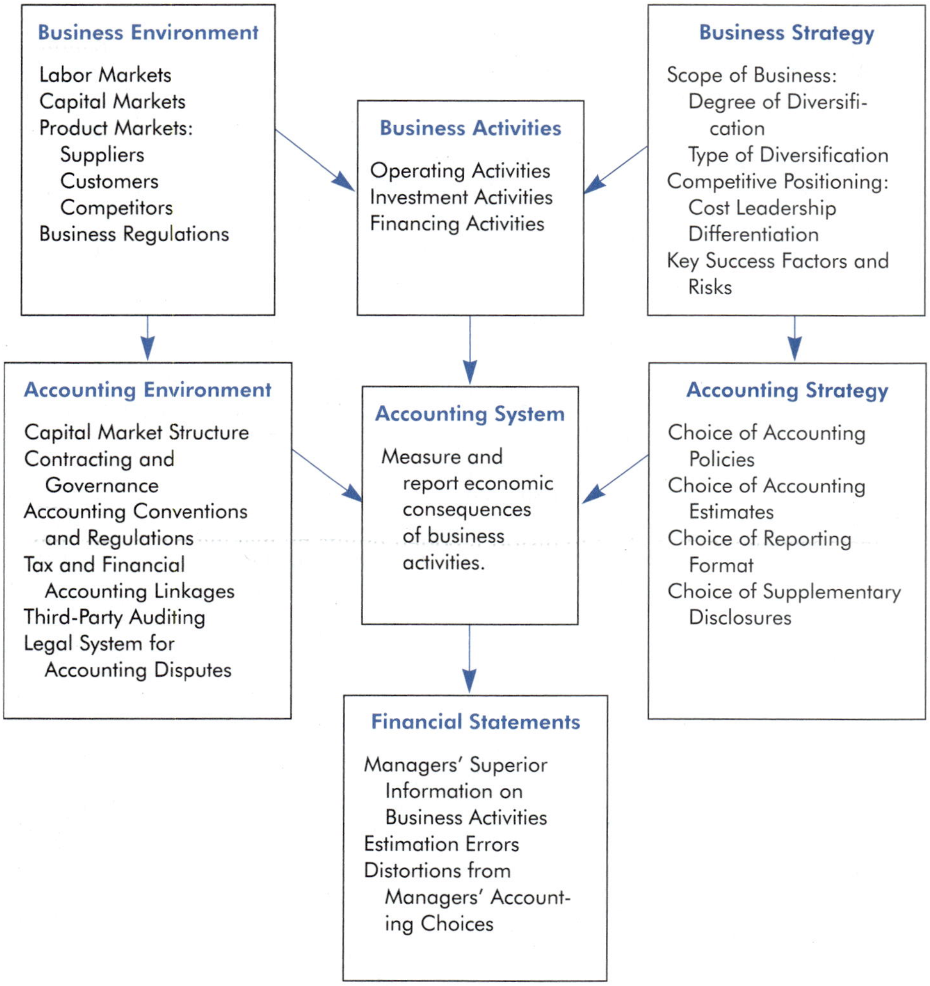

Business Environment

Labor Markets
Capital Markets
Product Markets:
    Suppliers
    Customers
    Competitors
Business Regulations

Business Activities

Operating Activities
Investment Activities
Financing Activities

Business Strategy

Scope of Business:
    Degree of Diversifi-
        cation
    Type of Diversification
Competitive Positioning:
    Cost Leadership
    Differentiation
Key Success Factors and
    Risks

Accounting Environment

Capital Market Structure
Contracting and
    Governance
Accounting Conventions
    and Regulations
Tax and Financial
    Accounting Linkages
Third-Party Auditing
Legal System for
    Accounting Disputes

Accounting System

Measure and
    report economic
    consequences
    of business
    activities.

Accounting Strategy

Choice of Accounting
    Policies
Choice of Accounting
    Estimates
Choice of Reporting
    Format
Choice of Supplementary
    Disclosures

Financial Statements

Managers' Superior
    Information on
    Business Activities
Estimation Errors
Distortions from
    Managers' Account-
    ing Choices

distinguishes between the recording of costs and benefits associated with economic activities and the actual payment and receipt of cash. Net income is the primary periodic performance index under accrual accounting. To compute net income, the effects of economic transactions are recorded on the basis of *expected,* not necessarily *actual,* cash receipts and payments. Expected cash receipts from the delivery of products or services are recognized as revenues, and expected cash outflows associated with these revenues are recognized as expenses.

The need for accrual accounting arises from investors' demand for financial reports on a periodic basis. Because firms undertake economic transactions on a continual basis, the arbitrary closing of accounting books at the end of a reporting period leads to a fundamental measurement problem. Since cash accounting does not report the full economic consequence of the transactions undertaken in a given period, accrual accounting is designed to provide more complete information on a firm's periodic performance.

Accounting System Feature 2: Accounting Standards and Auditing

The use of accrual accounting lies at the center of many important complexities in corporate financial reporting. Because accrual accounting deals with *expectations* of future cash consequences of current events, it is subjective and relies on a variety of assumptions. Who should be charged with the primary responsibility of making these assumptions? A firm's managers are entrusted with the task of making the appropriate estimates and assumptions to prepare the financial statements because they have intimate knowledge of their firm's business.

The accounting discretion granted to managers is potentially valuable because it allows them to reflect inside information in reported financial statements. However, since investors view profits as a measure of managers' performance, managers have incentives to use their accounting discretion to distort reported profits by making biased assumptions. Further, the use of accounting numbers in contracts between the firm and outsiders provides another motivation for management manipulation of accounting numbers. Income management distorts financial accounting data, making them less valuable to external users of financial statements. Therefore, the delegation of financial reporting decisions to corporate managers has both costs and benefits.

A number of accounting conventions have evolved to ensure that managers use their accounting flexibility to summarize their knowledge of the firm's business activities, and not to disguise reality for self-serving purposes. For example, the measurability and conservatism conventions are accounting responses to concerns about distortions from managers' potentially optimistic bias. Both these conventions attempt to limit managers' optimistic bias by imposing their own pessimistic bias.

Accounting standards known as Generally Accepted Accounting Principles (GAAP), promulgated by the Financial Accounting Standards Board (FASB) and similar standard-setting bodies in other countries, also limit potential distortions that managers can introduce into reported numbers. Uniform accounting standards attempt to reduce managers' ability to record similar economic transactions in dissimilar ways, either over time or across firms.

Increased uniformity from accounting standards, however, comes at the expense of reduced flexibility for managers to reflect genuine business differences in their firm's financial statements. Rigid accounting standards work best for economic transactions whose accounting treatment is not predicated on managers' proprietary information. However, when there is significant business judgment involved in assessing a transaction's economic consequences, rigid standards which prevent managers from using their superior business knowledge would be dysfunctional. Further, if accounting standards are too rigid, they may induce managers to expend economic resources to restructure business transactions to achieve a desired accounting result.

Auditing, broadly defined as a verification of the integrity of the reported financial statements by someone other than the preparer, ensures that managers use accounting rules and conventions consistently over time, and that their accounting estimates are reasonable. Therefore, auditing improves the quality of accounting data.

Third-party auditing may also reduce the quality of financial reporting because it constrains the kind of accounting rules and conventions that evolve over time. For example, the FASB considers the views of auditors in the standard-setting process. Auditors are likely to argue against accounting standards producing numbers that are difficult to audit, even if the proposed rules produce relevant information for investors.

The legal environment in which accounting disputes between managers, auditors, and investors are adjudicated can also have a significant effect on the quality of reported numbers. The threat of lawsuits and resulting penalties have the beneficial effect of improving the accuracy of disclosure. However, the potential for a significant legal liability might also discourage managers and auditors from supporting accounting proposals requiring risky forecasts, such as forward-looking disclosures.

Accounting System Feature 3: Managers' Reporting Strategy

Because the mechanisms that limit managers' ability to distort accounting data add noise, it is not optimal to use accounting regulation to eliminate managerial flexibility completely. Therefore, real-world accounting systems leave considerable room for managers to influence financial statement data. A firm's reporting strategy, that is, the manner in which managers use their accounting discretion, has an important influence on the firm's financial statements.

Corporate managers can choose accounting and disclosure policies that make it more or less difficult for external users of financial reports to understand the true economic picture of their businesses. Accounting rules often provide a broad set of alternatives from which managers can choose. Further, managers are entrusted with making a range of estimates in implementing these accounting policies. Accounting regulations usually prescribe *minimum* disclosure requirements, but they do not restrict managers from *voluntarily* providing additional disclosures.

A superior disclosure strategy will enable managers to communicate the underlying business reality to outside investors. One important constraint on a firm's disclosure strategy is the competitive dynamics in product markets. Disclosure of proprietary information about business strategies and their expected economic consequences may hurt the firm's competitive position. Subject to this constraint, managers can use financial statements to provide information useful to investors in assessing their firm's true economic performance.

Managers can also use financial reporting strategies to manipulate investors' perceptions. Using the discretion granted to them, managers can make it difficult for investors to identify poor performance on a timely basis. For example, managers can choose accounting policies and estimates to provide an optimistic assessment of the firm's true performance. They can also make it costly for investors to understand the true performance by controlling the extent of information that is disclosed voluntarily.

The extent to which financial statements are informative about the underlying business reality varies across firms—and across time for a given firm. This variation in accounting quality provides both an important opportunity and a challenge in doing business analysis. The process through which analysts can separate noise from information in financial statements, and gain valuable business insights from financial statement analysis, is discussed next.

FROM FINANCIAL STATEMENTS TO BUSINESS ANALYSIS

Because managers' insider knowledge is a source both of value and distortion in accounting data, it is difficult for outside users of financial statements to separate true information from distortion and noise. Not being able to undo accounting distortions completely, investors "discount" a firm's reported accounting performance. In doing so, they make a probabilistic assessment of the extent to which a firm's reported numbers reflect economic reality. As a result, investors can have only an imprecise assessment of an individual firm's performance. Financial analysts can add value by improving investors' understanding of a firm's current performance and its future prospects.

Effective financial statement analysis is valuable because it attempts to get at managers' inside information from public financial statement data. Because analysts do not have direct access to this information, they rely on their knowledge of the firm's industry and its competitive strategies to interpret financial statements. Successful analysts have at least as good an understanding of the industry economics as do the firm's managers, and a reasonably good understanding of the firm's competitive strategy. Although outside analysts have an information disadvantage relative to the firm's managers, they are more objective in evaluating the economic consequences of the firm's investment and operating decisions. Figure 1-2 provides a schematic overview of how business analysts use financial statements to accomplish four key steps: (1) business strategy analysis, (2) accounting analysis, (3) financial analysis, and (4) prospective analysis.

Analysis Step 1: Business Strategy Analysis

The purpose of business strategy analysis is to identify key profit drivers and business risks, and to assess the company's profit potential at a qualitative level. Business strategy analysis involves analyzing a firm's industry and its strategy to create a sustainable competitive advantage. This qualitative analysis is an essential first step because it enables the analyst to frame the subsequent accounting and financial analysis better. For example, identifying the key success factors and key business risks allows the identification of key accounting policies. Assessment of a firm's competitive strategy facilitates eval-

Figure 1-2 Doing Business Analysis Using Financial Statements

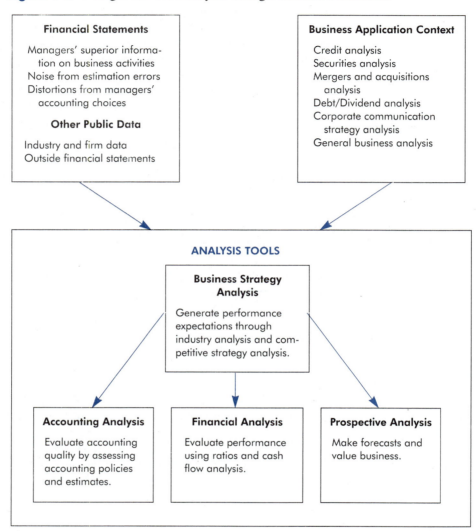

uating whether current profitability is sustainable. Finally, business analysis enables the analyst to make sound assumptions in forecasting a firm's future performance.

Analysis Step 2: Accounting Analysis

The purpose of accounting analysis is to evaluate the degree to which a firm's accounting captures the underlying business reality. By identifying places where there is accounting flexibility, and by evaluating the appropriateness of the firm's accounting policies and estimates, analysts can assess the degree of distortion in a firm's accounting numbers. Another important step in accounting analysis is to "undo" any accounting distortions by recasting a firm's accounting numbers. Sound accounting analysis improves the reliability of conclusions from financial analysis, the next step in financial statement analysis.

Analysis Step 3: Financial Analysis

The goal of financial analysis is to use financial data to evaluate the current and past performance of a firm and to assess its sustainability. There are two important skills related to financial analysis. First, the analysis should be systematic and efficient. Second, the analysis should allow the analyst to use financial data to explore business issues. Ratio analysis and cash flow analysis are the two most commonly used financial tools. Ratio analysis focuses on evaluating a firm's product market performance and financial policies; cash flow analysis focuses on a firm's liquidity and financial flexibility.

Analysis Step 4: Prospective Analysis

Prospective analysis, which focuses on forecasting a firm's future, is the final step in business analysis. Two commonly used techniques in prospective analysis are financial statement forecasting and valuation. Both these tools allow the synthesis of the insights from business analysis, accounting analysis, and financial analysis in order to make predictions about a firm's future.

The predictions from a sound business analysis are useful to a variety of parties and can be applied in various contexts. The exact nature of the analysis will depend on the context. The contexts that we will examine include securities analysis, credit evaluation, mergers and acquisitions, evaluation of debt and dividend policies, and assessing corporate communication strategies. The four analytical steps described above are useful in each of these contexts. Appropriate use of these tools, however, requires a familiarity with the economic theories and institutional factors relevant to the context.

SUMMARY AND CONCLUSIONS

Financial statements provide the most widely available data on public corporations' economic activities; investors and other stakeholders rely on them to assess the plans and performance of firms and corporate managers. Accrual accounting data in financial statements are noisy, and unsophisticated investors can assess firms' performance only imprecisely. Financial analysts who understand managers' disclosure strategies have an opportunity to create inside information from public data, and they play a valuable role in enabling outside parties to evaluate a firm's current and prospective performance.

This chapter has outlined the framework for doing business analysis with financial statements, using the four key steps: business strategy analysis, accounting analysis, financial analysis, and prospective analysis. The remainder of the chapters in this book describe these steps in greater detail and discuss how they can be used in a variety of business contexts.

DISCUSSION QUESTIONS

1. John, who has just completed his first finance course, is unsure whether he should take a course in Business Analysis and Valuation Using Financial Statements, since he believes that financial analysis adds little value, given the efficiency of capital markets. Explain to John when financial analysis can add value, even if capital markets are efficient.
2. Accounting statements rarely report financial performance without error. List three types of errors that can arise in financial reporting.
3. Joe Smith argues that "learning how to do business analysis and valuation using financial statements is not very useful, unless you are interested in becoming a financial analyst." Comment.
4. Four steps for business analysis are discussed in the chapter (strategy analysis, accounting analysis, financial analysis, and prospective analysis). As a financial analyst, explain why each of these steps is a critical part of your job, and how they relate to one another.

CASE

CUC International, Inc. (A)

p a r t

Business Analysis Tools

chapter 2

Business Strategy Analysis

$\mathbf{B}$usiness strategy analysis is an important starting point for the analysis of financial statements. Strategy analysis allows the analyst to probe the economics of the firm at a qualitative level so that the subsequent accounting and financial analysis is grounded in business reality. Business strategy analysis also allows the identification of the firm's profit drivers and key risks. This, in turn, enables the analyst to assess the sustainability of the firm's performance and make realistic forecasts of future performance.

A firm's value is determined by its ability to earn a return on its capital in excess of the cost of capital. What determines whether or not a firm is able to accomplish this goal? While a firm's cost of capital is determined by the capital markets, its profit potential is determined by its own strategic choices: (1) the choice of an industry or a set of industries in which the firm operates (industry choice), and (2) the manner in which the firm intends to compete with other firms in its chosen industry or industries (competitive positioning). Business strategy analysis, therefore, involves industry analysis and competitive strategy analysis.[1] In this chapter, we will briefly discuss both these steps, and use information from Compaq Computer Corporation to illustrate the application of the concepts discussed.[2]

INDUSTRY ANALYSIS

In analyzing a firm's profit potential, an analyst has to first assess the profit potential of each of the industries in which the firm is competing, because the profitability of various industries differs systematically and predictably over time. For example, the annual after-tax returns on equity (ROE) for all U.S. manufacturing companies between 1971 and 1990 was 12.6 percent. However, the average returns varied widely across specific industries: the average annual ROE during the period 1971–1990 was 15.2 percent for the food and kindred products industry, 12.5 percent for the paper and allied products industry, and 3.9 percent for the iron and steel industry.[3] What causes these profitability differences?

There is a vast body of research in industrial organization on the influence of industry structure on profitability.[4] Relying on this research, strategy literature suggests that the average profitability of an industry is influenced by the "five forces" shown in Figure 2-1.[5] According to this framework, the intensity of competition determines the potential for creating abnormal profits by the firms in an industry. Whether or not the potential profits are kept by the industry is determined by the relative bargaining power of the

Figure 2-1 Industry Structure and Profitability

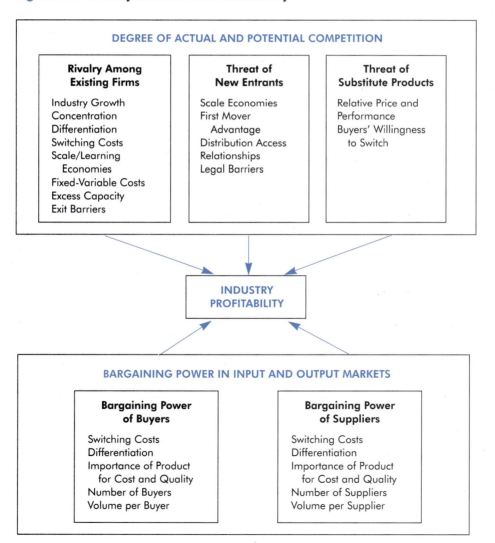

firms in the industry and their customers and suppliers. We will discuss each of these industry profit drivers in more detail below.

DEGREE OF ACTUAL AND POTENTIAL COMPETITION

At the most basic level, the profits in an industry are a function of the maximum price that customers are willing to pay for the industry's product or service. One of the key determinants of the price is the degree to which there is competition among suppliers of the same or similar products. At one extreme, if there is a state of perfect competition in the industry, micro-economic theory predicts that prices will be equal to marginal cost, and there will be few opportunities to earn super-normal profits. At the other extreme, if the industry is dominated by a single firm, there will be potential to earn monopoly profits. In reality, the degree of competition in most industries is somewhere in between perfect competition and monopoly.

There are three potential sources of competition in an industry: (1) rivalry between existing firms, (2) threat of entry of new firms, and (3) threat of substitute products or services. We will discuss each of these competitive forces in the following paragraphs.

Competitive Force 1: Rivalry among Existing Firms

In most industries, the average level of profitability is primarily influenced by the nature of rivalry among existing firms in the industry. In some industries, firms compete aggressively, pushing prices close to (and sometimes below) the marginal cost. In other industries, firms do not compete aggressively on price. Instead, they find ways to coordinate their pricing, or compete on non-price dimensions, such as innovation or brand image. Several factors determine the intensity of competition between existing players in an industry:

INDUSTRY GROWTH RATE.   If an industry is growing very rapidly, existing firms need not grab market share from each other to grow. In contrast, in stagnant industries, the only way existing firms can grow is by taking share away from the other players. In this situation, one can expect price wars among firms in the industry.

CONCENTRATION AND BALANCE OF COMPETITORS.   The number of firms in an industry and their relative sizes determine the degree of concentration in an industry.[6] The degree of concentration influences the extent to which firms in an industry can coordinate their pricing and other competitive moves. For example, if there is one dominant firm in an industry (such as IBM in the mainframe computer industry in the 1970s), it can set and enforce the rules of competition. Similarly, if there are only two or three equal-sized players (such as Coke and Pepsi in the U.S. soft-drink industry), they can implicitly cooperate with each other to avoid destructive price competition. If an industry is fragmented, price competition is likely to be severe.

DEGREE OF DIFFERENTIATION AND SWITCHING COSTS. The extent to which firms in an industry can avoid head-on competition depends on the extent to which they can differentiate their products and services. If the products in an industry are very similar, customers are ready to switch from one competitor to another purely on the basis of price. Switching costs also determine customers' propensity to move from one product to another. When switching costs are low, there is a greater incentive for firms in an industry to engage in price competition.

SCALE/LEARNING ECONOMIES AND THE RATIO OF FIXED TO VARIABLE COSTS. If there is a steep learning curve or there are other types of scale economies in an industry, size becomes an important factor for firms in the industry. In such situations, there are incentives to engage in aggressive competition for market share. Similarly, if the ratio of fixed to variable costs is high, firms have an incentive to reduce prices to utilize installed capacity. The airline industry, where price wars are quite common, is an example of this type of situation.

EXCESS CAPACITY AND EXIT BARRIERS. If capacity in an industry is larger than customer demand, there is a strong incentive for firms to cut prices to fill capacity. The problem of excess capacity is likely to be exacerbated if there are significant barriers for firms to exit the industry. Exit barriers are high when the assets are specialized, or if there are regulations which make exit costly.

Competitive Force 2: Threat of New Entrants

The potential for earning abnormal profits will attract new entrants to an industry. The very threat of new firms entering an industry potentially constrains the pricing of existing firms within it. Therefore, the ease with which new firms can enter an industry is a key determinant of its profitability. Several factors determine the height of barriers to entry in an industry:

ECONOMIES OF SCALE. When there are large economies of scale, new entrants face the choice of having either to invest in a large capacity which might not be utilized right away, or to enter with less than the optimum capacity. Either way, new entrants will at least initially suffer from a cost disadvantage in competing with existing firms. Economies of scale might arise from large investments in research and development (the pharmaceutical or jet engine industries), in brand advertising (soft-drink industry), or in physical plant and equipment (telecommunications industry).

FIRST MOVER ADVANTAGE. Early entrants in an industry may deter future entrants if there are first mover advantages. For example, first movers might be able to set industry standards, or enter into exclusive arrangements with suppliers of cheap raw materials. They may also acquire scarce government licenses to operate in regulated industries. Finally, if there are learning economies, early firms will have an absolute cost advantage over new entrants. First mover advantages are also likely to be large when there are significant switching costs for customers once they start using existing products. For example, switching costs faced by the users of Microsoft's DOS operating system make it difficult for software companies to market a new operating system.

ACCESS TO CHANNELS OF DISTRIBUTION AND RELATIONSHIPS.   Limited capacity in the existing distribution channels and high costs of developing new channels can act as a powerful barriers to entry. For example, a new entrant into the domestic auto industry in the U.S. is likely to face formidable barriers because of the difficulty of developing a dealer network. Similarly, new consumer goods manufacturers find it difficult to obtain supermarket shelf space for their products. Existing relationships between firms and customers in an industry also make it difficult for new firms to enter an industry. Industry examples of this include auditing, investment banking, and advertising.

LEGAL BARRIERS.   There are many industries in which legal barriers, such as patents and copyrights in research-intensive industries, limit entry. Similarly, licensing regulations limit entry into taxi services, medical services, broadcasting, and telecommunications industries.

Competitive Force 3: Threat of Substitute Products

The third dimension of competition in an industry is the threat of substitute products or services. Relevant substitutes are not necessarily those that have the same form as the existing products, but those that perform the same function. For example, airlines and car rental services might be substitutes for each other when it comes to travel over short distances. Similarly, plastic bottles and metal cans substitute for each other as packaging in the beverage industry. In some cases, threat of substitution comes not from customers' switching to another product but from utilizing technologies that allow them to do without, or use less of, the existing products. For example, energy conserving technologies allow customers to reduce their consumption of electricity and fossil fuels.

The threat of substitutes depends on the relative price and performance of the competing products or services, and on customers' willingness to substitute. Customers' perception of whether two products are substitutes depends to some extent on whether they perform the same function for a similar price. If two products perform an identical function, then it would be difficult for them to differ from each other in price. However, customers' willingness to switch is often the critical factor in making this competitive dynamic work. For example, even when tap water and bottled water serve the same function, many customers may be unwilling to substitute the former for the latter, enabling bottlers to charge a price premium. Similarly, designer label clothing commands a price premium even if it is not superior in terms of basic functionality, because customers place a value on the image offered by designer labels.

RELATIVE BARGAINING POWER IN INPUT AND OUTPUT MARKETS

While the degree of competition in an industry determines whether or not there is *potential* to earn abnormal profits, the *actual profits* are influenced by the industry's bargaining power with its suppliers and customers. On the input side, firms enter into transactions with suppliers of labor, raw materials and components, and finances. On the output side, firms either sell directly to the final customers, or enter into contracts with intermediaries in the distribution chain. In all these transactions, the relative economic power of the two sides is important to the overall profitability of the industry firms.

Competitive Force 4: Bargaining Power of Buyers

Two factors determine the power of buyers: price sensitivity and relative bargaining power. Price sensitivity determines the extent to which buyers care to bargain on price; relative bargaining power determines the extent to which they will succeed in forcing the price down.[7]

PRICE SENSITIVITY.   Buyers are more price sensitive when the product is undifferentiated and there are few switching costs. The sensitivity of buyers to price also depends on the importance of the product to their own cost structure. When the product represents a large fraction of the buyers' cost (for example, the packaging material for soft-drink producers), the buyer is likely to expend the resources necessary to shop for a lower cost alternative. In contrast, if the product is a small fraction of the buyers' cost (for example, windshield wipers for automobile manufacturers), it may not pay to expend resources to search for lower-cost alternatives. Further, the importance of the product to the buyers' product quality also determines whether or not price becomes the most important determinant of the buying decision.

RELATIVE BARGAINING POWER.   Even if buyers are price sensitive, they may not be able to achieve low prices unless they have a strong bargaining position. Relative bargaining power in a transaction depends, ultimately, on the cost to each party of not doing business with the other party. The buyers' bargaining power is determined by the number of buyers relative to the number of suppliers, volume of purchases by a single buyer, number of alternative products available to the buyer, buyers' costs of switching from one product to another, and the threat of backward integration by the buyers. For example, in the automobile industry, car manufacturers have considerable power over component manufacturers because auto companies are large buyers, with several alternative suppliers to choose from, and switching costs are relatively low. In contrast, in the personal computer industry, computer makers have low bargaining power relative to the operating system software producers because of high switching costs.

Competitive Force 5: Bargaining Power of Suppliers

The analysis of the relative power of suppliers is a mirror image of the analysis of the buyer's power in an industry. Suppliers are powerful when there are only a few companies and there are few substitutes available to their customers. For example, in the soft-drink industry, Coke and Pepsi are very powerful relative to the bottlers. In contrast, metal can suppliers to the soft drink industry are not very powerful because of intense competition among can producers and the threat of substitution of cans by plastic bottles. Suppliers also have a lot of power over buyers when the suppliers' product or service is critical to buyers' business. For example, airline pilots have a strong bargaining power in the airline industry. Suppliers also tend to be powerful when they pose a credible threat of forward integration. For example, IBM is powerful relative to mainframe computer leasing companies because of IBM's unique position as a mainframe supplier, and its own presence in the computer leasing business.

APPLYING INDUSTRY ANALYSIS: THE PERSONAL COMPUTER INDUSTRY

Let us consider the above concepts of industry analysis in the context of Compaq's industry—the IBM and compatible personal computer (PC) industry—in 1993.[8] The industry began in 1981 when IBM announced its PC with Intel's microprocessor and Microsoft's DOS operating system, and grew by 1992 to become a $62 billion dollar industry. Despite this spectacular growth, however, the industry in 1993 was characterized by low profitability. Even the largest companies in the industry, such as IBM, Compaq, and Dell, reported poor performance in the early 1990s, and were forced to undergo internal restructuring. What accounted for this low profitability? What was the industry's future profit potential?

COMPETITION IN THE PERSONAL COMPUTER INDUSTRY.   The competition was very intense for a number of reasons:

- The industry was highly fragmented, with many firms producing virtually identical products. Even the largest firm in the industry, IBM, had only about a 15 percent market share, and the ten largest firms in the industry accounted for only 53 percent of the industry.
- Component costs accounted for 80–90 percent of total costs of a personal computer, and volume purchases of components reduced these costs. Therefore, there was intense competition for market share among competing manufacturers.
- Products produced by different firms in the industry were virtually identical, and there were few opportunities to differentiate the products. While brand name and service were dimensions that customers valued in the early years of the industry, they became less important as PC buyers became more informed about the technology.

- Switching costs across different brands of personal computers were relatively low because the clones were essentially identical to IBM computers.
- Access to distribution was not a significant barrier, as demonstrated by Dell Computers, which distributed its computers through direct mail. The advent of computer superstores like CompUSA also mitigated this constraint, since these stores were willing to carry several brands.
- Since virtually all the components needed to produce a personal computer were available for purchase, there were very few barriers to entering the industry. In fact, Michael Dell started Dell Computer Company in the early 1980s by assembling PCs in his University of Texas dormitory room.
- Apple's Macintosh computers offered significant competition as a substitute product. Work stations produced by Sun, DEC, and other vendors were also potential substitutes at the higher end of the personal computer market.

THE POWER OF SUPPLIERS AND BUYERS.   Suppliers and buyers had significant power over firms in the industry for these reasons:

- Key hardware and software components for personal computers were controlled by firms with virtual monopoly. Intel dominated the microprocessor production for the personal computer industry, and Microsoft controlled the operating system market with its DOS and Windows operating systems.
- Buyers gained more power during the ten years from 1983 to 1993. Corporate buyers, who represented a significant portion of the customer base, were highly price sensitive since the expenditure on PCs represented a significant cost to their operations. Further, as they became knowledgeable about personal computer technology, customers were less influenced by brand name in their purchase decision. Buyers increasingly viewed PCs as commodities, and used price as the most important consideration in their buying decision.

As a result of the intense rivalry and low barriers to entry in the personal computer industry, there was severe price competition among different manufacturers. Further, there was tremendous pressure on firms to spend large sums of money to introduce new products rapidly, maintain high quality, and provide excellent customer support. Both these factors led to a low profit potential in the industry. The power of suppliers and buyers reduced the profit potential further. Thus, while the personal computer industry represented a technologically dynamic industry, its profit potential was poor.

Because there were few indications of change in the basic structure of the personal computer industry, there was little likelihood of viable competition emerging to challenge the domination of Microsoft and Intel in the input markets. Attempts by industry leaders like IBM to create alternative proprietary technologies have not succeeded, and barriers to entry are likely to continue. Threats from Apple are only likely to increase with the development of the PowerPC chip, as well as Apple's willingness to license its own operating system to clone manufacturers. As a result, the profitability of the PC industry may not improve significantly any time in the near future.

Limitations of Industry Analysis

A potential limitation of the industry analysis framework discussed in this chapter is the assumption that industries have clear boundaries. In reality, it is often not easy to clearly demarcate industry boundaries. For example, in analyzing Compaq's industry, should one focus on the IBM-compatible personal computer industry or the personal computer industry as a whole? Should one include workstations in the industry definition? Should one consider only the domestic manufacturers of personal computers, or also manufacturers abroad? Inappropriate industry definition will result in incomplete analysis and inaccurate forecasts.

COMPETITIVE STRATEGY ANALYSIS

The profitability of a firm is influenced not only by its industry structure but also by the strategic choices it makes in positioning itself in the industry. While there are many ways to characterize a firm's business strategy, as Figure 2-2 shows, there are two generic

Figure 2-2 Strategies for Creating Competitive Advantage

Cost Leadership

Supply same product or service at a lower cost.

Economies of scale and scope
Efficient production
Simpler product designs
Lower input costs
Low-cost distribution
Little research and development or brand advertising
Tight cost control system

Differentiation

Supply a unique product or service at a cost lower than the price premium customers will pay.

Superior product quality
Superior product variety
Superior customer service
More flexible delivery
Investment in brand image
Investment in research and development
Control system focus on creativity and innovation

Competitive Advantage

- Match between firm's core competencies and key success factors to execute strategy
- Match between firm's value chain and activities required to execute strategy
- Sustainability of competitive advantage

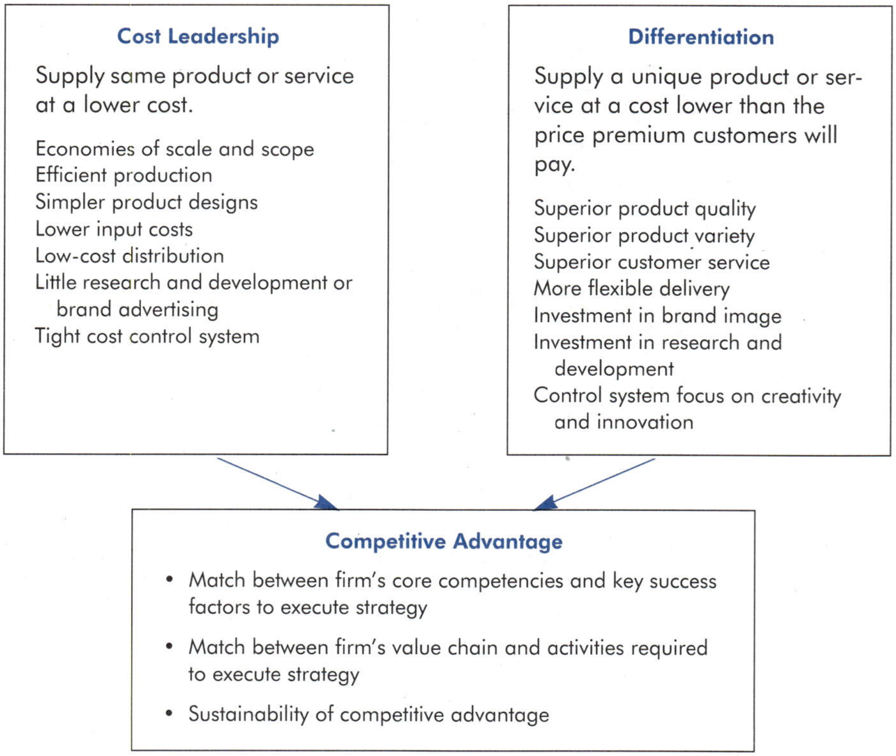

competitive strategies: (1) cost leadership and (2) differentiation.[9] Both these strategies can potentially allow a firm to build a sustainable competitive advantage.

Strategy researchers have traditionally viewed cost leadership and differentiation as mutually exclusive strategies. Firms that straddle the two strategies are considered to be "stuck in the middle" and are expected to earn low profitability.[10] These firms run the risk of not being able to attract price conscious customers because their costs are too high; they are also unable to provide adequate differentiation to attract premium price customers.[11]

SOURCES OF COMPETITIVE ADVANTAGE

Cost leadership enables a firm to supply the same product or service offered by its competitors at a lower cost. Differentiation strategy involves providing a product or service that is distinct in some important respect valued by the customer. For example, in retailing, Nordstrom has succeeded on the basis of differentiation by emphasizing exceptionally high customer service. In contrast, Filene's Basement Stores is a discount retailer competing purely on a low cost basis.

Competitive Strategy 1: Cost Leadership

Cost leadership is often the clearest way to achieve competitive advantage. In industries where the basic product or service is a commodity, cost leadership might be the only way to achieve superior performance. There are many ways to achieve cost leadership, including economies of scale and scope, economies of learning, efficient production, simpler product design, lower input costs, and efficient organizational processes. If a firm can achieve cost leadership, then it will be able to earn above-average profitability by merely charging the same price as its rivals. Conversely, a cost leader can force its competitors to cut prices and accept lower returns, or to exit the industry.

Firms that achieve cost leadership focus on tight cost controls. They make investments in efficient scale plants, focus on product designs that reduce manufacturing costs, minimize overhead costs, make little investment in risky research and development, and avoid serving marginal customers. They have organizational structures and control systems that focus on cost control.

Competitive Strategy 2: Differentiation

A firm following the differentiation strategy seeks to be unique in its industry along some dimension that is highly valued by customers. For differentiation to be successful, the firm has to accomplish three things. First, it needs to identify one or more attributes of a product or service that customers value. Second, it has to position itself to meet the chosen customer need in a unique manner. Finally, the firm has to achieve differentiation at a cost that is lower than the price the customer is willing to pay for the differentiated product or service.

Drivers of differentiation include providing superior intrinsic value via product quality, product variety, bundled services, or delivery timing. Differentiation can also be achieved by investing in signals of value, such as brand image, product appearance, or reputation. Differentiated strategies require investments in research and development, engineering skills, and marketing capabilities. The organizational structures and control systems in firms with differentiation strategies need to foster creativity and innovation.

While successful firms choose between cost leadership and differentiation, they cannot completely ignore the dimension on which they are not primarily competing. Firms which target differentiation still need to focus on costs, so that the differentiation can be achieved at an acceptable cost. Similarly, cost leaders cannot compete unless they achieve at least a minimum level on key dimensions on which competitors might differentiate, such as quality and service.

ACHIEVING AND SUSTAINING COMPETITIVE ADVANTAGE

The choice of competitive strategy does not automatically lead to the achievement of competitive advantage. To achieve competitive advantage, the firm has to have the capabilities needed to implement and sustain the chosen strategy. Both cost leadership and differentiation strategy require that the firm make the necessary commitments to acquire the core competencies needed, and structure its value chain in an appropriate way. Core competencies are the economic assets that the firm possesses, whereas the value chain is the set of activities that the firm performs to convert inputs into outputs. The uniqueness of a firm's core competencies and its value chain and the extent to which it is difficult for competitors to imitate them determines the sustainability of a firm's competitive advantage.[12]

To evaluate whether or not a firm is likely to achieve its intended competitive advantage, the analyst should ask the following questions:

- What are the key success factors and risks associated with the firm's chosen competitive strategy?
- Does the firm currently have the resources and capabilities to deal with the key success factors and risks?
- Has the firm made irreversible commitments to bridge the gap between its current capabilities and the requirements to achieve its competitive advantage?
- Has the firm structured its activities (such as research and development, design, manufacturing, marketing and distribution, and support activities) in a way that is consistent with its competitive strategy?
- Is the company's competitive advantage sustainable? Are there any barriers that make imitation of the firm's strategy difficult?
- Are there any potential changes in the firm's industry structure (such as new technologies, foreign competition, changes in regulation, changes in customer requirements) that might dissipate the firm's competitive advantage? Is the company flexible enough to address these changes?

APPLYING BUSINESS STRATEGY ANALYSIS

Once again, let us consider the concepts of business strategy analysis in the context of Compaq Computers. Compaq was the leading IBM compatible computer maker, with a market share of approximately 10 percent by 1993. After several years of strong performance, the company reported a decline in profits in 1992. However, with new management and a fine-tuning of its strategy, Compaq reported a strong profit performance once again in 1993.

Bill Gurley of CS First Boston summarized Compaq's business strategy that led to this superior performance in a difficult industry as follows:

> *Compaq Computer Corporation has emerged as the leading independent vendor of IBM/PC compatible computers, second only to the IBM PC Company itself in shipments and revenues. The company has achieved this position by establishing itself as a low cost producer without sacrificing its commitment to quality. As part of its strategy, Compaq has focused on revenue growth and market share gains rather than margin increases. Compaq has converted these market share gains into further volume-driven cost advantages. The company has then passed these cost advantages on to the customer in terms of lower pricing, thus generating further growth. The strategy is working, and we expect Compaq will continue to outperform its competitors and Wall Street's earnings forecasts in the process.*[13]

As Gurley's analysis suggests, Compaq distinguished itself from IBM by being a low cost producer, and it differentiated itself from other PC clone makers by investing in a brand name with an image of high quality, industry leading service, and continual introduction of new products. Compaq's competitive strategy produced these results:

- As a result of its brand image, Compaq commanded a slight price premium of about 5–6 percent over other IBM clones.
- Compaq had a significant cost advantage because of its ability to purchase components in large volumes. These components account for 80–90 percent of PC manufacturing costs. For example, Gurley suggests that Compaq followed a low-cost manufacturing strategy by creating vertically integrated manufacturing lines which significantly reduce direct labor costs and overhead costs. As a result of both lower input costs and manufacturing efficiencies, Compaq's cost of goods sold was approximately 70 percent, several percentage points lower than the ratio for Dell and other IBM compatible manufacturers.
- Compaq also lowered its operating expenses in 1992 and 1993 by focusing on tight cost controls.

In an industry with very small gross margins, the price premium and lower costs enabled Compaq to earn one of the highest net profit margins.

Although Compaq's strategy gave it a competitive advantage over both IBM and other PC clone makers, the long-term sustainability of Compaq's position was questionable. For example, if IBM's PC operations were better managed under its new management,

Compaq could be dominated by IBM in terms of technical innovation, customer service, and brand image. Similarly, it ran the risk of being dominated by low-cost clone makers like Packard-Bell and Gateway 2000, which avoided some of the costs incurred by Compaq without significantly sacrificing product quality and features. In either case, Compaq is likely to lose its current price premium, leading to significantly lower profits. How soon this happens will be determined to some extent by the strategies and actions taken by Compaq's competitors, something not in the control of Compaq's management.

SUMMARY AND CONCLUSIONS

Business strategy analysis is an important starting point for the analysis of financial statements because it allows the analyst to probe the economics of the firm at a qualitative level. Strategy analysis also allows the identification of the firm's profit drivers and key risks, enabling the analyst to assess the sustainability of the firm's performance and make realistic forecasts of future performance.

Whether or not a firm is able to earn a return on its capital in excess of its cost of capital is determined by its own strategic choices: (1) the choice of an industry or a set of industries in which the firm operates (industry choice) and (2) the manner in which the firm intends to compete with other firms in its chosen industry or industries (competitive positioning). Business strategy analysis involves both of these choices.

Industry analysis consists of identifying the economic factors which drive the industry profitability. In general, an industry's average profit potential is influenced by the degree of rivalry among existing competitors, the ease with which new firms can enter the industry, the availability of substitute products, the power of buyers, and the power of suppliers. To perform industry analysis, the analyst has to assess the current strength of each of these forces in an industry and make forecasts of any likely future changes.

Competitive strategy analysis involves identifying the basis on which the firm intends to compete in its industry. In general, there are two potential strategies that could provide a firm with a competitive advantage: cost leadership and differentiation. Cost leadership involves offering the same product or service that other firms offer at a lower cost. Differentiation involves satisfying a chosen dimension of customer need better than the competition, at an incremental cost that is less than the price premium that customers are willing to pay. To perform strategy analysis, the analyst has to identify the firm's intended strategy, assess whether or not the firm possesses the competencies required to execute the strategy, and recognize the key risks that the firm has to guard against. The analyst also has to evaluate the sustainability of the firm's strategy.

The insights gained from industry analysis can be useful in performing the remainder of the financial statement analysis. In accounting analysis, the analyst can examine whether a firm's accounting policies and estimates are consistent with its stated business strategy. For example, a firm's choice of functional currency in accounting for its international operations should be consistent with the level of integration between domestic and international operations that the business strategy calls for. Similarly, a firm that mainly sells housing to low income customers should have higher bad debts expenses.

Strategy analysis is also useful in guiding financial analysis. For example, in a cross-sectional analysis the analyst should expect firms with cost leadership strategy to have lower gross margins and higher asset turnover than firms that follow differentiated strategies. In a time series analysis, the analyst should closely monitor any increases in expense ratios and asset turnover ratios for low cost firms, and any decreases in investments critical to differentiation for firms that follow differentiation strategy.

Business strategy analysis also helps in prospective analysis. First, it allows the analyst to assess whether, and for how long, differences between the firm's performance and its industry performance are likely to persist. Second, strategy analysis facilitates forecasting investment outlays the firm has to make to maintain its competitive advantage.

DISCUSSION QUESTIONS

1. Judith, an accounting major, states: "Strategy analysis seems to be an unnecessary detour in doing financial statement analysis. Why can't we just get straight to the accounting issues? " Explain to Judith why she might be wrong.
2. What are the critical drivers of industry profitability?
3. One of the fastest growing industries in the last twenty years is the memory chip industry, which supplies memory chips for personal computers and other electronic devices. Yet the average profitability for this industry has been very low. Using the industry analysis framework, list all the potential factors that might explain this apparent contradiction.
4. Rate the pharmaceutical and lumber industries as high, medium, or low on the following dimensions of industry structure:

	Pharmaceutical Industry	Lumber Industry
Rivalry		
Threat of new entrants		
Threat of substitute products		
Bargaining power of buyers		
Bargaining power of suppliers		

Given your ratings, which industry would you expect to earn the highest returns?

5. Joe Smith argues: "Your analysis of the five forces that affect industry profitability is incomplete. For example, in the banking industry, I can think of at least three other factors that are also important; namely, government regulation, demographic trends, and cultural factors." His classmate Jane Brown disagrees and says: "These three factors are important only to the extent that they influence one of the five forces." Explain how, if at all, the three factors discussed by Joe affect the five forces for the banking industry.

6. Coca-Cola and Pepsi are both very profitable soft drinks. Inputs for these products include sugar, bottles/cans, and soft drink syrup. Coca-Cola and Pepsi produce the syrup themselves and purchase the other inputs. They then enter into exclusive contracts with independent bottlers to produce their products. Use the five forces framework and your knowledge of the soft drink industry to explain how Coca-Cola and Pepsi are able to retain most of the profits in this industry.

7. In the early 1980s, United, Delta, and American Airlines each started frequent flier programs as a way to differentiate themselves in response to excess capacity in the industry. Many industry analysts, however, believe that this move had only mixed success. Use the competitive advantage concepts to explain why.

8. What are the ways that a firm can use to create barriers to entry to deter competition in its business? What factors determine whether these barriers are likely to be enduring?

9. Explain why you agree or disagree with each of the following statements:
   a. It's better to be a differentiator than a cost leader, since you can then charge premium prices.
   b. It's more profitable to be in a high technology than a ow technology industry.
   c. The reason why industries with large investments have high barriers to entry is because it is costly to raise capital.

10. There are very few companies that are able to be both cost leaders and differentiators. Why? Can you think of a company that has been successful at both?

CASE

America Online, Inc.

NOTES

1. The discussion presented here is intended to provide a basic background in business strategy analysis. For a more complete discussion of the strategy concepts, see, for example, *Contemporary Strategy Analysis* by Robert M. Grant (Cambridge, MA: Blackwell Publishers, 1991).

2. Most of the 1992 annual report for Compaq Computer Corporation is in Part 5 at the end of the text.

3. These data are taken from *Selected Profitability Data on U.S. Industries and Companies* by Anita M. McGahan (Boston: Harvard Business School Publishing Division, 9-792-066).

4. For a summary of this research, see *Industrial Market Structure and Economic Performance*, second edition, by F. M. Scherer (Chicago: Rand McNally College Publishing Co., 1980).

5. See *Competitive Strategy* by Michael E. Porter (New York: The Free Press, 1980).

6. The four-firm concentration ratio is a commonly used measure of industry concentration; it refers to the market share of the four largest firms in an industry.

7. While the discussion here uses the buyer to connote industrial buyers, the same concepts also apply to buyers of consumer products. Throughout this chapter, we use the terms buyers and customers interchangeably.

8. The data on the personal computer (PC) industry discussed here and elsewhere in this chapter is drawn from a survey by Bill Gurley, "PC Profile 1993," CS First Boston, November 1993.

9. For a more detailed discussion of these two sources of competitive advantage, see Michael E. Porter, *Competitive Advantage: Creating and Sustaining Superior Performance* (New York: The Free Press, 1985).

10. Ibid.

11. In recent years, one of the strategic challenges faced by corporations is having to deal with competitors who achieve differentiation with low cost. For example, Japanese auto manufacturers have successfully demonstrated that there is no necessary trade-off between quality and cost. Similarly, in recent years several highly successful retailers like Wal-Mart and Home Depot have been able to combine high quality, high service, and low prices. These examples suggest that combining low cost and differentiation strategies is possible when a firm introduces a significant technical or business innovation. However, such cost advantage and differentiation will be sustainable only if there are significant barriers to imitation by competitors.

12. See *Competing for the Future* by Gary Hammel and C. K. Prahalad (Boston: Harvard Business School Press, 1994) for a more detailed discussion of the concept of core competencies and their critical role in corporate strategy.

13. "Compaq Computer Corporation" by J. Gurley, CS First Boston, November 29, 1993, p. 4.

chapter 3

Accounting Analysis

The purpose of accounting analysis is to evaluate the degree to which a firm's accounting captures its underlying business reality.[1] By identifying places where there is accounting flexibility, and by evaluating the appropriateness of the firm's accounting policies and estimates, analysts can assess the degree of distortion in a firm's accounting numbers. Another important skill is recasting a firm's accounting numbers using cash flow and footnote information to "undo" any accounting distortions. Sound accounting analysis improves the reliability of conclusions from financial analysis, the next step in financial statement analysis.

OVERVIEW OF THE INSTITUTIONAL FRAMEWORK FOR FINANCIAL REPORTING

There is typically a separation between ownership and management in public corporations. Financial statements serve as the vehicle through which owners keep track of their firms' financial situation. On a periodic basis, firms typically produce three financial reports : (1) an income statement that describes the operating performance during a time period, (2) a balance sheet that states the firm's assets and how they are financed, and (3) a cash flow statement (or in some countries, a funds flow statement) that summarizes the cash flows of the firm. These statements are accompanied by several footnotes and a message and narrative discussion written by the management.

To evaluate effectively the quality of a firm's financial statement data, the analyst needs to first understand the basic features of financial reporting and the institutional framework that governs them, as discussed in the following sections.

Building Blocks of Accrual Accounting

One of the fundamental features of corporate financial reports is that they are prepared using accrual rather than cash accounting. Unlike cash accounting, accrual accounting distinguishes between the recording of costs and benefits associated with economic activities and the actual payment and receipt of cash. Net income is the primary periodic performance index under accrual accounting. To compute net income, the effects of economic transactions are recorded on the basis of *expected*, not necessarily *actual*, cash receipts and payments. Expected cash receipts from the delivery of products or services are recognized as revenues, and expected cash outflows associated with these revenues are recognized as expenses.

While there are many rules and conventions that govern a firm's preparation of financial statements, there are only a few conceptual building blocks that form the foundation of accrual accounting. The principles that define a firm's assets, liabilities, equities, revenues, and expenses are as follows[2]:

- **Assets** are economic resources owned by a firm that (a) are likely to produce future economic benefits and (b) are measurable with a reasonable degree of certainty.
- **Liabilities** are economic obligations of a firm arising from benefits received in the past that are (a) required to be met with a reasonable degree of certainty and (b) at a reasonably well-defined time in the future.
- **Equity** is the difference between a firm's net assets and its liabilities.

These definitions lead to the fundamental relationship that governs a firm's balance sheet:

Assets = Liabilities + Equity

While the balance sheet is a summary at one point in time, the income statement summarizes a firm's revenues and expenses and its gains and losses arising from changes in assets and liabilities in accord with the following definitions:

- **Revenues** are economic resources earned during a time period. Revenue recognition is governed by the realization principle, which proposes that revenues should be recognized when (a) the firm has provided all, or substantially all, the goods or services to be delivered to the customer and (b) the customer has paid cash or is expected to pay cash with a reasonable degree of certainty.
- **Expenses** are economic resources used up in a time period. Expense recognition is governed by the matching and the conservatism principles. Under these principles, expenses are (a) costs directly associated with revenues recognized in the same period, or (b) costs associated with benefits that are consumed in this time period, or (c) resources whose future benefits are not reasonably certain.
- **Profit** is the difference between a firm's revenues and expenses in a time period.[3]

Delegation of Reporting to Management

While the basic definitions of the elements of a firm's financial statements are simple, their application in practice often involves complex judgments. For example, how should revenues be recognized when a firm sells land to customers and also provides customer financing? If revenue is recognized before cash is collected, how should potential defaults be estimated? Are the outlays associated with research and development activities, whose payoffs are uncertain, assets or expenses when incurred? Do frequent flyer reward programs create accounting liabilities for airline companies? If so, when and at what value?

Because corporate managers have intimate knowledge of their firms' businesses, they are entrusted with the primary task of making the appropriate judgments in portraying myriad business transactions using the basic accrual accounting framework. The accounting discretion granted to managers is potentially valuable because it allows them to reflect inside information in reported financial statements. However, since investors view profits as a measure of managers' performance, managers have an incentive to use their accounting discretion to distort reported profits by making biased assumptions. Further, the use of accounting numbers in contracts between the firm and outsiders provides a motivation for management manipulation of accounting numbers.

Income management distorts financial accounting data, making them less valuable to external users of financial statements. Therefore, the delegation of financial reporting decisions to managers has both costs and benefits. Accounting rules and auditing are mechanisms designed to reduce the cost and preserve the benefit of delegating financial reporting to corporate managers.

Generally Accepted Accounting Principles

Given that it is difficult for outside investors to determine whether managers have used their accounting flexibility to signal their proprietary information or merely to disguise reality, a number of accounting conventions have evolved to mitigate the problem. Accounting conventions and standards promulgated by the standard-setting bodies limit potential distortions that managers can introduce into reported accounting numbers. In the United States, the Securities and Exchange Commission (SEC) has the legal authority to set accounting standards. The SEC typically relies on private sector accounting bodies to undertake this task. Since 1973, accounting standards in the United States have been set by the Financial Accounting Standards Board (FASB). There are similar private sector or public sector accounting standard-setting bodies in many other countries. In addition, the International Accounting Standards Committee (IASC) has been attempting to set worldwide accounting standards, though IASC's pronouncements are not legally binding as of now.

Uniform accounting standards attempt to reduce managers' ability to record similar economic transactions in dissimilar ways either over time or across firms. Thus they create a uniform accounting language and increase the credibility of financial statements by limiting a firm's ability to distort them. Increased uniformity from accounting standards, however, comes at the expense of reduced flexibility for managers to reflect genuine business differences in a firm's accounting decisions. Rigid accounting standards work best for economic transactions whose accounting treatment is not predicated on managers' proprietary information. However, when there is a significant business judgment involved in assessing a transaction's economic consequences, rigid standards are likely to be dysfunctional, because they prevent managers from using their superior business knowledge. Further, if accounting standards are too rigid, they may induce managers to expend economic resources to restructure business transactions to achieve a desired accounting result.

External Auditing

Broadly defined as a verification of the integrity of the reported financial statements by someone other than the preparer, external auditing ensures that managers use accounting rules and conventions consistently over time, and that their accounting estimates are reasonable. In the United States, all listed companies are required to have their financial statements audited by an independent public accountant. The standards and procedures to be followed by independent auditors are set by the American Institute of Certified Public Accountants (AICPA). These standards are known as Generally Accepted Auditing Standards (GAAS). While auditors issue an opinion on published financial statements, it is important to remember that the primary responsibility of the statements still rests with corporate managers.

Auditing improves the quality and credibility of accounting data by limiting a firm's ability to distort financial statements to suit its own purposes. However, third-party auditing may also reduce the quality of financial reporting because it constrains the kind of accounting rules and conventions that evolve over time. For example, the FASB considers the views of auditors in the standard-setting process. Auditors are likely to argue against accounting standards that produce numbers which are difficult to audit, even if the proposed rules produce relevant information for investors.

Legal Liability

The legal environment in which accounting disputes between managers, auditors, and investors are adjudicated can also have a significant effect on the quality of reported numbers. The threat of lawsuits and resulting penalties have the beneficial effect of improving the accuracy of disclosure. However, the potential for a significant legal liability might also discourage managers and auditors from supporting accounting proposals requiring risky forecasts, such as forward-looking disclosures This type of concern is often expressed by the auditing community in the U.S.

Limitations of Accounting Analysis

Because the mechanisms that limit managers' ability to distort accounting data themselves add noise, it is not optimal to use accounting regulation to eliminate managerial flexibility completely. Therefore, real-world accounting systems leave considerable room for managers to influence financial statement data. The net result is that information in corporate financial reports is noisy and biased, even in the presence of accounting regulation and external auditing.[4] The objective of accounting analysis is to evaluate the degree to which a firm's accounting captures its underlying business reality and to "undo" any accounting distortions. When potential distortions are large, accounting analysis can add considerable value.[5]

Factors Influencing Accounting Quality

There are three potential sources of noise and bias in accounting data: (1) the noise and bias introduced by rigidity in accounting rules, (2) random forecast errors, and (3) systematic reporting choices made by corporate managers to achieve specific objectives. Each of these factors is discussed below.

ACCOUNTING RULES.   Accounting rules introduce noise and bias because it is often difficult to restrict management discretion without reducing the information content of accounting data. For example, the Statement of Financial Accounting Standards No. 2 issued by the FASB requires firms to expense research outlays when they are incurred. Clearly, some research expenditures have future value while others do not. However, because SFAS No. 2 does not allow firms to distinguish between the two types of expenditures, it leads to a systematic distortion of reported accounting numbers. Broadly speaking, the degree of distortion introduced by accounting standards depends on how well uniform accounting standards capture the nature of a firm's transactions.

FORECAST ERRORS.   Another source of noise in accounting data arises from pure forecast error, because managers cannot predict future consequences of current transactions perfectly. For example, when a firm sells products on credit, accrual accounting requires managers to make a judgment on the probability of collecting payments from customers. If payments are deemed "reasonably certain," the firm treats the transactions as sales, creating accounts receivable on its balance sheet. Managers then make an estimate of the proportion of receivables that will not be collected. Because managers do not have perfect foresight, actual defaults are likely to be different from estimated customer defaults, leading to a forecast error. The extent of errors in managers' accounting forecasts depends on a variety of factors, including the complexity of the business transactions, the predictability of the firm's environment, and unforeseen economy-wide changes.

MANAGERS' ACCOUNTING CHOICES.   Corporate managers also introduce noise and bias into accounting data through their own accounting decisions. Managers have a variety of incentives to exercise their accounting discretion to achieve certain objectives, leading to systematic influences on their firms' reporting[6]:

- *Accounting-based debt covenants.* Managers may make accounting decisions to meet certain contractual obligations in their debt covenants. For example, firms' lending agreements with banks and other debt holders require them to meet covenants related to interest coverage, working capital ratios, and net worth, all defined in terms of accounting numbers. Violation of these constraints may be costly because it allows lenders to demand immediate payment of their loans. Managers of firms close to violating debt covenants have an incentive to select accounting policies and estimates to reduce the probability of covenant violation. The debt covenant motivation for managers' accounting decisions has been analyzed by a number of accounting researchers.[7]
- *Management compensation.* Another motivation for managers' accounting choice comes from the fact that their compensation and job security are often tied to reported profits. For example, many top managers receive bonus compensation if they exceed certain prespecified profit targets. This provides motivation for managers to choose accounting policies and estimates to maximize their expected compensation.[8]
- *Corporate control contests.* In corporate control contests, including hostile takeovers and proxy fights, competing management groups attempt to win over the firm's shareholders. Accounting numbers are used extensively in debating managers' performance in these contests. Therefore, managers may make accounting decisions to influence investor perceptions in corporate control contests.[9]
- *Tax considerations.* Managers may also make reporting choices to trade off between financial reporting and tax considerations. For example, U.S. firms are required to use LIFO inventory accounting for shareholder reporting in order to use it for tax reporting. Under LIFO, when prices are rising, firms report lower profits, thereby reducing tax payments. Some firms may forgo the tax reduction in order to report higher profits in their financial statements.[10]
- *Regulatory considerations.* Since accounting numbers are used by regulators in a variety of contexts, managers of some firms may make accounting decisions to influence regulatory outcomes. Examples of regulatory situations where accounting numbers are used include antitrust actions, import tariffs to protect domestic industries, and tax policies.[11]
- *Capital market considerations.* Managers may make accounting decisions to influence the perceptions of capital markets. When there are information asymmetries between managers and outsiders, this strategy may succeed in influencing investor perceptions, at least temporarily.[12]
- *Stakeholder considerations.* Managers may also make accounting decisions to influence the perception of important stakeholders in the firm. For example, since labor unions can use healthy profits as a basis for demanding wage increases, managers may make accounting decisions to decrease income when they are facing union contract negotiations. In countries like Germany, where labor unions are

strong, these considerations appear to play an important role in firms' accounting policy. Other important stakeholders that firms may wish to influence through their financial reports include suppliers and customers.

- *Competitive considerations.* The dynamics of competition in an industry might also influence a firm's reporting choices. For example, a firm's segment disclosure decisions may be influenced by its concern that disaggregated disclosure may help competitors in their business decisions. Similarly, firms may not disclose data on their margins by product line for fear of giving away proprietary information. Finally, firms may discourage new entrants by making income-decreasing accounting choices.

In addition to accounting policy choices and estimates, the level of disclosure is also an important determinant of a firm's accounting quality. Corporate managers can choose disclosure policies that make it more or less costly for external users of financial reports to understand the true economic picture of their businesses. Accounting regulations usually prescribe minimum disclosure requirements, but they do not restrict managers from voluntarily providing additional disclosures. Managers can use various parts of the financial reports, including the Letter to the Shareholders, Management Discussion and Analysis, and footnotes, to describe the company's strategy, its accounting policies, and the firm's current performance. There is wide variation across firms in how managers use their disclosure flexibility.[13]

DOING ACCOUNTING ANALYSIS

In this section we will discuss a series of steps that an analyst can follow to evaluate a firm's accounting quality. Later in the chapter, an analysis of Compaq's accounting quality in 1992 is presented to illustrate the application of the concepts discussed.

Step 1: Identify Key Accounting Policies

As discussed in the chapter on business strategy analysis, a firm's industry characteristics and its own competitive strategy determine its key success factors and risks. One of the goals of financial statement analysis is to evaluate how well these success factors and risks are being managed by the firm. In accounting analysis, therefore, the analyst should identify and evaluate the policies and the estimates the firm uses to measure its critical factors and risks.

For example, one of the key success factors in the leasing business is to make accurate forecasts of residual values of the leased equipment at the end of the lease terms. For a firm in the equipment leasing industry, therefore, one of the most important accounting policies is the way residual values are recorded. Residual values influence the company's reported profits and its asset base. If residual values are over-estimated, the firm runs the risk of having to take large write-offs in the future.

Key success factors in the banking industry include interest and credit risk management; in the retail industry, inventory management is a key success factor; and for a manufacturer competing on product quality and innovation, research and development and product defects after the sale are key areas of concern. In each of these cases, the analyst has to identify the accounting measures the firm uses to capture these business constructs, the policies that determine how the measures are implemented, and the key estimates embedded in these policies. For example, the accounting measure a bank uses to capture credit risk is its loan loss reserves, and the accounting measure that captures product quality for a manufacturer is its warranty expenses and reserves.

Step 2: Assess Accounting Flexibility

Not all firms have equal flexibility in choosing their key accounting policies and estimates. Some firms' accounting choice is severely constrained by accounting standards and conventions. For example, even though research and development is a key success factor for biotechnology companies, managers have no accounting discretion in reporting on this activity. Similarly, even though marketing and brand building are key to the success of consumer goods firms, they are required to expense all their marketing outlays. In contrast, managing credit risk is one of the critical success factors for banks, and bank managers have the freedom to estimate expected defaults on their loans. Similarly, software developers have the flexibility to decide at what points in their development cycles the outlays can be capitalized.

If managers have little flexibility in choosing accounting policies and estimates related to their key success factors (as in the case of biotechnology firms), accounting data are likely to be not as informative for understanding the firm's economics. In contrast, if managers have considerable flexibility in choosing the policies and estimates (as in the case of software developers), accounting numbers have the potential to be informative, depending upon how managers exercise this flexibility.

Regardless of the degree of accounting flexibility a firm's managers have in measuring their key success factors and risks, they will have some flexibility with respect to several other accounting policies. For example, all firms have to make choices with respect to depreciation policy (straight-line or accelerated methods), inventory accounting policy (LIFO, FIFO, or Average Cost), policy for amortizing goodwill (write-off over forty years or less), and policies regarding the estimation of pension and other post-employment benefits (expected return on plan assets, discount rate for liabilities, and rate of increase in wages and health care costs). Since all these policy choices can have a significant impact on the reported performance of a firm, they offer an opportunity for the firm to manage its reported numbers.

Step 3: Evaluate Accounting Strategy

When managers have accounting flexibility, they can use it either to communicate their firm's economic situation or to hide true performance. Some of the strategy questions one could ask in examining how managers exercise their accounting flexibility include the following:

- How do the firm's accounting policies compare to the norms in the industry? If they are dissimilar, is it because the firm's competitive strategy is unique? For example, consider a firm that reports a lower warranty allowance than the industry average. One explanation is that the firm competes on the basis of high quality and has invested considerable resources to reduce the rate of product failure. An alternative explanation is that the firm is merely understating its warranty liabilities.
- Does management face strong incentives to use accounting discretion for earnings management? For example, is the firm close to violating bond covenants? Or, are the managers having difficulty meeting accounting-based bonus targets? Does management own significant stock? Is the firm in the middle of a proxy fight or union negotiations? Managers may also make accounting decisions to reduce tax payments, or to influence the perceptions of the firm's competitors.
- Has the firm changed any of its policies or estimates? What is the justification? What is the impact of these changes? For example, if warranty expenses decreased, is it because the firm made significant investments to improve quality?
- Have the company's policies and estimates been realistic in the past? For example, firms may overstate their revenues and understate their expenses during the year by manipulating quarterly reports, which are not subject to a full-blown external audit. However, the auditing process at the end of the fiscal year forces such companies to make large fourth-quarter adjustments, providing an opportunity for the analyst to assess the quality of the firm's interim reporting. Similarly, firms that expense acquisition goodwill too slowly will be forced to take a large write-off later. A history of write-offs may be, therefore, a sign of prior earnings management.
- Does the firm structure any significant business transactions so that it can achieve certain accounting objectives? For example, leasing firms can alter lease terms (the length of the lease or the bargain purchase option at the end of the lease term) so that the transactions qualify as sales-type leases for the lessors. Firms may structure a takeover transaction (equity financing rather than debt financing) so that they can use the pooling of interests method rather than the purchase method of accounting. Finally, a firm can alter the way it finances (coupon rate and the terms of conversion for a convertible bond issue) so that its reported earnings per share is not diluted. Such behavior may suggest that the firm's managers are willing to expend economic resources merely to achieve an accounting objective.

Step 4: Evaluate the Quality of Disclosure

Managers can make it more or less easy for an analyst to assess the firm's accounting quality and to use its financial statements to understand business reality. While accounting rules require a certain amount of minimum disclosure, managers have considerable choice in the matter. Disclosure quality, therefore, is an important dimension of a firm's accounting quality.

In assessing a firm's disclosure quality, an analyst could ask the following questions:

- Does the company provide adequate disclosures to assess the firm's business strategy and its economic consequences? For example, some firms use the Letter to the Shareholders in their annual report to clearly lay out the firm's industry conditions, its competitive position, and management's plans for the future. Others use the Letter to puff up the firm's financial performance and gloss over any competitive difficulties the firm might be facing.

- Do the footnotes adequately explain the key accounting policies and assumptions and their logic? For example, if a firm's revenue and expense recognition policies differ from industry norms, the firm can explain its choices in a footnote. Similarly, when there are significant changes in a firm's policies, footnotes can be used to disclose the reasons.

- Does the firm adequately explain its current performance? The Management Discussion and Analysis section of the firm's annual report provides an opportunity to help analysts understand the reasons behind the firm's performance changes. Some firms use this section to link financial performance to business conditions. For example, if profit margins went down in a period, was it because of price competition or because of increases in manufacturing costs? If the selling and general administrative expenses went up, was it because the firm is investing in a differentiation strategy, or because unproductive overhead expenses were creeping up?

- If accounting rules and conventions restrict the firm from measuring its key success factors appropriately, does the firm provide adequate additional disclosure to help outsiders understand how these factors are being managed? For example, if a firm invests in product quality and customer service, accounting rules do not allow the management to capitalize these outlays, even when the future benefits are certain. The firm's Management Discussion and Analysis can be used to highlight how these outlays are being managed and their performance consequences. For example, the firm can disclose physical indexes of defect rates and customer satisfaction so that outsiders can assess the progress being made in these areas and the future cash flow consequences of these actions.

- If a firm is in multiple business segments, what is the quality of segment disclosure? Some firms provide excellent discussion of their performance by product segments and geographic segments. Others lump many different businesses into one broad segment. The level of competition in an industry and management's willingness to share desegregated performance data influence a firm's quality of segment disclosure.

- How forthcoming is the management with respect to bad news? A firm's disclosure quality is most clearly revealed by the way management deals with bad news. Does it adequately explain the reasons for poor performance? Does the company clearly articulate its strategy, if any, to address the company's performance problems?

- How good is the firm's investor relations program? Does the firm provide fact books with detailed data on the firm's business and performance? Is the management accessible to analysts?

Step 5: Identify Potential Red Flags

In addition to the above analysis, a common approach to accounting quality analysis is to look for "red flags" pointing to questionable accounting quality. These indicators suggest that the analyst should examine certain items more closely or gather more information on them. Some common red flags are:

- *Unexplained changes in accounting, especially when performance is poor.* This may suggest that managers are using their accounting discretion to "dress up" their financial statements.[14]
- *Unexplained transactions that boost profits.* For example, firms might undertake balance sheet transactions, such as asset sales or debt for equity swaps, to realize gains in periods when operating performance is poor.[15]
- *Unusual increases in accounts receivable in relation to sales increases.* This may suggest that the company might be relaxing its credit policies or artificially loading up its distribution channels to record revenues during the current period. If credit policies are relaxed unduly, the firm may face receivable write-offs in the subsequent periods as a result of customer defaults. If the firm accelerates shipments to the distribution channels, it may either face product returns or reduced shipments in the subsequent periods.
- *Unusual increases in inventories in relation to sales increases.* If the inventory build-up is due to an increase in finished goods inventory, it could be a sign that the demand for the firm's products is slowing down, suggesting that the firm may be forced to cut prices (and hence earn lower margins) or write down its inventory. A build-up in work-in-progress inventory tends to be good news on average, probably signaling that managers expect an increase in sales. If the build-up is in raw materials, it could suggest manufacturing or procurement inefficiencies, leading to an increase in cost of goods sold (and hence lower margins).[16]
- *An increasing gap between a firm's reported income and its cash flow from operating activities.* While it is legitimate for accrual accounting numbers to differ from cash flows, there is usually a steady relationship between the two if the company's accounting policies remain the same. Therefore, any *change* in the relationship between reported profits and operating cash flows might indicate subtle changes in the firm's accrual estimates. For example, a firm undertaking large construction contracts might use the percentage-of-completion method to record revenues. While earnings and operating cash flows are likely to differ for such a firm, they should bear a steady relationship to each other. Now suppose the firm increases revenues in a period through an aggressive application of the percentage-of-comple-

tion method. Then its earnings will go up, but its cash flow remains unaffected. This change in the firm's accounting quality will be manifested by a *change* in the relationship between the firm's earnings and cash flows.

- *An increasing gap between a firm's reported income and its tax income.* Once again, it is quite legitimate for a firm to follow different accounting policies for financial reporting and tax accounting, as long as the tax law allows it.[17] However, the relationship between a firm's book and tax accounting is likely to remain constant over time, unless there are significant changes in tax rules or accounting standards. Thus, an *increasing* gap between a firm's reported income and its tax income may indicate that the firm's financial reporting to shareholders has become more aggressive. As an example, consider that warranty expenses are estimated on an accrual basis for financial reporting, but are recorded on a cash basis for tax reporting. Unless there is a big change in the firm's product quality, these two numbers bear a consistent relationship to each other. Therefore, a change in this relationship can be an indication either that the product quality is changing significantly or that financial reporting estimates are changing.

- *A tendency to use financing mechanisms like research and development partnerships and the sale of receivables with recourse.* While these arrangements may have a sound business logic, they can also provide management with an opportunity to understate the firm's liabilities and/or overstate its assets.[18]

- *Unexpected large asset write-offs.* This may suggest that management is slow to incorporate changing business circumstances into its accounting estimates. Asset write-offs may also be a result of unexpected changes in business circumstances.[19]

- *Large fourth-quarter adjustments.* A firm's annual reports are audited by the external auditors, but its interim financial statements are usually only reviewed. If a firm's management is reluctant to make appropriate accounting estimates (such as provisions for uncollectable receivables) in its interim statements, it could be forced to make adjustments at the end of the year as a result of pressure from its external auditors. A consistent pattern of fourth-quarter adjustments, therefore, may indicate an aggressive management orientation towards interim reporting.[20]

- *Qualified audit opinions or changes in independent auditors that are not well justified.* These may indicate a firm's aggressive attitude or a tendency to "opinion shop."

- *Related-party transactions or transactions between related entities.* These transactions may lack the objectivity of the marketplace, and managers' accounting estimates related to these transactions are likely to be more subjective and potentially self-serving.

While the preceding list provides a number of red flags for potentially poor accounting quality, it is important to do further analysis before reaching final conclusions. Each of the red flags has multiple interpretations; some interpretations are based on sound business reasons, and others indicate questionable accounting. It is, therefore, best to use the red flag analysis as a starting point for further probing, not as an end point in itself.[21]

Step 6: Undo Accounting Distortions

If the accounting analysis suggests that the firm's reported numbers are misleading, analysts should attempt to restate the reported numbers to reduce the distortion to the extent possible. It is, of course, virtually impossible to undo all the distortion using outside information alone. However, some progress can be made in this direction by using the cash flow statement and the financial statement footnotes.

A firm's cash flow statement provides a reconciliation of its performance based on accrual accounting and cash accounting. If the analyst is unsure of the quality of the firm's accrual accounting, the cash flow statement provides an alternative benchmark of its performance. The cash flow statement also provides information on how individual line items in the income statement diverge from the underlying cash flows. For example, if an analyst is concerned that the firm is aggressively capitalizing certain costs that should be expensed, the information in the cash flow statement provides a basis to make the necessary adjustment.

Financial statement footnotes also provide a lot of information that is potentially useful in restating reported accounting numbers. For example, when a firm changes its accounting policies, it provides a footnote indicating the effect of that change if it is material. Similarly, some firms provide information on the details of accrual estimates such as the allowance for bad debts. The tax footnote usually provides information on the differences between a firm's accounting policies for shareholder reporting and tax reporting. Since tax reporting is often more conservative than shareholder reporting, the information in the tax footnote can be used to estimate what the earnings reported to shareholders would be under more conservative policies.

ACCOUNTING ANALYSIS PITFALLS

There are several potential pitfalls in accounting analysis that an analyst should avoid. First, it is important to remember that from an analyst's perspective, conservative accounting is not the same as "good" accounting. Financial analysts are interested in evaluating how well a firm's accounting captures business reality in an unbiased manner, and conservative accounting can be as misleading as aggressive accounting in this respect. Further, conservative accounting often provides managers with opportunities for "income smoothing." Income smoothing may prevent analysts from recognizing poor performance in a timely fashion.

A second potential mistake is to confuse unusual accounting with questionable accounting. While unusual accounting choices might make a firm's performance difficult to compare with other firms' performance, such an accounting choice might be justified if the company's business is unusual. For example, firms that follow differentiated strategies, or firms that structure their business in an innovative manner to take advantage of particular market situations may make unusual accounting choices to properly reflect their business. Therefore, it is important to evaluate a company's accounting choices in the context of its business strategy.

Another potential pitfall in accounting analysis arises when an analyst attributes all changes in a firm's accounting policies and accruals to earnings management motives.[22] Accounting changes might be merely reflecting changed business circumstances. For example, as already discussed, a firm that shows unusual increases in its inventory might be preparing for a new product introduction. Similarly, unusual increases in receivables might merely be due to changes in a firm's sales strategy. Unusual decreases in the allowance for uncollectable receivables might be reflecting a firm's changed customer focus. It is therefore important for an analyst to consider all possible explanations for accounting changes and investigate them using the qualitative information available in a firm's financial statements.

APPLICATION OF ACCOUNTING ANALYSIS CONCEPTS TO COMPAQ COMPUTER CORPORATION

As discussed in the prior chapter on Business Strategy Analysis, Compaq's strategy in the personal computer industry in 1992 was to compete as a low-cost producer with a high quality and service image. Compaq sold its computers through large computer retailers. The key success factors for Compaq, therefore, were: (1) keeping manufacturing costs and administrative overhead low, (2) investing in product quality and service, and (3) keeping good relations with its retailers. In this section, we will analyze Compaq's accounting quality in its 1992 financial statements as a way to apply the concepts discussed above.[23]

Since Compaq's business was essentially assembling components into a personal computer and marketing it, its operating cycle (the time from purchasing materials to collecting cash from its customers) was relatively short. As a result, the firm faced few complex choices in its accrual accounting. Some of Compaq's key accounting policies and estimates were:

- *Accounting for inventory.* Compaq used FIFO accounting, which is normally a less conservative policy than LIFO. However, since prices of inputs and outputs in the personal computer industry have been decreasing, FIFO is a more conservative accounting choice for Compaq.
- *Revenue recognition.* Compaq sold computers to retailers, and recognized revenue upon shipping the computers. While this is standard practice, Compaq faced some risks with this policy. First, Compaq allowed for returns of computers sold, and it had to estimate them properly. In the personal computer industry, where technology changes rapidly, there was a risk of inventory obsolescence being borne by Compaq. Second, Compaq guaranteed financing of the inventory by some of its distributors. (See the footnote on Commitments and Contingencies in Compaq's annual report.) As a result, the company was essentially financing its distributors and hence was bearing the risk of customer defaults to an extent greater than indicated by its accounts receivable on the balance sheet.
- *Outlays on new product development, quality, and customer service.* While these

are some of the critical success factors for Compaq, accounting rules provided little flexibility to Compaq's management in dealing with these outlays, so Compaq expensed all such outlays when incurred. As a result, an analyst has to rely on information outside the financial statements in assessing how effective these activities were.

- *Warranty expenses.* The company had a policy of producing high quality products. To assure customers of its confidence in its product quality, Compaq offered warranties on its products. The warranty liability associated with current period sales, therefore, was an important accounting estimate for Compaq. The warranty reserve, as indicated in the Note 7, Other Current Liabilities, increased by 87 percent from $39 million in 1991 to $73 million in 1992, even though sales increased by only 25 percent. Some of the increase in warranty reserve in 1992 was attributable to a new three-year warranty Compaq began offering that year. It is also possible that the reserve in 1991 was unusually low. It would be useful to probe this issue further to fully understand the nature of this estimate.

- *Allowance for doubtful accounts.* As mentioned earlier, since the company recognized revenues when it shipped products to computer retailers, there was some default risk associated with its receivables. The allowance for doubtful accounts was 2.9 percent of the receivables in 1991, but it dropped to 2.5 percent in 1992. What was the reason for this change? Did the company take steps to improve its credit screening, or was the company not providing for adequate reserves? Or, was the company merely responding to the improved credit situation of its customers because of the overall improvement in the economy?

In addition to the above items, the following red flags could be investigated further:

- Compaq's accounts receivable to sales ratio increased from 19 percent in 1991 to 24 percent in 1992. Similarly, the inventory to sales ratio increased from 13 to 20 percent in 1992. While both these increases may be attributable to the many new products that Compaq introduced in 1992, it would be useful to probe this issue further.

- Compaq sold its equity interest in Connor Peripherals in 1992, recording a gain of about $85.7 million dollars. This gain accounts for a large part of the $141 million increase in Compaq's pre-tax income between 1991 and 1992. The company did not provide a sound explanation for the timing of this asset sale.

- The company's tax footnote shows that the difference between warranty expense recognized for financial reporting and tax reporting changed dramatically between 1990, 1991, and 1992. Deferred taxes arising out of this item were negative $2.95 million in 1990, $.098 million in 1991, and negative $6.68 million in 1992, consistent with our prior analysis that the provision in financial reports was unusually low in 1991. Once again, this issue needs to be investigated further.

Compaq's disclosure was generally adequate, but not excellent. The company provided a good description of its strategy, why its gross margins declined in 1992, how it managed its operating expenses during that year, and the factors that were likely to influence the company's future performance. However, Compaq did not provide a good explanation for a number of issues raised above. For example, why did Compaq's accounts receivable and inventory increase significantly in 1992? Why did it reduce its allowance for doubtful accounts as a proportion of accounts receivable? Why did it sell its stake in Connor Peripherals in 1992? Also, the company provided neither an adequate discussion of the potential threats to the sustainability of its competitive advantage in its industry, nor the steps the company was taking to protect its position.

In reaching a final conclusion on Compaq's accounting quality, it is important to assess management's motivations in 1992. The company reported a dramatic drop in earnings in 1991, and a new management team was subsequently put in place. The new management was implementing a turnaround strategy during 1992. It is likely that Compaq's managers were keen on showing that their restructuring strategy was paying off so that they could rally the company's suppliers, customers, employees, and investors behind the new management team. Compaq's top managers were also compensated based on the company's accounting profits. All these factors could have motivated Compaq's managers to use their accounting discretion to increase reported income in 1992. Therefore, while there may have been a real improvement in the company's fundamentals, reported results in 1992 may have also been helped by its accounting.

SUMMARY AND CONCLUSIONS

In summary, accounting analysis is an important step in the process of analyzing corporate financial reports. The purpose of accounting analysis is to evaluate the degree to which a firm's accounting captures the underlying business reality. Sound accounting analysis improves the reliability of conclusions from financial analysis, the next step in financial statement analysis.

There are six key steps in accounting analysis. The analyst begins by identifying the key accounting policies and estimates, given the firm's industry and its business strategy. The second step is to evaluate the degree of flexibility available to managers, given the accounting rules and conventions. Next, the analyst has to evaluate how managers exercise their accounting flexibility and the likely motivations behind managers' accounting strategy. The fourth step involves assessing the depth and quality of a firm's disclosures. The analyst should next identify any red flags needing further investigation. The final accounting analysis step is to restate accounting numbers to remove any noise and bias introduced by the accounting rules and management decisions.

DISCUSSION QUESTIONS

1. A finance student states: "I don't understand why anyone pays any attention to accounting earnings numbers, given that a 'clean' number like cash from operations is readily available." Do you agree? Why or why not?

2. Most airlines have frequent flyer programs that promise customers free flights, once they have accumulated 25,000 miles of travel with the same airline. Using the simple definitions of assets, liabilities, revenues, and expenses presented in this chapter, how should these programs be reflected in the airlines' financial statements?

3. If there are no accounting standards on reporting for frequent flyer programs, what incentives are likely to drive management's choice of accounting for these transactions?

4. Fred argues: "The standards that I like most are the ones that eliminate all management discretion in reporting—that way I get uniform numbers across all companies and don't have to worry about doing accounting analysis." Do you agree? Why or why not?

5. Bill Simon says: "We should get rid of the FASB and SEC, since free market forces will make sure that companies report reliable information." Do you agree? Why or why not?

6. Many firms recognize revenues at the point of shipment. This provides an incentive to accelerate revenues by shipping goods at the end of the quarter. Consider two companies, one of which ships its product evenly throughout the quarter, and the second of which ships all its products in the last two weeks of the quarter. Each company's customers pay thirty days after receiving shipment. How can you distinguish these companies, using accounting ratios?

7. a. If management reports truthfully, what economic events are likely to prompt the following accounting changes?
   - Increase in the estimated life of depreciable assets
   - Decrease in the allowance for uncollectibles as a percentage of gross receivables
   - Recognition of revenues at the point of delivery, rather than at the point cash is received
   - Capitalization of a higher proportion of software R&D costs

   b. What features of accounting, if any, would make it costly for dishonest managers to make the same changes without any corresponding economic changes?

8. The conservatism principle arises because of concerns about management's incentives to overstate the firm's performance. Joe Banks argues: "We could get rid of conservatism and make accounting numbers more useful if we delegated financial reporting to independent auditors, rather than to corporate managers." Do you agree? Why or why not?"

9. A fund manager states: "I refuse to buy any company that makes a voluntary accounting change, since it's certainly the case that its management is trying to hide bad news." Can you think of any alternative interpretation?

CASES

America Online, Inc.
Kansas City Zephyrs Baseball Club, Inc.

NOTES

1. Accounting analysis is sometimes also called quality of earnings analysis. We prefer to use the term accounting analysis, since we are discussing a broader concept than merely a firm's earnings quality.

2. These definitions paraphrase the definitions by the Financial Accounting Standards Board, Statement of Financial Accounting Concepts No. 6, "Elements of Financial Statements" (1985). Our intent is to present the definitions at a conceptual, not technical, level. For more complete discussion of these and related concepts, see the FASB's *Statements of Financial Accounting Concepts*.

3. Strictly speaking, the comprehensive net income of a firm also includes gains and losses from increases and decreases in equity from non-operating activities or extraordinary items.

4. Thus, although accrual accounting is theoretically superior to cash accounting in measuring a firm's periodic performance, the distortions it introduces can make accounting data less valuable to users. If these distortions are large enough, current cash flows may measure a firm's periodic performance better than accounting profits. The relative usefulness of cash flows and accounting profits in measuring performance, therefore, varies from firm to firm. For empirical evidence on this issue, see "Accounting earnings and cash flows as measures of firm performance: The role of accounting accruals" by Patricia M. Dechow, *Journal of Accounting and Economics* 18, 1994.

5. For example, Abraham Brilloff published a series of accounting analyses of public companies in *Barron's* magazine over several years. On average, the stock prices of the analyzed companies changed by about 8 percent on the day these articles were published, indicating the potential value of performing such analysis. For a more complete discussion of this evidence, see "Brilloff and the Capital Market: Further Evidence" by George Foster, Stanford University working paper, 1985.

6. For a complete discussion of these motivations, see *Positive Accounting Theory* by Ross L. Watts and Jerold L. Zimmerman (Englewood Cliffs, NJ: Prentice-Hall, 1986).

7. The most convincing evidence supporting the covenant hypothesis is reported in a study of the accounting decisions by firms in financial distress: "Debt-covenenat violations and managers' accounting responses," Amy Patricia Sweeney, *Journal of Accounting and Economics* 17, 1994.

8. A number of studies examine the bonus hypothesis and report evidence consistent with the view that managers' accounting decisions are influenced by compensation considerations. See, for example, "The effect of bonus schemes on accounting decisions," Paul M. Healy, *Journal of Accounting and Economics* 12, 1985.

9. "Managerial competition, information costs, and corporate governance: The use of accounting performance measures in proxy contests," Linda DeAngelo, *Journal of Accounting and Economics* 10, 1988.

10. The trade-off between taxes and financial reporting in the context of managers' accounting decisions is discussed in detail in *Taxes and Business Strategy* by Myron Scholes and Mark Wolfson (Englewood Cliffs, NJ: Prentice-Hall, 1992). Many empirical studies have examined firms' LIFO/FIFO choice.

11. Several researchers have documented that firms affected by such situations have a motivation to influence regulators' perceptions through their accounting decisions. For example, Jones documents that firms seeking import protections make income-decreasing accounting decisions in "Earnings management during import relief investigations," J. Jones, *Journal of Accounting Research* 29, 1991.

12. "The effect of firms' financial disclosure strategies on stock prices," Paul Healy and Krishna Palepu, *Accounting Horizons* 7, 1993. See also "Causes and consequences of aggressive finan-

cial reporting," P. Dechow, R. Sloan, and A. Sweeney, *Contemporary Accounting Research,* forthcoming.

13. Financial analysts pay considerable attention to managers' disclosure strategies; the Financial Analysts' Federation publishes annually a report evaluating U.S. firms' disclosure strategies. For a discussion of these ratings, see "Cross-sectional Determinants of Analysts' Ratings of Corporate Disclosures" by Mark Lang and Russ Lundholm, *Journal of Accounting Research* 31, Autumn 1993: 246–271.

14. For a detailed analysis of a company that made such changes, see "Anatomy of an Accounting Change" by Krishna Palepu in *Accounting & Management: Field Study Perspectives,* edited by William J. Bruns, Jr., and Robert S. Kaplan (Boston: Harvard Business School Press, 1987).

15. An example of this type of behavior is documented by John Hand in his study, "Did Firms Undertake Debt-Equity Swaps for an Accounting Paper Profit or True Financial Gain?," *The Accounting Review* 64, October 1989.

16. For an empirical analysis of inventory build-ups, see "Do Inventory Disclosures Predict Sales and Earnings?" by Victor Bernard and James Noel, *Journal of Accounting, Auditing, and Finance,* Fall 1991.

17. This is true by and large in the United States and in several other countries. However, in some countries, such as Germany and Japan, tax accounting and financial reporting are closely tied together, and this particular red flag is not very meaningful.

18. For research on accounting and economic incentives motivating the formation of R&D partnerships, see "Motives for Forming Research and Development Financing Organizations," by Anne Beatty, Philip G. Berger, and Joseph Magliolo, *Journal of Accounting & Economics* 19, 1995.

19. For an empirical examination of asset-write-offs, see "Write-offs as Accounting Procedures to Manage Perceptions" by John A. Elliott and Wayne H. Shaw, *Journal of Accounting Research,* Supplement, 1988.

20. Richard R. Mendenhall and William D. Nichols report evidence consistent with the hypothesis that managers take advantage of their discretion to postpone reporting bad news until the fourth quarter. See "Bad News and Differential Market Reactions to Announcements of Earlier-Quarter versus Fourth-Quarter Earnings," *Journal of Accounting Research,* Supplement, 1988.

21. This type of analysis is presented in the context of provisions for bad debts by Maureen McNichols and G. Peter Wilson in their study, "Evidence of Earnings Management from the Provisions for Bad Debts," *Journal of Accounting Research,* Supplement, 1988.

22. This point has been made by several accounting researchers. For a summary of research on earnings management, see "Earnings Management" by Katherine Schipper, *Accounting Horizons,* December 1989: 91–102.

23. Most of the 1992 Annual Report for Compaq Computer Corporation is given in Part 5 at the end of the text.

chapter 4

Financial Analysis

The goal of financial analysis is to assess the performance of a firm in the context of its stated goals and strategy. There are two principal tools of financial analysis: ratio analysis and cash flow analysis. Ratio analysis involves assessing how various line items in a firm's financial statements relate to one another. Cash flow analysis allows the analyst to examine the firm's liquidity and how the firm is managing its operating, investing, and financing cash flows.

Financial analysis is used in a variety of contexts. As we will discuss in later chapters, financial analysis is useful in credit evaluation, financial distress prediction, security analysis, mergers and acquisitions analysis, and corporate financial policy analysis. In all these contexts, financial analysis is a key input for making sound predictions about a company's future prospects.

RATIO ANALYSIS

The value of a firm is determined by its profitability and growth. As Figure 4-1 shows, a firm's profitability and growth are influenced by its product market and financial market strategies. The product market strategy is implemented through the firm's operating policies and investment strategies. Financial market strategies are implemented through financing and dividend policies.

The four levers managers can use to achieve their growth and profit targets are (1) operating management, (2) investment management, (3) financing strategy, and (4) dividend policies. The objective of ratio analysis is to evaluate the effectiveness of the firm's policies in each of these areas. Effective ratio analysis involves relating the financial numbers to the underlying business factors in as much detail as possible. While ratio analysis may not give an analyst all the answers regarding a firm's performance, it will help the analyst frame questions for further probing.

Figure 4-1 Drivers of a Firm's Profitability and Growth

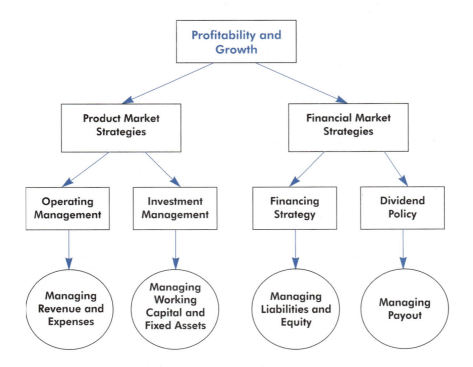

In ratio analysis, the analyst can (1) compare ratios for a firm over several years (a time-series comparison), (2) compare ratios for the firm and other firms in the industry (cross-sectional comparison), and/or (3) compare ratios to some absolute benchmark. In a time-series comparison, the analyst can hold firm-specific factors constant and examine the effectiveness of a firm's strategy over time. Cross-sectional comparison facilitates examining the relative performance of a firm within its industry, holding industry-level factors constant. For most ratios, there are no absolute benchmarks. The exceptions are measures of rates of return, which can be compared to the cost of the capital associated with the investment. For example, subject to distortions caused by accounting, the rate of return on equity (ROE) can be compared to the cost of equity capital.

In our discussion below, we will use Compaq Computer Corporation to illustrate these approaches. We will compare Compaq's ratios in 1992 with its own ratios in 1991 and with the 1992 ratios for Apple and Dell, two other prominent personal computer companies.[1] Recall from Chapter 2 that Compaq was the leading seller of IBM-compatible personal computers, and followed a volume-driven low-cost strategy. Compaq tried to differentiate itself from other personal computer makers through quality, innovation, and service. Dell was the second largest producer of IBM clones. Unlike Compaq, Dell competed purely on a cost basis. Apple, in contrast, competed on the basis of differentiation. Apple's computers were not IBM compatible, and they used a distinct microprocessor and software.

Measuring Overall Profitability: Return on Equity

The starting point for a systematic analysis of a firm's performance is its return on equity (ROE), defined as:

$$\text{ROE} = \frac{\text{Net income}}{\text{Shareholders equity}}$$

ROE is a comprehensive indicator of a firm's performance because it provides an indication of how well managers are employing the funds invested by the firm's shareholders to generate returns. On average over long periods, large publicly traded firms in the U.S. generate ROEs in the range of 11 to 13 percent.

In the long run, the value of the firm's equity is determined by the relationship between its ROE and its cost of equity capital.[2] That is, those firms that are expected over the long run to generate ROEs in excess of the cost of equity capital should have market values in excess of book value, and vice versa. (We will return to this point in more detail in Chapter 6.)

A comparison of ROE with the cost of capital is useful not only for contemplating the value of the firm, but also in considering the path of future profitability. The generation of consistent supernormal profitability will, absent significant barriers to entry, attract competition. For that reason, ROEs tend over time to be driven by competitive forces toward a "normal" level—the cost of equity capital. Thus, one can think of the cost of equity capital as establishing a benchmark for the ROE that would be observed in a long-run competitive equilibrium. Deviations from this level arise for two general reasons. One is the industry conditions and competitive strategy that cause a firm to generate supernormal (or subnormal) economic profits, at least over the short run. The second is distortions due to accounting.

Table 4-1 shows the ROE for Compaq, Apple Computer, and Dell. The first row in the table displays ROE based on reported earnings. In the second row, we recalculate ROE, excluding some gains and losses that are unlikely to reoccur and that do not reflect the product of ongoing operations. For Compaq, we exclude its gain on the sale of Conner Peripherals, Inc. in 1992, and its restructuring charges in 1991 and 1992.[3] These adjustments are only intended to be illustrative, and are not the only ones an analyst might make. The approach presented in Chapter 3 raises several issues that, depending on investigation, might cause an analyst to make further adjustments. There are no adjustments for Apple or Dell, because they disclosed no unusual, nonoperating gains or losses for 1992.

Regardless of whether we look at adjusted or unadjusted amounts in either 1991 or 1992, Compaq's ROE was lower than reasonable estimates of the cost of equity capital

Table 4-1 Return on Equity for Compaq and Selected Competitors

Ratio	Compaq 1991	Compaq 1992	Apple 1992	Dell 1992
Return on equity	6.8%	10.6%	24.2%	27.5%
Return on equity, adjusted for unusual gains/losses	11.0%	10.2%	24.2%	27.5%

for a firm in an industry as risky as the PC industry. (In Chapter 6, we will estimate that Compaq's cost of equity capital lies in the range of 12 to 15 percent.) Moreover, even though the *reported* earnings suggest a major improvement at Compaq, there is none evident in the adjusted amounts. The reason is that the reported improvement was largely due to a reduction in restructuring charges and a gain on the sale of Conner, as opposed to an improvement in operations.

Understanding Profit Drivers: Decomposing ROE

Compaq's ROE in 1992 was not only less than the cost of capital, it was also less than that of Apple (24.2%) and Dell (27.5%). In the following paragraphs we will attempt to gain a deeper understanding of why Compaq's ROE in 1992 differs from its own ROE in 1991, and from the ROEs of Apple and Dell.

A company's ROE is affected by two factors: how profitably it employs its assets and how big the firm's asset base is relative to shareholders' investment. To understand the effect of these two factors, ROE can be decomposed into return on assets (ROA) and a measure of financial leverage, as follows:

$$\text{ROE} = \text{ROA} \times \text{Financial leverage}$$

$$= \frac{\text{Net income}}{\text{Assets}} \times \frac{\text{Assets}}{\text{Shareholders' equity}}$$

ROA tells us how much profit a company is able to generate for each dollar of assets invested. Financial leverage indicates how many dollars of assets the firm is able to deploy for each dollar invested by its shareholders.

The measure of ROA shown above is commonly used, but it involves an internal inconsistency. Specifically, the denominator includes the assets claimed by all providers of capital to the firm, but the numerator includes only the earnings available to equity holders. An alternative measure of ROA begins to deal with this problem by expressing profits on a pre-interest basis. The numerator then can be labeled EBILAT, or earnings before interest, less adjusted taxes. The term "adjusted taxes" reflects the fact that we add back to net income the tax benefit of the interest expense deduction[4]:

$$\text{Pre-interest ROA} \; = \; \frac{\text{EBILAT}}{\text{Assets}} \; = \; \frac{\text{Net income} + \text{Interest expense} \times (1 - \text{tax rate})}{\text{Assets}}$$

Even the pre-interest ROA suffers from a shortcoming, in that the numerator reflects the returns available only to equity holders and holders of interest-bearing debt, and yet the denominator includes *all* assets—even those financed with non-interest-bearing debt. Another alternative measure is return on net assets (RONA), or return on capital (ROC), which uses EBILAT in the numerator and places equity and interesting-bearing debt in the denominator[5]:

$$\text{RONA (or ROC)} \; = \; \frac{\text{Net income} + \text{Interest expense} \times (1 - \text{Tax rate})}{\text{Equity} + \text{Debt}}$$

The appropriate benchmark for evaluating RONA (or ROC) is the weighted average cost of debt and equity capital, or WACC. In the long run, the value of the firm is determined by where RONA (or ROC) stands relative to this norm. Moreover, over the long run, and absent some barrier to competitive forces, RONA will tend to be pushed towards the weighted average cost of capital. Since the WACC is lower than the cost of equity capital, RONA (or ROC) tends to be pushed to a level lower than that to which ROE tends. The average RONA (or ROC) for large firms in the U.S., over long periods of time, is in the range of 9 to 11 percent.

A fourth measure of asset returns, called operating ROA, focuses on operating returns only and excludes any income earned by the firm from its cash and short-term investments. The appropriate denominator for this return is debt plus equity minus cash and short-term investments.[6]

$$\text{Operating ROA} \; = $$

$$\frac{\text{Net income} + (\text{Interest expense} - \text{Interest income}) \times (1 - \text{Tax rate})}{\text{Equity} + \text{Debt} - \text{Cash and short-term investments}}$$

The four alternative return on asset measures are presented in Table 4-2 for Compaq, Apple, and Dell. The pre-interest ROA does not differ significantly from the ROA because none of the firms have much interest-bearing debt. However, RONA and Operating ROA differ significantly from ROA for all the firms.

We can see that Compaq's RONA and its operating ROA were less than any reasonable estimate of its weighted average cost of capital in 1991.[7] While there was an increase in this ratio between 1991 and 1992, this increase was attributable to unusual and non-operating items. When these items are excluded, Compaq showed little improvement in any return on asset measure in Table 4-2. Moreover, all the return on asset measures were significantly lower than those for Apple and Dell. For Apple and Dell, there was a large difference between ROA (or pre-interest ROA) and RONA (or operating ROA) because both these firms had large cash and short-term investments. This shows that, at least for some firms, it is important to make adjustments to the simple ROA measure to take into account the interest expense, interest income, and financial assets.

Table 4-2 Return on Assets for Compaq, Apple, and Dell

Ratio	Compaq		Apple	Dell
	1991	1992	1992	1992
Return on assets (ROA)	4.6%	6.8%	12.6%	11.0%
Pre-interest ROA	5.4	7.6	12.0	11.5
RONA or ROC	7.6	11.9	22.6	25.5
Operating ROA	8.6	13.3	54.0	30.6
Amounts adjusted for unusual, non-operating gains:				
Return on assets (ROA)	7.5%	6.5%	12.6%	11.0%
Pre-interest ROA	8.3	7.3	12.7	11.5
RONA or ROC	11.7	11.5	22.6	25.5
Operating ROA	10.7	10.5	54.0	30.6

To begin our investigation of *why* the return on assets was so low for Compaq, we decompose ROA, showing it as a product of two factors:

$$ROA = \frac{\text{Net income}}{\text{Sales}} \times \frac{\text{Sales}}{\text{Assets}}$$

The ratio of net income to sales is called net profit margin or return on sales (ROS). The ratio of sales to assets is known as asset turnover. The profit margin ratio indicates how much the company is able to keep as profits for each dollar of sales it makes. Asset turnover indicates how many sales dollars the firm is able to generate for each dollar of its assets. In the above decomposition, we use the traditional measure of ROA, but analogous decompositions are possible for pre-interest ROA, RONA, and operating ROA.

Table 4-3 displays the three drivers of ROE for our computer firms: profit margin, asset turnover, and financial leverage. Compaq's ROE increased between 1991 and 1992 in part because its net profit margin increased from 4 percent to 5.2 percent. However, this increase in ROS based on *reported* earnings was entirely due to unusual gains and losses. The profit margin excluding the effects of unusual gains and losses actually eroded in 1992, from 6.5 to 5.3 percent. Compaq's ROE improved in 1992 also because its asset turnover and financial leverage increased marginally. However, as discussed below, relative to Apple and Dell, Compaq's asset turnover was not impressive; nor did it take advantage of as much leverage.

Both Apple and Dell had an ROA that was almost twice as large as Compaq's ROA, though for different reasons. Apple's ROA was larger than Compaq's primarily because of its higher net profit margins. In contrast, Dell's superior ROA was entirely due to its larger asset turnover. Apple's higher net profit margins were a result of its successful differentiation strategy, and Dell's higher asset turnover suggests that its low-cost strategy was working well.

Table 4-3 Key Drivers of Return on Equity

Ratio	Compaq 1991	Compaq 1992	Apple 1992	Dell 1992
Net profit margin (or ROS)	4.0%	5.2%	7.48%	5.05%
× Asset turnover	1.16	1.30	1.68	2.17
= Return on assets	4 .64%	6.76%	12.57%	10.96%
× Financial leverage	1.46	1.57	1.93	2.51
= Return on equity	6.8%	10.6%	24.2%	27.5%

In addition, both Apple and Dell had higher financial leverage relative to Compaq. Thus, Dell had a higher ROE than Compaq because it used its assets more productively and relied less on equity financing. Apple had a higher ROE than Compaq because its sales were more profitable, and it also leveraged its shareholders' investment more effectively. Below, we explore further the factors that are behind the ratios in Table 4-3.

Assessing Operating Management: Decomposing Net Profit Margins

A firm's net profit margin or return on sales (ROS) shows the profitability of the company's operating activities. Further decomposition of a firm's ROS allows an analyst to assess the efficiency of the firm's operating management. A popular tool used in this analysis is the common-sized income statement in which all the line items are expressed as a ratio of sales revenues.

Common-sized income statements make it possible to compare trends in income statement relationships over time for a firm, and trends across different firms in an industry. Income statement analysis allows the analyst to ask the following types of questions: (1) Are the company's margins consistent with its stated competitive strategy? (For example, a differentiation strategy should usually lead to higher gross profit margins than a low-cost strategy.) (2) Are the company's margins changing? Why? What are the underlying business causes—changes in competition, changes in input costs, or poor overhead cost management? (3) Is the company managing its overhead and administrative costs well? What are the business activities driving these costs? Are these activities necessary?

To illustrate how the income statement analysis can be used, we show common-sized income statements for Compaq, Apple, and Dell in Table 4-4.

GROSS PROFIT MARGINS.   The difference between a firm's sales and cost of sales is gross profit. Gross profit margin indicates the extent to which revenues exceed direct costs associated with sales. It is computed as:

$$\text{Gross profit margin} \quad = \quad \frac{\text{Sales} - \text{Cost of sales}}{\text{Sales}}$$

Gross profit margin is influenced by two factors: (1) the price premium that a firm's products or services command in the marketplace and (2) the efficiency of the firm's procurement and production process. The price premium a firm's products or services can command is influenced by the degree of competition and the extent to which its products are unique. A firm's cost of sales can be low when it can purchase its inputs at a lower cost than competitors and/or run its production processes efficiently. This is generally the case when a firm has a low-cost strategy.

Table 4-4 indicates that Compaq's gross profit margins in 1992 decreased to 29.1 percent from 37.2 percent in 1991. The company explained in its annual report that this decline was prompted by price competition in the PC industry. Dell's gross profit margins in 1992 were even lower at 22.3 percent. This suggests that Compaq was able to either charge a premium relative to Dell's prices, or to reduce its input and manufacturing costs. Both are consistent with Compaq's stated strategy of volume-driven cost leadership and premium pricing based on differentiation on service and quality.

Table 4-4 Common-Sized Income Statements

Line Item	Compaq 1991	Compaq 1992	Apple 1992	Dell 1992
Sales revenue	100.0%	100.0%	100.0%	100.0%
Cost of goods sold	62.8	70.9	56.3	77.7
Gross profit	**37.2**	**29.1**	**43.7**	**22.3**
Research and development	6.0	4.2	8.5	2.1
Selling, general, and administrative costs	22.1	17.0	23.8	13.3
Earnings before other income and expense	**9.1**	**7.9**	**12.8**	**7.3**
Other expense (income)	4.4	0.7	0.7	(0.2)
Earnings before taxes	**4.7**	**7.2**	**12.1**	**7.1**
Provision for taxes	1.3	2.4	4.6	2.1
Earnings from consolidated companies	3.4	4.8	7.5	5.0
Equity in net income of affiliated companies and other items	0.6	0.4	–	–
Net income	**4.0**	**5.2**	**7.5**	**5.0**
Net income excluding restructuring costs and gain on sale of investments	**6.5**	**5.0**	**7.5**	**5.0**

In contrast to Dell, Apple had a significantly larger gross profit margin than Compaq's. This is probably attributable to the fact that Apple followed a differentiation strategy in the PC industry. Its computers used software and hardware that was distinctly different from the IBM and compatible computers; they competed on the basis of ease in using and networking capabilities. Apple's differentiation strategy apparently allowed it to earn superior gross profit margins relative to both Compaq and Dell, primarily because of the price premium Apple's products commanded in the marketplace.

OPERATING EXPENSES.   A company's operating expenses are influenced by the activities it needs to undertake to implement its competitive strategy. As discussed in Chapter 2, firms with differentiation strategies have to undertake specific activities to achieve differentiation. A company competing on the basis of quality and rapid introduction of new products is likely to have higher research and development (R&D) costs relative to a company competing purely on a cost basis. Similarly, a company that attempts to build a brand image, distributes its products through full-service retailers, and provides after-sales service is likely to have higher selling and administrative costs than a company that sells through warehouse retailers or direct mail and does not provide much customer support.

A company's operating expenses are also influenced by the way it manages its overhead activities. The efficiency with which operating expenses are controlled is likely to be especially important for firms competing on the basis of low cost. However, even for differentiators, it is important to assess whether the cost of differentiation is commensurate with the price premium earned in the marketplace.

Focusing once again on Table 4-4, one can see that Compaq's operating expenses, including R&D and selling, general, and administrative (SG&A) costs, decreased significantly between 1991 and 1992. In its annual report, Compaq's management attributed this decline to the success of its new cost control efforts. Compaq also had significantly higher "other expenses" in 1991, primarily because of a large restructuring charge. While Compaq also had a restructuring charge in 1992, this charge was offset by a gain from the sale of its stock in Connor Peripherals, as discussed in Chapter 3. Thus, even though Compaq achieved significant cost reductions in R&D, and SG&A, its profits before other income and expenses went down from 9.1 percent to 7.9 percent of sales. This suggests that Compaq's operating cost reduction efforts in 1992 were not adequate to cover the decline in the company's gross profit margin. Only because Compaq had a one-time gain from the sale of its stake in Connor, the company's profit before taxes as a percent of sales went up from 4.7 percent to 7.2 percent.

Relative to Compaq, Dell had significantly lower operating expenses as a percent of sales, because Dell invested less both in R&D and in selling expenses. This is consistent with Dell's strategy of competing purely on a cost basis and selling its computers through direct mail. In fact, Compaq's higher operating expenses appear to fully offset the higher gross profit margin it was able to earn by emphasizing quality and service. As a result, earnings before taxes as a percent of sales for Dell and Compaq were similar, even though they achieved this through different business strategies.

Apple's operating expenses were significantly higher than Compaq's. Once again, this is consistent with Apple's differentiation strategy, which required additional expenses for R&D and marketing. Even with these additional expenses, Apple was able to achieve higher pre-tax earnings because its price premium more than offset its cost of differentiation.

TAX EXPENSE.   Taxes are an important element of a firm's total expenses. A wide variety of tax planning techniques allows a firm to attempt to reduce its tax expenses. There are two measures one can use to evaluate a firm's tax expense. One is the ratio of tax expense to sales. The second measure is the ratio of tax expense to earnings before taxes (also known as the average tax rate). The firm's tax footnote provides a detailed account of why its average tax rate differs from the statutory tax rate.

When evaluating a firm's tax planning, the analyst should ask two questions: (1) Are the company's tax policies sustainable? Or is the current tax rate influenced by one-time tax credits? (2) Do the firm's tax planning strategies lead to other business costs? For example, if the operations are located in tax havens, how does this affect the company's profit margins and asset utilization? Are the benefits of tax planning strategies (reduced taxes) greater than the increased business costs, such as lower labor productivity and higher transportation costs?

Table 4-4 shows that Compaq's tax rate did not change significantly between 1991 and 1992. Compaq's taxes as a percent of sales was also comparable to Dell's ratio. Apple's tax expense as a percent of sales was significantly higher than for Compaq, but it was because Apple's pre-tax earnings were also higher. The average tax rate for Compaq (33%) and Apple (29%) were indeed comparable.

Evaluating Investment Management: Decomposing Asset Turnover

Asset turnover is the second driver of a company's return on equity. Since firms invest considerable resources in their assets, using them productively is critical to a firm's overall profitability. A detailed analysis of asset turnover allows the analyst to evaluate the effectiveness of a firm's investment management.

There are two primary areas of asset management: (1) working capital management and (2) management of long-term assets. Working capital is the difference between a firm's current assets and current liabilities. The components of working capital that analysts focus on primarily are accounts receivable, inventory, and accounts payable. A certain amount of investment in working capital is necessary for a firm to run its normal operations. For example, a firm's credit policies and distribution policies determine its optimal level of accounts receivable. The nature of the production process and the need for buffer stocks determine the optimal level of inventory. Finally, accounts payable is a routine source of financing for a firm's working capital, and payment practices in an industry determine the normal level of accounts payable.

The following ratios are useful in analyzing a firm's working capital management:

$$\text{Current asset turnover} \ = \ \frac{\text{Sales}}{\text{Current assets}}$$

$$\text{Working capital turnover} \ = \ \frac{\text{Sales}}{\text{Current assets} \ - \ \text{Current liabilities}}$$

$$\text{Accounts receivable turnover} \ = \ \frac{\text{Sales}}{\text{Accounts receivable}}$$

$$\text{Inventory turnover} \ = \ \frac{\text{Cost of goods sold}}{\text{Inventory}}$$

$$\text{Accounts payable turnover} \ = \ \frac{\text{Purchases}}{\text{Accounts payable}} \quad or \quad \frac{\text{Cost of goods sold}}{\text{Accounts payable}}$$

$$\text{Days' receivables} \ = \ \frac{\text{Accounts receivable}}{\text{Average sales per day}}$$

$$\text{Days' inventory} \ = \ \frac{\text{Inventory}}{\text{Average cost of goods sold per day}}$$

$$\text{Days' payables} \ = \ \frac{\text{Accounts payable}}{\text{Average purchases (or cost of goods sold) per day}}$$

Current asset turnover and working capital turnover indicate how many dollars of sales a firm is able to generate for each dollar invested in current assets or working capital. Accounts receivable turnover, inventory turnover, and accounts payable turnover allow the analyst to examine how productively the three principal components of working capital are being used. Days' receivables, days' inventory, and days' payables are another way to evaluate the efficiency of a firm's working capital management. These reflect the number of days of operating activity (sales, production, and purchases, respectively) that are supported by the level of investment in the firm's receivables, inventory, and payables.[8]

Property, plant, and equipment (PP&E) is the most important long-term asset in a firm's balance sheet. The amount of sales generated by a dollar invested in PP&E is measured by the ratio:

$$\text{PP\&E turnover} \ = \ \frac{\text{Sales}}{\text{Property, plant, and equipment}}$$

The ratios listed above allow the analyst to explore a number of business questions: (1) How well does the company manage its inventory? Does the company use modern manufacturing techniques? Does it have good vendor and logistics management systems? If inventory ratios are changing, what is the underlying business reason? Are new products being planned? Is there a mismatch between demand forecasts and actual sales? (2) How well does the company manage its credit policies? Are these policies consistent with its marketing strategy? Is the company artificially increasing sales by loading distribution channels? (3) Is the company taking advantage of trade credit? Is it relying too much on trade credit? If so, what are the implicit costs? (4) Is the company's investment in plant and equipment consistent with its competitive strategy? Does the company have a sound policy of acquisitions and divestitures?

We present in Table 4-5 the asset turnover ratios for Compaq, Apple, and Dell. Recall that Compaq's asset turnover remained relatively stagnant between 1991 and 1992. Table 4-5 shows that Compaq's current asset turnover worsened in 1992 relative to 1991. The principal reason is that the company's receivables and inventory turned more slowly in 1992. Days' receivables increased from 70 to 88, and days' inventory increased from 78 to 105. The slow turnover of receivables and inventory are important to Compaq's overall asset productivity because these two items accounted for 79 percent of the company's current assets and 58 percent of its total assets in 1992.

Despite the worsening of current asset turnover, Compaq's working capital turnover improved marginally in 1992 because of an increase in days' payables from 35 to 65. Thus, while Compaq increased its investments in receivables and inventory significantly in 1992, its net investment in working capital did not increase correspondingly because the company also stretched its payables. These patterns in the company's working capital ratios were not well explained in the company's 1992 annual report, making it difficult for an outside analyst to understand the business reasons behind them without further probing.

Compaq's 1992 asset turnover ratios were also significantly different from Apple's and Dell's ratios, principally because both Dell and Apple had significantly higher turnovers of current assets and working capital. Apple turned its inventories and receivables faster and paid its suppliers sooner than did Compaq. Dell also had better receivables and inventory turnovers, though its payables turnover was comparable to Compaq's.

Table 4-5 Asset Management Ratios

Ratio	Compaq 1991	Compaq 1992	Apple 1992	Dell 1992
Current asset turnover	1.84	1.77	1.99	2.36
Working capital turnover	2.85	3.02	3.32	5.61
Accounts receivable turnover	5.24	4.15	6.52	5.38
Inventory turnover	4.70	3.48	6.88	5.16
Accounts payable turnover	10.50	5.63	9.35	5.30
Days' receivables	70	88	56	68
Days' inventory	78	105	53	71
Days' payables	35	65	39	69
PP&E turnover	3.71	5.08	15.33	28.6

In terms of PP&E utilization, Compaq showed a significant improvement between 1991 and 1992. However, relative to Apple and Dell, Compaq's PP&E productivity was significantly lower. In 1992, while Compaq realized five dollars in sales for each dollar invested in PP&E, Apple realized fifteen dollars and Dell realized more than twenty-eight dollars. The impact of these differences on the overall profitability of the three companies, however, was not very large because PP&E represented only a small fraction of the total assets for all three companies.

Evaluating Financial Management: Examining Financial Leverage

Financial leverage enables a firm to have an asset base larger than its equity. The firm can augment its equity through borrowing and the creation of other liabilities, such as accounts payable, accrued liabilities, and deferred taxes. Financial leverage increases a firm's ROE as long as the cost of the liabilities is less than the return from investing these funds. Financial leverage, however, also increases the firm's risk. Unlike equity, liabilities have predefined payment terms, and the firm faces risk of financial distress if it fails to meet these commitments.

There are a number of ratios to evaluate the degree of risk arising from a firm's financial leverage. These ratios are described in the following sections.

CURRENT LIABILITIES AND SHORT-TERM LIQUIDITY.   The following ratios are useful in evaluating the risk related to a firm's current liabilities:

$$\text{Current ratio} \quad = \quad \frac{\text{Current assets}}{\text{Current liabilities}}$$

$$\text{Quick ratio} \quad = \quad \frac{\text{Cash} + \text{Short-term investments} + \text{Accounts receivable}}{\text{Current liabilities}}$$

$$\text{Cash ratio} \quad = \quad \frac{\text{Cash} + \text{Short-term investments}}{\text{Current liabilities}}$$

$$\text{Operating cash flow ratio} \quad = \quad \frac{\text{Cash flow from operations}}{\text{Current liabilities}}$$

All the above ratios attempt to measure the firm's ability to repay its current liabilities. The first three compare a firm's current liabilities with its short-term assets, which can be used to repay the current liabilities. The fourth ratio focuses on the ability of the firm's operations to generate the resources needed to repay its current liabilities.

Since both current assets and current liabilities have comparable duration, the current ratio is a key index of a firm's short-term liquidity. Analysts view a current ratio of more than 1 to be an indication that the firm can cover its current liabilities with the cash realized from its current assets. However, the firm can face a short-term liquidity problem even with a current ratio exceeding 1 when some of its current assets are not easy to liquidate. The quick ratio and the cash ratio capture the firm's ability to cover its current liabilities from liquid assets. The quick ratio assumes that the firm's accounts receivable are liquid. This is true in industries where the credit-worthiness of the customers is beyond dispute, or when receivables are collected in a very short period. However, when these conditions do not prevail, the cash ratio, which considers only cash and marketable securities, is a better indication of a firm's ability to cover its current liabilities in an emergency. Operating cash flow is another measure of the firm's ability to cover its current liabilities with cash generated from operations of the firm.

We report the liquidity ratios for Compaq, Apple, and Dell in Table 4-6. Compaq's liquidity situation in 1992 was very comfortable, as indicated by a current ratio of 2.4 and a quick ratio of 1.40. However, both these ratios and the cash ratio deteriorated in 1992 relative to 1991. Further, because Compaq had a negative cash flow from operations in 1992, its operating cash flow ratio worsened significantly. Apple's liquidity in 1992 was certainly stronger than Compaq's. Apple had a cash ratio of 1, suggesting that it could meet all its current liabilities by merely liquidating its cash and marketable securities. Dell was in the weakest liquidity position among the three computer makers, in part due to the company's attempt to minimize its investment in working capital as part of its low-cost strategy.

DEBT AND LONG-TERM SOLVENCY.   A company's financial leverage is also influenced by its debt financing policy. There are several potential benefits from debt financing. First, debt is typically cheaper than equity because the firm promises predefined payment terms to debt holders. Second, in most countries, interest on debt financing is tax deductible, whereas dividends to shareholders are not tax deductible. Third, debt financing can impose discipline on the firm's management and motivate it to reduce wasteful expenditures. Fourth, it is often easier for management to communicate its proprietary information on the firm's strategies and prospects to private lenders than to public capital markets. Such communication can potentially reduce a firm's cost of capital.

Table 4-6 Liquidity Ratios

Ratio	Compaq 1991	Compaq 1992	Apple 1992	Dell 1992
Current ratio	2.79	2.41	2.50	1.72
Quick ratio	1.68	1.40	1.77	0.95
Cash ratio	0.71	0.37	1.00	0.19
Operating cash flow ratio	0.62	*	0.62	*

* Not meaningful because cash flow from operations was negative.

For all these reasons, it is optimal for firms to use at least some debt in their capital structure.

Too much reliance on debt financing is, however, potentially costly to the firm's shareholders. The firm will face financial distress if it defaults on the interest and principal payments. Debt holders also impose covenants on the firm, restricting the firm's operating, investing, and financing decisions.

The optimal capital structure for a firm is determined primarily by its business risk. A firm's cash flows are easier to predict when there is little competition or little threat of technological changes. Such firms have low business risk, and hence they can rely heavily on debt financing. In contrast, if a firm's operating cash flows are highly volatile and its capital expenditure needs are unpredictable, it may have to rely primarily on equity financing. Managers' attitudes toward risk and financial flexibility also often determine a firm's debt policies.

There are a number of ratios which help the analyst in this area. To evaluate the mix of debt and equity in a firm's capital structure, the following ratios are useful:

$$\text{Liabilities-to-equity ratio} \ = \ \frac{\text{Total liabilities}}{\text{Shareholders' equity}}$$

$$\text{Debt-to-equity ratio} \ = \ \frac{\text{Short-term debt} \ + \ \text{Long-term debt}}{\text{Shareholders' equity}}$$

$$\text{Debt-to-capital ratio} \ = \ \frac{\text{Short-term debt} \ + \ \text{Long-term debt}}{\text{Short-term debt} \ + \ \text{Long-term debt} \ + \ \text{Shareholders' equity}}$$

The first ratio restates the assets-to-equity ratio (one of the three primary ratios underlying ROE) by subtracting 1 from it. The second ratio provides an indication of how many dollars of debt financing the firm is using for each dollar invested by its shareholders. The third ratio gives the proportion of debt in the total capital of the firm.

The ease with which a firm can meet its interest payments is an indication of the degree of risk associated with its debt policy. The interest coverage ratio provides a measure of this construct:

$$\text{Interest coverage (earnings basis)} \ = \ \frac{\text{Net income} \ + \ \text{Interest expense} \ + \ \text{Tax expense}}{\text{Interest expense}}$$

$$\text{Interest coverage (cash basis)} \ = $$
$$\frac{\text{Cash flow from operations} \ + \ \text{Interest paid} \ + \ \text{Taxes paid}}{\text{Interest paid}}$$

The earnings-based coverage ratio indicates the dollars of earnings available for each dollar of required interest payment. The cash flow-based coverage ratio indicates the dollars of cash generated by operations for each dollar of required interest payment. In both these ratios, the denominator is the interest expense. In the numerator, we add taxes back because taxes are computed only after interest expense is deducted. A coverage ratio of 1 implies that the firm is barely covering its interest expense through its operating activities, which is a very risky situation. The larger the coverage ratio, the greater the cushion the firm has to meets its interest obligations.[9]

Some of the business questions to ask when the analyst is examining a firm's debt policies are: (1) Does the company have enough debt? Is it exploiting the potential benefits of debt—interest tax shields, management discipline, easier communication? (2) Given its business risk, does the company have too much debt? What type of debt covenant restrictions does the firm face? Is it bearing the costs of too much debt and risking potential financial distress and reduced business flexibility? (3) What is the company doing with the borrowed funds? Investing in working capital? Investing in fixed assets? Are these investments profitable? (4) Is the company borrowing money to pay dividends? If so, what is the justification?

We report the debt and coverage ratios for Compaq, Apple, and Dell in Table 4-7. The financial leverage for all three companies primarily comes from current liabilities. For example, in 1992, while Compaq had 57 cents in liabilities for each dollar of equity, it had no interest-bearing debt.[10] In fact, while Compaq increased its reliance on non-interest-bearing liabilities in 1992, the company paid off all its interest-bearing debt. Relative to Compaq, Apple and Dell had higher liabilities as a proportion of their equity. However, once again, most of these liabilities were non-interest-bearing. Both the firms had only a modest amount of interest-bearing debt. The low debt ratios for all three companies are a result of the high business risk associated with the PC industry.

Compaq had a comfortable interest coverage ratio in 1991, and it improved further in 1992 if one takes into account earnings-based coverage. However, if reported earnings are adjusted for unusual items, Compaq's coverage remained flat at approximately 8 in both 1991 and 1992. Further, the company's cash flow-based coverage deteriorated dramatically in 1992. Apple and Dell had a significantly better interest coverage position relative to Compaq.

Table 4-7 Debt and Interest Coverage Ratios

Ratio	Compaq 1991	Compaq 1992	Apple 1992	Dell 1992
Liabilities-to-equity	0.46	0.57	0.93	1.51
Debt-to-equity	0.04	0	0.08	0.13
Debt-to-capital	0.04	0	0.08	0.12
Interest coverage (earnings based)	5.7	8.4	98.1	19.1
Interest coverage (cash flow based)	14.5	−0.34	112.9	−7.8

Putting It All Together: Assessing Sustainable Growth Rate

Analysts often use the concept of sustainable growth as a way to evaluate a firm's ratios in a comprehensive manner. A firm's sustainable growth rate is defined as:

$$\text{Sustainable growth rate} = \text{ROE} \times (1 - \text{Dividend payout ratio})$$

We discussed the analysis of ROE in the previous four sections. The dividend payout ratio is defined as:

$$\text{Dividend payout ratio} = \frac{\text{Cash dividends paid}}{\text{Net income}}$$

A firm's dividend payout ratio is a measure of its dividend policy. As we will discuss in detail in a later chapter, firms pay dividends for several reasons. Dividends are a way for the firm to return to its shareholders any cash generated in excess of its operating and investment needs. When there are information asymmetries between a firm's managers and its shareholders, dividend payments can serve as a signal to shareholders about managers' expectations of the firm's future prospects. Firms may also pay dividends to attract a certain type of shareholder base.

The sustainable growth rate is the rate at which a firm can grow, keeping its profitability and financial policies unchanged. A firm's return on equity and its dividend payout policy determine the pool of funds available for growth. Of course, the firm can grow at a rate different from its sustainable growth rate if either its profitability, or payout policy, or financial leverage changes. Therefore, the sustainable growth rate is a benchmark against which a firm's growth plans can be evaluated. Figure 4-2 shows how a firm's sustainable growth rate can be linked to all the ratios discussed in this chapter. These linkages allow an analyst to examine the drivers of a firm's current sustainable growth rate. If the firm intends to grow at a rate higher than its sustainable growth rate, one could assess which of the ratios are likely to change in the process. Such an analysis can lead to asking these kinds of business questions: Where is the change going to take place? Is management expecting profitability to increase? Or is it expecting asset productivity to improve? Are these expectations realistic? Is management planning adequately for these changes? If the profitability is not likely to go up, will the firm increase its financial leverage or cut dividends? What is the likely impact of these financial policy changes?

Table 4-8 shows the sustainable growth rate and its components for Compaq, Apple, and Dell. Compaq's sustainable growth rate was equal to its return on equity because the firm did not pay cash dividends in either 1991 or in 1992. The sustainable growth rate for Compaq went up in 1992 relative to 1991 because its ROE increased. The analysis presented in the previous sections shows how Compaq has been able improve its ROE. For example, an important reason for the ROE increase was the difference in unusual gains and losses Compaq reported in the two years. If these gains and losses were excluded, Compaq's sustainable growth rate declined from 11 percent to 10.2 percent.

Figure 4-2 Sustainable Growth Rate Framework for Financial Ratio
Analysis

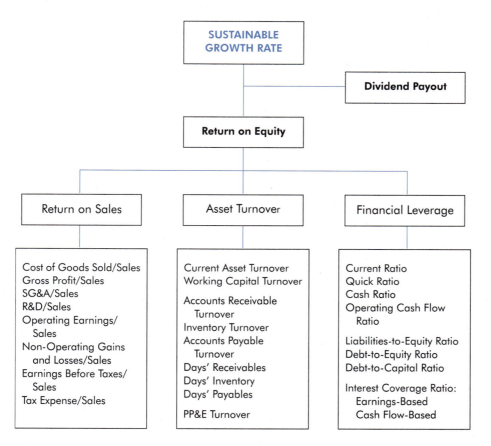

The analysis also shows that Compaq's sustainable growth rate in 1992 was positively influenced by its cost cutting and its increase in accounts payable. It was adversely influenced by the decrease in gross profit margins and the increase in receivables and inventory. Thus, if Compaq was to grow faster in 1993 than its 1992 sustainable growth rate, it had to improve its gross profit margins or reduce its inventory and receivables or further reduce its operating costs. Compaq could also grow by further increasing its days' payables, but this could strain the company's relations with its suppliers. The final option for Compaq to grow faster than its sustainable growth rate was to increase its debt. Since Compaq had no debt in 1992, this was feasible. However, Compaq's cash flow coverage of its interest in 1992 was only 1. A significant improvement in operating cash flow would have been needed to service the additional borrowing.

Table 4-8 Sustainable Growth Rate

Ratio	Compaq		Apple	Dell
	1991	1992	1992	1992
ROE	6.8%	10.6%	24.2%	27.5%
Dividend payout ratio	0	0	0.11	0
Sustainable growth rate	6.8%	10.6%	21.5%	27.5%

Like Compaq, Dell also did not pay cash dividends. Hence, Dell's sustainable growth rate was also equal to its ROE. Apple, however, paid modest dividends, equal to 11 percent of its earnings in 1992. As a result, the company's sustainable growth rate was less than its ROE. However, relative to Compaq, both Apple and Dell had significantly higher room for growth without having to alter any of their financial and operating policies.

CASH FLOW ANALYSIS

Ratio analysis focuses on analyzing a firm's income statement (net profit margin analysis) or its balance sheet (asset turnover and financial leverage). The analyst can get further insights into the firm's operating, investing, and financing policies by examining its cash flows. Cash flow analysis also provides an indication of the quality of the information in the firm's income statement and balance sheet. As before, we will use Compaq's cash flows to illustrate the concepts discussed in this section.

Cash Flow and Funds Flow Statements

All U.S. companies are required to include a statement of cash flows in their financial statements under Statement of Financial Accounting Standard No. 95 (SFAS 95). In the reported cash flow statement, firms classify their cash flows into three categories: cash flow from operations, cash flow related to investments, and cash flow related to financing activities. Cash flow from operations is the cash generated by the firm from the sale of goods and services after paying for the cost of inputs and operations. Cash flow related to investment activities shows the cash paid for capital expenditures, intercorporate investments and acquisitions, and cash received from the sales of long-term assets. Cash flow related to financing activities shows the cash raised from (or paid to) the firm's stockholders and debt holders.

Firms use two cash flow statement formats: the direct format and the indirect format. The key difference between the two formats is the way they report cash flow from operating activities. In the direct cash flow format, which is used by only a small number of firms in practice, operating cash receipts and disbursements are reported directly. In the indirect format, firms derive their operating cash flows by making adjustments to net income. Because the indirect format links the cash flow statement with the firm's income statement and balance sheet, many analysts and managers find this format more useful. As a result, current U.S. accounting rules require firms using the direct format to report operating cash flows in the indirect format as well.

Recall from Chapter 3 that net income differs from operating cash flows because revenues and expenses are measured on an accrual basis. There are two types of accruals embedded in net income. First, there are current accruals, such as credit sales and unpaid expenses. Current accruals result in changes in a firm's current assets (such as accounts receivable, inventory, and prepaid expenses), and current liabilities (such as accounts payable and accrued liabilities). The second type of accruals included in the income statement is non-current accruals, such as depreciation, deferred taxes, and equity income from unconsolidated subsidiaries. To derive cash flow from operations from net income, adjustments have to be made for both these types of accruals. In addition, adjustments have to be made for non-operating gains and losses included in net income, such as profits from asset sales.

Most firms outside the U.S. report a funds flow statement rather than a cash flow statement. Prior to SFAS No. 95, U.S. firms also reported a similar statement. It is useful for analysts to know how to convert a funds flow statement into a cash flow statement.

Funds flow statements typically provide information on a firm's working capital from operations, defined as net income adjusted for non-current accruals and gains from the sale of long-term assets. As discussed above, cash flow from operations essentially involves a third adjustment, the adjustment for current accruals. Thus, it is relatively straightforward to convert working capital from operations to cash flow from operations by making the relevant adjustments for current accruals related to operations.

Information on current accruals can be obtained by examining changes in the firm's current assets and current liabilities Typically, operating accruals represent changes in all the current asset accounts other than cash and cash equivalents, and changes in all the current liabilities other than notes payable and the current portion of long-term debt.[11] Cash from operations can be calculated as:

Working capital from operations
− Increase (or + decrease) in accounts receivable
− Increase (or + decrease) in inventory
− Increase (or + decrease) in other current assets, excluding cash and cash equivalents
+ Increase (or − decrease) in accounts payable
+ Increase (or − decrease) in other current liabilities excluding notes payable and debt

Funds flow statements also often do not classify investing and financing flows. In this case, the analyst has to classify the line items in the funds flow statement into these two categories by evaluating the nature of the business transactions that give rise to the flow represented by the line items.

Analyzing Cash Flow Information

Cash flow analysis can be used to address a variety of questions regarding the firm's cash flow dynamics:

- How strong is the firm's internal cash flow generation? Is the cash flow from operations positive or negative? If it is negative, why? Is it because the company is growing? Is it because its operations are unprofitable? Or is it having difficulty managing its working capital properly?
- Does the company have the ability to meet its short-term financial obligations, such as interest payments, from its operating cash flow? Can it continue to meet these obligations without reducing its operating flexibility?
- How much cash did the company invest in growth? Are these investments consistent with its business strategy? Did the company use internal cash flow to finance growth, or did it rely on external financing?
- Does the company have excess cash flow after investing in capital investments? Is it a long-term trend? What plans does management have to deploy the free cash flow?
- Did the company pay dividends from internal free cash flow, or did it have to rely on external financing? If the company had to fund its dividends from external sources, is the company's dividend policy sustainable?
- What type of external financing does the company rely on—equity, short-term debt, or long-term debt? Is the financing consistent with the company's overall business risk?

While the information in reported cash flow statements can be used to answer these questions directly for some firms, it may not always be easy to do so for several reasons. First, even though SFAS No. 95 provides broad guidelines on the format of a cash flow statement, there is still significant variation across firms in how cash flow data are disclosed. Therefore, to facilitate a systematic analysis and comparison across firms, analysts often recast the information in the cash flow statement, using their own cash flow model. Second, firms include interest expense and interest income in computing their cash flow from operating activities. However, these two items are not strictly related to a firm's operations. Interest expense is a function of financial leverage, and interest income is derived from financial assets rather than operating assets. Therefore, it is useful to restate the cash flow statement to take this into account.

Analysts use a number of different approaches to restate the cash flow data. One popular model, called the Total Cash Flow Analysis, is given in Table 4-9. This model shows clearly what one would expect from a firm that is healthy and has a sound financial management.

The Total Cash Flow Analysis presents cash flow from operations in two stages. The first step computes cash flow from operations before working capital investments. In computing this cash flow, the model excludes interest expense and interest income. A firm should generate a positive cash flow from operations in steady state, provided it col-

Table 4-9 Total Cash Flow Analysis of Compaq Computer Corporation

Cash Flow Effects of Various Activities	1991	1992
Net income	**130.9**	**213.2**
Adjustments for non-current operating accruals and non-operating items:		
Depreciation	165.8	159.5
Deferred taxes	(9.6)	34.1
Equity (income)/loss in affiliated companies	(19.8)	(15.2)
(Gain)/Loss on sale of assets and investments	4.2	(71.3)
Interest expense less interest and dividend income (net of related taxes)	2.7	5.9
Other*	204.8	(69.8)
Total	348.1	43.2
Cash flow from operations before working capital investments and interest payments	**479.0**	**256.4**
Cash flow effects of investment in working capital:		
(Increase)/Decrease in accounts receivable	2.2	(362.3)
(Increase)/Decrease in inventories	106.8	(397.6)
Increase/(Decrease) in accounts payable	(96.8)	320.7
(Increase)/Decrease in other current assets, excluding cash and cash equivalents	(186.1)	128.1
Increase/(Decrease) in other current liabilities, excluding debt	91.8	1.2
Total	(82.1)	(309.9)
Cash flow from operations after investment in working capital, before interest payments	**396.9**	**(53.5)**
Interest expense (net of taxes)	(22.1)	(25.3)
Interest income (net of taxes)	19.4	19.4
Cash flow from operations after investment in working capital and interest payments	**394.2**	**(59.4)**
Cash flow effects of investment in long-term assets:		
(Purchase)/Sale of property, plant, and equipment	(188.8)	(159.2)
(Purchase)/Sale of investments	(135.0)	376.4
Other	(16.6)	13.0
Total	(340.4)	230.2
Free cash flow before dividend payments and external financing activities	**53.8**	**170.8**
Dividend payments	0	0
Free cash flow after dividend payments	**53.8**	**170.8**
Cash flow effects of external financing activities:		
Stock repurchase	(82.2)	(215.5)
Sale of equity	22.6	56.8
Repayment of debt	(0.5)	(73.5)
Exchange rate gains (losses) on cash and cash equivalents	23.8	(34.1)
Total	(36.3)	(266.3)
Net cash flow after external financing	**17.5**	**(95.5)**

*Derived as a plug number because Compaq's cash flow statement does not disclose all details necessary to calculate this figure. It includes provision for restructuring costs.

lects more cash from its customers than it spends on its operating expenses. Most firms, however, use some of this cash flow for working capital items, such as accounts receivable, inventories, and accounts payable. A firm's net investment in working capital is a function of its credit policies (accounts receivable), payment policies (payables, pre-paid expenses, and accrued liabilities), and expected growth in sales (inventories). Thus, in interpreting a firm's cash flow from operations after working capital, it is important to keep in mind the firm's growth strategy, its industry characteristics, and its credit policies.

The next step in the Total Cash Flow Analysis is to compare the cash flow from operations after working capital investments with the firm's interest payments. If cash flow from operations is less than a firm's interest payments, it has to liquidate its assets or raise external capital to meet its interest obligations. Clearly, such a situation is unhealthy from a financial management perspective.

The Total Cash Flow Analysis focuses next on cash flows related to long-term investments. These investments take the form of capital expenditures, intercorporate investments, and mergers and acquisitions. Any positive operating cash flow after making interest payments allows the firm to pursue long-term growth opportunities. If the firm's operating cash flows after interest are not sufficient to finance its long-term investments, it has to rely on external financing to fund its growth. Such firms have less flexibility to pursue long-term investments than firms that can fund their growth internally. There are both costs and benefits from being able to fund growth internally. The cost is that managers can use the internally generated free cash flow to fund unprofitable investments. Such wasteful capital expenditures are less likely if managers are forced to rely on external capital suppliers. However, reliance on external capital markets may make it difficult for managers to undertake long-term risky investments if it is not easy to communicate to the capital markets the benefits from such investments.

Any excess cash flow after these long-term investments is free cash flow available for dividend payments. It is not prudent for a firm to pay dividends unless it has a positive free cash flow on a sustained basis. Thus, the Total Cash Flow Analysis compares cash flow after long-term investments with the firm's dividend payments. A negative cash flow after dividend payments is a signal that the firm's dividend policy may be subject to change. If the firm has a positive free cash flow after dividend payments, it can be used for repayment of debt or for repurchase of shares.

The Total Cash Flow Analysis suggests that the analyst should focus on a number of cash flow measures: (1) cash flow from operations before investment in working capital and interest payments, to examine whether or not the firm is able to generate a cash surplus from its operations; (2) cash flow from operations after investment in working capital to assess how the firm's working capital is being managed; (3) cash flow from operations after interest payments to assess the firm's ability to meet its interest obligations; (4) free cash flow before dividend payments to assess the firm's financial flexibility to finance long-term investments internally; (5) free cash flow after dividend payments to examine whether or not the firm's dividend policy is sustainable; and (6) net cash flow after external financing to examine the firm's financing policies. These measures have to be evaluated in the context of the company's business, its growth strategy, and its financial policies. Further, changes in these measures from year to year provide valuable information on the stability of the cash flow dynamics of the firm.

The Total Cash Flow Analysis can also be used to assess a firm's earnings quality, as discussed in Chapter 3. The reconciliation of a firm's net income with its cash flow from operations facilitates this exercise. Some of the questions an analyst can probe in this respect are:

- Are there significant differences between a firm's net income and its operating cash flow? Is it possible to clearly identify the sources of this difference? Which accounting policies contribute to it? Are there any one-time events contributing to the difference?
- Is the relationship between cash flow and net income changing over time? Why? Is it because of changes in business conditions or because of changes in the firm's accounting policies and estimates?
- What is the time lag between the recognition of revenues and expenses and the receipt and disbursement of cash flows? What type of uncertainties need to be resolved in between?
- Are the changes in receivables, inventories, and payables normal? If not, is there adequate explanation for the changes?

Analyzing Compaq's Cash Flow

In its 1992 annual report, Compaq used the direct format to report its cash flows. This statement shows that Compaq's 1992 operations led to a cash deficit of $59.4 million. At the bottom of the statement, the firm showed why there was a negative cash flow from operations, even though the firm reported a net income of over $213 million during 1992. Compaq's cash flow statement shows that the difference in its operating cash flow and net income arose from the three types of adjustments discussed above. For example, the company adjusted the net income for depreciation expense, deferred taxes, and equity in income of an affiliated company, all non-current accruals. It also adjusted for changes in a number of current assets and current liabilities. Finally, the company adjusted for non-operating gains from the sale of an investment in an affiliated company and losses on disposal of assets.

Compaq also reported that its investment activities resulted in a positive cash flow of $230 million in 1992. While the company invested $159.2 million in new plant and equipment, it was able to offset this investment with cash flows realized from the sale of stock in Connor Peripherals, Inc. and in Silicon Graphics, Inc. Compaq's financing activities in 1992 consumed $232.1 million, primarily as a result of stock repurchases and debt repayments.

Compaq's reported cash flow statement does not provide adequate information to address the types of questions raised at the beginning of the previous section. For example,

Compaq reported that its cash flow from operations was negative, largely because of a $456 million increase in its net current assets. However, it provided few details on the nature of these increases. To facilitate further analysis, we show in Table 4-9 the cash flow data for Compaq in 1991 and 1992, using the Total Cash Flow Analysis model.

Compaq generated $256.4 million in cash from operations in 1992 before its investments in working capital and the net interest payments are considered. However, because of significant investments in accounts receivable and inventories, Compaq's cash flow from operations after working capital investments became negative, even after a very large increase in its accounts payable. As a result, Compaq had a negative cash flow from operations before its interest payments. The firm paid its interest payments in part out of its interest income, and in part by drawing down its cash balance.

Compaq's cash flow pattern in 1992 differed significantly from the pattern in 1991. In that year, the firm generated a positive cash flow from operations, even after considering its investments in working capital and interest payments. This suggests that something changed in the firm's cash flow dynamics. Did the firm lose control of its inventory and receivables? Or were these increases merely a result of a surge in the firm's production and sales activities in the fourth quarter of 1992? Unfortunately, the firm provided few explanations. While it is not uncommon for growth firms like Compaq to have a negative cash flow from operations, the difference between 1991 and 1992 suggests that further investigation is warranted.

Another interesting aspect of Compaq's operating cash flow in 1992 was the large gap between its cash flow and net income. This gap was caused to some extent by one-time events, such as the gain on the sale of investments. It was also caused by a significant increase in accounts receivable. As discussed in Chapter 3, both these aspects, which were not present in 1991, raise questions about the sustainability of Compaq's 1992 earnings.

The negative cash flow from operations was not a major concern for Compaq's liquidity in 1992 because Compaq generated $376.4 million in cash by shrinking its long-term investments in affiliated companies. Thus, even after spending $159.2 million on plant and equipment, the firm had a positive cash flow from investment activities. It is unlikely, however, that Compaq could repeat this performance in subsequent years, since it did not have other investments it could liquidate, and its growth plans called for additional investments in plant and equipment.

As a result of its investment sales in 1992, Compaq had a free cash flow of $170.8 million before dividend payments and external financing activities. Compaq was not paying a regular cash dividend. However, the firm used its free cash flow to pay down its debt and repurchase its stock.

Overall, Compaq's liquidity was strong, and given the firm's low financial leverage, there was little cause for concern regarding the firm's financial risk. The one area that merits further analysis is the firm's working capital management. This conclusion is consistent with the ratio analysis of Compaq presented earlier.

SUMMARY AND CONCLUSIONS

There are two key tools of financial analysis: ratio analysis and cash flow analysis. Both these tools allow the analyst to examine the firm's performance and its financial condition, given its strategy and goals. Ratio analysis involves assessing the firm's income statement and balance sheet data. Cash flow analysis relies on the firm's cash flow statement.

The starting point for ratio analysis is the company's ROE. The next step is to evaluate the three drivers of ROE—net profit margin, asset turnover, and financial leverage. Net profit margin reflects a firm's operating management, asset turnover reflects its investment management, and financial leverage reflects its liability management. Each of these areas can be further probed by examining a number of ratios. For example, common-sized income statement analysis allows a detailed examination of a firm's net margins. Similarly, turnover of key working capital accounts, such as accounts receivable, inventory, and accounts payable, and turnover of the firm's fixed assets allows further examination of a firm's asset turnover. Finally, short-term liquidity ratios, debt policy ratios, and coverage ratios provide a means of examining a firm's financial leverage.

A firm's sustainable growth rate, the rate at which it can grow without altering its operating, investing, and financing policies, is determined by its ROE and its dividend policy. Therefore, the concept of sustainable growth provides a way to integrate the ratio analysis and to evaluate whether or not a firm's growth strategy is sustainable. If a firm's plans call for growing at a rate above its current sustainable rate, then the analyst can examine which of the firm's ratios is likely to change in the future.

Cash flow analysis supplements ratio analysis in examining a firm's operating activities, investment management, and financial risks. Firms in the U.S. are currently required to report a cash flow statement summarizing their operating, investing, and financing cash flows. Firms in other countries typically report working capital flows, but it is possible to use this information to create a cash flow statement.

Since there are wide variations across firms in the way cash flow data are reported, analysts often use a standard format to recast cash flow data. We discussed in this chapter a popularly used cash flow model called the Total Cash Flow Analysis. This model allows the analyst to assess whether a firm's operations generate cash flow before investments in working capital, and how much cash is being invested in the firm's working capital. It also enables the analyst to calculate the firm's free cash flow after investments in long-term investments, an indication of the firm's ability to sustain its dividend payments. Finally, the Total Cash Flow Analysis shows how the firm is financing itself and whether or not its financing patterns are too risky.

The insights gained from analyzing a firm's financial ratios and its cash flows are valuable in making forecasts about a firm's future prospects. We turn to this topic in the next three chapters.

DISCUSSION QUESTIONS

1. Which of the following types of firms do you expect to have particularly high or low asset turnover? Explain why.
   - a supermarket
   - a pharmaceutical company
   - a jewelry retailer
   - a steel company
2. Which of the following types of firms do you expect to have high or low sales margins? Why?
   - a supermarket
   - a pharmaceutical company
   - a jewelry retailer
   - a software company
3. James Broker, an analyst with an established brokerage firm, comments: "The critical number I look at for any company is operating cash flow. If cash flows are less than earnings, I consider a company to be a poor performer and a poor investment prospect. " Do you agree with this assessment? Why or why not?
4. In 1995 Chrysler has a return on equity of 20 percent, whereas Ford's return is only 8 percent. Use the decomposed ROE framework to provide possible reasons for this difference.
5. Joe Investor claims: "A company cannot grow faster than its sustainable growth rate. " True or false? Explain why.
6. What are the reasons for a firm having lower cash from operations than working capital from operations? What are the possible interpretations of these reasons?
7. ABC Company recognizes revenue at the point of shipment. Management decides to increase sales for the current quarter by filling all customer orders. Explain what impact this decision will have on:
   - Days receivable for the current quarter
   - Days receivable for the next quarter
   - Sales growth for the current quarter
   - Sales growth for the next quarter
   - Return on sales for the current quarter
   - Return on sales for the next quarter
8. What ratios would you use to evaluate operating leverage for a firm?
9. What are the potential benchmarks that you could use to compare a company's financial ratios? What are the pros and cons of these alternatives?

10. In a period of rising prices, how would the following ratios be affected by the accounting decision to select LIFO, rather than FIFO, for inventory valuation?
   - Gross margin
   - Current ratio
   - Asset turnover
   - Debt-to-equity ratio
   - Average tax rate

CASE

The Home Depot, Inc.

NOTES

1. We use the financial statements for the years ending December 31, 1991 and 1992 for Compaq, the year ending September 25, 1992 for Apple, and the year ending January 31, 1993 for Dell. The differences in the fiscal years for the three companies introduce some noise in the comparison of their ratios.

2. In computing ROE, one can either use the beginning equity, ending equity, or an average of the two. Conceptually, the average equity is appropriate, particularly for rapidly growing companies. However, for most companies, this computational choice makes little difference as long as the analyst is consistent. Therefore, analysts most often use ending balances for simplicity. This comment applies to all ratios discussed in this chapter, where one of the items in the ratio is a flow variable (items in the income statement or cash flow statement) and the other item is a stock variable (items in the balance sheet). Throughout this chapter, we use the ending balances of the stock variables for computational simplicity.

3. These adjustments to earnings are made assuming a 40 percent tax effect. Throughout this chapter we use a 40 percent tax rate based on a 34 percent federal tax rate for corporations and a 6 percent state and local tax rate.

4. When ROA is defined in this way, it can be reconciled with ROE as follows:

$$\text{ROE} = \text{Pre-interest ROA} \times \frac{\text{Earnings}}{\text{EBILAT}} \times \text{Financial leverage}$$

5. ROE can be expressed as a function of RONA, as follows:

$$\text{ROE} = \text{RONA} \times \frac{\text{Earnings}}{\text{EBILAT}} \times \frac{\text{Equity + Debt}}{\text{Assets}} \times \text{Financial leverage}$$

6. Strictly speaking, part of a cash balance is needed to run the firm's operations, so only the excess cash balance should be subtracted in the denominator of this ratio. However, firms do not provide this information, so we subtract all cash balances in our definition and computations. An alternative possibility is to subtract only short-term investments and ignore the cash balance completely.

7. Compaq has no debt, so its WACC is equal to its cost of equity capital. Thus, it is estimated to be in the range of 12 to 15 percent. See Chapter 6 for further discussion.

8. There are a number of practical issues related to the calculation of the above ratios. First, in calculating all the turnover ratios, the assets used in the calculations can be either year-end values or an average of the beginning and ending balances in a year. We use the year-end values here for simplicity. Second, strictly speaking, one should use credit sales to calculate accounts receivable turnover and days' receivables. However, since it is usually difficult to obtain data on credit sales, total sales are used instead. Similarly, in calculating accounts payable turnover or days' payables, cost of goods sold is substituted for purchases because of data availability.

9. One could also construct coverage ratios to take into account not only interest expense but also other fixed charges, such as lease payment obligations and required debt repayments.

10. As mentioned in Chapter 3, Compaq had some off-balance-sheet liabilities that are not included in the calculation of these debt ratios. In fact, some of Compaq's interest expense was related to these off-balance-sheet liabilities, including dealer-financing arrangements.

11. Changes in cash and marketable securities are excluded because this is the amount being explained by the cash flow statement. Changes in short-term debt and the current portion of long-term debt are excluded because these accounts represent financing flows, not operating flows.

chapter 5

Prospective Analysis: Forecasting

Most financial statement analysis tasks are undertaken with a forward-looking decision in mind. And much of the time, it is useful to summarize the view developed in the analysis with an explicit forecast. Managers need forecasts for planning and to provide performance targets. Analysts need forecasts to help communicate their view of the firm's prospects to investors. Bankers and debt market participants need forecasts to assess the likelihood of loan repayment. Moreover, there are a variety of contexts (including but not limited to security analysis) where the forecast is usefully summarized in the form of an estimate of the firm's value—an estimate that can be viewed as the best attempt to reflect in a single summary statistic the manager's or analyst's view of the firm's prospects.

Prospective analysis includes two tasks—forecasting and valuation—that together represent approaches to explicitly summarizing the analyst's forward-looking views. In this chapter, we focus on forecasting. Valuation is the topic of the following two chapters.

RELATION OF FORECASTING TO OTHER ANALYSES

Forecasting is not so much a separate analysis as it is a way of summarizing what has been learned through business strategy analysis, accounting analysis, and financial analysis. For example, a projection of the future profitability of Compaq as of early 1993 must be grounded ultimately in an understanding of questions such as:

 • *From business strategy analysis:* What will Compaq's shift in business strategy in 1992 mean for future margins and sales volume? Can Compaq continue to command price premiums even as it emphasizes cost leadership and market share? What will Compaq's drive for market share imply about the need for working capital and capital expenditures?

① • *From accounting analysis:* Are there any aspects of Compaq's accounting that suggest past earnings are either stronger or weaker than they appear on the surface? If so, what are the implications for future earnings?

③ • *From financial analysis:* What are the sources of the improvement in Compaq's net margin in 1992? Do they suggest that the improvement is sustainable? Has Compaq's shift in business strategy translated into improvements in asset utilization in 1992? Can any such improvements in efficiency be sustained or enhanced? Why is Compaq so conservative in its design of capital structure? Would a more aggressive stance enhance profitability enough to offset the increased risk of distress?

THE TECHNIQUES OF FORECASTING

A forecast can be no better than the business strategy analysis, the accounting analysis, and the financial analysis underlying it. However, there are certain techniques and knowledge that can help a manager or analyst to structure the best possible forecast, conditional on what has been learned in the previous steps. Below, we summarize an approach to structuring the forecast, some information useful in getting started, and some detailed steps used to forecast earnings, balance sheet data, and cash flows.

The Overall Structure of the Forecast

The best way to forecast future performance is to do it comprehensively, by producing not only an earnings forecast, but a forecast of cash flows and the balance sheet as well. A comprehensive approach is useful, even in cases where one might be interested primarily in a single facet of performance, because it guards against unrealistic implicit assumptions. For example, if an analyst forecasts growth in sales and earnings for several years without explicit consideration of the required increases in working capital and plant assets and the associated financing, the forecast might possibly imbed unreasonable assumptions about asset turnover, leverage, or equity capital infusions.

A comprehensive approach involves many forecasts, but in most cases they are all linked to the behavior of a few key "drivers." The drivers vary according to the type of business involved, but for businesses outside the financial services sector, the sales forecast is nearly always one of the key drivers, profit margin is another. When asset turnover is expected to remain stable—an often realistic assumption—working capital accounts and investment in plant should track the growth in sales closely. Most major expenses also track sales, subject to expected shifts in profit margins. By linking forecasts of such amounts to the sales forecast, one can avoid internal inconsistencies and unrealistic implicit assumptions.

In many contexts, the manager or analyst is interested ultimately in a forecast of cash flows, not earnings per se. Nevertheless, even forecasts of cash flows tend to be grounded in practice on forecasts of accounting numbers, including sales and earnings. Of course, it would be possible in principle to move *directly* to forecasts of cash flows—

inflows from customers, outflows to suppliers and laborers, and so forth—and in some businesses, this is a convenient way to proceed. In most cases, however, the growth prospects and profitability of the firm are more readily framed in terms of accrual-based sales and operating earnings. These amounts can then be converted to cash flow measures by adjusting for the effects of non-cash expenses and expenditures for working capital and plant.

Getting Started: Points of Departure

Every forecast has, at least implicitly, an initial "benchmark" or point of departure— some notion of how a particular amount, such as sales or earnings, would be expected to behave in the absence of detailed information. For example, in beginning to contemplate 1993 profitability for Compaq, one must start somewhere. A possibility is to begin with the 1992 performance; another starting point might be the 1992 performance, adjusted for recent trends. A third possibility that might seem reasonable—but one that generally turns out not to be very useful—is the average performance over several prior years.

By the time one has completed a business strategy analysis, an accounting analysis, and a detailed financial analysis, the resulting forecast might differ significantly from the original point of departure. Nevertheless, simply for purposes of having a starting point that can help anchor the detailed analysis, it is useful to know how certain key financial statistics behave "on average."

In the case of some key statistics, such as earnings, a point of departure or benchmark based only on prior behavior of the number is more powerful than one might expect. Research demonstrates that some such benchmarks for earnings are not much less accurate than the forecasts of professional security analysts, who have access to a rich information set. (We return to this point in more detail below.) Thus, the benchmark is often not only a good starting point, but also close to the amount forecast after detailed analysis. Large departures from the benchmark could be justified only in cases where the firm's situation is demonstrably unusual.

Reasonable points of departure for forecasts of key accounting numbers can be based on the evidence summarized below. Such evidence may also be useful for checking the reasonableness of a completed forecast.

THE BEHAVIOR OF SALES.   For typical firms, annual sales follow approximately a process labeled a "random walk with drift."[1] For such a process, the forecast for year $t+1$ is simply the amount observed for year t, plus a "drift" that reflects the average change in the series over prior years. Thus, the evidence indicates that for typical firms, sales behavior is very much a reflection of "what you have done for me lately." Sales information more than one year old is useful only to the extent that it contributes to the average annual trend.

The implication of the evidence is that, in beginning to contemplate future sales possibilities, a useful number to start with is last year's sales. Long-term trends in sales tend to be sustained on average, and so they are also worthy of consideration. The average level of sales over several prior years is not. If quarterly data are also considered, then some consideration should usually be given to any departures from the long-run trend that occurred in the most recent quarter. For most firms, these most recent changes tend to be partially repeated in subsequent quarters.[2]

THE BEHAVIOR OF EARNINGS.   Earnings have also been shown, on average, to follow a process that can be approximated by a "random walk" or "random walk with drift." Thus, the prior year's earnings is a good starting point in considering future earnings potential. As will be explained in more detail later in the chapter, it is reasonable to adjust this simple benchmark for the earnings changes of the most recent quarter (that is, changes versus the comparable quarter of the prior year, and after controlling for the long-run trend in the series). However, even a simple random walk forecast—one that predicts next year's earnings will be equal to last year's earnings—is surprisingly useful. One study documents that professional analysts' year-ahead forecasts are only 22 percent more accurate (on average) than a simple random walk forecast.[3] Thus, early in a year, an earnings forecast will *usually* not differ dramatically from a random walk benchmark.

THE BEHAVIOR OF RETURNS ON INVESTMENT.   Given that prior earnings serves as a useful benchmark for future earnings, one might expect the same to be true of rates of return on investment, such as return on equity (ROE). That, however, is not the case, for two reasons. First, even though the *average* firm tends to sustain the current earnings level, that is not true of firms with unusual levels of ROE. Firms with abnormally high (or low) ROE tend to experience earnings declines (or increases).[4]

Second, firms with higher ROEs tend to expand their investment bases more quickly than others, which causes the denominator of the ROE to increase. Of course, if firms could earn returns on the new investments that match the returns on the old ones, then the level of ROE would be maintained. However, firms have difficulty pulling that off. Firms with higher ROEs tend to find that, as time goes by, their earnings growth does not keep pace with growth in their investment base, and ROE ultimately falls.

The resulting behavior of ROE and other measures of return on investment is characterized as "mean reverting": firms with above-average or below-average rates of return tend to revert over time to a "normal" level within three to ten years (for ROE, historically in the range of 10 to 14 percent for U.S. firms).[5] Figure 5-1 documents this effect for U.S. firms for 1972–1991. In each year, firms are divided into ten groups based on their ROEs. The ROEs of each group are then traced through subsequent years. The most profitable group of firms initially, with ROEs of 34 percent, experience a decline to 15 percent within three years and are never above 13 percent after 5 years. Those with the lowest initial ROEs (–21 percent) experience an increase to breakeven within four years.

Figure 5-1 Path of ROE Over Time

Return on Equity

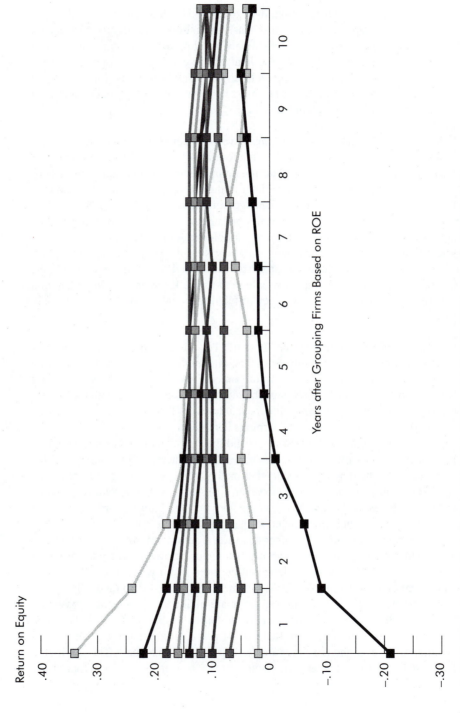

Years after Grouping Firms Based on ROE

Explanation: Firms are grouped in deciles in year 0, based on ROE. The graph then plots ROE for each of the ten groups for the subsequent ten years. Based on data for U.S. industrial firms, 1972–1991; the number of firms per year varies from 1640 to 2306.

All but the three initially most unprofitable groups revert to "normal" levels of ROE—within the range of 10 to 14 percent—by the fifth year.

The pattern in Figure 5-1 is not a coincidence. It is exactly what the economics of competition would predict. The tendency of high ROEs to fall is a reflection of high profitability attracting competition. The tendency of low ROEs to rise reflects the mobility of capital away from unproductive ventures and toward more profitable ones.

Despite the general tendencies documented in Figure 5-1, there are some firms whose ROEs may remain at above- or below-normal levels for long periods of time. In some cases, the phenomenon reflects the strength of a strong brand name (e.g., Coca-Cola), but often it is purely an artifact of accounting methods. Good examples in the U.S. are pharmaceutical firms, whose major economic asset (the intangible value of research and development) is not recorded on the balance sheet and is therefore excluded from the denominator of ROE. For those firms, one could reasonably expect high ROEs—in excess of 20 percent—over the long run, even in the face of strong competitive forces.

THE BEHAVIOR OF PROFIT MARGINS.   The behavior of rates of return on investment offers a lesson for the behavior of profit margins as well. Recall from Chapter 4 that ROEs and profit margins are linked as follows:

ROE = Profit margin $\times$ Asset turnover $\times$ Adjusted leverage

Asset turnover tends to be rather stable, in part because it is so much a function of the technology of an industry. Leverage also tends to be stable, simply because management policies on capital structure aren't often changed. Profit margins stand out as the most variable component of ROE. If the forces of competition drive abnormal ROEs toward more normal levels, the change is most likely to arrive in the form of changes in profit margins.

The implication is that profit margins, like ROEs, tend to be driven by competition to "normal" levels over time. However, what constitutes "normal" varies widely according to the technology employed within an industry and the corporate strategy pursued by a firm—both of which influence turnover and leverage.[6] For example, assume that asset turnover hovers around 1.5 and that there is no leverage (i.e., financial leverage = assets/equity = 1.0). Then if competition drives ROE toward a "normal" level of, say, 13 percent, the profit margin must be driven to about 8.7 percent:

ROE = Profit margin $\times$ Asset turnover $\times$ Financial leverage

13% = Profit margin $\times$ 1.5 $\times$ 1.0

Profit margin = 8.7%

However, if the technology in the industry were such that asset turnover could be sustained at 2.5, then competition would tend to drive the profit margin lower, to 5.2 percent (13% = 5.2% $\times$ 2.5 $\times$ 1.0). In a fully competitive equilibrium, profit margins should remain high for firms that must operate with a low turnover, and vice versa.

The implication of the above discussion of rates of return and profit margins is that a reasonable point of departure for a forecast of such a statistic should consider more than just the most recent observation. One should also consider whether that rate or margin is above or below a normal level. If so, and absent detailed information to the contrary, one would expect some movement over time toward the norm. Of course, this centralizing tendency might be overcome in some cases where, for example, the firm has erected barriers to competition that can protect margins, even for extended periods. The lesson from the evidence, however, is that such cases are the exceptional ones.

As we proceed with the steps involved in producing a detailed forecast, the reader will note that we draw to some extent on the above evidence of the behavior of accounting numbers. However, it is important to keep in mind that a knowledge of *average* behavior will not apply to all firms well. The art of financial statement analysis requires not only knowing what the "normal" patterns are but also knowing how to identify those firms that will *not* follow the norm.

Elements of the Detailed Forecast

The steps that could be followed in producing a comprehensive forecast are summarized in the following paragraphs. We assume that the firm being analyzed is among the vast majority for which the forecast would reasonably be anchored by a sales forecast.

THE SALES FORECAST.   The first step in most forecasting exercises is the sales prediction. There is no generally accepted approach to forecasting sales. The approach should be tailored to the context and should reflect the factors considered in the prior steps of the analysis. For example, for a large retail firm, a sales forecast would normally consider the prior year's sales, increases due purely to expansion of the number of retail outlets, and "comparable store growth," which captures growth in sales in already existing stores. The forecast of growth might consider such factors as customer acceptance of new product lines, marketing plans, changes in pricing strategies, competitors' behavior, and the expected state of the economy. Another approach—and possibly the only feasible one when little history exists—is to estimate the size of the target market, project the degree of market penetration, and then consider how quickly that degree of penetration can be achieved.

Table 5-1 presents a forecast of sales and earnings for Compaq Computer Corporation, produced by an analyst at Duff & Phelps in February 1993. The 1993 sales forecast, a 30 percent increase over the prior year, is approximately consistent with a continuation of sales levels achieved by Compaq in the latter half of 1992, after the introduction of a major set of new products. Thus, the forecast is roughly a random walk forecast, but based only on the last two quarters' sales. In commenting on the forecast, the analyst recognized at least three factors that might support a more optimistic view on sales: (1) Compaq's large sales backlog at the end of 1992; (2) the firm's shift in its corporate strategy towards higher unit volume through more aggressive pricing; and (3) the existence

Table 5-1 Analyst's Forecast of Compaq 1993 Earnings

	1992 Actual Results		1993 Forecast	
	$ millions	% of sales	$ millions	% of sales
Sales	$4,100	100%	$5,330	100%
Cost of sales	2,905	71%	3,944	74%
Gross margin	1,195	29%	1,386	26%
Research and development costs	173	4%	160	3%
Selling, general, and administrative expense	699	17%	746	14%
Other income and expense	28	1%	0	0%
Earnings before taxes	295	7.2%	479	9.0%
Provision for taxes	97	2.4%	158	3.0%
Earnings from consolidated companies	198	4.8%	321	6.0%
Equity in net income of affiliated company	15	0.4%	0	0.0%
Net income	$213	5.2%	$321	6.0%
ROE	.11		.15	
EPS: primary	$2.58		NA	
EPS: fully diluted	$2.52		$3.80	

Source: *Common Stock Summary: Compaq Computer Corporation*, Duff & Phelps Investment Research Company (Chicago, Illinois), February 1993.

of enough excess manufacturing capacity to accommodate a sales increase of nearly 40 percent without adding facilities. Nevertheless, the forecast was for no further improvement in earnings over the last two quarters, with higher unit sales being offset by lower prices, because (1) competitors were selling what the analyst considered similar products at comparable or lower prices; (2) overall industry growth was expected to slow; and (3) price pressure was expected to intensify even further as firms in the industry engaged in their ongoing "struggle for low-cost producer status."

The Duff & Phelps forecast appears to be based largely on analysis that views the firm as a whole. An alternative approach—not feasible for all firms—is to build a sales forecast on a product-by-product basis. Table 5-2 presents such a forecast, produced by First Boston analyst Bill Gurley in late 1993, about nine months after the Duff & Phelps forecast was released. By this time, it was clear that Compaq was performing much better than expected early in the year—1993 sales were now expected to be up 73 percent over the prior year.

Table 5-2 Analyst's Detailed Sales Forecast for Compaq, November 1993

Revenue Calculation for 1993

	First Quarter, A			Second Quarter, A			Third Quarter, A			Fourth Quarter, A			Year 1993, E		
	Units	Price	Revenue	Units	Price	Revenue	Units	Price	Revenue	Units	Price	Revenue	Units	Price	Revenue
Servers:															
ProLiant	0		$0	0		$0	2	$14,600	$26	7	$15,400	$108	9	$15,236	$134
Systempro	5	$14,500	65	5	$14,500	73	5	$13,475	67	2	$12,200	24	17	$13,911	230
Prosignia	12	6,400	74	15	6,425	96	16	6,800	109	19	6,900	131	62	6,665	410
	16	8,678	139	20	8,444	169	23	8,880	202	28	9,404	263	87	8,911	773
Desktop:															
Deskpro/M	155	2,776	430	151	2,695	407	150	2,710	407	160	2,800	448	616	2,746	1,692
Deskpro/I-/XE	135	1,751	236	137	1,700	233	135	1,685	227	145	1,750	254	552	1,722	951
Prolinea	208	1,421	296	210	1,380	290	225	1,350	304	245	1,300	319	888	1,360	1,208
Presario	0		0	0		0	30	1,210	38	100	1,195	120	130	1,198	156
	498	1,932	962	498	1,867	930	540	1,804	974	650	1,753	1,140	2186	1,832	4,006
Portable:															
Portable 486	5	4,700	24	5	4,900	25	4	4,950	20	4	4,950	20	18	4,867	88
Concerto	0	0	0	0	0	0	8	2,300	18	32	2,250	72	40	2,260	90
LTE Lite	105	2,635	277	103	2,750	283	105	2,750	289	115	2,750	316	428	2,722	1,165
Contura	106	1,736	184	110	1,810	199	115	1,900	219	130	1,950	254	461	1,855	855
Sub-Notebook	0		0	0		0	0		0	0		0	0		0
PDA	0		0	0		0	0		0	0		0	0		0
	216	2,242	484	218	2,325	507	232	2,351	545	281	2,354	662	947	2,321	2,198
Peripherals:															
Pagemarq Printers	9	2,895	26	10	2,700	27	11	2,200	24	12	2,000	24	42	2,411	101
Total	739	$2,180	$1,611	746	$2,188	$1,632	806	$2,167	$1,746	971	$2,151	$2,089	3262	$2,170	$7,078

Revenue Calculation for 1994

	First Quarter, A			Second Quarter, A			Third Quarter, A			Fourth Quarter, A			Year 1994, E		
	Units	Price	Revenue	Units	Price	Revenue	Units	Price	Revenue	Units	Price	Revenue	Units	Price	Revenue
Servers:															
ProLiant	8	$16,000	$128	9	$16,600	$141	9	$16,500	$149	11	$16,300	$179	37	$16,353	$597
Systempro	1		0	0		0	0		0	0		0	1		0
Prosignia	20	7,040	141	21	7,040	144	22	6,900	152	28	6,850	192	91	6,947	629
	29	9,432	269	29	9,842	285	31	9,687	300	39	9,515	371	128	9,613	1,226
Desktop:															
Deskpro/M	155	2,850	442	155	2,850	442	155	2,800	434	165	2,750	454	630	2,812	1,771
Deskpro/I-/XE	145	1,800	261	150	1,750	263	150	1,700	255	155	1,650	256	600	1,724	1,034
Prolinea	235	1,300	306	210	1,350	284	205	1,350	277	235	1,300	306	885	1,323	1,171
Presario	115	1,250	144	130	1,190	155	145	1,134	164	210	1,080	227	600	1,149	690
	650	1,772	1,152	645	1,771	1,143	655	1,724	1,130	765	1,623	1,242	2715	1,719	4,666
Portable:															
Portable 486	4	5,050	20	5	4,810	24	4	4,581	18	5	4,362	22	18	4,688	84
Concerto	50	2,400	120	65	2,350	153	70	2,238	157	80	2,132	171	265	2,264	600
LTE Lite	105	2,750	289	100	2,750	275	100	2,750	275	115	2,750	316	420	2,750	1,155
Contura	115	1,800	207	105	1,850	194	105	1,850	194	110	1,800	198	435	1,824	794
Sub-Notebook	5	1,100	6	15	1,100	17	20	1,050	21	30	1,000	30	70	1,043	73
PDA	0	0	0	0	0	0	10	1,300	13	30	1,250	38	40	1,263	51
	279	2,299	641	290	2,285	663	309	2,195	678	370	2,092	774	1248	2,209	2,756
Peripherals:															
Pagemarq Printers	15	1,900	29	20	1,800	36	22	2,400	53	29	2,286	68	86	2,135	184
Total	973	$2,150	$2,091	984	$2,161	$2,126	1017	$2,125	$2,161	1203	$2,039	$2,453	4177	$2,115	$8,832

Source: B. Gurley, "Compaq Computer Corporation: Initiation of Coverage," C S First Boston (November 29, 1993).

In Table 5-2, Gurley presents estimates of *actual* units sold and prices for each of 14 major Compaq product lines for the first three quarters of 1993, and associated *forecasts* for the fourth quarter of 1993 and for each quarter of 1994. Compaq management releases some breakdown of sales activity, but not at this level of detail. Gurley's estimates are based on information from a variety of sources in addition to management, including suppliers, competitors, retail outlets, and other firms that research the industry (such as Dataquest). The forecasts incorporate a detailed understanding of the various products and their features, distribution networks, and the prices that can be commanded in light of competition and the Compaq brand name. Overall, while Gurley recognizes that a repeat of 1993's expected 73 percent sales increase is not likely, he still projects a 25 percent jump in 1994. Following the normal increase during the holiday season in 1993, sales are projected to be maintained at that level during 1994 and to jump again in the fourth quarter of 1994.

Although built product by product, Gurley's projections are supported by thinking at both the product and overall firm level. Gurley explains that his projection of 1994 sales growth in excess of the industry average is based on three factors: (1) the benefits of consolidation as "natural selection plays out," (2) strong positioning, thanks to new products in the hot markets for servers and portables, and (3) opportunities for increased penetration in the fast-growing home PC market, resulting from favorable pricing and a popular product (Presario) introduced in the latter half of 1993. The explanation is offered in the context of a view that Compaq's new emphasis on a low-cost, high-volume approach is "the single most sustainable corporate strategy for a PC vendor that wishes to compete on a global basis,"[7] and that Compaq's brand image will help make this strategy succeed.

THE FORECAST OF EXPENSES AND EARNINGS. Expenses should be forecast item by item, since different expenses may be driven by different factors. However, most major expenses are clearly related to sales and are therefore naturally framed as fractions of sales. These include cost of sales and selling, general, and administrative expenses. Research and deveolpment need not track current sales closely; however, research and development generally tracks sales at least roughly over the long run. Other expenses are more closely related to drivers other than sales. Interest expense is driven by debt levels and interest rates. Depreciation expense should be forecast in a way consistent with the firm's depreciation policy. Under straight-line depreciation, the expense would tend to be a fairly stable fraction of beginning depreciable plant. Tax provisions are driven by pretax income and factors that have a permanent impact on tax payments (such as tax rates applicable to certain foreign subsidiaries). Equity in the income of affiliates is determined by whatever drives the affiliate's earnings.

In the case of Compaq, the three largest expenses—cost of sales, research and development, and selling, general and administrative expense—were all forecast by Duff & Phelps as fractions of sales (see Table 5-1). Cost of sales was expected to increase as a fraction of sales, causing the gross margin percentage to decline to 26 percent from 29 percent. This projected decline reflects a continuation of a trend in gross margin that existed for five consecutive quarters, based on Compaq's shift in corporate strategy and increasing competition based on price. By the last quarter of 1992, the gross margin percentage had already fallen to 26.9 percent, down from 37 percent a year earlier. Thus, the forecast of 26 percent for 1993 is only slightly lower than the margin already experienced recently. In Table 5-1, research and development and selling, general, and administrative are both expected to decline in 1993 as fractions of sales, because some economies are expected from Compaq's increased emphasis on sales volume and market share.

In long-range forecasts (to be presented in detail in Chapter 6), Duff & Phelps projected a continuing decline in gross margins, to 20 percent: "what the IBM PC company is living with now and appears to expect to live with in the future."[8] This view is consistent with our statements in Chapter 2 that, over the long run, it is not clear that Compaq can sustain a competitive advantage over IBM and some other PC assemblers. The decline in gross margin is projected to be accompanied by reductions in selling, general, and administrative costs as a fraction of sales, so as to leave Compaq with a competitive net margin. Thus, the forecasts are consistent with the behavior of margins described previously; that is, they are expected over several years to revert to a more normal level.

Remaining expenses are not driven directly by sales. The "other" category includes interest income, interest expense, and a number of transitory gains and losses that are nearly offsetting in 1992. The analyst projected zero for 1993, or grouped the items within another expense category. Tax expense is forecast as a fraction of pretax income, assuming that fraction will continue to hold at 33 percent. Equity in the income of an affiliate will fall to zero because the associated investment was liquidated in 1992.

The forecasts of sales and expenses produce an expected net margin of 6 percent and a return on equity of approximately 15 percent. Both are improvements over 1992's rather ordinary overall performance, but are slightly weaker than the performance of late 1992, when ROEs hit 19 percent after new product lines were introduced. The producer of the forecast notes that "though Compaq has a large backlog going into the first quarter, which we do not like to bet against, we do not believe that a 19%+ ROE is sustainable in an industry where elasticity [of demand is high]—[we expect] flat revenues on more units for 1993." The expected reversion to a more normal level of ROE is consistent with the average behavior of ROE described previously. It is also consistent with Chapter 2's statements about the difficulty of maintaining a competitive advantage in this industry.

THE FORECAST OF BALANCE SHEET ACCOUNTS.   Since various balance sheet accounts may be driven by different factors, they are usually best forecast individually. However, several accounts, including operating working capital accounts and plant assets, are driven over the long run by sales activity. Thus, these accounts can be forecast as fractions of sales, allowing for any expected changes in the efficiency of asset utilization. If management plans for capital expenditures are known, they would clearly be useful in forecasting plant assets. Other accounts may depend on a variety of factors, including policies on capital structure and dividends.

Table 5-3 presents Duff & Phelps' December 1993 forecast of 1994 income statement and balance sheet accounts for Compaq.[9] This forecast was produced around the same time as the First Boston sales forecast given in Table 5-2, and it reflects the stronger-than-anticipated experience of the first three quarters of 1993. The actual results for

Table 5-3 Analyst's Forecast of Compaq 1994 Earnings and Balance Sheet

	1993 Actual Results		1994 Forecast	
	$ millions	% of sales	$ millions	% of sales
Statement of earnings				
Sales	$7,191	100.0%	$8,712	100.0%
Cost of sales	5,493	76.4%	6,774	77.8%
Gross margin	1,698	23.6%	1,938	22.2%
Research and development	169	2.4%	218	2.5%
Selling, general, and administrative expense	837	11.6%	994	11.4%
Other expense (income)	76	1.1%	36	0.4%
Earnings before taxes	616	8.6%	690	7.9%
Provision for taxes	154	2.1%	173	2.0%
Net income	$462	6.4%	$517	5.9%
Balance sheet				
Cash and equivalents	$ 627	9%	$1,151	13%
Receivables	1,377	19%	1,500	17%
Inventories	1,123	16%	1,238	14%
Prepaid expenses and other	164	2%	157	2%
Total current assets	3,291	46%	4,046	46%
Property, plant, & equipment	779	11%	801	9%
Other assets	14	0%	25	0%
Total assets	4,084	57%	4,872	56%
Accounts payable	637	9%	813	9%
Income tax payable	69	1%	94	1%
Other current liabilities	538	7%	624	7%
Total current liabilities	1,244	17%	1,531	18%
Deferred income taxes	186	3%	220	3%
Shareholders equity	2,654	37%	3,121	36%
Total liabilities and equity	$4,084	57%	$4,872	56%

Sources: Actual results from Compaq Computer 1993 Annual Report; forecasts from *Company Analysis: Compaq Computer Corporation*, Duff & Phelps Investment Research Company (Chicago, Illinois), December 1993.

1993 are presented in Table 5-3 for purposes of comparison. Those results were not yet known at the forecast date, but analysts were able to project them with a high level of accuracy.

Most balance sheet account forecasts maintain relations to sales that are consistent from 1993 to 1994. In particular, total asset utilization is nearly constant. Receivables, inventory, and plant are forecast to decline slightly, relative to sales, reflecting increased efficiency as Compaq's shift to a high-volume strategy is more fully realized. However, this efficiency is largely offset by a dramatic projected increase in cash balances. The net effect is that total assets as a fraction of sales decline only slightly.

An alternative approach to balance sheet projection would be to assume the *change* in each balance sheet account is linked to the *change* in sales. For example, one might forecast that inventory balances will increase by 15 to 20 percent of sales increases. The weakness of this approach is that it takes the beginning balances as given and adjusts from those points. The approach is problematic because working capital accounts at a given point in time often reflect some unusual deviation from the norm. (For example, beginning-of-year accruals might have ballooned, depending on where payday falls on the calendar.) More importantly, the firm's strategy may suggest a shift from the beginning-of-year position. In Compaq's case, the shift to a high-volume strategy is expected by Duff & Phelps to reduce the amounts of inventory and receivables needed per dollar of sales.

Liability and equity accounts are maintained at nearly identical fractions of sales, reflecting a presumed maintenance of the current capital structure policy. Both Duff & Phelps and First Boston assume that Compaq will continue to shun debt. But First Boston analyst Gurley notes that ROE could improve substantially if Compaq began to take on more leverage. We will return to the question of what capital structure would be best for Compaq in Chapter 11.

THE FORECAST OF CASH FLOWS. The forecast of earnings and balance sheet accounts implies a forecast of cash flows, which can be constructed as described in Chapter 4. Table 5-4 illustrates the projection of cash flows for Compaq for 1994. Most of the amounts can be calculated from the earnings and balance sheet data already presented in Table 5-3. The exceptions are the projections of capital expenditures, interest expense, depreciation expense, and deferred taxes, all of which are provided in (or can be calculated from) the Duff & Phelps report.

Duff & Phelps forecasts capital expenditures for 1994 at $218 million, up from 1993's $145 million. Capital expenditures are difficult to forecast without some guidance from management, and Compaq announced only after the release of the Duff & Phelps forecast that 1994 capital expenditures would probably be closer to $250 million. In the absence of such information, a good rule of thumb is to assume that the ratio of plant to sales will remain relatively stable, and that capital expenditures will be whatever amount is needed to maintain that ratio. If sales are growing, then capital expenditures will exceed depreciation.

Table 5-4 Forecast of Compaq 1994 Free Cash Flows

	Dollars in Millions
Net income	**$517**
Adjustments for non-current operating accruals:	
Deferred taxes	34
Depreciation	211
	762
Adjustment for interest expense less interest income (net of related tax effect)	22
Cash flow from operations before working capital investments and interest payments	**784**
Investment in working capital:	
Receivables	(123)
Inventories	(115)
Prepaid expenses and other	7
Accounts payable	176
Income tax payable	25
Other current liabilities	87
Other adjustments	(76)
	(19)
Cash from operations after investment in working capital, before interest payments	**765**
Interest expense less interest income (net of tax)	22
Cash from operations after investment in working capital, after interest payments	**743**
Capital expenditures	(218)
Free cash flow	**$525**

Based on earnings and balance sheet data in Table 5-3 and detailed income statement and capital expenditure projections from Duff & Phelps December 1993 report. Cash flow projection does not match that published by Duff & Phelps due to differences between expected and actual 1993 balance sheet amount (not yet published at time of Duff & Phelps report).

    For purposes of producing a cash flow forecast from earnings, the two noncash expenses, depreciation and deferred taxes, are required. Of course, both of these are already embedded in our earnings forecast, but they were not made explicit in Table 5-3. Compaq has $1,310 million in gross depreciable plant at the beginning of 1994, and depreciation expense has been running at about 13 percent of gross plant—suggesting an average depreciable life of about 8 years. Thus, one might expect depreciation in 1994 to be about .13 × $1,310, or $170 million, plus some modest increase for the increment added to plant in 1994. The Duff & Phelps forecast of depreciation ($211 million) seems high relative to this amount.[10] The Duff & Phelps forecast of the increase in deferred taxes maintains a constant ratio of the balance of deferred taxes to sales. This represents a reasonable approximation, although with knowledge of the details of Compaq's tax situation, one might be able to produce a more accurate forecast. For example, a key determinant of the change in deferred taxes is warranty expenses that are not deductible until paid. Such amounts can change dramatically when the pace of sales changes.

The forecast suggests Compaq's earnings will translate into a nearly equivalent amount of free cash flow. At first blush, this is surprising, because Compaq is expected to grow so fast, and growth requires additional investment. The key to the projection is that receivables and inventory will increase more slowly than sales, and that the increases can be financed largely through increases in payables and other current liabilities. First Boston analyst Gurley was not as optimistic as Duff & Phelps about Compaq's ability to contain working capital increases in the face of higher sales. However, if the projection in Table 5-4 materializes, Compaq will generate a substantial amount of free cash flow—$525 million—even while supporting increased sales volume. Duff & Phelps forecasts for 1995 and beyond suggest continued high levels of cash generation, in the range of $295 to $450 million per year. Unless accumulation of billions of dollars of cash is efficient for Compaq (which seems doubtful), some reconsideration of Compaq's no-dividend policy or consideration of share buybacks may be in order. We will return to the question of what dividend policy might be best for Compaq in Chapter 11.

Sensitivity Analysis

The projections discussed thus far represent nothing more than a "best guess." Managers and analysts are typically interested in a broader range of possibilities. For example, in considering the likelihood that short-term financing will be necessary, it would be wise to produce projections based on a more pessimistic view of profit margins and asset turnover. Alternatively, an analyst estimating the value of Compaq should consider the sensitivity of the estimate to the key assumptions about sales growth, profit margins, and asset utilization. What if competitor reaction to Compaq's high-volume strategy requires more dramatic price cuts than anticipated? What if the anticipated improvements in inventory turnover do not materialize? What if Compaq begins to include some debt in its capital structure?

There is no limit to the number of possible scenarios that can be considered. However, to provide some feel for the range of possible profit and cash flow outcomes that could arise for Compaq in 1994, Table 5-5 considers sales growth rates from 10 to 30 percent, and profit margins from 4 to 8 percent. These assumptions bracket the expected values used above—21 percent sales growth and 5.9 percent profit margin. All the projections hold asset turnover constant, and they assume no use of debt.

Judgments about what alternative scenarios are reasonably possible are difficult to make, but history can provide some guidance. The lowest profit margin considered in Table 5-5, 4 percent, is equal to the lowest level experienced in Compaq's recent history (in 1991). While weaker performance may be unlikely, margins below that level have

Table 5-5 Forecast of Compaq 1994 Earnings and Cash Flows: Sensitivity Analysis

Alternative Scenarios Considered

Sales growth	10%	10%	10%	21%	21%	21%	30%	30%	30%
Profit margin	4%	5.9%	8%	4%	5.9%	8%	4%	5.9%	8%

Implied Sales, Earnings, and Free Cash Flows (millions of dollars)

Sales	$7,910	$7,910	$7,910	$8,712	$8,712	$8,712	$9,348	$9,348	$9,348
Earnings	316	469	633	348	517	697	374	555	748
Free cash flow	506	659	822	356	525	705	238	419	612

Notes: The base case (with 21% sales growth and 5.9% profit margin) is that presented in detail in Tables 5-3 and 5-4.
Alternative scenarios assume that asset turnover and leverage remain constant.

clearly been experienced by others in the industry, even as recently as 1993. Note that if Compaq's gross margin fell to the 20 percent that IBM generates in its PC division, with no decline in selling, general, and administrative expense, Compaq's net profit margin would vanish entirely. The lowest sales increase considered in Table 5-5 is 10 percent. Coming off a year where sales increased by 75 percent and new product lines were very successful late in the fourth quarter, and in light of Compaq's corporate strategy and overall industry growth rates, sales growth of 10 percent appears to be quite pessimistic.

Turning to the more optimistic projections, we could note that an 8 percent net profit margin may appear at first glance to be well within the range of achievable performance. It is lower than the double-digit performance turned in by Compaq in every year from 1987 through 1990. However, in light of Compaq's shift in corporate strategy and the increased price pressure in the industry, a return to those high margin days seems extremely unlikely. An 8 percent margin would require holding the line on gross margin while continuing to achieve efficiencies in selling, general, and administrative expense—not very likely in light of industry competition and Compaq's new strategy. Looking at sales growth, a 30 percent increase for the year is only 6 percent higher than what one would project if fourth-quarter 1993 sales volumes were maintained throughout 1994. Even much higher sales growth rates are not out of the question.

Sensitivity analysis can be useful in helping to identify the key drivers of profits and cash flows. An interesting (and not unusual) feature of the analysis in Table 5-5 is that the stronger the sales growth, the *weaker* the free cash flows. The reason is that greater sales growth requires larger investments in working capital. Overall, free cash flow estimates range from a low of $238 million with the combination of high growth and low margins, to a high of $822 million with low growth and high margins. Although one should also contemplate the possibility of slower inventory and receivables turns than considered thus far, the analysis suggests that Compaq is not likely to face a "cash squeeze" during 1994—and that the firm may well have to confront the question of what to do with excess cash.

SEASONALITY AND INTERIM FORECASTS

Thus far, we have concerned ourselves with annual forecasts. However, especially for security analysts in the U.S., forecasting is very much a quarterly game. Forecasting quarter-by-quarter raises a new set of questions. How important is seasonality? What is a useful point of departure: the most recent quarter's performance? the comparable quarter of the prior year? some combination of the two? How should quarterly data be used in producing an annual forecast? Does the item-by-item approach to forecasting used for annual data apply equally well to quarterly data? Full consideration of these questions lies outside the scope of this chapter, but we can begin to answer some of them.

Seasonality is a more important phenomenon in sales and earnings behavior than one might guess. It is present for more than just the retail sector firms that benefit from holiday sales. Seasonality also results from weather-related phenomena (e.g., for electric and gas utilities, construction firms, and motorcycle manufacturers), new product introduction patterns (e.g., for the automobile industry), and other factors. Analysis of the time series behavior of earnings for U.S. firms suggests that at least some seasonality is present in nearly every major industry.

The implication for forecasting is that one cannot focus only on performance of the most recent quarter as a point of departure. In fact, the evidence suggests that, in forecasting earnings, if one had to choose only one quarter's performance as a point of departure, it would be the comparable quarter of the prior year, not the most recent quarter. Note how consistent this finding is with the reports of analysts or the financial press. When they discuss a quarterly earnings announcement, it is nearly always evaluated relative to the performance of the comparable quarter of the prior year, not the most recent quarter.

Research has produced models that forecast sales, earnings, and earnings per share, based solely on prior quarters' observations. Such models are not used by many analysts, since analysts have access to much more information than such simple models contain. However, the models are useful for helping those unfamiliar with the behavior of earnings data to understand how it tends to evolve through time. Such an understanding can provide useful general background, a point of departure in forecasting that can be adjusted to reflect details not revealed in the history of earnings, or a "reasonableness" check on a detailed forecast.

Using Q_t to denote earnings (or EPS) for quarter t, and $E[Q_t]$ as its expected value, one model of the earnings process that fits well across a variety of industries is the so-called Foster model[11]:

$$E(Q_t) = Q_{t-4} + \delta + \phi(Q_{t-1} - Q_{t-5})$$

Foster shows that a model of the same form also works well with sales data. The form of the Foster model confirms the importance of seasonality, because it shows that the starting point for a forecast for quarter t is the earnings four quarters ago (Q_{t-4}). It states that, when constrained to using only prior earnings data, a reasonable forecast of earnings for quarter t includes the following elements:

the earnings of the comparable quarter of the prior year (Q_{t-4});

a long-run trend in year-to-year quarterly earnings increases (δ); and

a fraction (ϕ) of the year-to-year increase in quarterly earnings experienced most recently $(Q_{t-1} - Q_{t-5})$.

The parameters δ and ϕ can easily be estimated for a given firm with a simple linear regression model available in most spreadsheet software.[12] For most firms, the parameter ϕ tends to be in the range of .25 to .50, indicating that 25 to 50 percent of an increase in quarterly earnings tends to persist in the form of another increase in the subsequent quarter. The parameter δ reflects, in part, the average year-to-year change in quarterly earnings over past years, and it varies considerably from firm to firm.

Research indicates that the Foster model produces one-quarter-ahead forecasts that are off, on average, by $.30 to $.35 per share.[13] Such a degree of accuracy stacks up surprisingly well with that of security analysts, who obviously have access to much information ignored in the model. As one would expect, most of the evidence supports analysts' being more accurate, but the models are good enough to be "in the ball park" in most circumstances. Thus, while it would certainly be unwise to rely completely on such a naive model, an understanding of the typical earnings behavior reflected by it is useful.

Compaq's quarterly EPS for years prior to 1994 behaved as shown in Table 5-6. Note the strong presence of seasonality. The fourth quarter of the year has been the strongest in every year except 1989 and 1991. On average, the fourth quarter accounts for 36 percent of annual earnings.

If we used the Foster model to forecast EPS for the first quarter of 1994, we would start with EPS of the comparable quarter of 1993, or $1.23. We would then expect some additional upward trend in EPS, and a partial repetition of the most recent quarter's increase ($1.74 − $1.11). More specifically, when the parameters δ and ϕ are estimated with the data in Table 5-6,[14] the Foster model predicts EPS of $1.62.

$$E(Q_t) = Q_{t-4} + .08 + .49(Q_{t-1} - Q_{t-5})$$

Table 5-6 Compaq Quarterly Earnings per Share, 1987–1993

Quarter ended:	1993	1992	1991	1990	1989	1988	1987
March	$1.23	$0.50	$1.26	$1.08	$0.99	$0.60	$0.27
June	1.21	0.35	0.23	1.17	0.99	0.72	0.39
September	1.26	0.59	−0.82	1.38	1.02	0.69	0.48
December	1.74	1.11	0.77	1.50	0.93	1.08	0.63
Annual EPS	$5.45	$2.58	$1.49	$5.14	$3.89	$3.15	$1.80

$$= 1.23 + .08 + .49(1.74 - 1.11) = 1.62$$

The model can be extended to forecast earnings two quarters ahead, and even to produce a forecast for all quarters of the next year. The issue that arises here is that, in forecasting earnings two quarters ahead, one needs earnings one quarter ahead, and yet next quarter's earnings are still unknown. The proper resolution of the issue is to substitute the *forecast* of next quarter's earnings. Our forecast of earnings for Compaq for the second quarter of 1994, based on data through the fourth quarter of 1993, is $1.48:

$$\begin{aligned} E(Q_{t+1}) &= Q_{t-3} + .08 + .49[E(Q_t) - Q_{t-4}] \\ &= 1.21 + .08 + .49(1.62 - 1.23) = 1.48 \end{aligned}$$

The $1.62 forecast for the first quarter of 1994, naive as it is, is not far from the $1.69 average analyst forecast for Compaq in the March/April 1994 time frame (just after the 1993 earnings were announced). It is not surprising that the naive model produces a lower forecast, in light of the detailed information that we considered earlier. The model assumes that only 49 percent of the EPS increase of the most recent quarter will carry forward into 1994, but there are sound reasons to expect more at this point in Compaq's history. The most recent quarter's EPS reflects a long-term shift in the firm's corporate strategy and the profitability of hot new products that are still very early in their product life cycle.

The Foster model is not intended as a potential substitute for the hard work of producing a detailed forecast. Forecasting quarterly earnings should be done using the same approach used earlier for annual earnings, a line-item by line-item projection. However, the model does remind us of some important issues. First, it underscores that, due to seasonality, a reasonable starting point in quarterly forecasting is usually the comparable quarter of the prior year, not the most recent quarter. Second, it indicates that recent increases in profitability should *usually* not be extrapolated fully into the future—for Compaq's EPS, on average, only 49 percent of such changes tend to persist.

SUMMARY AND CONCLUSIONS

Forecasting represents the first step of prospective analysis, and serves to summarize the forward-looking view that emanates from business strategy analysis, accounting analysis, and financial analysis. Although not every financial statement analysis is accompanied by such an explicit summarization of a view of the future, forecasting is still a key tool for managers, consultants, security analysts, commercial bankers and other credit analysts, investment bankers, and others.

The best approach to forecasting future performance is to do it comprehensively: produce not only an earnings forecast but a forecast of cash flows and the balance sheet as well. Such a comprehensive approach provides a safeguard against internal inconsistencies and unrealistic implicit assumptions. The approach described here involves line-by-line analysis, so as to recognize that different items on the income statement and balance sheet are influenced by different drivers. Nevertheless, it remains true that a few key projections, such as sales growth and profit margin, usually drive most of the projected numbers.

The forecasting process should be embedded in an understanding of how various financial statistics tend to behave on average, and what might cause a firm to deviate from that average. Absent detailed information to the contrary, one would expect sales and earnings numbers to persist at their current levels, adjusted for overall trends of recent years. However, rates of return on investment (ROEs) tend, over several years, to move from abnormal to normal levels—close to the cost of equity capital—as the forces of competition come into play. Profit margins also tend to shift to normal levels, but for this statistic "normal" varies widely across firms and industries, depending on the levels of asset turnover and leverage. Some firms are capable of creating barriers to entry that enable them to fight these tendencies toward normal returns, even for many years, but these firms are the unusual cases.

For some purposes, including short-term planning and security analysis, forecasts for quarterly periods are desirable. One important feature of quarterly data is seasonality. At least some seasonality exists in the sales and earnings data of nearly every industry. An understanding of a firm's peaks and valleys throughout the year is a necessary ingredient of a good forecast of performance on a quarterly basis.

There are a variety of contexts (including but not limited to security analysis) where the forecast is usefully summarized in the form of an estimate of the firm's value—an estimate that, after all, can be viewed as the best attempt to reflect in a single summary statistic the manager's or analyst's view of the firm's prospects. That process of converting a forecast into a value estimate is labeled valuation. It is to that topic that we turn in the following two chapters.

DISCUSSION QUESTIONS

1. Merck is one of the largest pharmaceutical firms in the world. In the period 1985 to 1995 Merck consistently earned higher ROEs than the pharmaceutical industry as a whole. As a pharmaceutical analyst, what factors would you consider to be important in making projections of future ROEs for Merck? In particular, what factors would lead you to expect Merck to continue to be a superior performer in its industry, and what factors would lead you to expect Merck's future performance to revert to that of the industry as a whole?

2. John Right, an analyst with Stock Pickers Inc., claims: "It is not worth my time to develop detailed forecasts of sales growth, profit margins, etcetera, to make earnings projections. I can be almost as accurate, at virtually no cost, using the random walk model to forecast earnings." What is the random walk model? Do you agree or disagree with John Right's forecast strategy? Why or why not?

3. Which of the following types of businesses do you expect to show a high degree of seasonality in quarterly earnings? Explain why.
   - a supermarket
   - a pharmaceutical company
   - a software company
   - an auto manufacturer
   - a clothing retailer

4. What factors are likely to drive a firm's outlays for new capital (such as plant, property, and equipment) and for working capital (such as receivables and inventory)? What ratios would you use to help generate forecasts of these outlays?

5. How would the following events (reported this year) affect your forecasts of a firm's future net income?
   - an asset write-down
   - a merger or acquisition
   - the sale of a major division
   - the initiation of dividend payments

6. Consider the following two earnings forecasting models:

   Model 1: $\quad E_t(EPS_{t+1}) \;=\; EPS_t$

   Model 2: $\quad E_t(EPS_{t+1}) \;=\; \dfrac{1}{5}\sum_{t=1}^{5} EPS_t$

   $E_t(EPS)$ is the expected forecast of earnings per share for year $t+1$, given information available at t. Model 1 is usually called a random walk model for earnings, whereas Model 2 is called a mean-reverting model. The earnings per share for Ford Motor Company for the period 1990 to 1994 are as follows:

Year	1990	1991	1992	1993	1994
EPS	$0.93	$(2.40)	$(0.73)	$2.27	$4.97

   a. What would be the 1995 forecast for earnings per share for each model?
   b. Actual earnings per share for Ford in 1995 were $3.58. Given this information, what would be the 1996 forecast for earnings per share for each model? Why do the two models generate quite different forecasts? Which do you think would better describe earnings per share patterns? Why?

7. Joe Fatcat, an investment banker, states: "It is not worth my while to worry about detailed long-term forecasts. Instead, I use the following approach when forecasting cash flows beyond three years. I assume that sales grow at the rate of inflation, capital expenditures are equal to depreciation, and that net profit margins and working cap-

ital to sales ratios stay constant." What pattern of return on equity is implied by these assumptions? Is this reasonable?

CASES

The Home Depot, Inc.
The Gap, Inc.

NOTES

1. Among the few to have studied the statistical behavior of sales are Foster (1977) and Hopwood and McKeown (1985). They examine quarterly data, but their evidence is roughly consistent with annual sales behaving as indicated here.

2. See George Foster, "Quarterly Accounting Data: Time Series Properties and Predictive Ability Results," *The Accounting Review* (January 1977): 1–21; and William Hopwood and James McKeown, "The Incremental Information Content of Expenses over Sales," *Journal of Accounting Research* (Spring 1985): 161–174.

3. See Patricia O'Brien, "Analysts' Forecasts as Earnings Expectations," *Journal of Accounting and Economics* (January 1988): 53–83.

4. See Robert Freeman, James Ohlson, and Stephen Penman, "Book Rate-of-Return and Prediction of Earnings Changes: An Empirical Investigation," *Journal of Accounting Research* (Autumn 1982): 639–653.

5. See Stephen H. Penman, "An Evaluation of Accounting Rate-of-Return," *Journal of Accounting, Auditing, and Finance* (Spring 1991): 233–256; Eugene Fama and Kenneth French, "Size and Book-to-Market Factors in Earnings and Returns," *Journal of Finance* (March 1995): 131–156; and Victor Bernard, "Accounting-Based Valuation Methods: Evidence on the Market-to-Book Anomaly and Implications for Financial Statements Analysis," working paper, University of Michigan (1994). Ignoring the effects of accounting artifacts, ROEs should be driven in a competitive equilibrium to a level approximating the cost of equity capital.

6. A "normal" profit margin is that which, when multiplied by the turnover achievable within an industry through a viable corporate strategy, yields a return on investment that just covers the cost of capital. However, as mentioned above, accounting artifacts can cause returns on investment to deviate from the cost of capital for long periods, even in a competitive equilibrium.

7. B. Gurley, "Compaq Computer Corporation: Initiation of Coverage," C S First Boston (November 29, 1993).

8. M. G. Brandon, "Compaq Computer Corporation: Company Analysis," Duff & Phelps Investment Research Company (December 1993).

9. We present forecasts of balance sheet accounts and cash flows as of December 1993, because such details were not made available in the February 1993 forecast discussed above.

10. Duff & Phelps does not discuss its forecast of depreciation or the underlying rationale. Indeed, they do not publish a forecast of depreciation expense per se, but it can be inferred from capital expenditures and the forecast change in net plant.

11. See Foster, op. cit. A somewhat more accurate model is furnished by Brown and Rozeff, but it requires iterative statistical techniques for estimation. See Lawrence D. Brown and Michael

Rozeff, "Univariate Time Series Models of Quarterly Accounting Earnings per Share," *Journal of Accounting Research* (Spring 1979): 179–89.

12. To estimate the model, we write it in terms of realized earnings (as opposed to expected earnings), and move Q_{t-4} to the left-hand side:

$$Q_t - Q_{t-4} = \delta + \phi(Q_{t-1} - Q_{t-5}) + e_t$$

We now have a regression where $(Q_t - Q_{t-4})$ is the dependent variable, and its lagged value—$(Q_{t-1} - Q_{t-5})$—is the independent variable. Thus, to estimate the equation, prior earnings data must first be expressed in terms of year-to-year changes. The change for one quarter is then regressed against the change for the most recent quarter. The intercept provides an estimate of δ, and the slope is an estimate of ϕ. The equation is typically estimated using 24 to 40 quarters of prior earnings data.

13. See O'Brien, op. cit.

14. See note 12 for a description of the estimation process. The series for the dependent variable would be $(1.74 - 1.11)$, $(1.26 - 0.59)$, $(1.21 - 0.35)$, and so on. The series for the independent variable would be the corresponding lagged values: $(1.26 - 0.59)$, $(1.21 - 0.35)$, $(1.23 - 0.50)$, and so on.

chapter 6

Prospective Analysis: Valuation Based on Discounted Cash Flows

The previous chapter introduced forecasting, the first stage of prospective analysis. In this and the following chapter we will describe the second and final stage of prospective analysis—valuation.

Valuation is the process of converting a forecast into an estimate of the value of a firm or some component of the firm. At some level, nearly every business decision involves valuation (at least implicitly). Within the firm, capital budgeting involves consideration of how a particular project would affect firm value. Strategic planning focuses on how value would be influenced by larger sets of actions. Outside the firm, security analysts conduct valuation to support their buy/sell decisions, and potential acquirers (often with the assistance of their investment bankers) estimate the value of target firms and the synergies they might offer. Valuation is necessary to price an initial public offering and to inform parties to sales, estate settlements, and divisions of property involving ongoing business concerns. Even credit analysts, who typically do not explicitly estimate firm value, must at least implicitly consider the value of the firm's equity "cushion" if they are to maintain a complete view of the risk associated with lending activity.

In practice, a wide variety of valuation approaches are employed. For example, in evaluating the fairness of a takeover bid, investment bankers commonly use five to ten different methods of valuation. Among the available methods are the following:

- *Discounted cash flow (DCF) analysis.* This approach involves the production of detailed, multiple-year forecasts of cash flows. The forecasts are discounted at an estimated cost of capital to arrive at an estimated present value.
- *Discounted abnormal earnings.* In principle, this approach is equivalent to DCF analysis, but it is more directly linked to accounting numbers. The approach expresses the value of the firm's equity as the sum of the book value and the discounted forecasts of abnormal earnings.

- *Valuation based on price multiples.* This family of approaches does not involve a detailed, multi-year forecast. Instead, a current measure of performance or single forecast of performance is converted into a price through application of some price multiple for other presumably comparable firms. For example, firm value can be estimated by applying a price-to-earnings ratio to a forecast of the firm's earnings for the coming year. Other commonly used multiples include price-to-book ratios and price-to-sales ratios.

Here we discuss valuation based on discounted cash flow analysis. The next chapter deals with accounting-based valuation techniques, including both discounted abnormal earnings valuation and valuation based on price multiples.

OVERVIEW OF DISCOUNTED CASH FLOW (DCF) ANALYSIS

It is well accepted among financial theorists that the value of the firm should be equal to the present value of future dividends. Thus, all valuation approaches should ultimately be consistent with this principle. DCF analysis is the most popular way of operationalizing this principle.[1] It focuses on discounting cash flows from operations after investment in working capital, less capital expenditures.

Valuation based on DCF analysis can be structured in either of two ways:

- Forecast cash flows available to *equity holders,* and then discount the expected cash flows at the cost of equity capital. The result is an estimated value of equity.
- Forecast cash flows available to *all providers of capital* (debt and equity), and then discount the expected cash flows at the weighted average cost of (debt and equity) capital. Under this approach, one arrives at an estimated value of the firm, which must be reduced by the value of debt to arrive at an equity value.

The second approach is more widely used in practice because it does not require explicit forecasts of changes in debt balances. (A good forecast, however, would be grounded in an understanding of these changes as well as all other key elements of the firm's financial picture.) Based on its widespread use in practice, we will describe the second approach to DCF analysis. It involves the following steps:

Step 1: Forecast free cash flows available to debt and equity holders over a finite forecast horizon (usually 5 to 10 years). The final year of the horizon is called the "terminal year."

Step 2: Forecast free cash flows beyond the terminal year, based on some simplifying assumption.

Step 3: Discount free cash flows at the weighted average cost of capital (WACC)—that is, the required return on the combination of debt and equity capital. The discounted amount represents the estimated value of free cash flows available to debt and equity holders as a group.

Step 4: To arrive at the estimated value of equity, subtract from the discounted free cash flows the estimated current market value of debt. If there are non-operating assets held by the firm that have been ignored in the previous cash flow forecasts (e.g., marketable securities or real estate held for sale), then add their value.

Below, we illustrate the four steps as we convert an analyst's long-range forecasts for Compaq into an estimate of the firm's value at the end of 1993. The long-range forecasts are those of the same Duff & Phelps analyst whose year-ahead forecast was examined in Chapter 5. Thus, the valuation serves as an illustration of how the analyst could determine whether his specific forecasts imply a price for Compaq that is higher or lower than the existing market price at the time.

For purposes of applying DCF valuation techniques, Compaq represents a special case in that it has no debt at the end of 1993. Thus, our calculations will be the same, whether we compute the value of debt and equity (based on cash flows *before* debt service, discounted at the weighted average cost of capital) or compute the value of equity directly (based on discounted cash flows *after* debt service, discounted at the cost of equity capital). However, our discussion will include guidance on how to value firms with debt.

STEP 1 OF DCF: FORECAST FREE CASH FLOWS

Under DCF analysis, free cash flows are defined as cash flows from operations after investment in working capital, less capital expenditures. Since the DCF approach described here calls for cash flows available to *all* providers of capital—holders of short-term debt,[2] long-term debt, and equity—cash from operations should be expressed on a *pre-interest* but *post-tax* basis. That is, interest expense on debt should not be deducted in arriving at free cash flow, and amounts deducted for taxes should reflect what tax payments would be due if the firm had no interest deduction.[3]

Table 6-1 presents forecasts, as of December 1993, of free cash flows for Compaq Computer for 1994 through 2000. The forecasts are based largely on those of Duff & Phelps but include some augmentations and adjustments.[4] In Table 5-4 we calculated free cash flows for 1994; but Table 6-1 presents data for several additional years as well.

There are a number of factors an analyst would have to consider carefully in producing long-range forecasts like those in Table 6-1. They are included in many of the questions raised in our discussion of business strategy analysis and financial analysis. For example, the analyst must ask:

- To what extent is Compaq's currently above-normal profit margin dependent on its brand name, and how long can the associated price premium be sustained? Can a brand name established when Compaq focused on a product differentiation strategy command a substantial price premium now that the company is shifting toward producing computers more like the industry standard? How well insulated is the competitive advantage of all vendors of personal computers from the power of two key suppliers, Microsoft (producer of software) and Intel (producer of processors)?

Table 6-1 Analyst Forecast of Compaq Earnings, Cash Flows, and Balance Sheets: 1994–2000

	1993	1994F	1995F	1996F	1997F	1998F	1999F	2000F
			(all amounts other than ratios in millions of dollars)					
Sales	$7,191	$8,712	$10,454	$12,023	$13,225	$14,547	$16,002	$17,601
Net earnings	$462	$517	$565	$609	$628	$639	$702	$773
Earnings before noncash expenses	$580	$762	$848	$922	$970	$949	$1044	$1148
Investment in working capital and other adjustments	(340)	(19)	(293)	(264)	(206)	(215)	(237)	(260)
Cash from operations	$240	$743	$555	$658	$764	$734	$807	$888
Capital expenditures	(145)	(218)	(261)	(301)	(331)	(364)	(400)	(441)
Free cash flows	$95	$525	$294	$357	$433	$370	$407	$448
Key forecast drivers and other statistics:								
Sales growth rate	75.3%	21.2%	20.0%	15.0%	10.0%	10.0%	10.0%	10.0%
Gross margin percentage	23.6%	22.2%	21.5%	21.0%	20.5%	20.0%	20.0%	20.0%
R&D expense/Sales	2.4%	2.5%	2.5%	2.5%	2.5%	2.5%	2.5%	2.5%
SG&A expense/Sales	11.6%	11.4%	11.3%	11.2%	11.1%	11.1%	11.1%	11.1%
Net profit margin	6.4%	5.9%	5.4%	5.1%	4.7%	4.4%	4.4%	4.4%
Cash/Sales	8.7%	7.8%	6.5%	5.6%	5.1%	4.7%	4.2%	3.8%
Receivables/Sales	19.1%	17.2%	17.2%	17.2%	17.2%	17.2%	17.2%	17.2%
Inventory/Sales	15.6%	14.2%	14.4%	14.4%	14.5%	14.5%	14.5%	14.5%
Current assets/Sales	45.8%	41.0%	39.9%	39.1%	38.7%	38.2%	37.8%	37.4%
Net plant/Sales	10.8%	9.2%	7.9%	7.1%	6.6%	6.6%	6.6%	6.6%
Current liabilities/Sales	17.3%	17.6%	17.6%	17.6%	17.6%	17.6%	17.6%	17.6%
Sales turnover	1.990	2.054	2.220	2.267	2.279	2.313	2.336	2.357
Leverage	1.551	1.600	1.693	1.743	1.777	1.798	1.812	1.825
Return on average equity	0.198	0.195	0.203	0.200	0.192	0.183	0.186	0.189
Return on beginning equity	0.230	0.195	0.214	0.209	0.198	0.190	0.193	0.197
Total assets	$4,084	$4,398	$5,019	$5,586	$6,022	$6,556	$7,144	$7,791
Shareholders' equity	$2,654	$2,646	$2,917	$3,169	$3,364	$3,633	$3,928	$4,253

Forecasts of earnings and balance sheet details for 1994-1997 are based on Company Analysis: Compaq Computer Corporation, Duff & Phelps Investment Research Company (Chicago, Illinois), December 1993. Forecasts for 1998-1999 are based on Duff & Phelps forecasts of 20% gross margin beyond 1997, an assumed constant ratio of sales to expenses other than cost of sales, and maintenance of 1997 sales growth rate. Balances of cash and shareholders' equity as forecast by Duff & Phelps have been reduced to reflect distribution of all free cash flow beginning in 1994, and a $50 adjustment for the difference between actual 1993 earnings and amounts expected by Duff & Phelps at the time forecasts were prepared. However, cash balances of at least 3.8% of sales are assumed necessary to support operations.

- To what extent is Compaq's above-normal profit margin a function of cost advantages? Can these advantages be sustained? If Compaq's vertically integrated manufacturing is an advantage, how quickly could it be mimicked? Compaq also enjoys an agreement with IBM that exempts them from royalty patents, giving them a 2 to 3 percent cost advantage over most competitors—but that advantage lasts only until the late 1990s and, of course, gives Compaq no advantage over IBM itself.
- How much longer can Compaq's sales grow at above-industry rates? How much more market share can be garnered through Compaq's shift to cost leadership and more competitively priced products? Where does Compaq stand in the life cycle of its major products? What are the opportunities for expansion into markets beyond those where Compaq is already a leader (U.S., Canada, and Europe)?

Taking these and other considerations into account, Duff & Phelps forecasts that sales growth will decline from 25 percent in 1994 to 20 percent in 1995, and that Compaq will ultimately grow at a pace more in keeping with the industry. Compaq's strategy and the forces of competition are expected to drive gross margin down to 20 percent by 1998, similar to IBM's current gross margin on PCs. The declining gross margin leaves a forecast of net margin that falls to 4.4 percent by 1998.

Most balance sheet accounts are forecast to grow proportionately with sales. One exception is net plant; Compaq is forecast to utilize plant more efficiently, perhaps because of the ongoing improvements in their production operations and the excess capacity they had in 1993.[5] We also assume cash balances will decline as a fraction of sales, relative to the cash-rich position held at the end of 1993. (This implies initiation of dividends in 1994.[6]) The combination of the above effects—declining margins and increased asset utilization—produces an ROE that remains high (about 19 percent) by current industry norms, and probably higher than the cost of equity capital. Thus, one would expect Compaq might have difficulty extrapolating that rate of return over an even larger investment base, moving beyond 2000.

Table 6-1 includes not only sales and earnings forecasts, but also cash flow forecasts. Recall that the free cash flows needed for our DCF valuation are those available to equity *and* debt holders; normally it would be necessary to adjust cash flows so that they are forecast on a before-interest basis (net of associated tax benefit). In Compaq's case, there is no debt, so adding back interest expense is not required. Compaq does report an expense it labels as interest, but its unusual nature makes it more practical to treat it here like an operating expense and forecast cash flows after this expense.[7]

STEP 2 OF DCF: FORECAST CASH FLOWS BEYOND THE "TERMINAL YEAR"

The forecasts in Table 6-1 extend only through the year 2000, and thus 2000 is the "terminal year." (Selection of an appropriate terminal year is discussed later.) Since the value of the firm depends on cash flows over the remainder of Compaq's life, the analyst must adopt some assumption that simplifies the process of forecasting cash flows beyond the year 2000.

The Competitive Equilibrium Assumption

Duff & Phelps projects that by the year 2000, Compaq's sales, earnings, and cash flows from operations will all be growing at an annual rate of 10 percent. What should we assume beyond 2000? Can we assume a continuation of the 10 percent growth rate or is some other pattern more reasonable?

Clearly a continuation of a 10 percent sales growth rate is unrealistic over a very long horizon. That rate would likely outstrip inflation in the dollar and the real growth rate of the world economy. Over many years, it would imply that Compaq would grow to a size greater than that of all other firms in the world combined. But what would be a suitable alternative assumption? Should we expect the firm's sales growth rate to ultimately settle down to the rate of inflation? To a higher rate, the nominal growth rate in GNP? Or to some other rate?

Ultimately, the answers to such questions depend on the kinds of long-range considerations raised earlier. One must consider how much longer the rate of growth in industry sales can outstrip the general growth in the world economy, and how long Compaq's competitive advantages can enable it to grow faster than the overall industry. Clearly, looking seven or more years into the future, any forecasts of sales growth rates are likely to be subject to considerable error.

Fortunately, in many if not most situations, how we deal with the seemingly imponderable questions about long-range growth in sales simply *does not matter very much!* In fact, under plausible economic assumptions, there is no practical need to consider sales growth beyond the terminal year. Such growth may be *irrelevant* so far as the firm's current value is concerned.

How can long-range growth in sales *not* matter? The reasoning revolves around the forces of competition. Competition tends to constrain firms' ability to identify, on a consistent basis, growth opportunities that generate super-normal profits. (Recall the evidence in Chapter 5 concerning the reversion of ROEs to normal levels over horizons of five to ten years.) Certainly, a firm may at a point in time maintain a competitive advantage that permits it to achieve returns in excess of the cost of capital. When that advantage is protected with patents or a strong brand name, the firm may even be able to maintain it for many years—perhaps indefinitely. With hindsight, we know that some such firms—like Coca Cola and Wal-Mart—were able not only to maintain their competitive edge, but to expand it across dramatically increasing investment bases. But in the face of competition, one would typically not expect a firm to continue to extend its supernormal profitability to new, *additional* projects *year after year*. Ultimately, we would expect high profits to attract enough competition to drive the firm's return down to a normal level. Each new project would generate cash flows with a present value no greater than the cost of the investment—the investment would be a "zero net present value" project. Since the benefits of the project are offset by its costs, it does nothing to enhance the current value of the firm, and the associated growth can be ignored.

The appendix to this chapter presents a simple illustration to clarify the point. In the appendix, we consider a wide range of growth in sales for the year 2001: from no growth at all to $3 billion of additional sales. The amount of investment needed to support an additional $1.00 of sales is assumed to be $0.242, which holds the ratio of operating assets to sales constant at the year 2000 levels. We also assume that the impact of *incremental* sales on earnings is 3.15 percent of sales. Under these assumptions, and using a cost of capital of 13 percent (discussed later), the appendix shows that the additional sales—whether zero, $1 billion, or $3 billion—do *nothing* to enhance the current value of the firm.

The key assumption is that the incremental profit margin is 3.15 percent of the sales increase. Under that assumption, $1.00 of additional sales yields $.0315 of additional annual cash flow—just enough to cover the required 13 percent return on the investment of $0.242 in net working capital, plant, and other assets needed to support the higher sales level. The benefit of the added cash inflow is thus equal to its cost, and the incremental value of the added sales is zero.

The assumption about incremental profits is not arbitrary but based on the notion that over the long run, competitive forces drive incremental margins to the point of incremental costs. Margins any higher than this attract competition that forces the margins down. Margins below this level drive investment away until the margins recover.

Note that if we ignore sales increases beyond 2000, we are *not* assuming that Compaq's abnormal profitability will be driven away completely. In fact, if we treat sales and earnings as if they will remain constant after 2000, we are treating Compaq as if it will preserve its higher-than-normal margin on its year-2000 sales base *forever.* Another way to say this is that we assume the abnormally high year-2000 ROE (19 percent) is maintained on the equity base that exists in 2000, but that the incremental return on any added equity will be equal to the cost of capital, so that the aggregate ROE will fall slowly from 19 percent toward the cost of capital.

DCF valuation does not *require* this "competitive equilibrium assumption." If the analyst expects that supernormal margins can be extended to new markets for many years, it can be accommodated within the context of a DCF analysis. At a minimum, as we will discuss later, the analyst may expect that supernormal margins can be maintained on markets that grow at the rate of inflation. However, the important lesson here is that the rate of growth in sales beyond the forecast horizon is not a relevant consideration *unless* the analyst believes that the growth can be achieved while generating supernormal incremental margins—competition may make that a difficult trick to pull off.

Terminal Value As If There Is No Sales Growth Beyond Terminal Year

If we invoke the competitive equilibrium assumption as of the year 2001, then it does not matter what sales growth rate we use beyond that year, and we may as well simplify our arithmetic by treating sales as if they will be constant at the year 2000 level. Earnings will remain at $773 million; free cash flow will also be $773 million per year[8]:

Earnings (for firms with debt, add back interest, net of tax)	$773
Deferred taxes (balance sheet account remains constant)	0
Depreciation ($369), less capital expenditures ($369)	0
Investment in incremental working capital (balances constant)	0
Free cash flow	$773

Since the cash flows are constant beginning in 2001, it is simple to discount those flows. Again assuming a discount rate of 13 percent, the present value of the cash flows for the years beyond 2000 is thus equal to the 2001 flow of $773 million, divided by .13:

$$\text{Present value of cash flows beyond 2000} \quad = \quad \frac{\$773}{.13} \quad = \quad \$5,943$$

This represents the value of the cash flows as of the end of the year 2000. The value as of the end of 1993 would be obtained by discounting $5,943 million for seven years:

$$\text{Present value of cash flows beyond 2000, as of 1993} \quad = \quad \frac{\$5,943}{(1.13)^7} \quad = \quad \$2,526$$

The amount $2,526 million is the so-called "terminal value" of the firm. It represents a large fraction of the total value of the firm, as we will see shortly.

Terminal Value Based on a Price Multiple

An alternative approach to terminal value calculation is to apply a multiple to cash flows or earnings in the terminal period. In its most simple form, the analyst simply capitalizes earnings (before interest, less adjusted taxes) by a "normal" PE ratio.

The approach is not so ad hoc as it might at first appear. Note that under the assumption of no sales growth, cash flows beyond 2000 remain constant and equal to earnings. Capitalizing this cash flow in perpetuity by dividing by the cost of capital (.13) is equivalent to multiplying earnings by a PE of 7.7. Thus, applying a multiple in this range is similar to discounting all free cash flows beyond 2000, while invoking the competitive equilibrium assumption.

The mistake to avoid here is to capitalize the future earnings or cash flows using a multiple that is too high. The PE multiple might be high currently because the market anticipates much abnormally profitable growth. However, once that growth is realized, the PE multiple should fall to a normal level. It is that normal PE, applicable to a stable firm or one that can grow only through zero net present value projects, that should be used in the terminal value calculation. Thus, multiples in the range of 7 to 10—close to the reciprocal of the WACC—should be used here.[9] Higher multiples are justifiable only when the terminal year is closer and there are still abnormally profitable growth opportunities beyond that point.

Allowing for Growth Beyond the Terminal Year, and Dealing with Long-Run Inflation

The approaches described above each appeal in some way to the "competitive equilibrium assumption." However, there are circumstances where the analyst is willing to assume that the firm may defy competitive forces and earn abnormal rates of return on new projects for many years. In the case of Compaq, we could ask whether its current competitive advantage is protected by barriers that will allow it to extend its supernormal profitability well beyond its current market, and even into the 21st century. Note that some of the advantages mentioned earlier—for example, the unique exemptions from royalty payments to IBM—will definitely dissipate within a decade, on not only incremental sales but also the existing sales base. Compaq's vertically integrated approach to manufacturing, if it does involve advantages, could be mimicked by others, given enough time. What about Compaq's other advantages, including its brand name? Does it offer any competitive edge as Compaq extends its sales well beyond the current base and into new markets?

If the analyst believes supernormal profitability can be extended to larger markets for many years, one possibility is to project earnings and cash flows over a longer horizon, until the competitive equilibrium assumption can reasonably be invoked.

Another possibility is to project growth in cash flows at some constant rate. Consider the following. By treating Compaq as if its competitive advantage can be maintained only on the *nominal* sales level achieved in the year 2000, we were assuming that in *real* terms its competitive advantage would shrink. Let's say that the analyst expects Compaq can maintain its advantage (through supplies of new and more advanced products to a similar customer base) on a sales base that remains constant in real terms—that grows beyond the year 2000 at the expected long-run inflation rate of 3.5 percent. The computations implied by these assumptions are described below. The approach is more aggressive than the one described earlier, but it may be more realistic. After all, there is no obvious reason why the *real* size of the investment base on which Compaq earns abnormal returns during the twenty-first century should depend on inflation rates.

The approach just described still relies to some extent on the competitive equilibrium assumption. The assumption is now invoked to suggest that supernormal profitability can be extended only to an investment base that remains constant in real terms. However, there is nothing about the DCF method that requires any reliance on the competitive equilibrium assumption. The calculations described below could be used with *any* rate of growth in sales. The question is not whether the arithmetic is available to handle such an approach, but rather how realistic it is.

Let's stay with the approach that assumes Compaq will extend its supernormal margins to sales that grow beyond 2000 at the rate of inflation. How would free cash flows beyond 2000 behave? There are two incorrect approaches that are easy to fall into at this point. One might think that since free cash flows in the year 2001 were $773 million under our no-growth assumption, they would simply grow from that point at a 3.5 percent rate under our new assumptions. Alternatively, one might note that free cash flows in the year 2000 were $448 million (see Table 6-1), and then apply a 3.5 percent growth factor to that amount. Both approaches are wrong: the first one overstates value and the second one understates it. They ignore the fact that 3.5 percent growth in *sales* does not necessarily imply 3.5 percent growth in *cash flows*. The latter is heavily influenced by changes in amounts invested in net working capital and plant, and those shift dramatically when sales growth rates change.

Table 6-2 correctly projects free cash flows for the years 2000 through 2003, assuming that sales increase by 3.5 percent in 2001 and beyond, and that profit margins, asset turnover, and leverage remain constant. Note that in 2001, earnings increase at the same rate as sales: by 3.5 percent. In contrast, free cash flows jump 45 percent! Why? Because free cash flows reflect not just the firm's earnings experience, but also the amount invested to support growth. As the firm's growth slows from 10 percent in 2000 to 3.5 percent in 2001, the cash required to support working capital growth is slashed (by more

Table 6-2 Forecast of Free Cash Flows Beyond 2000, with 3.5 Percent Sales Growth and Constant Profit Margins

	Forecast for terminal year	Forecast beyond terminal year *as if* sales growth only keeps pace with inflation		
	2000	2001	2002	2003
Sales growth	10.0%	3.5%	3.5%	3.5%
Profit margin	4.4%	4.4%	4.4%	4.4%
Earnings (for firm with debt, add back interest, net of tax:	$773	$800	$828	$857
Earnings growth	10.0%	3.5%	3.5%	3.5%
Earnings before depreciation and deferred taxes	$1,148	$1,184	$1,225	$1,268
Investment in net working capital[a]	(260)	(122)	(126)	(131)
Capital expenditures[b]	(441)	(409)	(424)	(438)
Free cash flow	$448	$651	$674	$697
Free cash flow growth	10.0%	45.0%	3.5%	3.5%

Present value of free cash flows in 2001 and beyond:

$$\text{Present value in 2000} = \frac{2001 \text{ free cash flow}}{(\text{cost of capital} - \text{growth rate})} = \frac{\$651}{(.13 - .035)} = \$6,850$$

$$\text{Present value in 1993} = \frac{\$6,850}{(1.13)^7} = \$2,912$$

a. *Net working capital accounts (including cash balances needed to support operations) are maintained at the same ratio to sales as in 1988 (19.8 percent) through 2000 (see Table 6-1).*

b. *Capital expenditures are amounts necessary to maintain net plant at 6.6 percent of sales. Depreciation is projected at 31.9 percent of beginning net plant.*

than half), and capital expenditures fall as well (by about 7 percent). The upshot is a free cash flow growth rate that is much higher than the earnings growth rate in that year. However, beyond 2001, as the sales growth rate remains constant, the growth in earnings and working capital remains constant, and therefore the growth in free cash flows also remains constant, at 3.5 percent.

Since the rate of cash flow growth is constant beginning in 2001, it is simple to discount those flows. For a given discount rate r, any cash flow stream growing at the constant rate g can be discounted by dividing the cash flows in the first year by the amount $(r - g)$. Once again assuming a discount rate of 13 percent and our cash flow growth rate of 3.5 percent, the present value of the cash flows for the years beyond 2000 is as follows:

$$\text{Present value of cash flows beyond 2000} \quad = \quad \frac{\$651}{(.13 - .035)} \quad = \quad \$6,850$$

This is the present value as of the end of the year 2000; when we discount that amount to the end of 1993, we obtain $2,912 (see Table 6-2). This represents our terminal value estimate under the new set of assumptions. It is about $400 million higher than our terminal value estimate based on no growth in abnormal profitability.

Selecting the Terminal Year

A question begged by the above discussion is how long the forecast horizon should be. When the competitive equilibrium assumption is used, the answer is whatever time is required for the firm's returns on incremental investment projects to reach that equilibrium—an issue that turns on the sustainability of the firm's competitive advantage. As indicated in Chapter 5, the historical evidence indicates that most firms in the U.S. should expect ROEs to revert to normal levels within five to ten years. But for the typical firm, we can justify ending the forecast horizon even earlier—note that the return on *incremental* investment can be normal even while the return on *total* investment (and therefore ROE) remains abnormal. Thus, a five- to ten-year forecast horizon should be more than sufficient for most firms. Exceptions would include firms so well insulated from competition (perhaps due to the power of a brand name) that they can extend their investment base across new markets for many years and still expect to generate supernormal returns. In 1995 the Wrigley Company, producer of chewing gum that is still extending its brand name to untapped markets in other nations, appears to be such a firm.

In the case of Compaq, the terminal year used is seven years beyond the current one. Table 6-1 shows that the return on capital (in this case, ROE) is forecast to decline only gradually over these seven years, from the unusually high 20 percent in 1993 to a level that holds steady at 18 to 19 percent by the late 1990s. If profit margins could be maintained at the projected 4.4 percent on ever-increasing sales, this high ROE could be achieved even on new investment in 2001 and beyond. However, even a slight decline in the margin—in the initial year, to about 4.3 percent—would, in the face of continued 10 percent sales growth, be enough to render the return on the *incremental* investment no higher than the cost of capital. Thus, the performance we have already projected for the terminal year 2000 is not far removed from a competitive equilibrium, and extending the forecast horizon by a few more years would have little impact on the calculated value. Even if we project continuation of the 4.4 percent margin through 2003 with 10 percent annual sales increases (and with the competitive equilibrium assumption invoked thereafter), the final estimated firm value would increase by only about 5 percent. Large changes in our value estimate would arise only if the analyst is willing to assume abnormal rates of return on investments well into the twenty-first century—and in light of our analysis of industry conditions, such an assumption would be tenuous indeed. The upshot is that an analyst could argue that the terminal year used here for Compaq should be extended from the seventh year to, say, the tenth year or even a few years beyond that point, depending on the perceived sustainability of its competitive advantage. However, because we are already assuming Compaq is close to a competitive equilibrium in the year 2000, the final value estimate would not be particularly sensitive to this change.

STEP 3 OF DCF: DISCOUNT EXPECTED FREE CASH FLOWS

Table 6-3 illustrates how the projected cash flows from the previous tables should be discounted to the present, using a range of weighted average costs of capital from 11 to 15 percent. The terminal value used in Table 6-3 is the one that assumes Compaq can maintain its abnormal rate of return forever on the sales volume achieved in the terminal

Table 6-3 Valuation of Compaq Based on Discounted Free Cash Flows, December 1993

		1994	1995	1996	1997	1998	1999	2000	beyond 2000
		(dollar amounts in millions)							
Free cash flow		$525	$294	$357	$433	$370	$407	$448	$773*
Discount factor, at 13%		1.13	1.28	1.44	1.63	1.84	2.08	2.35	
Discounted free cash flow		$465	$230	$247	$266	$201	$195	$190	$2,526*
Sum of discounted free cash flows, at 13%	$4,320								
Discounted value at 11%	$5,293								
Discounted value at 12%	$4,763								
Discounted value at 14%	$3,946								
Discounted value at 15%	$3,625								

> The present value calculations treat all cash flows as if they occur at the end of the year. To assume that, on average, cash flows occur half way through the year, multiply the discounted value by $(1 + r/2)$, where r is the discount rate. When $r = 13\%$, the discounted value would be adjusted from $4,320 to $4,600.

*Terminal value calculation: When sales are treated as if they will not grow beyond 2000 while margins stay constant, cash flows rise to $773 in 2001 and remain at that level (see text). The present value of the $773 in perpetuity is $5,943 ($773/.13) at the end of 2000, and $2,526 ($5,943 / (1.13)^7) at the end of 1993.

If we allow for growth in sales beyond 2000 at the rate of expected inflation (3.5 percent), the terminal value based on a 13 percent discount rate rises to $2,912 (see Table 6-2). Estimated firm value rises to $4,706 and, when adjusted to reflect the arrival of cash flows halfway through the year, becomes $5,012.

year 2000, but not on any sales growth beyond that point. We will also discuss value estimates that allow for long-range growth in sales at the rate of inflation.

Computing a Discount Rate

Thus far, the discount rates used have been offered without explanation. How would they be estimated by the analyst?

Since Compaq is debt-free, there is no distinction between the cost of equity capital and the weighted average cost of capital (WACC). However, in general, the proper discount rate to use here is the WACC, because we are discounting cash flows available to both debt and equity holders. The WACC is calculated by weighting the costs of debt and equity capital according to their respective market values:.

$$\text{WACC} \quad = \quad \frac{V_D}{V_D + V_E} \times r_D(1 - T) + \frac{V_E}{V_D + V_E} \times r_E$$

where V_D = the market value of debt; V_E = the market value of equity
$\quad r_D$ = the cost of debt capital; r_E = the cost of equity capital
$\quad T$ = the tax rate reflecting the marginal tax benefit of interest

WEIGHTING THE COSTS OF DEBT AND EQUITY.   The weights assigned to debt and equity represent their respective fractions of total capital provided, measured in terms of market values. Computing a market value for debt should not be difficult. It is reasonable to use book values if interest rates have not changed significantly since the time the debt was issued. Otherwise, the value of the debt can be estimated by discounting the future payouts at current market rates of interest applicable to the firm.

What is included in debt? Should short-term as well as long-term debt be included? Should payables and accruals be included? The answer is revealed by considering how we calculated free cash flows. Those free cash flows are the returns to the providers of the capital to which the WACC applies. The cash flows are those available *before* servicing short-term and long-term debt, which indicates that both short-term and long-term debt should be considered a part of capital when computing the WACC. Servicing of other liabilities, such as accounts payable or accruals, should already have been considered when computing free cash flows. Thus, internal consistency requires that operating liabilities not be considered a part of capital when computing the WACC.

The tricky problem we face is assigning a market value to equity. That is the very amount we are trying to estimate in the first place! How can the analyst possibly assign a market value to equity at this intermediate stage, given that the estimate will not be known until all steps in the DCF analysis are completed?

One common approach to the problem is to insert "target" ratios of debt to capital $[V_D/(V_D + V_E)]$ and equity to capital $[V_E/(V_D + V_E)]$ at this point. For example, one might expect that a firm will, over the long run, maintain a capital structure that is 40 percent debt and 60 percent equity. The long-run focus is reasonable, because we are discounting cash flows over a long horizon.

Another way around the problem is to use some reasonable guess for the value of equity at this stage—perhaps based on some multiple of next year's earnings forecast. The guess can be used as a weight for purposes of calculating an initial estimate of the WACC, which in turn can be used in the discounting process to generate an initial estimate of the value of equity. That initial estimate can then be used in place of the guess to arrive at a new WACC, and a second estimate of the value of equity can be produced. This process can be repeated until the value used to calculate the WACC and the final estimated value converge.

ESTIMATING THE COST OF DEBT.   The cost of debt (r_D) should be based on current market rates of interest. For privately-held debt, such rates are not quoted, but stated interest rates may provide a suitable substitute if interest rates have not changed much since the debt was issued. The cost of debt should be expressed on a net-of-tax basis, because it is after-tax cash flows that are being discounted. In most settings, the market rate of interest can be converted to a net-of-tax basis by multiplying by one minus the marginal corporate tax rate.

ESTIMATING THE COST OF EQUITY.   Estimating the cost of equity (r_E) can be difficult, and a full discussion of the topic lies beyond the scope of this chapter. At any rate, even an extended discussion would not supply answers to all the questions that might be raised in this area, because the field of finance is in a state of flux over what constitutes an appropriate measure of the cost of equity.

One possibility is to use the capital asset pricing model (CAPM), which expresses the cost of equity as the sum of a required return on riskless assets, plus a premium for systematic risk:

$$r_E = r_F + \beta[E(r_M) - r_F]$$

where r_F is the riskless rate;

[$E(r_M) - r_F$] is the risk premium expected for the market as a whole, expressed as the excess of the expected return on the market index over the riskless rate;

and β is the systematic risk of the equity.

To compute r_E, one must estimate three parameters: the riskless rate r_F; the market risk premium [$E(r_M) - r_F$], and systematic risk, β. For r_F, analysts often use the rate on intermediate-term Treasury bonds, based on the observation that it is cash flows beyond the short term that are being discounted.[10] When r_F is measured in that way, then average common stock returns (based on the returns to Standard and Poor's 500 index) have exceeded that rate by 7.6 percent over the 1926–1993 period.[11] This excess return constitutes an estimate of the market risk premium [$E(r_M) - r_F$]. Finally, systematic risk

(β) reflects the sensitivity of the firm's value to economy-wide market movements. Historically, Compaq's stock price has changed 1.2 percent for each 1 percent change in the market index, indicating that Compaq's β is approximately 1.2.[12] Putting these estimates together and noting that in late 1993 rates on ten-year U.S. government bonds were 5.8 percent, we estimate that Compaq's cost of equity capital is about 15 percent:

$$r_E \;=\; r_F + \beta[\,E(r_M) - r_F\,] \;=\; .058 + 1.20(.076) \;=\; .149$$

Although the above CAPM is often used to estimate the cost of capital, the evidence indicates that the model is incomplete. Assuming stocks are priced competitively, stock returns should be expected just to compensate investors for the cost of their capital. Thus, long-run average returns should be close to the cost of capital and should (according to the CAPM) vary across stocks according to their systematic risk. However, factors beyond only systematic risk seem to play some role in explaining variation in long-run average returns. The most important such factor is labeled the "size effect": smaller firms (as measured by market capitalization) tend to generate higher returns in subsequent periods. Why this is so is unclear. It could either indicate that smaller firms are riskier than indicated by the CAPM, or that they are underpriced at the point their market capitalization is measured, or some combination of both. Average stock returns for U.S. firms (including NYSE, AMEX, and NASDAQ firms) varied across size deciles from 1926–1993, as shown in Table 6-4.

In the case of Compaq, we have a firm that is large. Based on any reasonable multiple of earnings, Compaq's market value would lie in either the largest or next-largest decile of the distribution above. On that basis alone, one might expect that equity holders

Table 6-4 Stock Returns and Firm Size

Size decile	Market value of largest company in decile, in 1993 (millions of dollars)	Average annual stock return, 1926–1993	Fraction of total NYSE value represented by decile (in 1993)
1–smallest	$ 60.3	22.3%	0.1%
2	146.3	18.2	0.4
3	253.5	17.1	0.9
4	406.0	16.2	1.4
5	612.3	15.7	2.1
6	1,017.6	15.7	3.4
7	1,537.5	14.7	5.0
8	2,812.7	14.1	8.5
9	5,311.2	13.3	16.1
10–largest	81,891.3	11.2	62.0

Source: Ibbotson Associates (1994).

would be satisfied with a return on equity that is relatively low. The table indicates that historically, investors in firms in the top two deciles of the size distribution have realized returns of only 11.2 to 13.3 percent. If we place Compaq close to the breakpoint between the top two deciles, based on reasonable estimates of its size, then the value-weighted average of the two deciles' returns, 11.6 percent, would be the best indicator of Compaq's cost of capital. Note, however, that if we use firm size as an indicator of the cost of capital, we are implicitly assuming that large size is indicative of lower risk. Yet finance theorists have not developed a well-accepted explanation for why that should be the case.

One method for combining the cost of capital estimates is based on the CAPM and the "size effect."[13] The approach calls for adjustment of the CAPM-based cost of capital, based on the difference between the average return on the market index used in the CAPM (Standard and Poor's 500) and the average return on firms of the size comparable to the firm being evaluated. Thus, since firms of Compaq's size have, on average, earned returns of 11.6 percent, or 0.7 percent less than the 12.3 percent return on the market index, we would adjust the cost of capital downward by the difference. Our resulting cost of capital estimate is about 14 percent:

$$r_E = r_F + \beta[E(r_M) - r_F] + r_{size} = [.058 + 1.2(.076) - .007] = .142$$

In light of the continuing debate on how to measure the cost of capital, it is not surprising that managers and analysts often consider a range of estimates. We will present estimates based on costs of capital from 11 to 15 percent, which bracket the estimates based on size alone and those based on either CAPM or the combined CAPM and size model. The 13 percent amount used thus far in our discussion lies between these estimates. However, we will also refer in our discussion to computations based on 14 percent, which comes closest to the estimate based on the CAPM adjusted for the size effect.

The Discounted Amount

In Table 6-3, we discounted Compaq's projected cash flows using the previously discussed range of cost of capital estimates. Since there is no debt, the weighted average cost of capital is equal to the cost of equity capital.

Table 6-3 indicates that, based on a cost of capital of 13 percent, we estimate Compaq's value at about $4.3 billion. If we allow for abnormally profitable growth in sales beyond the year 2000 at the rate of inflation, the estimate rises to $4.7 billion. Using a cost of capital of 14 percent would of course produce lower estimates ($3.9 billion and $4.2 billion, respectively). Note that Compaq's terminal value always represents a large fraction of the total discounted cash flows. It is not unusual for the terminal value to be so important. Since the terminal value estimate is hinged on the long-run earnings forecast, the latter thus becomes key to a good valuation.

That the terminal value is so large can leave an analyst feeling quite uncomfortable about a DCF-based estimate. After all, most of the value of Compaq is being attributed to cash flows that won't be realized until at least seven years go by—and few analysts would feel confident about forecasts that far into the future. Unfortunately for our nerves, that's just the way the world is. Growing companies chew up cash in the near term, and most of their value is derived from cash flows well out in the horizon. We can use simpler valuation techniques (such as the application of multiples to current earnings) that may not make this issue explicit, but those techniques don't make the underlying reality go away. Equity valuation is very much a game of projecting what earnings and cash flows will be years from now, and such projections are inherently uncertain. DCF valuation techniques can't eliminate that uncertainty, but they can produce estimates of value that are at least consistent with the best long-run projections the analyst can generate.

The primary calculations in Table 6-3 treat all cash flows as if they arrive at the end of the year. Of course, they are likely to arrive throughout the year. If we assume for the sake of simplicity that cash flows will arrive mid-year, then we should adjust our value estimates upward by the amount $1 + r/2$, where r is the discount rate. For the case of a 13 percent discount rate, the value estimate rises from \$4,320 million to \$4,600 million. Using a 14 percent cost of capital would yield an adjusted estimate of approximately \$4,220 million. Comparable amounts that allow for growth in sales beyond 2000 at the rate of inflation are \$5,012 million (based on a 13 percent discount rate) and \$4,512 (using 14 percent).

STEP 4 OF DCF: CALCULATE THE VALUE OF EQUITY

In general, the present value calculated above is the value of both debt and equity. The final step in the calculation is to convert this amount to the value of equity by subtracting the market value of debt (short-term and long-term). Note that we do not subtract the value of other liabilities, such as accounts payable. Their influence on firm value has already been considered in the process of forecasting free cash flows.

If the firm maintains any nonoperating assets that will generate cash flows not considered in our forecasts, the value of those assets must be added at this stage. Common examples are marketable securities, land held for sale, and excess pension fund assets (to the extent the benefit of the latter has not already been reflected in earnings projections). Adjustments should also be made for the expected cost of any obligations not recorded on the balance sheet and not already considered in earnings projections. For example, if the firm faced a possible cost to repair environmental damage and that amount was not accrued in the accounts, such a cost should be considered here. On the other hand, unrecorded obligations on operating leases need not be considered here, assuming that the earnings projections already reflect expected rent payments on such leases.

In Compaq's case there is no debt, and no major unrecorded liabilities exist for which adjustments are needed. Also, Compaq has no major nonoperating assets, with the possible exception of its cash balance. Should the value of cash be added as an adjustment to our existing present value estimate? The answer depends on whether we have already considered the earnings generated by cash in our projections of future cash flows. Although we did not present the detailed breakdown of earnings in the Table 6-1 forecasts from Duff & Phelps, the forecast does include interest income from cash equivalents. (The amount in 1994 is $45 million.) In addition, since some cash balances are required simply to keep operations running, cash contributes to the generation of cash from operations. The value of cash is thus already embedded in our present value estimate, and to make a further adjustment now would constitute double-counting. An alternative approach would be to treat at least some portion of cash and cash equivalents as a nonoperating asset, exclude the interest income on that asset from the cash flow projections, and add its current value to the present value of the projected cash flows. However, since some cash is necessary just to maintain operations, only the "excess" cash should be a candidate for such treatment.

A final set of adjustments would be required in cases where the firm has potentially dilutive securities outstanding. The market value of options and warrants, as well as the market value of the conversion feature of convertible securities, should be deducted from firm value. Estimation of such amounts can be quite complex and lies outside the scope of this chapter. However, for many if not most firms, the amounts involved are relatively small. Compaq, like most firms, has employee stock options outstanding, but they represent claims to shares constituting only $2/10$ of one percent of the firm's outstanding stock. Their value would be an even smaller fraction of the *value* of outstanding shares, because there is a cost (the exercise price) associated with exercising the options.

To summarize, the value of equity (based on a 13 percent cost of capital and treating cash flows as if they arrive mid-year) is calculated as follows:

Value of free cash flows to debt and equity holders	$4,600
− Value of debt	0
+ Value of nonoperating assets	0
− Expected cost of unrecorded obligations	0
− Value of options, warrants, and conversion features	0
Value of currently outstanding equity	$4,600

The value of currently outstanding equity is divided by the number of outstanding shares to arrive at an estimated per-share value of the stock. Given our previous estimated equity value of $4.6 billion for Compaq and their 84.3 million shares outstanding, our estimate of the per-share value is $54. The indicated per-share value falls to $50 on the basis of a cost of capital of 14 percent.

Had we used the more aggressive terminal value assumptions presented in Table 6-2 —which allowed for abnormally profitable long-run growth in sales at the rate of inflation and are probably more realistic—our per-share estimate based on a 13 percent cost of capital would have been $59. The price estimate would be $53, based on a 14 percent cost of capital.

Taking a Look at the Estimate

The estimates are lower than the $74 market price at the time of the release of the forecasts on which we relied. There can be only two explanations. One is that the market is using a lower cost of capital. An 11 percent cost of capital with the more aggressive terminal value assumptions of Table 6-2 implies a per-share value of $76. However, this explanation is difficult to justify because it ignores any premium for systematic risk.

The other possibility is simply that the market was more optimistic than the Duff & Phelps analyst on whose forecasts we have built.[14] The Duff & Phelps forecasts for 1994 are close to those of the median of the 33 analysts who issued forecasts for Compaq during the last two months of 1993. However, there was divergence about that median, and during this period of quickly rising expectations (the price had been below $60 just two months earlier), the median could be outdated relative to the expectations of market agents "driving" the stock price. Some analysts were forecasting 1994 EPS at levels nearly 20 percent higher than Duff & Phelps' forecast. One of Compaq's lead analysts (at C.S. First Boston) issued an EPS forecast that was only 6 percent higher than Duff & Phelps for 1994 but at least 15–20 percent higher over the longer term.

In order to "justify" the price at which Compaq traded in late 1993, the most plausible scenarios would involve a combination of forecasts more optimistic than Duff & Phelps' and a cost of capital below 15 percent. (We return to this point in more detail in Chapter 8.)

With hindsight, we know that the optimists proved correct in this case, as Compaq's stock rose to over $100 during the months after our forecast. During this period it became clear that Compaq would likely overtake IBM as the market share leader in personal computers, while still maintaining strong profit margins. By March of 1994, consensus EPS forecasts for 1994 were 35 percent higher than reflected in our valuation.

SUMMARY AND CONCLUSIONS

Valuation is the process by which forecasts of performance are converted into estimates of price. A variety of valuation techniques are employed in practice, and there is no single method that clearly dominates others. In fact, since each technique involves different advantages and disadvantages, there are gains to considering several approaches simultaneously.

In this chapter, we discussed one of the most widely used valuation techniques—discounted cash flow analysis. The method involves forecasting future free cash flows over a finite horizon, discounting them at an estimated cost of capital, and adding an appropriate terminal value estimate to reflect the value of cash flows beyond the forecast horizon.

Discounted cash flow analysis is, in practice, typically grounded in forecasts of earnings and other accounting numbers. In the following chapter, we discuss methods of valuation that are based more directly on accounting forecasts.

APPENDIX

The Competitive Equilibrium Assumption: How can sales growth NOT affect current firm value?

A key step in DCF valuation is the invoking of the competitive equilibrium assumption. When we invoke that assumption beyond the final year of the forecast (the year 2000 in our Compaq example), any additional growth in sales is assumed to have no impact on the current value of the firm. How can this be?

In Table 6-A, we take the forecasts of Table 6-1 as a given. Those forecasts carry us through the year 2000. Then we consider four different sales projections for the year 2001, ranging from no increase to a $3 billion increase (17 percent growth). We assume that the ratio of net working capital, net plant, and other assets, minus deferred taxes, remains as it stood in 2000, at .242.[15] Thus, the incremental investment to support, say, a $3 billion sales increase is $3 billion × .242, or $726 million.

If sales rise, projected earnings should also rise. The key assumption in Table 6-A—and one we explain momentarily—is that the *increment* to earnings is equal to 3.15 percent of sales. When added to the existing profits, this produces an overall margin that is slightly lower at higher sales levels. For example, the margin is 4.4 percent if sales remain constant, but only 4.2 percent if sales rise by $3 billion to $20.6 billion.

Now we consider the impact of the various sales projections on the cash flows and estimated value of the firm. To focus attention for the time being on the impact of *only* the change in sales experienced in 2001, let's assume that sales beyond 2001 stay constant at the levels projected for that year. Then annual free cash flows beyond 2001 will also stay constant and equal to the earnings for 2001. Why? Consider the adjustments necessary to move from earnings to free cash flows. The adding back of depreciation is offset exactly by capital expenditures, as the firm's net plant balance will be held constant (because sales beyond 2001 are held constant). With no further change in the scale of the firm, the change in deferred taxes will be zero, as will be the investment in additional working capital. The upshot is a perpetuity of free cash flow equal to earnings. The implied annual cash flows for the various sales levels are shown in Table 6-A, and are compared with the cash flows ($773 million) in the base case of no growth in sales. For example, if sales grow by $3 billion, free cash flows are $94 million higher than the

Table 6-A Impact on Value of Different Sales Projections for 2001

Projected sales level in 2001:	$17,601	$18,601	$19,601	$20,601
Projected sales increase	0	1,000	2,000	3,000
Projected earnings, assuming incremental margin is 3.15 % of incremental sales	$773	$804	$836	$867
Project net profit margin	4.4%	4.3%	4.3%	4.2%
Implied annual free cash flow, holding sales constant at new level*	$773	$804	$836	$867
Incremental annual free cash flow due to sales increase (ignoring impact of initial investment)	0	31	63	94
Present value of perpetuity of incremental free cash flow at 13%	0	242	484	726
Cash flow impact of investment required to support higher sales	0	−242	−484	−726
Enhancement of current firm value caused by increase in sales (present value of cash flow, less investment)	$ 0	$ 0	$ 0	$ 0

*Beyond 2001, with sales and earnings held constant at the level achieved in 2001, earnings and free cash flows will be equal to each other (and equal to earnings of 2001), as explained in the text. In the year 2001, free cash flows for the four different sales levels will be as follows:

Earnings	$773	$ 804	$ 836	$ 867
+ Depreciation (.319 of beginning net plant)	369	369	369	369
+ Deferred tax change (.025 of sales change)	0	25	50	75
− Investment in net working capital and other assets (.201 of change in sales)	0	−201	−402	−605
− Capital expenditures (sufficient to bring net plant to 6.6 % of sales)	−369	−435	−501	−567
Free cash flow	$773	$ 562	$ 352	$ 141
Incremental free cash flow versus base case	$ 0	$−211	$−421	$−632

Note that the incremental free cash flows in 2001 reflect two impacts:

Incremental free cash flow due to additional profits caused by sales increase in 2001	$ 0	$ 31	$ 63	$ 94
Reduction in free cash flow due to added investment required in 2001	0	−242	−484	−726
	$ 0	$−211	$−421	$−632

In Table 6-A, the present value of the perpetuity of incremental free cash flow includes the effect in 2001 of the second-to-last row above. The next-to-last row is treated separately, as the impact of investment.

base case in all years beyond 2001. The same increment to cash flows is present in 2001 as well, although bottom-line free cash flows in that year will also reflect the cost of investment needed to generate the higher sales levels. (See notes to Table 6-A). The upshot in the case of the $3 billion sales increase is that $726 million of cash investment generates a perpetuity of $94 million of additional annual cash flow.

So what is the value of the incremental cash flow generated by the various levels of sales growth in 2001? Given that the increment is constant over all future years, we can calculate its present value simply by dividing by the discount rate. Using a discount rate of 13 percent, the value of the $94 million increment to free cash flows caused by a $3 billion growth in sales is $726 million. How does that growth influence the current value of the firm's equity? *Not at all!* The value of the additional cash flows—$726 million—is offset precisely by the cost of the investment needed to support the higher sales level. The increment to sales—whether $1 billion or $2 billion or $3 billion—is zero net present value project. We can ignore it altogether and still arrive at the same estimate of the value of the firm. We could extend the same logic to additional sales growth in 2002, 2003, and so on, but the final conclusion would be the same: the rate of sales growth would have no impact on the current value of the firm.

DISCUSSION QUESTIONS

1. Free cash flows (FCF) used in DCF valuations discussed in the chapter are defined as follows:

   FCF to debt and equity = earnings before interest and taxes $\times$ (1 − tax rate) + depreciation and deferred taxes − capital expenditures −/+ increase/decrease in working capital

   FCF to equity = net income + depreciation and deferred taxes − capital expenditures −/+ increase/decrease in working capital +/− increase/decrease in debt

   Which of the following items affect free cash flows to debt and equity holders? Which affect free cash flows to equity alone? Explain why and how?
   • An increase in accounts receivable
   • A decrease in gross margins
   • An increase in property, plant, and equipment
   • An increase in inventory
   • Interest expense
   • An increase in prepaid expenses
   • An increase in notes payable to the bank

2. What factors would you consider in deciding when to stop computing detailed year-by-year cash flows and to use a terminal value in a valuation?

3. Starite Company is valued at $20 per share. Analysts expect that it will generate free cash flows to equity of $4 per share for the foreseeable future. What is the firm's implied cost of equity capital?

4. Cleanup Company has sales of $100 million (compared to $90 million for one year ago), net income to sales of 10 percent, capital expenditures to sales of 10 percent, depreciation and deferred taxes to sales of 6 percent, working capital to sales of 20 percent, a 40 percent tax rate, interest expense of $2 million, and no change in its debt obligations. What are the free cash flows to debt and equity holders? What are the free cash flows to equity holders alone?

5. In some cases the rate of sales growth does not affect a firm's value using DCF valuation. Explain how this may happen.

6. Can the cost of equity ever be lower than the cost of debt? Why or why not?

7. Joseph Kreps, an investment banker, has been asked to value Rears and Soeback, a retail chain. He makes detailed cash flow forecasts for the first five years and estimates a terminal value in year 6, using the following assumptions:
   - sales grow at the rate of 3% per year,
   - net income to sales remain constant at 8%,
   - capital expenditures are equal to depreciation ($25 million per year),
   - debt-to-equity is constant at 80%, and
   - the current assets to sales ratio is 25%.

   Kreps estimates that in year 5 sales will be $200 million, current assets will be $50 million, and fixed assets will be $50 million, implying that asset turnover is 2. Given the above assumptions, what will be the forecasted asset turnover and return on equity in years 6 through 10?

8. When do you think that the pattern in ROE and asset turnover observed in Question 7 will be reversed? Do you think that this pattern is consistent with the concept of competitive equilibrium discussed in the chapter? What is the key assumption that is driving the ROE and asset turnover pattern? What changes, if any, would you suggest to help Kreps improve his valuation?

9. Janet Stringer argues: "The DCF valuation method has increased managers' focus on short-term rather than long-term performance, since the discounting process places much heavier weight on short-term cash flows than on long-term flows." Comment.

10. What is the cost of retained earnings?

CASE

The Gap, Inc.

NOTES

1. The present value of future dividends and the present value of future cash flows generate identical firm valuations, provided free cash flows are equivalent in value to those ultimately distributed by the firm to its owners. This requirement holds as long as any cash flows not used for reinvestment in operations are held in what are *expected* to be zero net present value projects, such as fairly priced marketable securities.

2. Short-term debt excludes operating liabilities, such as accounts payable and most accruals.

3. Compaq's situation on this dimension is unusual, in that they report interest expense even though they have no debt. For reasons discussed below, it is more practical to treat Compaq's interest expense as an operating expense, and to forecast cash flows net of this expense.

4. The forecasts of earnings and cash flow through 1997 are based on those of Duff and Phelps, reformatted to conform to the approach described here. To produce forecasts for 1998 through 2000, it is assumed that sales continue to grow at the same pace maintained in 1997, while gross margins fall to the 20 percent level forecast by Duff & Phelps for "the out years." Balance sheet forecasts are also based on those of Duff & Phelps (with extrapolations beyond 1997), except for cash balances. As explained, we assume distribution of cash (as dividends) and lower cash balances beginning in 1994.

5. Even though Duff & Phelps forecasts a decline in the ratio of net plant to sales, it forecasts capital expenditures to remain relatively constant as a fraction of sales. This seems unusual, in that it implies a decline in the average useful life of plant, and a corresponding increase in the rate of depreciation. In our forecasts beyond 1997, net plant is held constant as a fraction of sales at the 1997 level (6.6 percent). Depreciation is forecast at 31.9 percent of beginning net plant, roughly consistent with the average experience projected over 1994–1996. Capital expenditures are projected at amounts sufficient to maintain net plant at 6.6 percent of sales.

6. Perhaps in the interest of simplicity and because cash balances were not relied on explicitly by Duff & Phelps, their forecast of cash assumed that all free cash flows would be retained. As a result, the cash balance rises as a fraction of total assets from 11 percent in 1992 to a forecasted 29 percent in 1997. In Table 6-1, we assume that cash balances beyond 1994 remain at their 1994 level, which implies that all free cash flows are distributed to owners. Holding the cash balance constant causes the ratio of cash to total assets to fall from 15 percent in 1994 to 9 percent in 2000. For valuation purposes, the key is to maintain internally consistent treatment of cash balances and interest income. We could assume higher cash balances *and* higher interest income if we reduced distributions to owners, but in principle a similar valuation should be obtained.

7. Most of Compaq's interest expense represents reimbursements of dealers' cost of financing their payments to Compaq for inventory still on the dealer floor. Compaq's expense is thus a marketing cost that comes in a form similar to interest on factored receivables. Duff and Phelps forecasts the expense in amounts roughly proportional to sales. In valuing Compaq, one could either discount cash flows *before* this expense and arrive at the value of the commitment to dealers plus the value of equity, or discount cash flows *after* this expense and arrive at the value of equity directly. Because this interest expense is so closely tied to sales volume, we include it with other operating expenses, discount cash flows *net* of this expense, and arrive at a value of equity directly. In most other situations, interest expense is associated with debt, in which case we would discount cash flows *before* interest expense to arrive at the value of debt plus equity.

8. In the forecasts for 2001 and beyond, we continue to maintain the same ratio between balance sheet accounts and sales that was assumed for 2000 (see Table 6-1). Thus, with no change in sales, there is no required investment in net working capital. Depreciation ($369 million) is forecast at 31.9 percent of beginning net plant, consistent with the year 2000, and capital expenditures ($369 million) are forecast in the amount necessary to maintain net plant at 6.6 percent of sales.

9. If the analyst expects the firm to maintain abnormally profitable rates of return on sales that grow at the rate of inflation, a higher capitalization rate (based on the reciprocal of the weighted average cost of capital measured in *real* terms) could be justified. However, the amount capitalized must reflect the cash investment necessary to support the sales growth.

10. See Copeland, T. T. Koller, and J. Murrin, *Valuation: Measuring and Managing the Value of Companies,* 2nd edition (New York: John Wiley and Sons, 1994). Theory calls for the use of a short-term rate, but if that rate is used here, a difficult practical question rises: How does one reflect the premium required for expected inflation over long horizons? While the premium could, in principle, be treated as a portion of the term $[E(r_M) - r_F]$, it is probably easier to use an intermediate- or long-term riskless rate that presumably reflects expected inflation.

11. The average return reported here is the arithmetic mean, as opposed to the geometric mean. Ibbotson and Associates explain why this estimate is appropriate in this context. See Ibbotson and Associates, *Stocks, Bonds, Bills, and Inflation 1993 Yearbook,* (Chicago, 1994).

12. One way to estimate systematic risk is to regress the firm's stock returns over some recent time period against the returns on the market index. The slope coefficient represents an estimate of β. More fundamentally, systematic risk depends on the firm's degree of leverage and how sensitive the firm's operating profits are to shifts in economy-wide activity. Financial analysis that assesses these financial and operating risks should be useful in arriving at reasonable estimates of β.

13. Ibbotson and Associates, op. cit.

14. The Duff & Phelps report was issued in conjunction with a downgrade in their recommendation to investors from "buy" to "accumulate." Since the preponderance of analysts' recommendations are "buys," this could be viewed as a relatively negative signal.

15. As indicated in Table 6-1, the ratio of current assets to sales for 2000 is forecast at .374; the ratio of current liabilities to sales is .176. Net working capital is thus .198 times sales. The ratio of net plant to sales is .066, and the ratio of other long-lived assets to sales is .003. The deferred tax liability is .025 times sales. Total net investment required to support $1 of additional sales is thus .198 + .066 + .003 − .025, or .242.

chapter 7

Prospective Analysis: Accounting-Based Valuation Techniques

W‌e conclude our discussion of prospective analysis with a description of accounting-based valuation techniques. In the previous chapter on discounted cash flow analysis, we noted that as the method is typically applied, its cash flow projections are grounded in forecasts of sales, profit margins, and other accounting numbers. Here, we describe an alternative valuation technique that is consistent with DCF but which is linked more directly to accounting measures. This approach expresses the value of the firm's equity as the sum of the book value of equity and discounted expectations of future abnormal earnings.

Another set of valuation techniques based directly on accounting numbers involves the use of price multiples: price-earnings multiples, price-to-book multiples, and others. Intelligent application of these techniques requires an understanding of the determinants of the various multiples. Valuation based on discounted abnormal earnings provides a framework for describing those determinants.

OVERVIEW OF DISCOUNTED EARNINGS ANALYSIS

The recognition that DCF valuation is often grounded in forecasts of accounting measures raises a question: Is there a way to estimate value by discounting some accounting measure directly? For years, the finance literature suggested that there is no acceptable way to map accounting numbers into an estimate of firm value without first converting the accounting numbers into cash flows. Many have argued that the limitations of accounting numbers make this impossible. For example, accounting numbers often fail to reflect the timing of cash inflows and the investments necessary to generate them, and are affected by earnings management, which should not affect firm value. More recently, a number of practitioners and academics have rediscovered a notion that has long existed in the literature: It is possible to estimate equity value by discounting accounting numbers directly, so long as the proper technique is used.[1]

In principle, the accounting-based valuation described below should deliver the same estimate as DCF. The DCF method values the total expected cash inflows generated by a firm, whereas the abnormal earnings method values the firm at book value plus or minus adjustments for expected abnormal earnings. The major difference in the methods is the way that they frame the valuation, which can potentially cause the analyst to focus attention on different issues. We will return to this point after having laid out the calculations.

Estimating Value Based on Discounted Abnormal Earnings

As we noted in Chapter 6, it is well recognized among financial theorists that the market value of a firm's equity should equal the present value of its future dividends. There are two key steps to reformulating this dividend discount model in terms of accounting numbers. First, we must redefine dividends. This is straightforward provided we use "clean surplus" accounting, whereby all charges to equity go through the income statement. Dividends in any period can then be rewritten as follows:

> Dividends = Beginning book value + Earnings + Capital contributions (− Withdrawals)
> − Ending book value

The second step separates earnings into two components: normal and abnormal earnings. Normal earnings for a firm are its normal return multiplied by the beginning book value of equity. The normal rate of return is equal to the cost of equity capital—the same cost of equity that we use (along with the cost of debt) in the context of DCF valuation. Abnormal earnings are then the difference between earnings and normal earnings:

> Abnormal earnings = Earnings − (Cost of equity × Beginning book value)

If we substitute the earnings and book value expression for dividends into the dividend discount model and rearrange some of the terms, we can view the value of the firm's equity as the sum of its current book value plus its discounted expected future abnormal earnings. Using the operation $E_t[\,\cdot\,]$ to represent the expected value as of time t, the value of equity can be expressed as:

$$\text{Value of equity at time } t = \text{Book value of equity at time } t + \sum_{\tau=t+1}^{\infty} \frac{E_t(\text{Abnormal earnings for year } \tau)}{(1 + \text{Cost of equity})^{\tau}}$$

This formulation has intuitive appeal. It implies that if a firm can earn only a normal rate of return on its book value, then investors should be willing to pay no more than book value to acquire an interest. Investors should pay more or less than book value if earnings are above or below this normal level. Thus, the deviation of the firm's market value from its book value depends on the firm's power to generate "abnormal earnings."

Estimating Value Based on Discounted Abnormal ROE

We can reformat the abnormal earnings valuation by scaling all of the terms in the above accounting valuation equation by book value. Our job is now to estimate the price-to-book ratio, as opposed to the price itself. Under this approach, the valuation task would be described by the equation shown below. As before, we use the operator $E_t[\cdot]$ to indicate the expected value as of time t.

$$\frac{V_t}{b_t} = 1 + \frac{E_t(ROE_t - r_e)}{(1 + r_e)} + \frac{E_t[(ROE_{t+1} - r_e)(1 + g_{t+1})]}{(1 + r_e)^2} +$$

$$\frac{E_t[(ROE_{t+3} - r_e)(1 + g_{t+1})(1 + g_{t+2})]}{(1 + r_e)^3} + \cdots$$

where V_t = estimated value of equity at time t
b_t = book value at time t
r_e = cost of equity capital
g_{t+n} = growth in book value from year $t+n-1$ to year $t+n$ $= \dfrac{(b_{t+n} - b_{t+n-1})}{b_{t+n-1}}$

The ratio of market value to book value is expressed directly in terms of future abnormal ROE, which is simply future ROE less the cost of equity capital ($ROE_{t+n} - r_e$). Firms with expected positive abnormal ROE are assigned price-to-book ratios greater than one, and those with below-normal ROEs take on ratios below one. The deviation about one depends not only on the amount of abnormal ROE, but also the amount of growth in book value.

The valuation task can now be framed in terms of two key questions about the firm's "value drivers":

- How much greater (or smaller) than normal will the firm's ROE be?
- How quickly will the firm's investment base (book value) grow?

If desired, the equation can be rewritten so that future ROEs are expressed as the product of their components: profit margins, sales turnover, and leverage. Thus, the approach permits us to build directly on projections of the same accounting numbers utilized in financial analysis (see Chapter 4), without the need to convert projections of those numbers into cash flows. Yet in the end, the estimate of value should be the same as that from DCF.[2]

A "Shortcut" Technique for Estimating Value Based on Discounted Abnormal ROE

One advantage of the abnormal ROE approach is that it is amenable to producing quick and simple estimates of value without relying on assumptions as restrictive as, say, those implicit in the simple application of a PE multiple. "Back of the envelope" estimates are useful in a variety of contexts where the cost and time involved in a detailed DCF analysis is not justifiable. More than that, such estimates can provide a good "sanity check" on the detailed analysis. It is easy in the detailed analysis to become "so preoccupied by the trees that one loses sight of the forest"—inadvertently introducing internally inconsistent or unreasonable assumptions.

To illustrate the shortcut technique, assume that the analyst expects a firm to generate a constant $\overline{ROE}$ for the foreseeable future, and that sales and book value will grow at a constant rate $\overline{g}$ forever. The ratio of market to book value is then as follows:

$$\frac{V_t}{b_t} = 1 + \frac{(\overline{ROE} - r_e)}{r_e - \overline{g}}$$

The shortcut approach can easily be modified if the analyst expects that in the near term the firm will earn higher returns than the long-term expected ROE, or have higher book value growth than the long-term rate. For example, if a firm is expected to generate an unusually high ROE and rate of growth in book value for the first year of the valuation, and to then earn a constant return, $\overline{ROE}$, and have stable book value growth of $\overline{g}$ forever, the market to book value is:

$$\frac{V_t}{b_t} = 1 + \frac{[E(ROE_{t+1}) - r_e]}{(1 + r_e)} + \frac{(\overline{ROE} - r_e)(1 + g_{t+1})}{(r_e - \overline{g})(1 + r_e)}$$

The shortcut is not much more difficult than applying a PE multiple, and yet it provides the flexibility to entertain any desired combination of abnormal profitability, growth, and discount rates. For example, if desired, we could have allowed for a longer period of abnormally profitable growth and/or for ROEs that revert to more normal levels through time. The technique can be used to gain a quick feel for what a reasonable value might be, or for considering how value would be impacted by various "what if" scenarios. In fact, armed with information about current ROE, an understanding of how ROE is likely to change in the future, and a sense for likely sales growth rates, one can produce a "back of the envelope" estimate of firm value very quickly. Such an approach should not, however, be viewed as a perfect substitute for the more detailed analyses described below.

Illustration of Earnings-Based Valuation

How can an earnings-based approach generate the same estimate of value as the DCF method? After all, the earnings-based approach discounts abnormal earnings, which differ in both timing and magnitude from the free cash flows discounted under the DCF approach. To see the relation between these methods and to confirm that they do indeed provide identical estimates of value, consider the following simplified example.

An all-equity firm owns $60 million of inventory (with no other assets) and expects to sell the inventory over a two-year period and to then be dissolved. Analysts forecast that the firm will sell half of its inventory in the coming year for $50 million cash, and the other half for the same amount in cash in two years. If the firm's tax rate is zero, the free cash flows to equity used for valuation under DCF are $50 million in each year, whereas earnings are only $20 million per year (assuming inventory is valued using the average cost method). Consequently, there is a timing difference between earnings and free cash flows. Nonetheless, as we show below, earnings-based approaches yield the same estimates of value as DCF.

Under the discounted cash flow approach, the market value of equity is the present value of free cash flows to equity. Given a cost of equity of 15 percent, the DCF method estimates the market value to be $81 million, as follows:

	Year 1	Year 2
	(dollar amounts in millions)	
Forecasted free cash flow to equity	$50	$50
PV factor (at 15%)	0.8696	0.7561
PV of free cash flows	43.5	37.8
Sum of discounted free cash flows	$81.3	

Using the abnormal earnings valuation approach, the market value of equity is the sum of the beginning book value and the present value of forecasted abnormal earnings. Abnormal earnings for each year are expected earnings less the cost of capital multiplied by the beginning book value. To keep the problem simple, our firm pays out all of its surplus cash as dividends. At the end of the first year, forecasted book value is therefore $30 million, comprising the opening balance of $60 million, plus forecasted earnings of $20, less dividends of $50 million. Despite the difference in timing between earnings and cash flows, the estimated value under the discounted abnormal earnings approach is identical to the DCF value, and is computed as follows:

		Year 1	Year 2
		(dollar amounts in millions)	
Book value, year 0	$60.0		
Earnings forecast		$20	$20
Beginning book value		60	30
Abnormal earnings:			
Earnings − r × book value (r = 15%)		11.0	15.5
PV factor (at 15%)		0.8696	0.7561
PV of abnormal earnings	21.3	9.6	11.7
Opening book value plus sum of discounted abnormal earnings	$81.3		

Finally, we show that the abnormal ROE estimate of equity is also identical to that under DCF. The abnormal ROE method estimates the market to book ratio as one plus the present value of abnormal ROEs scaled by growth in book value. ROE is computed using forecasted earnings and beginning book value. Given a 15 percent cost of equity, abnormal ROEs are 18 percent in year 1 and 52 percent in year 2. The estimate of market value is then computed as follows:

		Year 1	Year 2
		(dollar amounts in millions)	
Book value, year 0	$60.0		
Earnings forecast		$20	$20
Beginning book value		60	30
ROE		0.333	0.667
Abnormal ROE:			
ROE − r		0.183	0.517
Cumulative growth in book value since year 1		1.00	0.50
Abnormal ROE × cumulative book value growth		0.183	0.259
PV factor (at 15%)		0.8696	0.7561
PV of abnormal ROE × cumulative book value growth		0.159	0.195
Market to book ratio	× 1.354*		
Market value	$81.2		

*sum of discounted abnormal ROE (0.159 + 0.195 + 1)

This approach yields a market-to-book ratio of 1.35 and a market value estimate of $81, identical to that using DCF.

In other words, it doesn't matter for valuation purposes that the earnings-based approach discounts only abnormal earnings, since normal earnings are captured by book values. The DCF method provides the same value by unraveling book value and discounting the full cash flow stream.

The above example also shows that timing differences between earnings and cash flows do not lead to a difference in estimated values under DCF and earnings-based approaches. Timing differences affect both earnings and book values. Thus, any earnings realized prior to the receipt of cash are included in subsequent book values, thereby lowering future abnormal earnings by a discount factor. This effect is undone once cash is received, since the timing difference no longer affects book values. This point is discussed in more detail below as we show how earnings-based valuations are affected by accounting decisions.

How Do Accounting Decisions Affect Value Under the Discounted Earnings Approach?

One common question that arises for earnings-based valuation is how value is affected by accounting decisions. If earnings are subject to manipulation by management through use of accounting discretion, how can the valuation approach deliver correct estimates?

Because accounting choices must affect both earnings and book values (a requirement of "clean surplus" accounting), and because of the self-correcting nature of double-entry bookkeeping (all "distortions" of accounting must ultimately reverse), estimated values based on discounted abnormal earnings or ROE will not be affected by accounting choices. To see how this works, consider how the valuation of the hypothetical company discussed above would change if managers use FIFO instead of average cost to value inventory. Assume that under FIFO the cost of inventory sold is $20 million in year 1 and $40 million in year 2. This change in accounting has no tax consequences for our firm, since it doesn't pay taxes. However, it increases year 1 earnings and ending book value by $20 million. In year 2, the higher-valued inventory is sold, leading to a $20 million decline in earnings relative to the average cost inventory method. For the time being, let's assume that this accounting effect is transparent and has no influence on the analyst's view of the firm's real performance. The revised book values, earnings, and abnormal earnings for years 1 and 2 are now as follows:

	Year 1	Year 2
	(in millions)	
Effect of accounting decision on:		
Earnings	$10	−$10
Opening book value		10
Abnormal earnings (earnings − 15% × book value)	10	−11.5
Discounted abnormal earnings	10	−10

The accounting decision increases earnings by $10 million in year 1 and decreases them by the same amount in year 2. This change has no effect on the opening book value for year 1, but it causes the year 2 value to decline by $10 million. Abnormal earnings thus increase by the full $10 million in year 1. However, in year 2 abnormal earnings decline by $11.5 million, representing the $10 million from the earnings reversal and the incremental normal earnings of $1.5 million from the higher opening book value. The net effect on market value is zero, since the present value of the increase in abnormal earnings in year 1 ($10 million) is exactly offset by the decline in discounted abnormal earnings in year 2 ($10 million).

Consequently, provided the analyst is aware of biases in accounting data as a result of the use of aggressive or conservative accounting choices by management, abnormal earnings-based valuations are unaffected by the variation in accounting decisions. This implies that strategic and accounting analyses are critical precursors to abnormal earnings valuation. As we discuss below, strategic and accounting analyses help the analyst to identify whether abnormal earnings or ROEs arise from sustainable competitive advantage or from unsustainable accounting manipulations.

Cash-Flow-Based Valuation Versus Accounting-Based Valuation

In principle, valuation based on discounted abnormal earnings delivers exactly the same estimate as DCF-based methods. However, the analyst could still consider the differences between the two approaches important. First, the alternatives frame the valuation task differently and can in practice focus the analyst's attention on different issues. The accounting-based approach can be framed in a way that immediately focuses attention on the same key measure of performance, ROE, that is decomposed in a standard financial analysis. Second, if it is more natural to think about future performance in terms of accounting returns, and if the analyst faces a context where a "back of the envelope" estimate of value would be of use, the accounting-based technique can be simplified to deliver such an estimate. Such an estimate could also be easily generated through, say, an application of some PE multiple, but that approach would involve restrictive assumptions not required here.

STEPS IN DISCOUNTED EARNINGS VALUATION

There are seven key steps in implementing abnormal earnings, or abnormal ROE, valuation:

Step 1:   Analyze strategy to understand factors driving the performance of an industry and firm, and to assess whether those factors are likely to persist or be easily imitated.

Step 2:   Analyze accounting to assess whether management has made conservative or aggressive accounting decisions for reporting earnings and book values. This knowledge can help the analyst to assess whether reported abnormal earnings or ROE performance is likely to be sustained, is understated because of accounting conservatism, or is likely to be reversed because of aggressive accounting.

Step 3:   Forecast future earnings or ROEs for the firm for a finite horizon. The final year of this horizon is termed the "terminal year."

Step 4:   Forecast the future growth in book value for the firm until the terminal year.

Step 5:   Forecast earnings/ROEs and book value growth rates beyond the terminal year using a simplifying assumption.

Step 6:   Estimate the cost of equity for the firm.

Step 7:   Use the cost of equity to estimate abnormal earnings or ROEs and to discount these values. Under the abnormal earnings approach, the market value of the firm is the current book value plus discounted abnormal earnings. Under the abnormal ROE method, the market value is the current book value plus book value multiplied by the discounted product of abnormal ROEs and growth in book value.

Below we illustrate these steps, using the long-term earnings and book value forecasts for Compaq made by the analyst at Duff & Phelps. The forecasts were made at the end of 1993, when the stock price was $74. These forecasts, as well as the details of the abnormal earnings valuation, are shown in Table 7-1. Forecasts of ROE and growth in book value, as well as details of abnormal ROE valuation, are presented in Table 7-2. The illustration has been constructed to preserve the equivalence between DCF and earnings-based valuation methods.[3]

Step 1: Analyze Strategy

As we discussed in Chapters 3 and 5, a firm's industry and positioning within that industry are key drivers of its long-term earnings, ROEs, and growth in book values. It is therefore important that the analyst develop an understanding of these strategic factors. With respect to Compaq, the analyst could ask:

- What are the expected growth prospects for the personal computer hardware business? For how long can the historically high levels of growth in this industry be sustained?
- Is Compaq's mixed strategy of being both a low cost provider and continuing to stress its high product quality and brand likely to be successful in the long term? Or will Compaq be dominated by low cost providers in that segment of the market, and by manufacturers that focus exclusively on product innovation and quality?

As shown by the earnings and ROE forecasts reported in Tables 7-1 and 7-2, the Duff & Phelps analyst expects that Compaq's low cost strategy will continue to be successful in driving high rates of sales growth and maintaining high and stable ROEs at least until the year 2000. Sales are predicted to grow at 21 percent in 1994, and to stabilize at 10 percent in 1997. Growth rates for book values are considerably lower, especially prior to 1997, primarily because the analyst assumes that much of the early sales growth comes from improvements in asset productivity, reflected in growing asset turnover.

Step 2: Analyze Accounting

Accounting analysis is an especially important step in accounting-based valuation. A thorough analysis of the firm's accounting decisions will help the analyst decide whether the firm's underlying economics is being reported aggressively, conservatively, or in an

Table 7-1 Valuation of Compaq Based on Book Value and Abnormal Earnings, December 1993

	1994	1995	1996	1997	1998	1999	2000	beyond 2000
				(dollar amounts in millions)				
Book value, 1993	$2,654							
Earnings forecast	$517	$565	$609	$628	$639	$702	$773	$773*
Book value, beginning	$2,654	$2,646	$2,917	$3,169	$3,364	$3,633	$3,928	$4,253*
Residual earnings:								
Earnings – r (book value)	$172	$221	$230	$216	$202	$230	$262	$220*
Discount factor, at 13%	1.13	1.28	1.44	1.63	1.84	2.08	2.35	
Discounted abnormal earnings	$152	$173	$159	$132	$109	$110	$112	$718*
Book value plus sum of discounted abnormal earnings	$4,320							

*Terminal value calculation: When sales are treated as if they will not grow beyond 2000 while margins stay constant, earnings remain at $773 in 2001 and beyond. Book value, which rises to $4,253 at the end of 2000 to accommodate the growth occurring during that year, remains at this level thereafter. Abnormal earnings are thus $773 – (.13 × $4253), or $220 per year. The present value of the $220 in perpetuity is $1,690 at the end of 2000 ($220/.13) and $718 at the end of 1993 [$1,690 / (1.13)⁷].

If sales were treated as if they grew at a 3.5 percent rate beyond 2000 while holding margins constant, earnings would rise 3.5 percent each year, to $800 in 2001, $828 in 2002, and so on. Book value would be $4,253 at the beginning of 2001 and would also rise by 3.5 percent each year. Abnormal earnings would be $247 in 2001 [$800 – (.13 × $4,253)], and would rise 3.5 percent each year. The present value of the growing abnormal earnings stream would be $2,597 in 2000 [$247/(.13-.035)] and $1,104 as of the end of 1993. The sum of book value and discounted abnormal earnings would be $4,706—or $5,012 after multiplication by [1 + (.13/2)] to account for cash flows arriving halfway through the year, rather than at year's end. Indicated per-share value would be $59.

When adjusted to assume that cash flows occur halfway through the year, the amount is $4,320 × (1 + .13/2) = $4,600, or $54 per share.

Table 7-2 Valuation of Compaq Based on Growth in Book Value and Abnormal ROE, December 1993

	1994	1995	1996	1997	1998	1999	2000	beyond 2000
				(dollar amounts in millions)				
Book value, 1993	$2,654							
ROE forecast	0.195	0.214	0.209	0.198	0.190	0.193	0.197	0.182*
Residual ROE:								
ROE − r (book value)	0.065	0.084	0.079	0.068	0.060	0.063	0.067	0.052*
Book value growth factor	1.00	1.00	1.10	1.19	1.27	1.37	1.48	1.60*
Residual ROE × book value growth	0.065	0.083	0.087	0.081	0.076	0.087	0.099	0.083
Discount factor, at 13%	1.13	1.28	1.44	1.63	1.84	2.08	2.35	
Discount residual ROE × book value growth	0.057	0.065	0.060	0.050	0.041	0.042	0.042	0.271*
Market to book ratio	1.628		When adjusted to assume that cash flows occur halfway through the year,					
Market value	$4,320		the amount is $4,320 × (1 + .13/2) = $4,600, or $54 per share.					

*Terminal value calculation: When sales are treated as if they will not grow beyond 2000 while margins stay constant, ROE remains at 18.2 percent in 2001 and beyond. There is also no growth in book value beyond 2000. Abnormal ROE times the growth in book value factor are thus 8.3 percent per year. The present value of this residual ROE times book value growth in perpetuity is 0.638 (0.083/.13) and 0.271 at the end of 1993 [0.638/ (1.13)^7].

If sales were treated as if they grew at a 3.5 percent rate beyond 2000 while holding margins constant, earnings would rise by 3.5 percent per year, to $800 in 2001, $828 in 2002, and so on. Book value would be $4,253 at the beginning of 2001 and would also rise by 3.5 percent each year. ROE would then be 18.8 percent (and abnormal ROE would be 5.8 percent) in 2001 and each year thereafter. The present value of the abnormal ROE stream, given ongoing growth in book value of 3.5 percent per year, would be 0.611 in 2000 [0.058/(.13−.035)] and 0.417 as of the end of 1993. The market-to-book value would then be 1.774, implying a market value of $4,706—or $5,012 after multiplication by [1 + (.13/2)] to account for cash flows arriving halfway through the year, rather than at year's end. Indicated per-share value would be $59.

"unbiased" manner. The illustration of earnings-based valuation discussed above shows that unbiased valuations can only be made if the analyst's forecasts of future earnings and ROEs reflect any future write-downs or lower earnings likely to arise for firms that report aggressively. Similarly, for firms that use conservative accounting the analyst must recognize that it will report future superior profits as the conservative accounting unwinds.

Of course, as we discuss in Chapter 3, there are multiple interpretations of management's accounting estimates and method choices. Management that makes a seemingly aggressive accounting estimate may do so either because it believes that this decision is warranted by the firm's business economics and strategy, or as a way to conceal poor performance. For example, if management anticipates that investments to improve product quality are likely to be highly effective, it may decide to report this improvement in performance by lowering its estimate of the provision for product returns. Alternatively, it may lower the provision for product returns as a way of window dressing. Accounting analysis provides the analyst with a basis for distinguishing between these possibilities. If the analyst decides that a firm's accounting estimates are unbiased and provide new information from management on the effectiveness of a quality improvement program, current earnings and ROE should be seen as sustainable. However, if the analyst suspects that management has lowered return provisions as a window-dressing tactic, subsequent losses arising when defective products are actually returned will lower future earnings and ROEs and will need to be incorporated in the valuation analysis.

Once an overview of the firm's accounting decisions is completed, the analyst has to adjust forecasts of earnings and book values for any accounting bias identified.[4] Two forms of adjustment are possible. The simplest is to adjust the current book value to make it unbiased. If accounting is deemed to be aggressive, this adjustment requires a write-down of assets or recognition of unrecorded liabilities to reflect a neutral or unbiased book value. Alternatively, the analyst can make adjustments to future earnings directly as a way of correcting for the bias.

Accounting analysis can also be important if there are deviations from "clean surplus" accounting. Remember that this accounting requires the following relation:

End-of-period book value =
Beginning book value + Earnings − Dividends + Capital contributions (− Withdrawals)

Clean surplus accounting rules out situations where some gain or loss is excluded from earnings but is still used to adjust the book value of equity. For example, under U.S. GAAP, gains and losses on foreign currency translations are handled this way. In applying the valuation technique described here, the analyst would need to deviate from GAAP in producing forecasts and treat such gains/losses as a part of earnings. However, the technique does not require clean surplus accounting to have been applied in the past. So the existing book value, based on U.S. GAAP or any other set of principles, can still serve as the starting point. All the analyst needs to do is apply clean surplus accounting in his or her forecasts. That much is not only easy, but is usually the natural thing to do anyway. The Duff & Phelps forecasts, for example, were consistent with clean surplus accounting.

Step 3: Forecast Earnings/ROEs

Strategy and accounting analysis are critical precursors to forecasting earnings and ROEs under the accounting-based valuation. They help the analyst to identify whether current abnormal earnings or ROEs arise from sustainable competitive advantage or from unsustainable accounting manipulations. For a detailed valuation, forecasts should be made until the firm is expected to earn a stable ROE. The shortcut approach simplifies the analysis by using average ROE values for the near and long term.

Table 7-1 shows the Duff & Phelps forecasts of Compaq's earnings and book values, and Table 7-2 shows forecasts of ROE and book value growth using data from Table 6-1. The forecasts show that Duff & Phelps expects ROE to fluctuate between 19 and 21 percent from 1994 to 2000, implying that Compaq will continue to show high abnormal earnings and returns.

Step 4: Forecast Growth in Book Values

Strategy and accounting analysis also help the analyst to assess expected future growth in book values through the terminal year. Strategy analysis helps the analyst forecast whether the firm will retain all of its earnings to reinvest in profitable new investments, implying that book value growth will be the same as return on equity. Of course, a firm can grow its book value at an even higher rate than its return on equity if it also issues new equity to finance its growth. Alternatively, the firm may have reached a steady state, where profits more than cover replacement investment. A significant proportion of annual profits or ROEs are then paid out as dividends or stock repurchases, implying that book values will be stable, or grow at only the rate of inflation. Finally, if the industry is in decline, the firm's book value may actually fall, since there will be no new investment. Accounting analysis can help the analyst to assess whether the firm is making aggressive accounting estimates and will be subsequently required to take write-downs, lowering book value.

The forecasts of book values, presented in Tables 7-1 and 7-2, show that Duff & Phelps expects Compaq's book value to be stable for one year, and to then grow at between 6 and 10 percent from 1994 to 2000. These are significantly lower than the ROE forecasts of 19 to 21 percent, and imply that Duff & Phelps expects that Compaq's earnings and cash flows will exceed its investment requirements and that the firm will begin paying dividends. The dividend payouts reflected in the forecasts reported in Tables 7-1 and 7-2 assume that the firm maintains a cash balance of 3.8 percent of sales for working capital uses and pays out any surplus cash as dividends.[5]

Step 5: Forecast Earnings/ROEs and Book Values Beyond the Terminal Year

When valuation is based on abnormal earnings, the terminal value is the present value of abnormal earnings beyond the terminal year. There are several approaches to estimating this terminal value. One is to assume that sales, margins, book values, and hence abnormal earnings and ROEs, remain constant beyond the terminal year. For Compaq, this approach leads to projections of abnormal earnings beyond 2000 of $220 per year, equivalent to an 18.1 percent ROE.[6] Alternatively, the analyst can allow for modest growth in sales (perhaps at the rate of inflation or GNP growth). For example, for Compaq, we could let sales grow by 3.5 percent and hold margins constant at 4.4 percent.

A second approach is to project a "normal" market-to-book ratio at the terminal date. This represents an estimate of the difference between the market value and the book value of equity in that year and is equivalent to projecting the future market-to-book premium. An appropriate "normal" multiple would be one that that allows for the possibility of supernormal profits on assets in place, but not for further growth with abnormal profitability. Average price-to-book ratios in the U.S. have been about 1.6 over the years. Applying this ratio to Compaq's projected book value for 2000 would have produced a terminal value estimate of $2,552 million [$4,253 million × (1.6 − 1.0)].

Finally, we could adopt the shortcut approach and make simplifying assumptions about Compaq's long-term average ROE and growth in sales (and hence book values). For example, the analyst could assume that Compaq will continue to generate an ROE in the range of 19 percent for the foreseeable future, and that sales and book value will grow at a rate of 20 percent. However, beyond three years, any growth is ignored, assuming it comes only in the form of zero net present value projects.

Step 6: Estimate the Cost of Equity

Since the accounting-based valuation provides an estimate of the market value of equity directly, as opposed to the market value of the firm, the appropriate cost of capital for earnings is the cost of equity. A more detailed discussion of how to estimate the cost of equity is provided in Chapter 6. Here we provide only a recap of that discussion.

The most popular approach for estimating the cost of equity is to use the capital asset pricing model (CAPM). Under this model the cost of equity is the sum of the required return on riskless assets plus a premium for systematic (or beta) risk. However, many finance theorists now view the CAPM as incomplete in light of evidence that returns are related to firms' characteristics other than beta risk, such as their size and market-to-book ratios.

For Compaq, we showed in Chapter 6 that the cost of equity is approximately 15 percent, using a CAPM approach, and only 11 to 12 percent when benchmarked against firms of comparable size. We use a rate of 13 percent, which lies between the CAPM and size values, to estimate and then discount abnormal earnings. However, any comprehensive analysis would also examine the sensitivity of market value estimates to this assumption.

Step 7: Estimate and Discount Abnormal Earnings/ROEs

Once we have forecasted earnings and book values and have estimated the cost of equity, we can compute and discount abnormal earnings. Remember that normal earnings for a firm are its cost of equity multiplied by the beginning book value of equity, and abnormal earnings are simply the difference between earnings and normal earnings. Similarly, abnormal ROEs are the difference between forecasted ROEs and the cost of equity.

For Compaq, the present value of abnormal earnings from 1994 to 2000 (at 13 percent) is $947. The present value of forecasted abnormal earnings beyond 2000 in perpetuity is $718 million as of the end of 1993. When we add these values to the initial book value, we arrive at an indicated value per share of $54. (See Table 7-1 for details.)

If we had assumed that sales beyond 2000 would grow by 3.5 percent, with margins holding constant at 4.4 percent, the terminal value would have been $2,597 million as of 2000, and $1,104 million as of the end of 1993. (See the notes to Table 7-1.) Price per share would be $59, as opposed to our base case of $54. Alternatively, we can use a projected "normal" market-to-book premium for Compaq in 2000 as an estimate of terminal value. As noted above, this produces a terminal value estimate of $2,552 million—nearly identical to our more optimistic estimate above.

As shown in Table 7-2, the abnormal ROE method generates exactly the same equity value as the DCF and abnormal earnings approaches. The forecasts of ROEs and book value growth generate a market-to-book ratio of 1.628. Given the opening book value of $2,654, this is equivalent to a market value of $4,320.

Finally, we can also use the "shortcut" approach to value Compaq. For example, if we expect that Compaq will earn an ROE of 19 percent for the foreseeable future, and sales and book value will grow at a rate of 20 percent for three years and zero thereafter, we can adapt the formula shown earlier in this section. The implied ratio of market value to book value is 1.72, as shown below.[7]

$$\frac{V_t}{b_t} = 1 + \frac{(.19 - .13)}{(1.13)} + \frac{(.19 - .13)(1.20)}{(1.13)^2} + \frac{(.19 - .13)(1.20)^2}{(1.13)^3}$$

$$+ \frac{(.19 - .13)(1.20)^3 / (.13)}{(1.13)^3} = 1.72$$

A price-to-book ratio of 1.72 suggests a current price per share of $54. We could easily have allowed for growth in abnormal earnings of 3.5 percent for all years beyond the third, raising our implied price to $60.[8]

COMPARISON OF ABNORMAL EARNINGS/ROE AND DCF APPROACHES

The market value for Compaq, estimated using the discounted abnormal earnings method, is identical to that obtained with the DCF method, $4.3 billion, when we treat sales as constant beyond 2000. Nearly two-thirds of this value is already represented in the beginning book value reported by Compaq. Another fraction is reflected in the discounted abnormal earnings for 1994 through 2000. Only about 17 percent of the value is attributed to abnormal earnings from years beyond 2000. Contrast this with the terminal value calculated under DCF, which represented 58 percent of total value. On the surface, this would appear to mitigate concerns about the aspect of valuation that leaves the analyst most uncomfortable. Is this apparent advantage real? As explained below, the answer turns on how well value is already reflected in the accountant's book value.

Earnings-based valuation does not make DCF's terminal value problem go away, but it does reframe it. DCF terminal values include the present value of *all* expected cash flows beyond the forecast horizon. Under accounting-based valuation, that value is broken into two parts: the present values of both *normal* and *abnormal* earnings beyond the terminal year. The terminal value in the accounting-based technique includes only the abnormal earnings; the present value of normal earnings is already reflected in the original book value or growth in book value over the forecast horizon.

The accounting-based approach, then, recognizes that current book value and earnings over the forecast horizon already reflect many of the cash flows expected to arrive after the forecast horizon. The accounting-based approach builds on these products of accrual accounting directly. The DCF approach, on the other hand, starts by writing off the original investment and makes forecasts of all future returns. The essential difference between the two approaches is that accounting-based valuation recognizes that the accrual process may already have performed a portion of the valuation task, whereas the DCF approach ultimately moves back to the primitive cash flows underlying the accruals.

As we discussed above, the usefulness of the accounting-based perspective hinges on how well the accrual process reflects future cash flows. The approach is most convenient when accounting is "unbiased," so that ROEs can be abnormal only as the result of economic rents and not as a product of the accounting itself.[9] In that case, as the forecast horizon extends to the point where the firm is expected to approach a competitive equilibrium and earn only a normal return on its projects, expected ROE would approach the cost of capital. Subsequent abnormal earnings would be zero, and the terminal value at that point would be nil. In this extreme case, all of the firm's value is reflected in the book value and earnings projected over the forecast horizon.

TECHNIQUES OF VALUATION BASED ON PRICE MULTIPLES

Both the DCF valuation method and valuation based on discounted abnormal earnings require detailed, multi-year forecasts. In that sense, the methods place heavy demands on the analyst. Moreover, given that the valuation depends so heavily on forecasts of performance several years into the future, the analyst may feel less than confident about the final range of estimates. An alternative approach is to value the firm based on price multiples of "comparable" firms. Under this approach, one relies on the market to undertake the difficult task of considering the short- and long-term prospects for growth and profitability and their implications for the values of the seemingly comparable firms. Then the analyst *assumes* that the pricing of those other firms is applicable to the firm at hand.

Application of price multiples for comparable firms seems straightforward on the surface. One simply identifies firms in the same industry, calculates the desired multiple—e.g., price-earnings or price-to-book—and then applies the multiple to the firm being valued.

Unfortunately, application of price multiples is not so simple as it would appear. Identification of firms that are really comparable is often quite difficult. There are also some choices to be made concerning how the multiples will be calculated. Finally, explaining why multiples vary across firms, and how applicable another firm's multiple is to the one at hand, requires a sound understanding of the determinants of each multiple.

Below, we address some of these issues with the aid of Table 7-3, which compares various multiples for Compaq with those of three other industry players. One could view Table 7-3 as a foundation for assessing how favorably priced Compaq is relative to others. Alternatively, if one imagined that Compaq were a private firm with no observable market price, one could consider the multiples for other firms as indicators of how one might price Compaq.

Selecting Comparable Firms

Ideally, price multiples used in a comparable firm analysis would be those for firms with the most similar operating and financial characteristics. Firms within the same industry

Table 7-3 Selected Price Multiples for Compaq and "Comparable" Firms

Price multiple	Compaq Computer	Comparable Firms		
		AST Research	Apple Computer	Dell Computer
Trailing PE based on four most recently reported quarters' EPS	14.3	17.4	12.7	NM
Leading PE based on forecast 1994 EPS	11.5	12.6	18.1	12.6
Unlevered[a] **price/sales ratio** based on four most recently reported quarters' sales	.89	.50	.44	.36
Unlevered[a] **price/sales ratio** based on forecast 1994 sales	.75	.34	.39	.27
Price-to-book ratio based on book value as reported in most recent quarter	2.48	2.22	1.72	2.61
Unlevered[b] **price-to-"cash flow" ratio** based on 1993 EBITDA	6.7	9.5	4.6	NM

a. Unlevered price/sales ratio $= \dfrac{(\text{Market value of equity } + \text{ Debt})}{\text{Sales}}$

b. Unlevered price/"cash flow" ratio $= \dfrac{(\text{Market value of equity } + \text{ Debt})}{\text{Earnings before interest, depreciation, and amortization}}$

are the most obvious candidates. However, even within narrowly defined industries, it is often difficult to find multiples for similar firms. Compaq's closest competitor in the personal computer (PC) market is IBM, but IBM is involved in much more than the production and sale of PCs. Moreover, IBM does not reveal financial data for its PC division; even if it did, there is no observable market price for only that part of the business.

Similar issues arise with DEC and Hewlett-Packard. Another close competitor, NCR, cannot be used in the comparison because it exists as a division within ATT. Yet another player, NEC, produces more than just PCs and presents another difficulty as well: Even though its financials are converted to U.S. GAAP, it is unlikely that, as a Japanese firm, its accounting policies are truly similar to those that would be used by a U.S. firm. Gateway and Packard Bell are also close competitors but, as private firms in 1993, they had no price data. Commodore International produces desktop computers, but it was facing so much financial difficulty in late 1993 that its price multiples are difficult to interpret and probably not applicable to a healthy company like Compaq.

Compaq competitors that are publicly held and that focus almost primarily on production of desktop computers include Apple, AST Research, and Dell—the firms whose multiples appear in Table 7-3. Even among this small set, there are some problems in drawing comparisons. Dell is coming off losses in 1993, and so its trailing price/earnings ratio is not meaningful. AST Research does not have the strength of brand that Compaq has developed, and so its profit margins are lower. As explained below, this affects the comparability of some ratios but not others. Apple has maintained a strong brand image and high margins in the past, but is adjusting later than Compaq to new market realities. Thus, while Compaq's earnings are already on the rebound in 1993, Apple may still face another year or two of mediocre earnings growth.

Differences such as those found here inevitably arise in valuation based on price multiples. One way of dealing with the problem is to average across *all* firms in the industry. However, the analyst using that approach can only hope that various sources of noncomparability cancel each other out, so that the firm being valued is a "typical" industry member. Another approach is to focus on those firms within the industry that are most similar, as we do in Table 7-3. As explained below, this should be done with the recognition that what constitutes comparability varies according to which multiple is being applied. We will return to this topic after discussing some technical issues.

Use of Forecasts Versus Past Performance

Price multiples can include, in the denominator, measures of either past or future performance. Which is best? Note that prices should be based on expected future performance. Thus, using historical data in the denominator of a price multiple is justified only in the sense that the denominator is viewed as an indicator of the future. If a reliable forecast is directly available, it would generally be preferred as the basis for a multiple. However, such forecasts are typically available only for larger firms.

Table 7-3 presents PE ratios based on both past earnings (a *trailing* PE multiple) and on forecasts of fiscal 1994 earnings (a *leading* PE multiple). In the interests of using the

latest data in the trailing PE multiple, the denominator includes the EPS of the most recent four quarters, even though those quarters may span different fiscal years.

Trailing PE multiples can be distorted substantially by the transitory gains and losses
or other unusual performance of the most recent year. With that in mind, we have excluded from the denominator of Apple's PE multiple a large nonrecurring loss. Absent
such an adjustment, Apple's PE would have been nearly 50! Even after eliminating such
nonrecurring items, PEs can still be distorted, however. For example, Dell suffered an
operating loss in 1993 that analysts do not expect to see repeated, rendering their trailing
PE nonmeaningful.

Leading multiples can also be distorted, but are less likely to include one-time gains
and losses in the denominator, simply because such items are difficult to anticipate in
forecasts. All of the leading PE multiples in Table 7-3 are within a "normal" range, 11.5
to 18.1.

Adjusting Multiples for Leverage

Price multiples should be calculated in a way that preserves consistency between the numerator and denominator. Consistency is an issue for those ratios where the denominator reflects performance *before* servicing debt. Examples include the price-to-sales
multiple and any multiple of operating earnings or operating cash flows. When calculating these multiples, the numerator should include not just the market value of equity, but
the value of debt as well. This is not an issue for Compaq or Apple, neither of which
carry any debt. However, both AST Research and Dell do have debt in their capital structure. In the case of AST Research, the trailing price-to-sales multiple was adjusted for
debt as follows:

$$\frac{(\text{Market value of equity} + \text{Debt})}{\text{Sales}} = \frac{(\text{Stock price} \times \text{Shares}) + \text{Debt}}{\text{Sales}}$$

$$= \frac{(\$23 \times 31.6 \text{ million}) + \$92 \text{ million}}{\$1,645 \text{ million}} = .50$$

Interpreting and Comparing Multiples

Even across these relatively closely related firms, some of the price multiples vary considerably. For example, Compaq's unlevered price-to-sales ratio is much higher than that
of any of the "comparable" firms. Does this suggest that Compaq is relatively overpriced? Or is there some other explanation? If Compaq had no observable market price,
how appropriate would it be to apply the price-to-book multiples of the other firms to
estimate the value of Compaq?

Careful analysis of such questions requires consideration of the determinants of each
multiple, the factors that might explain why some firms' multiples should be higher than
others:

- *Price-earnings ratios* should vary positively with differences in expected future growth in (abnormal) earnings, and negatively with risk.[10] In the special case where no growth is expected in the current level of earnings, or where such growth will come only as the product of additional investment in zero net present value projects, the PE ratio should be approximately equal to the reciprocal of the cost of equity capital, thus placing it in the range of 6 to 10.[11] In early 1995, the market priced U.S. auto manufacturers at multiples in the range of 5 to 7, reflecting an expectation of essentially no growth in abnormal earnings.

  The leading PE ratios for Compaq, AST Research, and Dell all indicate that market agents expect moderate growth in (abnormal) earnings beyond the coming year. The ratios are all within the range of 11.5 to 12.6. Apple holds a higher multiple of forecast 1994 earnings, at 18.1. The higher multiple reflects the market's expectation that much of Apple's rebound will not occur until *after* 1994. In fact, Apple stands as the only firm in the set for which analysts are projecting a decline in earnings in 1994. The upshot is that Apple's higher multiple should *not* be taken as an indication that it is overpriced, or that Compaq is underpriced. The difference is expected, based on the likely path of earnings growth for the two firms.

- *Price-to-book ratios.* The theoretical determinants of a price-to-book ratio are provided in the previous discussion of valuation based on discounted abnormal earnings. Price-to-book ratios should vary across firms according to differences in their future ROEs, growth in book value, and risk (the driver of differences in discount rates).

  Compaq and Dell have relatively high price-to-book ratios. That should be expected, because analysts are expecting high ROEs (in the upper teens) for both firms in the future, along with strong growth in book value. Apple's price-to-book ratio is relatively low, but that again is to be expected. *Value Line* forecasts ROE for Apple to be only about 10 percent in 1994, rising to about 13.5 percent over a four-year horizon. AST Research sits in the middle of the price-to-book distribution, as does its forecast long-range ROE (15 percent).

- *Price-to-sales ratios* can be viewed as the product of price-earnings ratios and earnings-to-sales ratios. Thus, in addition to the factors that explain variation in PE ratios, price-to-sales ratios should vary with expected profit margins. Firms with higher expected margins should be worth more in dollar sales. This is why one would expect, for example, a pharmaceutical company to have a higher price-to-sales ratio than a grocery store chain; or why one would expect the price-to-sales ratio to be higher when a firm carries a strong brand name.

  The price-to-sales ratio is the one multiple for which Compaq appears on the surface to be most out of line with its competitors. Its ratio is more than twice as large as the average of the others. Given that differences in the PE ratios were much smaller, the differences in price-to-sales ratios are explainable only if Compaq can maintain a higher profit margin. Indeed, that is expected. Projected operating margins are (according to *Value Line*) substantially larger than those of the other firms.

This is consistent with the view of Compaq's strength of brand name and cost efficiencies, expressed earlier.

• *Price-to-cash flow ratios,* as used in practice, rarely employ a pure cash flow measure in the denominator. Cash flow from operations is often affected by temporary fluctuations in working capital accounts, and thus provides a noisy indicator of value as it stands alone. Instead, the price-cash flow multiples used in practice usually refer to a multiple of earnings before depreciation, or some similar measure. A commonly used denominator is EBITDA, or operating earnings before interest, taxes, depreciation, and amortization. Note that such a ratio should be unlevered (including the value of debt in the numerator) because the denominator reflects earnings before interest.

Table 7-3 presents the unlevered multiple of trailing EBITDA for the most recent year. Leading multiples are not presented because forecasts of EBITDA are not widely available. Compaq's "cash flow" multiple lies between that of AST and Apple; Dell's multiple is not meaningful. The pattern is consistent with the trailing PE multiples; it reflects the market's expectation of a large rebound from 1993 for AST and continuing difficulties at Apple.

The above discussion helps highlight that a firm can be high on one multiple and low on another, because they are determined by different factors. Consider the two most commonly used multiples, price-earnings (PE) and price-to-book (PB).[12] Both multiples vary positively with future earnings prospects. However, PB is determined by the future level of earnings *relative to book value,* and the growth in book value. PE is determined by growth in future earnings *relative to the earnings* in the denominator of PE. Apple has a relatively high leading PE, because earnings are expected to grow substantially from the depressed level forecast for the coming year. However, even after the rebound occurs, earnings are not expected to be high *relative to book value* (i.e., ROE is not expected to be high), and thus the PB ratio is lower than that for the other firms in Table 7-3.

In general, as illustrated in Table 7-3, the PB and PE ratios are *both* high only when a firm is expected to grow quickly and to enjoy abnormally high ROEs during the growth period and/or after the growth occurs. These are the "rising stars." Other firms, which might be called "falling stars," may still be enjoying high ROEs on existing investments but are no longer growing fast. Such firms would have high PBs but relatively low PEs. Many recovering firms, like Apple, are expected to rebound from temporarily low earnings levels but will be prevented by competition from returning to a point of abnormally high ROEs. They should have high PEs and relatively low PBs. Finally, firms whose earnings have little prospect for either growth or high ROEs—the "dogs"—will carry low PBs and low PEs.

What Can Be Learned from Analysis of Price Multiples

Overall, the variation in multiples across the firms in Table 7-3 appears explainable and therefore not necessarily indicative that Compaq's pricing is either more or less favorable than that of other firms. If Compaq had no market price and we were turning to the multiples of the other firms to suggest how it should be priced, the differences in the determinants of multiples discussed above should be taken into account. For example, given Compaq's relatively high expected margins, it would be unreasonable to apply the other firms' sales multiples directly to Compaq. Some upward adjustment would be in order. In terms of future earnings growth, the firms are more similar, and thus an application to Compaq of other firms' PE multiples—with the possible exception of Apple's—would be more reasonable.

Note that the multiples in Table 7-3 do not provide us with a great deal of confidence in statements about Compaq's pricing. Even if Compaq were, for example, underpriced by 10 percent, the sort of analysis in Table 7-3 would probably not make that evident. Alternatively, if Compaq had no market price and we were attempting to estimate it, the multiples in Table 7-3 would only be suggestive of a reasonable *range* of values rather than a pinpoint estimate.

The differences that exist across firms—even firms as closely related as those in Table 7-3—render pricing based on multiples an inherently crude technique. The analyst can reduce the impact of such differences by focusing on *average* multiples across the comparable firms, but there is still no guarantee that the average applies perfectly to the firm being valued. Valuations based on detailed forecasts may take on the appearance of delivering more precision, but there is nearly always a high degree of uncertainty surrounding the long-run forecasts.

The bottom line is that valuation of firms is a difficult and uncertain business, and no technique can alter that underlying reality. The analyst can only apply the techniques as intelligently as possible, so that estimation error results only from underlying economic uncertainties and not from avoidable misjudgments in applying the valuation method.

Multiples Based on Formulae

Our discussion thus far has focused on price multiples based on comparable firms, but it is also possible to construct multiples based on various formulae. Perhaps the most widely known example is the "Gordon-Shapiro growth formula," which expresses the price (P) as a function of the current dividend (*d*), based on estimates of the cost of equity capital (*r*) and future dividend growth (*g*):

$$P = \frac{d}{(r - g)}$$

If the firm retains the fraction *k* of the firm's earnings (*E*), and thus $d = E(1 - k)$, then the implied price-earnings multiple should be:

$$\frac{P}{E} = \frac{(1 - k)}{(r - g)}$$

This formula assumes dividends can grow at the same rate in perpetuity. Almost inevitably, that assumption is so unrealistic as to call into question the practical value of the formula. It is obviously of no use in pricing Compaq, which currently pays no dividends and for which expectations of dividends in the near term are quite uncertain.

Miller and Modigliani provide a somewhat less restrictive approach.[13] They consider a setting where growth may continue for a period of any length but is relevant to the firm's current value for only T years, because beyond that point the expected return on investment (r^*) will be driven by competition to the cost of capital (r). That is, we expect the firm to find abnormally profitable projects for only T years. Beyond that point, only zero net present value projects are expected. If over the T-year horizon the firm reinvests the fraction k of its earnings, then the price-earnings ratio should be:

$$\frac{P}{E} = \frac{1 + Tk(r^* - r)}{r}$$

This formula also has shortcomings. For example, it implicitly assumes that the rate of return on investment r^* expected in the future is equal to that which generated the earnings E.[14] As explained in Chapter 5, it is generally unrealistic to assume that rates of return on investment will remain constant.

Price-earnings multiples based on restrictive formulae like those above are probably best viewed as useful devices for thinking about valuation. They should not be used as methods of estimating value in practical situations. The previously discussed "shortcut" technique based on discounted abnormal earnings provides an alternative that is less restrictive.

DETAILED VALUATION VERSUS USE OF MULTIPLES

Valuation based on either DCF or discounted abnormal earnings requires detailed, multiple-year forecasts about a variety of parameters, including growth, profitability, and cost of capital. These techniques supply the proper conceptual template for thinking about what creates value, and they offer the advantage of forcing the analyst to make his or her forecasts explicit. Doing so can help avoid unrealistic or internally inconsistent assumptions, but it places high demands on the analyst. Moreover, the detailed approaches are vulnerable to the analyst's idiosyncratic estimation errors. Recall how great an impact on estimated value can arise from a 2 percent shift in the cost of capital—and errors of that magnitude are understandable given the current uncertainty about how the cost of capital should be measured.

Valuation based on multiples for comparable firms is less demanding. It can also avoid some vulnerability to the analyst's idiosyncratic estimation error by "letting the market decide" some of the valuation parameters. For example, application of a price-earnings multiple does not require explicit specification of a firm's cost of capital or growth rate. It simply assumes that whatever such parameters' values may be, they are similar to those for firms deemed "comparable." Of course, how much is gained (or lost!) by relying on the market's pricing of other firms depends critically on how closely comparable those firms are. Such reliance also involves a certain circularity. If all equity valuation were based solely on comparables, then mispricing of one firm would translate into mispricing in another firm, and so on. To avoid this never-ending spiral, someone must ultimately conduct an analysis based on something other than mere comparables.

Each of the alternatives offers its own set of advantages. There is no "best" valuation method, which explains why analysts tend to "triangulate" by applying several methods in the same context.

SUMMARY AND CONCLUSIONS

In this chapter we described several accounting-based valuation techniques. One approach expresses the value of the firm's equity as book value plus discounted expectations of future abnormal earnings. The approach is conceptually sound, consistent with DCF analysis, and it offers the advantage of being framed directly in terms of the drivers of firm value (ROE, profit margins, growth, and so forth).

Valuation techniques based on price multiples are commonly used in practice. They place fewer demands on the analyst; they also take direct advantage of information known in the marketplace and embedded in other firms' prices, even when that information may not be known to the analyst using the multiple. The primary difficulty with using price multiples lies in identifying firms that are truly comparable. An understanding of the determinants of various multiples can help the analyst assess the degree of comparability and explain why differences in multiples should be expected across firms.

The various alternatives to valuation each offer their own strengths and weaknesses. In a given setting, some are more useful than others. However, there are typically gains to be had by considering several approaches simultaneously.

DISCUSSION QUESTIONS

1. Joe Watts, an analyst at EMH Securities, states: "I don't know why anyone would ever try to value earnings. Obviously, the market knows that earnings can be manipulated, and it only values cash flows." Discuss.

2. Construct a two-period numerical example to show that the accounting-based valuation of a firm is the same, whether R&D is capitalized or expensed.

3. Explain why terminal values in accounting-based valuation are significantly less than those for DCF valuation.

4. Can accounting analysis improve accounting-based valuations? Explain why or why not.

5. Manufactured Earnings is a "darling" of Wall Street analysts. Its current market price is $15 per share, and its book value is $5 per share. Analysts forecast that the firm's book value will grow by 10 percent per year indefinitely, and the cost of eq-

uity is 15 percent. Given these facts, what is the market's expectation of the firm's long-term average ROE?

6. Given the information in Question 5, what will be Manufactured Earnings' stock price if the market revises its expectations of long-term average ROE to 20 percent?

7. Analysts reassess Manufactured Earnings' future performance as follows: growth in book value increases to 12 percent per year, but the ROE of the incremental book value is only 15 percent. What is the impact on the market-to-book ratio?

8. How can a company with a high ROE have a low PE ratio?

9. What type of companies have:
   a. a high PE ratio and a low market-to-book ratio?
   b. a high PE ratio and a high market-to-book ratio?
   c. a low PE ratio and a high market-to-book ratio?
   d. a low PE ratio and a low market-to-book ratio?

10. Explain how two companies with the same market-to-book ratios could have different sales-to-price ratios.

CASES

The Computer Industry in 1992
The Gap, Inc.

NOTES

1. See G. A. D. Preinreich,"Annual Survey of Economic Theory: The Theory of Depreciation," *Econometrica* (July 1938): 219–241; Edgar O. Edwards and Philip W. Bell, *The Theory and Measurement of Business Income* (Berkeley: University of California Press, 1961); Victor L. Bernard,"Accounting-Based Valuation Techniques, Market-to-Book Ratios, and Implications for Financial Statements Analysis," working paper, University of Michigan (1994); James Ohlson, "Earnings, Book Value, and Dividends in Security Valuation," *Contemporary Accounting Research* (Spring 1995); G. Bennett Stewart, *The Quest for Value*, second edition (New York: HarperCollins, 1994).

One version of the approach, based on Stewart's economic value added (EVA) model, has quickly gained acceptance in practice since 1990. Stewart's approach could be viewed as an application or extension of a valuation technique first described by Preinreich and then reintroduced to the literature by Edwards and Bell, Bernard, and especially Ohlson, among others.

2. It may seem surprising that one can estimate value with no explicit attention to two of the cash flow streams considered in DCF analysis: investments in working capital and capital expenditures. The accounting-based technique recognizes that these investments cannot possibly contribute to value without impacting abnormal earnings, and that therefore only their earnings impacts need be considered. For example, the benefit of an increase in inventory turnover surfaces in terms of its impact on ROE (and thus, abnormal earnings), without the need to consider explicitly the cash flow impacts involved.

3. Some special aspects of Compaq's case make it easier to preserve this equivalence. First, there is no debt, so there is no question about maintaining internally consistent estimates of the WACC (used in DCF to discount cash flows) and the cost of equity capital (used here for discounting abnormal earnings). Second, beginning in 1994, we treat all free cash flows as if they are distributed as dividends, not reinvested. The DCF method *assumes* that free cash flows are reinvested in zero net present value projects. As implemented here, the accounting-based valuation method permits but does not assume this. Third, our approach to long-range forecasting assures that once sales growth reaches a steady state beyond the terminal year, both abnormal earnings growth and free cash flow growth do so as well.

4. In his book on EVA valuation, Bennett Stewart (op. cit.) recommends a number of accounting adjustments, including the capitalization of research and development.

5. An alternative approach is to assume no change in dividend payout. Cash and marketable securities and book value will then grow steadily over the forecast period. However, this has several unintended consequences. First, Compaq's leverage (net debt to equity) would continuously decline over the forecast period. Second, the firm's ROE would steadily decline as returns from cash assets are likely to be lower than those earned on operating assets. In the extreme, Compaq will end up looking more like a mutual fund than a computer manufacturer. Note, that while this approach will lead to different earnings and book values, investments in marketable securities earn only a normal return, and hence do not change Compaq's market value. In other words, as long as they are accounted for correctly in the forecasts of earnings and book values, changes in dividend policy do not affect firm value.

6. The abnormal earnings drop in 2001 despite earnings remaining constant. The reason is that book value during 2000 was still growing at a 10 percent rate, so that the benchmark for normal earnings—based on beginning book value—is higher in 2001 than in 2000.

7. The first three terms to the right of the 1 include abnormal ROE, scaled up by the amount of prior growth in book value and discounted to the present. The final term recognizes that the scaled abnormal ROE of the third year—$(.19 - .13)(1.20)^2$—is now assumed to remain constant in perpetuity, and so it can be capitalized by dividing by (.13) and then discounted to the present with the factor $(1.13)^3$. Given that book value is assumed to grow at a rate that exceeds the ROE, the calculation implicitly assumes some (small) capital infusions.

8. To do this, simply capitalize the fourth term by (.13 − .035) rather than .13. The indicated market-to-book ratio would then be 1.93, and the implied price per share would be $60.

9. Unbiased accounting is that which, in a competitive equilibrium, produces an expected ROE equal to the cost of capital. The actual ROE thus reveals the presence of economic rents. Market-value accounting is a special case of unbiased accounting that produces an expected ROE equal to the cost of capital, even when the firm is not in a competitive equilibrium. That is, market-value accounting reflects the present value of future economic rents in book value, driving the expected ROEs to a normal level. For a discussion of unbiased and biased accounting, see Gerald Feltham and James Ohlson,"Valuation and Clean Surplus Accounting for Operating and Financial Activities," *Contemporary Accounting Research* (Spring 1995).

10. An underappreciated point is that PE ratios vary according to expected changes in *abnormal* earnings, not earnings per se. If earnings will grow *only* as the result of additional investment that will produce normal rates of return, that should have no impact on the current *price* of the firm and therefore no impact on the PE ratio as a whole. See Patricia Fairfield, "P/E, P/B, and the Present Value of Future Dividends," *Financial Analysts Journal* (July/August 1994): 23–31; and Stephen Penman, "The Articulation of Price-Earnings Ratios and Market-to-Book Ratios and the Evaluation of Growth," working paper, University of California at Berkeley (1994).

11. More precisely, a trailing PE ratio for a no-growth firm should be equal to $\left(\frac{1 + r}{r} - \frac{\text{div}}{E}\right)$ where r = cost of equity capital and $\frac{\text{div}}{E}$ = dividend payout ratio during the period over which earnings were measured. Thus, with a 50 percent dividend payout and a 13 percent cost of capital, the PE ratio in the no-growth case would be $(1.13/.13) - .50$, or 8.2. See Fairfield (op. cit.) and Penman (op. cit.).

12. For a more detailed explication of the points drawn here, see Penman (op. cit.).

13. See Merton Miller and Franco Modigliani, "Dividend Policy, Growth, and the Valuation of Shares," *Journal of Business* 34 (1961): 411–433.

14. See Penman (op. cit.) for further discussion.

p a r t 3

Business Analysis Applications

chapter 8

Equity Security Analysis

Equity security analysis is the evaluation of a firm and its prospects from the perspective of a current or potential investor in the firm's stock. Security analysis is one step in a larger investment process that involves (1) establishing the objectives of the investor or fund, (2) forming expectations about the future returns and risks of individual securities, and then (3) combining individual securities into portfolios to maximize progress toward the investment objectives. Security analysis is the foundation for the second step, projecting future returns and assessing risk. Security analysis is typically conducted with an eye towards identification of mispriced securities, in hopes of generating returns that more than compensate the investor for risk. However, that need not be the case. For analysts who do not have a comparative advantage in identifying mispriced securities, the focus should be on gaining an appreciation for how a security would affect the risk of a given portfolio, and whether it fits the profile that the portfolio is designed to maintain.

Security analysis is undertaken by individual investors, by analysts at brokerage houses (sell-side analysts), by analysts that work at the direction of funds managers for various institutions (buy-side analysts), and others. The institutions employing buy-side analysts include mutual funds, pension funds, insurance companies, universities, and others.

A variety of questions are dealt with in security analysis:

- A sell-side analyst asks: How do my forecasts compare to those of the analysts' consensus? Is the observed market price consistent with that consensus? Given my expectations for the firm, does this stock appear to be mispriced? Should I recommend this stock as a buy, a sell, or a hold?
- A buy-side analyst for a "value stock fund" offered to mutual fund investors asks: Does this stock possess the characteristics we seek in our fund? That is, does it have a relatively low ratio of price to earnings, book value, and other fundamental indicators? Do its prospects for earnings improvement suggest good potential for high future returns on the stock?

- An individual investor asks: Does this stock offer the risk profile that suits my investment objectives? Does it enhance my ability to diversify the risk of my portfolio? Is the firm's dividend payout rate low enough to help shield me from taxes while I continue to hold the stock?

As the above questions underscore, there is more to security analysis than estimating the value of stocks. Nevertheless, for most sell-side and buy-side analysts, the key goal remains the identification of mispriced stocks.

MARKET EFFICIENCY AND THE PRICING OF EQUITY SECURITIES

How a security analyst should invest his or her time depends on how quickly and efficiently information flows through markets and becomes reflected in security prices. In the extreme, information would be reflected in security prices fully and immediately upon its release. This is essentially the condition posited by the *efficient markets hypothesis*. This hypothesis states that security prices reflect all available information, as if such information could be costlessly digested and translated immmediately into demands for buys or sells without regard to frictions imposed by transactions costs. Under such conditions, it would be impossible to identify mispriced securities on the basis of public information.

In a world of efficient markets, the expected return on any equity security is just enough to compensate investors for the unavoidable risk the security involves. Unavoidable risk is that which cannot be "diversified away" simply by holding a portfolio of many securities. Given efficient markets, the investor's strategy shifts away from the search for mispriced securities and focuses instead on maintaining a well diversified portfolio. Aside from this, the investor must arrive at the desired balance between risky securities and short-term government bonds. The desired balance depends on how much risk the investor is willing to bear for a given increase in expected returns.

The above discussion implies that investors who accept that stock prices already reflect available information have no need for analysis involving a search for mispriced securities. Of course, if all investors adopted this attitude, no such analysis would be conducted, mispricing would go uncorrected, and markets would no longer be efficient! This is why the efficient markets hypothesis cannot represent an equilibrium in a strict sense. In equilibrium, there must be just enough mispricing to provide incentives for the investment of resources in security analysis.

The existence of some mispricing, even in equilibrium, does not imply that it is sensible for just anyone to engage in security analysis. Instead, it suggests that securities analysis is subject to the same laws of supply and demand faced in all other competitive industries: it will be rewarding only for those with the strongest comparative advantage. How many analysts are in that category is a question that cannot be settled at a theoretical level, but it need not be many. In the case of Compaq, which is among the larger companies in the United States, there are only about 30 professional analysts who formally track and report on the firm. Only a subset of these analysts are considered the "key movers" of the stock. There are many others, however, including most buy-side analysts, who track the firm on their own account without issuing any formal reports to outsiders. For the smallest publicly traded firms in the U.S., there is typically no formal following by analysts, and would-be investors and their advisors are left to themselves to conduct securities analysis.

Market Efficiency and the Role of Financial Statement Analysis

The degree of market efficiency that arises from competition among analysts and other market agents is an empirical issue addressed by a large body of research spanning the last three decades. Such research has important implications for the role of financial statements in security analysis. Consider, for example, the implications of an extremely efficient market, where information is fully impounded in prices within minutes of its revelation. In such a market, agents could profit from digesting financial statement information in two ways. First, the information would be useful to the select few who receive newly-announced financial data, interpret it quickly, and trade on it within minutes. Second, and probably more important, the information would be useful for gaining an understanding of the firm, so as to place the analyst in a better position to interpret other news (from financial statements as well as other sources) as it arrives.

On the other hand, if securities prices fail to reflect financial statement data fully, even days or months after its public revelation, there is a third way in which market agents could profit from such data. That is to create trading strategies designed to exploit any systematic ways in which the publicly available data are ignored or discounted in the price-setting process.

Market Efficiency and Managers' Financial Reporting Strategies

The degree to which markets are efficient also has implications for managers' approaches to communicating with their investment communities. The issue becomes most important when the firm pursues an unusual strategy, or when the usual interpretation of financial statements would be misleading in the firm's context. In such a case, the communication avenues managers can successfully pursue depend not only on management's credibility, but also on the degree of understanding present in the investment community. We will return to the issue of management communications in more detail in Chapter 12.

Evidence on Market Efficiency

There is an abundance of evidence consistent with a high degree of efficiency in the primary U.S. securities markets.[1] In fact, during the 1960s and 1970s, the evidence was so one-sided that the efficient markets hypothesis gained widespread acceptance within the academic community and had a major impact on the practicing community as well.

Evidence pointing to very efficient securities markets comes in several forms:

- When information is announced publicly, the markets react *very* quickly.
- It is difficult to identify specific funds or analysts who have consistently generated abnormally high returns.
- A number of studies suggest that stock prices reflect a rather sophisticated level of fundamental analysis.

While a large body of evidence consistent with efficiency exists, recent years have witnessed a re-examination of the once widely accepted thinking. A sampling of the research includes the following:

- On the issue of the speed of stock price response to news, a number of studies suggest that even though prices react quickly, the initial reaction tends to be incomplete.[2]
- A number of studies point to trading strategies that could have been used to outperform market averages.[3]
- Some related evidence—still subject to ongoing debate about its proper interpretation—suggests that, even though market prices reflect some relatively sophisticated analyses, prices still do not fully reflect all the information that could be garnered from publicly available financial statements.[4]

The controversy over the efficiency of securities markets is unlikely to end soon. However, there are some lessons that are accepted by most researchers. First, securities markets not only reflect publicly available information, they also anticipate much of it before it is released. The open question is what fraction of the response remains to be impounded in price once the day of the public release comes to a close. Second, even in most studies that suggest inefficiency, the degree of mispricing is relatively small for large stocks.

Finally, even if some of the evidence is currently difficult to align with the efficient markets hypothesis, it remains a useful benchmark (at a minimum) for thinking about the behavior of security prices. The hypothesis will continue to play that role unless it can be replaced by a more complete theory. Some researchers are developing theories that encompass the existence of market agents who trade for inexplicable reasons, and prices that differ from so-called "fundamental values," even in equilibrium.

APPROACHES TO FUND MANAGEMENT AND SECURITIES ANALYSIS

Approaches used in practice to manage funds and analyze securities are quite varied. One dimension of variation is the extent to which the investments are actively or passively managed. Another variation is whether a quantitative or a traditional fundamental approach is used. Security analysts also vary considerably in terms of whether they produce formal or informal valuations of the firm.

Active Versus Passive Management

Active portfolio management relies heavily on security analysis to identify mispriced securities. The passive portfolio manager serves as a price taker, avoiding the costs of security analysis and turnover while typically seeking to hold a portfolio designed to match some overall market index or sector performance. Combined approaches are also possible. For example, one may actively manage 20 percent of a fund balance while passively managing the remainder. The widespread growth of passively managed funds in the U.S. over the past twenty years serves as testimony to many fund managers' belief that earning superior returns is a difficult thing to do.

Quantitative Versus Traditional Fundamental Analysis

Actively managed funds must depend on some form of security analysis. Some funds employ "technical analysis," which attempts to predict stock price movements on the basis of market indicators (prior stock price movements, volume, etc.). In contrast, "fundamental analysis," the primary approach to security analysis, attempts to evaluate the current market price relative to projections of the firm's future earnings and cash-flow generating potential. Fundamental analysis involves all the steps described in the previous chapters of this book: business strategy analysis, accounting analysis, financial analysis, and prospective analysis (forecasting and valuation).

In recent years, some analysts have supplemented traditional fundamental analysis, which involves a substantial amount of subjective judgment, with more quantitative approaches. The quantitative approaches themselves are quite varied. Some involve simply "screening" stocks on the basis of some set of factors, such as trends in analysts' earnings revisions, price-earnings ratios, price-book ratios, and so on. Whether such approaches are useful depends on the degree of market efficiency relative to the screens. Quantitative approaches can also involve implementation of some formal model to predict future stock returns. Longstanding statistical techniques such as regression analysis and probit analysis can be used, as can more recently developed, computer-intensive techniques such as neural network analysis. Again, the success of these approaches depends on the degree of market efficiency and whether the analysis can exploit information in ways not otherwise available to market agents as a group.

Quantitative approaches play a more important role in security analysis today than they did a decade or two ago. However, by and large, analysts still rely primarily on the kind of fundamental analysis involving complex human judgments, as outlined in our earlier chapters.

Formal Versus Informal Valuation

Full-scale, formal valuations based on the kind of discounted cash flow methods described in Chapter 6 have become more common, especially in recent years. However, less formal approaches are also possible. For example, an analyst can compare his or her long-term earnings projection with the consensus forecast to generate a buy or sell recommendation. Alternatively, an analyst might recommend a stock because his or her earnings forecast appears relatively high in comparison to the current price. Another possible approach might be labeled "marginalist." This approach involves no attempt to value the firm. The analyst simply assumes that if he or she has unearthed favorable (unfavorable) information believed not to be recognized by others, the stock should be bought (sold).

Unlike many security analysts, investment bankers produce formal valuations as a matter of course. Investment bankers, who estimate values for purposes of bringing a private firm to the public market, for evaluating a merger or buyout proposal, or for purposes of periodic managerial review, must document their valuation in a way that can readily be communicated to management and (if necessary) to the courts.

THE PROCESS OF A COMPREHENSIVE SECURITY ANALYSIS

Given the variety of approaches practiced in security analysis, it is impossible to summarize all of them here. Instead, we briefly outline steps to be included in a comprehensive security analysis. The amount of attention focused on any given step varies among analysts.

Selection of Candidates for Analysis

No analyst can effectively investigate more than a small fraction of the securities on a major exchange, and thus some approach to narrowing the focus must be employed. Sell-side analysts are often organized within an investment house by industry or sector. Thus, they tend to be constrained in their choices of firms to follow. However, from the perspective of a fund manager or an investment firm as a whole, there is usually the freedom to focus on any firm or sector.

Some fund managers direct the energies of their analysts toward identification of stocks that fit some desired risk profile. Individual investors who seek to maintain a well diversified portfolio without holding many stocks also need information about the nature of a firm's risks. Thus, the analyst could first ask:

- What is the risk profile of this firm? How volatile are its earnings stream and its stock price? What are the key possible bad outcomes? What is the upside potential? How closely linked are the firm's risks to the health of the overall economy? Are the risks largely diversifiable, or are they systematic?

For the manager of funds with certain desired characteristics (e.g., growth stocks, "value" stocks, technology stocks, cyclical stocks), the following questions might also be raised:

- Does this firm possess the characteristics of a growth stock? What is the expected pattern of sales and earnings growth for the coming years? Is the firm reinvesting most or all of its earnings?
- Does the firm match the characteristics desired in our "income funds"? Is it a mature or maturing company, prepared to "harvest" profits and distribute them in the form of high dividends?
- Is the firm a candidate for a "value fund"? Does it offer measures of earnings, cash flow, and book value that are high relative to the price?

An alternative approach is to screen firms on the basis of some hypothesis about mispricing—perhaps with follow-up detailed analysis of stocks that meet the specified criteria. For example, one fund managed by a large U.S. insurance company screens stocks on the basis of recent "earnings momentum," as reflected in revisions in the earnings projections of sell-side and buy-side analysts. Upward revisions trigger investigations for possible purchase. The fund operates on the belief that earnings momentum is a positive signal of future price movements. Another fund complements the earnings momentum screen with one based on recent short-term stock price movements, in the hopes of identifying earnings revisions not yet reflected in stock prices.

Inferring Market Expectations

If the security analysis is conducted with an eye toward the identification of mispricing, it must ultimately involve a comparison of the analyst's expectations with those of "the market." One possibility is to view the observed stock price as the reflection of market expectations and to compare the analyst's own estimate of value with that price. However, a stock price is only a "summary statistic." It is useful to have a more detailed idea of the market's expectations about a firm's future performance, expressed in terms of sales, earnings, and other measures. For example, assume an analyst has developed potentially unrecognized information about near-term sales. Whether in fact the information is unrecognized and whether a buy recommendation is appropriate can be easily determined if the analyst knows the market consensus sales forecast.

Around the world, a number of agencies summarize analysts' forecasts of sales and earnings. Forecasts for the next year or two are commonly available, and for many firms a long-run earnings growth projection is also available—typically for three-to-five years. In the U.S., some agencies provide continuous on-line updates to such data, so that if an analyst revises a forecast, that can be made known to fund managers and other analysts within seconds.

As useful as analysts' forecasts of sales and earnings are, they do not represent a complete description of expectations about future performance, and there is no guarantee that consensus analyst forecasts are the same as those reflected in market prices. However, armed with the model in Chapters 6 and 7 that expresses price as a function of future cash flows or earnings, an analyst can draw some educated inferences about the expectations embedded in stock prices.

In Chapter 6, our primary estimate of the value of Compaq stock in December 1993 was $59, based on analyst forecasts from Duff & Phelps—forecasts that were very close to the consensus analyst forecast at the time.[5] However, the observed stock price was substantially higher, at $74. The discrepancy raises questions about what the market is really expecting, and whether a particular projection of future earnings has already been impounded in the market price. What if an analyst had information suggesting expected long-run earnings should be 10 percent higher than the median published analyst forecast? Does that suggest the analyst should label the stock a "buy"? Or have market agents already embedded such information in the price, even though the published consensus does not yet reflect it?

By altering the amounts assumed for key value drivers and arriving at combinations that generate an estimated value equal to the observed market price, the analyst can infer what the market may have been expecting for Compaq in late 1993. Table 8-1 below summarizes the "base case" combinations from Chapter 6 as well as other combinations that generate higher values. The lightly shaded cells represent combinations of assumptions that are consistent with market prices close to the observed price (in the range of $70 to $80). The more darkly shaded cells indicate combinations that produce an estimated price much higher than the market price (above $80).

Table 8-1 indicates that in order to explain an observed market price of $74 while holding the cost of capital at 13 percent, one must project a *combination* of higher sales growth *and* higher margins than we projected in Chapter 6. However, the strong competition in the industry would probably make margins any higher than 5 percent difficult to achieve over such a long period. Five percent is sufficient to produce ROEs in the range of about 22 percent, in excess of long-run industry norms and the cost of capital. More optimistic sales forecasts would be easier to justify. Although the industry is expected to grow at a rate of only 10 to 15 percent in the short run, and at a slower pace in the long run, Compaq is currently expanding market share to remain above that rate. First Boston analyst Gurley expects that the future will be harsh on the less efficient clone assemblers that produce 40 percent of PCs, and projects that low-cost producers with a recognized brand name may continue to take market share from those firms for several years. In the most optimistic scenario above, Compaq achieves *average* 17 percent growth over 1993–2000, implying nearly 16 percent in the late 1990s—substantially higher than the expected long-run industry growth rate. Progress toward such growth appears to be already reflected in the price.

Another lesson from the table is that none of the cases considered produce an estimated value as high as the observed price when the cost of capital is as high as 14 percent—which, in turn, is still slightly lower than our estimate in Chapter 6, based on the capital asset pricing model (CAPM) and the size effect. Thus, either market agents perceive Compaq as less risky than our model in Chapter 6 assumed, or market agents are even more optimistic than the most optimistic scenario considered above.

Table 8-1 Alternative Assumptions about Value Drivers for Compaq, Including Combinations Consistent with Observed Market Price of $74

| | Average annual sales growth, 1993 to 2000 | | | | | |
| | Base case: Sales growth =13.6% | | Projected sales growth = 15%* | | Projected sales growth = 17%* | |
	Base case	Other case	Base case	Other case	Base case	Other case
Profit margin declines by year 2000 to:	4.4%	5.0%	4.4%	5.0%	4.4%	5.0%
Implied earnings level in year 2000:	$773	$880	$840	$960	$950	$1,080
Implied price, based on cost of capital of:						
14 percent	$ 54	$ 60	$ 56	$ 66	$ 60	$ 68
13 percent	$ 59	$ 67	$ 63	$ 73	$ 67	$ 76
12 percent	$ 67	$ 75	$ 71	$ 83	$ 76	$ 87

*The base case was altered to produce average sales growth of 15 percent (17 percent) from 1993 to 2000, by altering projected growth rates in 1997 through 2000 from 10 percent to 12.31 percent (15.75 percent). Sales in the year 2000 are projected at $19,128 ($21,581).

Security analysis need not involve such a detailed attempt to infer market expectations. However, whether the analysis is made explicit or not, a good analyst understands what economic scenarios could plausibly be reflected in the observed price. It is useful to know, for example, that the price is *already* reflecting expectations of supernormal margins for Compaq, and that any further price appreciation is more likely to be hinged on spreading those high margins over an even larger market share. The market appears to be quite optimistic about Compaq's future, despite how difficult it is to sustain a competitive advantage in the PC industry.

Developing the Analyst's Expectations

Ultimately, a security analyst must compare his or her own view of a stock with the view embedded in the market price. The analyst's own view is generated using the same tools discussed in Chapters 2 through 7: business strategy analysis, accounting analysis, financial analysis, and prospective analysis. Thus, key questions in the analysis will be:

- How profitable is the firm? In light of industry conditions, the firm's corporate strategy, and its barriers to competition, how sustainable is that rate of profitability?
- What are the opportunities for growth for this firm?
- How risky is this firm? How vulnerable are operations to general economic down-

turns? How highly levered is the firm? What does the riskiness of the firm imply about its cost of capital?

- How do answers to the above questions compare to the expectations embedded in the observed stock price?

The final product of the work described in Chapters 2 through 7 is, of course, a forecast of the firm's future earnings and cash flows and an estimate of the firm's value. However, that final product is less important than the understanding of the business and its industry that the analysis provides. It is such understanding that positions the analyst to interpret new information as it arrives and to infer its implications. A good illustration is provided by our Compaq analyst, Bill Gurley.

By early April of 1994, it was apparent that sales volume at Compaq was running well in excess of the expectations analysts held at the end of 1993. Not only were sales expanding more quickly than projected, but profit margins were *increasing* at the same time! Accordingly, Compaq's stock price had shot up to $100. The consensus earnings forecasts for 1994 and 1995 were running at $7.03 per share and $8.19 per share, respectively, up from 1993's actual EPS of $5.44.[6]

As optimistic as the market was about Compaq at the time, analyst Gurley saw reason for even further optimism. The basis for Gurley's view lay in signals about future sales volume. One signal came directly from management: its announced intention to increase worldwide market share to 14 percent in 1994. However, a second confirming signal was inferred. It was based on Gurley's understanding of Compaq's cash position, its recent decision to issue $300 million of debt, and its statement that the proceeds would be used in part to finance working capital. Given its cash balance at the end of 1993 and the relation between its sales and working capital, Gurley estimated that Compaq could not possibly require more cash to finance inventory and receivables unless it were planning for sales volume in excess of $11.4 billion—a nearly 60 percent increase over 1993. On that basis, Gurley forecast 1994 sales "conservatively" at $10.5 billion, 1994 EPS at $7.95, and 1995 EPS at $10.00. Assuming that Compaq's growth prospects beyond 1995 would justify a higher-than-industry-average PE multiple of 15 in 1995, Gurley projected the price would reach $150 per share in that year. He rated the stock a "buy," even at $100. In fact, the stock did rise to over $110 within the month and to over $125 (on a split-adjusted basis) later in 1994.[7]

Gurley's work illustrates how the understanding developed from a thorough fundamental analysis can enhance one's ability to recognize the import of newly arriving information. Viewed in isolation, a debt issue would not necessarily have any implications for sales volume. However, in the context of an understanding of Compaq's current cash position, its relation of working capital to sales, and other factors, Gurley saw in the debt issue an action that confirmed management's optimistic disclosures about future sales.

The Final Product of Security Analysis

For sell-side analysts like Bill Gurley, or buy-side analysts who must communicate with fund managers, the final product of security analysis is a recommendation to buy, sell, or hold the stock (or some more refined ranking). The recommendation is supported by a set of forecasts and a report summarizing the foundation for the recommendation. Analysts' reports often delve into significant detail. For example, Gurley's April 1994 buy recommendation was supported by a 10-page report, complete with line-by-line income statement forecasts for each quarter of 1994 and for the year 1995.

FINANCIAL STATEMENT DATA AND SECURITY PRICES

While security analysis clearly involves much information beyond the financial statements, those statements play an important role. Much research over the past three decades has helped describe the role of financial statement data in the setting of security prices. An understanding of that role provides an appreciation for the importance of that data in security analysis, as well as market agents' ability to digest such data.

A thorough review of research on financial statement data and security prices lies well outside the scope of this chapter. However, we can summarize a few of the key findings from the literature.

Earnings and book value are good indicators of stock prices.

Accounting earnings and book values ignore important aspects of the firm's economic landscape, are subject to distortion by managers, and are not adjusted for inflation in the U.S. and most other countries. One could (and the financial press frequently does) reasonably question whether accounting numbers are good indicators of the expected cash flows that should drive stock prices.

It turns out that, in spite of the widely discussed shortcomings of accounting systems, earnings and book value offer a good reflection of much of the information in security prices. In the U.S., the combination of book value (per-share) and earnings explains, in a typical year, nearly two-thirds of the cross-sectional variation in stock prices.[8] Such a finding indicates that book value and earnings provide good starting points for predicting the cash flows that should drive prices.

That book value and earnings do not summarize the information in prices more completely should not be surprising. There are a number of factors that influence prices that accounting systems are not designed to capture well, including, for example, the value of brand assets, growth opportunities, and research and development.

Explaining variation in the *level* of a firm's stock prices is one thing; explaining stock returns, which depend on *changes* in those levels, is quite another. The latter is clearly the more challenging task. It is necessary to not only identify factors that explain value, but also to determine to what extent information about the factors became known to market agents within the interval over which the price changes are measured. Researchers have in fact had difficulty explaining more than a small fraction of the variance in stock returns over years or shorter intervals. Earnings data are the most powerful of the factors that have been studied, but even so, the explanatory power is relatively low. A combination of earnings and earnings changes (both expressed relative to price at the beginning of the year) explains only about 5–15 percent of the variation in annual stock returns.[9]

To summarize, the picture that emerges is that earnings data provide somewhat noisy indicators of value—good enough to approximate whether the stock price should be closer to, say, $10 than $5, but not sufficiently precise to provide clear indications of whether that price level might have changed by, for example, 10 percent rather than 5 percent over the past year. Thus, while the earnings number is a good starting point for analysis, more information is certainly required to track stock prices.

Market agents can anticipate much of the information in earnings.

To say that financial statement data *reflect* much of the information in prices does not necessarily mean that when those data are reported, they convey *new* information. Indeed, market agents have access to a variety of information sources more timely than financial statements, and they use these sources to anticipate the data ultimately revealed in financial statements.

Figure 8-1 describes the extent to which the key financial statement datum—earnings—is anticipated by market agents.[10] In the figure, firms are divided into 10 groups, based on the extent to which quarterly earnings have changed from prior quarters. (The earnings change is labeled SUE, for standardized unexpected earnings.) The importance of the earnings information is evident in how much the stock price performance differs across the groups. The top performers experience a three-month stock price increase 4.2 percent greater than a control group, while those at the bottom underperform by 6.1 percent. However, note that most (about 60 percent) of this movement occurs *before* the week of the earnings announcement. This underscores that there are sources more timely than earnings that reflect the same information that will ultimately be reflected in earnings.

How does the market anticipate the earnings announcement? In some cases, management itself reveals information. For example, on several occasions in 1993 and 1994, Compaq's management made statements to the press and in financial analysts' meetings about their progress in gaining market share. That information should improve market agents' ability to forecast earnings. Sometimes management will make explicit statements about the range in which earnings are likely to be. Even in the absence of such direct information channels, however, it should be possible to anticipate to some extent how well a firm is performing. In the case of Compaq, one could learn through discussions with retail outlets, suppliers, competitors, and industry news sources. Even general information about the state of the economy, the retail sector, and the computer industry should permit more educated guesses about how well the firm is performing.

The findings summarized in Figure 8-1 offer an important lesson for security analysts. Specifically, it's not good enough to be aware of earnings as soon as they are announced. A good analyst also tracks more timely information sources.

A final comment on Figure 8-1 pertains to stock price movements *after* the earnings are announced. Note that for those firms with earnings increases, the stock prices continue to rise, and for those with earnings decreases, the prices continue to fall (relative to the control group). This is the phenomenon that was mentioned briefly in the section

Figure 8-1 Stock Price Movements Before and After Quarterly Earnings Announcements

Stock return relative to control group (%)

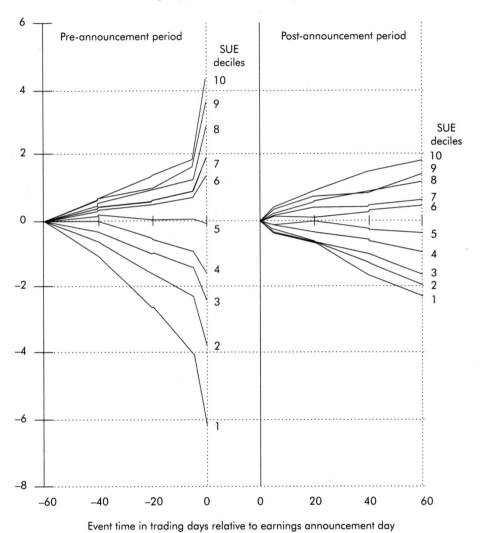

Event time in trading days relative to earnings announcement day

Explanation: Firms are grouped into ten portfolios based on "standardized unexpected earnings," or SUE: actual earnings less a statistical forecast, and scaled by the standard deviation of past unexpected earnings. Stock returns (less those for a size control group) are then cumulated over the 60 days before and after the earnings announcement for each of the ten groups.

on market efficiency. The figure suggests that even though most of the response to earnings occurs on a timely basis, some portion of the response appears to be delayed.

Financial statement details matter.

Throughout our discussion of business strategy analysis, accounting analysis, financial analysis, and prospective analysis, we drew on financial statement information beyond simply earnings. Moreover, in the chapter on accounting analysis, we pointed to a number of items in the financials that could temper one's view of the quality of earnings. Assuming market agents are capable of conducting similar analyses, we would expect stock prices to reflect financial statement details beyond just earnings.

A large number of studies have examined the relation between stock prices and financial statement data beyond earnings. For example, one study focused on roughly a dozen financial statement variables that could be useful in assessing the quality of earnings: disproportionate inventory and receivables buildups, increases in gross margin percentage, and other factors.[11] The results confirm that stock prices reflect such variables. In other words, one can explain variation in stock prices better when armed not just with earnings but also with the factors that help analysts interpret the quality of earnings.

Many studies have also examined the extent to which footnote disclosures are related to stock price behavior. For example, one study examined the extent to which unrealized gains in banks' investment portfolios are reflected in stock prices.[12] The conclusion of most studies in this area is that prices at least approximately reflect the details in footnotes. Thus, the evidence is consistent with the footnotes presenting important data and with analysts "doing their homework." Whether market agents do a *complete* job of digesting footnote data is less clear.

Research on the relation of stock prices to financial statement details continues, and many of the questions in the area remain unsettled.[13] A few general comments on the current state of understanding can be offered. First, many financial statement details are important, in the sense that they reflect factors that drive stock prices. Second, whether market agents learn about such details from the financial statements themselves or from more timely sources is difficult to know. (Most studies are not sharp enough to answer this question.) Third, whether stock prices reflect financial statement details completely and immediately remains a subject of debate, with some studies on both sides of the issue. One implication of the research for security analysts is that to stay abreast of the market one must be able to gather and interpret the kind of information reflected in the financial statement details—either by going directly to the statements or (preferably) to more timely sources.

SUMMARY AND CONCLUSIONS

Equity security analysis is the evaluation of a firm and its prospects from the perspective of a current or potential investor in the firm's stock. Security analysis is one component of a larger investment process that involves (1) establishing the objectives of the investor or fund, (2) forming expectations about the future returns and risks of individual securities, and then (3) combining individual securities into portfolios to maximize progress toward the investment objectives.

Some security analysis is devoted primarily to assuring that a stock possesses the proper risk profile and other desired characteristics prior to inclusion in an investor's portfolio. However, especially for many professional buy-side and sell-side security analysts, the analysis is also directed toward the identification of mispriced securities. In equilibrium, such activity will be rewarding for those with the strongest comparative advantage. They will be the ones able to identify any mispricing at the lowest cost and exert pressure on the price so as to correct the mispricing. What kinds of efforts are productive in this domain depends on the degree of market efficiency. A large body of evidence exists that is supportive of a high degree of efficiency in the U.S. market, but recent evidence has reopened the debate on this issue.

In practice, a wide variety of approaches to fund management and security analysis are employed. However, at the core of the analyses are the same steps outlined in Chapters 2 through 7 of this book: business strategy analysis, accounting analysis, financial analysis, and prospective analysis (forecasting and valuation). For the professional analyst, the final product of the work is, of course, a forecast of the firm's future earnings and cash flows, and an estimate of the firm's value. However, that final product is less important than the understanding of the business and its industry, which the analysis provides. It is such understanding that positions the analyst to interpret new information as it arrives and infer its implications.

While security analysis clearly involves much information beyond the financial statements, those statements play an important role. Much research over the past three decades has helped describe the role of financial statement data in the setting of security prices. The research shows conclusively that financial statements reflect much of the information that drives prices. However, whether market agents acquire the information directly from the financial statements themselves or from more timely sources is less clear. Much of the information in financial statements appears to be anticipated before its release. Finally, whether stock prices reflect financial statement details completely and immediately remains a subject of debate. One implication of the research for security analysts is that to stay abreast of the market, one must be able to gather and interpret the kind of information reflected in the financial statement details—either by going directly to the statements or (preferably) to more timely sources.

DISCUSSION QUESTIONS

1. Despite many years of research, the evidence on market efficiency described in this chapter appears to be inconclusive. Some argue that this is because researchers have been unable to link company fundamentals to stock prices precisely. Comment.

2. Geoffrey Henley, a professor of finance, states: "The capital market is efficient. I don't know why anyone would bother devoting their time to following individual stocks and doing fundamental analysis. The best approach is to buy and hold a well-diversified portfolio of stocks." Do you agree? Why or why not?

3. What is the difference between fundamental and technical analysis? Can you think of any trading strategies that use technical analysis? What are the underlying as-

sumptions made by these strategies?

4. Investment funds follow many different types of investment strategies. Income funds focus on stocks with high dividend yields, growth funds invest in stocks that are expected to have high capital appreciation, value funds follow stocks that are considered to be undervalued, and short funds bet against stocks they consider to be overvalued. What types of investors are likely to be attracted to each of these types of funds? Why?

5. Three months ago, Intergalactic Software Company went public. You are a sophisticated investor who devotes time to fundamental analysis as a way of identifying mispriced stocks. Which of the following characteristics would you focus on in deciding whether to follow this stock?
   • The market capitalization
   • The average number of shares traded per day
   • The bid–ask spread for the stock
   • Whether the underwriter that brought the firm public is a Top Five investment banking firm
   • Whether its audit company is a Big Six firm
   • Whether there are analysts from major brokerage firms following the company
   • whether the stock is held mostly by retail or institutional investors

6. There are two major types of financial analysts: buy-side and sell-side. Buy-side analysts work for investment firms and make stock recommendations that are available only to the management of funds within that firm. Sell-side analysts work for brokerage firms and make recommendations that are used to sell stock to the brokerage firms' clients, which include individual investors and managers of investment funds. What would be the differences in tasks and motivations of these two types of analysts?

7. Many market participants believe that sell-side analysts are too optimistic in their recommendations to buy stocks, and too slow to recommend sells. What factors might explain this bias?

8. Joe Klein is an analyst for an investment banking firm that offers both underwriting and brokerage services. Joe sends you a highly favorable report on a stock that his firm recently helped go public and for which it currently makes the market. What are the potential advantages and disadvantages in relying on Joe's report in deciding whether to buy the stock?

9. Intergalactic Software Company's stock has a market price of $20 per share and a book value of $12 per share. If its cost of equity capital is 15 percent and its book value is expected to grow at 5 percent per year indefinitely, what is the market's assessment of its steady state return on equity? If the stock price increases to $35 and the market does not expect the firm's growth rate to change, what is the revised steady state ROE? If instead the price increase was due to an increase in the market's assessments about long-term book value growth, rather than long-term ROE, what would the price revision imply for the steady state growth rate?

10. Joe states: "I can see how ratio analysis and valuation help me do fundamental analysis, but I don't see the value of doing strategy analysis." Can you explain to him how strategy analysis could be potentially useful?

CASES

America Online, Inc.
The Gap, Inc.

NOTES

1. For a recent review of evidence on market efficiency, see Eugene Fama, "Efficient Capital Markets: II," *Journal of Finance* (December 1991): 1575–1618.

2. For example, see V. Bernard and J. Thomas, "Evidence that Stock Prices Do Not Fully Reflect the Implications of Current Earnings for Future Earnings," *Journal of Accounting and Economics* (December 1990): 305–341.

3. A good example, in which a "value stock" strategy is examined, is in Josef Lakonishok, Andre Shleifer, and Robert Vishny, "Contrarian Investment, Extrapolation, and Risk," *Journal of Finance* (December 1994): 1541–1578.

4. For example, see J. Ou and S. Penman, "Financial Statement Analysis and the Prediction of Stock Returns," *Journal of Accounting and Economics* (November 1989a): 295–330; R. Holthausen and D. Larcker, "The Prediction of Stock Returns Using Financial Statement Information," *Journal of Accounting and Economics* (June/September 1992): 373–412; and Richard Sloan, "Do Stock Prices Fully Impound Information in Accruals about Future Earnings?" working paper, University of Pennsylvania (1995).

5. The $59 estimate is based on a 13 percent discount rate, and it allows for growth in sales and abnormal earnings beyond 2000 at the rate of inflation.

6. Consensus forecasts are from the March/April 1994 edition of I/B/E/S Quarterly Company Data.

7. Compaq's sales volume for 1994 ultimately reached $10.9 billion. EPS was $9.63 on a split-adjusted basis. The stock price peaked at $133 during early 1995 (on a split-adjusted basis), and fell back to $90 in the spring of 1995.

8. On average across time, 66 percent of the variance in price per share is explained by book value per share and the rank of earnings per share. See Victor Bernard, "Accounting-Based Valuation, the Determinants of Market-to-Book Ratios, and Implications for Financial Statements Analysis," working paper, University of Michigan (January 1994).

9. For two of several discussions of research in this area, see Baruch Lev, "On the Usefulness of Earnings and Earning Research: Lessons and Directions from Two Decades of Empirical Research," *Journal of Accounting Research*, supplement 1989: 153–197; and Peter Easton, Trevor Harris, and James Ohlson, "Aggregate Accounting Earnings Can Explain Most of Security Returns," *Journal of Accounting and Economics* (June/September 1992): 119–142.

10. V. Bernard and J. Thomas, "Post-Earnings-Announcement Drift: Delayed Price Response or Risk Premium?" *Journal of Accounting Research* (Supplement 1989): 1–36. For seminal work on the timeliness of earnings information, see R. Ball and P. Brown, "An Empirical Evaluation of Accounting Income Numbers," *Journal of Accounting Research* (Autumn 1968): 159–178; and William H. Beaver, "The Information Content of Annual Earnings Announcements," *Journal of Accounting Research* (Supplement, 1968), 67–92.

11. Baruch Lev and Ramu Thiagarajan, "Fundamental Information Analysis," *Journal of Accounting Research* (Autumn 1993): 190–215.

12. M. Barth, "Fair value accounting: Evidence from investment securities and the market valuation of banks," *The Accounting Review* (January 1994), 1–25.

13. For some incomplete reviews of work in this area, see Victor Bernard, "Capital Markets Research in Accounting During the 1980's: A Critical Review," in *The State of Accounting Research As We Enter the 1990's,* Thomas J. Frecka, editor. (Urbana: University of Illinois Press, 1989): 72–120; and Victor Bernard and Katherine Schipper, "Recognition and Disclosure in Financial Reporting," working paper, University of Michigan (November 1994).

chapter 9

Credit Analysis and Distress Prediction

Credit analysis is the evaluation of a firm from the perspective of a holder or potential holder of its debt, including trade payables, loans, and public debt securities. A key element of credit analysis is the prediction of the likelihood a firm will face financial distress.

Credit analysis is involved in a wide variety of decision contexts:

- A potential supplier asks: Should I sell products or services to this firm? The associated credit will be extended only for a short period, but the amount is large and I should have some assurance that collection risks are manageable.
- A commercial banker asks: Should we extend a loan to this firm? If so, how should it be structured? How should it be priced?
- If the loan is granted, the banker must later ask: Are we still providing the services, including credit, that this firm needs? Is the firm still in compliance with the loan terms? If not, is there a need to restructure the loan, and if so, how? Is the situation serious enough to call for accelerating the repayment of the loan?
- A pension fund manager, insurance company, or other investor asks: Are these debt securities a sound investment? What is the probability that the firm will face distress and default on the debt? Does the yield provide adequate compensation for the default risk involved?
- An investor contemplating purchase of debt securities in default asks: How likely is it that this firm can be turned around? In light of the high yield on this debt, relative to its current price, can I accept the risk that the debt will not be repaid in full?

Although credit analysis is typically viewed from the perspective of the financier, it is obviously important to the borrower as well:

- A manager of a small firm asks: What are our options for credit financing? Would the firm qualify for bank financing? If so, what type of financing would be possible? How costly would it be? Would the terms of the financing constrain our flexibility?

- A manager of a large firm asks: "What are our options for credit financing? Is the firm strong enough to raise funds in the public market? If so, what is our debt rating likely to be? What required yield would that rating imply?

Finally, there are third parties—those other than borrowers and lenders—who are interested in the general issue of how likely it is that a firm will avoid financial distress:

- An auditor asks: How likely is it that this firm will survive beyond the short run? In evaluating the firm's financials, should I consider it a going concern?
- An actual or potential employee asks: How confident can I be that this firm will be able to offer employment over the long term?
- A potential customer asks: What assurance is there that this firm will survive to provide warranty services, replacement parts, product updates, and other services?
- A competitor asks: Will this firm survive the current industry shakeout? What are the implications of potential financial distress at this firm for my pricing and market share?

THE MARKET FOR CREDIT

An understanding of credit analysis requires an appreciation for the various players in the market for credit. We describe those players briefly here, and discuss the suppliers of credit to Compaq and its competitors.

Suppliers of Credit

The major suppliers in the market for credit are described below.

COMMERCIAL BANKS. Commercial banks are very important players in the market for credit. Since banks tend to provide a range of services to a client, and have intimate knowledge of the client and its operations, they have a comparative advantage in extending credit in settings where (1) knowledge gained through close contact with management reduces the perceived riskiness of the credit and (2) credit risk can be contained through careful monitoring of the firm.

A constraint on bank lending operations is that the credit risk be relatively low, so that the bank's loan portfolio will be of acceptably high quality to bank regulators. Because of the importance of maintaining public confidence in the banking sector and the desire to shield government deposit insurance from risk, governments have incentives to constrain banks' exposure to credit risk. Banks also tend to shield themselves from the risk of shifts in interest rates by avoiding fixed-rate loans with long maturities. Since most of banks' capital comes from short-term deposits, such long-term loans leave them exposed to increases in interest rates, unless the risk can be hedged with derivatives.

Thus, banks are less likely to play a role when a firm requires a very long-term commitment to financing. However, in some such cases they assist in providing a placement of the debt with, say, an insurance company, a pension fund, or a group of private investors.

OTHER FINANCIAL INSTITUTIONS.   Banks face competition in the commercial lending market from a variety of sources. In the U.S., there is competition from savings and loans, even though the latter are relatively more involved in financing mortgages. Finance companies compete with banks in the market for asset-based lending (i.e., the secured financing of specific assets, such as receivables, inventory, or equipment). Insurance companies are involved in a variety of lending activities. Since life insurance companies face obligations of a long-term nature, they often seek investments of long duration (e.g., long-term bonds or loans to support large, long-term commercial real estate and development projects). Investment bankers are prepared to place debt securities with private investors or in the public markets (discussed below). Various government agencies are another source of credit.

PUBLIC DEBT MARKETS.   Some firms have the size, strength, and credibility necessary to bypass the banking sector and seek financing directly from investors, either through sales of commercial paper or through the issuance of bonds. Such debt issues are facilitated by the assignment of a debt rating. In the U.S., Moody's and Standard and Poor's are the two largest rating agencies. A firm's debt rating influences the yield that must be offered to sell the debt instruments. After the debt issue, the rating agencies continue to monitor the firm's financial condition. Changes in the rating are associated with fluctuation in the price of the securities.

Banks often provide financing in tandem with a public debt issue or other source of financing. In highly-levered transactions, such as leveraged buyouts, banks commonly provide financing along with a public debt issue that would have a lower priority in case of bankruptcy. The bank's "senior financing" would typically be scheduled for earlier retirement than the public debt, and it would carry a lower yield. For smaller or startup firms, banks often provide credit in conjunction with equity financing from venture capitalists. Note that in the case of both the leveraged buyout and the startup company, the bank helps provide the cash needed to make the deal happen, but does so in a way that shields it from risks that would be unacceptably high in the banking sector.

SELLERS WHO PROVIDE FINANCING.   Another sector of the market for credit are manufacturers and other suppliers of goods and services. As a matter of course, such firms tend to finance their customers' purchases on an unsecured basis for periods of 30 to 60 days. Suppliers will, on occasion, also agree to provide more extended financing, usually with the support of a secured note. A supplier may be willing to grant such a loan in the expectation that the creditor will survive a cash shortage and remain an important customer in the future. However, the customer would typically seek such an arrangement only if bank financing is unavailable, because it could constrain flexibility in selecting among and/or negotiating with suppliers.

Sources of Credit for Compaq and Its Competitors

In our prior discussion of Compaq Computer, we indicated that the firm had no debt, but that it had the capacity to assume leverage if desired. In March of 1994, Compaq did assume $300 million of debt. At that time, Compaq had a $300 million line of credit on which it could have drawn. However, not surprisingly, Compaq bypassed its financial institutions and went directly to the public debt markets to raise the funds. Despite the volatility in the computer industry, Compaq's strong balance sheet and earnings potential allowed it to issue debt with an investment grade rating. The issue included $150 million of 5-year notes with a yield of 6.5 percent and $150 million of 10-year notes at 7.25 percent—rates that were quite favorable, even relative to most other investment-grade bonds trading at the time.

Compaq's direct competitors discussed in Chapter 7 include two with debt: AST Research and Dell Computer. Neither firm matches Compaq's size or financial strength and, accordingly, their arrangements for financing are quite different. AST Research relies on a revolving credit facility from a consortium of eight major international banks. Dell appealed to the public debt markets for financing in 1993, but was forced to offer a yield of 11 percent to facilitate the issue (at a time when investment grade bonds were selling for yields in the range of 7 to 8 percent).

THE CREDIT ANALYSIS PROCESS

At first blush, credit analysis might appear less difficult than the valuation task discussed in Chapters 6 and 7. After all, a potential creditor ultimately cares only about whether the firm is strong enough to pay its debts at the scheduled times. The firm's exact value, its upside potential, or its distance from the threshold of credit-worthiness may not appear so important. Viewed in that way, credit analysis may seem more like a "zero-one" decision: either the credit is extended, or it is not.

It turns out, however, that credit analysis involves more than "just" establishing credit-worthiness. First, there are ranges of credit-worthiness, and it is important to understand where a firm lies within that range for purposes of pricing and structuring a loan. Moreover, if the creditor is a bank or other financial institution with an expected continuing relationship with the borrower, the borrower's upside potential is important, even though downside risk must be the primary consideration in credit analysis. A firm that offers growth potential also offers opportunities for income-generating financial services.

Given this broader view of credit analysis, it should not be surprising that it involves most of the same issues already discussed in the prior chapters on business strategy analysis, accounting analysis, financial analysis, and prospective analysis. Perhaps the greatest difference is that credit analysis rarely involves any explicit attempt to estimate the value of the firm's equity. However, the determinants of that value are relevant in credit analysis, because a larger equity cushion translates into lower risk for the creditor.

Below we describe one series of steps that is used by commercial lenders in credit analysis. Of course, not all commercial lenders follow the same process, but the steps are representative of typical approaches. The approach used by commercial lenders is of interest in its own right and illustrates a comprehensive credit analysis. However, analysis by others who grant credit often differs. For example, even when a manufacturer conducts some credit analysis prior to granting credit to a customer, it is typically much less extensive than the analysis conducted by a banker because the credit is very short-term and the manufacturer is willing to bear some credit risk in the interest of generating a profit on the sale.

We present the steps in a particular order, but they are in fact all interdependent. Thus, analysis at one step may need to be rethought, depending on the analysis at some later step.

Step 1: Consider the Nature and Purpose of the Loan

Understanding the purpose of a loan is important not just for deciding whether it should be granted, but also for structuring the loan. Loans might be required for only a few months, for several years, or even as a permanent part of a firm's capital structure. Loans might be used for replacement of other financing, to support working capital needs, or to finance the acquisition of long-term assets or another firm.

The required amount of the loan must also be established. In the case of small and medium-sized companies, a banker would typically prefer to be the sole financier of the business, in which case the loan would have to be large enough to retire existing debt. The preference for serving as the sole financier is not just to gain an advantage in providing a menu of financial services to the firm. It also reflects the desirability of not permitting another creditor to maintain a superior interest that would give it a higher priority in case of bankruptcy. If other creditors are willing to subordinate their positions to the bank, that would of course be acceptable so far as the bank is concerned.

In many cases, the commercial lender deals with firms that may have parent-subsidiary relations. The question of to whom one should lend then arises. The answer is usually the entity that owns the assets that will serve as collateral (or that could serve as such if needed in the future). If this entity is the subsidiary and the parent presents some financial strength independent of the subsidiary, a guarantee of the parent could be considered.

Step 2: Consider the Type of Loan and Available Security

The type of loan considered is a function of not only its purpose, but also the financial strength of the borrower. Thus, to some extent, the loan type will be dictated by the financial analysis described in the following step in the process. Some of the possibilities are as follows:

- *Open line of credit.* An open line of credit permits the borrower to receive cash up to some specified maximum on an as-needed basis for a specified term, such as one year. To maintain this option, the borrower pays a fee (e.g., 3/8 of 1 percent) on the unused balance, in addition to the interest on any used amount. An open line of credit is useful in cases where the borrower's cash needs are difficult to anticipate.

- *Revolving line of credit.* When it is clear that a firm will need credit beyond the short run, financing may be provided in the form of a "revolver." Sometimes used to support working capital needs, the borrower is scheduled to make payments as the operating cycle proceeds and inventory and receivables are converted to cash. However, it is also expected that cash will continue to be advanced so long as the borrower remains in good standing. In addition to interest on amounts outstanding, a fee is charged on the unused line.
- *Working capital loan.* Such a loan is used to finance inventory and receivables, and is usually secured. The maximum loan balance may be tied to the balance of the working capital accounts. For example, the loan may be allowed to rise to no more than 80 percent of receivables less than 60 days old.
- *Term loan.* Term loans are used for long-term needs and are often secured with long-term assets, such as plant or equipment. Typically, the loan will be amortized, requiring periodic payments to reduce the loan balance.
- *Mortgage loan.* Mortgages support the financing of real estate, have long terms, and require periodic amortization of the loan balance.
- *Lease financing.* Lease financing can be used to facilitate the acquisition of any asset, but is most commonly used for equipment, including vehicles. Leases may be structured over periods of 1 to 15 years, depending on the life of the underlying asset.

Much bank lending is done on a secured basis, especially with smaller and more highly levered companies. Security will be required unless the loan is short-term and the borrower exposes the bank to minimal default risk. When security is required, one consideration is whether the amount of available security is sufficient to support the loan. The amount that a bank will lend on given security involves business judgment, and it depends on a variety of factors that affect the liquidity of the security in the context of a situation where the firm is distressed. The following are some rules of thumb often applied in commercial lending to various categories of security:

- *Receivables.* Accounts receivable are usually considered the most desirable form of security because they are the most liquid. One large regional bank allows loans of 50 to 80 percent of the balance of nondelinquent accounts. The percentage applied is lower when (1) there are many small accounts that would be costly to collect in the case the firm is distressed; (2) there are a few very large accounts, such that problems with a single customer could be serious; and/or (3) the customer's financial health is closely related to that of the borrower, so that collectibility is endangered just when the borrower is in default. On the latter score, banks often refuse to accept receivables from affiliates as effective security.
- *Inventory.* The desirability of inventory as security varies widely. The best case scenario is inventory consisting of a common commodity that can easily be sold to other parties if the borrower defaults. More specialized inventory, with appeal to only a limited set of buyers, or inventory that is costly to store or transport, is less desirable. The large regional bank mentioned above lends up to 60 percent on raw materials, 50 percent on finished goods, and 20 percent on work in process.

- *Machinery and equipment.* Machinery and equipment is less desirable as collateral. It is likely to be used, and it must be stored, insured, and marketed. Keeping the costs of these activities in mind, banks typically will loan only up to 50 percent of the estimated value of such assets in a forced sale, such as an auction.
- *Real estate.* The value of real estate as collateral varies considerably. Banks will often lend up to 80 percent of the appraised value of readily salable real estate. However, a factory designed for a unique purpose would be much less desirable.

When security is required to make a loan viable, a commercial lender will estimate the amounts that could be loaned on each of the assets available as security. Unless the amount exceeds the required loan balance, the loan would not be extended.

Even when a loan is not secured initially, a bank can require a "negative pledge" on the firm's assets—a pledge that the firm will not use the assets as security for any other creditor. In that case, if the borrower begins to experience difficulty and defaults on the loan, and if there are no other creditors in the picture, the bank can demand the loan become secured if it is to remain outstanding.

Step 3: Analyze the Potential Borrower's Financial Status

This portion of the analysis involves all the steps discussed in our chapters on business strategy analysis, accounting analysis, and financial analysis. The emphasis, however, is on the firm's ability to service the debt at the scheduled rate. The focus of the analysis depends on the type of financing under consideration. For example, if a short-term loan is considered to support seasonal fluctuations in inventory, the emphasis would be on the ability of the firm to convert the inventory into cash on a timely basis. In contrast, a term loan to support plant and equipment must be made with confidence in the long-run earnings prospects of the firm.

Some of the questions to be addressed in this analysis are:

- *Business strategy analysis*:
  How does this business work? Why is it valuable? What is its strategy for sustaining or enhancing that value? How well qualified is the management to carry out that strategy effectively? Is the viability of the business highly dependent on the talents of the existing management team?
- *Accounting analysis*:
  How well do the firm's financial statements reflect its underlying economic reality? Are there reasons to believe that the firm's performance is stronger or weaker than reported profitability would suggest? Are there sizable off-balance-sheet liabilities (e.g., operating leases) that would affect the potential borrower's ability to repay the loan?
- *Financial analysis*:
  Is the firm's level of profitability unusually high or low? What are the sources of any unusual degree of profitability? How sustainable are they? What risks are associated with the operating profit stream?

How highly levered is the firm?

What is the firm's funds flow picture? What are its major sources and uses of funds? Are funds required to finance expected growth? How great are fund flows expected to be, relative to the debt service required? Given the possible volatility in those fund flows, how likely is it that they could fall to a level insufficient to service debt and meet other commitments?

Ultimately, the key question in the financial analysis is how likely it is that cash flows will be sufficient to repay the loan. With that question in mind, lenders focus much attention on solvency ratios: the magnitude of various measures of profits and cash flows relative to debt service and other requirements. To the extent such a ratio exceeds one, it indicates the "margin of safety" the lender faces. When such a ratio is combined with an assessment of the variance in its numerator, it provides an indication of the probability of nonpayment.

Ratio analysis from the perspective of a creditor differs somewhat from that of an owner. For example, there is greater emphasis on cash flows and earnings available to *all* claimants (not just owners) *before* taxes (since interest is tax-deductible and paid out of pre-tax dollars). To illustrate, the creditor's perspective is apparent in the following solvency ratio, called the "funds flow coverage ratio":

$$\text{Funds flow coverage} = \frac{\text{EBIT} + \text{Depreciation}}{\text{Interest} + \dfrac{\text{Debt repayment}}{(1 - \text{tax rate})} + \dfrac{\text{Preferred dividends}}{(1 - \text{tax rate})}}$$

We see earnings before both interest and taxes in the numerator. This measures the numerator in a way that can be compared directly to the interest expense in the denominator, because interest expense is paid out of pre-tax dollars. In contrast, any payment of principal scheduled for a given year is nondeductible and must be made out of after-tax profits. In essence, with a 50 percent tax rate, one dollar of principal payment is "twice as expensive" as a one-dollar interest payment. Scaling the payment of principal by (1 - tax rate) accounts for this. The same idea applies to preferred dividends, which are not tax deductible.

The funds flow coverage ratio provides an indication of how comfortably the funds flow can cover unavoidable expenditures. The ratio excludes payments such as common dividends and capital expenditures on the premise that they could be reduced to zero to make debt payments if necessary.[1] Clearly, however, if the firm is to survive in the long run, funds flow must be sufficient to not only service debt but also maintain plant assets. Thus, long-run survival requires a funds flow coverage ratio well in excess of 1.[2]

It would be overly simplistic to establish any particular threshold above which a ratio indicates a loan is justified. However, a creditor clearly wants to be in a position to be repaid on schedule, even when the borrower faces a reasonably foreseeable difficulty. That argues for lending only when the funds flow coverage is expected to exceed 1, even in a recession scenario—and higher if some allowance for capital expenditures is prudent.

The financial analysis should produce more than an assessment of the risk of nonpayment. It should also identify the nature of the significant risks. At many commercial banks, it is standard operating procedure to summarize the analysis of the firm by listing the key risks that could lead to default and factors that could be used to control those risks if the loan were made. That information can be used in structuring the detailed terms of the loan so as to trigger default when problems arise, at a stage early enough to permit corrective action.

Step 4: Utilize Forecasts to Assess Payment Prospects

Already implicit in some of the above discussion is a forward-looking view of the firm's ability to service the loan. Good credit analysis should also be supported by explicit forecasts. The basis for such forecasts is usually management, but, not surprisingly, lenders do not accept such forecasts without question.

In forecasting, a variety of scenarios should be considered—including not just a "best guess" but also a "pessimistic" scenario. Ideally, the firm should be strong enough to repay the loan even in this scenario. Ironically, it is not necessarily a decline in sales that presents the greatest risk to the lender. If managers can respond quickly to the dropoff in sales, it should be accompanied by a liquidation of receivables and inventory, which enhances cash flow for a given level of earnings. The nightmare scenario is one that involves large negative profit margins, perhaps because managers are caught by surprise by a downturn in demand and are forced to liquidate inventory at substantially reduced prices.

At times, it is possible to reconsider the structure of a loan so as to permit it to "cash flow." That is, the term of the loan might be extended, or the amortization pattern changed. Often, a bank will grant a loan with the expectation that it will be continually renewed, thus becoming a permanent part of the firm's financial structure. (Such a loan is labeled an "evergreen.") In that case, the loan will still be written as if it is due within the short term, and the bank must assure itself of a viable "exit strategy." However, the firm would be expected to service the loan by simply covering interest payments.

Step 5: Assemble the Detailed Loan Structure, Including Loan Covenants

If the analysis thus far indicates that a loan is in order, it is then time to pull together the detailed structure: type of loan, repayment schedule, loan covenants, and pricing. The first two items were discussed above. Here we discuss loan covenants and pricing.

WRITING LOAN COVENANTS.   Loan covenants specify mutual expectations of the borrower and lender by specifying actions the borrower will and will not take. Some covenants require certain actions (such as regular provision of financial statements); others preclude certain actions (such as undertaking an acquisition without the permission of the lender); still others require maintenance of certain financial ratios. Violation of a covenant represents an event of default that could cause immediate acceleration of the debt payment, but in most cases the lender uses the default as an opportunity to re-examine the situation and either waive the violation or renegotiate the loan.

Loan covenants must strike a balance between protecting the interests of the lender and providing the flexibility management needs to run the business. The covenants represent a mechanism for insuring that the business will remain as strong as the two parties anticipated at the time the loan was granted. Thus, required financial ratios are typically based on the levels that existed at that time, perhaps with some allowance for deterioration but often with some expected improvement over time.

The particular covenants included in the agreement should contain the significant risks identified in the financial analysis, or to at least provide early warning that such risks are surfacing. Some commonly used financial covenants include:

- *Maintenance of minimum net worth.* This covenant assures that the firm will maintain an "equity cushion" to protect the lender. Covenants typically require a level of net worth rather than a particular level of income. In the final analysis, the lender may not care whether that net worth is maintained by generating income, cutting dividends, or issuing new equity. Tying the covenant to net worth offers the firm the flexibility to use any of these avenues to avoid default.
- *Minimum coverage ratio.* Especially in the case of a long-term loan, such as a term loan, the lender may want to supplement a net worth covenant with one based on coverage of interest or total debt service. The funds flow coverage ratio presented above would be an example. Maintenance of some minimum coverage helps assure that the ability of the firm to generate funds internally is strong enough to justify the long-term nature of the loan.
- *Maximum ratio of total liabilities to net worth.* This ratio constrains the risk of high leverage and prevents growth without either retaining earnings or infusing equity.
- *Minimum net working capital balance or current ratio.* Constraints on this ratio force a firm to maintain its liquidity by using cash generated from operations to retire current liabilities (as opposed to acquiring long-lived assets).
- *Maximum ratio of capital expenditures to earnings before depreciation.* Constraints on this ratio help prevent the firm from investing in growth (including the illiquid assets necessary to support growth) unless such growth can be financed internally, with some margin remaining for debt service.

In addition to such financial covenants, loans sometimes place restrictions on other borrowing activity, pledging of assets to other lenders, selling of substantial parts of assets, engaging in mergers or acquisitions, and payment of dividends.

Covenants are included in not only private lending agreements with banks, insurance companies, and others, but also in public debt agreements. However, public debt agreements tend to have less restrictive covenants, for two reasons. First, negotiations resulting from a violation of public debt covenants are costly (possibly involving not just the trustee, but also bondholders), and so they are written to be triggered only in serious circumstances. Second, public debt is usually issued by stronger, more creditworthy firms. (The primary exception would be high-yield debt issued in conjunction with leveraged buyouts.) For the most financially healthy firms, with strong debt ratings, very few covenants will be used—only those necessary to limit dramatic changes in the firm's operations, such as a major merger or acquisition.

Earlier, we indicated that Dell Computer's debt financing came in the form of publicly issued notes. The major covenants on the notes impose limitations on future borrowing and restrictions on dividends. However, if Dell's debt achieves an investment-grade rating in the future, those covenants are to be relaxed.

LOAN PRICING.   A detailed discussion of loan pricing falls outside the scope of this text. The essence of pricing is to assure that the yield on the loan is sufficient to cover (1) the lender's cost of borrowed funds; (2) the lender's costs of administering and servicing the loan; (3) a premium for exposure to default risk; and (4) at least a normal return on the equity capital necessary to support the lending operation. The price is often stated in terms of a deviation from a bank's prime rate—the rate charged to stronger borrowers. For example, a loan might be granted at prime plus 1 percent. An alternative base is LIBOR, or the London Interbank Offer Rate, the rate at which large banks from various nations lend large blocks of funds to each other.

Banks compete actively for commercial lending business, and it is rare that a yield includes more than 2 percentage points to cover the cost of default risk. If the spread to cover default risk is, say, 1 percent, and the bank recovers only 50 percent of amounts due on loans that turn out bad, then the bank can afford only 2 percent of their loans to fall into that category. This underscores how important it is for banks to conduct a thorough analysis and to contain the riskiness of their loan portfolio.

FINANCIAL STATEMENT ANALYSIS AND PUBLIC DEBT

Fundamentally, the issues involved in analysis of public debt are no different from those of bank loans and other private debt issues. Institutionally, however, the contexts are different. Bankers can maintain very close relations with clients so as to form an initial assessment of their credit risk and monitor their activities during the loan period. In the case of public debt, the investors are distanced from the issuer. To a large extent, they must depend on professional debt analysts, including debt raters, to assess the riskiness of the debt and monitor the firm's ongoing activities. Such analysts and debt raters thus serve an important function in closing the information gap between issuers and investors.

The Meaning of Debt Ratings

As indicated above, the two major debt rating agencies in the U.S. are Moody's and Standard and Poor's. Using the Standard and Poor's labeling system, the highest possible rating is AAA. Firms with this rating are large and have strong and steady earnings and little leverage. Only about 1 to 2 percent of the public industrial companies rated by Standard & Poor's have the financial strength to merit this rating. Among the few in 1995 are Exxon, Merck, General Electric, and Nippon Telegraph and Telephone—all among the largest, most profitable firms in the world. Proceeding downward from AAA, the ratings are AA, A, BBB, BB, B, CCC, CC, C, and D, where "D" indicates debt in default. To be considered investment grade, a firm must achieve a rating of BBB or higher. Many funds are precluded by their charters from investing in any bonds below that grade. Table 9-1 presents examples of firms in rating categories AAA through CCC, as well as average values for selected financial ratios across all firms in each category.

Note that even to achieve a grade of BBB is difficult. General Motors, the second most profitable corporation in the U.S. in 1994, and with rising earnings in early 1995, was still rated as "only" BBB—barely investment grade—in 1995. In this case, the bond raters recalled the string of losses that GM suffered in the early 1990s, recognizing the riskiness of the GM profit stream. Sears Roebuck is another large, profitable firm ranked "only" as BBB—and, like GM, it has suffered losses in the recent past. Overall, firms in the BBB class are only moderately leveraged, with about 40 percent of long-term capitalization coming in the form of debt. Earnings tend to be relatively strong, as indicated by a pre-tax interest coverage (EBIT/interest) of 2.5 and a funds flow debt coverage (working capital from operations/total debt) of nearly 30 percent.

The difficulty of achieving an investment-grade rating is also revealed by Compaq's experience in the debt markets in 1994. Consider this: Compaq's debt represents only 7.4 percent of long-term capital, and even if Compaq's $300 million debt issue had been outstanding for the entire year, pre-tax earnings would have been *56 times* interest expense. In fact, Compaq's cash balances were more than sufficient to retire the entire debt issue immediately! On the basis of such information, one might expect Compaq would easily qualify as AAA. However, Standard and Poor's classified the debt as BBB, and Moody's gave it a comparable rating. The reason is that the bond raters do not focus on a single year's performance. They consider the volatility of earnings in the past and the risk of downturns in the future. In commenting on the rating, Standard and Poor's stated, "Compaq Computer Corp.'s rating reflects the volatile nature of the personal computer hardware industry, offset by Compaq's competitive cost position in an environment of aggressive price competition; technological leadership in an industry characterized by short product cycles; improved customer focus; and strong balance sheet."[3]

Interestingly, the debt markets were apparently more confident in Compaq than the debt raters. The debt was issued at par at rates of 6.5 percent and 7.25 percent (depending on maturity) at a time when other BBB issues were yielding about 8 percent. The rates faced by Compaq were similar to those carried by AAA debt.

Firms with below investment-grade ratings tend to face some significant risk, even though many are quite profitable. Table 9-1 places United Airlines in the BB category. In 1995 it is the leading U.S. airline in terms of revenues, but one that was profitable in 1994 and 1995 only after having suffered severe losses in the early 1990s. The B category includes Stone Container Corporation, a highly leveraged producer of corrugated containers that experienced losses from 1991 through early 1995. The CCC category includes firms whose long-term capital is three-fourths debt, on average. An illustrative CCC firm is Spectravision, a provider of in-room movies to the lodging industry. Spectravision emerged from bankruptcy in 1992 and has since operated at a loss, with negative book value.

Table 9-1   Debt Ratings: Example Firms and Median Financial Ratios by Category

S&P debt rating	Example firms in 1995	Percentage of public industrials given same rating by S&P*	Median ratios for overall category over three years prior to rating—1991–1993 (industrials only)			
			Pre-tax return on long-term capital	Pre-tax interest coverage	Working capital from operations to total debt	Long-term debt to total capital
AAA	General Electric Merck and Co. Nippon T & T	1.2%	24.5%	19.9	136.8%	11.0%
AA	McDonald's Corp. Wal-Mart Stores, Inc. J. P. Morgan	5.4	18.4	8.9	75.1	19.3
A	Ford Motor Company Citicorp	16.2	13.7	4.7	44.3	30.9
BBB	General Motors Sears Roebuck and Co.	19.5	9.7	2.5	29.3	39.5
BB	Revco United Airlines	26.1	9.6	1.6	17.9	50.5
B	Stone Container Corp. Northwest Airlines	28.6	6.4	0.7	8.5	58.9
CCC	Spectravision, Inc. Presidio Oil Co.	1.1	5.5	0.5	1.5	75.4

*Ratings are as of September 1994; firms included in set for analysis only if data were publicly available 1989–1993.
Source: Standard and Poor's *Global Sector Review* (October 1994).

Factors That Drive Debt Ratings

The Compaq illustration seems to suggest that it would be difficult to predict debt ratings purely on the basis of financial statement data. In turns out that the Compaq example is unusual, however. Research demonstrates that a majority of the variation in debt ratings can be explained as a function of selected financial statement ratios, even as used within a quantitative model that incorporates no subjective human judgment. Some debt rating agencies rely heavily on quantitative models, and such models are commonly used by insurance companies, banks, and others to assist in the evaluation of the riskiness of debt issues for which a public rating is not available.

Table 9-2 lists the factors used by three different firms in their quantitative debt-rating models. The firms include one insurance company and one bank, which use the models in their private placement activities, and an investment research firm, which employs the

Table 9-2 Factors Used in Quantitative Models of Debt Ratings

	Insurance Firm 1	*Bank* Firm 2	*Investmt research* Firm 3
Profitability measures	Return on long-term capital	Return on long-term capital	Return on long-term capital
Leverage measures	Long-term debt to capitalization	Long-term debt to capitalization Total debt to total capital	Long-term debt to capitalization
Profitability and leverage	Interest coverage Cash flow to long-term debt	Interest coverage Cash flow to long-term debt	Fixed charge coverage Coverage of short-term debt and fixed charges
Firm size	Sales	Total assets	
Other		Standard deviation of return Subordination status	

model in evaluating its own debt purchases and holdings. In each case, profitability and leverage play an important role in the rating. One firm also uses firm size as an indicator, with larger size associated with higher ratings.

Several researchers have estimated quantitative models used for debt ratings. Two of these models, developed by Kaplan and Urwitz and shown in Table 9-3, highlight the relative importance of the factors.[4] Model 1 has the greater ability to explain variation in bond ratings. However, it includes some factors based on stock market data, which are not available for all firms. Model 2 is based solely on financial statement data.

The factors in Table 9-3 are listed in the order of their statistical significance in Model 1. An interesting feature is that the most important factor explaining debt ratings is not a financial ratio at all—it is simply firm size! Large firms tend to get better ratings than small firms. Whether the debt is subordinated or unsubordinated is next most important, followed by a leverage indicator. Profitability appears less important, but in part that reflects the presence in the model of multiple factors (ROA and interest coverage) that capture profitability. It is only the explanatory power that is *unique* to a given variable that is indicated by the ranking in Table 9-3. Explanatory power common to the two variables is not considered.

When applied to a sample of bonds that were not used in the estimation process, the Kaplan-Urwitz model (1) predicted the rating category correctly in 44 of 64 cases, or 63 percent of the time. Where it erred, the model was never off by more than one category, and in about half of those cases its prediction was more consistent with the market yield on the debt than was the actual debt rating. Interestingly, application of the model to Compaq (using 1993 data and assuming that $300 million of debt had been incorporated in Compaq's capital structure during the year) produces a predicted AAA rating—incon-

Table 9-3 Kaplan-Urwitz Models of Debt Ratings

Firm or debt characteristic	Variable reflecting characteristic	Coefficients	
		Model 1	Model 2
	Model intercept	5.67	4.41
Firm size	Total assets[a]	.0010	.0012
Subordination status of debt	1 = subordinated; 0 = unsubordinated	−2.36	−2.56
Leverage	Long-term debt to total assets	−2.85	−2.72
Systematic risk	Market model beta, indicating sensitivity of stock price to market-wide movements (1 = average)[b]	−.87	NA
Profitability	Net income to total assets	5.13	6.40
Unsystematic risk	Standard deviation of residual from market model (average = .10)[b]	−2.90	NA
Riskiness of profit stream	Coefficient of variation in net income over 5 years (standard deviation / mean)	NA	−.53
Interest coverage	Pre-tax funds flow before interest to interest expense	.007	.006

The score from the model is converted to a bond rating as follows:
If score > 6.76, predict AAA
  score > 5.19, predict AA
  score > 3.28, predict A
  score > 1.57, predict BBB
  score < 0.00, predict BB

a. The coefficient in the Kaplan-Urwitz model was estimated at .005 (Model 1) and .006 (Model 2). Its scale has been adjusted to reflect that the estimates were based on assets measured in dollars from the 1960s and 1970s. Given that $1 from 1970 is approximately equivalent to $5 in 1995, the original coefficient estimate has been divided by 5.
b. Market model is estimated by regressing stock returns against the return on the market index, using monthly data for prior five years.

sistent with the actual rating, but consistent with the market yield on the debt issued in early 1994.[5]

Given that debt ratings can be explained so well in terms of a handful of financial ratios, one might question whether ratings convey any *news* to investors—anything that could not already have been garnered from publicly available financial data. The answer to the question is yes, at least in the case of debt rating downgrades. That is, downgrades are greeted with drops in both bond and stock prices.[6] To be sure, the capital markets anticipate much of the information reflected in rating changes. However, that is not surprising, given that the changes often represent reactions to recent known events, and that the rating agencies typically indicate in advance that a change is being considered.

PREDICTION OF DISTRESS AND TURNAROUND

The key task in credit analysis is assessing the probability that a firm will face financial distress and fail to repay a loan. A related analysis, relevant once a firm begins to face distress, involves considering whether it can be turned around. In this section, we consider evidence on the predictability of these states.

The prediction of either distress or turnaround is a complex, difficult, and subjective task that involves all of the steps of analysis discussed throughout this book: business strategy analysis, accounting analysis, financial analysis, and prospective analysis. Purely quantitative models of the process can rarely serve as substitutes for the hard work the analysis involves. However, research on such models does offer some insight into which financial indicators are most useful in the task. Moreover, there are some settings where extensive credit checks are too costly to justify, and where quantitative distress prediction models are useful. For example, the commercially available "Zeta" model is used by some manufacturers and other firms to assess the credit-worthiness of their customers.[7]

Several distress prediction models have been developed over the years.[8] They are similar to the debt rating models, but instead of predicting ratings, they predict whether a firm will face some state of distress within one year, typically defined as bankruptcy. One study suggests that the factors most useful (on a stand-alone basis) in predicting bankruptcy one year in advance are[9]:

1. Profitability $= \left[\dfrac{\text{Net income}}{\text{Net worth}} \right]$

2. Volatility $= \left[\text{Standard deviation of} \left(\dfrac{\text{Net income}}{\text{Net worth}} \right) \right]$

3. Financial leverage $= \left[\dfrac{\text{Market value of equity}}{(\text{Market value of equity } + \text{ Book value of debt})} \right]$

The evidence indicates that the key to whether a firm will face distress is its level of profitability, the volatility of that profitability, and how much leverage it faces. Interestingly, liquidity measures turn out to be much less important. Current liquidity won't save an unhealthy firm if it is losing money at a fast pace.

Of course, if one were interested in predicting distress, there would be no need to restrict attention to one variable at a time. A number of multi-factor models have been designed to predict financial distress. One such model is the Altman Z-score model[10]:

$$Z = .717(X_1) + .847(X_2) + 3.11(X_3) + .420(X_4) + .998(X_5)$$

where X_1 = net working capital/total assets
X_2 = retained earnings/total assets
X_3 = EBIT/total assets
X_4 = shareholders' equity/total liabilities
X_5 = sales/total assets

The model predicts bankruptcy when Z < 1.20. The range between 1.20 and 2.90 is labeled the "gray area." As an example, and not surprisingly, Compaq stands well above the threshold for survival, based on its 1993 data:

$$Z = .717(.50) + .847(.51) + 3.11(.15) + .420(2.13) + .998(1.76) = 3.91$$

Such models have some ability to predict failing and surviving firms. Altman reports that when the model was applied to a holdout sample containing 33 failed and 33 nonfailed firms (the same proportion used to estimate the model), it correctly predicted the outcome in 63 of 66 cases. However, the performance of the model would degrade substantially if applied to a holdout sample where the proportion of failed and nonfailed firms was not forced to be the same as that used to estimate the model.

Simple distress prediction models like the Altman model cannot serve effectively as a replacement for in-depth analysis of the kind discussed throughout this book. But they provide a useful reminder of the power of financial statement data to summarize important dimensions of the firm's performance. Even in the absence of direct information about management expertise, corporate strategy, engineering know-how, and market position, financial ratios can reveal much about who will make it and who will not.

SUMMARY AND CONCLUSIONS

Credit analysis is the evaluation of a firm from the perspective of a holder or potential holder of its debt. Credit analysis is important to a wide variety of economic agents—not just bankers and other financial intermediaries, but also public debt analysts, industrial companies, service companies, and others.

At the heart of credit analysis lie the same techniques described in Chapters 2 through 5: business strategy analysis, accounting analysis, financial analysis, and portions of prospective analysis. The purpose of the analysis is not just to assess the likelihood that a potential borrower will fail to repay the loan. It is also important to identify the nature of the key risks involved, and how the loan might be structured to mitigate or control those risks. A well-structured loan provides the lender with a viable "exit strategy," even in the case of default. A key to this structure is properly designed accounting-based covenants.

Fundamentally, the issues involved in analysis of public debt are no different from those involved in evaluating bank loans or other private debt. Institutionally, however, the contexts are different. Investors in public debt are usually not close to the borrower and must rely on other agents, including debt raters and other analysts, to assess creditworthiness initially, and on a continuing basis. Debt ratings, which depend heavily on firm size and financial measures of performance, have an important influence on the market yields that must be offered to issue debt.

The key task in credit analysis is the assessment of the probability of default. The task is complex, difficult, and to some extent, subjective. Nevertheless, a small number of key financial ratios are sufficient to predict financial distress with impressive accuracy. The most important financial indicators for this purpose are profitability, volatility of profits, and leverage.

DISCUSSION QUESTIONS

1. What are the critical performance dimensions for (a) a retailer and (b) a financial services company that should be considered in credit analysis? What ratios would you suggest looking at for each of these dimensions?

2. Why would a company pay to have its public debt rated by a major rating agency (such as Moody's or Standard and Poors)? Why might a firm decide not to have its debt rated?

3. Some have argued that the market for original-issue junk bonds developed in the late 1970s as a result of a failure in the rating process. Proponents of this argument suggest that rating agencies rated companies too harshly at the low end of the rating scale, denying investment grade status to some deserving companies. What are proponents of this argument effectively assuming were the incentives of rating agencies? What economic forces could give rise to this incentive?

4. Many debt agreements require borrowers to obtain the permission of the lender before undertaking a major acquisition or asset sale. Why would the lender want to include this type of restriction?

5. Betty Li, the CFO of a company applying for a new loan, argues: "I will never agree to a debt covenant that restricts my ability to pay dividends to my shareholders, because it reduces shareholder wealth." Do you agree with this argument?

6. Cambridge Construction Company follows the percentage-of-completion method for reporting long-term contract revenues. The percentage of completion is based on the cost of materials shipped to the project site as a percentage of total expected materials costs. Cambridge's major debt agreement includes restrictions on net worth, interest coverage, and minimum working capital requirements. A leading analyst claims that "the company is buying its way out of these covenants by spending cash and buying materials, even when they are not needed." Explain how this may be possible.

7. Can Cambridge improve its Z score by behaving as the analyst claims in Question 6? Is this change consistent with economic reality?

8. A banker argues: "I avoid lending to companies with negative cash from operations because they are too risky." Is this a sensible lending policy?

9. A leading retailer finds itself in a financial bind. It doesn't have sufficient cash flow from operations to finance its growth, and is close to violating the maximum debt-to-assets ratio allowed by its covenants. The Vice-President for Marketing suggests: "We can raise cash for our growth by selling the existing stores and leasing them back. This source of financing is cheap, since it avoids violating either the debt-to-assets or interest coverage ratios in our covenants." Do you agree with his analysis? Why or why not? As the firm's banker, how would you view this arrangement?

CASES

Debt Ratings in the Chemical Industry
Pageturner Bookstores, Inc.

NOTES

1. The same is true of preferred dividends. However, when preferred stock is cumulative, any dividends missed must be paid later, when and if the firm returns to profitability.

2. Other relevant coverage ratios are discussed in Chapter 4.

3. *Standard and Poor's Credit Week* (March 14, 1994), p. 73.

4. Robert Kaplan and G. Urwitz, "Statistical Models of Bond Ratings: A Methodological Inquiry," *Journal of Business* (April 1979): 231–261.

5. Using Model 2 and assuming that the debt issue increases leverage without changing total assets, we obtain:

$$4.41 + .0012(4084) - 2.56(0) - 2.72(.07) + 6.4(.11) - .53(.46) + .006(29.9) = 9.77$$

6. See Robert Holthausen and Richard Leftwich, "The Effect of Bond Rating Changes on Common Stock Prices," *Journal of Financial Economics* (September 1986): 57–90; and John Hand, Robert Holthausen, and Richard Leftwich, "The Effect of Bond Rating Announcements on Bond and Stock Prices," *Journal of Finance* (June 1992): 733–752.

7. See Edward Altman, *Corporate Financial Distress* (New York: John Wiley, 1983).

8. See Edward Altman, "Financial Ratios, Discriminant Analysis, and the Prediction of Corporate Bankruptcy," *Journal of Finance* (September 1968): 589–609; Altman, 1983, op. cit.; William Beaver, "Financial Ratios as Predictors of Distress," *Journal of Accounting Research,* supplement, 1966: 71–111; James Ohlson, "Financial Ratios and the Probabilistic Prediction of Bankruptcy," *Journal of Accounting Research* (Spring 1980): 109–131; and Mark Zmijewski, "Predicting Corporate Bankruptcy: An Empirical Comparison of the Extant Financial Distress Models," working paper, SUNY at Buffalo, 1983.

9. Zmijewski, op. cit.

10. Altman, 1983, op. cit.

chapter 10

Mergers and Acquisitions

Mergers and acquisitions have long been a popular form of corporate investment, particularly in countries with Anglo-American forms of capital markets. There is no question that these transactions provide a healthy return to target stockholders. However, their value to acquiring shareholders is less understood. Many skeptics point out that given the hefty premiums paid to target stockholders, acquisitions tend to be negative-valued investments for acquiring stockholders.

A number of questions can be examined using financial analysis for mergers and acquisitions:

- Securities analysts can ask: Does a proposed acquisition create value for the acquiring firm's stockholders?
- Risk arbitrageurs can ask: What is the likelihood that a hostile takeover offer will ultimately succeed, and are there other potential acquirers likely to enter the bidding?
- Acquiring management can ask: Does this target fit our business strategy? If so, what is it worth to us, and how can we make an offer that can be successful?
- Target management can ask: Is the acquirer's offer a reasonable one for our stockholders? Are there other potential acquirers that would value our company more than the current bidder?
- Investment bankers can ask: How can we identify potential targets that are likely to be a good match for our clients? And how should we value target firms when we are asked to issue fairness opinions?

In this chapter we focus primarily on the use of financial statement data and analysis by financial analysts interested in evaluating whether a merger creates value for the acquiring firm's stockholders. However, our discussion can also be applied to these other merger contexts.

Our discussion of whether acquisitions create value for acquirers focuses on evaluating motivations for acquisitions, the pricing of offers, and the methods of financing, as well as assessing the likelihood that an offer will be successful. Throughout the chapter we use AT&T's $7.5 billion acquisition of NCR in 1991 to illustrate how financial analysis can be used in a merger context.[1]

MOTIVATION FOR MERGER OR ACQUISITION

There are a variety of reasons that firms merge or acquire other firms. Some acquiring managers may want to increase their own power and prestige. Others, however, realize that business combinations provide an opportunity to create new economic value for their stockholders. New value can be created in the following ways:

1. *Taking Advantage of Economies of Scale.* Mergers are often justified as a means of providing the two participating firms with increased economies of scale. Economies of scale arise when one firm can perform a function more efficiently than two. For example, AT&T and NCR both design and manufacture UNIX-based personal computers. Following a merger, they will probably be able to take advantage of economies of scale in research and development by reducing the number of researchers working on similar new products. The combined firm may also be able to economize on management costs, including accounting and corporate finance functions and corporate management.

2. *Improving Target Management.* Another common motivation for acquisition is to improve target management. A firm is likely to be a target if it has systematically under-performed its industry. Historical poor performance could be due to bad luck, but it could also be due to the firm's managers making poor investment and operating decisions, or deliberately pursuing goals which increase their personal power but cost stockholders.

3. *Combining Complementary Resources.* Firms may decide that a merger will create value by combining complementary resources of the two partners. For example, a merger between a firm with a strong research and development unit, such as AT&T, and a firm in the same industry with a strong distribution unit, such as NCR, may benefit both firms. Of course, they could both separately invest to strengthen their respective distribution and R&D units. However, it may well be cheaper to combine resources through a merger.

4. *Capturing Tax Benefits.* In the U.S. the 1986 Tax Reform Act eliminated many of the tax benefits from mergers and acquisitions. However, several merger tax benefits remain. The major benefit is the acquisition of operating tax losses. If a firm does not expect to earn sufficient profits to fully utilize operating loss carryforward benefits, it may decide to buy another firm which is earning profits. The operating losses and loss carryforwards of the acquirer can then be offset against the target's taxable income.[2] A second tax benefit often attributed to mergers is the

tax shield that comes from increasing leverage for the target firm. This was particularly relevant for leveraged buyouts in the 1980s.

5. *Providing Low-Cost Financing to a Financially Constrained Target.* If capital markets are imperfect, perhaps because of information asymmetries between management and outside investors, firms can face capital constraints. Information problems are likely to be especially severe for newly formed, high-growth firms. These firms can be difficult for outside investors to value since they have short track records, and their financial statements provide little insight into the value of their growth opportunities. Further, since they typically have to rely on external funds to finance their growth, capital market constraints for high-growth firms are likely to affect their ability to undertake profitable new projects. Public capital markets are therefore likely to be costly sources of funds for these types of firms. An acquirer that understands the business and is willing to provide a steady source of finance may therefore be an attractive option.

6. *Increasing Product-Market Rents.* Firms also can have incentives to merge to increase product-market rents. By merging and becoming a dominant firm in the industry, two smaller firms can collude to restrict their output and raise prices, thereby increasing their profits. This circumvents problems that arise in cartels of independent firms, where firms have incentives to cheat on the cartel and increase their output.

   While product-market rents make sense for firms as a motive for merging, the two partners are unlikely to announce their intentions when they explain the merger to their investors, since most countries have anti-trust laws which regulate mergers between two firms in the same industry. For example, in the U.S. there are three major anti-trust statutes—The Sherman Act of 1890, The Clayton Act of 1914, and The Hart Scott Rodino Act of 1976.

While many of the motivations for acquisitions are likely to create new economic value for shareholders, some are not. Firms that are flush with cash but have few new profitable investment opportunities are particularly prone to using their surplus cash to make acquisitions. Stockholders of these firms would probably prefer that managers pay out any surplus or "free" cash flows as dividends, or use the funds to repurchase their firm's stock. However, these options reduce the size of the firm and the assets under management's control. Management may therefore prefer to invest the free cash flows to buy new companies, even if they are not valued by stockholders. Of course, managers will never announce that they are buying a firm because they are reluctant to pay out funds to stockholders. They may explain the merger using one of the motivations discussed above, or they may argue that they are buying the target at a bargain price.

Another motivation for mergers that is valued by managers but not stockholders is diversification. Diversification was a popular motivation for acquisitions in the 1960s and early 1970s. Acquirers sought to dampen their earnings volatility by buying firms in unrelated businesses. Diversification as a motive for acquisitions has since been widely discredited. Modern finance theorists point out that in a well functioning capital market, investors can diversify for themselves and do not need managers to do so for them. In addition, diversification has been criticized for leading firms to lose sight of their major competitive strengths and to expand into businesses where they do not have expertise.

Financial Analysis of Merger Motivations

In evaluating a proposed merger, financial analysts are interested in determining whether the merger creates new wealth for acquiring and target stockholders, or whether it is motivated by managers' desires to increase their own power and prestige. Financial analysis is likely to include:

- *Learning about the motivation(s) for an acquisition and any anticipated benefits through public disclosures by acquirers or targets.*
- *Comparing the industries of the target and acquirer.* Are the firms related horizontally or vertically? How close are the business relations between them? If the businesses are unrelated, is the acquirer cash-rich and reluctant to return free cash flows to stockholders?
- *Evaluating the key operational strengths of the target and the acquirer.* Are these strengths complementary? For example, does one firm have a renowned research group and the other a strong distribution network?
- *Assessing whether the acquisition is a friendly one, supported by target management, or hostile.* A hostile takeover is more likely to occur for targets with poor-performing management who oppose the acquisition to preserve their jobs.
- *Comparing the pre-merger performance of the two firms.* Performance metrics are likely to include ROE, gross margins, general and administrative expenses to sales, and working capital management ratios. On the basis of these measures, is the target a poor performer in its industry, implying that there are opportunities for improved management? Is the acquirer in a declining industry and searching for new directions?
- *Assessing the tax position of both firms.* What are the average and marginal current tax rates for the target and the acquirer? Does the acquirer have operating loss carryforwards and the target taxable profits?

This analysis should help the analyst understand what specific benefits, if any, the merger is likely to generate.

Motivation for AT&T's Acquisition

Prior to 1984, AT&T was a regulated utility providing telephone services and manufacturing-related equipment. However, in 1982 the company signed a Consent Agreement with the Department of Justice (DOJ) to divest its Bell operating companies, which provided short-distance telephone services. This agreement followed eight years of negotiations with the DOJ over allegations that AT&T monopolized the telephone services and telephone equipment industries. In return for agreeing to this divestiture, AT&T was granted permission to enter the computer industry, which had previously been off-limits to the company.

Management argued that the Consent Agreement permitted the firm to concentrate on linking its telecommunications with computer and information services. The company could finally begin to take advantage of advances in computer science, particularly the development of UNIX operating systems that had been made at its renowned research park, Bell Labs. However, prior to 1990, the company had not been particularly successful in implementing this strategy. The financial press estimated that the firm's computer operations lost at least $2 billion between 1984 and 1990. Losses for 1990 alone were estimated at between $10 million and $300 million on sales of $1.5 billion.

AT&T's management decided that the best approach to its computer problems involved increasing its presence in computer operations and began searching for a suitable acquisition candidate. NCR, which had a corporate culture similar to AT&T's, emerged as the ideal target from this search. It also had compatible product lines and a similar policy of using UNIX operating systems. However, NCR was stronger than AT&T in networking and had an international computer marketing presence and customer base. Consistent with its desire to use NCR to develop its expertise in computer operations, AT&T announced that it would combine both companies' computer operations under NCR's management.

In summary, given AT&T's strategy of combining telecommunications and computer technologies and services, the acquisition of NCR appeared to make some economic sense. However, some analysts who were critical of AT&T's overall strategy argued that the acquisition would probably not create value for AT&T's stockholders, and that AT&T should concede that its entry into the computer business was a costly mistake.

ACQUISITION PRICING

A well thought-out economic motivation for a merger or acquisition is a necessary but not sufficient condition for it to create value for acquiring stockholders. The acquirer must be careful to avoid overpaying for the target. Overpayment makes the transaction highly desirable and profitable for target stockholders, but it diminishes the value of the deal to acquiring stockholders. A financial analyst can use the following methods to assess whether the acquiring firm is overpaying for the target.

Analyzing Premium Offered to Target Stockholders

One popular way to assess whether the acquirer is overpaying for a target is to compare the premium offered to target stockholders to premiums offered in similar transactions. If the acquirer offers a relatively high premium, the analyst is typically led to conclude that the transaction is less likely to create value for acquiring stockholders.

Premiums differ significantly for friendly and hostile acquisitions. Premiums tend to be about 30 percent higher for hostile deals than for friendly offers, implying that hostile acquirers are more likely to overpay for a target.[3] There are several reasons for this. First, a friendly acquirer has access to the internal records of the target, making it much less likely that it will be surprised by hidden liabilities or problems once it has completed the deal. In contrast, a hostile acquirer does not have this advantage in valuing the target and is forced to make assumptions, which may later turn out to be false. Second, the delays that typically accompany a hostile acquisition often provide opportunities for competing bidders to make an offer for the target, leading to a bidding war.

Comparing a target's premium to values for similar types of transactions is straight-forward to compute, but it has several practical problems. First, it is not obvious how to define a comparable transaction. Figure 10-1 shows the average premiums paid for U.S. targets between 1989 and 1993 relative to stock prices one month and one week prior to the first acquisition announcement. Average one-month premiums have varied dramati-cally during this period, ranging from 53 percent in 1989 to 72 percent in 1993.

Figure 10-1 Average Premium Paid for Mergers and Acquisitions in the Period 1989 to 1993

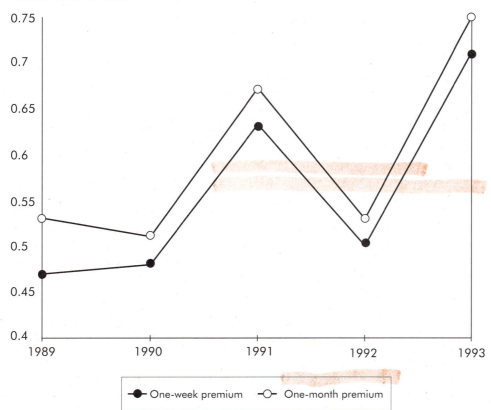

A second problem in using premiums offered to target stockholders to assess whether an acquirer overpaid is that measured premiums can be misleading if an offer is anticipated by investors. The stock price run-up for the target will then tend to make estimates of the premium appear relatively low. This limitation can be partially offset by using target stock prices one month prior to the acquisition offer as the basis for calculating premiums. However, in some cases offers may have been anticipated for even longer than one month.

Finally, using target premiums to assess whether an acquirer overpaid ignores the value of the target to the acquirer after the acquisition. This value can be viewed as:

$$\text{Value of target after acquisition} = \text{Value as independent firm} + \text{Value of merger benefits}$$

The value of the target before acquisition is the present value of the free cash flows for the target if it were to remain an independent entity. This is likely to be somewhat different from the firm's stock price prior to any merger announcement, since the pre-takeover price is a weighted average of the value of the firm as an independent unit and its value in the event of a takeover. The benefits of the merger include such effects as improvements in target operating performance from economies of scale, improved management, or tax benefits, as well as any spillover benefits to the acquirer from the acquisition. Clearly, acquirers will be willing to pay higher premiums for targets which are expected to generate higher merger benefits. Thus, examining the premium alone cannot determine whether the acquisition creates value for acquiring stockholders.

Analyzing Value of the Target to the Acquirer

A second and more reliable way of assessing whether the acquirer has overpaid for the target is to compare the offer price to the estimated value of the target to the acquirer. This latter value can be computed using the valuation techniques discussed in Chapters 6 and 7. The most popular methods of valuation used for mergers and acquisitions are earnings multiples and discounted cash flows. Since a comprehensive discussion of these techniques is provided earlier in the book, we focus here on implementation issues that arise for valuing targets in mergers and acquisitions. We recommend first computing the value of the target as an independent firm. This provides a way of checking whether the valuation assumptions are reasonable, since for publicly listed targets we can compare our estimate with pre-merger market prices. It also provides a useful benchmark for thinking about how the target's performance, and hence its value, is likely to change once it is acquired.

EARNINGS MULTIPLES.   To estimate the value of a target to an acquirer using earnings multiples, we have to forecast earnings for the target and decide on an appropriate earnings multiple.

Step One: Forecasting Earnings. Earnings forecasts are usually made by first forecasting next year's net income for the target, assuming no acquisition. Historical sales growth rates, gross margins, and average tax rates are useful in building a pro forma income model. Once we have forecasted the income for the target prior to an acquisition, we can incorporate into the pro forma model any improvements in earnings performance that we expect to result from the acquisition. Performance improvements can be modeled as:

- Higher operating margins through economies of scale in purchasing, or increased market power;
- Reductions in expenses as a result of consolidating research and development staffs, sales forces, and/or administration; or
- Lower average tax rates from taking advantage of operating tax loss carryforwards.

Forecasting earnings after acquisition requires some caution since, as we discuss later, an acquisition accounted for using purchase accounting will typically lead to increased goodwill amortization and depreciation expenses for revalued assets after the acquisition. These effects should be ignored in estimating future earnings for price-earnings valuation.

Step Two: Determining Price-Earnings Multiple. How do we determine the earnings multiple to be applied to our earnings forecasts? If the target firm is listed, it may be tempting to use the pre-acquisition price-earnings multiple to value post-merger earnings. However, there are several limitations to this approach. First, for many targets, earnings growth expectations are likely to change after a merger, implying that there will be a difference between the pre- and post-merger price-earnings multiples. Post-merger earnings should then be valued using a multiple for firms with comparable growth and risk characteristics. (See discussion in Chapter 7.) A second problem is that pre-merger price-earnings multiples are unavailable for unlisted targets. Once again, it becomes necessary to decide which types of listed firms are likely to be good comparables. Finally, if a pre-merger price-earnings multiple is appropriate for valuing post-merger earnings, care is required to ensure that the multiple is calculated prior to any acquisition announcement, since the price will increase in anticipation of the premium to be paid to target stockholders.

The following table summarizes how price-earnings multiples are used to value a target firm before an acquisition (assuming it will remain an independent entity), and to estimate the value of a target to a potential acquirer:

Summary of Price-Earnings Valuation for Targets

Value of target as an independent firm	Target earnings forecast for the next year, assuming no change in ownership, multiplied by its *pre-merger* PE multiple.
Value of target to potential acquirer	Target *revised* earnings forecast for the next year, incorporating the effect of any operational changes made by the acquirer, multiplied by its *post-merger* PE multiple.

LIMITATIONS OF PRICE-EARNINGS VALUATION.   As explained in Chapter 6, there are serious limitations to using earnings multiples for valuation. In addition to these limitations, the method has several more that are specific to merger valuations:

1. PE multiples assume that merger performance improvements come either from an immediate increase in earnings or from an increase in earnings growth (and hence an increase in the post-merger PE ratio). In reality, improvements and savings can come in many forms—gradual increases in earnings from implementing new operating policies, elimination of over-investment, better management of working capital, or paying out excess cash to stockholders. These types of improvements are not naturally reflected in PE multiples.

2. PE models do not easily incorporate any spillover benefits from an acquisition for the acquirer, since they focus on valuing the earnings of the target.

DISCOUNTED CASH FLOWS OR ABNORMAL EARNINGS.   As discussed in Chapters 6 and 7, we can also value a company using the discounted free cash flow and discounted abnormal earnings methods. These require us to first forecast the free cash flows or abnormal earnings for the firm and then discount them at the cost of capital.

Step One: Forecast Free Cash Flows/Abnormal Earnings. A pro forma model of expected future income and cash flows for the firm provides the basis for forecasting free cash flows/abnormal earnings. As a starting point, the model should be constructed under the assumption that the target remains an independent firm. The model should reflect our best estimates of future sales growth, cost structures, working capital needs, investment and research and development needs, and cash requirements for known debt retirements, developed from financial analysis of the target. Under the free cash flow approach, the pro forma model will forecast free cash flows to either the firm or to equity, typically for a period of five to ten years. The abnormal earnings method requires that we forecast abnormal earnings for as long as the firm expects new investment projects to earn more than their cost of capital. Once we have a model of the free cash flows or abnormal earnings, we can incorporate any improvements in free cash flows/earnings that we expect to result from the acquisition. These will include the cost savings, cash received from asset sales, benefits from eliminating over-investment, improved working capital management, and paying out excess cash to stockholders.

Step Two: Compute the Discount Rate. If we are valuing the target's post-acquisition cash flows to the firm, the appropriate discount rate is the weighted average cost of capital for the target, using its expected *post-acquisition* capital structure. Alternatively, if the target equity cash flows are being valued directly or if we are valuing abnormal earnings, the appropriate discount rate is the target's *post-acquisition cost of equity* rather than its weighted average cost of capital (WACC). Two common mistakes are to use the acquirer's cost of capital or the target's *pre-acquisition* cost of capital to value the post-merger cash flows/abnormal earnings from the target.

The computation of the target's post-acquisition cost of capital can be complicated if the acquirer plans to make a change to the target's capital structure after the acquisition, since the target's costs of debt and equity will change. However, the net effect of these changes on the weighted average cost of capital is likely to be quite small unless the revision in leverage has a significant effect on the target's interest tax shields or its likelihood of financial distress.

The following table summarizes how the discounted cash flow/abnormal earnings methods can be used to value a target before an acquisition (assuming it will remain an independent entity), and to estimate the value of a target firm to a potential acquirer.

Summary of Discounted Cash Flow/Abnormal Earnings Valuation for Targets

Value of target without an acquisition	(a) Present value of free cash flows to target equity assuming no acquisition, discounted at *pre-merger* cost of equity; or
	(b) Present value of free cash flows to target debt and equity assuming no acquisition, discounted at *pre-merger* WACC, less value of debt; or
	(c) Present value of abnormal earnings to target stockholders assuming no acquisition, discounted at *pre-merger* cost of equity.
Value of target to potential acquirer	(a) Present value of free cash flows to target equity, *including benefits from merger,* discounted at *post-merger* cost of equity; or
	(b) Present value of free cash flows to target, *including benefits from merger,* discounted at *post-merger* WACC, less value of debt; or
	(c) Present value of abnormal earnings to target stockholders, *including benefits from merger,* discounted at *post-merger* cost of equity.

Step Three: Analyze Sensitivity. Once we have estimated the expected value of a target, we will want to examine the sensitivity of our estimate to changes in the model assumptions. For example, answering the following questions can help the analyst assess the risks associated with an acquisition.

- What happens to the value of the target if it takes longer than expected for the benefits of the acquisition to materialize?
- What happens to the value of the target if the acquisition prompts its primary competitors to respond by also making an acquisition? Will such a response affect our plans and estimates?

AT&T's Pricing of NCR

AT&T's $7.5 billion price for NCR represents a 120 percent premium to target stockholders (adjusted for market-wide changes during the merger negotiation period). This is certainly substantially higher than typical premiums during this period and in part reflects opposition to the acquisition from NCR's management. AT&T's initial offer for the firm was $85 per share. The final price, which was accepted by target management, was $110.

AT&T's pricing of NCR also appears to be aggressive in terms of traditional forms of valuation. At the time of the announcement of AT&T's offer, the typical PE value for firms in the computer industry was 12.9 and NCR's PE was 11.5, yet AT&T's final offer valued NCR at 18 times current earnings. If these benefits are realized immediately, the total annual performance improvements from the acquisition for the new firm is equivalent to 50 percent of NCR's pre-merger earnings, a challenging target. Of course AT&T's management believed some of these benefits would come from increased earnings from its own operations.

The market reaction to acquisition announcements suggests that analysts believed that AT&T overpaid for NCR—AT&T's stock price dropped by 13 percent (again adjusted for market-wide changes), or $4.9 billion, during the negotiation period. Given the $3.7 billion premium that AT&T paid for NCR, this decline in AT&T equity implies that analysts believed that AT&T would actually destroy value in NCR! Subsequent short-term financial results for AT&T's computer operations (which includes NCR) support the market's skepticism. NCR's 1991 earnings were $100 million (26 percent) below projections made to AT&T. AT&T's loss from computer operations in 1993 was $99 million (including a $190 million restructuring charge). For the first quarter of 1994 the firm reported an operating loss of $61 million (including another restructuring charge of $120 million).

In summary, it appears from preliminary results and market assessments of the acquisition that AT&T overpaid for NCR. Indeed, the market believed that AT&T would actually destroy NCR's value as an independent firm, raising questions about the merits of AT&T's overall technology strategy.

ACQUISITION FINANCING

Even if an acquisition is undertaken to create new economic value and is priced judiciously, it may still destroy shareholder value if it is inappropriately financed. Several financing options are available to acquirers, including issuing stock or warrants to target stockholders, or acquiring target stock using surplus cash or proceeds from new debt. The trade-offs between these options from the standpoint of target stockholders usually hinge on their tax and transaction cost implications. For acquirers, they can affect the firm's capital structure and the financial reporting of the transaction and provide new information to investors.

As we discuss below, the financing preferences of target and acquiring stockholders can diverge. Financing arrangements can therefore increase or reduce the attractiveness of an acquisition from the standpoint of acquiring stockholders. As a result, a complete analysis of an acquisition will include an examination of the implications of the financing arrangements for the acquirer.

Effect of Form of Financing on Target Stockholders

As noted above, the key financing considerations for target stockholders are the tax and transaction cost implications of the acquirer's offer.

TAX EFFECTS OF DIFFERENT FORMS OF CONSIDERATION. Target stockholders care about the after-tax value of any offer they receive for their shares. In the U.S., whenever target stockholders receive cash for their shares, they are required to pay capital gains tax on the difference between the takeover offer price and their original purchase price. Alternatively, if they receive shares in the acquirer as consideration and the acquisition is undertaken as a tax-free reorganization, they can defer any taxes on the capital gain until they sell the new shares.

U.S. tax laws appear to cause target stockholders to prefer a stock offer to a cash one. This is certainly likely to be the case for a target founder who still has a significant stake in the company. If the company's stock price has appreciated over its life, the founder will face a substantial capital gains tax on a cash offer and will therefore probably prefer to receive stock in the acquiring firm. However, cash and stock offers can be tax-neutral for some groups of stockholders. For example, consider the tax implications for risk arbitrageurs, who take a short-term position in a company that is a takeover candidate in the hope that other bidders will emerge and increase the takeover price. They have no intention of holding stock in the acquirer once the takeover is completed, and will pay ordinary income tax on any short-term trading gain. Cash and stock offers therefore have identical after-tax values for risk arbitrageurs. Similarly, tax-exempt institutions are likely to be indifferent to whether an offer is in cash or stock.

TRANSACTION COSTS AND THE FORM OF FINANCING. Transaction costs are another factor related to the form of financing that can be relevant to target stockholders. Transaction costs are incurred when target stockholders sell any stock received as consideration for their shares in the target. These costs will not be faced by target stockholders if the bidder offers them cash. Transaction costs are unlikely to be significant for investors who intend to hold the acquirer's stock following a stock acquisition. However, they may be relevant for investors who intend to sell, such as risk arbitrageurs.

Effect of Form of Financing on Acquiring Stockholders

For acquiring stockholders, the costs and benefits of different financing options usually depend on how the offer affects their firm's capital structure, any information effects associated with different forms of financing, and the accounting methods of recording the acquisition.

CAPITAL STRUCTURE EFFECTS OF FORM OF FINANCING. In acquisitions where debt financing or surplus cash are the primary form of consideration for target shares, the acquisition increases the financial leverage of the acquirer. This increase in leverage may be part of the acquisition strategy, since one way an acquirer can add value to an inefficient firm is to lower its taxes by increasing interest tax shields. However, in many acquisitions an increase in post-acquisition leverage is a side effect of the method of financing and not part of a deliberate tax-minimizing strategy. The increase in leverage can then potentially reduce shareholder value for the acquirer by increasing the risk of financial distress.

To assess whether an acquisition leads an acquirer to have too much leverage, financial analysts can assess the acquirer's financial risk following the proposed acquisition by these methods:

- Assessing the pro forma financial risks for the acquirer under the proposed financing plan. Popular measures of financial risk include debt-to-equity and interest-coverage ratios, as well as projections of cash flows available to meet debt repayments. The ratios can be compared to similar performance metrics for the acquiring and target firms' industries. Do post-merger ratios indicate that the firm's probability of financial distress has increased significantly?
- Examining whether there are important off-balance sheet liabilities for the target and/or acquirer which are not included in the pro forma ratio and cash flow analysis of post-acquisition financial risk.
- Determining whether the pro forma assets for the acquirer are largely intangible, and therefore sensitive to financial distress. Measures of intangible assets include such ratios as market to book equity and tangible assets to the market value of equity.

INFORMATION PROBLEMS AND THE FORM OF FINANCING. As we discuss in Chapter 11, information asymmetries between managers and external investors can make managers reluctant to raise equity to finance new projects. Managers' reluctance arises from their fear that investors will interpret the decision as an indication that the firm's stock is overvalued. In the short term, this effect can lead managers to deviate from the firm's long-term optimal mix of debt and equity. As a result, acquirers are likely to prefer to use internal funds or debt to finance an acquisition, since these forms of consideration are less likely to be interpreted negatively by investors.

The information effects imply that firms forced to use stock financing are likely to face a stock price decline when investors learn of the method of financing. From the viewpoint of financial analysts, the financing announcement may therefore provide valuable news about the pre-acquisition value of the acquirer. However, it should have no implications for analysis of whether the acquisition creates value for acquiring shareholders, since the news reflected in the financing announcement is about the *pre-acqui-sition* value of the acquirer and not about the *post-acquisition* value of the target to the acquirer.

A second information problem arises if the acquiring management does not have good information about the target. Stock financing then provides a way for acquiring stockholders to share the information risks with target shareholders. If the acquirer finds out after the acquisition that the value of the target is less than previously anticipated, the accompanying decline in the acquirer's equity price will be partially borne by target stockholders who continue to hold the acquirer's stock. In contrast, if the target's shares were acquired in a cash offer, any post-acquisition loss would be fully borne by the acquirer's original stockholders. The risk-sharing benefits from using stock financing appears to be widely recognized for acquisitions of private companies, where public in-formation on the target is largely unavailable. In practice, it appears to be considered less important for acquisitions of large public corporations.

FORM OF FINANCING AND POST-ACQUISITION ACCOUNTING.   Finally, the form of financing has an effect on the acquirer's financial statements following the ac-quisition. Two methods of reporting for the acquisition are permitted under U.S. ac-counting—purchase and pooling of interests.

Under the *purchase method,* the acquirer writes up the assets of the target to their market value, and records the difference between the purchase price and the market value of the target's tangible net assets as goodwill. In the U.S. and most other countries, goodwill is subsequently amortized to earnings over a period of from 5 to 40 years. In contrast, U.K. companies typically write off any goodwill against shareholders' equity.

The *pooling-of-interests method* of accounting for mergers, which is rarely used out-side the U.S., requires acquirers to show the target's assets, liabilities, and equity at their original book values. Thus, no goodwill is recorded, and subsequent earnings need not be reduced by the amortization of goodwill.

An acquirer's decision on a method of financing an acquisition largely determines its method of accounting for the transaction. A number of conditions must be satisfied for an acquirer to use the pooling-of-interests method to account for an acquisition. If these conditions are not satisfied, the acquirer is required to use purchase accounting. The most significant of these conditions are that: (1) the acquirer issues voting common shares (not cash) in exchange for substantially all of the voting common shares (at least 90 percent) of the acquired company; and (2) the acquisition occurs in a single trans-action.

Some managers seem to believe that there is a benefit to shareholders from using the pooling-of-interests method for recording an acquisition. They argue that investors use earnings to value a firm's stock. Since the pooling-of-interests method leads to higher earnings than the purchase method by avoiding amortization of goodwill (at least until the asset is fully depleted), pooling must therefore lead to higher stock prices. However, while the two methods do have different earnings implications for the firm, they do not lead to different cash flows. They therefore do not alter the economic value of the firm. Thus, for the financial analyst, the choice of financing largely determines the accounting methods used to prepare an acquirer's pro forma balance sheets and income statements. But these accounting effects are not relevant to the question of whether the acquisition creates value for acquiring stockholders.

In summary, the form of financing has important tax and transaction cost implications for target stockholders. It can also have important capital structure, information, and merger accounting implications for acquirers. From the perspective of the financial analyst, the effect of any corporate tax benefits from debt financing should already be reflected in the valuation of the target. Information and accounting effects are not relevant to the value of the acquisition. However, the analyst does need to consider whether demands by target stockholders for consideration in cash lead the acquirer to have a post-acquisition capital structure which increases the risk of financial distress to a point that is detrimental for stockholders. Thus, part of the financial analyst's task in analyzing the value of an acquisition is to determine how it affects the acquirer's capital structure and its risks of financial distress.

AT&T's Financing of NCR

AT&T offered NCR's shareholders the right to exchange 100 percent of their shares for AT&T stock, valued at $110 per NCR share, unless AT&T was not satisfied that an all-stock merger could be accounted for as a pooling of interests. In that case, target stockholders would exchange 40 percent of their shares for AT&T stock and 60 percent for cash, where both stock and cash were valued at $110 per share. High and low collars were added to the stock deal to ensure that NCR's stockholders were protected in the event of a decline in AT&T's stock price. In either event the acquisition was to be treated as a tax-free purchase of stock.

AT&T's offer is unusual because it indicates that the firm had a strong preference for having the acquisition accounted for under the pooling-of-interests method. AT&T's managers argued that it was important for the firm to use pooling-of-interests accounting to avoid any goodwill amortization, which would hurt the firm's earnings and stock price. And certainly, goodwill amortization would have hurt earnings: pro forma estimates indicate that 1990 earnings per share for AT&T (including the earnings of NCR) would have been $2.42 under the pooling-of-interests method and only $1.97 under the purchase method. However, it is not so obvious that this earnings decline would have affected the stock price.

In summary, AT&T chose to finance NCR with a 100 percent stock offer, primarily to ensure that it could use pooling-of-interests accounting. Because this is a very conservative approach, the financing of the acquisition does not impose additional financial risks on AT&T's stockholders. However, AT&T's explanation of the offer should raise questions for analysts about whether the form of the offer really maximized value for AT&T's existing shareholders.

ACQUISITION OUTCOME

The final question of interest to the analyst evaluating a potential acquisition is whether it will indeed be completed. If an acquisition has a clear value-based motive, the target is priced appropriately, and its proposed financing does not create unnecessary financial risks for the acquirer, it may still fail because the target receives a higher competing bid or because of opposition from entrenched target management. Therefore, to evaluate the likelihood that an offer will be accepted, the financial analyst has to understand whether there are potential competing bidders who could pay an even higher premium to target stockholders than is currently offered. They also have to consider whether target management is entrenched and, to protect their jobs, likely to oppose an offer.

Other Potential Acquirers

If there are other potential bidders for a target, especially ones who place a higher value on the target, there is a strong possibility that the bidder in question will be unsuccessful. Target management and stockholders have an incentive to delay accepting the initial offer to give potential competitors time to also submit a bid. From the perspective of the initial bidder, this means that the offer could potentially reduce stockholder value by the cost of making the offer (including substantial investment banking and legal fees). In practice, a losing bidder can usually recoup these losses, and sometimes even make healthy profits from selling to the successful acquirer any shares it has accumulated in the target.

How can the financial analyst determine whether there are other potential acquirers for a target and how they value the target? There are several ways:

- Identify other firms that could also implement the initial bidder's acquisition strategy. For example, if this strategy relies on developing benefits from complementary assets, look for potential bidders who also have assets complementary to the target. If the goal of the acquisition is to replace inefficient management, what other firms in the target's industry could provide management expertise?
- Examine competitors of the acquirer. Could any of these firms provide an even better fit for the target?

Target Management Entrenchment

If target managers are entrenched and fearful for their jobs, it is likely that they will oppose a bidder's offer. Some firms have implemented "golden parachutes" for top managers to counteract their concerns about job security at the time of an offer. Golden parachutes provide top managers of a target firm with attractive compensation rewards should the firm get taken over. However, many firms do not have such schemes, and opposition to an offer from entrenched management is a very real possibility.

What indicators of entrenched management can financial analysts use in assessing the likely success of an acquisition? One indicator is the existence of a golden parachute plan for target management. A second indicator is the existence of takeover defenses for the target. Many such defenses were used during the turbulent 1980s, when mergers and acquisitions were at their peak. Some of the most widely adopted include poison pills, staggered boards, super-majority rules, dual-class recapitalizations, fair-price provisions, ESOP plans, and changes in firms' states of incorporation (to states with more restrictive anti-takeover laws)

While the existence of takeover defenses for a target indicates that its management is likely to fight a bidding firm's offer, defenses have typically not prevented an acquisition from taking place. Instead, they tend to cause delays, which increase the likelihood that there will be competing offers made for the target, including offers by friendly parties solicited by target management, called "white knights." Takeover defenses therefore increase the likelihood that the bidder in question will be outbid for the target, or that it will have to increase its offer significantly to win a bidding contest. Given these risks, some have argued that acquirers are now less likely to embark on a potentially hostile acquisition.

Analysis of Outcome of AT&T's Offer for NCR

AT&T had good reason to be concerned about the outcome of an offer for NCR. NCR had rejected AT&T's preliminary friendly offers made to the company before any public announcement, indicating that target management intended to oppose the offer and use whatever anti-takeover measures were at their disposal. NCR followed up this opposition by creating a qualified ESOP and announcing a special dividend of $1 and a $.02 per share regular dividend increase, all intended to prohibit AT&T from using pooling of interests to account for the acquisition. NCR's opposition certainly increased the likelihood that either AT&T would overpay for NCR, or that it would be forced to drop its offer. No competing offers for NCR emerged, probably because the high price offered by AT&T scared off any competitors. The acquisition was finally completed on September 19, 1991, ten months after AT&T's initial offer.

SUMMARY AND CONCLUSIONS

This chapter summarizes how financial statement data and analysis can be used by financial analysts interested in evaluating whether an acquisition creates value for an acquiring firm's stockholders. Obviously, much of this discussion is also likely to be relevant to other merger participants, including target and acquiring management and their investment banks.

For the external analyst, the first task is to identify the acquirer's acquisition strategy. We discuss a number of strategies. Some of these are consistent with maximizing acquirer value, including acquisitions to: take advantage of economies of scale; improve target management; combine complementary resources; capture tax benefits; provide low-cost financing to financially constrained targets; and increase product-market rents.

However, other strategies appear to benefit managers more than stockholders. For example, some unprofitable acquisitions are made because managers are reluctant to return free cash flows to shareholders, or because managers want to lower the firm's earnings volatility by diversifying into unrelated businesses.

The financial analyst's second task is to assess whether the acquirer is offering a reasonable price for the target. Even if the acquirer's strategy is based on increasing shareholder value, it can overpay for the target. Target stockholders will then be well rewarded but at the expense of acquiring stockholders. We show how the ratio, pro forma, and valuation techniques discussed earlier in the book can all be used to assess the worth of the target to the acquirer.

The method of financing an offer is also relevant to a financial analyst's review of an acquisition proposal. If a proposed acquisition is financed with surplus cash or new debt, it increases the acquirer's financial risk. Financial analysts can use ratio analysis of the acquirer's post-acquisition balance sheet and pro forma estimates of cash flow volatility and interest coverage to assess whether demands by target stockholders for consideration in cash lead the acquirer to increase its risk of financial distress.

Finally, the financial analyst is interested in assessing whether a merger is likely to be completed once the initial offer is made, and at what price. This requires the analyst to determine whether there are other potential bidders, and whether target management is entrenched and likely to oppose a bidder's offer.

DISCUSSION QUESTIONS

1. It is 1992, and Mary Saxon, a U.K. investment banker, is advising a local client on a potential foreign acquisition in the U.S. Currently, there is a competing cash bid for the target by a U.S. competitor. However, Saxon argues that the target should be worth more to the U.K. client than to the U.S. competitor, since U.K. accounting rules permit the considerable goodwill from the transaction to be written off against owners' equity, thus avoiding any ongoing charges against income. In contrast, U.S. rules require goodwill to be written off over 40 years or less. What would you recommend to the U.K. bidder?

2. During the early 1990s there was a noticeable increase in mergers and acquisitions between firms in different countries (termed cross-border acquisitions). What factors could explain this increase? What special issues can arise in executing a cross-border acquisition and in ultimately meeting your objectives for a successful combination?

3. In the 1980s leveraged buyouts (LBOs) were a popular form of acquisition. Under a leveraged buyout, a buyout group (which frequently includes target management)

makes an offer to buy the target firm at a premium over its current price. The buyout group finances much of the acquisition with debt capital, leading the target to become a highly leveraged private company following the acquisition.

   a. What types of firms would make ideal candidates for LBOs? Why?

   b. How might the acquirer add sufficient value to the target to justify a high buyout premium?

4. Kim Silverman, CFO of the First Public Bank Company, notes: "We are fortunate to have a cost of capital of only 10 percent. We want to leverage this advantage by acquiring other banks that have a higher cost of funds. I believe that we can add significant value to these banks by using our lower cost financing." Do you agree with Silverman's analysis? Why or why not?

5. The Boston Tea Company plans to acquire Hi Flavor Soda Co. for $60 per share, a 50 percent premium over current market price. John E. Grey, the CFO of Boston Tea, argues that this valuation can easily be justified, using a price-earnings analysis. "Boston Tea has a price-earnings ratio of 15, and we expect that we will be able to generate long-term earnings for Hi Flavor Soda of $5 per share. This implies that Hi Flavor is worth $75 to us, well below our $60 offer price." Do you agree with this analysis? What are Grey's key assumptions?

6. You have been hired by GS Investment Bank to work in the merger department. The analysis required for all potential acquisitions includes an examination of the target for any off-balance-sheet assets or liabilities that have to be factored into the valuation. Prepare a checklist for your examination.

7. Company T is currently valued at $50 in the market. A potential acquirer, A, believes that it can add value in two ways: $15 of value can be added through better working capital management, and an additional $10 of value can be generated by making available a unique technology to expand T's new product offerings. In a competitive bidding contest, how much of this additional value will A have to pay out to T's shareholders to emerge as the winner?

8. In 1995 Disney acquired ABC television at a significant premium. Disney's management justified much of this premium by arguing that the acquisition would guarantee access for Disney's programs on ABC's television stations. Evaluate the economic merits of this claim.

9. A leading oil exploration company decides to acquire an electronics company at a 50 percent premium. The acquirer argues that this move creates value for its own stockholders because it can use its excess cash flows from the oil business to help finance growth in the new electronics segment. Evaluate the economic merits of this claim.

10. a. How would the following ratios differ for a company that used the purchase method to account for an acquisition versus the pooling-of-interests method in the year following the acquisition?
  - Return on sales
  - Return on assets
  - Asset turnover

b. Two years after the acquisition, the company decides that it was a failure and sells the target at a price substantially below its original price but above the original book value. What effect will this transaction have on the earnings of the acquirer in the two cases (purchase versus pooling)?

CASE

Schneider and Square D

NOTES

1. Much of our discussion is based on analysis of the acquisition presented by Thomas Lys and Linda Vincent in "An Analysis of the Value Destruction in AT&T's Acquisition of NCR," *Journal of Financial Economics,* forthcoming.

2. Of course, another possibility is for the profitable firm to acquire the unprofitable one. However, in the U.S., the IRS will disallow the use of tax loss carryforwards by an acquirer if it appears that an acquisition was tax-motivated.

3. See Paul Healy, Krishna Palepu, and Richard Ruback, "Which Mergers Are Profitable—Strategic or Financial?," unpublished working paper, 1992, MIT Sloan School of Management and Harvard Business School.

chapter 11

Corporate Financing Policies

In this chapter, we discuss how firms set their capital structure and dividend policies to maximize shareholder value. There is a strong relation between these two decisions. For example, a firm's decision to retain internally-generated funds rather than paying them out as a dividend can also be thought of as a financing decision. It is not surprising, therefore, to find that many of the factors that are important in setting capital structure (such as taxes, costs of financial distress, agency costs, and information costs) are also relevant for dividend policy decisions. In the following sections we discuss these factors, how they affect capital structure and dividend policy, as well as how the financial analysis tools, discussed in Part 2 of this book, can be used to evaluate capital structure and dividend policy decisions.

A variety of questions are dealt with in analysis of corporate financing policies:

- Securities analysts can ask: Given its capital structure and dividend policy, how should we position a firm in our fund—as a growth or income stock?
- Takeover specialists can ask: Can we improve stockholder value for a firm by changing its financial leverage or by increasing dividend payouts to owners?"
- Management can ask: Have we selected a capital structure and dividend policy which supports our business objectives?
- Credit analysts can ask: What risks do we face in lending to this company, given its business and current financial leverage?

Throughout our discussion, we take the perspective of an external analyst who is evaluating whether a firm has selected a capital structure and dividend policy that maximize shareholder value. However, our discussion obviously also applies to management's decisions about what debt and dividend policies it should implement.

FACTORS THAT DETERMINE FIRMS' DEBT POLICIES

When financial analysts evaluate a firm's capital structure, two related questions typically emerge. First, in the long term, what is the best mix of debt and equity for creating stockholder value? And second, if managers are considering new investment initiatives in the short-term, what type of financing should they use? Two popular models of capital structure provide help in thinking about these questions. The static model of capital structure examines how trade-offs between the benefits and costs of debt determine a firm's long-term optimal mix of debt and equity. And the dynamic model examines how information effects can lead a firm to deviate from its long-term optimal capital structure as it seeks financing for new investments. We discuss both models, since they have somewhat different implications for thinking about capital structure.

To show how financial analysis can be used to help managers make capital structure decisions, we examine financial leverage for Compaq Computer, the company we have discussed throughout these chapters. Throughout the section we discuss factors that are relevant to Compaq's optimal long-term mix of debt and equity and its financing of new capital projects. As you can see from the table below, Compaq has a very conservative capital structure. Its cash and marketable securities actually outweigh interest-bearing debt, so that reported financial leverage is negative. This low leverage is somewhat offset by modest off-balance-sheet liabilities for noncancelable operating leases, factored receivables, and guarantees on finance company loans to the company's resellers. It is difficult to quantify the effects of these liabilities on Compaq's leverage.

THE OPTIMAL LONG-TERM MIX OF DEBT AND EQUITY

To determine the best long-term mix of debt and equity capital for a firm, we need to consider the benefits and costs of financial leverage. By trading off these benefits and costs, we can decide whether a firm should be financed mostly with equity or mostly with debt.

TABLE 11-1 Net Interest-Bearing Debt and Equity for Compaq Computer for the Years Ended December 31, 1991 and 1992

	1992	1991
Interest-bearing debt	0	73,456
Less: cash and short-term investments	356,747	452,174
Net debt	(356,747)	(378,718)
Book stockholders' equity	2,006,691	1,930,704
Net interest-bearing debt to book equity	(18%)	(20%)

Benefits of Leverage

The major benefits of financial leverage typically include corporate tax shields on interest and improved incentives for management.

CORPORATE INTEREST TAX SHIELDS.   In the U.S., and in many other countries for that matter, tax laws provide a form of government subsidy for debt financing which does not exist for equity financing. This arises from the corporate tax deductibility of interest against income. No such corporate tax shield is available for dividend payments or for retained earnings. Debt financing therefore has an advantage over equity, since the interest tax shields under debt provide additional income to debt- and equity-holders. This higher income translates directly into higher firm values for leveraged firms in relation to unleveraged firms.

Some practitioners and theorists have pointed out that the corporate tax benefit from debt financing is potentially offset by a personal tax disadvantage of debt. That is, since the holders of debt must pay relatively high tax rates on interest income, they require that corporations offer high pre-tax yields on debt. This disadvantage is particularly severe when interest income is taxed at a higher rate than capital gains on equity. However, under current U.S. tax laws, personal tax rates on interest income and capital gains are identical, implying that personal tax effects are unlikely to eliminate the corporate tax benefits of debt.

Therefore, the corporate tax benefits from debt financing should encourage firms with high effective tax rates and few forms of tax shield other than interest to have highly-leveraged capital structures. In contrast, firms that have tax shield substitutes for interest, such as depreciation, or that have operating loss carryforwards and hence do not expect to pay taxes, should have capital structures that are largely equity.

What tax benefits is Compaq forgoing? In evaluating Compaq's financial leverage, analysts would probably want to know how much the firm could save in taxes if management modified its current policy of zero debt. To evaluate the tax effects of additional debt, analysts can use accounting, financial ratio, and prospective analysis to answer the following types of questions:

- What is Compaq's average income tax rate? How does this rate compare with the average tax rate and financial leverage for the firm's major competitors?
- What portion of Compaq's tax expense is deferred taxes versus current taxes?
- What is Compaq's marginal corporate tax rate likely to be?
- Does Compaq have tax loss carryforwards or other tax benefits? How long are they expected to continue?
- What non-interest tax shields are currently available to the firm? For example, are there sizable tax shields from accelerated depreciation?
- Based on pro forma income and cash flow statements, what are our estimates for Compaq's taxable income for the next five to ten years? What non-interest tax

shields are available to the firm? Finally, what would be the tax savings from using some debt financing?

Analysis of Compaq's tax footnote indicates that the firm's average current tax rate in 1992 is 21.4 percent. This rate is lower than the statutory rate of 34 percent because the firm's Singapore operations receive a tax holiday, expected to continue through at least 1997. The firm has only a modest depreciation tax shield, since depreciable assets are a relatively small percentage of total assets. And as we discussed in Chapter 5, Compaq is likely to continue generating impressive taxable income in the foreseeable future. Thus, it certainly appears that the firm could reduce its tax burden and create additional value for stockholders by adding some debt to its capital structure.

MANAGEMENT INCENTIVES FOR VALUE CREATION.   A second benefit of debt financing is that it focuses management on value creation, thus reducing conflicts of interests between managers and shareholders. Conflicts of interest can arise when managers make investments that are of little value to stockholders and/or spend the firm's funds on perks, such as overly spacious office buildings and lavish corporate jets. Firms are particularly prone to these temptations when they are flush with cash but have few promising new investment opportunities, often referred to as a "free cash flow" situation. These firms' stockholders would generally prefer that their managers pay out any free cash flows as dividends or use the funds to repurchase stock. However, these options reduce the size of the firm and the assets under management's control. Management may therefore invest the free cash flows in new projects, even if they are not valued by stockholders, or spend the cash flows on management perks.

How can debt help reduce management's incentives to over-invest and to overspend on perks? The primary way is by reducing resources available to fund these types of outlays, since firms with relatively high leverage face pressures to generate cash flows to meet payments of interest and principal.

Could Compaq benefit from using debt to improve management focus? Compaq's lack of debt may increase opportunities for managers to spend free cash flows on perks or to invest in projects that are not valued by stockholders. Financial ratio and prospective analysis can help analysts assess whether there are currently free cash flow inefficiencies at Compaq as well as risks of future inefficiencies. Symptoms of excessive management perks and investment in unprofitable projects include the following:

- *Does Compaq have high ratios of general and administrative expenses and overhead to sales?* If its ratios are higher than those for its major competitors, one possibility is that management is wasting money on perks.
- *Is Compaq making significant new investments in unrelated areas?* If it is difficult to rationalize new investments, Compaq might have a free cash flow problem.
- *Does Compaq have high levels of expected operating cash flows (net of essential capital expenditures and debt retirements) from pro forma income and cash flow statements?*

- *Does Compaq have poor management incentives to create additional shareholder value,* evidenced by a weak linkage between management compensation and firm performance?

Currently Compaq does not appear to have any problems with inefficient investment of free cash flows. It operates in a highly competitive industry which has gone through a difficult few years, it has remained very focused and invested only in related businesses, and its selling, general and administrative expenses are only 17 percent of sales in 1992, down from 22 percent in 1991. Further, management indicates that it plans to keep a tight rein on administrative expenses as part of the firm's new strategy. Thus, there currently appears to be little value in using debt to improve management focus.

However, as shown in Chapter 5's prospective analysis of Compaq, if the firm's new strategy pays off, its cash flows will mushroom. Analysts have some concerns that, if this occurs, the firm might waste these resources on acquisitions instead of paying them out to stockholders. One way for management to ensure that it does not end up making unprofitable future investments with free cash flows is to increase leverage in 1993.

Costs of Leverage: Financial Distress

As a firm increases its leverage, it increases the likelihood of financial distress, where it is unable to meet interest or principal repayment obligations to creditors. This may force the firm to declare bankruptcy or to agree to restructure its financial claims.

Financial distress can be expensive, since restructurings of a firm's ownership claims typically involve costly legal negotiations. It can also be difficult for distressed firms to raise capital to undertake profitable new investment opportunities. Finally, financial distress can intensify conflicts of interest between stockholders and the firm's debtholders, increasing the cost of debt financing.

LEGAL COSTS OF FINANCIAL DISTRESS.   When a firm is in serious financial distress, its owners' claims are likely to be restructured. This can take place under formal bankruptcy proceedings or out of bankruptcy. Restructurings are likely to be costly, since the parties involved have to hire lawyers, bankers, and accountants to represent their interests, and they have to pay court costs if there are formal legal proceedings. These are often called the *direct* costs of financial distress.

COSTS OF FORGONE INVESTMENT OPPORTUNITIES.   When a firm is in financial distress and particularly when it is in bankruptcy, it may be very difficult for it to raise additional capital for new investments, even though they may be profitable for all the firm's owners. In some cases, bankrupt firms are run by court-appointed trustees, who are unlikely to take on risky new investments—profitable or not. Even for a firm whose management supports new investment, the firm is likely to be capital constrained. Creditors are unlikely to approve the sale of nonessential assets unless the proceeds are used to first repay their claims. Potential new investors and creditors will be wary of the firm because they do not want to become embroiled in the legal disputes themselves. Thus, in all likelihood the firm will be unable to make significant new investments, potentially diminishing its value.

COSTS OF CONFLICTS BETWEEN CREDITORS AND STOCKHOLDERS. When a firm is performing well, both creditors' and stockholders' interests are likely to coincide. Both want the firm's managers to take all investments which increase the value of the firm. However, when the firm is in financial difficulty, conflicts can arise between different classes of owners. Creditors become concerned about whether the firm will be able to meet its interest and principal commitments. Shareholders become concerned that their equity will revert to the creditors if the firm is unable to meet its outstanding obligations. Thus, managers are likely to face increased pressure to make decisions which serve the interests of only one form of owner, typically stockholders, rather than making decisions in the best interests of all owners. For example, managers have incentives to issue additional debt with equal or higher priority, to invest in riskier assets, or to pay liquidating dividends, since these actions reduce the value of outstanding creditors' claims and benefit stockholders. When it is costly to completely eliminate this type of game playing, creditors will simply reduce the amount they are willing to pay the firm for the debt when it is issued, increasing the costs of borrowing for the firm's stockholders.

OVERALL EFFECTS OF FINANCIAL DISTRESS. The costs of financial distress discussed above offset the tax and monitoring benefits of debt. As a result, firms that are more likely to fall into financial distress or for which the costs of financial distress are especially high should have relatively low financial leverage. Firms are more likely to fall into financial distress if they have high business risks, that is, if their revenues and earnings before interest are highly sensitive to fluctuations in the economy. Financial distress costs are also likely to be relatively high for firms whose assets are easily destroyed in financial distress. For example, firms with human capital and brand intangibles are particularly sensitive to financial distress since dissatisfied employees and customers can leave or seek alternative suppliers. In contrast, firms with tangible assets can sell their assets if they get into financial distress, providing additional security for lenders and lowering the costs of financial distress. Firms with intangible assets are therefore less likely to be highly leveraged than firms whose assets are mostly tangible.

FINANCIAL DISTRESS COSTS FOR COMPAQ. As the above discussion implies, Compaq's optimal financial leverage will depend on its underlying business risks and asset types. If the firm's business risks are relatively high or its assets can be easily destroyed by financial distress, changing the mix of debt and equity toward more debt may actually destroy shareholder value. Analysts can use ratio, cash flow, and pro forma analysis to assess Compaq's business risks and whether its assets are easily destroyed by financial distress. Their analysis should focus on:

- *Comparing indicators of business risk for Compaq and other firms in the computer industry with the economy.* Popular indicators of business risk include the ratio of fixed operating expenses (such as depreciation on plant and equipment) to sales, the volatility of return on assets, as well as the relation between indicators of Compaq's performance and indicators of performance for the economy as a whole.
- *Examining the competitive nature of the industry.* Since Compaq is in a highly competitive industry, its performance is very sensitive to changes in strategy by its competitors.
- *Determining whether the firm's assets are largely intangible and therefore sensitive to financial distress,* using such ratios as market to book equity.

Although Compaq is not highly capital intensive, it does face significant business risk because of the high degree of competition in the industry. There is intense pressure in the personal computer industry to develop more powerful machines and to lower prices. Thus, Compaq's business risks arise from shocks to the industry from introductions of new technology and price wars. To compound these risks, many of Compaq's research and development assets are human ones that can leave if the firm gets into financial difficulty. Therefore, for Compaq the risks of financial distress are relatively high.

Determining the Long-Term Optimal Mix of Debt and Equity

The above discussion implies that the optimal mix of debt and equity for a firm can be estimated by trading off the corporate interest tax shield and monitoring benefits of debt against the costs of financial distress. As the firm becomes more highly leveraged, the costs of leverage presumably begin to outweigh the tax and monitoring benefits of debt.

However, there are several practical difficulties in trying to estimate a firm's optimal financial leverage. One difficulty is quantifying some of the costs and benefits of leverage. For example, it is not easy to value the expected costs of financial distress or any management incentive benefits from debt. There are no easy answers to this problem. The best that we can do is to qualitatively assess whether the firm faces free cash flow problems, and whether it faces high business risks and has assets that are easily destroyed by financial distress. These qualitative assessments can then be used to adjust the more easily quantified tax benefits from debt to determine whether the firm's financial leverage should be relatively high, low, or somewhere in between.

A second practical difficulty in deciding whether a firm should have high, low, or medium financial leverage is quantifying what we mean by high, low, and medium. One way to resolve this question is to use indicators of financial leverage, such as debt-to-equity ratios, for the market as a whole as a guide on leverage ranges. To provide a rough sense of what companies usually consider to be high, medium, and low financial leverage, Figures 11-1 and 11-2 show ranges of debt-to-market-equity and debt-to-book-equity ratios for public firms in the period 1984 to 1993 for a variety of countries.

FIGURE 11-1 Ratio of Net Interest-Bearing Debt to Market Equity from 1984 to 1993 for the 25th, 50th, and 75th Percentiles of Public Firms by Country

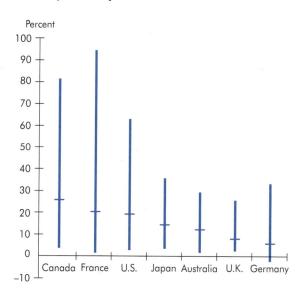

FIGURE 11-2 Ratio of Net Interest-Bearing Debt to Book Equity from 1984 to 1993 for the 25th, 50th, and 75th Percentiles of Public Firms by Country

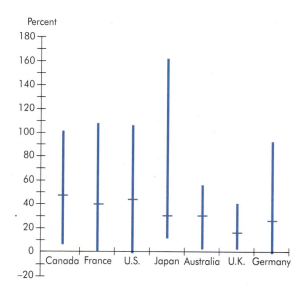

For U.S. firms, the median net interest-bearing debt-to-market-equity ratio from 1984 to 1993 is 19 percent. In contrast, the firm at the 25th percentile has zero net debt and the firm at the 75th percentile has a 63 percent ratio. Debt-to-book-equity ratios for U.S. firms are −6 percent for the firm at the 25th percentile, 44 percent for the median firm, and 106 percent for the firm at the 75th percentile.[1] It is interesting to note that for all the countries reported, more than 25 percent of the public firms have almost no net debt. In addition, firms in the U.S., Canada, and France appear to have systematically higher debt-to-equity ratios than firms in the U.K., Germany, and Australia.[2] However, some of these comparisons should not be taken too literally, since accounting practices vary considerably by country. For example, until relatively recently, reports for Japanese, German, and French companies were frequently unconsolidated, potentially understating their reported leverage.

THE OPTIMAL MIX OF DEBT AND EQUITY FOR COMPAQ.   Like other firms in its industry, Compaq's capital structure is currently quite conservative.[3] As we discussed above, Compaq could generate significant tax benefits from changing this policy and increasing financial leverage. However, given the current competitive situation in the industry, this would come at a cost—it would increase the likelihood of financial distress.

The personal computer industry is one of the most competitive in the U.S. By using equity financing, Compaq has ensured that it has "breathing room" to respond to any new technological or pricing challenges. This flexibility helped the firm to weather the financial problems faced in 1991. It also provides an important way for the firm to buttress itself against potential future problems as it embarks on its aggressive new strategy to cut prices and squeeze operating costs.

If Compaq's new strategy is successful, its cash position is likely to be impressive. Analysts raise concerns about whether the firm will use these free cash flows to make unprofitable acquisitions. One way for management to answer these concerns is to increase leverage, thereby reducing incentives to waste free cash flows on unprofitable acquisitions and investments.

THE FINANCING OF NEW PROJECTS

The second model of capital structure focuses on how firms make new financing decisions. Proponents of this dynamic model argue that there can be short-term frictions in capital markets which cause deviations from long-run optimal capital structure. One source of friction arises when managers have better information about their firm's future performance than outside investors. This could lead managers to deviate from their long-term optimal capital structure as they seek financing for new investments.

To see how information asymmetries between outside investors and management can create market imperfections and potentially affect short-term capital structure decisions, consider management's options for financing a proprietary new project that it expects to be profitable. One financing option is to use retained earnings to cover the investment outlay. However, what if the firm has no retained earnings available today? If it pays dividends, it could perhaps cut dividends to help pay for the project. But as we discuss later, investors usually interpret a dividend cut as an indication that the firm's management anticipates poor future performance. A dividend cut is therefore likely to lead to a stock price decline, albeit temporary, which management would probably prefer to avoid. Also, many firms do not pay dividends.

A second financing option is to borrow additional funds to finance the project. However, if the firm is already highly leveraged, the tax shield benefits from debt are likely to be relatively modest and the potential costs of financial distress relatively high, making additional borrowing unattractive.

The final financing option available to the firm is to issue new equity. However, if investors know that management has superior information on the firm's value, they are likely to interpret an equity offer as an indication that management believes that the firm's stock price is higher than the intrinsic value of the firm. The announcement of an equity offer is therefore likely to lead to a drop in the price of the firm's stock, raising the firm's cost of capital, and potentially leading management to abandon a perfectly good project.

The above discussion implies that if the firm has internal cash flows available or is not already highly-leveraged, it is relatively straightforward for it to arrange financing for the new project. Otherwise, management has to decide whether it is worthwhile undertaking the new project, given the costs of cutting dividends, issuing additional debt, or issuing equity to finance the project. The information costs of raising funds through these means lead managers to have a "pecking order" for new financing. Managers first use internal cash to fund investments, and only if this is unavailable do they resort to external financing. Further, if they have to use external financing, managers first use debt financing. New equity issues are used only as a last resort because of the difficulties that investors have in interpreting these issues.[4]

One way for management to mitigate the information problems of using external financing is to ensure that the firm has financial slack. Management can create financial slack by reinvesting free cash flows in marketable securities, so that it doesn't have to go to the capital market to finance a new project. It could also choose to have relatively low levels of debt, so that the firm can borrow easily in the future.

In summary, information asymmetries between managers and external investors can make managers reluctant to raise new equity to finance new projects. Managers' reluctance arises from their fear that investors will interpret the decision as an indication that the firm's stock is overvalued. In the short-term, this effect can lead managers to deviate from the firm's long-term optimal mix of debt and equity.

Compaq's Options for Raising Financing for New Investments

The above discussion implies that in the short-term Compaq should attempt to finance new projects primarily with retained earnings. Further, it suggests that the firm would be well advised to maintain financial slack to ensure that it is not forced to use costly external financing. To assess Compaq's financing options, we would ask the following types of questions:

- What is the value of current cash reserves (not required for day-to-day working capital needs) that could be used for new capital outlays? What operating cash resources are expected to become available in the coming few years? Do these internal resources cover Compaq's expected cash needs for new investment and working capital associated with its new operating strategy?
- How do Compaq's future cash needs for investment change as its operating performance deteriorates or improves? Are its investment opportunities relatively fixed, or are they related to current operating cash flow performance? Investment opportunities for many firms decline during a recession and increase during booms, enabling them to consistently use internal funds for financing. However, firms with stable investment needs should build financial slack during booms so that they can support investment during busts.
- If internal funds are not readily available, what opportunities does Compaq have to raise low-cost debt financing? Normally, a firm which has virtually zero debt could do this without difficulty. However, if it is in a volatile industry or has mostly intangible assets, debt financing may be costly.

- If Compaq has to raise costly equity capital, are there ways to focus investors on the value of the firm's assets and investment opportunities to lower any information asymmetries between managers and investors? For example, management might be able to disclose additional information about the uses and expected returns from the new funds.

Compaq's long-term optimal mix of debt and equity should continue to be mostly equity. Given its expected continued growth in operating cash flows, the need for external financing is likely to be minimal in the foreseeable future. Further, if the firm does face a future short-term cash shortfall—perhaps because of difficulties in implementing its new business strategy or the financing of new growth—it could easily raise additional low-cost debt. In 1993, Compaq actually registered $300 million of debt and negotiated a $300 million line of credit to provide for additional working capital needs associated with its growth.

Summary of Debt Policy

There are no easy ways to quantify the best mix of debt and equity for a firm and its best financing options. However, some general principles are likely to be useful in thinking about these questions. We have seen that the benefits from debt financing are likely to be highest for firms with:

high marginal tax rates and few non-interest tax shields, making interest tax shields from debt valuable;

high, stable income/cash flows and few new investment opportunities, increasing the monitoring value of debt and reducing the likelihood that the firm will fall into financial distress or require costly external financing for new projects; and

high tangible assets that are not easily destroyed by financial distress.

As we illustrated with Compaq, the financial analysis tools developed in Part 2 of the book are useful in rating a firm's interest tax shield benefits, its business risk and investment opportunities, and its major asset types. This information can then be used to judge whether there are benefits from debt or whether the firm would be better off using equity financing to support its business strategies.

FACTORS THAT DETERMINE FIRMS' DIVIDEND POLICIES

What factors should a firm consider when setting its dividend policy? Do investors prefer firms to pay out profits as dividends or to retain them for reinvestment? As we noted above, many of the factors that affect dividends are similar to those examined in the section on capital structure decisions. This should not be too surprising, since a firm's dividend policies also affect its financing decisions. Thus, dividends provide a means of reducing free cash flow inefficiencies. They also have tax implications for investors and can reduce a firm's financial slack. Finally, lending contracts can affect a firm's dividend payouts to protect lenders' interests.

Below we discuss the factors that are relevant to managers' dividend decisions and how financial analysis tools can be used in this decision process. To provide a context for our discussion, we again consider the case of Compaq Computer, using our financial analysis tools to discuss factors that are relevant to Compaq's dividend policy.

Dividends as a Way of Reducing Free Cash Flow Inefficiencies

As we discussed earlier, conflicts of interest between managers and shareholders can affect a firm's optimal capital structure; they also have implications for dividend policy decisions. Stockholders of a firm with free cash flows and few profitable investment opportunities want managers to adopt a dividend policy with high payouts. This will deter managers from growing the firm by reinvesting the free cash flows in new projects that are not valued by stockholders or from spending the free cash flows on management perks. In addition, if managers of a firm with free cash flows wish to fund a new project, most stockholders would prefer that they do so by raising new external capital rather than cutting dividends. Stockholders can then assess whether the project is genuinely profitable or simply one of management's pet projects.

Compaq's Use of Dividends for Improving Management Focus

Earlier we discussed how ratio and cash flow analysis can help Compaq's management assess whether the firm faces free cash flow inefficiencies, and how pro forma analysis can help indicate the likelihood of future free cash flow problems. The same analysis can help management to decide whether Compaq should initiate dividends. As of December 31, 1992, Compaq had never paid a dividend. By committing to pay dividends, management can reduce opportunities to overspend on perks or invest in projects that do not create value for stockholders.

Compaq does not currently appear to have a serious free cash flow problem, so that there is little benefit from using dividends as a way to improve management focus. However, if its new strategy pays off, management may want to consider initiating a dividend to maintain pressure to lower administrative and operating costs, and to reduce the risk of investing free cash flows in unrelated businesses.

Tax Costs of Dividends

What are the implications for dividend policy if dividends and capital gains are taxed, particularly at different rates? Classical models of the tax effects of dividends predict that if the capital gains tax rate is less than the rate on dividend income, investors will prefer that the firm either pay no dividends, so that they subsequently take gains as capital accumulation, or that the firm undertakes a stock repurchase, which qualifies as a capital distribution. Even if capital gains are slightly higher than dividend tax rates, investors are still likely to prefer capital gains to dividends, since they do not actually have to realize their capital gains. They can delay selling their shares and thereby defer paying the taxes on any capital appreciation. The longer investors wait before selling their stock, the lower the value of the capital gains tax. Only if capital gains tax rates are substantially higher than the rates on ordinary income are investors likely to favor dividend distributions over capital gains.

Today many practitioners and theorists believe that taxes play only a minor role in determining a firm's dividend policy, since a firm can attract investors with different tax preferences. Thus, a firm that wishes to pay high dividend rates will attract stockholders that are tax-exempt institutions, which do not pay taxes on dividend income. In contrast, a firm that prefers to pay low dividend rates will attract stockholders who have high marginal tax rates and prefer capital gains to dividend income.

Dividends Relative to Financial Slack

We discussed earlier how managers' information advantage over dispersed investors can increase a firm's cost of external funds. One way to avoid having to raise costly external funds is to have a conservative dividend policy which creates financial slack in the organization. By paying only a small percentage of income as dividends and reinvesting the free cash flows in marketable securities, management reduces the likelihood that the firm will have to go to the capital market to finance a new project.

Managers of firms with high intangible assets and growth opportunities are particularly likely to have an information advantage over dispersed investors, since accounting information for these types of firms is frequently a poor indicator of future performance. Accountants, for example, do not attempt to value R&D, intangibles, or growth opportunities. These types of firms are therefore more likely to face information problems and capital market constraints. To compound this problem, high-growth firms are typically heavily dependent on external financing, since they are not usually able to fund all new investments internally. Any capital market constraints are therefore likely to affect their ability to undertake profitable new projects.

Because paying dividends reduces financial slack and is thus costly, a firm's dividend policy can help management communicate effectively with external investors. Investors recognize that managers will only increase their firm's dividend rate if they anticipate that the payout does not have a serious effect on the firm's future financing options. Thus, the decision to increase dividends can help investors appreciate management's optimism about the firm's future performance and its ability to finance growth.

Compaq's Financial Slack Costs and Dividend Initiation

As we discussed earlier, financial analysis tools can help assess how much financial slack Compaq should maintain. If the firm's projected cash needs for new investments are stable in relation to operating cash flows, management might decide that it is important to build significant financial slack during boom periods to help fund investments during busts. Similarly, if the firm's opportunities to raise low-cost debt are limited because it is in a volatile industry or has mostly intangible assets, financial slack may be valuable. Management may then decide that the initiation of dividend payments will not benefit stockholders, since it increases the risk that the firm will have to raise high-cost external capital in the future, lower dividends, or even forgo a profitable new project.

In Compaq's case, the cash flow needs for working capital are significant, because of its current high sales growth. Management might then decide that it is in the shareholders' best interests to delay initiating dividend payments until the growth has stabilized. This strategy protects against the risk of competitors' introductions of new technology and price wars. However, once growth stabilizes in the longer term, Compaq is more likely to have sufficient financial slack, so that management will almost surely have to initiate dividends to avoid holding huge cash balances.

Lending Constraints and Dividend Policy

One of the concerns of a firm's creditors is that when the firm is in financial distress, managers will pay a large dividend to stockholders. This problem is likely to be particularly severe for a firm with highly liquid assets, since its managers can pay a large dividend without selling assets. To limit these types of games, managers agree to restrict dividend payments to stockholders. Such dividend covenants usually require the firm to maintain certain minimum levels of retained earnings and current asset balances, which effectively limit dividend payments when it is facing financial difficulties. However, these constraints on dividend policy are unlikely to be severe for a profitable firm. Since Compaq does not have any significant debt, this constraint is not relevant.

Practical Difficulties in Determining Optimal Dividend Payouts

One difficulty that arises in using the above factors to determine dividend policy is defining what we mean by high, low, and medium dividend payouts. To provide a rough sense of what companies usually consider to be high, medium, and low dividend payouts and yields, Figures 11-3 and 11-4 show ranges of these ratios for public firms in the period 1984 to 1993 for a variety of countries.

In the U.S., more than 25 percent of publicly-listed firms do not pay dividends. The median payout is 16 percent and the rate for the firm at the 75th percentile is 49 percent. Payout rates in Germany, Australia, U.K., Japan, Canada, and France are somewhat

FIGURE 11-3 Dividend Payout Ratio from 1984 to 1993 for the 25th, 50th, and 75th Percentiles of Public Firms by Country

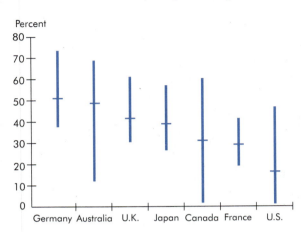

FIGURE 11-4 Dividend Yield from 1984 to 1993 for the 25th, 50th, and 75th Percentiles of Public Firms by Country

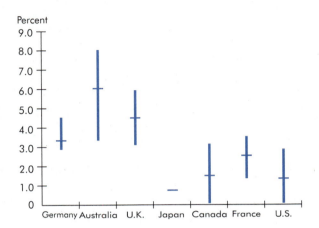

higher than in the U.S., with median firms paying out between 28 percent and 51 percent of profits. Dividend yields in the U.S. also tend to be somewhat lower than many other countries. The median dividend yield in the U.S. is about 1 percent, substantially lower than yields in Germany, Australia, the U.K., and France. It is interesting to see that dividend yields in Japan are less than 1 percent, with almost no variation between firms at the 75th and 25th percentiles.

Should Compaq Initiate Dividends?

Given its expected continued growth in operating cash flows for 1993 and 1994, Compaq should be able to afford to cover both moderate dividend payouts and new capital needs from internal funds. Further, the firm's conservative capital structure provides considerable financial slack in the event of a future short-term cash shortfall. Paying dividends also reduces the firm's free cash flows and thus maintains pressure on management to continue lowering operating and administrative costs.

If management is confident that the new business strategy will pay off, it might want to consider initiating a modest dividend as early as 1992. This could provide a strong optimistic signal to investors about the outcome of the strategy change. Otherwise, management might prefer to wait until the results of the strategy change become clearer.

In general, analysts predict that Compaq will not initiate dividends in the next few years. However, based on their forecasts of future growth, analysts presume that the firm will begin paying dividends within the coming five years. Otherwise, Compaq is likely either to have huge cash balances or to invest in unprofitable projects.

A Summary of Dividend Policy

Just as it is difficult to provide a simple formula to help management compute its optimal capital structure, it is difficult to formalize a firm's optimal dividend policy. However, we are able to identify several factors that appear to be important:

- High-growth firms should have low dividend payout ratios, and they should use their internally generated funds for reinvestment. This minimizes any costs from capital market constraints on financing growth options.
- Firms with high and stable operating cash flows and few investment opportunities should have high dividend payouts to reduce managers' incentives to reinvest free cash flows in unprofitable ventures.
- Firms should probably not worry too much about tax factors in setting dividend policy. Whatever their policy, they will be able to attract a clientele of investors. Firms that select high dividend payouts will attract tax-exempt institutions or corporations, and firms that pay low or no dividends will attract individuals in high tax brackets.
- Firms' financial covenants can have an impact on their dividend policy decisions. Firms will try to avoid being too close to their constraints in order to minimize the possibility of cutting their dividend.

SUMMARY AND CONCLUSIONS

This chapter examined how firms make optimal capital structure and dividend decisions. We show that a firm's optimal long-term capital structure is largely determined by its expected tax status, business risks, and types of assets. The benefits from debt financing are expected to be highest for firms with: high marginal tax rates and few non-interest tax shields, making interest tax shields valuable; high, stable income/cash flows and few new investment opportunities, increasing the monitoring value of debt and reducing the likelihood that the firm will fall into financial distress; and high tangible assets that are not easily destroyed by financial distress.

We also show that, in the short-term, managers can deviate from their long-term optimal capital structure when they seek financing for new investments. In particular, managers are reluctant to raise external financing, especially new equity, for fear that outside investors will interpret their action as meaning that the firm is overvalued. This information problem has implications for how much financial slack a firm is likely to need to avoid facing these types of information problems.

Optimal dividend policy is determined by many of the same factors—firms' business risks and their types of assets. Thus, dividend rates should be highest for firms with high and stable cash flows and few investment opportunities. By paying out relatively high dividends, these firms reduce the risk of managers investing free cash flows in unprofitable projects. Conversely, firms with low, volatile cash flows and attractive investment opportunities, such as start-up firms, should have relatively low dividend payouts. By reinvesting operating cash flows and reducing the amount of external financing required for new projects, these firms reduce their costs of financing.

Financial statement analysis can be used to better understand a firm's business risks, its expected tax status, and whether its assets are primarily assets in place or growth opportunities. Useful tools for assessing whether a firm's current capital structure and dividend policies maximize shareholder value include accounting analysis to determine off-balance-sheet liabilities, ratio analysis to help understand a firm's business risks, and cash flow and pro forma analysis to explore current and likely future investment needs.

DISCUSSION QUESTIONS

1. Financial analysts typically measure financial leverage as the ratio of debt to equity. However, there is less agreement on how to measure debt, or even equity. How would you treat the following items in computing this ratio? Justify your answers.
   - Revolving credit agreement with bank
   - Cash and marketable securities
   - Deferred tax liabilities
   - Preferred stock
   - Convertible debt

2. Until 1987 Master Limited Partnerships (MLPs) were treated as partnerships for tax purposes. This meant that no corporate taxes were paid by the entity. Instead, taxes were paid by partners (at their individual tax rates) on entity profits (both distributed and undistributed). The marginal tax rate for corporations in 1987 was 34 percent, compared to 33 percent for individuals in the highest tax bracket.

   a. If an entity distributes all after-tax earnings as dividends and generates before-tax earnings of $10 million, what would be the distribution to owners (after entity and personal taxes) if it is organized as (1) a corporation and (2) an MLP?

   b. What would be the optimal capital structure for the MLP discussed in (a)? Justify your answer.

   c. What types of dividend policy do you expect the MLP to follow? Why?

3. Finance theory implies that the debt-to-equity ratio should be computed using the market values of debt and equity. However, most financial analysts use book values of debt and equity to compute a firm's financial leverage. What are the limitations of using book values rather than market values for comparing leverage across industries or firms? For what types of industries/firms are book values likely to be most misleading?

4. One important driver of a firm's capital structure and dividend policy decisions is its business risk. What ratios would you look at to assess business risk? Name two industries with very high business risk and two industries with very low business risk.

5. As discussed in the chapter, U.S. public companies with "low" leverage have an interest-bearing net debt-to-equity ratio of 0 percent or less, firms with "medium" leverage have a ratio between 1 and 62 percent, and "high" leverage firms have a ratio of 63 percent or more. Given these data, how would you classify the following firms in terms of their optimal debt-to-equity ratio (high, medium, or low)?
   - a successful pharmaceutical company
   - an electric utility
   - a manufacturer of consumer durables
   - a commercial bank
   - a start-up software company

6. A rapidly growing Internet company, recently listed on NASDAQ, needs to raise additional capital to finance new research and development. What financing options are available, and what are the trade-offs between each?

7. The following table reports (in millions) earnings, dividends, capital expenditures, and R&D for Intel for the period 1990–95:

Year	Net Income	Dividends	Capital Expenditures	R&D
1990	$650	$0	$680	$517
1991	819	0	948	618
1992	1,067	43	1,228	780
1993	2,295	88	1,933	970
1994	2,288	100	2,441	1,111
1995	3,566	133	3,550	1,296

What are the dividend payout rates for Intel during these years? Is this payout policy consistent with the factors expected to drive dividend policy, as discussed in the chapter? What factors do you expect would lead Intel's management to increase its dividend payout? How do you expect the stock market to react to such a decision?

8. As discussed in the chapter, U.S. public companies with "low" dividend payouts have payout ratios of 0 percent or less, firms with "medium" payouts have ratios between 1 and 48 percent, and "high" payout firms have a ratio of 49 percent or more. Given these data, how would you classify the following firms in terms of their optimal payout policy (high, medium, or low)?
   - a successful pharmaceutical company
   - an electric utility
   - a manufacturer of consumer durables
   - a commercial bank
   - a start-up software company

9. It is frequently argued that Japanese and German companies can afford to have more financial leverage and to follow lower dividend payout policies than U.S. companies because they are largely owned by financial institutions that have long-

term horizons. Does this argument make economic sense? If so, explain why, and if not, why not. What other factors might explain differences in capital structure and dividend policy across countries.

10. In 1990 U.S. tax law increased capital gains rates from 20 percent to the same level as ordinary income rates, between 28 and 34 percent. What implications does this change have for corporate dividend policy and capital structure?

CASE

The Murray Ohio Manufacturing Co.

NOTES

1. Firms can have a negative ratio, since the denominator is net debt, that is, interest-bearing debt less cash and marketable securities. A negative ratio for a firm indicates that its cash holdings exceed debt.

2. Japanese firms appear to be relatively highly leveraged when leverage is measured using debt to book equity, but only modestly leveraged using debt to market equity.

3. Apple also has no debt, and both Dell and AST have debt-to-long-term-capital ratios of about 25%.

4. These issues are discussed by Stewart Myers and Nicholas Majluf in "Corporate Financing and Investment Decisions When Firms Have Information That Investors Do Not Have," *Journal of Financial Economics* (June 1984): 187–221.

chapter 12

Management Communications

M anagement communication is increasingly important as firms invest in complex product and production technologies and in intangible assets such as research and development. These outlays can be quite difficult for outsiders to value, since they do not have access to the same data as management. As we discuss in this chapter, financial reports provide a low-cost way for management to communicate with investors. However, financial reports are not always effective as a communication vehicle. We therefore examine how alternative forms of communication can be used by management to mitigate information problems with external investors.

Several questions can be addressed by analyzing management's communication strategy:

- Management can ask: Is our current communication strategy effective in helping investors understand the firm's business strategy and expected future performance, thereby ensuring that our stock price is not seriously over- or undervalued?
- Securities analysts can ask: Do management's communications provide us with credible information that is useful for forecasting a firm's future performance? What types of information can we reasonably expect management to provide us? And how should we interpret information provided by management?

Throughout this book we have focussed primarily on showing how financial statement data can be helpful for *analysts* and *outside investors* in making a variety of decisions. In this chapter we change our emphasis and focus primarily on *management's* use of financial analysis to help communicate effectively with external users. However, as we note above, analysis of management's communication strategy is also likely to be useful to securities analysts.

To illustrate how managers can use financial analysis to help set their communication strategy, we examine the communication issues facing Compaq Computer, the company we have discussed throughout this book. In 1992, Compaq's performance deteriorated significantly, and in response management changed the firm's operating strategy. As discussed below, this change raises several questions for Compaq's management as it communicates with outside investors.

COMMUNICATING WITH INVESTORS

Some managers argue that communication problems are not worth worrying about. They maintain that as long as managers make investment and operating decisions that enhance shareholder value, investors will value their performance and the firm's stock accordingly. While this is true in the long run, since all information is eventually public, it may not hold in the short or even medium term. If investors do not have access to the same information as management, they will probably find it difficult to value new and innovative investments. In an efficient capital market, they will not consistently over- or undervalue these new investments, but their valuations will tend to be noisy. This can make stock prices relatively noisy, leading management at various times to consider their firms to be either seriously over- or undervalued.

Does it matter if a firm's stock is over- or undervalued for a period? Most managers would prefer to not have their stock undervalued, since it makes it more costly to raise new financing. They may also worry that undervaluation is likely to increase the chance of a takeover by a hostile acquirer, with an accompanying reduction in their job security. Managers of firms that are overvalued may be concerned about the market's assessment, since they are legally liable for failing to disclose information relevant to investors. They may therefore not wish to see their stock seriously overvalued, even though overvaluation provides opportunities to issue new equity at favorable rates.

A Word of Caution

It is natural that many managers believe that firms are undervalued by the capital market. This frequently occurs because it is difficult for managers to be realistic about their company's future performance. After all, it is part of their job to sell the company to new employees, customers, suppliers, and investors. In addition, forecasting the firm's future performance objectively requires them to judge their own capabilities as managers. Thus, many managers may argue that investors are uninformed and that their firm is undervalued. Only some can back that up with solid evidence.

We recommend that before jumping to the conclusion that their firm is undervalued, managers should analyze their firm's performance and compare their own forecasts of future performance with those of analysts, using the following approach:

- *Is there a significant difference between internal management forecasts of future earnings and cash flows and those of outside analysts?*

- *Do any differences between managers' and analysts' forecasts arise because of different expectations about economy-wide performance?* Managers may understand their own businesses better than analysts, but they may not be any better at forecasting macroeconomic conditions.
- *Can managers identify any factors with the firm that might explain a difference between analysts' and managers' forecasts of future performance?* For example, are analysts unaware of positive new R&D results, do they have different information about customer responses to new products and marketing campaigns, etc.? These types of differences could indicate that the firm faces an information problem.

If management decides that the firm does face a genuine information problem, it can begin to consider whether and how this could be redressed. Is the problem potentially serious enough that it is worth doing something to alter investors' perceptions? Or is the problem likely to resolve itself within a short period? Does the firm have plans to raise new equity or to use equity to acquire another company? Is management's job security threatened? As we discuss below, there is a wide range of options for management in this situation.

Communication Issues for Compaq's Managers

As we discussed earlier, Compaq experienced deteriorating performance in 1991. In that year, the firm's sales declined by 9 percent, return on equity dropped to 7 percent (from 30 percent in 1990), and the stock price dropped from a high of $74.25 to a low of $22.13. As a result of this deterioration, the firm replaced its founding CEO and changed its business strategy to focus on increasing market share. This was to be accomplished by introducing new programs in pricing, product development, distribution and marketing, and service support.

Having decided to make management and strategy changes, Compaq's management faced several communication questions. One approach was to make no major effort to communicate the new plans to external investors, letting subsequent earnings and cash flow improvements speak for themselves. A second approach was to publicize the change in strategy, discuss the logic that underlay the decision—perhaps projecting how it would affect the firm's future earnings performance—and even implement financial policy changes to indicate that management was optimistic about the firm's future performance. Both approaches have pluses and minuses. By publicizing a strategy change, Compaq's management would be alerting the firm's competitors to the change, potentially increasing the likelihood of retaliation. However, this approach also reduces the risk that investors will misvalue Compaq, since they will have access to some of the same information as management about the firm's future prospects.

In making their decision about how to communicate the strategy change, management would want to consider the following questions:

- *What competitive retaliation is likely if Compaq provides a clear signal that management is optimistic about the firm's strategy change? How does this affect the value of the strategy?*
- *Do investors seriously undervalue the firm, given its new strategy?* This requires management to estimate pro forma earnings or cash flows for Compaq under the new strategy and then to use these projections to model the value of the firm's stock.
- *Is Compaq's strategy dependent on new financing? If so, can the firm raise new capital from low-cost debt, or will it be forced to raise new equity just when the market undervalues its stock?*

If Compaq's managers decide to follow a proactive communication strategy to explain the firm's new operating strategy to investors and analysts, they have several options. They can use the firm's financial reports to attempt to show that the long-term future is strong. Alternatively, they can use non-accounting forms of communication, such as increased disclosure of non-accounting data or the selection of financial policies that signal optimism to investors.

COMMUNICATION THROUGH FINANCIAL REPORTING

Financial reports are the least costly and the most popular format for management communication. Below we discuss the role of financial reporting as a means of investor communication, the institutions that make accounting information credible, and when it is likely to be ineffective.

Accounting as a Means of Management Communication

As we discussed in Chapter 3, financial reports are an important medium for management communication with external investors. Reports provide investors with an explanation of how their money has been invested, a summary of the performance of those investments, and a discussion of how current performance fits within the firm's overall philosophy and strategy.

Accounting reports not only provide a record of past transactions, they also reflect management estimates and forecasts of the future. For example, they include estimates of bad debts, forecasts of the lives of tangible assets, and implicit forecasts that outlays will generate future cash flow benefits that exceed their cost. Since management is likely to be in a position to make forecasts of these future events that are more accurate than these of external investors, financial reports are a potentially useful form of communicating with investors. However, investors are also likely to be skeptical of reports prepared by management, since managers have conflicts of interest in providing information that will be used to assess their own performance.

Investors' Concerns About the Credibility of Accounting Communication

It is difficult for managers to be truly impartial in providing external investors with information about their firm's performance. Management has a natural incentive to want to "sell" the company, in part because that is its job and in part because it is reluctant to provide information that jeopardizes its own job security. Reporting consistently poor earnings increases the likelihood that top management will be replaced, either by the board of directors or by an acquirer who takes over the firm to improve its management. Consequently, investors sometimes believe that accounting communications lack credibility.

Factors That Increase the Credibility of Accounting Communication

A number of mechanisms mitigate conflicts of interest in financial reporting and increase the credibility of accounting information that is communicated to stockholders. These include accounting standards, auditing, monitoring of management by financial analysts, and management reputation.

ACCOUNTING STANDARDS AND AUDITING.   Accounting standards promulgated by the Financial Accounting Standards Board (FASB) and the Securities Exchange Commission (SEC) provide guidelines for managers on how to make accounting decisions and provide outside investors with a way of interpreting these decisions. Uniform accounting standards attempt to reduce managers' ability to record similar economic transactions in different ways, either over time or across firms. Compliance with these standards is enforced by external auditors who attempt to ensure that managers' estimates are reasonable. Auditors therefore reduce the likelihood of earnings management.

MONITORING BY FINANCIAL ANALYSTS.   Financial intermediaries, such as analysts, also limit management's ability to manage earnings. Financial analysts specialize in developing firm- and industry-specific knowledge, enabling them to assess the quality of a firm's reported numbers and to make any necessary adjustments. Analysts evaluate the appropriateness of management's forecasts implicit in accounting method choices and reported accruals. This requires a thorough understanding of the firm's business and the relevant accounting rules used in the preparation of its financial reports. Superior analysts adjust reported accrual numbers, if necessary, to reflect economic reality, perhaps by using the cash flow statement and the footnote disclosures.

Analysts' business and technical expertise as well as their legal liability and incentives differ from those of auditors. Consequently, analyst reports can provide information to investors on whether the firm's accounting decisions are appropriate, or whether managers are overstating the firm's economic performance to protect their jobs.

MANAGEMENT REPUTATION.   A third factor that can counteract external investors' natural skepticism about financial reporting is management reputation. Managers that expect to have an ongoing relation with external investors and financial intermediaries may be able to build a track record for unbiased financial reporting. By making accounting estimates and judgments that are supported by subsequent performance, managers can demonstrate their competence and reliability to investors and analysts. As a result, managers' future judgments and accounting estimates are more likely to be viewed as credible sources of information.

Limitations of Financial Reporting for Investor Communication

While accounting standards, auditing, monitoring of management by financial analysts, and management concerns about its reputation increase the credibility and informativeness of financial reports, these mechanisms are far from perfect. Consequently, there are times when financial reporting breaks down as a means for management to communicate with external investors. These breakdowns can arise when: (1) there are no accounting rules to guide practice or the existing rules do not distinguish between poor and successful performers, (2) auditors and analysts do not have the expertise to judge new products or business opportunities, or (3) management faces credibility problems.

ACCOUNTING RULES.   Despite the rapid increase in new accounting standards, accounting rules frequently do not distinguish between good and poor performers. For example, current accounting rules do not permit managers to show on their balance sheets in a timely fashion. the benefits of investments in quality improvements, human resource development programs, research and development, and customer service.

Some of the problems with accounting standards arise because it takes time for standard setters to develop appropriate standards for many new types of economic transactions. Other difficulties arise because standards are the result of compromises between different interest groups (e.g., auditors, investors, corporate managers, and regulators).

AUDITOR AND ANALYST EXPERTISE.   While auditors and analysts have access to proprietary information, they do not have the same understanding of the firm's business as managers. The divergence between managers' and auditors'/analysts' business assessments is likely to be most severe for firms with distinctive business strategies, or firms that operate in emerging industries. In addition, auditors' decisions in these circumstances are likely to be dominated by concerns about legal liability, hampering management's ability to use financial reports to communicate effectively with investors.

MANAGEMENT CREDIBILITY.   When is management likely to face credibility problems with investors? There is very little evidence on this question. However, we expect that managers of new firms, firms with volatile earnings, firms in financial distress, and firms with poor track records in communicating with investors will find it difficult to be seen as credible reporters.

If management faces a credibility problem, financial reports are likely to be viewed with considerable skepticism. Investors will then view financial reporting estimates that increase income as evidence that management is padding earnings. This makes it very difficult for management to use financial reports to communicate positive news about future performance.

Compaq's Accounting Communication

For Compaq, the change in operating strategy is likely to have certain effects on future measures of accounting measures of performance:

1. The cost-cutting measures aimed at increasing manufacturing and administrative efficiency are likely to lead to layoffs and restructuring costs.
2. Given the elasticity of demand for PC products and Compaq's brand name, the more aggressive pricing policy should lead to a surge in demand for the company's products and hence superior revenue growth.
3. Plans to extend its current one-year product warranty to three years will increase warranty costs and customer satisfaction.
4. Plans to pursue an aggressive research and development strategy to ensure that it maintains its technological edge will lead R&D costs to continue to grow in the coming years.

Compaq's management is likely to be in the best position to understand how long it will take the company to successfully implement its strategy, and how long it will take for this success to be reflected in earnings performance. Financial reporting can provide management with a number of ways to convey its intentions to investors:

- Write-offs of major restructuring outlays indicate the costs of implementing the new strategy and the seriousness of management efforts to reorganize the firm. Write-offs are likely to be viewed positively by investors if they are one-time events which show management's commitment to increasing productivity and efficiency. They are likely to be less effective if management consistently understates write-offs, so that there are further write-offs in subsequent years.
- Outlays associated with implementing the strategy change and that have future benefits could be capitalized, signaling to investors that management and the firm's auditors are confident that the changes will be successful.
- Inventory build-ups can provide investors with information on how much of an increase in volume that management is anticipating as a result of its more aggressive pricing policy.
- Estimates of future costs associated with the new strategy, such as increased warranty expenses, are required to be reported as liabilities on the firm's balance sheet, helping investors to understand the financial implications of additional services provided.

Compaq faced restructuring costs associated with reducing its costs of manufacturing and administration. These included costs of $135 million in 1991 and $73 million in

1992, for layoffs of personnel and costs of reorganizing its operations to increase efficiency. These charges are likely to help investors appreciate management's commitment to making significant operational changes and the magnitude of the reorganization required. However, they do not provide much new information about the expected financial benefits of the changes. Given the limitations on capitalizing R&D and brand capital in the U.S., there are no opportunities for management to capitalize any outlays associated with increased customer service or R&D, despite their likely future benefits. However, estimated additional warranty costs could provide new information for investors on the financial implications of increased customer service. Compaq anticipated it had a strategic edge over generic PC manufacturers in providing two years of additional warranty, since its returns tended to be lower than those of the generics. Warranty liabilities therefore provide investors with management estimates of future returns and product quality, both good indicators of customer satisfaction. Finally, Compaq doubled its inventory in 1992, largely to prepare for expected sales growth from the introduction of new models and pricing reductions.

OTHER FORMS OF COMMUNICATING WITH INVESTORS

Given the limitations of accounting standards, auditing, and monitoring by financial analysts, as well as the reporting credibility problems faced by management, firms that wish to communicate effectively with external investors are often forced to use alternative media. Below we discuss three alternative ways that managers can communicate with external investors and analysts: meetings with analysts to publicize the firm, expanded voluntary disclosure, and using financing policies to signal management expectations. These forms of communication are typically not mutually exclusive. For example, at meetings with analysts, management usually discloses additional information that is helpful in valuing the firm.

Analyst Meetings

One popular way for managers to help mitigate communication problems is to meet regularly with financial analysts that follow the firm. At these meetings, management will field questions about the firm's current financial performance as well discuss its future business plans. As noted above, management typically provides additional disclosures to analysts at these meetings. In addition to holding analyst meetings, many firms appoint a director of public relations, who provides further regular contact with analysts seeking more information on the firm.

Voluntary Disclosure

One way for managers to improve the credibility of their financial reporting is through voluntary disclosure. Accounting rules usually prescribe minimum disclosure requirements, but they do not restrict managers from voluntarily providing additional information. These could include an articulation of the company's long-term strategy, specification of non-financial leading indicators which are useful in judging the effectiveness of the strategy implementation, explanation of the relation between the leading indicators and future profits, and forecasts of future performance. Voluntary disclosures can be reported in the firm's annual report, in brochures created to describe the firm to investors, in management meetings with analysts, or in investor relations responses to information requests.

One constraint on expanded disclosure is the competitive dynamics in product markets. Disclosure of proprietary information on strategies and their expected economic consequences may hurt the firm's competitive position. Managers then face a trade-off between providing information that is useful to investors in assessing the firm's economic performance, and withholding information to maximize the firm's product market advantage.

A second constraint in providing voluntary disclosure is management's legal liability. Forecasts and voluntary disclosures can potentially be used by dissatisfied shareholders to bring civil action against management for providing misleading information. This seems ironic, since voluntary disclosures should provide investors with additional information. Unfortunately, it can be difficult for courts to decide whether managers' disclosures were good-faith estimates of uncertain future events which later do not mateialize, or whether management manipulated the market. Consequently, many corporate legal departments recommend against management providing much voluntary disclosure.

Finally, management credibility can limit a firm's incentives to provide voluntary disclosures. If management faces a credibility problem in financial reporting, any voluntary disclosures it provides are also likely to be viewed skeptically. In particular, investors may be concerned about what management is not telling them, particularly since such disclosures are not audited.

Selected Financial Policies

Managers can also use financing policies to communicate effectively with external investors. Financial policies that are useful in this respect include dividend payouts, stock repurchases, financing choices, and hedging strategies.

DIVIDEND PAYOUT POLICIES.   As we discussed in Chapter 11, a firm's cash payout decisions can provide information to investors on managers' assessments of the firm's future prospects. This arises because dividend payouts tend to be sticky, in the sense that managers are reluctant to cut dividends. Thus, managers will only increase dividends when they are confident that they are able to sustain the increased rate in future years. Consequently, investors interpret dividend increases as signals of managers' confidence in the quality of current and future earnings.

STOCK REPURCHASES.   In some countries, such as the U.S. and the U.K., managers can use stock repurchases to communicate with external investors. Under a stock repurchase, the firm buys back its own stock, either through a purchase on the open market, through a tender offer, or through a negotiated purchase with a large stockholder. Of course a stock repurchase, particularly a tender offer repurchase, is an expensive way for management to communicate with outside investors. Firms typically pay a hefty premium to acquire their shares in tender offer repurchases, potentially diluting the value of the shares that are not tendered or not accepted for tender. In addition, the fees to investment banks, lawyers, and share solicitation fees are not trivial.

FINANCING CHOICES.   Firms that have problems communicating with external investors may be able to use financing choices to reduce them. For example, a firm that is unwilling to provide proprietary information to help dispersed public investors value it may be willing to provide such information to a knowledgeable private investor—which can become a large stockholder/creditor—or a bank that agrees to provide the company with a significant new loan. A firm with credibility problems in financial reporting can sell stock or issue debt to an informed private investor such as a large customer who has superior information about the quality of product or service.

   Such changes in financing and ownership can mitigate communication problems in two ways. First, the terms of the new financing arrangement and the credibility of the new lender or stockholder can provide investors with information to reassess the value of the firm. Second, the accompanying increased concentration of ownership and the role of large block holders in corporate governance can have a positive effect on valuation. If investors are concerned about management's incentives to increase shareholder value, the presence of a new block shareholder or significant creditor on the board can be reassuring. This type of monitoring arises in leveraged buyouts, start-ups backed by venture capital, and in firms with equity partnership investments. In Japanese and German corporations, it may also arise because large banks own both debt and equity and have close working relationships with firms' managers.

   Of course, in the extreme, management can decide that the best option for the firm is to no longer continue operating as a public company. This can be accomplished by a management buyout, where a buyout group (including management) leverages its own investment (using bank or public debt finance), buys the firm, and takes it private. The buyout firm hopes to run the firm for several years and then take the company public again, hopefully with a track record of improved performance that enables investors to value the firm more effectively.

HEDGING.   An important source of mispricing arises if investors are unable to distinguish between unexpected changes in reported earnings due to management performance and transitory shocks that are beyond managers' control (e.g., foreign currency translation gains and losses). Managers can counteract these effects by hedging such "accounting" risks. Even though hedging is costly, it may be valuable if it reduces information problems that potentially lead to misvaluation.

Compaq's Use of Other Communications

Many of the non-accounting forms of communication discussed above are available to Compaq's management. The firm can meet with analysts to explain the new strategy, present the logic that underlies it, provide analysts with information on leading indicators that will foretell the strategy's success, and even forecast future earnings.

Compaq's management can also change financial policies to indicate its optimism to investors. By repurchasing the firm's own stock, initiating a dividend, or raising new debt or equity financing from a respected and knowledgeable investor, Compaq's management may be able to persuade investors that the firm's future is bright. One important difference between this type of communication and additional disclosure is that the firm does not provide potentially proprietary information to competitors. The signal therefore indicates to competitors that Compaq's management is bullish on the new strategy, but it does not provide details of key dimensions of the strategy or implementation issues.

Compaq opted to use a relatively passive voluntary disclosure strategy in communicating with investors. The Financial Analysts Federation's ratings of the firm's voluntary disclosure actually declined between 1990 and 1991. Although analysts that rated the firm commended it for continuing to provide overall good coverage, despite the declining performance, the company's ratings dropped from above average for the industry in 1990 to average or slightly below average in 1991.

However, Compaq has been willing to use financial policies to communicate more effectively with investors. For example, on May 16, 1991, the Board of Directors voted to repurchase on the open market up to ten million shares of common stock, representing approximately 12 percent of the shares outstanding at the beginning of 1991.[1] This decision was made in response to the 30 percent stock price drop that occurred on May 15–16, following the announcement that second-quarter earnings had fallen by 15 percent. The announcement of the repurchase decision, made on May 17, was accompanied by a statement from top management and the Board that they were confident that the company's earnings problems were temporary. In contrast to typical repurchase announcements, the market reaction to this event was subdued—the stock held at $35.25. In 1992, Compaq announced that it had begun hedging its net income from foreign currency risks. This could potentially assist in communicating with investors if management was concerned that foreign currency risks might obscure earnings information about the outcome of the change in operating strategy.

It is interesting that the above communications by Compaq's management were largely ineffective in changing investors' perceptions of the firm's future performance. Indeed, it wasn't until late 1992, when there were actual earnings improvements, that the firm's stock price began to recover.

SUMMARY AND CONCLUSIONS

This chapter discussed firms' strategies for communicating with investors. Communication with investors can be useful because managers typically have better information on their firm's current and expected future performance than outside analysts and investors. By communicating effectively with investors, management can potentially reduce this information gap, lowering the likelihood that the stock will be mispriced or volatile. This can be important for firms that wish to raise new capital, avoid takeovers, or whose management is concerned that its true job performance is not reflected in the firm's stock.

The typical way for firms to communicate with investors is through financial reporting. Accounting standards and auditing make the reporting process a way for managers to not only provide information about the firm's current performance, but to indicate, through accounting estimates, where they believe the firm is headed in the future. However, financial reports are not always able to convey the types of forward-looking information that investors need. Accounting standards often do not permit firms to capitalize outlays that provide significant future benefits to the firm, such as R&D outlays.

A second way that management can communicate with investors is through non-accounting means. We discussed several such mechanisms, including: meeting with financial analysts to explain the firm's strategy, current performance and outlook; disclosing additional information, both quantitative and qualitative, to provide investors with similar information as management's; and using financial policies (such as stock repurchases, dividend increases, and hedging) to help signal management's optimism about the firm's future performance.

In this chapter we have stressed the importance of communicating effectively with investors. However, firms also have to communicate with other stakeholders, including employees, customers, suppliers, and regulatory bodies. Many of the same principles discussed here can also be applied to management communication with these other stakeholders.

DISCUSSION QUESTIONS

1. Apple's inventory increased from $1 billion on December 29, 1994, to $1.95 billion one year later. In contrast, sales for the fourth quarter in each of these years increased from $2 billion to $2.6 billion. What is the implied annualized inventory turnover for Apple for these years? What different interpretations about future performance could a financial analyst infer from this change? What information could Apple's management provide to investors to clarify the change in inventory turnover? What are the costs and benefits to Apple from disclosing this information?

2. a. What are likely to be the long-term critical success factors for the following types of firms?
   - a high technology company, such as Microsoft
   - a large low-cost retailer, such as Kmart

   b. How useful is financial accounting data for evaluating how well these two companies are managing their critical success factors? What other types of information would be useful in your evaluation? What are the costs and benefits to these companies from disclosing this type of information to investors?

3. Management frequently objects to disclosing additional information on the grounds that it is proprietary. Consider the recent FASB proposals on expanding disclosures on (a) executive stock compensation and (b) business segment performance. Many corporate managers expressed strong opposition to both proposals. What are the potential proprietary costs from expanded disclosures in each of these areas? If you conclude that proprietary costs are relatively low for either, what alternative explanations do you have for management's opposition?

4. Financial reporting rules in many countries outside the U.S. (e.g., the U.K., Australia, New Zealand, and France) permit management to revalue fixed assets (and in some cases even intangible assets) which have increased in value. Revaluations are typically based on estimates of realizable value made by management or independent valuers. Do you expect that these accounting standards will make earnings and book values more or less useful to investors? Explain why or why not. How can management make these types of disclosures more credible?

5. Under a management buyout, the top management of a firm offers to buy the company from its stockholders, usually at a premium over its current stock price. The management team puts up its own capital to finance the acquisition, with additional financing typically coming from a private buyout firm and private debt. If management is interested in making such an offer for its firm in the near future, what are its financial reporting incentives? How do these differ from the incentives of management that are not interested in a buyout?

6. You are approached by the management of a small start-up company that is planning to go public. The founders are unsure about how aggressive they should be in their accounting decisions as they come to the market. John Smith, the CEO, asserts: "We might as well take full advantage of any discretion offered by accounting rules, since the market will be expecting us to do so." What are the pros and cons of this strategy?

7. Two years after a successful public offering, the CEO of a bio-technology company is concerned about stock market uncertainty surrounding the potential of new drugs in the development pipeline. In his discussion with you, the CEO notes that even though they have recently made significant progress in their internal R&D efforts, the stock has performed poorly. What options does he have to help convince investors of the value of the new products? Which of these options are likely to be feasible?

8. Why might the CEO of the bio-technology firm discussed in Question 7 be concerned about the firm being undervalued? Would the CEO be equally concerned if the stock is overvalued? Do you believe that the CEO would attempt to correct the market's perception in this overvaluation case?

9. When companies decide to shift from private to public financing by making an initial public offering for their stock, they are likely to face increased costs of investor communications. Given this additional cost, why would firms opt to go public?

10. German firms are traditionally financed by banks, which have representatives on the companies' boards. How would communication challenges differ for these firms relative to U.S. firms, which rely more on public financing?

CASES

CUC International, Inc. (A)
Harnischfeger Corporation

NOTE

1. The company carried through on its repurchase commitment. Three million shares were acquired in 1991, at a cost of $95.5 million, and an additional seven million were acquired at a cost of $202.2 million in 1992

p a r t 4

Cases in Financial Statement Analysis

*W*hen it comes to technology companies, the stock market's current mania, it's hard to top America Online, Inc. Technology stocks are hot, up about 50 percent on average this year, but AOL is positively scalding, up about 135 percent. In fact, AOL's stock has soared more than 2,000 percent from its initial public offering, in 1992. The Vienna-based company has 35 times the customers and 20 times the revenue it had five years ago. It's the nation's biggest on-line company and is building a recognized brand.

But look closely and you see that AOL is as much about accounting technology as it is about computer technology. So make sure you understand the numbers before rushing out to buy AOL, which is valued at about $4 billion.

The above report written by Allan Sloan appeared on October 24, 1995, in *Newsweek*'s business section.[1]

COMPANY BACKGROUND

Founded in Vienna, VA, America Online, Inc. (AOL) was a leader in the development of a new mass medium that encompassed online services, the Internet, multimedia, and other interactive technologies. Through its America Online service the company offered members a broad range of features including real-time talk, electronic mail, electronic magazines and newspapers, online classes and shopping, and Internet access. In addition to its online service, AOL's business had expanded during 1995 to include access software for the Internet, production and distribution of original content, interactive marketing and transactions capabilities, and networks to support the transmission of data.

AOL generated revenues principally from consumers through membership fees, as well as from content providers and merchandisers through advertising, commissions on merchandise sales and other transactions, and from other businesses through the sale of network and production services. Through continued investment in the growth of its existing online service, the pursuit of related business opportunities, its ability to provide

This case was prepared by Professors Krisna Palepu and Amy Sweeney as the basis for class discussion rather than to illustrate eithe effective or ineffective handling of an administrative situation. Copyright © 1987 by the President and Fellows of Harvard College. Harvard Business School case 9-196-13.

1. "*Look Beyond the High-Tech Accounting To Measure America Online's Market Risk,*" Allan Sloan, Newsweek, October 24, 1995.

a full range of interactive services, and its technological flexibility, the company positioned itself to lead the development of the evolving mass medium for interactive services.

Stephen Case and James Kimsey founded America Online's predecessor, Quantum Computer Services, in 1985. Quantum offered its Q-Link service for Commodore computers. In 1989, the service was extended to Apple computers. The company changed its name to America Online in 1991 and went public in 1992. That same year, AOL licensed its on-line technology to Apple for use in eWorld and NewtonMail services for which AOL continues to receive a usage-based royalty. In 1993, the company expanded its market with a Windows version of its software and began developing a version for palmtop computer. In 1994, AOL's subscription base surpassed those of CompuServe and Prodigy, two rival online service providers, making AOL the number one consumer online service in the United States. By the end of October 1995, AOL had a subscriber base of more than four million members.

AOL's Products

a

1-2

The broad range of features offered by the America Online service was designed to meet the varied needs of its four million members. A key feature of the online service was the ease with which members with related interests could communicate through real-time conferences, e-mail, and bulletin boards. Members used the interactive communications facilities to share information and ideas, exchange advice, and socialize. It was America Online's goal to continue developing and adding new sources of information and content in support of these member activities. The range of features offered by America Online included the following:

- *Online Community*. In addition to its e-mail service, AOL promoted real-time online communications by scheduling conferences and discussions on specific topics, offering interactive areas that served as "meeting rooms" for members to participate in lively interactive discussions with other members, and providing public bulletin boards on which members could share information and opinions on subjects of general or specialized interest.
- *Computing*. AOL provided its members access to tens of thousands of public domain and "shareware" software programs, to online help from 300 hardware and software developers, and to online computer shopping and online computer magazines such as *MacWorld*, *PC World,* and *Computer Life*.
- *Education and References*. AOL's online educational services allowed adults and children to learn without leaving their homes. AOL contracted with professional instructors to teach real-time interactive classes in subjects of both general academic interest and adult education (such as creative writing and gourmet cooking). Regular tutoring sessions were offered in English, biology, and math. Education and reference services included the Library of Congress, College Board, CNN, Smithsonian, *Consumer Reports*, and *Compton's Encyclopedia*.

- *News and Personal Finance*. AOL offered a broad range of information services, including domestic and international news, weather, sports, stock market prices, and personalized portfolio tracking. Members could search news wires for stories of interest, access mutual fund information through Fidelity Online and Morningstar, and execute brokered trades online through PC Financial Network. Subscribers had access to over 70 newspapers, periodicals, and wire services, including *The New York Times*, *Chicago Tribune*, *San Jose Mercury News*, *Time*, *Scientific American*, *Investors Business Daily,* and Reuters.
- *Travel and Shopping*. AOL members also had access to travel and shopping reference materials and transaction services. Subscribers could send customized greeting cards through Hallmark Corporation, send flowers through 1-800-Flowers, shop for CDs and tapes online at Tower Records, book vacation packages with Preview Vacations, and access account data and travel information and services with American ExpressNet. Additionally, AOL had introduced its own interactive shopping service, 2Market, which featured goods and services from numerous catalogs and retailers.
- *Entertainment and Children's Programming*. AOL provided various clubs and forums for games and sports, multi-player games, and other related content for both adults and children. Specialized content was provided by such organizations as MusicSpace, the Games Channel, Disney Adventures, Comedy Clubs, Nintendo Power Source, Kids Only, Hollywood Online, Warner-Reprise Records, American Association for Retired Persons, MTV, Cooking Club, Environment Club, and Baby Boomers' Forum.

a

1-3

Customer Acquisition and Retention

AOL's biggest expenditure was the cost of attracting new subscribers. AOL aggressively marketed its online service using both independent marketing efforts, such as direct mail packets with AOL software disks and television and print advertising featuring a toll-free telephone number for ordering the AOL software, as well as co-marketing efforts with computer magazine publishers and personal computer hardware and software producers. These companies bundled the AOL software with their computer products, facilitating easy trial use by their customers. With the AOL software in hand, the customer needed only a personal computer, a telephone line, and a computer modem to gain access to AOL's online service. Accompanying each program disk was a unique registration number and password that could be used to generate a new AOL account. Customers could activate their accounts by providing AOL with their credit card account number. The first ten hours of access by this new account were free, after which AOL automatically billed the customer's credit card account the standard monthly rate until the customer canceled the AOL account.

These types of promotions were expensive, costing more than $40 per new subscriber in 1994. Thus, to retain these new subscribers and increase customer loyalty and satisfaction, AOL invested in specialized retention programs including regularly scheduled online events and conferences, online promotions of upcoming events and new features, and the regular addition of new content, services, and software programs. AOL's goal was to maximize customer subscription life.

Critical to customer retention and usage rates was the content available on AOL. To build and create unique content America Online participated in numerous joint ventures. During 1995 its alliances grew to include American Express, ABC, Reuters, Shoppers Express, Business Week, Fidelity, Vanguard, and the National Education Association. Also important to AOL were the newest stars of cyberspace, special-interest sites created by entrepreneurs such as Tom and David Gardner, who created Motley Fool and Follywood, two of the most popular sites offered on America Online. These hot special-interest sites kept customers on line, running up metered time and revenues. Traditionally, AOL had kept 80 percent or more of the revenues generated by these sites and had demanded exclusive contracts with the entrepreneurs creating them. However, content providers now had the option of setting up sites on the Internet World Wide Web. While they could not yet collect fees from Web browsers, this new distribution channel was changing the balance of power between AOL and its content providers.[2]

Compared to its competitors, AOL's rate structure was the easiest for consumers to understand and anticipate. A monthly fee of $9.95 provided access to all of America Online's services for up to five hours each month. Each additional hour was $2.95 and no additional downloading fees were charged. CompuServe and Prodigy offered the same standard pricing but charged additional fees for premium services and downloading. Microsoft Network (MSN), the newest entrant into the online services industry, offered a standard monthly plan of up to three hours for $4.95, with each additional hour costing $2.50. Content providers on MSN also applied charges to customers based on usage rates. The additional fees charged by AOL's competitors made it more difficult for their customers to anticipate their monthly spending.

Strategy for Future Growth

Through a tapestry of alliances and subsidiaries AOL's goal was to establish a central and defining leadership position in the worldwide market for interactive services. Toward this end, AOL had signed new strategic partnerships with American Express, Business Week Online, and NTN Communications; shipped the 2Market CD-ROM shopping service with an online connection; and completed its acquisitions of Internet software developers BookLink Technologies, Inc., NaviSoft, Inc., and Internet backbone developer Advanced Network & Services (ANS). These deals, along with AOL's growing membership base, its enhanced look and feel, and its ability to program content to appeal to users, uniquely positioned America Online to lead the development of the new interactive services industry. In implementing its strategy, AOL pursued a number of initiatives:

---

2. "On-Line Stars Hear Siren Calls to Free Agency," Steven Lohr, **New York Times**, November 25, 1995.

- *Invest in Growth of Existing Service.* America Online planned to continue to invest in the rapid growth of its existing online service. AOL believed it could attract and retain new members by expanding the range of content and services it offers, continuing to improve the engaging multimedia context of its service and building a sense of community online. At the same time, by offering access to a large, growing, and demographically attractive audience, together with software tools and services to develop content and programming for that audience, AOL believed it would continue to appeal to content and service providers.
- *Exploit New Business Opportunities.* AOL intended to leverage its technology, management skills, and content packaging skills to identify and exploit new business opportunities, such as electronic commerce, entry into international markets, and the "consumerization" of the Internet with its highly graphical interface software and its World Wide Web browser, which used high-speed compression technology to improve access speed and graphic display performance.
- *Provide a Full Range of Interactive Services.* Through acquisitions and internal development, AOL had assembled content development, distribution capabilities, access software, and its own communications network to become a full service, vertically integrated provider of interactive services. As a result, AOL believed it was well positioned to influence the evolution of the interactive services market.
- *Maintain Technological Flexibility.* AOL recognized the need to provide its services over a diverse set of platforms. Its software worked on different types of personal computers and operating systems (including Macintosh, Windows 3.xx and Windows 95) and supported a variety of different media, including online services, the Internet, and CD-ROM. AOL intended to adapt its products and services as new technologies become available.

While AOL currently generated revenues largely from membership fees, AOL's management believed that these initiatives would allow the company to increase the proportion of its revenues generated from other sources, such as advertising fees, commissions on merchandise sales to consumers, and revenues from the sale of production and network services to other enterprises.

INDUSTRY COMPETITION AND OUTLOOK

The online consumer services industry represented $1.1 billion in revenues in 1994 and was expected to grow by 30 percent to $1.4 billion in 1995. Eleven million customers subscribed to commercial online services worldwide and this number was expected to explode in the next five years. Industry leaders America Online, CompuServe, and Prodigy served about 8.5 million of the existing subscribers (4.0 million, 2.8 million, and 1.6 million, respectively). This oligopoly had very successfully acted as middlemen between thousands of content providers and millions of customers. They were the publishers, closely controlling the product and paying content providers, the writers, only modest royalties. However, with the advent of the Internet World Wide Web and the entrance of Microsoft Network, content providers now had alternative distribution channels which offered greater control over their products and potentially higher revenues.

Forbes discussed this topic in its August 28, 1995 issue:

> *Until recently the only way to reach cyberspace browsers was through one of the big three on-line services, America Online, CompuServe and Prodigy. That oligopoly is set to fade fast, and it's not just Microsoft that threatens. It's the whole Internet, the pulsating, undisciplined and rapidly expanding network of World Wide Web computers that contain public data bases.*[3]

While the big three acted as publishers, Microsoft had decided to act more like a bookstore, one in which every author (content provider) was his/her own publisher. Customers of MSN paid $4.95 per month for up to three hours (each additional hour was $2.50). Then, each content provider charged whatever it wanted for its material, so much per hour, per page, or per picture. Microsoft kept a 30 percent commission out of the provider's fee and passed along the rest to the content provider. In addition to offering content providers a larger share of the revenues, MSN also offered content providers greater control over their own products. In contrast to the standardized screen displays and icons of the big three, MSN permitted content providers to use any font and format they wished. Thus, while Microsoft still acted as a middleman, it played a very limited and passive role in determining content and fees charged for that content.

Beyond Microsoft lurked the vast potential of the Internet World Wide Web, where the middleman's role was shrunk still further. On the Internet, everyone with a computer was his/her own publisher. Customers would sign up for an Internet on-ramp service, of the sort offered by PST, Netcom, or MCI. Once on the net, the subscriber used browsing software like Netscape or Spyglass to roam the world's databases. While it remained difficult for self-publishers on the Internet to collect fees from browsers who read their pages, that was expected to change quickly as banks, Microsoft, and other intermediaries worked on systems to provide on-line currency.

Many content providers were beginning to take advantage of these alternative distribution channels. For example, *Wired* magazine, unwilling to settle for just 20 percent of the revenues from subscribers spending time on its pages on AOL, created HotWired on the Internet. Andrew Anker, chief technologist at *Wired*, believed that HotWired would soon be more lucrative than the America Online venture and he noted that on the Internet his firm had greater control of its own product. General Electric's NBC decided to switch from AOL to Microsoft Network. "While we had many users visiting us on America Online, we weren't making much revenue," explained Martin Yudkovitz, a senior vice-president at NBC.[4]

With the migration of proprietary services and content to Web sites, the unique offerings of the big three services were declining. However, the online services were still bet-

3. *"Who Needs the Middleman?,"* Nikhil Hutheesing, **Forbes**, August 28, 1995.
4. *Ibid.*

ter for interactive communications with full-fledged message boards and live chat. The Web, on the other hand, was mainly a publication environment for reading. The question remained, what would be the role of online service providers in the future? Would they become just another Internet access provider with their own look and browsers or could they continue to offer something unique to users?

Some analysts were projecting that the U.S. online services market would grow 30–35 percent annually through the year 2000, and that the Internet market would grow even faster. These analysts expected America Online to retain about a 20 percent market share.[5] On the other hand, Forrester Research of Cambridge, Mass., predicted that the big three, America Online, CompuServe, and Prodigy, would continue to add subscribers only through 1997. After that, Forrester predicted, it would be all downhill for the big three.[6]

AOL'S RECENT PERFORMANCE

For the fourth quarter ended June 30, 1995, America Online announced that its earnings were $0.16, excluding $0.01 merger expenses and $0.02 amortization of goodwill. This was a significant improvement over 1994's fourth-quarter earnings, $0.02, and above analysts' estimate, $0.14. Service revenues surged to $139 million, versus analysts' estimate of $132 million, and total revenues rose to $152 million versus $40.4 in the fourth quarter of 1994. For the fiscal year ended June 30, 1995, AOL reported a loss of $33.6 million on revenues of $394 million compared with a profit of $2.5 million on revenues of $116 million a year earlier. New charges recorded for the first time in 1995 included $50.3 million for acquired R&D, $1.7 million amortization of goodwill, and $2.2 million in merger expenses. (See Exhibit 3, America Online's 1995 Abridged Annual Report.)

New subscriber momentum continued to be strong, increasing 233 percent year-over-year and adding 691,000 new net subscribers during the fourth quarter. All major metrics used by analysts to evaluate AOL's franchise and gauge the "health" of its rapidly growing subscriber base also improved during the quarter: projected retention rates rose to 41 months from 39 months; paid usage grew to 2.93 hours from 2.73, and projected lifetime revenues per subscriber increased to $714 from $667. (See Exhibit 2 for the history of America Online's User Metrics.) However, analysts were projecting lower gross margins in the future as subscribers continued to transition to higher-speed access and as AOL introduced a heavy-usage pricing plan in response to Microsoft's lower per-hour pricing.

On November 8, 1995, America Online announced its results for the first quarter of fiscal 1996 ended September 30, 1995. Even though revenues rose to $197.9 million from $56 million a year earlier, America Online reported a loss of $10.3 million com-

5.   "America Online, Inc. — Company Report," A. Pooley, The Chicago Corporation, April 18, 1995.
6.   Op. cit., Forbes, August 28, 1995.

pared with a profit of $1.5 million a year earlier. America Online took a $16.9 million charge to reflect research and development taking place at Ubique, a company it acquired on September 21, 1995, as well as to pay off other recently acquired assets. It took another charge of $1.7 million for amortization of goodwill. These charges were partially offset by AOL's decision to increase the period over which it amortized subscriber acquisition costs. Effective July 1, 1995, these costs would be amortized over 24 months rather than 12–18 months. The effect of the change in accounting estimates for the three months ended September 30, 1995, was to decrease the reported loss by $1.95 million. AOL also announced that it added 711,000 subscribers in the first quarter of 1996, bringing its total subscriber base to four million.[7]

America Online's stock price had been on the move since the company's initial public offering (IPO) in March 1992. The stock price appreciated from the IPO price of $2.90 to $7.31, $14.63, and $28.00 at calendar year end 1992, 1993, and 1994, respectively. At its current price of $81.63 (dated November 8, 1995), the company's market value was around $4.0 billion. (See Exhibit 1 for the stock price history of America Online, its equity beta, and additional market-based data.)

THE CONTROVERSY SURROUNDING AOL

America Online's stock was one of the most controversial of this period. Some analysts promoted the stock's potential for price appreciation, while others recommended selling the shares short to profit from a decline in price. Bulls saw America Online as part of a revolution in communication, like cellular phones and cable television in the early days. They considered AOL's graphical interface software, its high-speed Web browser, and Mr. Case's marketing genius (subscribership had quadrupled to over four million in a little over a year) to be major competitive advantages. Bears, on the other hand, anticipating new entrants competing in the online services industry and a migration of subscribers to the Internet, questioned whether AOL would continue to experience high growth in its subscriber base or be able to retain existing subscribers.

Shortsellers had sold around seven million America Online shares, betting that the stock's price would not go up forever. Shortsellers pointed to the recent hedging activities by Apple Computer to lock in profits on its 5.7 percent stake as an indication that AOL's stock was overvalued. Adding fuel to the shortsellers' fire, corporate insiders at AOL had sold some of their shareholdings. Between March 9 and March 15 of 1995, seventeen insiders sold approximately 200,000 shares, including the company founders, President Steven Case (25,000 shares for $2.1 million) and Chairman James Kimsey (40,000 shares for $3.3 million).[8]

---

7. *"America Online Posts $10.3 Million Loss But Says Revenue Rose 250% in Quarter,"* The Washington Post, Nov. 8, 1995.

8. As of August 15, 1995 all executive officers and directors as a group continued to own 3,729,547 shares, Steven Case owned 1,036,790 shares and James Kimsey owned 679,616 shares.

Adding to the controversy, some analysts labeled AOL's accounting "aggressive." AOL amortized its software development costs over five years, a long time in the fast-changing, uncertain online services industry, and AOL capitalized subscriber acquisition costs when its number one competitor, CompuServe, did not. Furthermore, effective July 1, 1995, AOL extended the amortization period for its subscriber acquisition costs from about 15 months to 24 months. Given the uncertainties surrounding AOL's subscriber retention rates and revenue growth as competition emerged in the young industry, analysts questioned the wisdom of AOL's accounting decisions. The big risk AOL faced was that eventually customers could switch on-line services as frequently as they now move among long-distance carriers.

While America Online expensed the free trial expenses (i.e., those charges incurred from the ten free hours given away in the initial month), it capitalized the marketing costs associated with acquiring a customer including direct mail, advertising, start-up kits, and bundling costs. As indicated in its annual report, prior to July 1, 1995, the capitalization had occurred on two schedules depending on the acquisition method. Costs for subscribers acquired through direct marketing programs were amortized over a 12-month period. Costs for subscribers acquired through co-marketing efforts with personal computer producers and magazine publishers were amortized over an 18-month period, as these bundling campaigns had historically shown a longer response time. However, effective July 1, 1995, AOL increased the period over which it amortized subscriber acquisition costs to 24 months for both acquisition methods.

Defending AOL's accounting choices, Lennert Leader, the Chief Financial Officer of America Online, Inc., said that the company was following standard accounting procedures in matching the timing of expenses with the period over which the revenues would be received. He argued that the company's marketing and software development expenses produced customer accounts that last a long time. Thus, he said, it was appropriate to write off the costs over a period of years, even though AOL had spent the cash.[9]

However, some analysts raised red flags about AOL's accounting choices. As noted in the October 24, 1995 *Newsweek* article:

> *One of AOL's hidden assets is the brilliant accounting decision it made to treat its marketing and research and development costs as capital items rather than expenses. . . .*
>
> *AOL charges R&D expenses over a five-year period, a very long time in the online biz. In July, AOL began charging off marketing expenses over two years, up from about 15 months.*
>
> *Why change to 24 months from 15? Leader said it's because the average life of an AOL account has climbed to 41 months from 25 months in 1992. How many AOL customers have been around for 41 months? Almost none, as Leader concedes. That's understandable, considering that AOL has added virtually all its*

a

1-9

---

9.   *Op. cit.,* **Newsweek**, *October 24, 1995.*

customers in the past 36 months. Leader says the 41-month average live number comes from projections. Of course, it will take years to find out if he's right. . . .[10]

Analysts were also concerned about AOL's cash flow situation and the signal sent by the timing of its latest equity offering. The *Newsweek* article continued:

Accounting is terribly important to AOL. The better the numbers look, the more Wall Street loves it and the easier AOL can sell new shares to raise cash to pay its bills. . . . On October 10 [AOL] raised about $100 million by selling new shares. AOL sold the stock even though its shares had fallen to $58.37 from about $72 in September, when the sale plans were announced. Most companies would have delayed the offering, waiting for the price to snap back. AOL didn't, prompting cynics to think the company really needed the money. . . .

Some analysts believed that AOL issued shares when its stock price was low because the company needed the cash immediately. Others argued that AOL was building a war chest needed because deep-pocketed rivals such as Microsoft were about to start an online price war and because increasingly information providers were going directly to the Internet, rather than using middlemen such as AOL. Some analysts interpreted CompuServe's recent adoption of more aggressive accounting techniques as a sign that it too was readying for war. Beginning the first quarter of fiscal 1996, CompuServe would capitalize direct response advertising costs associated with customer acquisition activity.[11]

While AOL's stock price rebounded to $81.63 by November 8, 1995, there were many questions concerning AOL's future. How would the demand for AOL's services be affected by the entry of Microsoft Network and the growth of Internet? Would AOL's accounting choices stand the test of time? What if AOL's subscription growth rates slowed or subscriber renewal rates fell? Did AOL have the financial flexibility to face these competitive pressures and accounting risks?

---

10. Op. cit., **Newsweek**, October 24, 1995.

11. Op. cit., **Newsweek**, October 24, 1995.

EXHIBIT 1

Stock Price History for America Online, Inc.

Exhibit 1   Stock Price History for America Online, Inc.

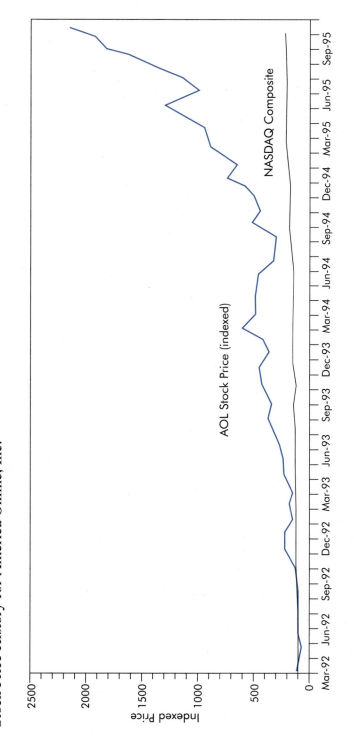

Additional market-based data:

America Online's equity beta	1.4
Moody's AAA corporate debt in November 1995 (%)	7.02
Treasury bills rate in November 1995 (%)	5.35
Government 30-year treasury rates in November 1995 (%)	6.26

Sources: Datastream International, Standard and Poor's Compustat, and the *Wall Street Journal.*

a

Exhibit 2   America Online, Inc. User Metrics to June 30, 1995

a

EXHIBIT 2
America Online, Inc. User Metrics to June 30, 1995

	Dec-93	Mar-94	Jun-94	Sep-94	Dec-94	Mar-95	Jun-95
Paid usage (hours)	1.85	2	2.1	2.27	2.46	2.73	2.93
Projected average months' retention	30	32	32+	34	36	39	41
Projected average lifetime revenue	$443	$496	$496	$551	$612	$667	$714
Internet usage (% time)	1%	1%	3%	4%	5%	6%	9%

Source: Alex Brown & Sons, Inc., August 24, 1995.

Exhibit 3   America Online 1995 Abridged Annual Report

EXHIBIT 3

America Online 1995 Abridged Annual Report

REPORT OF INDEPENDENT AUDITORS

Board of Directors and Stockholders
America Online, Inc.

We have audited the accompanying consolidated balance sheets of America Online, Inc., as of June 30, 1995 and 1994, and the related consolidated statements of operations, changes in stockholders' equity and cash flows for each of the three years in the period ended June 30, 1995. These financial statements are the responsibility of the Company's management. Our responsibility is to express an opinion on these financial statements based on our audits.

We conducted our audits in accordance with generally accepted auditing standards. Those standards require that we plan and perform the audit to obtain reasonable assurance about whether the financial statements are free of material misstatement. An audit includes examining, on a test basis, evidence supporting the amounts and disclosures in the financial statements. An audit also includes assessing the accounting principles used and significant estimates made by management, as well as evaluating the overall financial statement presentation. We believe that our audits provide a reasonable basis for our opinion.

In our opinion, the financial statements referred to above present fairly, in all material respects, the consolidated financial position of America Online, Inc. at June 30, 1995 and 1994, and the consolidated results of their operations and their cash flows for each of the three years in the period ended June 30, 1995, in conformity with generally accepted accounting principles.

As discussed in Note 9 to the consolidated financial statements, in fiscal 1994 the Company changed its method of accounting for income taxes. As discussed in Note 2 to the consolidated financial statements, in fiscal 1995 the Company changed its method of accounting for short-term investments in certain debt and equity securities.

Ernst & Young LLP

Vienna, Virginia
August 25, 1995

a

1-13

Exhibit 3   America Online 1995 Abridged Annual Report

SELECTED CONSOLIDATED FINANCIAL AND OTHER DATA
(In Thousands, Except Per Share Data)

	Year Ended June 30,				
	1995	1994	1993	1992	1991
Statements of Operations Data:					
Online service revenues	$358,498	$100,993	$38,462	$26,226	$19,515
Other revenues	35,792	14,729	13,522	12,527	10,646
Total Revenues	394,290	115,722	51,984	38,753	30,161
Income (loss) from operations	(19,294)	4,608	1,925	3,685	1,341
Income (loss) before extraordinary items	(33,647)	2,550	399	2,344	1,100
Net income (loss) [1]	(33,647)	2,550	1,532	3,768	1,761
Income (loss) per common share:					
Income (loss) before extraordinary item	$ (0.99)	$ 0.07	$ 0.01	$ 0.10	$ 0.06
Net income (loss)	$ (0.99)	$ 0.07	$ 0.05	$ 0.17	$ 0.09
Weighted average shares outstanding	33,986	34,208	29,286	22,828	19,304

	As of June 30,				
	1995	1994	1993	1992	1991
Balance Sheet Data:					
Working capital (deficiency)	$ (456)	$47,890	$10,498	$12,363	$ (966)
Total assets	406,464	154,584	39,279	31,144	11,534
Total debt	21,810	9,302	2,959	2,672	1,865
Stockholders' equity (deficiency)	217,944	98,297	23,785	21,611	(8,623)
Other data (at fiscal year end):					
Subscribers	3,005	903	303	182	131

(1) Net loss in the fiscal year ended June 30, 1995, includes charges of $50.3 million for acquired research and development and $2.2 million for merger expenses. See Note 3 of the Notes to Consolidated Financial Statements.

MANAGEMENT'S DISCUSSION AND ANALYSIS OF FINANCIAL CONDITIONS AND RESULTS OF OPERATIONS

Overview

The Company has experienced a significant increase in revenues over the past three fiscal years. The higher revenues have been principally produced by increases in the Company's subscriber base resulting from growth of the online services market, the introduction of a Windows version of America Online in the middle of fiscal 1993, which greatly increased the available market for the Company's service, as well as the expansion of its services and content. Additionally, revenues have increased as the average monthly revenue per subscriber has risen steadily during the past three years, primarily as a result of an increase in the average monthly paid hours of use per subscriber.

The Company's online service revenues are generated primarily from subscribers paying a monthly member's fee and hourly charges based on usage in excess of the number of hours of usage provided as part of the monthly fee. Through December 31, 1994, the Company's standard monthly membership fee, which includes five hours of service, was $9.95, with a $3.50 hourly fee for usage in excess of five hours per month. Effective January 1, 1995, the hourly fee for usage in excess of five hours per month decreased from $3.50 to $2.95, while the monthly membership fee remained unchanged at $9.95.

The Company's other revenues are generated primarily from providing new media and interactive marketing services, data network services, and multimedia and CD-ROM production services. Additionally, the Company generates revenues related to online transactions and advertising, as well as development and licensing fees.

In fiscal 1995 the Company acquired RCC, NaviSoft, BookLink, ANS, WAIS, Medior and Global Network Navigator, Inc. Additionally, in August 1995, the Company entered into an agreement to acquire Ubique. For additional information relating to these acquisitions, refer to Notes 3 and 13 of the Notes to Consolidated Financial Statements.

The online services market is highly competitive. The Company believes that existing competitors, which include, among others, CompuServe, Prodigy and MSN, are likely to enhance their service offerings. In addition, new competitors have announced plans to enter the online services market, resulting in greater competition for the Company. The competitive environment could require new pricing programs and increased spending on marketing, content procurement and product development; limit the Company's opportunities to enter into and/ or renew agreements with content providers and distribution partners; limit the Company's ability to grow its subscriber base; and result in increased attrition in the Company's subscriber base. Any of the foregoing events could result in an increase in costs as a percentage of revenues, and may have a material adverse effect on the Company's financial condition and operating results.

During September 1995, the Company modified the components of subscriber acquisition costs deferred and will be expensing certain subscriber acquisition cost as incurred, effective July 1, 1995. All costs capitalized before this change will continue to be amortized. The effect of this change for the year ended June 30, 1995 (including the amortization of amounts capitalized as of June 30, 1994) would have been to increase marketing costs by approximately $8 million. This change will have a greater impact on the Company's marketing costs in fiscal 1996, as the Company expects to significantly increase subscriber acquisition activity, including those subscriber acquisition expenditures which the Company will be expensing as incurred.

In addition, effective July 1, 1995, the Company changed the period over which it amortizes subscriber acquisition cost from twelve and eighteen months to twenty-four months. Based on the Company's historical average customer life experience, the change in amortization period is being made to more appropriately match subscriber acquisition costs with associated online service revenues. The effect of this change in accounting estimate for the year ended June 30, 1995 would have been to

Exhibit 3   America Online 1995 Abridged Annual Report

decrease the amount of the amortization of sub-scriber acquisition costs by approximately $27 million. While this change will thereby positively impact operating margins, the Company expects that any such positive impact will be partially offset by increased investments in marketing and other business activities during fiscal 1996 and the decision, effective July 1, 1995, to expense certain subscriber acquisition costs as incurred.

Results of Operations

Fiscal 1995 Compared to Fiscal 1994

Online Service Revenues. For fiscal 1995, online service revenues increased from $100,993,000 to $358,498,000, or 255%, over fiscal 1994. This increase was primarily attributable to a 289% increase in revenues from IBM-compatible subscribers and a 196% increase in revenues from Macintosh subscribers as a result of a 273% increase in the number of IBM-compatible subscribers and a 143% increase in the number of Macintosh subscribers. The percentage increase in online service revenues in fiscal 1995 was greater than the percentage increase in subscribers principally due to an increase in the average monthly online service revenue per subscriber, which increased from $15.00 in fiscal 1994 to $17.10 in fiscal 1995.

Other Revenues. Other revenues, consisting principally of new media and interactive marketing services, data network services, multimedia and CD-ROM production services, and development and licensing fees, increased from $14,729,000 in fiscal 1994 to $35,792,000 in fiscal 1995. This increase was primarily attributable to data network revenues and multimedia and CD-ROM production service revenues from companies acquired during fiscal 1995.

Cost of Revenues. Cost of revenues includes network-related costs, consisting primarily of data and voice communication costs, costs associated with operating the data center and providing customer support, royalties paid to information and service providers and other expenses related to marketing and production services. For fiscal 1995, cost of revenues increased from $69,043,000 to $229,724,000, or 233%, over fiscal 1994, and

decreased as a percentage of total revenues from 59.7% to 58.3%.

The increase in cost of revenues was primarily attributable to an increase in data communication costs, customer support costs and royalties paid to information and service providers. Data communication costs increased primarily as a result of the larger customer base and more usage by customers. Customer support costs, which include personnel and telephone costs associated with providing customer support, were higher as a result of the larger customer base and a large number of new subscriber registrations. Royalties paid to information and service providers increased as a result of a larger customer base and more usage and the Company's addition of more service content to broaden the appeal of the America Online service.

The decrease in cost of revenues as a percentage of total revenues is primarily attributable to a decrease in expenses related to marketing services and personnel related costs as a percentage of total revenues, partially offset by an increase in data communication costs as a percentage of total revenues, primarily resulting from an increase in higher baud speed usage at a higher variable rate as well as lower hourly pricing for online service revenue which became effective January 1, 1995.

Marketing. Marketing expenses include the costs to acquire and retain subscribers and other general marketing expenses. Subscriber acquisition costs are deferred and charged to operations over a twelve or eighteen month period, using the straight-line method, beginning the month after such costs are incurred. For additional information regarding the accounting for deferred subscriber acquisition costs, refer to Note 2 of the Notes to Consolidated Financial Statements. For fiscal 1995, marketing expenses increased from $23,548,000 to $77,064,000, or 227%, over fiscal 1994, and decreased as a percentage of total revenues from 20.3% to 19.5%. The increase in marketing expenses was primarily due to an increase in the number and size of marketing programs to expand the Company's subscriber base. The decrease in marketing expenses as a percentage of total revenues is primarily attributable to a decrease as a percentage of total revenues in personnel related costs.

Exhibit 3   America Online 1995 Abridged Annual Report

Product Development. Product development costs include research and development expenses, other product development costs and the amortization of software costs. For fiscal 1995, product development expenses increased from $4,961,000 to $12,842,000, or 159%, over fiscal 1994, and decreased as a percentage of total revenues from 4.3% to 3.3%. The increase in product development costs was primarily attributable to an increase in personnel costs related to an increase in the number of technical employees. The decrease in product development costs as a percentage of total revenues was principally a result of the substantial growth in revenues, which more than offset the additional product development costs. Product development costs, before capitalization and amortization, increased by 126% in fiscal 1995.

General and Administrative. Fiscal 1995 general and administrative costs increased from $13,562,000 to $41,966,000, or 209%, over fiscal 1994, and decreased as a percentage of total revenues from 11.7% to 10.6%. The increase in general and administrative expenses was principally attributable to higher office and personnel expenses related to an increase in the number of employees. The decrease in general and administrative costs as a percentage of total revenues was a result of the substantial growth in revenues, which more than offset the additional general and administrative costs, combined with the semi-variable nature of many of the general and administrative costs.

Acquired Research and Development. Acquired research and development costs, totaling $50,335,000, relate to in-process research and development purchased pursuant to the Company's acquisition of two early-stage Internet technology companies, BookLink and NaviSoft. The purchased research and development relating to the BookLink and NaviSoft acquisitions was the foundation of the development of the Company's Internet related products.

Amortization of Goodwill. Amortization of goodwill relates to the Company's acquisition of ANS, which resulted in approximately $44 million in goodwill. The goodwill related to the ANS acquisition is being amortized on a straight-line basis over a ten-year period.

Other Income. Other income consists primarily of investment and rental income net of interest expense. For fiscal 1995, other income increased from $1,774,000 to $3,023,000. This increase was primarily attributable to an increase in interest income generated by higher levels of cash available for investment, partially offset by a decrease in rental income and an increase in interest expense.

Merger Expenses. Non-recurring merger expenses totaling $2,207,000 were recognized in fiscal 1995 in connection with the mergers of the Company with RCC, WAIS and Medior.

Provisions for Income Taxes. The provision for income taxes was $3,832,000 and $15,169,000 in fiscal year 1994 and fiscal 1995, respectively. For additional information regarding income taxes, refer to Note 9 of the Notes to Consolidated Financial Statements.

Net Loss. The net loss in fiscal 1995 totaled $33,647,000. The net loss in fiscal 1995 included charges of $50,335,000 for acquired research and development and $2,207,000 for merger expenses.

Liquidity and Capital Resources

The Company has financed its operations through cash generated from operations, sale of its common stock and funding by third parties for certain product development activities. Net cash provided by operating activities was $2,205,000, $1,884,000 and $15,891,000 for fiscal 1993, fiscal 1994 and fiscal 1995, respectively. Included in operating activities were expenditures for deferred subscriber acquisition costs of $10,685,000, $37,424,000 and $111,761,000 in fiscal 1993, fiscal 1994 and fiscal 1995, respectively. Net cash used in investing activities was $8,915,000, $41,870,000 and $85,725,000 in fiscal 1993, fiscal 1994 and fiscal 1995, respectively. Investing activities included $20,523,000 in fiscal 1995 related to business acquisitions, substantially all of which were related to the acquisition of ANS.

In December 1993 the Company completed a public stock offering of 4,000,000 shares of common stock which generated net cash proceeds of approximately $62.7 million.

a

1-17

Exhibit 3   America Online 1995 Abridged Annual Report

In April 1995 the company entered into a joint venture with Bertelsmann to offer interactive online services in Europe. In connection with the agreement, the Company received approximately $54 million through the sale of approximately 5% of its common stock to Bertelsmann.

The Company leases the majority of its equipment under noncancelable operating leases, and as part of its network portfolio strategy is building AOLnet, its data communications network. The buildout of this network requires a substantial investment in telecommunication equipment, which the Company plans to finance principally though leasing. In addition, the Company has guaranteed minimum commitments under certain data and voice communication agreements. The Company's future lease commitments and guaranteed minimums are discussed in Note 6 of the Notes to Consolidated Financial Statements.

The Company uses its working capital to finance ongoing operations and to fund marketing and content programs and the development of its products and services. The Company plans to continue to invest aggressively in acquisition marketing and content programs to expand its subscriber base, as well as in computing and support infrastructure. Additionally, the Company expects to use a portion of its cash for the acquisition and subsequent funding of technologies, products or businesses complementary to the Company's current business. Apart from its agreement to acquire Ubique, as discussed below, the Company has no agreements or understandings to acquire any businesses. The Company anticipates that available cash and cash provided by operating activities will be sufficient to fund its operations for the next fiscal year.

Various legal proceedings have arisen against the Company in the ordinary course of business. In the opinion of management, these proceedings will not have a material effect on the financial position of the Company.

The Company believes that inflation has not had a material effect on its results of operations.

On August 23, 1995, the Company entered into a stock purchase agreement to purchase Ubique, an Israeli company. The Company has agreed to pay approximately $15 million ($1.5 million in cash and $13.5 million in common stock) in the transaction, which is to be accounted for as a purchase. Subject to the results of an in-process valuation, a substantial portion of the purchase price may be allocated to in-process research and development and charged to the Company's operations in the first quarter of fiscal 1996.

Exhibit 3   America Online 1995 Abridged Annual Report

CONSOLIDATED STATEMENTS OF OPERATIONS
(Amounts in Thousands, Except Per Share Data)

	Year ended June 30,		
	1995	1994	1993
Revenues:			
Online service revenues	$358,498	$100,993	$ 38,462
Other revenues	35,792	14,729	13,522
Total revenues	394,290	115,722	51,984
Costs and expenses:			
Cost of revenues	229,724	69,043	28,820
Marketing	77,064	23,548	9,745
Product development	12,842	4,961	2,913
General and administrative	41,966	13,562	8,581
Acquired research and development	50,335	—	—
Amortization of goodwill	1,653	—	—
Total costs and expenses	413,584	111,114	50,059
Income (loss) from operations	(19,294)	4,608	1,925
Other income, net	3,023	1,774	371
Merger expenses	(2,207)	—	—
Income (loss) before provision for income taxes and extraordinary item	(18,478)	6,382	2,296
Provision for income taxes	(15,169)	(3,832)	(1,897)
Income (loss) before extraordinary item	(33,647)	2,550	399
Extraordinary item—tax benefit arising from net operating loss carryforward	—	—	1,133
Net income (loss)	$ (33,647)	$ 2,550	$ 1,532
Earnings (loss) per share:			
Income (loss) before extraordinary item	$ (0.99)	$ 0.07	$ 0.01
Net income (loss)	$ (0.99)	$ 0.07	$ 0.05
Weighted average shares outstanding	33,986	34,208	29,286

See accompanying notes.

a

1-19

Exhibit 3   America Online 1995 Abridged Annual Report

CONSOLIDATED STATEMENTS OF CASH FLOWS
(Amounts in Thousands)

	Year ended June 30,		
	1995	1994	1993
Cash flows from operating activities:			
Net income (loss)	$ (33,647)	$ 2,550	$ 1,532
Adjustments to reconcile net income to net cash provided by operating activities:			
Depreciation and amortization	11,136	2,965	1,957
Amortization of subscriber acquisition costs	60,924	17,922	7,038
Loss/(Gain) on sale of property and equipment	37	5	(39)
Charge for acquired research and development	50,335	—	—
Changes in assets and liabilities:			
Trade accounts receivable	(14,373)	(4,266)	(936)
Other receivables	(9,057)	(681)	(966)
Prepaid expenses and other current assets	(19,641)	(2,867)	(1,494)
Deferred subscriber acquisition costs	(111,761)	(37,424)	(10,685)
Other assets	(8,432)	(2,519)	(89)
Trade accounts payable	60,824	10,204	2,119
Accrued personnel costs	1,846	367	336
Other accrued expenses and liabilities	5,703	9,526	1,492
Deferred revenue	7,190	2,322	1,381
Deferred income taxes	14,763	3,832	759
Deferred rent	44	(52)	(200)
Total adjustments	49,538	(666)	673
Net cash provided by operating activities	15,891	1,884	2,205
Cash flows from investing activities:			
Short-term investments	5,380	(18,947)	(5,105)
Purchase of property and equipment	(57,751)	(17,886)	(2,041)
Product development costs	(13,011)	(5,132)	(1,831)
Sale of property and equipment	180	95	62
Purchase costs of acquired businesses	(20,523)	—	—
Net cash used in investing activities	(85,725)	(41,870)	(8,915)
Cash flows from financing activities:			
Proceeds from issuance of common stock, net	61,253	67,372	609
Principal and accrued interest payments on line of credit and long-term debt	(3,298)	(7,716)	(6,924)
Proceeds from line of credit and issuance of long-term debt	13,741	14,200	7,181
Tax benefit from stock option exercises	—	—	6
Principal payments under capital lease obligations	(375)	(142)	(112)

Exhibit 3   America Online 1995 Abridged Annual Report

CONSOLIDATED STATEMENT OF CASH FLOWS (continued)

	Year ended June 30,		
	1995	1994	1993
Net cash provided by financing activities	71,321	73,714	760
Net increase (decrease) in cash and cash equivalents	1,487	33,728	(5,950)
Cash and cash equivalents at beginning of period	43,891	10,163	16,113
Cash and cash equivalents at end of period	$ 45,378	$ 43,891	$ 10,163
Supplemental cash flow information			
Cash paid during the period for:			
Interest	1,067	575	193
Income taxes	—	—	15

See accompanying notes.

CONSOLIDATED BALANCE SHEETS
(Amounts in Thousands, Except Per Share Data)

	June 30,	
	1995	1994
ASSETS		
Current assets:		
Cash and cash equivalents	$ 45,378	$ 43,891
Short-term investments	18,672	24,052
Trade accounts receivable	32,176	8,547
Other receivables	11,103	2,036
Prepaid expenses and other current assets	25,527	5,753
Total current assets	132,856	84,279
Property and equipment at cost, net	70,466	20,306
Other assets:		
Product development costs, net	18,914	7,912
Deferred subscriber acquisition costs, net	77,229	26,392
License rights, net	5,537	53
Other assets	11,479	2,800
Deferred income taxes	35,627	12,842
Goodwill, net	54,356	—
	$406,464	$154,584

(continued)

Exhibit 3 America Online 1995 Abridged Annual Report

CONSOLIDATED BALANCE SHEETS (continued)

	June 30,	
	1995	1994
LIABILITIES AND STOCKHOLDERS' EQUITY		
Current liabilities:		
Trade accounts payable	$ 84,639	$ 15,642
Accrued personnel costs	2,829	896
Other accrued expenses and liabilities	23,509	13,076
Deferred revenue	20,021	4,488
Line of credit	484	1,690
Current portion of long-term debt and capital lease obligations	1,830	597
Total current liabilities	133,312	36,389
Long-term liabilities:		
Notes payable	17,369	5,836
Capital lease obligations	2,127	1,179
Deferred income taxes	35,627	12,842
Deferred rent	85	41
Total liabilities	188,520	56,287
Stockholders' equity:		
Preferred stock, $.01 par value; 5,000,000 shares authorized, none issued	—	—
Common stock, $.01 par value; 100,000,000 shares authorized, 37,554,849 and 30,771,212 shares issued and outstanding at June 30, 1995 and 1994, respectively	375	308
Additional paid-in capital	251,539	98,836
Accumulated deficit	(33,970)	(847)
Total stockholders' equity	217,944	98,297
	$406,464	$154,584

See accompanying notes.

Exhibit 3   America Online 1995 Abridged Annual Report

NOTES TO CONSOLIDATED FINANCIAL STATEMENTS

1. Organization

America Online, Inc. ("the Company") was incorporated in the State of Delaware in May 1985. The Company, based in Vienna, Virginia, is a leading provider of online services, offering its subscribers a wide variety of services, including e-mail, online conferences, entertainment, software, computing support, interactive magazines and newspapers, and online classes, as well as easy and affordable access to services of the Internet. In addition, the Company is a provider of data network services, new media and interactive marketing services, and multimedia and CD-ROM production services.

2. Summary of Significant Accounting Policies

Principles of Consolidation – The consolidated financial statements include the accounts of the Company and its subsidiaries. All significant intercompany accounts and transactions have been eliminated. Investments in affiliates owned twenty percent or more and corporate joint ventures are accounted for under the equity method. Other securities in companies owned less than twenty percent are accounted for under the cost method.

Business Combinations – Business combinations which have been accounted for under the purchase method of accounting include the results of operations of the acquired business from the date of acquisition. Net assets of the companies acquired are recorded at their fair value to the Company at the date of acquisition.

Other business combinations have been accounted for under the pooling of interests method of accounting. In such cases, the assets, liabilities, and stockholders' equity of the acquired entities were combined with the Company's respective accounts at recorded values. Prior period financial statements have been restated to give effect to the merger unless the effect of the business combination

is not material to the financial statements of the Company.

Revenue and cost recognition – Online service revenue is recognized over the period services are provided. Other revenue, consisting principally of marketing, data network and multimedia production services, as well as development and royalty revenues, are recognized as services are rendered. Deferred revenue consists principally of third-party development funding not yet recognized and monthly subscription fees billed in advance.

Property and equipment – Property and equipment are depreciated or amortized using the straight-line method over the estimated useful life of the asset, which ranges from 5 to 40 years, or over the life of the lease.

Property and equipment under capital leases are stated at the lower of the present value of minimum lease payments at the beginning of the lease term or fair value at inception of the lease.

Deferred subscriber acquisition costs – Subscriber acquisition costs are deferred and charged to operations over a twelve or eighteen month period (straight-line method) beginning the month after such costs are incurred. These costs, which relate directly to subscriber solicitations, principally include printing, production and shipping of starter kits and the costs of obtaining qualified prospects by various targeted direct marketing programs (i.e., direct marketing response cards, mailing lists) and from third parties, and are recorded separately from ordinary operating expenses. No indirect costs are included in subscriber acquisition costs. To date, all subscriber acquisition costs have been incurred for the solicitation of specific identifiable prospects. Costs incurred for other than those targeted at specific identifiable prospects for the Company's services, and general marketing, are expensed as incurred.

The Company's services are sold on a monthly subscription basis. Subscriber acquisition costs incurred to obtain new subscribers are recoverable from revenues generated by such subscribers within a short period of time after such costs are incurred.

a

1-23

Exhibit 3   America Online 1995 Abridged Annual Report

Effective July 1, 1992, the Company changed, from twelve months to eighteen months, the period over which it amortizes the costs of deferred subscriber acquisition costs relating to marketing activities in which the Company's starter kit is bundled and distributed by a third-party marketing company. The change in accounting estimate was made to more accurately match revenues and expenses. Based on the Company's experience and the distribution channels used in such marketing activities, there is a greater time lag between the time the Company incurs the cost for the starter kits and the time the starter kits begin to generate new customers than with direct marketing activities. Also, the period over which new subscribers (and related revenues) are generated is longer than that experienced with the use of traditional independent, direct marketing activities. The effect of this change in accounting estimate for the year ended June 30, 1993 was to increase income before extraordinary item and net income by $264,000 ($.01 per share).

In the first quarter of fiscal 1995 the Company adopted the provisions of Statement of Position ("SOP") 93-7, "Reporting on Advertising Costs," which provides guidance on financial reporting on advertising costs. The adoption of SOP 93-7 had no effect on the Company's financial position or results of operations.

Product development costs – The Company capitalizes cost incurred for the production of computer software used in the sale of its services. Costs capitalized include direct labor and related overhead for software produced by the Company and the costs of software purchased from third parties. All costs in the software development process which are classified as research and development are expensed as incurred until technological feasibility has been established. Once technological feasibility has been established, such costs are capitalized until the software is commercially available. To the extent the Company retains the rights to software development funded by third parties, such costs are capitalized in accordance with the Company's normal accounting policies. Amortization is provided on a product-by-product basis, using the greater of the straight-line method or current year revenue as a percent of total

revenue estimates for the related software product not to exceed five years, commencing the month after the date of product release.

Product development costs consist of the following:

	Year ended June 30,	
	1995	1994
	(in thousands)	
Balance, beginning of year	$ 7,912	$3,915
Cost capitalized	13,011	5,132
Cost amortized	(2,009)	(1,135)
Balance, end of year	$18,914	$7,912

The accumulated amortization of product development costs related to the production of computer software totaled $7,894,000, and $5,885,000 at June 30, 1995 and 1994, respectively.

Included in product development costs are research and development costs totaling $3,856,000, $2,126,000, and $1,130,000 and other product development costs totaling $6,977,000, $1,050,000 and $579,000 in the years ended June 30, 1995, 1994 and 1993, respectively.

License rights – The cost of acquired license rights is amortized using the straight-line method over the term of the agreement for such license rights, ranging from one to three years.

Goodwill – Goodwill consists of the excess of cost over the fair value of net assets acquired and certain other intangible assets relating to purchase transactions. Goodwilll and intangible assets are amortized over periods ranging from 5–10 years.

Operating lease costs – Rent expense for operating leases is recognized on a straight-line basis over the lease term. The difference between rent expense incurred and rental payments is charged or credited to deferred rent.

Cash, cash equivalents and short-term investments – The Company considers all highly liquid investments with an original maturity of three months or less to be cash equivalents. In fiscal 1995, the Company adopted Statement of Financial

Exhibit 3   America Online 1995 Abridged Annual Report

Accounting Standards No. 115 ("SFAS 115"), "Accounting for Certain Investments in Debt and Equity Securities." The adoption was not material to the Company's financial position or results of operations. The Company has classified all debt and equity securities as available-for-sale. Available-for-sale securities are carried at fair value, with unrealized gains and losses reported as a separate component of stockholders' equity. Realized gains and losses and declines in value judged to be other-than-temporary on available-for-sale securities are included in other income. Available-for-sale securities at June 30, 1995, consisted of U.S. Treasury Bills and other obligations of U.S. Government agencies totaling $7,579,000 and U.S. corporate debt obligations totaling $11,093,000. At June 20, 1995, the estimated fair value of these securities approximated cost.

Net income (loss) per common share – Net income (loss) per share is calculated by dividing income (loss) before extraordinary item and net income (loss) by the weighted average number of common and, when dilutive, common equivalent shares outstanding during the period.

Reclassification – Certain amounts in prior years' consolidated financial statements have been reclassified to conform to the current year presentation.

3. Business Combination

Pooling Transactions

On August 19, 1994, Redgate Communications Corporation ("RCC") was merged with and into a subsidiary of the Company. The Company exchanged 1,789,300 shares of common stock for all of the outstanding common and preferred stock and warrants of RCC. Additionally, 401,148 shares of the Company's common stock were reserved for outstanding stock options issued by RCC and assumed by the Company. The merger was accounted for under the pooling of interests method of accounting, and accordingly, the accompanying consolidated financial statements have been restated for all periods prior to the acquisition to include the financial position, results of operations and cash flows of RCC. Effective August 1994, RCC's fiscal year-end has been changed from December 31 to June 30 to conform to the Company's fiscal year-end.

Revenues and net earnings (loss) for the individual entities are as follows:

	Three months ended September 30, 1994 (unaudited)	Year ended June 30, 1994	1993
		(in thousands)	
Total revenues:			
AOL	$50,783	$104,410	$40,019
RCC	3,813	11,312	11,965
Less intercompany sales	(173)	—	—
	$54,423	$115,722	$51,984
Net income (loss):			
AOL	$ 3,018	$ 6,210	$ 4,210
RCC	(42)	(3,660)	(2,678)
Merger expenses	(1,710)	—	—
	$ 1,266	$ 2,550	$ 1,532

Exhibit 3   America Online 1995 Abridged Annual Report

In connection with the merger of the Company and RCC, merger expenses of $1,710,000 were recognized during 1995.

During fiscal 1995, Medior, Inc. and Wide Area Information Servers, Inc. were merged into subsidiaries of the Company. The Company issued 1,082,019 shares of its common stock in the transactions. The transactions were accounted for under the pooling of interests method of accounting. Prior year financial statements have not been restated for the transactions because the effect would not be material to the operations of the Company.

Purchase Transactions

During fiscal 1995, the Company acquired NaviSoft, Inc. ("NaviSoft"), BookLink Technologies, Inc. ("BookLink"), Advanced Network & Services, Inc. ("ANS") and Global Network Navigator, Inc., in transactions accounted for under the purchase method of accounting. The Company paid a total of $97,669,000, of which $75,697,000 was in stock and $21,972,000 was in cash for the acquisitions. Of the aggregate purchase price, approximately $50,335,000 was allocated to in-process research and development and $55,314,000 was allocated to goodwill and other intangible assets.

The following unaudited pro forma information relating to the BookLink and ANS acquisitions is not necessarily an indication of the combined results that would have occurred had the acquisitions taken place at the beginning of the period, nor is necessarily an indication of the results that may occur in the future. Pro forma information for NaviSoft and Global Network Navigator, Inc. is immaterial to the operations of the consolidated entity. The amount of the aggregate purchase price allocated to in-process research and development for both the NaviSoft and BookLink acquisitions has been excluded from the pro forma information as it is a non-recurring item.

	Year ended June 30,	
	1995	1994
	(in thousands except per share data)	
Revenues	$410,147	$135,785
Income (loss) from operations	23,117	(5,465)
Pro forma income (loss)	11,205	(4,694)
Pro forma income (loss) per share	$ 0.25	$ (0.16)

4. Property and Equipment

Property and equipment consist of the following:

	June 30,	
	1995	1994
	(in thousands)	
Computer equipment	$49,167	$12,418
Furniture and fixtures	4,992	1,398
Buildings	13,800	5,648
Land	6,075	2,052
Building improvements	6,284	1,343
Property under capital leases	8,486	2,686
Leasehold improvements	3,059	306
	91,863	25,851
Less accumulated depreciation and amortization	(21,397)	(5,545)
Net property and equipment	$70,466	$20,306

5. License Rights

License rights consist of the following:

	June 30,	
	1995	1994
	(in thousands)	
License rights	$ 7,484	$ 954
Less accumulated amortization	(1,947)	(901)
	$ 5,537	$ 53

Exhibit 3   America Online 1995 Abridged Annual Report

6. Commitments and Contingencies

The Company leases equipment under several long-term capital and operating leases. Future minimum payments under capital leases and noncancelable operating leases with initial terms of one year or more consist of the following:

	Capital Leases	Operating Leases
	(in thousands)	
Year ending June 30,		
1996	$1,654	$20,997
1997	1,236	21,264
1998	641	19,450
1999	310	8,711
2000	103	3,511
Thereafter	—	2,636
Total minimum lease payments	3,944	$76,569
Less amount representing interest	(402)	
Present value of net minimum capital lease payments, including current portion of $1,415	$3,542	

The Company's rental expense under operating leases in the years ended June 30, 1995, 1994 and 1993 totaled approximately $10,001,000, $2,889,000, and $2,155,000, respectively.

Communication networks – The Company has guaranteed monthly usage levels of data and voice communications with one of its vendors. The remaining commitments are $113,400,000, $59,000,000, $9,000,000 and $6,750,000 for the years ending June 30, 1996, 1997, 1998 and 1999, respectively. The related expense for the years ended June 30, 1995, 1994 and 1993 was $138,793,000, $40,315,000 and $11,226,000, respectively.

Contingencies – Various legal proceedings have arisen against the Company in the ordinary course of business. In the opinion of management, these proceedings will not have a material effect on the financial position of the Company.

7. Notes Payable

Notes payable at June 30, 1995 totaled approximately $18 million and consist primarily of amounts borrowed to finance the purchases of two office buildings. The notes are collateralized by the respective properties. The notes have a variable interest rate equal to 105 basis points above the 30 day London Interbank Offered Rate and a fixed interest rate of 8.48% per annum at June 30, 1995. Aggregate maturities of notes payable for the years ended June 30, 1996, 1997, 1998, 1999, 2000 and thereafter are $415,000, $429,000, $445,000, $462,000, $480,000 and $15,553,000, respectively.

8. Other Income

The following table summarizes the components of other income:

	Year ended June 30,		
	1995	1994	1993
	(in thousands)		
Interest income	$3,920	$1,646	$572
Interest expense	(1,054)	(575)	(172)
Other	157	703	(29)
	$3,023	$1,774	$371

Exhibit 3   America Online 1995 Abridged Annual Report

9. Income Taxes

The provision for income taxes is attributable to:

	Year ended June 30,		
	1995	1994	1993
	(in thousands)		
Income before extraordinary item	$15,169	$3,832	$1,897
Tax benefit arising from net operating loss carryforward	—	—	(1,133)
	$15,169	$3,832	$ 764
Current	$ —	$ —	$ 5
Deferred	15,169	3,832	759
	$15,169	$3,832	$ 764

The provision for income taxes differs from the amount computed by applying the statutory federal income tax rate to income before provision for income taxes and extraordinary item. The sources and tax effects of the differences are as follows:

	Year ended June 30,		
	1995	1994	1993
	(in thousands)		
Income tax at the federal statutory rate of 34%	$ (6,283)	$2,170	$ 781
State income tax, net of federal benefit	1,597	403	200
Losses relating to RCC	—	1,259	916
Nondeductible merger expenses	750	—	—
Nondeductible charge for purchased research and development	17,114	—	—
Loss, for which no tax benefit was derived	1,632	—	—
Other	359	—	—
	$15,169	$3,832	$1,897

Deferred income taxes arise because of differences in the treatment of income and expense items for financial reporting and income tax purposes, primarily relating to deferred subscriber acquisition and product development costs.

As of June 30, 1995, the Company has net operating loss carryforwards of approximately $109 million for tax purposes which will be available, subject to certain annual limitations, to offset future taxable income. If not used, these loss carryforwards will expire between 2001 and 2010. To the extent that net operating loss carryforwards, when realized, relate to stock option deductions, the resulting benefits will be credited to stockholders' equity.

The Company's income tax provision was computed on the federal statutory rate and the average state statutory rates, net of the related federal benefit.

Effective July 1, 1993 the Company changed its method of accounting for income taxes from the deferred method to the liability method required by FASB Statement No. 109, "Accounting for Income Taxes." As permitted under the new rules, prior years' financial statements have not been restated.

No increase to net income resulted from the cumulative effect of adopting Statement No. 109 as of July 1, 1993. The deferred tax asset increased by approximately $5,965,000 as a result of the adoption. Similarly, the deferred tax liability, stockholders' equity and the valuation allowance increased by approximately $3,173,000, $759,000 and $2,033,000, respectively.

Deferred income taxes reflect the net tax effects of temporary differences between the carrying amounts of assets and liabilities for financial reporting purposes and the amounts used for income tax purposes. Significant components of the Company's deferred tax liabilities and assets are as follows:

Exhibit 3   America Online 1995 Abridged Annual Report

	Year ended June 30,	
	1995	1994
	(in thousands)	
Deferred tax liabilities:		
Capitalized software costs	$ 7,008	$ 2,962
Deferred member acquisi-		
tion costs	28,619	9,880
Net deferred tax liabilities	$35,627	$12,842
Deferred tax assets:		
Net operating loss carry-		
forwards	$39,000	$17,510
Total deferred tax assets	39,000	17,510
Valuation allowance for		
deferred assets	(3,373)	(4,668)
Net deferred tax assets	$35,627	$12,842

13. Subsequent Event

On August 23, 1995, the Company entered into a stock purchase agreement to purchase Ubique, Ltd., an Israeli company. The Company has agreed to pay approximately $15 million ($1.5 million in cash and $13.5 million in common stock) in the transaction, which is to be accounted for under the purchase method of accounting. Subject to the results of an in-process valuation, a substantial portion of the purchase price may be allocated to in-process research and development and charged to the Company's operations in the first quarter of fiscal 1996.

a

QUARTERLY INFORMATION (unaudited)

	Quarter Ended				
	September 30	December 31	March 31	June 30	Total
Fiscal 1995[a]					
Online service revenues	$50,056	$69,712	$99,814	$138,916	$358,498
Other revenues	6,880	6,683	9,290	12,939	35,792
Total revenues	56,936	76,395	109,104	151,855	394,290
Income (loss) from operations	4,623	(35,258)	233	11,108	(19,294)
Net income (loss)	1,481	(38,730)	(2,587)	6,189	(33,647)
Net income (loss) per share[b]	$ 0.04	$ (0.20)	$ (0.07)	$ 0.13	$ (0.99)
Fiscal 1994					
Online service revenues	$14,299	$20,292	$28,853	$37,549	$100,993
Other revenues	4,780	4,239	2,836	2,874	14,729
Total revenues	19,079	24,531	31,689	40,423	115,722
Income from operations	531	520	1,931	1,626	4,608
Net income	303	70	1,272	905	2,550
Net income per share[b]	$ 0.01	$ —	$ 0.03	$ 0.02	$ 0.07

a. *Historical financial information for amounts previously reported in fiscal 1995 has been adjusted to account for pooling of interest transactions.*

b. *The sum of per-share earnings (loss) does not equal earnings (loss) per share for the year due to equivalent share calculations which are impacted by the Company's loss in 1995 and by fluctuations in the Company's common stock market prices.*

It is mid-1992. The collection of industries under the heading "computer systems" (SIC 3571) grew dramatically during the 1970s and 1980s, but it is now in a state of turmoil. Most firms have suffered declines in earnings, and several—including industry giants IBM and Digital Equipment Corporation—have experienced large losses. Overall, profitability (as measured by return on equity) in the industry has fallen steadily from 23 percent in 1988 to 11 percent in 1991, and sales have been flat for the last two years. In the face of this turmoil, however, some firms with well-positioned product lines have managed to grow at a quick pace. For example, Sun Microsystems, a major player in the expanding market for workstations, experienced a 30 percent compounded annual growth rate from 1986 through 1991.

Standard and Poor's Corporation describes the situation as follows:

Computer manufacturers have become used to citing the reasons for the present malaise in the information technology business. These include the following:

1. The spread of open system computer networks based on standard industry components that cannot command the gross profit margins inherent in proprietary designs. The gross margin associated with a mainframe computer sale can be as high as 70 percent; for personal computers (PCs) and workstations, it can be less than 30 percent.

2. A seemingly never-ending decline in the cost, and growth in the power of data processing equipment, which has further squeezed manufacturers' margins. A high performance workstation can cost less than $1000 for every million instructions per second (mips) of computer power. Mainframes typically cost more than $100,000 per mip. For many tasks, but not all, it is possible to substitute low-cost workstation power for mainframe power.

3. A slackening of demand for computer systems . . . [due to] saturation in some areas of the market, dissatisfaction with the results of continued computerization, and (in some countries) high interest rates.[1]

To deal with the changes in the industry, some firms have abandoned product differentiation, cut prices, and focused on cost reduction. Some have undergone major restructurings. Several firms, including Apple and IBM, have formed new alliances.

....

This case was prepared by Professor Victor L. Bernard, and is based upon publicly available information. It was prepared as a basis for class discussion and is not intended to illustrate either an effective or ineffective management of a business situation.

1. *Standard and Poor's Industry Report Service (July 3, 1992), Vol. 3., No. 2, Sec. 2.*

The following brief sketches of four computing systems manufacturers help describe the variety of experience within the industry.

ATARI CORPORATION

Atari manufactures personal computers and video game systems. The firm's principle products are its Atari ST series of PCs, based on Motorola 68000 and 68030 series microprocessors and employing Atari's own TOS operating system with state-of-the-art graphical interface; its PC-compatible, MS-DOS based personal computers, including the one-pound Atari Portfolio and full-scale PCs driven by an 80386 microprocessor; Atari 8-bit microcomputers, which retail for less than $100; and video game systems. There are over 8000 software titles available for the ST computers, as well as a variety of peripherals. The fractions of net sales accounted for by the various product lines have been as follows:

	1991	1990	1989
Atari ST personal computers	.53	.59	.59
Atari PC compatible palm-top & personal computers	.10	.18	.17
Atari microcomputers	.03	.02	.06
Atari video game systems	.34	.21	.18

More than 80 percent of Atari's sales are in Europe, where it holds about 5 percent of the PC market, ranking behind IBM, Commodore, Olivetti, and Amstrad, and barely ahead of Apple Macintosh and Compaq. Until the second quarter of 1991, the company's principle products were manufactured in Taiwan, but that facility was sold. Since that time, various independent subcontractors have assembled the products, and some start-up problems were encountered. Atari intends to acquire another location for its manufacturing operations and resume in-house production.

Net sales declined 37 percent for Atari in 1991. In his letter to shareholders, Atari CEO Sam Tramiel (son of 46-percent owner Jack Tramiel) was straightforward: "I am quite displeased with the company's 1991 results, and hope that this message accurately conveys my dissatisfaction." Net income in 1991 reached its highest level since 1987, but only after inclusion of a $40.9 million pretax gain on the sale of its Taiwan manufacturing facility. Atari's ST sales continued the slide that began in 1990, as software producers—miffed by Atari's giveaway of prepackaged programs with ST computers—shifted their efforts to Apple and DOS systems.

Tramiel points to several corrections in Atari's strategy, all of which were in place or being put into place by the end of fiscal 1991. The changes include (1) cost reductions and careful monitoring of inventory levels, (2) refocusing of advertising to target specific audiences and reduce costs, and (3) redefining R&D, with a shift in emphasis to high volume production. Looking forward to late 1992, Atari is also ready to bring two new products to market. One is the Falcon 030, a more powerful version of the ST computer; the other is Jaguar, the next-generation video game console.

A summary of Atari's recent financial performance appears in Exhibit 1. The company experienced a loss in the first quarter of 1992 equal to 11 percent of beginning equity. Analysts' forecasts for future performance are not available.

CRAY RESEARCH

Cray is the leading manufacturer of supercomputers, used in weather forecasting, aircraft and automotive design, scientific research, and seismic analysis. At the end of 1991, 324 Cray supercomputer systems were in use, including 68 installed in 1991. Approximately half of Cray sales for 1991 were in the U.S.; remaining sales were primarily in Western Europe and Pacific Asia. Cray is clearly the world leader in supercomputers, holding a market share in excess of 50 percent. However, it faces competition not only from other supercomputer manufacturers but also from the increasing power of "mini-supercomputers."

Cray supercomputers have generally relied on a single microprocessor. However, there has been a shift in high-speed computing toward massively parallel processing (MPP), which allows the simultaneous employment of many microprocessors. Cray has recently developed a partnership with Digital Equipment Corporation (DEC), to produce MPP implementations for sale by 1993. Cray also announced that, beginning in 1992, their EL systems will be sold not only through existing channels, but also through DEC's distribution network. The EL systems are "low-end" supercomputers, selling for approximately $350,000; some of its purchasers may ultimately upgrade to larger systems. Cray's high-end C90 systems sell for $30 million.

Cray also formed an alliance with Sun Microsystems that would facilitate seamless linkage of Cray computers and Sun workstations, as well as allow the use of Sun's SPARC chip in new Cray hardware. In the meantime, Cray introduced five new supercomputer systems in 1991. In their letter to shareholders, the CEO and COO labeled the market's response as "enthusiastic," and reported 58 new customers in 1991, more than in any previous year.

During 1991, Cray's revenues increased by seven percent, while profits increased only slightly. While such performance might normally be viewed as disappointing, Cray's letter to shareholders placed it in context: "These results came during what many observers are describing as the worst year overall in the computer industry's history." Based on Cray's performance relative to the industry, management indicated that "these results mean that we will not have to divert our attention in 1992 to 'rebuilding' or 'restructuring' efforts that have become almost commonplace in the industry."

During the first quarter of 1992, Cray installed 11 new and 2 used systems, generating sales of $165 million, up 15 percent over the first quarter of 1991. Nevertheless, net income fell 26 percent, to $3.9 million, reflecting lower volume in high-end systems. In mid-1992, Cray is just beginning to ship its top-of-the-line C90 systems at the rate of

C

1-3

about one per month. Analysts expect that Cray, which tends to make a big push to install systems before years' end, will see a pickup in earnings in the latter half of the year. Analysts forecast sales increases of 10 percent and 11 percent for 1992 and 1993, respectively, and return on equity of 13 to 14 percent in each year.

A summary of Cray's financial statements for recent years appears in Exhibit 2.

TANDEM COMPUTERS

Tandem operates within the niche of fault-tolerant mainframe and mid-range computer systems. Its products (labeled NonStop systems) are used in on-line transaction processing (OLTP) in banking, manufacturing, communications, distribution, brokerage and securities, and other industries. NonStop systems feature multiple independent processors, and are designed to continue operating through any single processor failure. (This is referred to as "continuous availability.") Beginning in 1990, Tandem produced a new fault-tolerant, high performance UNIX-based system, based on the high-speed Reduced Instruction Set Computing (RISC) technology. Through its subsidiary, Ungermann-Bass, Tandem also produces general-purpose local area networks. Almost half of Tandem's sales are within the U.S.; the remainder are primarily in Europe, with some in the Pacific Rim and elsewhere.

Tandem pioneered the fault-tolerant market and remains the acknowledged worldwide leader in fault-tolerant systems, with a 70 percent market share. However, it faces competition from Digital Equipment, Hewlett-Packard, Fujitsu, and Hitachi—all of which have entered the market in recent years—and from Stratus, a much smaller manufacturer. Moreover, some standard mid-range systems (produced by IBM and others) now have fault-tolerant capabilities, and so lines are blurring between the fault-tolerant market and mainstream systems market.

Tandem's revenues increased only slightly in 1991, and earnings declined. In the Tandem Annual Report for 1991, President and CEO James Treybig stated that "we are not satisfied with our financial results," and attributed the firm's difficulties to "the length and severity of a widespread recession." He indicated that the firm would "change the basic cost structure of [its] business" by reducing the size of its workforce, eliminating redundancies, increasing the leverage of sales and marketing efforts, and realigning the organization. Treybig indicated that Tandem would capitalize on opportunities in an OLTP marketplace that would continue to grow by "extending leadership in price/performance, open networking, and continuous availability." However, with the product cycle just beginning for some new RISC-based systems, substantial growth in Tandem sales could be a few quarters away.

In the first quarter of 1992, Tandem recorded an after-tax restructuring charge of $80 million, while sales rose only slightly. Thanks to that change, analysts expect the ROE to be only 4.3 percent in 1992, but to rise to 8.1 percent in 1993. Sales growth is projected at 4 to 5 percent for the next two years.

A summary of Tandem's recent financial statement data appears in Exhibit 3.

STRATUS COMPUTER

Like Tandem, Stratus produces fault-tolerant computer systems for use in OLTP, and is introducing a new generation of RISC-based fault-tolerant computers. Stratus systems consists of up to 32 processing modules connected via a high-speed communications link. The systems are used in the securities industry, banking, distribution, plant management, hotel reservation systems, and communications. Stratus is the only computer company in the world totally focused on continuous availability for OLTP; its 1991 annual report claims that, of their 150 largest bids of the year, "not one situation was reported where a competitor could show higher availability than Stratus."

Stratus was but a minor player in the fault-tolerant market until the mid- to late 1980s, but it now holds a 21 percent market share, second only to Tandem. More than half of Stratus sales are within the U.S., with Europe accounting for most other sales. Sales to IBM—which sells Stratus equipment on an OEM basis—accounted for 23 percent of Stratus sales in 1991, down from 26 percent in 1990 and 35 percent in 1989. Stratus is attempting to diversify its customer base, and expects increases in its sales to NEC (1.5 percent of 1991 sales) and others.

Stratus revenues for 1991 were up 11 percent, while earnings rose 34 percent. In its upbeat annual report to shareholders, Stratus emphasized what it considers its systems' unparalleled record of online applications availability, and indicated that "the growth of critical online applications is outpacing the abilities of most vendors to provide the levels of availability that customers actually need. This presents Stratus with the opportunity to capitalize on the trend that more businesses are becoming increasingly reliant on their online computer systems."

In the first quarter of 1992, sales growth slowed to "only" 9 percent, largely because of a dropoff of sales to IBM. However, earnings rose 40 percent. Analysts are projecting ROE of about 17 percent for 1992 and 1993, on sales growth of 13 percent in 1992 and 17 percent in 1993.

A summary of Stratus's recent financial statement data appears in Exhibit 4.

C

1-5

EXHIBIT 1
Atari Corporation – Common-Size Financial Statements and Selected Ratios

	1991	1990	1989	1988	1987
Cash	0.275	0.135	0.166	0.272	0.200
Receivables	0.318	0.352	0.324	0.297	0.196
Inventory	0.321	0.419	0.393	0.348	0.380
Other current assets	0.030	0.026	0.046	0.041	0.007
Total current assets	0.944	0.933	0.928	0.958	0.783
Plant, property, equip	0.038	0.050	0.042	0.025	0.128
Other long-term assets	0.018	0.017	0.030	0.017	0.089
Total assets	1.000	1.000	1.000	1.000	1.000
Notes payable	0.001	0.000	0.000	0.000	0.003
Other current liabilities	0.312	0.449	0.506	0.532	0.416
Total current liabilities	0.313	0.449	0.506	0.532	0.419
Long term debt	0.191	0.180	0.234	0.222	0.258
Other liabilities	0.000	0.000	0.000	0.000	0.000
Total liabilities	0.505	0.629	0.740	0.754	0.677
Shareholders' equity	0.495	0.371	0.260	0.246	0.323
Total liabilities and equity	1.000	1.000	1.000	1.000	1.000
Total assets (millions)	$253	$273	$331	$338	$518
Sales	1.000	1.000	1.000	1.000	1.000
Cost of sales	0.725	0.766	0.725	0.616	0.608
SGA expense	0.338	0.284	0.261	0.248	0.250
Operating income before depreciation	−0.063	−0.050	0.015	0.136	0.142
Depreciation	0.010	0.012	0.006	0.005	0.009
Interest expense	0.017	0.016	0.015	0.011	0.011
Nonoperating gain/loss	0.024	0.030	0.012	0.008	0.029
Special gain/loss	0.156	0.000	0.000	0.000	0.000
Income before tax	0.091	−0.047	0.006	0.129	0.152
Income tax provision	0.000	0.004	−0.004	0.042	0.062
Income before extraordinary items	0.092	−0.051	0.009	0.087	0.090
Net income	0.099	0.036	0.009	−0.188	0.116
Sales (millions)	$258	$411	$424	$452	$493
EBI/Sales	0.098	−0.044	0.015	0.091	0.094
Earnings/EBI	0.933	1.144	0.615	0.954	0.955
Sales turnover = sales/average assets	0.981	1.364	1.266	1.056	
Leverage = assets/equity (average)	2.320	3.222	3.953	3.415	
ROE = product of above	0.209	−0.223	0.047	0.314	

EBI = earnings before interest, net of tax. Tax effect of interest is assumed to be 40 percent.

EXHIBIT 2
Cray Research – Common-Size Financial Statements and Selected Ratios

	1991	1990	1989	1988	1987
Cash	0.034	0.071	0.072	0.182	0.194
Receivables	0.226	0.124	0.188	0.118	0.107
Inventory	0.227	0.191	0.212	0.238	0.214
Other current assets	0.030	0.024	0.007	0.005	0.006
Total current assets	0.517	0.409	0.479	0.543	0.520
Plant, property, equip	0.333	0.367	0.325	0.291	0.242
Other long-term assets	0.150	0.224	0.196	0.166	0.238
Total assets	1.000	1.000	1.000	1.000	1.000
Notes payable	0.006	0.039	0.053	0.009	0.010
Other current liabilities	0.186	0.177	0.175	0.192	0.176
Total current liabilities	0.192	0.216	0.227	0.201	0.186
Long term debt	0.100	0.112	0.151	0.111	0.120
Other liabilities	0.006	0.006	0.000	0.005	0.017
Total liabilities	0.297	0.334	0.378	0.317	0.323
Shareholders' equity	0.703	0.666	0.622	0.683	0.677
Total liabilities and equity	1.000	1.000	1.000	1.000	1.000
Total assets (millions)	$1,079	$944	$956	$991	$902
Sales	1.000	1.000	1.000	1.000	1.000
Cost of sales	0.333	0.306	0.289	0.272	0.252
SGA expense	0.348	0.356	0.370	0.330	0.321
Operating income before depreciation	0.320	0.338	0.341	0.398	0.426
Depreciation	0.131	0.137	0.130	0.110	0.105
Interest expense	0.009	0.010	0.011	0.010	0.013
Nonoperating gain/loss	0.009	0.022	0.023	0.031	0.029
Special gain/loss	0.005	−0.004	−0.061	0.000	0.000
Income before tax	0.193	0.209	0.162	0.309	0.338
Income tax provision	0.062	0.068	0.049	0.102	0.124
Income before extraordinary items	0.131	0.140	0.113	0.207	0.214
Net income	0.131	0.140	0.113	0.207	0.214
Sales (millions)	$862	$804	$785	$756	$687
EBI/Sales	0.135	0.144	0.118	0.211	0.219
Earnings/EBI	0.973	0.972	0.964	0.980	0.976
Sales turnover = sales/average assets	0.852	0.847	0.806	0.799	
Leverage = assets/equity (average)	1.458	1.553	1.532	1.471	
ROE = product of above	0.163	0.185	0.140	0.243	

C

1-7

EBI = earnings before interest, net of tax. Tax effect of interest is assumed to be 40 percent.

EXHIBIT 3
Tandem Computers – Common-Size Financial Statements and Selected Ratios

	1991	1990	1989	1988	1987
Cash	0.059	0.049	0.122	0.095	0.328
Receivables	0.258	0.264	0.259	0.270	0.263
Inventory	0.080	0.100	0.089	0.098	0.095
Other current assets	0.054	0.047	0.063	0.026	0.024
Total current assets	0.452	0.460	0.533	0.488	0.711
Plant, property, equip	0.331	0.341	0.276	0.317	0.261
Other long-term assets	0.218	0.199	0.190	0.194	0.028
Total assets	1.000	1.000	1.000	1.000	1.000
Notes payable	0.022	0.016	0.024	0.007	0.002
Other current liabilities	0.243	0.248	0.249	0.270	0.197
Total current liabilities	0.265	0.263	0.273	0.277	0.198
Long term debt	0.048	0.051	0.066	0.044	0.009
Other liabilities	0.041	0.045	0.050	0.029	0.047
Total liabilities	0.354	0.359	0.389	0.350	0.255
Shareholders' equity	0.646	0.641	0.611	0.650	0.745
Total liabilities and equity	1.000	1.000	1.000	1.000	1.000
Total assets (millions)	$1,932	$1,877	$1,619	$1,318	$967
Sales	1.000	1.000	1.000	1.000	1.000
Cost of sales	0.328	0.294	0.306	0.309	0.298
SGA expense	0.575	0.541	0.516	0.517	0.489
Operating income before depreciation	0.097	0.165	0.178	0.174	0.213
Depreciation	0.066	0.064	0.065	0.062	0.048
Interest expense	0.011	0.010	0.007	0.007	0.002
Nonoperating gain/loss	0.010	0.010	0.008	0.013	0.015
Special gain/loss	0.000	0.000	0.000	−0.007	0.000
Income before tax	0.030	0.100	0.114	0.111	0.179
Income tax provision	0.011	0.035	0.042	0.039	0.077
Income before extraordinary items	0.018	0.065	0.072	0.072	0.102
Net income	0.018	0.065	0.072	0.072	0.102
Sales (millions)	$1,922	$1,866	$1,633	$1,315	$1,035
EBI/Sales	0.023	0.069	0.075	0.075	0.102
Earnings/EBI	0.812	0.940	0.964	0.961	0.993
Sales turnover = sales/average assets	1.009	1.067	1.112	1.150	
Leverage = assets/equity (average)	1.554	1.595	1.591	1.449	
ROE = product of above	0.029	0.111	0.128	0.120	

EBI = earnings before interest, net of tax. Tax effect of interest is assumed to be 40 percent.

EXHIBIT 4
Stratus Computer – Common-Size Financial Statements and Selected Ratios

	1991	1990	1989	1988	1987
Cash	0.256	0.133	0.117	0.142	0.223
Receivables	0.348	0.379	0.417	0.375	0.356
Inventory	0.169	0.217	0.166	0.228	0.190
Other current assets	0.023	0.026	0.019	0.016	0.016
Total current assets	0.796	0.755	0.719	0.760	0.786
Plant, property, equip	0.171	0.199	0.245	0.209	0.196
Other long-term assets	0.033	0.046	0.036	0.030	0.018
Total assets	1.000	1.000	1.000	1.000	1.000
Notes payable	0.010	0.014	0.015	0.014	0.013
Other current liabilities	0.157	0.210	0.207	0.240	0.240
Total current liabilities	0.167	0.224	0.222	0.253	0.254
Long term debt	0.007	0.044	0.107	0.051	0.042
Other liabilities	0.010	0.014	0.000	0.000	0.000
Total liabilities	0.184	0.283	0.329	0.304	0.296
Shareholders' equity	0.816	0.717	0.671	0.696	0.704
Total liabilities and equity	1.000	1.000	1.000	1.000	1.000
Total assets (millions)	$385	$321	$274	$200	$145
Sales	1.000	1.000	1.000	1.000	1.000
Cost of sales	0.340	0.361	0.342	0.354	0.319
SGA expense	0.457	0.463	0.451	0.436	0.470
Operating income before depreciation	0.203	0.176	0.207	0.210	0.211
Depreciation	0.064	0.049	0.049	0.040	0.044
Interest expense	0.004	0.007	0.005	0.000	0.000
Nonoperating gain/loss	0.010	0.008	0.009	0.003	0.005
Special gain/loss	0.002	0.000	0.000	0.000	0.000
Income before tax	0.146	0.127	0.162	0.173	0.172
Income tax provision	0.035	0.036	0.058	0.062	0.066
Income before extraordinary items	0.111	0.092	0.104	0.111	0.105
Net income	0.111	0.092	0.104	0.111	0.105
Sales (millions)	$449	$404	$341	$265	$184
EBI/Sales	0.112	0.094	0.106	0.111	0.105
Earnings/EBI	0.985	0.970	0.982	1.000	1.000
Sales turnover = sales/average assets	1.271	1.357	1.441	1.537	
Leverage = assets/equity (average)	1.297	1.437	1.467	1.430	
ROE= product of above	0.183	0.179	0.219	0.243	

EBI = earnings before interest, net of tax. Tax effect of interest is assumed to be 40 percent.

CUC International, Inc. (A)

In March 1989 Stuart Bell, Executive Vice President and CFO of CUC International, Inc., was concerned that the company's stock was seriously undervalued. He attributed the undervaluation to the investment community's concern about the quality of CUC's earnings:

> I am afraid our accounting is misunderstood by many investors. Recently, we have been forced to spend a lot of top management time and energy defending our policy in analysts' meetings. As a result we have been unable to focus investors' attention on our innovative business strategy and the tremendous cash-flow generating potential of our business. Concerns about our earnings quality are scaring new institutional investors from investing in our business. Many money managers tell me that they love our business concept but are afraid to buy our stock because they are worried about our accounting. The accounting is also giving short sellers an excuse to scare our current investors and drive down the stock price.

While Bell was convinced that CUC's accounting was appropriate, he wondered whether it was actually hurting, rather than helping, the company. What, if anything, should CUC do to shore up investors' confidence in the company?

BUSINESS HISTORY AND OPERATIONS

CUC International, located in Stamford, Connecticut, was a membership-based consumer services company. CUC marketed its membership programs to credit cardholders of major financial, retailing, and oil companies, including Chase Manhattan, Citibank, Sears, JC Penney, and Amoco. The company was formed in 1973 as Comp-U-Card of America, went public in 1983, and was renamed CUC International in 1987. As a result of its strong performance, the company was included in *Inc.* magazine's list of the fastest growing public companies in 1984 and 1986.

CUC's most popular product was Shoppers Advantage, introduced in 1981. Consumers paid an annual membership fee for this service, which entitled them to call the company's operators on a toll-free line, or to use on-line computer access seven days a week

This case was prepared by Professor Paul Healy of M.I.T. Sloan School and Professor Krishna Palepu of Harvard Business School as the basis for class discussion rather than to illustrate either effective or ineffective handling of an administrative situation. Copyright © 1992 by the President and Fellows of Harvard College. Harvard Business School case 9-192-099.

to inquire about, price, and/or buy brand-name products. Shoppers Advantage offered more than 250,000 brand-name and specialty items. Many members used the service principally as a reference for comparison pricing, not necessarily to purchase items directly. The company's large membership base allowed it to negotiate attractive discounts on the products offered in its catalog. As a result, the company guaranteed its subscribers the lowest prices available on goods it sold. If a member, after purchasing merchandise through CUC, sent an advertisement from an authorized dealer with a lower price within 30 days of placing an order, the company agreed to refund the difference. Members' purchase orders were executed through independent vendors who shipped the merchandise directly to customers, enabling the company to carry no inventory.

The firm acquired a large share of its new members through agreements with major credit card issuers, who provided CUC access to its list of cardholders. These individuals were solicited by three direct marketing approaches: billing statement inserts, solo mailings, and telemarketing. In billing statement insert programs, membership applications were enclosed in the monthly billing statements of credit card issuers. Solo mailings were membership offers mailed directly. Telemarketing involved following up mailings with telephone calls to explain membership offers further. CUC paid 10 percent to 20 percent of initial and renewal membership fees as a commission to the credit card company.

CUC incurred a large one-time cost for new member solicitations. Because only a small fraction of people reached through direct mail solicitations purchased the service, membership acquisition costs typically exceeded membership fees in the first year. For example, in 1989 the annual membership fee for Shoppers Advantage was $39, the average solicitation cost per new member was $29.37, commissions to the credit card companies were $6.63, and the average operating service cost per member was $5.00. Thus on average for each new member acquired, CUC incurred a cash outflow of $2 in the first year.

Members subscribed to Shoppers Advantage for a single year at a time. Renewals were automatically billed each year through the credit card company, and members could elect to cancel the service. There were thus no direct solicitation costs for renewing members. In 1989 CUC had a net cash inflow of $27.37 for each renewing member—membership fees were $39, and the commissions to the credit card companies and operating service costs totaled $11.63.[1] Membership renewal rates were therefore a key determinant of the profitability of the Shoppers Advantage program. The average annual renewal rate for Shoppers Advantage in recent years was 71 percent, making the program very profitable. This average was based on eight years' experience with the product since 1981.

CUC capitalized on its Shoppers Advantage experience by introducing a variety of other membership-based products. These included: (1) Travellers Advantage—a travel membership created in 1988 to provide subscribers access to database information and reservations on discount airline travel, hotels and auto rental, tours, and cruises; (2) AutoVantage—provided subscribers with new car price and performance summaries,

---

1. The figures in this and the previous paragraph are from an analyst report by Brian E. Stack of Advest, Inc. dated October 30, 1989.

used car valuations, and parts and service discounts; and (3) Premier Dining—a service introduced in 1989 that offered subscribers two-for-one dining at mid- to upscale restaurants in major U.S. cities. The company made large marketing investments to build memberships in these new programs.

CUC's management explained the key elements of its business strategy as follows:

> The company's expansion has been built on a foundation of creating, developing, and marketing a broad array of valuable services to consumers. . . . Aggressive marketing is an important strength. We sell our goods and services directly to millions of customers of major credit card issuers. Because our consumer services are a natural enhancement to personal financial services, more than 40 of the top 50 money center banks and a growing number of retailers and oil companies find it advantageous to work with CUC. . . . As competition heats up in the financial services industry, demand for CUC's services is likely to increase. Credit card issuers rely upon our services to draw new customers, increase card use, and raise average balances. They also use our services to differentiate their cards from others, and to tailor what they offer to appeal to different life-style and geographic preferences. Finally, card issuers benefit from the stream of membership commissions they receive from CUC.[2]

By December 1988, CUC had approximately 12 million members enrolled in its programs. Revenues had grown from $45 million in the year ending January 31, 1984 (fiscal year 1984) to $198 million in the year ending January 31,1988 (fiscal 1988), and earnings had grown from $3 million to $17 million during this period. Exhibits 3 and 4 present the financial statements for the year ended January 31, 1988, and for the nine months ended October 31, 1988. Management expected the company to continue its rapid growth in the future, with revenues for the fiscal year ending January 31, 1989 projected to be approximately $270 million.

THE FINANCIAL REPORTING CONTROVERSY

CUC's management decided that because current marketing outlays provided significant future benefits, the company should capitalize membership solicitation costs in its financial statements, and amortize them over three years at rates of 40 percent, 30 percent, and 30 percent. This choice was endorsed by Ernst & Whinney, the company's auditors, and by the Securities and Exchange Commission when the company went public.

While it was unusual to capitalize marketing costs, CUC's managers believed that this decision was justified given the nature of the company's business and their confidence in future renewal rates. Bell explained the rationale behind CUC's accounting choice:

> Many companies spend money on acquiring plant and equipment, and they capitalize these costs. Our business does not require major investments in plant and

C
2-3

2. Source: CUC's 1988 Annual Report.

equipment. Instead, it requires investments in membership acquisitions. Because our membership renewal rates are so high and steady, I believe that it is important for accounting to reflect future benefits from spending money on membership acquisition in the current period. While expensing these costs is conservative, it fails to reflect their true nature.

In its accounting choice, CUC's management could not obtain much guidance from other companies' practices. Magazine publishers typically expensed costs of acquiring new subscribers, whereas insurance companies capitalized policy acquisition costs. Safecard Services, Inc., a credit-card registration company which also incurred large outlays for membership acquisition, capitalized its membership acquisition costs and amortized them over a ten-year period.

When CUC made the initial public stock offering, it had only a limited following among analysts and institutional investors. As the company grew larger, it sought to broaden its investor base. Some analysts, however, were concerned that capitalized marketing costs would subsequently have to be written off as losses because of high uncertainty about future renewal rates. They argued that deferring current marketing costs lowered the firm's earnings quality.

Analysts' concerns about the firm's accounting for marketing costs may have arisen from their experience with Safecard Services Inc. Safecard's capitalization of membership acquisition costs had been the subject of considerable controversy in the financial press. Safecard's decision to write off deferred marketing costs in 1987 may have heightened analysts' concerns about the value of CUC's capitalized marketing costs.

By early 1989 the company's stock had become a target of short sellers and its price began to suffer. As shown in Exhibit 1, short positions in the company rose from approximately 157,000 in November 1988 to more than 2,000,000 in March 1989.[3] While the stock market was generally on the upswing, CUC's stock price declined from $19.3 at the beginning of January 1988 to $16.3 at the beginning of March 1989. Exhibit 2 shows the stock price performance for CUC relative to the performance of the value-weighted OTC market index between January 1, 1988, and March 1, 1989. During this period CUC's stock price declined by 50 percent relative to the market. *Value Line Investment Survey* commented in its report on CUC dated March 17, 1989:

> *CUC International shares have taken a beating. The stock has fallen more than 35% since our last report three months ago. Wall Street's concern over the company's accounting methods . . . contributed to the stock price decline.*

Management believed that the decline in CUC's stock performance could not be explained by either disappointing current operating performance or by forecasts of slower growth. Quarterly revenues and earnings grew steadily throughout 1988, and were consistent with *Value Line* analyst forecasts. In its March 18, 1988, report, *Value Line* forecasted that the company would have earnings of $5.5 million, $6 million, and $6.6 million in the quarters ending in April 1988, July 1988, and October 1988. Actual earnings in these quarters were $6 million, $6.6 million, and $6.9 million, respectively. The

---

3. *Source:* Barron's Financial Weekly *(Down Jones News Service).*

company projected that its growth would continue in the future—sales were projected to grow by 30 percent per year and operating cash flows would grow by 60 percent per year during the next five years. Finally, the firm was able to fund its substantial marketing outlays solely from operating cash flows during this period.

POSSIBLE MANAGEMENT RESPONSES

At least three options were available to CUC's management in responding to investors' concerns. One approach would be to adopt a more conservative policy to account for membership acquisition costs. By writing off previously capitalized expenses and adopting a policy of expensing future outlays as incurred, the firm would eliminate the major source of analysts' criticisms. However, such a move would seriously affect the company's balance sheet and income statement. More importantly, the accounting change would be unlikely to help management convince investors that current marketing outlays have future benefits.

An alternative strategy would be to provide expanded disclosure to justify the firm's capitalization of membership acquisition costs. This approach would involve identifying what type of information is likely to be most relevant and credible to investors. Further, it would require assessing whether the additional disclosures would provide proprietary information to competitors.

Finally, CUC could use corporate finance policies to enhance its stock price. Investors typically interpret cash payouts in the form of dividends and share repurchases as an indication of management's optimism about the firm's future cash flows. Such payouts, however, need to be planned in the context of the firm's investment needs for membership acquisitions.

One of the items on the agenda of CUC's upcoming board meeting was to consider proposals for dealing with the firm's communication challenge. Stu Bell was wondering which of the above options he should recommend.

C
2-5

EXHIBIT 1
CUC International Shares Sold Short from January 1988 to March 1989

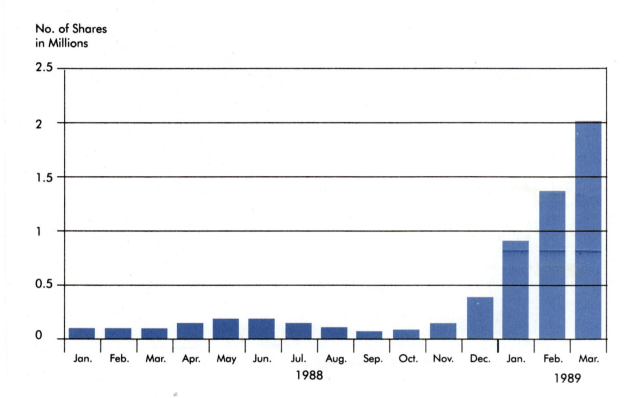

C

2-6

EXHIBIT 2

Cumulative Difference in Stock Returns for CUC International and the OTC Market Index in the Period January 4, 1988, to March 9, 1989

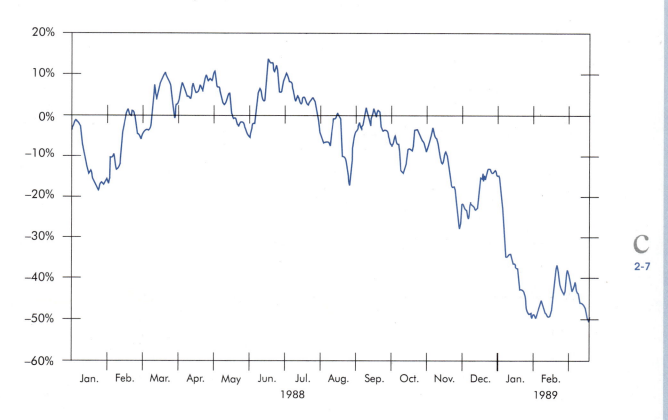

C

2-7

EXHIBIT 3

CUC International, Abridged Annual Report for the Year Ended January 31, 1988

CONSOLIDATED BALANCE SHEET

	January 31	
(Dollar amounts in thousands)	1988	1987
ASSETS		
Current Assets		
Cash and cash equivalents	$ 25,953	$ 14,810
Receivables, less allowance of $613 and $405	33,201	24,209
Prepaid expenses and other	3,468	3,288
Total Current Assets	62,622	42,307
Deferred membership charges, net	22,078	13,112
Prepaid solicitation costs	17,089	4,915
Prepaid commissions	6,267	8,127
Contract renewal rights, net	27,944	30,443
Excess of cost over net assets acquired, net	33,301	19,066
Properties, net	16,048	10,074
Other	1,519	4,416
Total Assets	$186,868	$132,460
LIABILITIES AND SHAREHOLDERS' EQUITY		
Current Liabilities		
Members' deposits	$ 4,997	$ 4,340
Accounts payable and accrued expenses	36,063	16,446
Federal and state income taxes	423	
Current portion of long-term obligations	1,404	5,011
Total Current Liabilities	42,887	25,797
Convertible subordinated debentures	12,000	22,000
Long-term obligations	3,767	5,120
Deferred income taxes	14,624	6,073
Other	1,229	1,268
Total Liabilities	74,507	60,258
Shareholders' Equity		
Common stock-par value $.01 per share; authorized 50 million shares; issued 19,683,567 and 17,820,338	197	178
Additional paid-in capital	82,271	59,550
Retained earnings	32,420	14,997
Treasury stock—398,230 and 398,091 shares, at cost	(2,527)	(2,523)
Total Shareholders' Equity	112,361	72,202
Total Liabilities and Shareholders' Equity	$186,868	$132,460

CONSOLIDATED STATEMENT OF INCOME

	Year Ended January 31		
(Dollar amounts in thousands, except per share amounts)	1988	1987	1986
Revenues			
Membership and service fees	$195,277	$138,149	$84,123
Other	3,180	3,610	3,342
Total Revenues	198,457	141,759	87,465
Expenses			
Operating	64,092	43,248	26,729
Marketing	68,937	56,496	35,042
General and administrative	31,729	23,342	14,572
Interest	2,259	2,663	1,507
Total Expenses	167,017	125,749	77,850
Operating Income	31,440	16,010	9,615
Acquisition costs			2,348
Income Before Income Taxes and Extraordinary Credit	31,440	16,010	7,267
Provision for income taxes	14,017	7,350	4,435
Income Before Extraordinary Credit	17,423	8,660	2,832
Extraordinary credit-utilization of tax loss carryforwards		1,041	3,589
Net Income	$ 17,423	$ 9,701	$ 6,421
Income Per Common Share			
Income before extraordinary credit	$.90	$.49	$.18
Extraordinary credit		.06	.23
Net Income Per Common Share	$.90	$.55	$.41

C

2-9

CONSOLIDATED STATEMENT OF CASH FLOWS

(Dollar amounts in thousands)	Year Ended January 31		
	1988	1987	1986
Operating Activities			
Net income	$17,423	$ 9,701	$ 6,421
Adjustments to reconcile net income to net cash provided by operating activities:			
Amortization of membership acquisition costs	44,641	35,501	20,237
Amortization of prepaid commissions	1,860	2,029	2,081
Amortization of contract rights and excess cost	3,423	2,199	
Deferred income taxes	11,712	5,553	442
Depreciation	2,506	2,582	1,969
Extraordinary credit and loss from discontinued operations			(1,475)
Change in operating assets and liabilities, net of acquisitions:			
Net (increase) decrease in receivables	(8,049)	(6,747)	3,795
Net increase (decrease) in members' deposits, accounts payable and accrued expenses and federal and state income taxes	12,755	(3,649)	(586)
Deferred membership income	9,629	14,366	9,052
Membership acquisition costs	(63,236)	(43,720)	(42,564)
Prepaid solicitation costs	(12,174)	(4,915)	
Prepaid commissions			(409)
Other, net	2,576	(1,748)	39
Net cash from (used in) operating activities	23,066	11,152	(998)
Investing Activities			
Acquisitions, net of cash acquired	(4,625)	(18,341)	
Acquisitions of properties	(7,586)	(5,078)	(4,345)
Proceeds from disposal of properties net of $3.2 million note receivable		783	
Disposals of marketable securities		1,933	2,724
Other, net			240
Net cash from (used in) investing activities	(12,211)	(20,703)	(1,381)

(continued)

(Dollar amounts in thousands)	Year Ended January 31		
	1988	1987	1986
Financing Activities			
Issuance of Common Stock	5,326	6,220	613
Issuance of convertible subordinated debentures			15,000
Purchase of treasury stock		(2,377)	
Repayments of long-term obligations	(4,960)	(2,955)	(795)
Other, net	(78)		
Net cash from financing activities	288	888	14,818
Net Increase (Decrease) in Cash and Cash Equivalents	11,143	(8,663)	12,439
Cash and cash equivalents at beginning of year	14,810	23,473	11,034
Cash and cash equivalents at end of year	$25,953	$14,810	$23,473

NOTES TO CONSOLIDATED FINANCIAL STATEMENTS

Note 1. Summary of Significant Accounting Policies

Principles of Consolidation: The consolidated financial statements include the accounts of CUC International Inc. (formerly Comp-U-Card International Incorporated) and its wholly-owned subsidiaries. The Company operates in one business segment, providing a variety of services through individual, financial institution, credit union and group memberships. All significant intercompany transactions have been eliminated in consolidation.

Deferred Membership Charges, Net: Deferred membership charges is comprised of (in thousands):

January 31,	1988	1987
Deferred membership income	$(52,834)	$(43,205)
Unamortized membership acquisition costs	74,912	56,317
Deferred membership charges, net	$ 22,078	$ 13,112

The related membership fees and membership acquisition costs have been between $30 and $39 per individual member during the years ended January 31, 1988 and 1987. In addition, the annual renewal costs have remained between ten and twenty percent of annual membership fees for the same period.

Renewal costs consist principally of charges from sponsoring institutions and are amortized over the renewal period. Individual memberships are principally for a one-year period. These membership fees are recorded, as deferred membership income, upon acceptance of membership, net of estimated cancellations, and pro-rated over the membership period. The related initial membership acquisition costs are recorded as incurred and charged to operations as membership fees are recognized, allowing for renewals, over a three-year period. Such costs are amortized commencing with the beginning of the membership period, at the annual rate of 40%, 30% and 30%, respectively. Membership renewal rates are dependent upon the nature of the benefits and services provided by the Company in its various membership programs. Through January 31, 1988, membership renewal rates have been sufficient to generate future revenue in excess of deferred membership acquisition costs over the remaining amortization period.

Amortization of membership acquisition costs, including deferred renewal costs, amounted to $44.6 million, $35.5 million and $20.2 million for the years ended January 31, 1988, 1987, and 1986, respectively.

Prepaid Solicitation Costs: Prepaid solicitation costs consist of initial membership acquisition costs pertaining to membership solicitation programs that were in process at year end. Accordingly, no membership fees had been received or recognized at year end.

Prepaid Commissions: Prepaid commissions consist of the amount to be paid in connection with the termination of contracts with the Company's field sales force ($4.9 million and $5.8 million at January 31, 1988 and 1987, respectively) and the termination of special compensation agreements with an officer and former officer ($1.3 million and $1.6 million at January 31, 1988 and 1987, respectively). The amount relating to the termination of the field sales force is being amortized, using the straight-line method, over eight years and the amount relating to the termination of the special compensation agreement is being amortized ratably over ten years.

Contract Renewal Rights: Contract renewal rights represent the value assigned to contracts acquired in acquisitions and are being amortized over 9 to 16 years using the straight-line method.

Excess of Cost Over Net Assets Acquired: The excess of cost over net assets acquired is being amortized over 15 to 25 years using the straight-line method.

Earnings Per Share: Amounts per share have been computed using the weighted average number of common and common equivalent shares outstanding. The weighted average number of common and common equivalent shares outstanding was 19.4 million, 17.8 million and 15.8 million for the years ended January 31, 1988, 1987, and 1986, respectively. Fully diluted earnings per share did not differ significantly from primary earnings per share in any year.

Statement of Cash Flows: The Company adopted Financial Accounting Standards Board (FASB) "Statement of Cash Flows" in its fiscal 1988 financial statements and restated previously reported statements of changes in financial position for fiscal years 1987 and 1986. For purposes of the consolidated statement of cash flows, the Company considers all investments with a maturity of three months or less to be cash equivalents.

Financial Highlights

(In thousands, except per share amounts)

Year Ended January 31	1988	1987	1986	1985	1984
Total Revenues	$198,457	$141,759	$87,465	$65,947	$45,468
Net Income	17,423	9,701	6,421	4,214	3,184
Per Common Share:					
Net Income	$ .90	$ .55	$ .41	$ .28	$ .23
Book Value	5.83	4.14	2.33	1.94	1.70
Shareholders' Equity	$112,361	$ 72,202	$34,859	$28,673	$24,806
Number of Active Members	10,000	8,400	4,700	1,200	450

REPORT OF INDEPENDENT AUDITORS

Six Landmark Square, Suite 500
Stamford, Connecticut 06901

Board of Directors and Shareholders
CUC International Inc.
Stamford, Connecticut

We have examined the consolidated balance sheet of CUC International Inc. as of January 31, 1988 and 1987, and the related consolidated statements of income, shareholders' equity and cash flows for each of the three years in the period ended January 31, 1988. Our examinations were made in accordance with generally accepted auditing standards and, accordingly, included such tests of the accounting records and such other auditing procedures as we considered necessary in the circumstances.

In our opinion, the consolidated financial statements referred to above present fairly the consolidated financial position of CUC International Inc. at January 31, 1988 and 1987, and the consolidated results of operations and cash flows for each of the three years in the period ended January 31, 1988, in conformity with generally accepted principles applied on a consistent basis.

Ernst & Whinney

Stamford, Connecticut
March 30, 1988

Exhibit 4   CUC International, Abridged Interim Financial Statements

EXHIBIT 4

CUC International, Abridged Interim Financial Statements for Nine Months Ended October 31, 1988

CONSOLIDATED BALANCE SHEET

(Dollar amounts in thousands)	October 31, 1988 (unaudited)	January 31, 1988
ASSETS		
Current Assets		
Cash and cash equivalents	$ 32,003	$ 25,953
Receivables	38,118	33,201
Other	4,164	3,468
Total Current Assets	74,285	62,622
Deferred membership charges, net	37,223	22,078
Prepaid solicitation costs	25,538	17,089
Prepaid commissions	5,397	6,267
Contract renewal rights and intangible assets, net	64,419	61,245
Properties, net	19,805	16,048
Other	2,040	1,519
Total Assets	$228,707	$186,868

Exhibit 4   CUC International, Abridged Interim Financial Statements

CONSOLIDATED BALANCE SHEET (continued)

(Dollar amounts in thousands)	October 31, 1988 (unaudited)	January 31, 1988
LIABILITIES AND SHAREHOLDERS' EQUITY		
Current Liabilities		
Members' deposits	$ 4,485	$ 4,997
Accounts payable and accrued expenses	50,017	36,063
Federal and state income taxes	1,264	423
Current portion of long-term obligations	1,494	1,404
Total Current Liabilities	57,260	42,887
Convertible subordinated debentures	12,000	12,000
Long-term obligations	2,673	3,767
Deferred income taxes	16,844	14,624
Other	1,402	1,229
Total Liabilities	90,179	74,507
Shareholders' Equity		
Common Stock	203	197
Other shareholders' equity	138,325	112,164
Total Shareholders' Equity	138,528	112,361
Total Liabilities and Shareholders' Equity	$228,707	$186,868

C

2-15

Exhibit 4   CUC International, Abridged Interim Financial Statements

CONSOLIDATED INCOME STATEMENT
(unaudited)

(In thousands, except per share amounts)	Three Months Ended October 31		Nine Months Ended October 31	
	1988	1987	1988	1987
Revenues				
Membership and service fees	$70,131	$50,696	$192,016	$143,409
Other	938	386	2,297	1,693
Total Revenues	71,069	51,082	194,313	145,102
Expenses				
Operating	24,320	16,258	64,123	47,608
Marketing	23,524	17,761	65,647	50,625
General and administrative	11,787	8,, 1	32,363	25,097
Total Expenses	59,631	42,740	162,133	123,330
Operating Income	11,438	8,342	32,180	21,772
Provision for income taxes	4,577	3,672	12,854	9,591
Net Income	$ 6,861	$ 4,670	$ 19,326	$ 12,181
Net Income Per Common Share	$.33	$.24	$.93	$.63
Weighted Average Number of Common and Common Equivalent Shares Outstanding	20,752	19,665	20,870	19,231

Debt Ratings in the Chemical Industry

R ichard Mandrell is a newly hired credit analyst, employed by a small but quickly growing insurance company that is becoming increasingly active in the market for private placements. In reviewing possible investments, the company considers what rating would have been assigned to similar bonds in the public markets. Such ratings play a significant role in determining the issues' yields and marketability. At this date, early 1991, AAA-rated corporate bonds are yielding, on average, about 9.4 percent, whereas BBB-rated corporates are yielding an average 10.2 percent. Some junk bonds are, of course, yielding much higher rates.

Analysis of prospective investments inevitably involves a degree of subjective business judgment. However, Mandrell is aware that, in the view of some, determination of an appropriate debt rating category for a particular issue is sometimes based largely on a few key financial ratios. In fact, several of Mandrell's competitors in the private placement market use purely quantitative debt scoring models as an important input to their credit analysis. Such an approach suggests that one could explain much of the variation in bond ratings based on a handful of financial ratios. Intrigued by that observation, Mandrell has decided to review a few recent public debt issues to see how well he can "predict" their current ratings based solely on a cursory review of the financial statements of the issuers.

The firms selected by Mandrell for analysis are all in the chemical industry: Fargo Chemical Company, Texas Gulf Corporation, MST Company, Boland Corporation, and Quotron Chemical Corporation. Despite their common industry membership, the five firms have widely varying capital structures and profitability.

The wide variation across the five firms' performance reflects the differences within the chemical industry. The prices of both inputs and outputs are volatile, and often they do not move in tandem. Thus, profitability critically depends on which prices are most important to a given firm. Some firms focus on basic chemicals—essentially, commodities that are similar across producers—and have little control over prices on either the input or output side of their market. Other firms focus on specialty chemicals. These firms tend to have highly differentiated products, specialized knowledge and processes, and close customer relations. In some cases, they are the sole supplier of a particular chemical. These firms are better insulated from changes in the prices of their inputs,

Prepared by Professor Victor L. Bernard, with the assistance of Mike Finn, Elise Kartchmar, and Hans Littooy. The firms on which the base is based are real, but the names have been disguised. The case was prepared as a basis for class discussion and is not intended to illustrate either an effective or ineffective management of a business situation. ·

because they have some ability to pass on such changes to their customers. Many chemical companies diversify across basic and speciality chemicals, sometimes achieving some manufacturing synergies in the process.

Profits in the chemical industry reached an all-time high in 1988 and 1989, due to favorable trends in prices. Sales grew by 10 percent, while net profit margins reached a healthy 8 percent and ROE moved to 17 percent. In 1990, however, the industry was not as fortunate. The prices in many input markets, including those for petroleum products, rose during the Gulf War. Simultaneously, a worldwide recession dampened demand for the outputs of chemical firms, including demand from the key sectors of construction and transportation. Sales growth in chemicals slowed significantly, and net profit margins fell below 7 percent. Several specialty chemical manufacturers maintained strong profits, but producers of basic chemicals struggled. With the world still in a recession in 1991, and the industry now facing some excess capacity due to the plant expansions that commenced during the highly profitable late 1980s, the near-term profitability picture for many chemical companies is only mediocre.

FARGO CHEMICAL COMPANY

Fargo Chemical is a leading international manufacturer and marketer of intermediate chemicals and specialty products. The company produces three principal chemicals: propylene oxide and derivatives, used in urethane foams and in solvents for furniture, auto, and construction industries; tertiary butyl alcohol and derivatives, used as an octane enhancer; and styrene, used in plastic and rubber components.

Fargo resulted from a spinoff of a major petroleum company in 1987; the majority of its shares remain in the control of that company. Earnings grew steadily in 1987 and 1988, but then fell in both 1989 and 1990, reflecting the generally difficult conditions in the chemical industry and the heightened price competition.

Fargo's long-term debt includes a half-dozen public and privately placed issues. The one for which Mandrell will attempt to "predict" a rating is a $100 million debenture, issued in 1990 and due in 2005. Like nearly all other long-term debt issued by Fargo, the debentures are unsecured, subordinated, and issued "for general corporate purposes." They are not callable.

Fargo's financial statements are presented in Exhibit 1.

TEXAS GULF CORPORATION

Texas Gulf Corporation is the smallest of the five chemical companies reviewed by Mandrell. It produces several highly integrated lines of commodity and specialty chemicals, and is a leading producer of chlorine, caustic soda, sodium chlorate, vinyl chloride monomer, and other chlorine-based and alcohol products. End uses for the products are diverse: housing and construction markets, solvents, plastics and fibers, consumer products, pulp and paper, and other uses.

Texas Gulf enjoyed extraordinary margins in 1988 and 1989. The profitability reflected not only the favorable relation of output to input prices, but also the efficiencies of Texas Gulf's highly integrated manufacturing process. Texas Gulf considers itself a low-cost producer of commodity and specialty chemicals, and claims that its productivity rates are among the highest in the industry. Nevertheless, Texas Gulf was not invulnerable to the downturn of 1990, with operating profits falling by nearly 25 percent.

In an effort to insulate itself from potential takeover, Texas Gulf undertook a recapitalization in April 1990, and followed that action with the adoption of a poison pill agreement. The recapitalization involved the distribution of a $30 dividend to shareholders, financed with a combination of $191 million of subordinated notes (issued to the shareholders), a $507 million term loan, and a smaller ($44 million) revolving credit agreement. The term loan and revolver were arranged with a group of financial institutions. The term loan is payable in quarterly installments through 1998.

The debt considered by Mandrell is the subordinated note issue. The notes are callable at par beginning 1995, and are due in 2000. Prepayment of the subordinated notes is prohibited while the bank debt remains outstanding. The notes are unsecured, but require that certain financial ratios be maintained.

Texas Gulf's financial statements are presented in Exhibit 2.

d

MST COMPANY

MST Company is the largest of the five firms considered here, and one of the largest chemical producers in the U.S. Its lines of business include agriculture, personal care products, food products, construction materials, plastics, resin products, rubber and process chemicals, and pharmaceuticals. In several of its lines of business, it holds major brand names.

MST is more widely diversified than others in the chemical industry, and therefore may be better insulated from the current industry conditions. Nevertheless, it experienced a decline in margins and a resulting dropoff in profits in 1990.

Among MST's many debt issues are $100 million of callable sinking fund debentures, issued for general corporate purposes. The debentures rank on a parity with nearly all of MST's other debt, and are unsecured and unsubordinated.

MST's financial statements appear in Exhibit 3.

BOLAND CORPORATION

Boland Corporation is a diversified manufacturer of chemicals, metals and materials, and defense-related products. Within its chemical operations, Boland produces industrial chemicals (including caustic soda, urethanes, and chlorines), performance chemicals, water sanitizing chemicals, and image-forming chemicals. Its metals products include a variety of copper and steel materials. The most important defense-related product is ammunition.

Boland's earnings grew steadily from 1985 through 1989. However, they fell by more than 30 percent in 1990, as Boland found itself selling products into those sectors of the economy most affected by the recession.

Boland's long-term debt consists of $341 million of notes, revolvers, and other debt arranged with a variety of financial institutions, plus $125 million of publicly held subordinated notes. It is the subordinated notes that Mandrell is attempting to rate. The notes were issued in 1987, are due in 1997, are not callable, and are unsecured. The notes were issued to reduce short-term bank debt incurred in early 1987 to finance working capital and long-term investments.

Boland's financial statements appear in Exhibit 4.

QUOTRON CHEMICAL CORPORATION

Quotron Chemical is a long-standing company engaged in the manufacturing and retailing of petrochemicals, propanes, and polyethylene products. Quotron ranks as the nation's largest propane retailer (24 percent of sales) and polyethylene producer (54 percent of sales). The polyethylene business tends to experience particularly volatile earnings, as the prices of the inputs (e.g., ethylene) and output (polyethylene) sometimes fail to move in tandem. The propane business is also subject to some randomness; for example, propane sales vary depending on the severity of winter weather.

Quotron's earnings, after having stagnated during the early and mid-1980s, grew dramatically in 1987 and 1988, largely as a product of strong demand and higher prices for polyethylene, polypropylene, and other petrochemical products. However, polyethylene margins fell in 1989 and a fire caused the shutdown of a major plant for the last half of the year—leaving Quotron operating profits down almost 40 percent. The plant resumed operations in the spring of 1990, but prices continued to swing in unfavorable directions, leading to another decline in operating profits.

In early 1989, the company undertook a number of actions to prevent a takeover. First, a leveraged recapitalization was arranged, involving the issue of a $50 per share dividend and a large increase in the firm's long-term debt. Secondly, a "poison pill" shareholders' rights plan was adopted. Third, an ESOP plan was adopted, resulting in the placement of 14 percent of the firm's shares in the hands of the ESOP trustee.

Quotron has more than a dozen issues of debt outstanding. Seven issues totaling $1.25 billion are unsubordinated; the remaining issues are subordinated. Mandrell has decided to consider one debt issue in each of these categories. The first is Quotron's largest debt issue: $500 million of unsecured subordinated debentures, issued in conjunction with the recapitalization in 1989 and due in 2004, callable after 1994 at prices that begin at 106.50 and decline over time to par. The other debt issue considered by Mr. Mandrell is Quotron's second largest: $300 million of unsecured unsubordinated sinking fund notes, dated 1988 and due in 2018, callable after 1991 at prices that begin at 108 and decline over the life of the issue to par.

Quotron's financial statements appear in Exhibit 5.

Exhibit 1 Fargo Chemical Company – Financial Statements

EXHIBIT 1

Fargo Chemical Company – Financial Statements

INCOME STATEMENT

($ millions, except per share data)	1990	1989	1988	1987
		Year Ended December 31		
Sales	2,830	2,663	2,700	1,952
Cost of Goods Sold	1,993 70%	1,749 66%	1,704 63%	1,335 68%
Gross Profit	837 30%	914 34%	996 37%	617 32%
SG & A Expense	281	238	191	152
Operating Income Before Depreciation	556	676	805	465
Depreciation, Depletion, & Amortization	117	93	83	67
Operating Profit	439	583	722	398
Interest Expense	75	37	51	41
Non-Operating Income/Expense	73	56	92	64
Special Items	30	−3	0	0
Pretax Income	467	599	763	421
Total Income Taxes	159	194	269	164
Income Before Extraordinary Items	308	405	494	257
Extraordinary Items	43	0	0	0
Net Income	351 12.4%	405 15.2%	494 18.3%	257 13%

d

1-5

Exhibit 1 Fargo Chemical Company – Financial Statements

BALANCE SHEET

	as of December 31			
($ millions)	1990	1989	1988	1987
Assets:				
Cash & Equivalents	486	144	410	709
Net Receivables	593	409	477	363
Inventories	289	286	271	207
Other Current Assets	38	13	12	12
Total Current Assets	1,406	852	1,170	1,291
Gross PP & E	2,467	1,851	1,565	1,427
Accumulated Depreciation	699	588	487	443
Net PP & E	1,768	1,263	1,078	984
Investments at Equity	132	118	99	76
Other Investments	270	11	8	0
Deferred Charges	163	182	193	183
Other Assets	0	229	0	0
Total Assets	3,739	2,655	2,548	2,534
Liabilities:				
LT Debt Due in One Year	39	29	4	0
Notes Payable	40	102	256	650
Accounts Payable	225	151	113	122
Taxes Payable	45	48	71	31
Accrued Expenses	192	84	141	134
Other Current Liabilities	0	0	52	39
Total Current Liabilities	541	414	637	976
Long-Term Debt	1,181	390	271	166
Deferred Taxes	208	221	217	239
Other Liabilities	51	39	48	37
Total Noncurrent Liabilities	1,440	650	536	442
Total Liabilities	1,981	1,064	1,173	1,418
Equity:				
Common Stock	100	100	100	100
Capital Surplus	864	864	864	869
Retained Earnings	907	740	520	147
Less: Treasury Stock	113	113	109	0
Common (Total) Equity	1,758	1,591	1,375	1,116
Total Liabilities & Equity	3,739	2,655	2,548	2,534

Exhibit 2   Texas Gulf Corporation – Financial Statements

EXHIBIT 2

Texas Gulf Corporation – Financial Statements

INCOME STATEMENT

	Year Ended December 31			
($ millions, except per share data)	1990	1989	1988	1987
Sales	932	1,104	1,061	707
Cost of Goods Sold	646 *69.3%*	742 *67.2%*	689 *64.9%*	498 *70.4%*
Gross Profit	286	362	371	209
SG & A Expense	41	48	46	28
Operating Income Before Depreciation	245	315	325	181
Depreciation, Depletion, & Amortization	16	16	12	9
Operating Profit	229	299	313	172
Interest Expense	63	1	3	11
Non-Operating Income/Expense	3	2	3	1
Special Items	−18	0	0	0
Pretax Income	150	300	312	163
Total Income Taxes	55	108	119	71
Including Before Extraordinary Items	95	192	194	92
Extraordinary Items	0	0	0	−10
Net Income	95 *10.2%*	192 *17.4%*	194 *18.3%*	82 *11.6%*

d

1-7

Exhibit 2   Texas Gulf Corporation – Financial Statements

BALANCE SHEET

($ millions)	as of December 31			
	1990	1989	1988	1987
Assets:				
Cash & Equivalents	6	46	40	24
Net Receivables	118	117	127	95
Inventories	86	75	85	55
Prepaid Expenses	8	7	8	8
Total Current Assets	218	244	260	182
Gross PP & E	316	300	245	184
Accumulated Depreciation	101	91	76	64
Net PP & E	215	209	169	120
Deferred Charges	21	0	0	0
Other Assets	3	20	28	6
Total Assets	457	473	457	309
Liabilities:				
LT Debt Due in One Year	43	0	0	0
Accounts Payable	75	63	81	56
Taxes Payable	8	9	19	24
Accrued Expenses	35	27	28	20
Other Current Liabilities	0	6	0	0
Total Current Liabilities	161	106	128	100
Long-Term Debt	683	1	42	42
Deferred Taxes	36	36	31	25
Total Noncurrent Liabilities	720	37	73	66
Total Liabilities	881	143	201	166
Equity:				
Common Stock	0	1	1	1
Capital Surplus	2	36	27	23
Retained Earnings	−427	427	302	125
Less: Treasury Stock	0	134	74	7
Common (Total) Equity	−424	330	256	143
Total Liabilities & Equity	457	473	457	309

Exhibit 3   MST Company – Financial Statements

EXHIBIT 3
MST Company – Financial Statements

INCOME STATEMENT

($ millions, except per share data)	Year Ended December 31			
	1990	1989	1988	1987
Sales	8,995	8,681	8,293	7,639
Cost of Goods Sold	4,901 *54%*	4,597 *53%*	4,537 *54%*	4,334 *56.7%*
Gross Profit	4,094 *45.5%*	4,084 *47%*	3,756 *45.3%*	3,305 *43.3%*
SG & A Expense	2,485	2,342	2,135	1,957
Operating Income Before Depreciation	1,609	1,742	1,621	1,348
Depreciation, Depletion, & Amortization	700	664	666	646
Operating Profit	909	1,078	955	702
Interest Expense	(208)	204	193	188
Non-Operating Income/Expense	120	151	138	136
Special Items	0	0	0	32
Pretax Income	821	1,025	900	682
Total Income Taxes	263	336	302	237
Minority Interest	12	10	7	9
Net Income	546 *6.1%*	679 *7.8%*	.591 *7.1%*	436 *5.7%*

d

1-9

Exhibit 3 MST Company – Financial Statements

BALANCE SHEET

($ millions)	as of December 31			
	1990	1989	1988	1987
Assets:				
Cash & Equivalents	204	253	221	223
Net Receivables	1,498	1,309	1,234	1,209
Inventories	1,270	1,197	1,170	1,081
Other Current Assets	541	489	472	490
Total Current Assets	3,513	3,248	3,097	3,003
Gross PP & E	7,620	6,937	6,926	6,730
Accumulated Depreciation	4,128	3,764	3,780	3,654
Net PP & E	3,492	3,173	3,146	3,076
Investments at Equity	248	204	205	240
Intangibles	1,425	1,682	1,790	1,953
Other Assets	558	297	223	183
Total Assets	9,236	8,604	8,461	8,455
Liabilities:				
LT Debt Due in One Year	118	44	128	119
Notes Payable	464	461	428	420
Accounts Payable	584	514	545	527
Taxes Payable	95	126	124	101
Accrued Expenses	929	777	755	633
Total Current Liabilities	2,190	1,922	1,980	1,800
Long-Term Debt	1,652	1,471	1,408	1,564
Deferred Taxes	640	621	588	584
Other Liabilities	665	649	685	606
Total Noncurrent Liabilities	2,957	2,741	2,681	2,754
Total Liabilities	5,147	4,663	4,661	4,554
Equity:				
Common Stock	329	164	164	164
Capital Surplus	714	877	874	872
Retained Earnings	4,609	4,144	3,714	3,382
Less: Treasury Stock	1,563	1,244	952	517
Common (Total) Equity	4,089	3,941	3,800	3,901
Total Liabilities & Equity	9,236	8,604	8,461	8,455

Exhibit 4　Boland Corporation – Financial Statements

EXHIBIT 4

Boland Corporation – Financial Statements

INCOME STATEMENT

($ millions, except per share data)	Year Ended December 31			
	1990	1989	1988	1987
Sales	2,592	2,509	2,308	1,930
Cost of Goods Sold	1,936 74.7%	1,811 72.2%	1,664 72.1%	1,337 69.3%
Gross Profit	656 25.3%	698 27.8%	644 27.9%	593 30.7%
SG & A Expense	382	353	347	326
Operating Income Before Depreciation	274	345	297	267
Depreciation, Depletion, & Amortization	123	122	117	118
Operating Profit	151	223	180	149
Interest Expense	56	57	44	34
Non-Operating Income/Expense	25	22	15	12
Special Items	−4	4	0	0
Pretax Income	116	192	151	127
Total Income Taxes	32	68	53	49
Net Income	84 3.2%	124 4.9%	98 4.2%	78 4.0%

d

1-11

Exhibit 4   Boland Corporation – Financial Statements

BALANCE SHEET

		as of December 31		
($ millions)	1990	1989	1988	1987
Assets:				
Cash & Equivalents	6	12	25	34
Net Receivables	419	453	437	362
Inventories	293	296	311	273
Other Current Assets	16	29	28	11
Total Current Assets	734	790	801	680
Gross PP & E	2,297	2,169	2,164	2,007
Accumulated Depreciation	1,468	1,388	1,363	1,280
Net PP & E	829	781	801	727
Investments at Equity	145	144	149	137
Intangibles	106	110	141	102
Other Assets	52	79	48	39
Total Assets	1,866	1,904	1,940	1,685
Liabilities:				
LT Debt Due in One Year	34	15	39	24
Notes Payable	70	140	172	26
Accounts Payable	222	255	223	200
Taxes Payable	9	4	4	11
Accrued Expenses	187	171	179	143
Total Current Liabilities	522	585	617	404
Long-Term Debt	466	501	474	392
Deferred Taxes	48	60	60	49
Other Liabilities	115	93	106	140
Total Noncurrent Liabilities	629	654	640	581
Total Liabilities	1,151	1,239	1,257	985
Equity:				
Common Stock	19	19	20	22
Capital Surplus	180	177	188	200
Retained Earnings	505	469	475	478
Common Equity	704	665	683	700
Preferred Stock	11	0	0	0
Total Equity	715	665	683	700
Total Liabilities & Equity	1,866	1,904	1,940	1,685

Exhibit 5   Quotron Chemical Corporation – Financial Statements

EXHIBIT 5

Quotron Chemical Corporation – Financial Statements

INCOME STATEMENT

($ millions, except per share data)	Year Ended December 31			
	1990	1989	1988	1987
Sales	2,618	2,637	2,884	2,525
Cost of Goods Sold	1,991 *76.1%*	1,790 *67.9%*	1,770 *61.4%*	1,772 *70.2%*
Gross Profit	627 *23.9%*	847 *32.1%*	1,114 *38.6%*	753 *29.8%*
SG & A Expense	217	224	207	232
Operating Income Before Depreciation	410	623	907	522
Depreciation, Depletion, & Amortization	155	147	147	142
Operating Profit	255	476	760	380
Interest Expense	269	297	116	83
Non-Operating Income/Expense	47	0	–26	6
Special Items	28	0	0	0
Pretax Income	61	178	618	303
Total Income Taxes	39	64	258	159
Income Before Discontinued Operations	21	114	360	144
Discontinued Operations	0	133	23	108
Net Income	21 *0.8%*	247 *9.4%*	383 *13.3%*	252 *10%*

d

1-13

Exhibit 5   Quotron Chemical Corporation – Financial Statements

BALANCE SHEET

($ millions)	as of December 31			
	1990	1989	1988	1987
Assets:				
Cash & Equivalents	13	104	219	25
Net Receivables	467	361	428	434
Inventories	366	304	339	316
Other Current Assets	51	99	354	61
Total Current Assets	897	868	1,339	836
Gross PP & E	2,905	2,513	1,943	2,037
Accumulated Depreciation	885	754	634	657
Net PP & E	2,020	1,759	1,309	1,380
Investments at Equity	32	129	60	60
Other Investments	34	39	39	107
Intangibles	83	94	26	62
Other Assets	156	115	135	137
Total Assets	3,222	3,004	2,908	2,581
Liabilities:				
LT Debt Due in One Year	14	8	3	21
Notes Payable	0	0	5	93
Accounts Payable	137	133	157	134
Taxes Payable	0	38	88	87
Accrued Expenses	277	324	326	242
Other Current Liabilities	0	0	1,141	0
Total Current Liabilities	428	503	1,720	577
Long-Term Debt	2,530	2,363	1,332	727
Deferred Taxes	230	160	174	150
Other Liabilities	135	151	88	82
Total Noncurrent Liabilities	2,895	2,674	1,594	959
Total Liabilities	3,323	3,176	3,315	1,536
Equity:				
Common Stock	220	159	57	75
Capital Surplus	0	0	0	29
Retained Earnings	-321	-331	-464	942
Common (Total) Equity	-101	-172	-407	1,045
Total Liabilities & Equity	3,222	3,004	2,908	2,581

Brenda Curtis, a buy-side analyst focusing on retail stocks, has watched her favorite industry suffer through turmoil and retrenchment during 1991. But while the industry faltered and Macy's filed for bankruptcy, one retailer—The Gap— was busy generating an almost-unheard-of ROE of 40 percent for the year ended January 1992. This San Francisco based marketer of casual clothing was labeled as "the nation's hottest retailer" by *Business Week* (March 9, 1992, cover story). Curtis has decided to take a harder look at The Gap to see what all the fuss is about.

The Gap's lofty P/E ratio of 35 and price-to-book ratio of 12 (based on a price in the $55 range) suggest that investors expect even more good things from The Gap in the future. Duff and Phelps analyst Carol I. Palmer labels The Gap a "buy," noting that relative to 1993 earnings forecasts, the P/E multiple was not unusually high, and yet five-year earnings growth was forecast "conservatively" at 17 percent, well above the 13 percent forecasted growth rate for the market as a whole. In speaking about The Gap's valuation, Palmer notes the following:

> *Discounting only five years of Gap cash flows (using a weighted average discount rate) and adding the residual value (present value of cash flows from 1996 on) and subtracting debt, we obtain a fair market value of $30 per share. However, since we feel strongly that The Gap is a long-term growth company, it is, therefore, appropriate to discount years beyond the next five, using a weighted average discount rate, into the "fair price"; a ten-year time-frame yields a fair market value of $55 per share. Note also that our forecast of fundamentals is conservative by the standards of both consensus opinion and the Company itself.[1]*

Palmer's optimism about the long run is buttressed by her view of The Gap's position within the industry. Few if any retailers had been so successful in recent years in executing their strategy and establishing their "look":

> *The Gap has established itself as a trend-setter in casual wear, at good prices, for younger consumers. Excellent management, systems, and merchandising support a continued leadership position. . . . We think the Company has mastered the right*

Prepared by Professor Victor L. Bernard, with the assistance of Elise Kartchmar. This case is based upon publicly available information. It was prepared as a basis for class discussion and is not intended to illustrate either an effective or ineffective management of a business situation.

1. *Duff and Phelps Company Analysis (April 1992). Duff & Phelps does not disclose the cost of capital estimate used in their model. However, analysts estimate The Gap's beta at approximately 1.30. Intermediate-term government bonds are yielding approximately 6.3 percent.*

mix of value-added, fashion merchandise and quality staples. This mix, combined with highly focused image-management (advertising, store layout, and locations), has made The Gap the definition of correctness in casual wear for a broad demographic group.[2]

Ironically, The Gap's notable success may be its greatest source of concern. *Business Week* notes that:

. . . plenty of rivals are regrouping to compete. Department store executives preach to employees about the need to "Gap-ize" the colors, fibers, and display of their wares. . . . Giorgio Armani is looking to skim The Gap's biggest-spending customers with its new A/X Armani Exchanges, which offer stripped-down fashions with a European look at prices much lower than those at the top of Armani's line. . . . The Limited Inc. has Gap-like "relaxed fit" jeans, sold in some stores with a sales tag whose design is strikingly like The Gap's. . . . Dayton Hudson is experimenting with a chain called Everyday Hero that will have a distinctly Gap-like approach.[3]

Despite concerns about competitive forces in the retail industry, analyst Curtis is intrigued enough by Palmer's optimism to press on with her investigation of The Gap. The following paragraphs summarize the information at her disposal.

BUSINESS AT THE GAP

The Gap, Inc. is a specialty retailer of casual and active apparel for men, women, and children. Incorporated in 1969 as a retailer of Levi's jeans, records, and tapes, The Gap was restructured in 1984 under the guidance of merchandiser Mickey Drexler. Under Drexler, The Gap sought to provide stylish yet affordable apparel, primarily for the 20- to 45-year-old customer. GapKids was introduced in 1986 to serve the market for boys and girls aged 2 through 12. Selected GapKids stores include "babyGap" sections offering clothing for infants and toddlers. The Gap also owns Banana Republic, Inc., another specialty retailer emphasizing rugged and casual men's and women's apparel.

Gap, GapKids, and Banana Republic stores are located primarily in shopping malls throughout the U.S. As of April 1992, there were 1226 such stores, 1176 of which were located in the U.S. The remainder were located in Canada and the U.K.

Drexler's motto for The Gap is "Good style, good quality, good value." Analyst Palmer characterized The Gap's formula this way:

. . . mostly staple/commodity apparel, with some differentiated fashion merchandise, at highly competitive prices (given the reliable quality), in convenient locations; while the s.k.u. count is limited, the inventory is deep. To summarize, using The Gap's self-description: "intensely focused."[4]

2. *Ibid.*
3. Business Week, *March 9, 1992. p. 63–64.*
4. *Duff and Phelps Company Analysis (April 1992)*

The Gap's formula begins with its own New York designers, Lisa Schultz and John Fumiatti, who attempt to anticipate consumer desires for clothing that is stylish but basic, and faithful to The Gap "look." The Gap relies more on the vision of its designers and quick market tests than on quantitative consumer research. Designs are created approximately one year in advance of sale, in sufficient numbers to assure that Gap stores will receive a new collection of styles every two months; older clothing still unsold at that point is moved out quickly by slashing prices.

All clothing is manufactured under The Gap's private label, by over 450 suppliers. To control manufacturing quality, The Gap establishes specifications for each order and maintains a staff of 200 inspectors at the factory sites. In 1991, 38 percent of the clothing was produced domestically, and the rest in Hong Kong and other foreign countries. No single manufacturer accounted for more than 5 percent of the supply.

The Gap maintains little replenishment merchandise at the retail outlets. Instead, large inventories are maintained in distribution centers in California, Kentucky, Canada, the U.K., and (beginning in 1992) Maryland. Point-of-sale scanners permit tracking of inventory needs at each retail outlet, so that distribution centers can replenish stock quickly.

Gap stores are usually leased in shopping malls and are company-controlled, not franchised. Most Gap stores tend to be small by industry standards—often no more than 4000 square feet—but many of the newer outlets are larger: about 7000 square feet. They are more sparse than some specialty clothing outlets, but are well-lit, clean, and "shopper friendly," with wide aisles and readily accessible merchandise. Store layout and operations are controlled tightly by the corporation; one observer states that "there's no more room for creative expression at a Gap store than there is at a McDonald's— maybe less."[5] Each week, store windows and displays are rearranged, according to a specified company design, to maintain a fresh, new look even to frequent customers.

The Gap "look" is reinforced through advertising in lifestyle and fashion magazines, and in various outdoor media: bus shelters, mass transit posters, telephone kiosks, and so forth. Advertising campaigns are designed by The Gap's own in-house staff. The ads feature such well-known faces as Spike Lee, Joan Didion, and James Dean. Some of the black-and-white prints used in this campaign have won advertising awards. In 1991, The Gap kicked off a black-and-white television ad campaign, and intended to expand this campaign in 1992. Advertising costs were 1.5 percent, 1.2 percent, and 1.4 percent of sales in fiscal 1989, 1990, and 1991. Comparable amounts for direct competitors, such as the Limited, are not available.

Growth at The Gap has been phenomenal. Sales, which stood at about $850 million in 1986, rose to $2.5 billion in 1991. Over that same period, annual earnings rose from $68 million to $230 million. In 1991, The Gap brand became the Number 2 private label in the clothing business, behind Levi Strauss.

Much of the sales growth at The Gap has resulted from new store openings; the number of stores rose from 960 in 1989 to 1092 in 1990, and to 1216 in 1991. In addition, however, much growth is attributable to enhanced utilization of existing floor space.

g
1-3

Sales per square foot increased from $250 in 1986 to $481 in 1991; comparable store growth (i.e., growth ignoring the effects of new store openings and expansions) has been much higher than that of competitors. Below is a comparison of growth at The Gap with each of two competitors, The Limited and Petrie Stores. The Limited Inc. (owner of The Limited Stores, Express, Lane Bryant, Victoria's Secret, Structure, and others) was the second-fastest growing specialty retailer in fiscal 1991, behind The Gap. Petrie Stores (owner of Petrie's, Marianne's, Stuarts, and others), was among the more slowly growing firms in the specialty retail category.

	Sales ($ billions)			Sales per Square Foot ($)			Comparable Store Growth		
	Gap	Limited	Petrie	Gap	Limited	Petrie	Gap	Limited	Petrie
1991	2.519	6.281	1.355	481	302	N/D	13%	3%	3.5%
1990	1.933	5.376	1.282	438	309	N/D	14%	3%	1.7%
1989	1.587	4.750	1.258	389	323	N/D	15%	9%	2.0%
1986	0.848	3.223	1.198	250	277	N/D	12%	18%	N/D

N/D = not publicly disclosed

INDUSTRY CONDITIONS AND COMPETITION

The Gap's performance in the early 1990s was highly unusual within the retail sector. Retail businesses were hit hard by weak consumer confidence and a slowly growing economy. In real terms, sales declined from 1989 to 1990, and again from 1990 to 1991. Particularly hard hit were department stores, which experienced "probably the most trying period in [their] history."[6] Performance by general merchandisers was stronger, but still not overly impressive; ROEs for a composite of general merchandisers (K-Mart, Penney's, Sears, and Wal-Mart) averaged about 12 to 15 percent over the 1987–1991 period, not much different from the average for U.S. corporations in a typical year. Profitability at speciality retailers was highly variable, but healthy on average. ROEs for a specialty retailer composite (Gap, Limited, Melville, Nordstrom, and Petrie) ranged from 20 to 23 percent in 1987–1991.

Those firms who managed to find paths to profitability were the so-called "power retailers" or "New Wave retailers."[7] Included in this category were some specialty retailers (e.g., The Gap, The Limited, and Toys-R-Us) and other general merchandisers, including discount retailer Wal-Mart. The innovations that made these firms successful were varied, and included higher-margin niche strategies as well as everyday low pricing

6. Standard and Poor's Industry Surveys, June 4, 1992, p. R77.
7. Ibid., p. R81. The term "New Wave" retailer is attributed to Dr. Carl Steidtmann, Chief Economist of Management Horizons, a division of Price Waterhouse.

("value pricing") strategies. Most success stories, however, involved high inventory turns and high sales volume per square foot.

The Gap's 1991 10-K characterizes the specialty retail industry as "highly competitive," and acknowledges that the success of the Company's operations has increased the likelihood of imitation. Indeed, *Fortune* magazine states that "If imitation is the sincerest form of you-know-what, then The Gap is in the middle of an outright lovefest."[8]

On the subject of competition within the industry, Gap Chairman and CEO Donald Fisher says, "We don't worry. We have a distinct advantage in our name, our merchandise, and the number and location of our stores."[9] Is President Drexler worried? "Sure, but hey look, there aren't too many secrets in this business. It's just going to make us run a little harder."[10]

OUTLOOK

In their 1991 Letter to Shareholders, President Drexler and CEO Fisher described The Gap's outlook as follows:

> *Our challenges for 1992 and beyond begin with increasing market share through continued sales growth. To start working toward this goal we will open approximately 135 new stores in 1992. We will also continue the program to expand our locations by enlarging approximately 100 existing stores.*
>
> *Along with building new stores and larger stores, . . . we plan to continue to grow our business through a concerted effort to increase consumer awareness of our four brands—Gap, GapKids, babyGap, and Banana Republic.*

The Gap has stated goals of at least 20 percent annual sales and EPS growth; 30 percent ROE; and pretax margins of 10.5 to 11 percent. The growth is to be supported through capital expenditures of over $200 million per year beyond 1992.[11] In the foreseeable future, most of this will be devoted to investment in the U.S. However, international sales may become increasingly important. By the end of 1993, The Gap expects to have approximately 100 stores outside the U.S., primarily in Canada, but with an increasing presence in the U.K. Longer term, there is some possibility of expansion to Europe and Asia.

Analyst Michael Schiffman rated The Gap a strong buy, based on his optimism about short-run earnings performance, but still expressed some reasons to constrain enthusiasm about the long run:

> *The Gap has been a big beneficiary of changes in spending habits in the 1990s. Recessionary times have altered consumers' attitudes over the last couple of years. Expensive, impressive "labels" are out; value is in. . . . In the current environment, consumers have decided that a logo is not worth the extra cost.*

g
1-5

....

8. Fortune, *December 2, 1991, p. 106.*
9. Business Week, *March 9, 1992, p. 60.*
10. Fortune, *op. cit.*
11. *Duff and Phelps Company Analysis (April 1992).*

Will these changes be long-lasting? That remains to be seen. It's not clear to us that people's attitudes have been permanently altered; that when prosperity returns, they will still flock to this retailer's stores in search of good quality at a value price. That's not to say the market for good-quality apparel at prices most people can afford to pay will disappear. We just don't think it will continue to grow by leaps and bounds over the next 3 to 5 years.[12]

Analyst Carol Palmer was more optimistic:

. . . The big question is whether The Gap can continue its recent record of success; more precisely, is its formula one for this recession (in which white-collar boomers are tightening their belts) or one for the decade of the '90s?

The market's worst fear about The Gap appears to be that, in an economic recovery, shoppers will trade up from The Gap for casual wear. In our opinion, consumers will merely complement Gap-shopping with more traditionally upscale shopping as they sense themselves gaining purchasing power. We think a better economy should serve to bolster The Gap's formidable consumer franchise.[13]

g

1-6

12. *Value Line report (February 28, 1992).*
13. *Duff and Phelps Company Analysis (April 1992).*

Exhibit 1   Excerpts from The Gap's 1991 Annual Report

EXHIBIT 1
Excerpts from The Gap's 1991 Annual Report

MANAGEMENT'S DISCUSSION AND ANALYSIS OF RESULTS OF OPERATIONS AND FINANCIAL CONDITION

RESULTS OF OPERATIONS

Net Sales

	Fiscal Year Ended		
	Feb. 1, 1992 (Fiscal 1991) 52 Weeks	Feb. 2, 1991 (Fiscal 1990) 52 Weeks	Feb. 3, 1990 (Fiscal 1989) 53 Weeks
Net Sales ($000)	$2,518,893	$1,933,780	$1,586,596
Total sales growth	30%	22%	27%
Growth in comparable store sales (52-week basis)	13%	14%	15%
Number of			
New stores	139	152	98
Expanded stores	79	56	7
Closed stores	15	20	38

The opening of new stores (less the effect of stores closed), and the expansion of existing stores, as well as the increase in comparable store sales contributed to total sales growth for the fiscal years 1991, 1990 and 1989.

Net sales per average square foot increased to $481 in 1991 from $438 in 1990 and $389 in 1989. Over the past two years, the Company has increased the average size of its new stores and expanded the size of some of its existing stores. This has resulted in a net increase in total square footage of 18% in 1991 and 17% in 1990.

Cost of Goods Sold and Occupancy Expenses

Cost of goods sold and occupancy expenses decreased as a percentage of net sales to 62.3% in 1991 from 64.2% in 1990 and 65.9% in 1989. The 1.9% decrease in 1991 was primarily a result of an increase in merchandise margins as a percentage of net sales. The 1.7% decrease in 1990 was the result of higher merchandise margins, somewhat offset by an increase in occupancy expenses as a percentage of net sales.

Operating Expenses

Operating expenses as a percentage of net sales were 22.9%, 23.4% and 22.9% for fiscal years 1991, 1990 and 1989. The .5% decrease in 1991 from 1990 was primarily due to lower payroll costs as a percentage of net sales, which reflected the positive leverage achieved on expenses through sales growth. The .5% increase in 1990 from 1989 was largely attributable to costs associated with the write off of fixed assets for store expansions and relocations.

Net Interest Expense

Net interest expense was $3,523,000 and $1,435,000 and $2,760,000 for fiscal years 1991, 1990 and 1989. The increase in 1991 over 1990 of $2,088,000 was due to increases in average net borrowings and average net interest rates. The decrease in 1990 from 1989 of $1,325,000 reflected lower average net borrowings and lower average net interest rates.

Hemisphere Closure

During the fourth quarter of 1989, the Company closed its Hemisphere stores resulting in a pretax charge to earnings of $10,785,000 ($.05 per share after tax). This charge represented the write down of related property and equipment, inventory, fourth quarter operating loss and a provision for occupancy expenses.

Income Taxes

The effective tax rate was 38.0% in 1991 compared with 39.0% in 1990 and 40.0% in 1989. The 1.0% decrease in the effective tax rate for 1991 was primarily due to a reduction in state taxes and net foreign taxes as a percentage of earnings before income taxes. The 1.0% decrease in 1990 was primarily due to a reduction in state taxes as a percentage of earnings before income taxes.

Exhibit 1   Excerpts from The Gap's 1991 Annual Report

LIQUIDITY AND CAPITAL RESOURCES

The following sets forth certain measures of the Company's liquidity:

	Fiscal Year		
	1991	1990	1989
Cash provided by operating activities ($000)	$333,696	$256,892	$118,093
Working capital ($000)	$235,537	$101,518	$129,139
Current ratio	1.71:1	1.39:1	1.69:1
Debt to equity ratio	.12:1	.04:1	.06:1

In 1991, capital expenditures totaled $227 million, net of construction allowances and dispositions (representing the addition of 139 new stores, the expansion of 79 stores and the remodeling of certain existing stores) which resulted in a net increase in store space of 876,100 square feet. The expenditures also included the construction of the Maryland distribution facility and an offsite data center. Capital expenditures were $200 million in 1990 and $94 million in 1989, a net increase in store space of 705,700 square feet in 1990 and 177,300 square feet in 1989.

In fiscal year 1992, the Company expects capital expenditures to total approximately $230 million, net of construction allowances, representing the addition of approximately 135 stores, the expansion of approximately 100 stores, and the remodeling of certain existing stores. Planned expenditures also include costs for administrative facilities and equipment. The Company expects to fund such capital expenditures by a combination of anticipated cash flow from operations, normal trade credit arrangements, and bank and other borrowings. New stores are generally expected to be leased.

In February 1991, the Company issued $75 million of 8.87% Senior Notes which are due in February 1995. Interest is payable quarterly. The Senior Notes are redeemable, in whole or in part, at any time after February 22, 1993, at the option of the Company.

The Company has a credit agreement which provides for a $250 million revolving credit facility until March 1995, at which time any outstanding borrowings can be converted to a four-year term loan. In addition, the credit agreement provides for the issuance of letters of credit during the three-year revolving period for up to $300 million at any one time.

Under the Company's 1988 program to repurchase up to 12,000,000 shares of its common stock, 40,460 shares were repurchased in 1991 for $1,004,000. To date, 10,484,528 shares have been repurchased for $92,454,000. Share amounts have been restated to reflect the two-for-one splits of common stock to stockholders of record on June 17, 1991 and September 17, 1990.

PER SHARE DATA

Fiscal	Market Prices[a]				Cash Dividends[a]	
	1991		1990		1991	1990
	High	Low	High	Low		
1st Quarter	$31½	$20	$17⅜	$12⁵⁄₃₂	$.062	$.048
2nd Quarter	36⅛	20³⁄₁₆	17⅜	13²¹⁄₃₂	.080	.048
3rd Quarter	47½	34¾	14¹⁄₃₂	10³⁄₃₂	.080	.062
4th Quarter	59	44¾	21¼	13¼	.080	.062
Year					$.302	$.22

The principal markets on which the Company's stock is traded are the New York and Pacific Stock Exchanges. The number of holders of record of the Company's common stock as of April 3, 1992 was 4,311.

(a) Restated to reflect the 2-for-1 splits of common stock to stockholders of record on June 17, 1991 and September 17, 1990.

Exhibit 1   Excerpts from The Gap's 1991 Annual Report

CONSOLIDATED STATEMENTS OF EARNINGS

($000 except per share amounts)	Fiscal 1991 52 Weeks		Fiscal 1990 52 Weeks		Fiscal 1989 53 Weeks	
Net sales	$2,518,893	100.0%	$1,933,780	100.0%	$1,586,596	100.0%
Costs and expenses						
Cost of goods sold and occupancy expenses	1,568,921	62.3%	1,241,243	64.2%	1,046,236	65.9%
Operating expenses	575,686	22.9%	454,180	23.4%	364,101	22.9%
Interest expense (net)	3,523	.1%	1,435	.1%	2,760	.2%
Hemisphere closure	—	—	—	—	10,785	.7%
Earnings before income taxes	370,763	14.7%	236,922	12.3%	162,714	10.3%
Income taxes	140,890	5.6%	92,400	4.8%	65,086	4.1%
Net earnings	$ 229,873	9.1%	$ 144,522	7.5%	$ 97,628	6.2%
Weighted average number of shares	142,139,577		141,500,888		141,080,200	
Earnings per share	$ 1.62		$ 1.02		$ .69	

See notes to consolidated financial statements.

g

1-9

Exhibit 1   Excerpts from The Gap's 1991 Annual Report

CONSOLIDATED BALANCE SHEETS

($000)	February 1, 1992	February 2, 1991
ASSETS		
Current Assets		
Cash and equivalents	$192,585	$66,716
Accounts receivable	7,962	9,609
Merchandise inventory	313,899	247,462
Prepaid expenses and other	51,402	41,268
Total Current Assets	565,848	365,055
Property and Equipment		
Leasehold improvements	394,835	289,266
Furniture and equipment	255,665	178,109
Construction-in-progress	86,967	60,992
	737,467	528,367
Accumulated depreciation and amortization	(189,727)	(144,819)
	547,740	385,548
Lease rights and other assets	33,826	28,297
Total Assets	$1,147,414	$776,900
LIABILITIES AND STOCKHOLDERS' EQUITY		
Current Liabilities		
Accounts payable	$ 158,317	$115,282
Accrued expenses	135,333	102,341
Income taxes payable	32,104	32,725
Current installments on long-term debt	2,500	12,500
Other current liabilities	2,057	689
Total Current Liabilities	330,311	263,537
Long-Term Liabilities		
Long-term debt	77,500	5,000
Other liabilities	16,773	18,945
Deferred lease credits	45,042	23,685
	139,315	47,630
Stockholders' Equity		
Common stock $.05 par value		
Authorized 240,000,000 shares; issued 153,007,862 and 151,708,098		
shares; outstanding 142,523,334 and 141,264,030 shares	7,650	7,585
Additional paid-in capital	124,683	91,185
Retained earnings	654,858	466,111
Foreign currency translation adjustment	575	5,667
Restricted stock plan deferred compensation	(17,524)	(13,365)
Treasury stock, at cost	(92,454)	(91,450)
	677,788	465,733
Total Liabilities and Stockholders' Equity	$1,147,414	$776,900

See notes to consolidated financial statements.

Exhibit 1   Excerpts from The Gap's 1991 Annual Report

CONSOLIDATED STATEMENTS OF CASH FLOWS

($000)	Fiscal 1991 52 Weeks	Fiscal 1990 52 Weeks	Fiscal 1989 53 Weeks
Cash Flows from Operating Activities			
Net earnings	$229,873	$144,522	$ 97,628
Adjustments to reconcile net earnings to net cash provided by operating activities			
Depreciation and amortization	82,133	61,473	43,769
Hemisphere closure	—	—	6,522
Deferred income taxes	(7,045)	(5,637)	(4,134)
Change in operating assets and liabilities			
Accounts receivable	1,643	(3,807)	108
Merchandise inventory	(66,559)	(3,980)	(50,214)
Prepaid expenses and other	(5,557)	(2,969)	(15,953)
Accounts payable	43,220	20,481	12,897
Accrued expenses	33,417	26,910	19,393
Income taxes payable	(574)	18,022	(27)
Other current liabilities	1,368	(26)	13
Other long-term liabilities	420	(2,802)	3,910
Deferred lease credits	21,357	4,705	4,181
Net cash provided by operating activities	333,696	256,892	118,093
Cash Flows from Investing Activities			
Net purchases of property and equipment	(236,521)	(193,734)	(88,398)
Net lease rights	(7,802)	(5,883)	(5,868)
Other assets	(1,382)	1,423	10,628
Net cash used for investing activities	(245,705)	(198,194)	(83,638)
Cash Flows from Financing Activities			
Issuance of long-term debt	75,000	—	—
Payments on long-term debt	(12,500)	(2,500)	(2,000)
Issuance of common stock	20,036	10,189	4,262
Repurchase of common stock	—	—	(213)
Purchase of treasury stock	(1,004)	(10,076)	(21,446)
Cash dividends paid	(41,126)	(29,625)	(22,857)
Net cash provided by (used for) financing activities	40,406	(32,012)	(42,254)
Effect of exchange rate changes on cash	(2,528)	1,245	219
Net increase (decrease) in cash and equivalents	125,869	27,931	(7,580)
Cash and equivalents at beginning of year	66,716	38,785	46,365
Cash and equivalents at end of year	$192,585	$ 66,716	$ 38,785

See notes to consolidated financial statements.

Exhibit 1   Excerpts from The Gap's 1991 Annual Report

NOTES TO CONSOLIDATED FINANCIAL STATEMENTS

For the Fifty-Two Weeks ended February 1, 1992 (Fiscal 1991), the Fifty-Two Weeks ended February 2, 1991 (Fiscal 1990) and the Fifty-Three Weeks ended February 3, 1990 (Fiscal 1989).

NOTE A: SUMMARY OF SIGNIFICANT ACCOUNTING POLICIES

The Company is an international specialty retailer selling casual and contemporary apparel. The consolidated financial statements include the accounts of the Company and its subsidiaries. Intercompany accounts and transactions have been eliminated.

Cash and equivalents represent cash and short-term, highly liquid investments with maturities of three months or less.

Merchandise inventory is stated at the lower of FIFO (first-in, first-out) cost or market.

Property and equipment are stated at cost. Depreciation and amortization are computed using the straight-line method over the estimated useful lives of the related assets or lease terms, whichever is less.

Lease rights are recorded at cost and are amortized over 12 years or the lives of the respective leases, whichever is less.

Costs associated with the opening of new stores are charged against earnings as incurred.

Deferred taxes are provided for those items reported in different periods for income tax and financial statement purposes. Tax credits reduce the current provision for income taxes in the year they are realized. The Company is required to adopt Statement of Financial Accounting Standards No. 109, Accounting for Income Taxes, during fiscal 1993. The impact on the current financial statements would have been immaterial if early adoption had been elected.

Foreign currency translation adjustments result from translating foreign subsidiaries' assets and liabilities to U.S. dollars using the exchange rates in effect at the balance sheet date. Resulting translation adjustments are included in stockholders' equity. Results of foreign operations are translated using the average exchange rates during the period.

Restricted stock awards represent deferred compensation and are shown as a reduction of stockholders' equity.

Earnings per share are based upon the weighted average number of shares of common stock outstanding during the period.

Certain reclassifications have been made to the 1990 and 1989 financial statements to conform with the classifications used in the 1991 financial statements.

NOTE B: LONG-TERM DEBT AND OTHER CREDIT ARRANGEMENTS

Long-Term Debt

($000)	Feb. 1, 1992	Feb. 2, 1991
8.87% Senior Notes, due February 1995	$75,000	$ —
Term Loan Agreement, unsecured, due in equal annual installments through July 1993	5,000	7,500
9.46% unsecured Term Loan due August 1991	—	10,000
	80,000	17,500
Less current installments	(2,500)	(12,500)
	$77,500	$ 5,000

Interest on the Senior Notes is payable quarterly. The Senior Notes are redeemable, in whole or in part, at anytime after February 22, 1993, at the option of the Company.

Interest on the Term Loan Agreement is at prime plus one-quarter of 1% or at LIBOR plus three-quarters of 1%, at the Company's option.

Other Credit Arrangements

The Company has a credit agreement with a syndicated bank group which provides for a $250 million revolving credit facility until March 2, 1995 at which time any outstanding borrowings can be converted to a four-year term loan. The revolving credit facility contains both auction and fixed spread borrowing options and serves as a back-up for the issuance of commercial paper. In addition, the credit agreement provides for the issuance of letters of credit during the three-year revolving period of up to $300 million at any one time.

At February 1, 1992, the Company had outstanding letters of credit totaling $148,634,000.

Borrowings under the Company's loan and credit agreements are subject to the Company maintain-

Exhibit 1 Excerpts from The Gap's 1991 Annual Report

ing certain levels of tangible net worth and financial ratios. Under the most restrictive covenant of these agreements, $376,918,000 of retained earnings were available for the payment of cash dividends at February 1, 1992.

Gross interest payments were $7,593,000, $4,477,000 and $4,501,000 in fiscal 1991,1990 and 1989.

NOTE C: INCOME TAXES

Income taxes consisted of the following:

($000)	Fiscal 1991 52 Weeks	Fiscal 1990 52 Weeks	Fiscal 1989 53 Weeks
Currently Payable			
Federal income taxes	$125,181	$79,951	$55,236
Less tax credits	(6,879)	(1,392)	(1,282)
	118,302	78,559	53,954
State income taxes	24,354	18,011	15,604
Foreign income taxes	6,733	2,142	1,731
	149,389	98,712	71,289
Deferred			
Federal	(9,920)	(5,879)	(4,471)
State	1,421	(433)	(1,732)
	(8,499)	(6,312)	(6,203)
Total provision	$140,890	$92,400	$65,086

The foreign component of earnings before income taxes in fiscal 1991,1990 and 1989 was $31,174,000, $23,377,000 and $11,974,000. Deferred federal and applicable state income taxes, net of applicable foreign tax credits, have not been provided for the undistributed earnings of foreign subsidiaries (approximately $38,791,000 at February 1, 1992) because the Company intends to permanently reinvest such undistributed earnings abroad.

The difference between the effective income tax rate and the United States federal income tax rate is summarized as follows:

	Fiscal 1991 52 Weeks	Fiscal 1990 52 Weeks	Fiscal 1989 53 Weeks
Federal tax rate	34.0%	34.0%	34.0%
State income taxes, less federal benefit	4.8	5.1	5.6
Other	(.8)	(.1)	.4
Effective tax rate	38.0%	39.0%	40.0%

In fiscal 1990 and 1989, accelerated depreciation decreased deferred tax assets by $4,719,000 and $2,797,000. In fiscal 1989, deferred compensation increased deferred tax assets by $4,547,000.

Income tax payments were $135,370,000, $74,790,000 and $73,682,000 in fiscal 1991,1990 and 1989.

NOTE D: LEASES

The Company leases substantially all of its store premises, distribution and office facilities.

Leases relating to store premises, distribution and office facilities expire at various dates through 2025. The aggregate minimum annual lease payments under leases in effect on February 1, 1992 are as follows:

Fiscal Year	($000)
1992	$ 143,780
1993	139,434
1994	134,414
1995	129,422
1996	125,761
Thereafter	624,070
Total minimum lease commitment	$1,296,881

For leases which contain predetermined fixed escalations of the minimum rentals, the Company recognizes the related rental expense on a straight-line basis and includes the difference between the expense charged to income and amounts payable under the leases in deferred lease credits. At February 1, 1992 and February 2, 1991, this liability amounted to $27,400,000 and $19,700,000.

Cash or rent abatements received upon entering into certain store leases are recognized on a straight-line basis as a reduction to rent expense over the lease term. The unamortized portion is included in deferred lease credits.

Some of the leases relating to stores in operation at February 1, 1992 contain renewal options for periods ranging up to 20 years. Most leases also provide for payment of operating expenses, real estate taxes, and for additional rent based on a percentage of sales. No lease directly imposes any restrictions relating to leasing in other locations (other than radius clauses).

g

1-13

Exhibit 1   Excerpts from The Gap's 1991 Annual Report

Net rental expense for all operating leases was as follows:

	Fiscal 1991 52 Weeks	Fiscal 1990 52 Weeks	Fiscal 1989 53 Weeks
Minimum rentals	$137,721	$106,754	$ 88,386
Contingent rentals	30,473	24,666	20,463
	$168,194	$131,420	$108,849

NOTE I: QUARTERLY FINANCIAL INFORMATION (UNAUDITED)

Fiscal 1991 Quarter Ended

($000 except per share amounts)	May 4, 1991	Aug. 3, 1991	Nov. 2, 1991	Feb.1, 1992	Fiscal 1991
Net sales	$490,300	$523,056	$702,052	$803,485	$2,518,893
Gross profit	183,254	179,413	277,731	309,574	949,972
Net earnings	40,913	34,222	70,796	83,942	229,873
Net earnings per share	.29	.24	.50	.59	1.62

Fiscal 1990 Quarter Ended

($000 except per share amounts)	May 5, 1990	Aug. 4, 1990	Nov. 3, 1990	Feb. 2, 1991	Fiscal 1990
Net sales	$402,368	$404,996	$501,690	$624,726	$1,933,780
Gross profit	132,575	131,127	196,283	232,552	692,537
Net earnings	21,154	19,162	47,726	56,480	144,522
Net earnings per share	.15	.14	.33	.40	1.02

EXHIBIT 2

Comparative Five-Year Financial Summaries for The Gap, The Limited, and Specialty Retailers

THE GAP, INC.

INCOME STATEMENT

($ millions)	Jan. 1992	Jan. 1991	Jan. 1990	Jan. 1989	Jan. 1988
Sales	$2,519	$1,934	$1,587	$1,252	$1,062
Cost of Goods Sold	1,499	1,190	1,008	814	654
Gross Profit	1,020	744	578	438	408
Selling, General, and Administrative Expense	576	454	364	271	254
Operating Income Before Depreciation	444	290	214	167	154
Depreciation & Amortization	70	51	38	31	25
Operating Profit	374	238	176	136	129
Interest Expense	4	1	3	3	4
Shut-down and Restructuring Costs	0	0	−11	−7	0
Pretax Income	371	237	163	126	125
Total Income Taxes	141	92	65	52	55
Net Income	$ 230	$ 145	$ 98	$ 74	$ 70
Earnings per Share	$1.62	$1.02	$0.69	$0.51	$0.49
Dividends per Share	$0.30	$0.22	$0.17	$0.13	$0.13

Note: Depreciation and amortization above is less than that disclosed in The Gap's cash flow statement because it excludes amortization of deferred compensation.

g

1-15

BALANCE SHEET

($ millions)	Jan. 1992	Jan. 1991	Jan. 1990	Jan. 1989	Jan. 1988
ASSETS					
Cash & Equivalents	$ 193	$ 67	$ 38	$ 46	$ 32
Net Receivables	8	10	6	6	9
Inventories	314	248	244	193	195
Other Current Assets	51	41	29	13	23
Total Current Assets	566	365	317	258	259
Gross Plant, Property & Equipment	738	528	352	286	234
Accumulated Depreciation	190	145	114	95	77
Net Plant, Property & Equipment	548	384	238	191	157
Other Assets	34	29	25	32	19
TOTAL ASSETS	$1,147	$777	$580	$481	$434
LIABILITIES					
Long-Term Debt Due in One Year	3	13	3	2	2
Notes Payable	0	0	0	0	5
Accounts Payable	158	115	94	81	68
Taxes Payable	32	33	15	15	6
Accrued Expenses	135	102	75	53	47
Other Current Liabilities	2	1	1	1	1
Total Current Liabilities	330	264	187	152	129
Long-Term Debt	78	5	18	20	12
Other Liabilities	62	43	37	33	21
TOTAL LIABILITIES	470	311	242	205	161
EQUITY					
Common Stock	8	4	2	2	2
Capital Surplus	125	95	73	57	51
Retained Earnings	638	458	345	277	221
Less: Treasury Stock	93	92	81	60	0
TOTAL EQUITY	678	466	338	276	273
TOTAL LIABILITIES & EQUITY	$1,147	$777	$580	$481	$434

THE LIMITED, INC.

COMMON SIZE INCOME STATEMENT

	Jan. 1992	Jan. 1991	Jan. 1990	Jan. 1989	Jan. 1988
Sales	1.000	1.000	1.000	1.000	1.000
CGS	0.658	0.640	0.640	0.654	0.671
Gross Profit	0.342	0.360	0.360	0.346	0.329
SGA	0.193	0.196	0.194	0.200	0.186
Operating Income Before Depreciation	0.149	0.164	0.165	0.146	0.143
Depreciation and Amortization	0.035	0.034	0.034	0.033	0.030
Operating Profit	0.113	0.130	0.132	0.112	0.113
Interest Expense	0.010	0.011	0.012	0.015	0.011
Non-op. and Special Items	0.002	0.002	0.001	−0.002	0.003
Pretax Income	0.105	0.122	0.121	0.095	0.105
Income Taxes	0.041	0.047	0.048	0.036	0.040
Minority Interest	0.000	0.000	0.000	0.000	0.000
Income Before Extra Items	0.064	0.074	0.073	0.059	0.065
Extra Items and Discontinued Operations	0.000	0.000	0.000	0.000	0.000
Net Income	0.064	0.074	0.073	0.059	0.065
EBI/Sales	0.070	0.080	0.080	0.068	
Asset Turnover	1.997	2.032	2.081	2.226	
Leverage = assets/equity (average)	1.830	1.889	2.087	2.228	
Net Income/EBI	0.913	0.921	0.909	0.866	
ROE = product of above	0.235	0.285	0.317	0.293	
ROA = EBI/Assets	0.140	0.163	0.167	0.152	
Sustainable Growth	0.175	0.222	0.264	0.241	

EBI = earnings before interest, net of assumed 40% tax effect.
Sustainable growth rate is equal to ROE, multiplied by earnings retention rate.

SELECTED FINANCIAL STATEMENT DATA

(millions of $)	Jan. 1992	Jan. 1991	Jan. 1990	Jan. 1989	Jan. 1988
Net Receivables	736	670	596	532	95
Inventory	730	585	482	407	354
Net Property and Equipment	1,657	1,395	1,173	1,067	889
Total Assets	3,419	2,872	2,419	2,146	1,588
Total Equity	1,877	1,560	1,241	946	729
Sales	6,281	5,376	4,750	4,155	3,616
Cost of Goods Sold	4,133	3,440	3,041	2,717	2,426
Selling, General, & Admin. Expense	1,212	1,056	923	832	672
Operating Income Before Depreciation	935	880	785	606	518
Net Income	403	398	347	245	235

g

1-17

SPECIALTY RETAILERS INDUSTRY COMPOSITE

(including Gap, Limited, Melville, Petrie, and Nordstrom)

COMMON SIZE INCOME STATEMENT

	Jan. 1992	Jan. 1991	Jan. 1990	Jan. 1989	Jan. 1988
Sales	1.000	1.000	1.000	1.000	1.000
CGS	0.638	0.635	0.630	0.632	0.637
Gross Profit	0.362	0.365	0.370	0.368	0.363
SGA	0.252	0.253	0.251	0.253	0.250
Operating Income Before Depreciation	0.110	0.112	0.119	0.115	0.113
Depreciation and Amortization	0.026	0.025	0.024	0.024	0.023
Operating Profit	0.084	0.087	0.094	0.091	0.090
Interest Expense	0.007	0.008	0.008	0.008	0.009
Non-op and Special Items	0.005	0.005	0.004	0.004	0.009
Pretax Income	0.082	0.085	0.091	0.087	0.091
Income Taxes	0.032	0.030	0.033	0.031	0.035
Minority Interest	0.002	0.002	0.002	0.003	0.003
Income Before Extra Items	0.049	0.052	0.056	0.053	0.053
Extra Items and Discontinued Operations	0.000	0.000	0.000	0.004	0.000
Net Income	0.049	0.052	0.056	0.057	0.053
EBI/Sales	0.053	0.057	0.060	0.061	
Asset Turnover	2.141	2.153	2.175	2.190	
Leverage = Assets/equity (average)	1.874	1.889	1.869	1.860	
Net income/EBI	0.919	0.919	0.923	0.921	
ROE = Product of above	0.196	0.211	0.226	0.230	
ROA = EBI/Assets	0.114	0.122	0.131	0.134	
Sustainable Growth	0.058	0.062	0.058	0.054	

EBI = earnings before interest, net of assumed 40% tax effect.
Sustainable growth = ROE × earnings retention rate.

SELECTED FINANCIAL STATEMENT DATA

(millions of $)	Jan. 1992	Jan. 1991	Jan. 1990	Jan. 1989	Jan. 1988
Net Receivables	1,604	1,430	1,290	1,156	631
Inventory	3,578	3,067	2,558	2,316	1,986
Net Property and Equipment	4,456	3,874	3,200	2,878	2,476
Total Assets	11,588	10,104	8,635	7,749	6,622
Total Equity	6,230	5,344	4,576	4,192	3,534
Sales	23,220	20,172	17,819	15,734	13,771
Cost of Goods Sold	14,804	12,817	11,226	9,946	8,769
Selling, General, & Administrative Expense	5,855	5,096	4,480	3,984	3,442
Operating Income Before Depreciation	2,561	2,259	2,113	1,805	1,560
Net Income	1,132	1,047	990	889	730

Harnischfeger Corporation

In February 1985, Peter Roberts, the research director of Exeter Group, a small Boston-based investment advisory service specializing in turnaround stocks, was reviewing the 1984 annual report of Harnischfeger Corporation (Exhibit 4). His attention was drawn by the $1.28 per share net profit Harnischfeger reported for 1984. He knew that barely three years earlier the company had faced a severe financial crisis. Harnischfeger had defaulted on its debt and stopped dividend payments after reporting a hefty $7.64 per share net loss in fiscal 1982. The company's poor performance continued in 1983, leading to a net loss of $3.49 per share. Roberts was intrigued by Harnischfeger's rapid turnaround and wondered whether he should recommend purchase of the company's stock (see Exhibit 3 for selected data on Harnischfeger's stock).

COMPANY BUSINESS AND PRODUCTS

Harnischfeger Corporation was a machinery company based in Milwaukee, Wisconsin. The company had originally been started as a partnership in 1884 and was incorporated in Wisconsin in 1910 under the name Pawling and Harnischfeger. Its name was changed to the present one in 1924. The company went public in 1929 and was listed on the New York Stock Exchange.

The company's two major segments were the P&H Heavy Equipment Group, consisting of the Construction Equipment and the Mining and Electrical Equipment divisions, and the Industrial Technologies Group, consisting of the Material Handling Equipment and the Harnischfeger Engineers divisions. The sales mix of the company in 1983 consisted of: Construction Equipment 32 percent; Mining and Electrical Equipment 33 percent, Material Handling Equipment 29 percent, and Harnischfeger Engineers 6 percent.

Harnischfeger was a leading producer of construction equipment. Its products, bearing the widely recognized brand name P&H, included hydraulic cranes and lattice boom cranes. These were used in bridge and highway construction and for cargo and other material handling applications. Harnischfeger had market shares of about 20 percent in hydraulic cranes and about 30 percent in lattice boom cranes. In the 1980s the construction equipment industry in general was experiencing declining margins.

Professor Krishna Palepu prepared this case as the basis for class discussion rather than to illustrate either effective or ineffective handling of an administrative situation. Copyright © 1985 by the President and Fellows of Harvard College. Harvard Business School case 9-186-160.

Electric mining shovels and excavators constituted the principal products of the Mining and Electrical Equipment Division of Harnischfeger. The company had a dominant share of the mining machinery market. The company's products were used in coal, copper, and iron mining. A significant part of the division's sales were from the sale of spare parts. Because of its large market share and the lucrative spare parts sales, the division was traditionally very profitable. Most of the company's future mining product sales were expected to occur outside the United States, principally in developing countries.

The Material Handling Equipment Division of Harnischfeger was the fourth largest supplier of automated material handling equipment, with a 9 percent market share. The division's products included overhead cranes, portal cranes, hoists, monorails, and components and parts. The demand for this equipment was expected to grow in the coming years as an increasing number of manufacturing firms emphasized cost reduction programs. Harnischfeger believed that the material handling equipment business would be a major source of its future growth.

Harnischfeger Engineers was an engineering services division engaged in design, custom software development, and project management for factory and distribution automation projects. The division engineered and installed complete automated material handling systems for a wide variety of applications on a fee basis. The company expected such automated storage and retrieval systems to play an increasingly important role in the "factory of the future."

Harnischfeger had a number of subsidiaries, affiliated companies, and licensees in a number of countries. Export and foreign sales constituted more than 50 percent of the total revenues of the company.

FINANCIAL DIFFICULTIES OF 1982

The machinery industry experienced a period of explosive growth during the 1970s. Harnischfeger expanded rapidly during this period, growing from $205 million in revenues in 1973 to $644 million in 1980. To fund this growth, the company relied increasingly on debt financing, and the firm's debt/equity ratio rose from 0.88 in 1973 to 1.26 in 1980. The worldwide recession in the early 1980s caused a significant drop in demand for the company's products starting in 1981 and culminated in a series of events that shook the financial stability of Harnischfeger.

Reduced sales and the high interest payments resulted in poor profit performance leading to a reported loss in 1982 of $77 million. The management of Harnischfeger commented on its financial difficulties:

There is a persistent weakness in the basic industries, both in the United States and overseas, which have been large, traditional markets for P&H products. Energy-related projects, which had been a major source of business of our Construction Equipment Division, have slowed significantly in the last year as a result of lower oil demand and subsequent price decline, not only in the U.S. but throughout the world. Lack of demand for such basic minerals as iron ore, copper and bauxite have decreased worldwide mining activity, causing reduced sales for mining equipment, although coal mining remains relatively strong worldwide. Difficult economic conditions have caused many of our normal customers to cut capital expenditures dramatically, especially in such depressed sectors as the steel industry, which has always been a major source of sales for all P&H products.

The significant operating losses recorded in 1982 and the credit losses experienced by its finance subsidiary caused Harnischfeger to default on certain covenants of its loan agreements. The most restrictive provisions of the company's loan agreements required it to maintain a minimum working capital of $175 million, consolidated net worth of $180 million, and a ratio of current assets to current liabilities of 1.75. On October 31, 1982, the company's working capital (after reclassification of about $115 million long-term debt as a current liability) was $29.3 million, the consolidated net worth was $142.2 million, and the ratio of current assets to current liabilities was 1.12. Harnischfeger Credit Corporation, an unconsolidated finance subsidiary, also defaulted on certain covenants of its loan agreements, largely due to significant credit losses relating to the financing of construction equipment sold to a large distributor. As a result of these covenant violations, the company's long-term debt of $124.3 million became due on demand, the unused portion of the bank revolving credit line of $25.0 million became unavailable, and the unused short-term bank credit lines of $12.0 million were canceled. In addition, the $25.1 million debt of Harnischfeger Credit Corporation also became immediately due. The company was forced to stop paying dividends and began negotiations with its lenders to restructure its debt to permit operations to continue. Price Waterhouse, the company's audit firm, qualified its audit opinion on Harnischfeger's 1982 annual report with respect to the outcome of the company's negotiations with its lenders.

CORPORATE RECOVERY PLAN

Harnischfeger responded to the financial crisis facing the firm by developing a corporate recovery plan. The plan consisted of four elements: (1) changes in the top management, (2) cost reductions to lower the break-even point, (3) reorientation of the company's business, and (4) debt restructuring and recapitalization. The actions taken in each of these four areas are described below.

To deal effectively with the financial crisis, Henry Harnischfeger, then Chairman and Chief Executive Officer of the company, created the position of Chief Operating Officer. After an extensive search, the position was offered in August 1982 to William Goessel, who had considerable experience in the machinery industry. Another addition to the management team was Jeffrey Grade, who joined the company in 1983 as Senior Vice President of Finance and Administration and Chief Financial Officer. Grade's appointment was necessitated by the early retirement of the previous Vice President of Finance in 1982. The engineering, manufacturing, and marketing functions were also restructured to streamline the company's operations (see Exhibits 1 and 2 for additional information on Harnischfeger's current management).

h
1-3

To deal with the short-term liquidity squeeze, the company initiated a number of cost reduction measures. These included (1) reducing the workforce from 6,900 to 3,800; (2) eliminating management bonuses and reducing benefits and freezing wages of salaried and hourly employees; (3) liquidating excess inventories and stretching payments to creditors; and (4) permanent closure of the construction equipment plant at Escanaba, Michigan. These and other related measures improved the company's cash position and helped to reduce the rate of loss during fiscal 1983.

Concurrent with the above cost reduction measures, the new management made some strategic decisions to reorient Harnischfeger's business. First, the company entered into a long-term agreement with Kobe Steel, Ltd., of Japan. Under this agreement, Kobe agreed to supply Harnischfeger's requirements for construction cranes for sale in the United States as Harnischfeger phased out its own manufacture of cranes. This step was expected to significantly reduce the manufacturing costs of Harnischfeger's construction equipment, enabling it to compete effectively in the domestic market. Second, the company decided to emphasize the high technology part of its business by targeting for future growth the material handling equipment and systems business. To facilitate this strategy, the Industrial Technologies Group was created. As part of the reorientation, the company stated that it would develop and acquire new products, technology, and equipment and would expand its abilities to provide computer-integrated solutions to handling, storing, and retrieval in areas hitherto not pursued—industries such as distribution warehousing, food, pharmaceuticals, and aerospace.

While Harnischfeger was implementing its turnaround strategy, it was engaged at the same time in complex and difficult negotiations with its bankers. On January 6, 1984, the company entered into agreements with its lenders to restructure its debt obligations into three-year term loans secured by fixed as well as other assets, with a one-year extension option. This agreement required, among other things, specified minimum levels of cash and unpledged receivables, working capital, and net worth.

The company reported a net loss of $35 million in 1983, down from the $77 million loss the year before. Based on the above developments during the year, in the 1983 annual report the management expressed confidence that the company would return to profitability soon:

> We approach our second century with optimism, knowing that the negative events of the last three years are behind us, and with a firm belief that positive achievements will be recorded in 1984. By the time the corporation celebrates its 100th birthday on December 1, we are confident it will be operating profitably and attaining new levels of market strength and leadership.

During 1984 the company reported profits during each of the four quarters, ending the year with a pre-tax operating profit of $5.7 million, and a net income after tax and extraordinary credits of $15 million (see Exhibit 4). It also raised substantial new capital through a public offering of debentures and common stock. Net proceeds from the offering, which totaled $150 million, were used to pay off all of the company's restruc-

h
1-4

tured debt. In the 1984 annual report the management commented on the company's performance as follows:

> *1984 was the Corporation's Centennial year and we marked the occasion by rededicating ourselves to excellence through market leadership, customer service and improved operating performance and profitability.*
>
> ⋮
>
> *We look back with pride. We move ahead with confidence and optimism. Our major markets have never been more competitive; however, we will strive to take advantage of any and all opportunities for growth and to attain satisfactory profitability. Collectively, we will do what has to be done to ensure that the future will be rewarding to all who have a part in our success.*

h

Exhibit 1   Harnischfeger Corporation Board of Directions in 1984

EXHIBIT 1
Harnischfeger Corporation Board of Directions in 1984

	Director Since	Current Term	Shares Owned
Edward W. Duffy Chairman of the Board and Chief Executive Officer of United States Gypsum Company, manufacturer of building materials and products used in industrial processes, since 1983; Vice Chairman from 1981 to 1983; President and Chief Operating Officer from 1971 to 1981. Director, American National Bank and Trust Company of Chicago, Walter E. Heller International Corporation, W. W. Grainger, Inc., and UNR Industries, Inc. Age 64.	1981	1985	100
Herbert V. Kohler, Jr. Chairman, Chief Executive Officer, and Director of Kohler Company, manufacturer of plumbing and specialty products, engines, and generators, since 1972; President since 1974. Age 44.	1973	1985	700
Taisuke Mori Executive Vice Chairman and Director of Kobe Steel, Ltd., a Japanese manufacturer of steel and steel products, industrial machinery, construction equipment, aluminum, copper and alloy products, and welding equipment and consumables. Age 63.	1981	1985	None
William W. Goessel President and Chief Operating Officer of the Corporation since 1982. Executive Vice President of Beloit Corporation from 1978 to 1982. Director, Goulds Pumps, Inc. Age 56.	1982	1986	15,000
Henry Harnischfeger Chairman of the Board and Chief Executive Officer of the Corporation since 1970; President from 1959 to 1982. Director, First Wisconsin Corporation and First Wisconsin National Bank of Milwaukee. Age 60.	1945	1986	611,362
Karl F. Nygren Partner in Kirkland & Ellis, attorneys, since 1959. Age 56.	1964	1986	2,000

Exhibit 1 Harnischfeger Corporation Board of Directions in 1984

	Director Since	Current Term	Shares Owned
John P. Gallagher Senior lecturer, Graduate School of Business, University of Chicago. Director, IC Industries, Inc., Stone Container Corporation, UNR Industries, Inc., American National Bank and Trust Company of Chicago, and Walter E. Heller International Corporation. Age 67.	1979	1987	500
Jeffrey T. Grade Senior Vice President/Finance and Administration and Chief Financial Officer of the Corporation since August 1, 1983. Vice President Corporate Finance of IC Industries from 1981 to 1983; Assistant Vice President from 1976 to 1981. Age 40.	1983	1987	3,750
Donald Taylor President, Chief Operating Officer, and Director of Rexnord, Inc., a major manufacturer of industrial components and machinery, since 1978. Director, Johnson Controls, Inc., Marine Corporation, and Marine Bank, N.A. Age 56.	1979	1987	100
Frank A. Lee Director of Foster Wheeler Corporation since 1971; Chairman of the Board from 1981 to 1982; President and Chief Executive Officer from 1978 to 1981. Director, Belco Pollution Control Corporation, International General Industries, Inc., and Banker's Life Insurance Co. Age 59.	1983	1987	None

Exhibit 2   Executive Compensation, Harnischfeger Corporation

EXHIBIT 2
Executive Compensation, Harnischfeger Corporation

The following table sets forth all cash compensation paid to each of the Corporation's five most highly compensated executive officers and to all executive officers as a group for services rendered to the Corporation and its subsidiaries during fiscal 1984.

		Cash Compensation
Henry Harnischfeger	Chairman of the Board and Chief Executive Officer	$ 364,004
William W. Goessel	President and Chief Operating Officer	280,000
C. P. Cousland	Senior Vice President and group executive, P&H Heavy Equipment	210,000
Jeffrey T. Grade	Senior Vice President-Finance and Administration and Chief Financial Officer	205,336
Douglas E. Holt	President, Harnischfeger Engineers, Inc.	152,839
All persons who were executive officers during the fiscal year as a group (14 persons)		2,159,066

1985 EXECUTIVE INCENTIVE PLAN

In December 1984, the board of directors established an Executive Incentive Plan for fiscal 1985 which provides an incentive compensation opportunity of 40% of annual salary for 11 senior executive officers only if the Corporation reaches a specific net after-tax profit objective; it provides an additional incentive compensation of up to 40% of annual salary for seven of those officers if the corporation exceeds the objective. The Plan covers the chairman, president, senior vice presidents; president, Harnischfeger Engineers, Inc.; vice president, P&H World Services; vice president, Material Handling Equipment; and secretary. Awards made in fiscal year 1984 are included in the compensation table above.

EXHIBIT 3
Harnischfeger Corporation, Selected Stock Price and Market Data

A. STOCK PRICES

	Harnischfeger's Stock Price			S&P 400 Industrials Index		
	High	Low	Close	High	Low	Close
January 4, 1985	9 1/8	8 6/8	9	186.4	181.8	182.2
January 11, 1985	10 6/8	8 7/8	10 5/8	188.2	182.2	182.8
January 18, 1985	11	10	10 4/8	191.9	186.9	191.3
January 25, 1985	11 2/8	10 1/8	11	199.7	191.3	198.6
February 1, 1985	11 5/8	10 7/8	11 2/8	201.8	198.6	200.0

Harnischfeger's stock beta = 0.95 (Value Line estimate)

B. MARKET DATA

	February 1985
Median P/E ratio of Dow Jones Industrials	10.9
Median P/E ratio of Value Line stocks	11.3
Median P/E ratio of machinery industry (construction and mining equipment)	10.0
Prime rate	10.5%
91-day Treasury bill rate	8.4%
30-year Treasury bond yield	11.4%
Moody's Aaa corporate bond yield	12.0%

Exhibit 4   Harnischfeger Corporation 1984 Annual Report (abridged)

EXHIBIT 4
Harnischfeger Corporation 1984 Annual Report (abridged)

TO OUR SHAREHOLDERS

The Corporation recorded gains in each quarter during fiscal 1984, returning to profitability despite the continued depressed demand and intense price competition in the world markets it serves.

For the year ended October 31, net income was $15,176,000 or $1.28 per common share, which included $11,005,000 or 93¢ per share from the cumulative effect of a change in depreciation accounting. In 1983, the Corporation reported a loss of $34,630,000 or $3.49 per share.

Sales for 1984 improved 24% over the preceding year, rising to $398.7 million from $321 million a year ago. New orders totaled $451 million, a $101 million increase over 1983. We entered fiscal 1985 with a backlog of $193 million, which compared to $141 million a year earlier.

ALL DIVISIONS IMPROVED

All product divisions recorded sales and operating improvements during 1984.

Mining equipment was the strongest performer with sales up over 60%, including major orders from Turkey and the People's Republic of China. During the year we began the implementation of the training, engineering and manufacturing license agreement concluded in November, 1983 with the People's Republic of China, which offers the Corporation long-term potential in modernizing and mechanizing this vast and rapidly developing mining market.

Sales of material handling equipment and systems were up 10% for the year and the increasingly stronger bookings recorded during the latter part of the year are continuing into the first quarter of 1985.

Sales on construction equipment products showed some signs of selective improvement. In the fourth quarter, bookings more than doubled from the very depressed levels in the same period a year ago, although the current level is still far below what is needed to achieve acceptable operating results for this product line.

FINANCIAL STABILITY RESTORED

In April, the financial stability of the Corporation was improved through a public offering of 2.15 million shares of common stock, $50 million of 15% notes due April 15, 1994, and $100 million of 12% subordinated debentures due April 15, 2004, with two million common stock purchase warrants.

Net proceeds from the offering totaled $149 million, to which we added an additional $23 million in cash, enabling us to pay off all of our long-term debt. As a result of the refinancing, the Corporation gained permanent long-term capital with minimal annual cash flow requirements to service it. We now have the financial resources and flexibility to pursue new opportunities to grow and diversify.

Furthermore, should we require additional funds, they will be available through a $52 million unsecured three-year revolving credit agreement concluded in June with ten U.S. and Canadian banks. An $80 million product financing capability was also arranged through a major U.S. bank to provide financing to customers purchasing P&H products.

OUTLOOK

Throughout 1985 we believe we will see gradual improvements in most of our U.S. and world markets.

For our mining excavator product line, coal and certain metals mining are expected to show a more favorable long-term outlook in selected foreign requirements and our capability to source equipment from the U.S., Japan or Europe places us in a strong marketing position. In the U.S., we see only a moderate strengthening in machinery requirements for coal, while metals mining will remain weak.

Continuing shipments of the Turkish order throughout 1985 will help to stabilize our plant utilization levels and improve our operating results for this product line.

In our material handling and systems markets, particularly in the U.S., we are experiencing a moderately strong continuation of the improved bookings which we began to see in the third and fourth quarters of last year.

Exhibit 4 Harnischfeger Corporation 1984 Annual Report (abridged)

In construction lifting equipment markets, we expect modest overall economic improvement in the U.S., which should help to absorb the large numbers of idle lifting equipment that have been manufacturer, distributor and customer inventories for the last three years. As this overhang on the market is reduced we will see gradual improvement in new sales. Harnischfeger traditionally exports half of its U.S.-produced lifting products. However, as with mining equipment, the continued strength of the U.S. dollar severely restricts our ability to sell U.S.-built products in world markets.

In addition to the strong dollar and economic instability in many foreign nations, overcapacity in worldwide heavy equipment manufacturing remains a serious problem in spite of some exits from the market as well as consolidations within the industry.

The Corporation continues to respond to severe price competition through systematic cost reduction programs and through expanded sourcing of P&H equipment from our European operation and, most importantly, through our 30-year association with our Japanese partner, Kobe Steel, Ltd. P&H engineering and technology have established world standards for quality and performance for construction cranes and mining equipment, which customers can expect from every P&H machine regardless of its source. More than a dozen new models of foreign-sourced P&H construction cranes will be made available for the first time in the U.S. during 1985, broadening our existing product lines and giving competitive pricing to our U.S. distributors and customers.

To improve our future operating results, we restructured our three operating divisions into two groups. All construction and mining related activities are in the new "P&H Heavy Equipment Group." All material handling equipment and systems activities are now merged into the "Industrial Technologies Group." More information on these Groups is reported in their respective sections.

We are pleased to announce that John P. Moran was elected Senior Vice President and Group Executive, Industrial Technologies Group, and John R. Teitgen was elected Secretary and General Counsel.

In September Robert F. Schnoes became a member of our Board of Directors. He is President and Chief Executive Officer of Burgess, Inc. and of Ultrasonic Power Corporation, and a member of the Board of Signode Industries, Inc.

BEGINNING OUR SECOND CENTURY

1984 was the Corporation's Centennial year and we marked the occasion by rededicating ourselves to excellence through market leadership, customer service and improved operating performance and profitability.

Our first century of achievement resulted from the dedicated effort, support and cooperation of our employees, distributors, suppliers, lenders, and shareholders, and we thank all of them.

We look back with pride. We move ahead with confidence and optimism. Our major markets have never been more competitive; however, we will strive to take advantage of any and all opportunities for growth and to attain satisfactory profitability. Collectively, we will do what has to be done to ensure that the future will be rewarding to all who have a part in our success.

Henry Harnischfeger
Chairman of the Board

William W. Goessel
President

January 31, 1985

Exhibit 4 Harnischfeger Corporation 1984 Annual Report (abridged)

MANAGEMENT'S DISCUSSION & ANALYSIS

RESULTS OF OPERATIONS

1984 Compared to 1983

Consolidated net sales of $399 million in fiscal 1984 increased $78 million or 24% over 1983. Sales increases were 62% in the Mining and Electrical Equipment Segment, and 10% in the Industrial Technologies Segment. Sales in the Construction Equipment Segment were virtually unchanged reflecting the continued low demand for construction equipment world-wide.

Effective at the beginning of fiscal 1984, net sales include the full sales price of construction and mining equipment purchased from Kobe Steel, Ltd. and sold by the Corporation, in order to reflect more effectively the nature of the Corporation's transactions with Kobe. Such sales aggregated $28.0 million in 1984.

The $4.0 million increase in Other Income reflected a recovery of certain claims and higher license and technical service fees.

Cost of Sales was equal to 79.1% of net sales in 1984 and 81.4% in 1983; which together with the increase in net sales resulted in a $23.9 million increase in gross profit (net sales less cost of sales). Contributing to this increase were improved sales of higher-margin replacement parts in the Mining Equipment and Industrial Technologies Segments and a reduction in excess manufacturing costs through greater utilization of domestic manufacturing capacity and economies in total manufacturing costs including a reduction in pension expense. Reductions of certain LIFO inventories increased gross profit by $2.4 million in 1984 and $15.6 million in 1983.

Product development selling and administrative expenses were reduced, due to the funding of R&D expenses in the Construction Equipment Segment pursuant to the October 1983 Agreement with Kobe Steel, Ltd., to reductions in pension expenses and provision for credit losses, and to the absence of the corporate financial restructuring expenses incurred in 1983.

Net interest expense in 1984 increased $2.9 million due to higher interest rates on the outstanding funded debt and a reduction in interest income.

Equity in Earnings (Loss) of Unconsolidated Companies included 1984 income of $1.2 million of Harnischfeger Credit Corporation, an unconsolidated finance subsidiary, reflecting an income tax benefit of $1.4 million not previously recorded.

The preceding items, together with the cumulative effect of the change in depreciation method described in Financial Note 2, were included in net income of $15.2 million or $1.28 per common share, compared with net loss of $34.6 million or $3.49 per share in 1983.

The sales orders booked and unshipped backlogs of orders of the Corporation's three segments are summarized as follows (in million of dollars):

Orders Booked	1984	1983
Industrial Technologies	$132	$106
Mining and Electrical Equipment	210	135
Construction Equipment	109	109
	$451	$350
Backlogs at October 31		
Industrial Technologies	$ 79	$ 71
Mining and Electrical Equipment	91	50
Construction Equipment	23	20
	$193	$141

1983 Compared to 1982

Consolidated net sales of $321 million in fiscal 1983 were $126 million or 28% below 1982. This decline reflected, for the second consecutive year, the continued low demand in all markets served by the Corporation's products, with exports even more severely depressed due to the strength of the dollar. The largest decline was reported in the Construction Equipment Segment, down 34%; Mining and Electrical Equipment Segment shipments were down 27%, and the Industrial Technologies Segment, 23%.

Cost of Sales was equal to 81.4% of net sales in 1983 and 81.9% in 1982. The resulting gross profit

Exhibit 4   Harnischfeger Corporation 1984 Annual Report (abridged)

was $60 million in 1983 and $81 million in 1982, a reduction equal to the rate of sales decrease.

The benefits of reduced manufacturing capacity and economies in total manufacturing costs were offset by reduced selling prices in the highly competitive markets. Reductions of certain LIFO inventories increased gross profits by $15.6 million in 1983 and $7.2 million in 1982.

Product development, selling and administrative expenses were reduced as a result of expense reduction measures in response to the lower volume of business and undertaken in connection with the Corporation's corporate recovery program, and reduced provisions for credit losses, which in 1982 included $4.0 million in income support for Harnischfeger Credit Corporation.

Net interest expense was reduced $9.1 million from 1982 to 1983, due primarily to increased interest income from short-term cash investments and an accrual of $4.7 million in interest income on refundable income taxes not previously recorded.

The Credit for Income Taxes included a federal income tax benefit of $5 million, based upon the recent examination of the Corporation's income tax returns and refund claims. No income tax benefits were available for the losses of the U.S. operations in 1983.

The losses from unconsolidated companies recorded in 1983 included $0.5 million in Harnischfeger Credit Corporation; $2.1 million in Cranetex, Inc., a Corporation-owned distributorship in Texas; and $0.8 million in ASEA Industrial Systems Inc., then a 49%-owned joint venture between the Corporation and ASEA AB and now 19%-owned with the investment accounted for on the cost method.

The preceding items were reflected in a net loss of $34.6 million or $3.49 per share.

LIQUIDITY AND FINANCIAL RESOURCES

In April 1984, the Corporation issued in public offerings 2,150,000 shares of Common Stock, $50 million principal amount of 15% Senior Notes due in 1994, and 100,000 Units consisting of $100 million principal amount of 12% Subordinated Debentures due in 2004 and 2,000,000 Common Stock Purchase Warrants.

The net proceeds from the sales of the securities of $149 million were used to prepay substantially all of the outstanding debt of the Corporation and certain of its subsidiaries.

During the year ended October 31, 1984, the consolidated cash balances increased $32 million to a balance of $96 million, with the cash activity summarized as follows (in million of dollars):

Funds provided by operations	$10
Funds returned to the Corporation upon restructuring of the Salaried Employees' Pension Plan	39
Debt repayment less the proceeds of sales of securities	(9)
Plant and equipment additions	(6)
All other changes—net	(2)
	$32

In the third quarter of fiscal 1984 the Corporation entered into a $52 million three-year revolving credit agreement with ten U.S. and Canadian banks. While the Corporation has adequate liquidity to meet its current working capital requirements, the revolver represents another step in the Corporation's program to strengthen its financial position and provide the required financial resources to respond to opportunities as they arise.

Exhibit 4 Harnischfeger Corporation 1984 Annual Report (abridged)

CONSOLIDATED STATEMENT OF OPERATIONS

(Dollar amounts in thousands except per share figures)	Year Ended October 31		
	1984	1983	1982
Revenues:			
Net sales	$398,708	$321,010	$447,461
Other income, including license and technical service fees	7,067	3,111	5,209
	405,775	324,121	452,670
Cost of Sales	315,216	261,384	366,297
Operating Income	90,559	62,737	86,373
Less:			
Product development, selling and administrative expenses	72,196	85,795	113,457
Interest expense—net	12,625	9,745	18,873
Provision for plant closing	—	—	23,700
Income (Loss) Before Provision (Credit) for Income Taxes, Equity Items and Cumulative Effect of Accounting Change	5,738	(32,803)	(69,657)
Provision (Credit) for Income Taxes	2,425	(1,400)	(1,600)
Income (Loss) Before Equity Items and Cumulative Effect of Accounting Change	3,313	(31,403)	(68,057)
Equity items:			
Equity in earnings (loss) of unconsolidated companies	993	(3,397)	(7,891)
Minority interest in (earnings) loss of consolidated subsidiaries	(135)	170	(583)
Income (Loss) Before Cumulative Effect of Accounting Change	4,171	(34,630)	(76,531)
Cumulative Effect of Change in Depreciation Method	11,005	—	—
Net Income (Loss)	$ 15,176	$(34,630)	$ (76,531)
Earnings (Loss) per Common and Common Equivalent Share:			
Income (Loss) before cumulative effect of accounting change	$ .35	$(3.49)	$(7.64)
Cumulative effect of change in depreciation method	.93	—	—
Net income (loss)	$1.28	$(3.49)	$(7.64)
Pro forma Amounts Assuming the Changed Depreciation Method Had Been Applied Retroactively:			
Net (loss)		$ (33,918)	$ (76,695)
(Loss) per common share		$(3.42)	$(7.65)

(The accompanying notes are an integral part of the financial statements.)

Exhibit 4   Harnischfeger Corporation 1984 Annual Report (abridged)

CONSOLIDATED BALANCE SHEET

	October 31	
(Dollar amounts in thousands except per share figures)	**1984**	1983
Assets		
Current Assets:		
Cash and temporary investments	**$ 96,007**	$ 64,275
Accounts receivable	**87,648**	63,740
Inventories	**144,312**	153,594
Refundable income taxes and related interest	**1,296**	12,585
Other current assets	**5,502**	6,023
Prepaid income taxes	**14,494**	14,232
	349,259	314,449
Investments and Other Assets:		
Investments in and advances to:		
Finance subsidiary, at equity in net assets	**8,849**	6,704
Other companies	**4,445**	2,514
Other assets	**13,959**	6,411
	27,253	15,629
Operating Plants:		
Land and improvements	**9,419**	10,370
Buildings	**59,083**	60,377
Machinery and equipment	**120,949**	122,154
	189,451	192,901
Accumulated depreciation	**(93,259)**	(107,577)
	96,192	85,324
	$472,704	$415,402

(continued)

h

Exhibit 4 Harnischfeger Corporation 1984 Annual Report (abridged)

CONSOLIDATED BALANCE SHEET (continued)

(Dollar amounts in thousands except per share figures)	October 31 1984	October 31 1983
Liabilities and Shareholders' Equity		
Current Liabilities:		
Short-term notes payable to banks by subsidiaries	$ 9,090	$ 8,155
Long-term debt and capitalized lease obligations payable within one year	973	18,265
Trade accounts payable	37,716	21,228
Employee compensation and benefits	15,041	14,343
Accrued plant closing costs	2,460	6,348
Advance payments and progress billings	20,619	15,886
Income taxes payable	1,645	3,463
Account payable to finance subsidiary	—	3,436
Other current liabilities and accruals	29,673	32,333
	117,217	123,457
Long-Term Obligations:		
Long-term debt payable to:		
Unaffiliated lenders	128,550	139,092
Finance subsidiary	—	5,400
Capitalized lease obligations	7,870	8,120
	136,420	152,612
Deferred Liabilities and Income Taxes:		
Accrued pension costs	57,611	19,098
Other deferred liabilities	5,299	7,777
Deferred income taxes	6,385	134
	69,295	27,009
Minority Interest	2,400	2,405
Shareholders' Equity:		
Preferred stock $100 par value—authorized 250,000 shares:		
Series A $7.00 cumulative convertible preferred shares: authorized, issued and outstanding 117,500 shares in 1984 and 100,000 shares in 1983	11,750	10,000
Common stock, $1 par value—authorized 25,000,000 shares: issued and outstanding 12,283,563 shares in 1984 and 10,133,563 shares in 1983	12,284	10,134
Capital in excess of par value of shares	114,333	88,332
Retained earnings	19,901	6,475
Cumulative translation adjustments	(10,896)	(5,022)
	147,372	109,919
	$472,704	$415,402

(The accompanying notes are an integral part of the financial statements.)

Exhibit 4　Harnischfeger Corporation 1984 Annual Report (abridged)

CONSOLIDATED STATEMENT OF CHANGES IN FINANCIAL POSITION

(Dollar amounts in thousands)	Year Ended October 31,		
	1984	1983	1982
Funds Were Provided by (Applied to):			
Operations:			
Income (loss) before cumulative effect of accounting change	$ **4,171**	$ (34,630)	$(76,531)
Cumulative effect of change in depreciation method	**11,005**	—	—
Net income (loss)	**15,176**	(34,630)	(76,531)
Add (deduct) items included not affecting funds:			
Depreciation	**8,077**	13,552	15,241
Unremitted (earnings) loss of unconsolidated companies	**(993)**	3,397	7, 891
Deferred pension contributions	**(500)**	4,834	—
Deferred income taxes	**6,583**	(3,178)	1,406
Reduction in accumulated depreciation resulting from change in depreciation method	**(17,205)**	—	—
Other—net	**(2,168)**	(67)	2,034
Decrease in operating working capital (see below)	**7,039**	11,605	72,172
Add (deduct) effects on operating working capital of:			
Conversion of export and factored receivable sales to debt	**—**	23,919	—
Reclassification to deferred liabilities:			
Accrued pension costs	**—**	14,264	—
Other liabilities	**—**	5,510	—
Foreign currency translation adjustments	**(6,009)**	(1,919)	(5,943)
Funds provided by operations	**10,000**	37,287	16,270
Financing, Investment and Other Activities:			
Transactions in debt and capitalized lease obligations —Long-Term debt and capitalized lease obligations:			
Proceeds from sale of 15% Senior Notes and 12% Subordinated Debentures, net of issue costs	**120,530**	—	—
Other increases	**1,474**	—	25,698
Repayments	**(161,500)**	(760)	(9,409)
Restructured debt	**—**	158,058	—
Debt replaced, including conversion of receivable sales of $23,919, and short-term bank notes payable of $9,028	**—**	(158,058)	—
	(39,496)	(760)	16,289
Net increase (repayment) in short-term bank notes payable	**2,107**	(3,982)	(2,016)

(continued)

h

1-17

Exhibit 4   Harnischfeger Corporation 1984 Annual Report (abridged)

CONSOLIDATED STATEMENT OF CHANGES IN FINANCIAL POSITION (continued)

(Dollar amounts in thousands)	Year Ended October 31,		
	1984	1983	1982
Net increase (repayment) in debt and capitalized lease obligations	**$(37,389)**	$ (4,742)	$ 14,273
Issuance of:			
Common stock	**21,310**	—	449
Common stock purchase warrants	**6,663**	—	—
Salaried pension assets reversion	**39,307**	—	—
Plant and equipment additions	**(5,546)**	(1,871)	(10,819)
Advances to unconsolidated companies	**(2,882)**	—	—
Other—net	**269**	1,531	848
Funds provided by (applied to) financing, investment and other activities	**21,732**	(5,082)	4,751
Increase in Cash and Temporary Investments Before Cash Dividends	**$ 31,732**	$ 32,205	$21,021
Cash Dividends	**—**	—	(2,369)
Increase in Cash and Temporary Investments	**$ 31,732**	$ 32,205	$ 18,652
Decrease (Increase) in Operating Working Capital (Excluding Cash Items, Debt and Capitalized Lease Obligations):			
Accounts receivable	**$ (23,908)**	$ (5,327)	$ 42,293
Inventories	**9,282**	56,904	26,124
Refundable income taxes and related interest	**11,289**	(2,584)	(6,268)
Other current assets	**259**	10,008	(439)
Trade accounts payable	**16,488**	(1,757)	(3,302)
Employee compensation and benefits	**698**	(15,564)	(3,702)
Accrued plant closing costs	**(3,888)**	(14,148)	20,496
Other current liabilities	**(3,181)**	(15,927)	(3,030)
Decrease in operating working capital	**$ 7,039**	$ 11,605	$ 72,172

(The accompanying notes are an integral part of the financial statements.)

CONSOLIDATED STATEMENT OF SHAREHOLDERS' EQUITY

(Dollar amounts in thousands except per share figures)	Preferred Stock	Common Stock	Capital in Excess of Par Value of Shares	Retained Earnings	Cumulative Translation Adjustments	Total
Balance at October 31, 1981	$10,000	$10,085	$ 87,932	$120,005	$ —	$228,022
Cumulative translation adjustments through October 31, 1981					(1,195)	(1,195)
Issuance of Common Stock:						
10,000 shares to Kobe Steel, Ltd.		10	91			101
38,161 shares under stock purchase and dividend reinvestment plans		39	309			348
Net (loss)				(76,531)		(76,531)
Cash dividends paid on:						
Preferred stock				(350)		(350)
Common stock $.20 per share				(2,019)		(2,019)
Translation adjustments, net of deferred income taxes of $128					(2,928)	(2,928)
Balance at October 31, 1982	10,000	10,134	88,332	41,105	(4,123)	145,448
Net (loss)				(34,630)		(34,630)
Translation adjustments, including deferred income taxes of $33					(899)	(899)
Balance at October 31, 1983	10,000	10,134	88,332	6,475	(5,022)	109,919
Issuance of:						
2,150,000 shares of common stock		2,150	19,160			21,310
2,000,000 common stock purchase warrants			6,663			6,663
17,500 shares of Series A $7.00 cumulative convertible preferred stock in discharge of dividends payable on preferred stock	1,750			(1,750)		—
Net income				15,176		15,176
Translation adjustments, net of deferred income taxes of $300					(5,874)	(5,874)
Other			178			178
Balance at October 31, 1984	$11,750	$12,284	$114,333	$ 19,901	$(10,896)	$147,372

(The accompanying notes are an integral part of the financial statements.)

Exhibit 4   Harnischfeger Corporation 1984 Annual Report (abridged)

Exhibit 4   Harnischfeger Corporation 1984 Annual Report (abridged)

FINANCIAL NOTES

Note 1

Summary of Significant Accounting Policies:

Consolidation—The consolidated financial statements include the accounts of all majority-owned subsidiaries except a wholly-owned domestic finance subsidiary, a subsidiary organized in 1982 as a temporary successor to a distributor, both of which are accounted for under the equity method, and a wholly-owned Brazilian subsidiary, which is carried at estimated net realizable value due to economic uncertainty. All related significant intercompany balances and transactions have been eliminated in consolidation.

Financial statements of certain consolidated subsidiaries, principally foreign, are included, effective in fiscal year 1984, on the basis of their fiscal years ending September 30; previously, certain of such subsidiaries had fiscal years ending July (See Note 2). Such fiscal periods have been adopted by the subsidiaries in order to provide for a more timely consolidation with the Corporation.

Inventories—The Corporation values its inventories at the lower of cost or market. Cost is determined by the last-in, first-out (LIFO) method for inventories located principally in the United States, and by the first-in, first-out (FIFO) method for inventories of foreign subsidiaries.

Operating Plants, Equipment and Depreciation—Properties are stated at cost. Maintenance and repairs are charged to expense as incurred and expenditures for betterments and renewals are capitalized. Effective in 1981, interest is capitalized for qualifying assets during their acquisition period. Capitalized interest is amortized on the same basis as the related asset. When properties are sold or otherwise disposed of, the cost and accumulated depreciation are removed from the accounts and any gain or loss is included in income.

Depreciation of plants and equipment is provided over the estimated useful lives of the related assets, or over the lease terms of capital leases, using, effective in fiscal year 1984, the straight-line method for financial reporting, and principally accelerated methods for tax reporting purposes. Previously, accelerated methods, where applicable, were also used for financial reporting purposes (See Note 2). For U.S. income tax purposes, depreciation lives are based principally on the Class Life Asset Depreciation Range for additions, other than buildings, in the years 1973 through 1980, and on the Accelerated Cost Recovery System for all additions after 1980.

Discontinued facilities held for sale are carried at the lower of cost less accumulated depreciation or estimated realizable value, which aggregated $4.9 million and $3.6 million at October 31, 1984 and 1983, respectively, and were included in Other Assets in the accompanying Balance Sheet.

Pension Plans—The Corporation has pension plans covering substantially all of its employees. Pension expenses of the principal defined benefit plans consist of current service costs of such plans and amortization of the prior service costs and actuarial gains and losses over periods ranging from 10 to 30 years. The Corporation's policy is to fund at a minimum the amount required under the Employee Retirement Income Security Act of 1974.

Income Taxes—The consolidated tax provision is computed based on income and expenses recorded in the Statement of Operations. Prepaid or deferred taxes are recorded for the difference between such taxes and taxes computed for tax returns. The Corporation and its domestic subsidiaries file a consolidated federal income tax return. The operating results of Harnischfeger GmbH are included in the Corporation's U.S. income tax returns.

Additional taxes are provided on the earnings of foreign subsidiaries which are intended to be remitted to the Corporation. Such taxes are not provided on subsidiaries' unremitted earnings which are intended to be permanently reinvested.

Investment tax credits are accounted for under the flow-through method as a reduction of the income tax provision, if applicable, in the year the related asset is placed in service.

Reporting Format—Certain previously reported items have been conformed to the current year's presentation.

Note 2

Accounting Changes:

Effective November 1, 1983, the Corporation includes in its net sales products purchased from

Exhibit 4   Harnischfeger Corporation 1984 Annual Report (abridged)

Kobe Steel, Ltd. and sold by the Corporation, to reflect more effectively the nature of the Corporation's transactions with Kobe. Previously only the gross margin on Kobe-originated equipment was included. During fiscal year 1984 such sales aggregated $28.0 million. Also, effective November 1, 1983, the financial statements of certain foreign subsidiaries are included on the basis of their fiscal years ending September 30 instead of the previous years ending July 31. This change had the effect of increasing net sales by $5.4 million for the year ended October 31, 1984. The impact of these changes on net income was insignificant.

In 1984, the Corporation has computed depreciation expense on plants, machinery and equipment using the straight-line method for financial reporting purposes. Prior to 1984, the Corporation used principally accelerated methods for its U.S. operating plants. The cumulative effect of this change, which was applied retroactively to all assets previously subjected to accelerated depreciation, increased net income for 1984 by $11.0 million or $.93 per common and common equivalent share. The impact of the new method on income for the year 1984 before the cumulative effect was insignificant.

As a result of the review of its depreciation policy, the Corporation, effective November 1, 1983, has changed its estimated depreciation lives on certain U.S. plants, machinery and equipment and residual values on certain machinery and equipment, which increased net income for 1984 by $3.2 million or $.27 per share. No income tax effect was applied to this change.

The changes in accounting for depreciation were made to conform the Corporation's depreciation policy to those used by manufacturers in the Corporation's and similar industries and to provide a more equitable allocation of the cost of plants, machinery and equipment over their useful lives.

Note 3

Cash and Temporary Investments:

Cash and temporary investments consisted of the following (in thousands of dollars):

| | October 31, | |
	1984	1983
Cash—in demand deposits	$ 2,155	$11,910
—in special accounts principally to support letters of credit	4,516	—
Temporary investments	89,336	52,365
	$96,007	$64,275

Temporary investments consisted of short-term U.S. and Canadian treasury bills, money market funds, time and certificates of deposit, commercial paper and bank repurchase agreements and bankers' acceptances. Temporary investments are stated at cost plus accrued interest, which approximates market value.

Note 4

Long-Term Debt, Bank Credit Lines and Interest Expense:

Outstanding long-term debt payable to unaffiliated lenders was as follows (in thousands of dollars):

| | October 31, | |
	1984	1983
Parent Company:		
15% Senior Notes due April 15, 1994	$ 47,700	$ —
12% Subordinated Debentures, with an effective interest rate of 16.3%; sinking fund redemption payments of $7,500 due annually on April 15 in 1994–2003, and final payment of $25,000 in 2004	100,000	—
Term Obligations—		
Insurance company debt:		
9% Notes	—	20,000
9 7/8 Notes	—	38,750
8 7/8 Notes	—	40,500
Bank debt, at 105% of prime	—	25,000
Paper purchase debt, at prime or LIBOR, plus 1¼%	—	18,519
9.23% Mortgage Note due monthly to April, 1998	4,327	4,481

(continued)

h

1-21

Exhibit 4   Harnischfeger Corporation 1984 Annual Report (abridged)

	October 31,	
	1984	1983
	152,027	147,250
Consolidated Subsidiaries:		
Notes payable to banks in German marks	—	9,889
Contract payable in 1985–1989, in South African rands, with imputed interest rate of 12%	**1,024**	—
Other	—	36
	153,051	157,175
Less: Amounts payable within one year	**644**	17,799
Unamortized discounts	**23,857**	284
Long-Term Debt—excluding amounts payable within one year	**$128,550**	$139,092

Note 5

Harnischfeger Credit Corporation and Cranetex, Inc.

Condensed financial information of Harnischfeger Credit Corporation ("Credit"), an unconsolidated wholly-owned finance subsidiary, accounted for under the equity method, was as follows (in thousands of dollars):

Balance Sheet	October 31,	
	1984	1983
Assets:		
Cash and temporary investments	**$ 404**	$19,824
Finance receivables—net	**4,335**	11,412
Factored account note and current account receivable from parent company	—	8,836
Other assets	**4,181**	661
	$8,920	$40,733
Liabilities and Shareholder's Equity:		
Debt payable	**$ —**	$32,600
Advances from parent company	**950**	—
Other liabilities	**71**	1,429
	1,021	34,029
Shareholder's equity	**7,899**	6,704
	$8,920	$40,733

Statement of Operations	Year Ended October 31,		
	1984	1983	1982
Revenues	**$1,165**	$2,662	$9,978
Less:			
Operating Expenses	**1,530**	3,386	14,613
Provision (credit) for income taxes	**(1,560)**	(222)	180
Net income (loss)	**$1,195**	$(502)	$(4,815)

Credit's purchases of finance receivables from the Corporation aggregated $1.1 million in 1984, $46.7 million in 1983 and $50.4 million in 1982. In 1982, Credit received income support of $4.0 million from the Corporation.

In 1982, the Corporation organized Cranetex, Inc. to assume certain assets and liabilities transferred by a former distributor of construction equipment, in settlement of the Corporation's and Credit's claims against the distributor and to continue the business on an interim basis until the franchise can be transferred to a new distributor. The Corporation recorded provisions of $2.5 million in 1983 and $2.3 million in 1982 and Credit recorded a provision of $6.7 million in 1982, for credit losses incurred in the financing of equipment sold to the former distributor.

The condensed balance sheet of Cranetex, Inc. was as follows (in thousand of dollars):

	October 31,	
	1984	1983
Assets:		
Cash	**$ 143**	$ 49
Accounts receivables	**566**	428
Inventory	**2,314**	3,464
Property and equipment	**1,547**	1,674
	$4,570	$5,615
Liabilities and Deficit:		
Loans payable	**$4,325**	$6,682
Other liabilities	**338**	620
	4,663	7,302
Shareholder's (deficit), net of accounts and advances payable to parent company	**(93)**	(1,687)
	$4,570	$5,615

Exhibit 4   Harnischfeger Corporation 1984 Annual Report (abridged)

The net losses of Cranetex, Inc. of $.2 million in 1984, $2.1 million in 1983 and $1.0 million in 1982 were included in Equity in Earnings (Loss) of Unconsolidated Companies in the Corporation's Statement of Operations.

Note 6

Transactions with Kobe Steel, Ltd. and ASEA Industrial Systems Inc.

Kobe Steel, Ltd. of Japan ("Kobe"), has been a licensee for certain of the Corporation's products since 1955, and has owned certain Harnischfeger Japanese construction equipment patents and technology since 1981. As of October 31, 1984, Kobe held 1,030,000 shares or 8.4% of the Corporation's outstanding Common Stock (See Note 13). Kobe also owns 25% of the capital stock of Harnischfeger of Australia Pty. Ltd., a subsidiary of the Corporation. This ownership appears as the minority interest on the Corporation's balance sheet.

Under agreements expiring in December 1990, Kobe pays technical service fees on P&H mining equipment produced and sold under license from the Corporation, and trademark and marketing fees on sales of construction equipment outside of Japan. Net fee income received from Kobe was $4.3 million in 1984, $3.1 million in 1983, and $3.9 million in 1982; this income is included in Other Income in the accompanying Statement of Operations.

In October 1983, the Corporation entered into a ten-year agreement with Kobe under which Kobe agreed to supply the Corporation's requirements for construction cranes for sale in the United States as it phases out its own manufacture of cranes over the next several years, and to make the Corporation the exclusive distributor of Kobe-built cranes in the United States. The Agreement also involves a joint research and development program for construction equipment under which the Corporation agreed to spend at least $17 million over a three-year period and provided it does so, Kobe agreed to pay this amount to the Corporation. Sales of cranes outside the United States continue under the contract terms described in the preceding paragraph.

The Corporation's sales to Kobe, principally components for mining and construction equipment, excluding the R&D expenses discussed in the preceding paragraph, approximated $5.2 million, $10.5 million and $7.0 million during the three years ended October 31, 1984, 1983 and 1982, respectively. The purchases from Kobe of mining and construction equipment and components amounted to approximately $33.7 million, $15.5 million and $29.9 million during the three years ended October 31, 1984, 1983 and 1982, respectively, most of which were resold to customers (See Note 2).

The Corporation owns 19% of ASEA Industrial Systems Inc. ("AIS"), an electrical equipment company controlled by ASEA AB of Sweden. The Corporation's purchases of electrical components from AIS aggregated $11.2 million in 1984 and $6.1 million in 1983 and its sales to AIS approximated $2.6 million in 1984 and $3.8 million in 1983.

The Corporation believes that its transactions with Kobe and AIS were competitive with alternative sources of supply for each party involved.

Note 7

Inventories

Consolidated inventories consisted of the following (in thousand of dollars):

| | October 31, | |
	1984	1983
At lower of cost or market (FIFO method):		
Raw materials	$ 11,003	$ 11,904
Work in process and purchased parts	88,279	72,956
Finished goods	79,111	105,923
	178,393	190,783
Allowance to reduce inventories to cost on the LIFO method	(34,081)	(37,189)
	$144,312	$153,594

Inventories valued on the LIFO method represented approximately 82% of total inventories at both October 31, 1984 and 1983.

Inventory reductions in 1984, 1983 and 1982 resulted in a liquidation of LIFO inventory quantities carried at lower costs compared with the current cost of their acquisitions. The effect of these liquidations was to increase net income by 2.4 million or $.20

Exhibit 4 Harnischfeger Corporation 1984 Annual Report (abridged)

per common share in fiscal 1984, and to reduce the net loss by approximately $15.6 million or $1.54 per share in 1983, and by $6.7 million or $.66 per share in 1982; no income tax effect applied to the adjustment in 1984 and 1983.

Note 8

Accounts Receivable

Accounts receivable were net of allowances for doubtful accounts of $5.9 million and $6.4 million at October 31, 1984 and 1983, respectively.

Note 9

Research and Development Expense

Research and development expense incurred in the development of new products or significant improvements to existing products was $5.1 million in 1984 (net of amounts funded by Kobe Steel, Ltd.) $12.1 million in 1983 and $14.1 million in 1982.

Note 10

Foreign Operations

The net sales, net income (loss) and net assets of subsidiaries located in countries outside the United States and Canada and included in the consolidated financial statements were as follows (in thousands of dollars):

| | Year Ended October 31, | | |
	1984	1983	1982
Net sales	$78,074	$45,912	$69,216
Net income (loss) after minority interests	828	(1,191)	3,080
Corporation's equity in total net assets	17,734	7,716	7,287

Foreign currency transaction losses included in Cost of Sales were $2.7 million in 1984, $1.2 million in 1983 and $1.3 million in 1982.

Note 11

Pension Plans and Other Postretirement Benefits

Pension expense for all plans of the Corporation and its consolidated subsidiaries was $1.9 million in 1984, $6.5 million in 1983 and $12.2 million in 1982.

Accumulated plan benefits and plan net assets for the Corporation's U.S. defined benefit plans, at the beginning of the fiscal years 1984 and 1983, with the data for the Salaried Employees' Retirement Plan as in effect on August 1, 1984, were as follows (in thousands of dollars):

	1984	1983
Actuarial present value of accumulated plan benefits:		
Vested	$52,639	$108,123
Nonvested	2,363	5,227
	$55,002	$113,350
Net assets available for benefits:		
Assets of the Pension Trusts	$45,331	$112,075
Accrued contributions not paid to the Trusts	16,717	12,167
	$62,048	$124,242

The Salaried Employees' Retirement Plan, which covers substantially all salaried employees in the U.S., was restructured during 1984 due to overfunding of the Plan. Effective August 1, 1984, the Corporation terminated the existing plan and established a new plan which is substantially identical to the prior plan except for an improvement in the minimum pension benefit. All participants in the prior plan became fully vested upon its termination. All vested benefits earned through August 1, 1984 were covered through the purchase of individual annuities at a cost aggregating $36.7 million. The remaining plan assets, which totaled $39.3 million, reverted to the Corporation in cash upon receipt of regulatory approval of the prior plan termination from the Pension Benefit Guaranty Corporation. For financial reporting purposes, the new plan is considered to be a continuation of the terminated plan. Accordingly, the $39.3 million actuarial gain which resulted from the restructuring is included in Accrued Pension Costs in the accompanying Balance Sheet and is being amortized to income over a ten-year period commencing in 1984. For tax reporting purposes, the asset reversion will be

Exhibit 4   Harnischfeger Corporation 1984 Annual Report (abridged)

treated as a fiscal 1985 transaction. The initial unfunded actuarial liability of the new plan, computed as of November 1, 1983, of $10.3 million is also included in Accrued Pension Costs.

In 1982 and 1983, the Pension Trusts purchased certain securities with effective yields of 13% and 12%, respectively, and dedicated these assets to the plan benefits of a substantial portion of the retired employees and certain terminated employees with deferred vested rights. These rates, together with 9% for active employees in 1984, 8% in 1983 and 7¼% in 1982, were the assumed rates of return used in determining the annual pension expense and the actuarial present value of accumulated plan benefits for the U.S. plans.

The effect of the changes in the investment return assumption rates for all U.S. plans, together with the 1984 restructuring of the U.S. Salaried Employees' Plan, was to reduce pension expense by approximately $4.0 million in 1984 and $2.0 million in 1983, and the actuarial present value of accumulated plan benefits by approximately $60.0 million in 1984. Pension expense in 1983 was also reduced $2.1 million from the lower level of active employees. Other actuarial gains, including higher than anticipated investment results, more than offset the additional pension costs resulting from plan changes and interest charges on balance sheet accruals in 1984 and 1983.

The Corporation's foreign pension plans do not determine the actuarial value of accumulated benefits or net assets available for retirement benefits as calculated and disclosed above. For those plans, the total of the plans' pension funds and balance sheet accruals approximated the actuarially computed value of vested benefits at both October 31, 1984 and 1983.

The Corporation generally provides certain health care and life insurance benefits for U.S. retired employees. Substantially all of the Corporation's current U.S. employees may become eligible for such benefits upon retirement. Life insurance benefits are provided either through the pension plans or separate group insurance arrangements. The cost of retiree health care and life insurance benefits, other than the benefits provided by the pension plans, is expensed as incurred; such costs approximated $2.6 million in 1984 and $1.7 million in 1983.

Note 12

Income Taxes

Domestic and foreign income (loss) before income tax effects was as follows (in thousands of dollars):

| | Year Ended October 31, | | |
	1984	1983	1982
Domestic	**$1,578**	$(35,412)	$(77,600)
Foreign:			
Harnischfeger GmbH	**432**	(2,159)	(475)
All other	**3,728**	4,768	8,418
	4,160	2,609	7,943
Total income (loss) before income tax effects, equity items and cumulative effect of accounting change	**$5,738**	$(32,803)	$(69,657)

Provision (credit) for income taxes, on income (loss) before income tax effects, equity items and cumulative effect of accounting change, consisted of (in thousands of dollars):

	1984	1983	1982
Currently payable (refundable):			
Federal	$ —	$(7,957)	$(9,736)
State	**136**	297	70
Foreign	**2,518**	3,379	5,376
	2,654	(4,281)	(4,290)
Deferred (prepaid):			
Federal	—	2,955	2,713
State and foreign	**(229)**	(74)	(23)
	(229)	2,881	2,690
Provision (credit) for income taxes	**$2,425**	$(1,400)	$(1,600)

During 1983 an examination of the Corporation's 1977–1981 federal income tax returns and certain refund claims was completed by the Internal Revenue Service, and as a result, a current credit for federal income taxes of $8.0 million was recorded in 1983, $3.0 million of which was applied to the reduction of prepaid income taxes.

h

1-25

Exhibit 4   Harnischfeger Corporation 1984 Annual Report (abridged)

In 1984, tax credits fully offset any federal income tax otherwise applicable to the year's income, and in 1983 and 1982, the relationship of the tax benefit to the pre-tax loss differed substantially from the U.S. statutory tax rate due principally to losses from the domestic operations for which only a partial federal tax benefit was available in 1982. Consequently, an analysis of deferred income taxes and variance from the U.S. statutory rate is not presented.

Unremitted earnings of foreign subsidiaries which have been or are intended to be permanently reinvested were $19.1 million at October 31, 1984. Such earnings, if distributed, would incur income tax expense of substantially less than the U.S. income tax rate as a result of previously paid foreign income taxes, provided that such foreign taxes would become deductible as foreign tax credits. No income tax provision was made in respect of the tax-deferred income of a consolidated subsidiary that has elected to be taxed as a domestic international sales corporation. The Deficit Reduction Act of 1984 provides for such income to become nontaxable effective December 31, 1984.

At October 31, 1984, the Corporation had federal tax operating loss carry-forwards of approximately $70.0 million, expiring in 1998 and 1999, for tax return purposes, and $88.0 million for book purposes. In addition, the Corporation had for tax purposes, foreign tax credit carry-forwards of $3.0 million (expiring in 1985 through 1989), and investment tax credit carry-forwards of $1.0 million (expiring in 1997 through 1999). For book purposes, tax credit carry-forwards approximately $8.0 million. The carry-forward will be available for the reduction of future income tax provisions, the extent and timing of which are not determinable.

Differences in income (loss) before income taxes for financial and tax purposes arise from timing differences between financial and tax reporting and relate to depreciation, consolidating eliminations for inter-company profits in inventories, and provisions, principally, for warranty, pension, compensated absences, product liability and plant closing costs.

REPORT OF INDEPENDENT ACCOUNTANTS

Milwaukee, Wisconsin
November 29, 1984

To the Directors and Shareholders of Harnischfeger Corporation:

In our opinion, the financial statements, which appear on pages 18 to 34 of this report, present fairly the consolidated financial position of Harnischfeger Corporation and its subsidiaries at October 31, 1984 and 1983, and the results of their operations and the changes in their financial position for each of the three years in the period ended October 31, 1984, in conformity with generally accepted accounting principles consistently applied during the period except for the change, with which we concur, in the method of accounting for depreciation expense as described in Note 2 on page 23 of this report. Our examinations of these statements were made in accordance with generally accepted auditing standards and accordingly included such tests of the accounting records and such other auditing procedures as we considered necessary in the circumstances.

Price Waterhouse

The Home Depot, Inc.

T*he difference between a company with a concept and one without is the difference between a stock that sells for 20 times earnings and one that sells for 10 times earnings. The Home Depot is definitely a concept stock, and it has the multiple to prove it – 27-28 times likely earnings in the current fiscal year ending this month. On the face of it, The Home Depot might seem like a tough one for the concept-mongers to work with. It's a chain of hardware stores. But, as we noted in our last visit to the company in the spring of '83, these hardware stores are huge warehouse outlets – 60,000 to 80,000 feet in space. You can fit an awful lot of saws in these and still have plenty of room left over to knock together a very decent concept.*

And in truth, the warehouse notion is the hottest thing in retailing these days. The Home Depot buys in quantum quantities, which means that its suppliers are eager to keep within its good graces and hence provide it with a lot of extra service. The company, as it happens, is masterful in promotion and pricing. The last time we counted, it had 22 stores, all of them located where the sun shines all the time.

Growth has been sizzling. Revenues, a mere $22 million in fiscal '80, shot past the quarter billion mark three years later. As to earnings, they have climbed from two cents in fiscal '80 to an estimated 60 cents in the fiscal year coming to an end [in January 1985].

Its many boosters in the Street, moreover, anticipate more of the same as far as the bullish eye can see. They're confidently estimating 30% growth in the new fiscal year as well. Could be. But while we share their esteem for the company's merchandising skills and imagination, we're as bemused now as we were the first time we looked at The Home Depot by its rich multiple. Maybe a little more now than then.[1]

The above report appeared on January 21, 1985, in "Up & Down Wall Street," a regular column in *Barron's* financial weekly.

COMPANY BACKGROUND

Bernard Marcus and Arthur Blank founded The Home Depot in 1978 to bring the warehouse retailing concept to the home center industry. The company operated retail "do-

This case was prepared by Professor Krishna Palepu as the basis for class discussion rather than to illustrate either effective or ineffective handling of an administrative situation. Copyright © 1988 by the President and Fellows of Harvard College. Harvard Business School case 9-188-148.1.

1. *Reprinted with permission from* Barron's, *January 21, 1985.*

it-yourself" (DIY) warehouse stores which sold a wide assortment of building materials and home improvement products. Sales, which were on a cash-and-carry basis, were concentrated in the home remodeling market. The company targeted as its customers individual homeowners and small contractors.

The Home Depot's strategy had several important elements. The company offered low and competitive prices, a feature central to the warehouse retailing concept. The Home Depot's stores, usually in suburbs, were also the warehouses, with inventory stacked over merchandise displayed on industrial racks. The warehouse format of the stores kept the overhead low and allowed the company to pass the savings to customers. Costs were further reduced by emphasizing higher volume and lower margins with a high inventory turnover. While offering low prices, The Home Depot was careful not to sacrifice the depth of merchandise and the quality of products offered for sale.

To ensure that the right products were stocked at all times, each Home Depot store carried approximately $4,500,000 of inventory, at retail, consisting of approximately 25,000 separate stock-keeping units. All these items were kept on the sales floor of the store, thus increasing convenience to the customer and minimizing out-of-stock occurrences. The company also assured its customers that the products sold by it were of the best quality. The Home Depot offered nationally advertised brands as well as lesser known brands carefully chosen by the company's merchandise managers. Every product sold by The Home Depot was guaranteed by either the manufacturer or by the company itself.

The Home Depot complemented the above merchandising strategy with excellent sales assistance. Since the great majority of the company's customers were individual homeowners with no prior experience in their home improvement projects, The Home Depot considered its employees' technical knowledge and service orientation to be very important to its marketing success. The company pursued a number of policies to address this need. Approximately 90% of the company's employees were on a full-time basis. To attract and retain a strong sales force, the company maintained salary and wage levels above those of its competitors. All the floor sales personnel attended special training sessions to gain thorough knowledge of the company's home improvement products and their basic applications. This training enabled them to answer shoppers' questions and help customers in choosing equipment and material appropriate for their projects. Often, the expert advice the sales personnel provided created a bond that resulted in continuous contact with the customer throughout the duration of the customer's project.

Finally, to attract customers, The Home Depot pursued an aggressive advertising program utilizing newspapers, television, radio, and direct mail catalogues. The company's advertising stressed promotional pricing, the broad assortment and depth of its merchandise, and the assistance provided by its sales personnel. The company also sponsored in-store demonstrations of do-it-yourself techniques and product uses. To increase customers' shopping convenience, The Home Depot's stores were open seven days a week, including weekday evenings.

Fortune magazine commented on The Home Depot's strategy as follows:

h
2-2

Warehouse stores typically offer shoppers deep discounts with minimal service and back-to-basics ambiance. The Home Depot's outlets have all the charm of a freight yard and predictably low prices. But they also offer unusually helpful customer service. Although warehouse retailing looks simple, it is not: As discounting cuts into gross profit margins, the merchant must carefully control buying, merchandising, and inventory costs. Throwing in service, which is expensive and hard to systematize, makes the job even tougher. In the do-it-yourself (DIY) segment of the industry – which includes old-style hardware stores, building supply warehouses, and the everything-under-one-roof home centers – The Home Depot is the only company that has successfully brought off the union of low prices and high service.[2]

The Home Depot's strategy was successful in fueling an impressive growth in the company's operations. The first three Home Depot stores, opened in Atlanta in 1979, were a quick success. From this modest beginning, the company grew rapidly and went public in 1981. The company's stock initially traded over-the-counter and was listed on the New York Stock Exchange in April 1984. Several new stores were opened in markets throughout the Sunbelt, and the number of stores operated by The Home Depot grew from 3 in 1979 to 50 by the end of fiscal 1985. As a result, sales grew from $7 million in 1979 to $700 million in 1985. Exhibit 1 provides a summary of the growth in the company's operations. The company's stock price performance during 1985 is summarized in Exhibit 2.

INDUSTRY AND COMPETITION

The home improvement industry was large and growing during the 1980s. The industry sales totaled approximately $80 billion in 1985 and strong industry growth was expected to continue, especially in the do-it-yourself (DIY) segment, which had grown at a compounded annual rate of 14 percent over the last 15 years. With the number of two-wage-earner households growing, there was an increase in families' average disposable income, making it possible to increase the frequency and magnitude of home improvement projects. Further, many homeowners were undertaking these projects by themselves rather than hiring a contractor. Research conducted by the Do-It-Yourself Institute, an industry trade group, showed that DIY activities had become America's second most popular leisure-time activity after watching television.

The success of warehouse retailing pioneered by The Home Depot attracted a number of other companies into the industry. Among the store chains currently operating in the industry were Builders Square (a division of K Mart), Mr. HOW (a division of Service Merchandise), The Home Club (a division of Zayre Corp.), Payless Cashways (a division of W.R. Grace), and Hechinger Co. Most of these store chains were relatively new and not yet achieving significant profitability.

....

2. *Reprinted with permission from Fortune, February 1988, p. 73.*

h
2-3

Among The Home Depot's competitors, the most successful was Hechinger, which had operated hardware stores for a long time and recently entered the do-it-yourself segment of the industry. Using a strategy quite different from The Home Depot's, Hechinger ran gleaming upscale stores and aimed at high profit margins. As of the end of fiscal 1985, the company operated 55 stores, located primarily in southeastern states. Hechinger announced that it planned to expand its sales by 20 to 25 percent a year by adding 10 to 14 stores a year. A summary of Hechinger's recent financial performance is presented in Exhibit 3.

THE HOME DEPOT'S FUTURE

While The Home Depot had achieved rapid growth every year since its inception, fiscal 1985 was probably the most important in the company's seven-year history. During 1985 the company implemented its most ambitious expansion plan to date by adding 20 new stores in eight new markets. Nine of these stores were acquired from Bowater, a competing store chain which was in financial difficulty. As The Home Depot engaged in major expansion, its revenues rose 62 percent from $432 million in fiscal 1984 to $700 million in 1985. However, the company's earnings declined in 1985 from the record levels achieved during the previous fiscal year. In fiscal 1985, The Home Depot earned $8.2 million, or $0.33 per share, as compared with $14.1 million or $0.56 per share in fiscal 1984.

Bernard Marcus, The Home Depot's chairman and chief executive officer, commented on the company's performance as follows:

Fiscal 1985 was a year of rapid expansion and continued growth for The Home Depot. Feeling the time was ripe for us to enhance our share of the do-it-yourself market, we seized the opportunity to make a significant investment in our long-term future. At the same time, we recognized that our short-term profit growth would be affected.

The Home Depot's 1985 annual report (Exhibit 4) provided more details on the firm's financial performance during the year.

As fiscal 1985 came to a close, The Home Depot faced some critical issues. The competition in the do-it-yourself industry was heating up. The fight for market dominance was expected to result in pressure on margins, and industry analysts expected only the strongest and most capable firms in the industry to survive. Also, The Home Depot had announced plans for further expansion that included the opening of nine new stores in 1986. The company estimated that site acquisition and construction would cost about $6.6 million for each new store, and investment in inventory (net of vendor financing) would require an additional $1.8 million per store. The company needed significant additional financing to implement these plans.

Home Depot relied on external financing—both debt and equity—to fund its growth in 1984 and 1985. However, the significant drop in its stock price in 1985 made further equity financing less attractive. While the company could borrow from its line of credit, it had to make sure that it could satisfy the interest coverage requirements (see Note 3 in Exhibit 4 for a discussion of debt covenant restrictions). Clearly, generating more cash from its own operations would be the best way for Home Depot to invest in its growth on a sustainable basis.

EXHIBIT 1

The Home Depot, Inc. – Summary of Performance During Fiscal Years 1981–1985

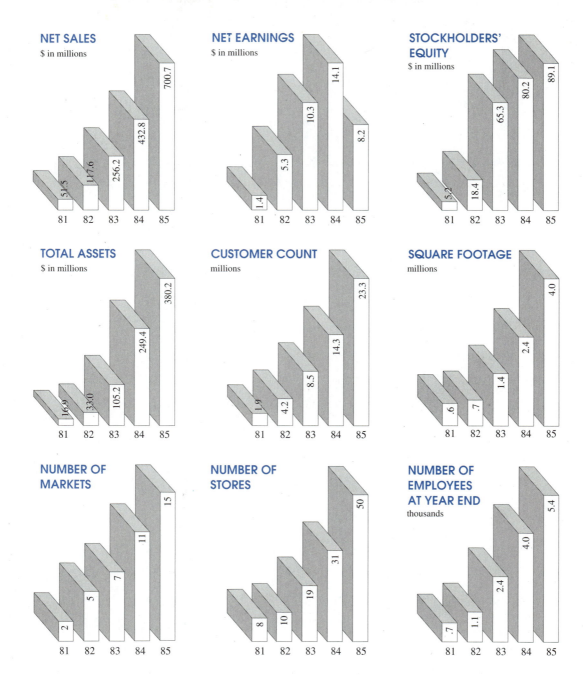

h
2-6

EXHIBIT 2

The Home Depot's Common Stock Price and Standard & Poor's 500
Composite Index from January 1985 to February 1986

Date	Home Depot Stock Price	S&P 500 Composite Index
1/2/85	$17.125	165.4
2/1/85	16.375	178.6
3/1/85	19.000	183.2
4/1/85	17.000	181.3
5/1/85	18.000	178.4
6/3/85	16.125	189.3
7/1/85	13.000	192.4
8/1/85	12.625	192.1
9/2/85	11.875	197.9
10/1/85	11.375	185.1
11/1/85	10.750	191.5
12/2/85	11.000	200.5
1/2/86	12.625	209.6
2/3/86	13.125	214.0
Cumulative Return:	−23.4%	29.4%

The Home Depot's β = 1.3 (Value Line estimate).

h

2-7

EXHIBIT 3

The Home Depot, Inc. – Summary of Financial Performance of Hechinger Company

I. HECHINGER'S FINANCIAL RATIOS

	Year Ending		
	February 1, 1986	February 2, 1985	January 28, 1984
Profit Before Taxes/Sales (%)	7.80	9.40	9.80
× Sales/Average Assets	1.48	1.72	2.02
× Average Assets/Average Equity	2.21	2.12	1.79
× (1 − Average Tax Rate)	0.62	0.55	0.54
= Return on Equity (%)	15.80	18.90	19.10
× (1 − Dividend Payout Ratio)	0.93	0.95	0.95
= Sustainable Growth Rate (%)	14.70	18.00	18.10
Gross Profit/Sales (%)	29.30	30.10	32.10
Selling, General and Administrative Expenses/Sales (%)	21.60	21.10	22.90
Interest Expenses/Sales (%)	2.10	1.30	0.70
Interest Income/Sales (%)	2.20	1.70	1.30
Inventory Turnover	4.50	4.50	4.40
Average Collection Period[a] (Days)	32.00	33.00	35.00
Average Accounts Payable Period[b] (Days)	58.00	61.00	63.00

a. Assumed 365 days in the fiscal year.
b. Payables also include accrued wages and expenses. Purchases are computed as cost of sales plus increase in inventory during the year. Assumed 365 days in the fiscal year.

II. HECHINGER'S CASH FLOW

	Year Ending		
(Dollars in Thousands)	February 1, 1986	February 2, 1985	January 28, 1984
Cash Provided from Operations			
Net earnings	$23,111	$20,923	$16,243
Items not requiring the use of cash or marketable securities:			
Depreciation and amortization	6,594	4,622	3,429
Deferred income taxes	1,375	2,040	1,515
Deferred rent expense	2,321	2,064	1,463
	33,401	**29,649**	**22,650**
Cash Invested in Operations			
Accounts receivable	4,657	7,905	7,954
Merchandise inventories	17,998	8,045	20,596
Other current assets	4,891	3,760	1,304
Accounts payable and accrued expenses	(6,620)	(12,099)	(9,767)
Taxes on income – current	285	3,031	(575)
	21,211	**10,642**	**19,512**
Net Cash Provided from Operations	**12,190**	**19,007**	**3,138**
Cash Used for Investment Activities			
Expenditures for property, furniture and equipment, net of disposals, and other assets	**(36,037)**	**(25,531)**	**(16,346)**
Cash Used to Pay Dividends to Shareholders	**(1,550)**	**(1,091)**	**(868)**
Cash Provided from Financing Activities			
Proceeds from public offering of 8½% converted subordinated debentures, net of expenses	—	85,010	—
Proceeds from public offering of common stock net of expenses	28,969	—	13,439
Proceeds from sale and leaseback transactions under operating leases	—	8,338	6,874
Increase (decrease) in long-term debt	—	(4,750)	6,366
Decrease in short-term debt	—	—	(318)
Exercise of stock options including income tax benefit	180	674	611
Decrease in capital lease obligations	(311)	(280)	(254)
	28,838	**88,992**	**26,718**
Increase in Cash and Marketable Securities	**$ 3,441**	**$81,377**	**$12,642**

EXHIBIT 4

The Home Depot, Inc.—Abridged Annual Report for Fiscal Year 1985

A Letter to Our Shareholders:

Fiscal 1985 was a year of rapid expansion and continued growth for The Home Depot. Feeling the time was ripe for us to enhance our share of the do-it-yourself market, we seized the opportunity to make a significant investment in our long-term future. At the same time, we recognized that our short-term profit growth would be affected.

The Home Depot intends to be the dominant factor in every market we serve. The key to our success has been that upon entering a new market, we make a substantial commitment—opening multiple stores, providing excellent customer service, creating highly visible promotions, and growing the entire market. We turn the novice into a do-it-yourselfer and enable the expert to do more for less money.

From shortly before the end of fiscal 1984 to the close of fiscal 1985, The Home Depot entered eight new markets—Dallas, Houston, Jacksonville, San Diego, Los Angeles, Shreveport, Baton Rouge and Mobile—in a period of approximately 13 months. In that time, the number of Home Depot stores rose dramatically, from 22 to 50, including 9 stores acquired in the Bowater acquisition which had not been in our original plan. Twenty of these stores were opened during the past fiscal year alone. During this time span, we have become the only national warehouse retailing chain serving markets across the Sunbelt.

This expansion program required a tremendous investment of capital expenditures and inventory, as well as in personnel. As a result, our net earnings declined from record levels achieved during the previous fiscal year. In fiscal 1985, The Home Depot earned $8,219,000, or $.33 per share, as compared with $14,122,000, or $.56 per share, in fiscal 1984. However, as The Home Depot engaged in this major thrust forward, it also increased its market share and market presence as revenues rose 62% from $432,779,000 in fiscal 1984 to $700,729,000 in fiscal 1985.

Despite our significant investments, we still continue to be in a very strong financial condition. In Decem-

ber, The Home Depot replaced a prior $100 million bank credit line with an eight-year decreasing revolving credit agreement of $200 million. In addition, we are pursuing sale-and-leaseback negotiations for an aggregate of approximately $50 million for ten of our stores. These sources of additional funds, along with internally generated cash flow, will provide us with an ample financial foundation to continue to underwrite our growth over the next several years.

We are also quite proud that The Home Depot achieved its substantial gain in sales and market share in what turned out to be a very difficult year for our industry and retailing in general. The do-it-yourself "warehouse" industry, which we pioneered only a few short years ago, has recently attracted many competitors, some of whom have already fallen by the wayside, having mistaken our dramatic success as a path towards easy profits. Now the industry is faced with a situation when only the strongest and most capable will survive. As this process continues, we expect to encounter additional cost competition in the fight for market dominance. However, with our strengths—both financial and our successful ability to develop a loyal customer base—we are confident that The Home Depot will emerge an even stronger company.

We have never doubted The Home Depot's ability to be a leader in our business. We have the market dominance, the superior retailing concepts and the necessary foundation of experienced management. Further, we have the determination to maintain our position.

Looking at some of our markets individually, clearly our most difficult environment has been in Houston, where the oil-related economy is undergoing painful contractions combined with particularly fierce industry competition. This has caused our newly-opened stores to operate at a sub par level. In Dallas/Fort Worth, the stores we acquired at the end of fiscal 1984 have not yet generated the profits we expect. Such difficult market conditions demand a flexible reaction both in merchandising and operations. Recognizing the future potential of both of these markets, our management team is addressing the issues and feels confident that the final outcome will be positive.

In the other markets entered this year, the situation has been considerably more positive. There, our stores are experiencing growth much closer to our historical patterns.

In support of our California and Arizona operations, a West Coast division was inaugurated to facilitate a timely response to the demands of that marketplace. With management personnel in place, this division is now responsible for the merchandising and operations of all stores in the western states.

Other highlights of the past year's activities include the progress we have made in expanding our management team, and the computer systems we installed into our operations to enhance our efficiency.

During the year, we completed the store price look-up phase of our management information system. This facilitates tracking individual items' sales through our registers, resulting in a more concise method of inventory reorder and margin management with the information now available.

During the coming year we will be testing a perpetual inventory tie-in with our price look-up system, eliminating pricing of our merchandise at the store level. The latter is being tested in several stores presently and hopefully will be expanded to include all of our stores by year end. This will have a significant effect on labor productivity at the store level.

The Home Depot is always looking for ways in which to do things better, priding ourselves on our flexibility and ability to innovate and to react to changing conditions. Whether it is a matter of developing state-of-the-art computer systems, reevaluating our store layouts or adapting to fast-changing markets and new types of merchandising, flexibility has always been a Home Depot characteristic.

In fiscal 1986, The Home Depot will continue to expand, but at a much more moderate pace. We plan to open nine new stores. These stores will be in existing markets except for two locations in the new market of San Jose, California.

When we open stores in existing markets, sharing advertising costs and operational expenses, we achieve a faster return than stores in new markets. With this in mind, in January 1986, we withdrew from the Detroit market and delayed the opening of stores in San Francisco. These stores were targeted for a substantial initial loss in earnings that would have been necessary to achieve market dominance. From our standpoint, these new markets would have had the combined effect of diluting our personnel and negatively affecting our earnings.

It has always been Home Depot's philosophy to maintain orderly growth and achieve market dominance as we expand to new markets. Indeed, growth for growth's sake has never been and never will be our objective. We intend to invest prudently and expand aggressively in our business and our markets only when such expenditures meet our criteria for long-term profitability.

We are quite optimistic about our company's future—both for fiscal 1986 and for the years to follow. Essential to this optimism is the fact that The Home Depot has consistently proven that we can grow the market in every geographical area we enter. Simply, this means that we do not have to take business away from hardware stores and other existing home-improvement outlets, but rather, to create new do-it-yourselfers out of those who have never done their own home improvements.

Our philosophy is to educate our customers on how to be do-it-yourselfers. Our customers have come to expect The Home Depot's knowledgeable sales staff to guide them through any project they care to undertake, whether it be installing kitchen cabinets, constructing a deck, or building an entire house. Our sales staff knows how to complete each project, what tools and material to include, and how to sell our customers everything they need.

The Home Depot traditionally holds clinics for its customers in such skills as electrical wiring, carpentry, and plumbing, to name a few. Upon the successful completion of such clinics, our customers are confident in themselves and in The Home Depot. This confidence allows them to attempt increasingly advanced and complex home improvements.

Concerning our facilities, Home Depot's warehouse retailing concept allows us to carry a truly fantastic

h

selection of merchandise and offer it at the lowest possible prices. Each of our stores ranges from about 65,000 to over 100,000 square feet of selling space, with an additional 4,000 to 10,000 square feet of outdoor selling area. In these large stores, we are able to stock all the materials and tools needed to build a house from scratch, and to landscape its grounds. With each store functioning as its own warehouse, with a capacity of over 25,000 different items, we are able to keep our prices at a minimum while providing the greatest selection of building materials and name brand merchandise.

For the majority of Americans, their home is their most valuable asset. It is an asset that consistently appreciates. It is also an asset in need of ongoing care and maintenance. By becoming do-it-yourselfers, homeowners can significantly enhance the value of their homes. We at The Home Depot have found that by successfully delivering this message, we have created loyal and satisfied customers. And by maintaining leadership in our markets, we have established a sound basis on which to build a future of growth with profitability.

The Home Depot management and staff are dedicated to the proposition that we are—and will remain—America's leading do-it-yourself retailer.

Bernard Marcus
Chairman and
Chief Executive Officer

Arthur M. Blank
President and
Chief Operating Officer

h

CONSOLIDATED STATEMENTS OF EARNINGS F/S

	Fiscal Year Ended		
	February 2, 1986 (52 weeks)	February 3, 1985 (53 weeks)	January 29, 1984 (52 weeks)
Net Sales (note 2)	$700,729,000	$432,779,000	$256,184,000
Cost of Merchandise Sold	519,272,000	318,460,000	186,170,000
Gross Profit	181,457,000	114,319,000	70,014,000
Operating Expenses:			
Selling and store operating expenses	134,354,000	74,447,000	43,514,000
Preopening expenses	7,521,000	1,917,000	2,456,000
General and administrative expenses	20,555,000	12,817,000	7,376,000
Total Operating Expenses	162,430,000	89,181,000	53,346,000
Operating Income	19,027,000	25,138,000	16,668,000
Other Income (Expense):			
Net gain on disposition of property and equipment (note 7)	1,317,000	—	—
Interest income	1,481,000	5,236,000	2,422,000
Interest expense (note 3)	(10,206,000)	(4,122,000)	(104,000)
	(7,408,000)	1,114,000	2,318,000
Earnings Before Income Taxes	11,619,000	26,252,000	18,986,000
Income Taxes (note 4)	3,400,000	12,130,000	8,725,000
Net Earnings	$ 8,219,000	$ 14,122,000	$ 10,261,000
Earnings per Common and Common Equivalent Share (note 5)	$ .33	$ .56	$ .41
Weighted Average Number of Common and Common Equivalent Shares	25,247,000	25,302,000	24,834,000

h
2-13

CONSOLIDATED BALANCE SHEETS

	February 2, 1986	February 3, 1985
ASSETS		
Current Assets:		
Cash, including time deposits of $43,374,000 in 1985	$ 9,671,000	$ 52,062,000
Accounts receivable, net (note 7)	21,505,000	9,365,000
Refundable income taxes	3,659,000	—
Merchandise inventories	152,700,000	84,046,000
Prepaid expenses	2,526,000	1,939,000
Total current assets	190,061,000	147,412,000
Property and Equipment, at Cost (note 3):		
Land	44,396,000	30,044,000
Buildings	38,005,000	3,728,000
Furniture, fixtures, and equipment	34,786,000	18,162,000
Leasehold improvements	23,748,000	11,743,000
Construction in progress	27,694,000	14,039,000
	168,629,000	77,716,000
Less accumulated depreciation and amortization	7,813,000	4,139,000
Net property and equipment	160,816,000	73,577,000
Cost in Excess of the Fair Value of Net Assets Acquired, net of accumulated amortization of $730,000 in 1985 and $93,000 in 1984 (note 2)	24,561,000	25,198,000
Other	4,755,000	3,177,000
	$380,193,000	$249,364,000

(continued)

	February 2, 1986	February 3, 1985
LIABILITIES AND STOCKHOLDERS' EQUITY		
Current Liabilities:		
Accounts payable	$ 53,881,000	$ 32,356,000
Accrued salaries and related expenses	5,397,000	3,819,000
Other accrued expenses	13,950,000	10,214,000
Income taxes payable (note 4)	—	626,000
Current portion of long-term debt (note 3)	10,382,000	287,000
Total current liabilities	83,610,000	47,302,000
Long-Term Debt, Excluding Current Installments (note 3):		
Convertible subordinated debentures	100,250,000	100,250,000
Other long-term debt	99,693,000	17,692,000
	$199,943,000	$117,942,000
Other Liabilities	861,000	1,320,000
Deferred Income Taxes (note 4)	6,687,000	2,586,000
Stockholders' Equity (note 5):		
Common stock, par value $.05. Authorized: 50,000,000 shares; issued and outstanding – 25,150,063 shares at February 2, 1986 and 25,055,188 shares at February 3, 1985	1,258,000	1,253,000
Paid-in capital	48,900,000	48,246,000
Retained earnings	38,934,000	30,715,000
Total stockholders' equity	89,092,000	80,214,000
Commitments and Contingencies (notes 5, 6 and 8)	$380,193,000	$249,364,000

h
2-15

CONSOLIDATED STATEMENTS OF CHANGES IN FINANCIAL POSITION

Fiscal Year Ended:	February 2, 1986	February 3, 1985	January 29, 1984
Sources of Working Capital:			
Net earnings	$8,219,000	$14,122,000	$ 10,261,000
Items which do not use working capital:			
Depreciation and amortization of property and equipment	4,376,000	2,275,000	903,000
Deferred income taxes	3,612,000	1,508,000	713,000
Amortization of cost in excess of the fair value of net assets required	637,000	93,000	—
Net gain on disposition of property and equipment	(1,317,000)	—	—
Other	180,000	77,000	59,000

(continued)

CONSOLIDATED STATEMENTS OF CHANGES IN FINANCIAL POSITION (continued)

Fiscal Year Ended:	February 2, 1986	February 3, 1985	January 29, 1984
Working capital provided by operations	**15,707,000**	18,075,000	11,936,000
Proceeds from disposition of property and equipment	**9,469,000**	861,000	3,000
Proceeds from long-term borrowings	**92,400,000**	120,350,000	4,200,000
Proceeds from sale of common stock, net	**659,000**	814,000	36,663,000
	$118,235,000	$140,100,000	$ 52,802,000
Uses of Working Capital:			
Additions to property and equipment	**$ 99,767,000**	$50,769,000	$ 16,081,000
Current installments and repayments of long-term debt	**10,399,000**	6,792,000	52,000
Acquisition of Bowater Home Center, Inc., net of working capital of $9,227,000 (note 2):			
Property and equipment	**—**	4,815,000	—
Cost in excess of the fair value of net assets acquired	**—**	25,291,000	—
Other assets, net of liabilities	**—**	(913,000)	—
Other, net	**1,728,000**	2,554,000	252,000
Increase in working capital	**6,341,000**	50,792,000	36,417,000
	$118,235,000	$140,100,000	$ 52,802,000
Changes in Components of Working Capital:			
Increase (decrease) in current assets:			
Cash	**(42,391,000)**	$29,894,000	$ 13,917,000
Receivables, net	**15,799,000**	7,170,000	1,567,000
Merchandise inventories	**68,654,000**	25,334,000	41,137,000
Prepaid expenses	**587,000**	1,206,000	227,000
	42,649,000	63,604,000	56,848,000
Increase (decrease) in current liabilities:			
Accounts payable	**21,525,000**	10,505,000	17,150,000
Accrued salaries and related expenses	**1,578,000**	(93,000)	2,524,000
Other accrued expenses	**3,736,000**	2,824,000	341,000
Income taxes payable	**(626,000)**	(657,000)	406,000
Current portion of long-term debt	**10,095,000**	233,000	10,000
	36,308,000	12,812,000	20,431,000
Increase in Working Capital	**$ 6,341,000**	$ 50,792,000	$ 36,417,000

SELECTED FINANCIAL DATA

	Fiscal Year Ended				
	February 2, 1986	February 3, 1985[a]	January 29, 1984	January 30, 1983	January 31, 1982
Selected Consolidated Statement of Earnings Data:					
Net sales	$700,729,000	$432,779,000	$256,184,000	$117,645,000	$51,542,000
Gross profit	181,457,000	114,319,000	70,014,000	33,358,000	14,735,000
Earnings before income taxes and extraordinary item	11,619,000	26,252,000	18,986,000	9,870,000	1,963,000
Earnings before extraordinary item	8,219,000	14,122,000	10,261,000	5,315,000	1,211,000
Extraordinary item-reduction of income taxes arising from carryforward of prior years' operating losses	—	—	—	—	234,000
Net earnings	$ 8,219,000	$ 14,122,000	$10,261,000	$5,315,000	$1,445,000
Per Common and Common Equivalent Share:					
Earnings before extraordinary item	$ .33	$ .56	$ .41	$ .24	$.06
Extraordinary item	—	—	—	—	.01
Net earnings	$ .33	$ .56	$ .41	$ .24	$ .07
Weighted average number of common and common equivalent shares	25,247,000	25,302,000	24,834,000	22,233,000	21,050,000
Selected Consolidated Balance Sheet Data:					
Working capital	$106,451,000	$100,110,000	$ 49,318,000	$ 12,901,000	$ 5,502,000
Total assets	380,193,000	249,364,000	105,230,000	33,014,000	16,906,000
Long-term debt	199,943,000	117,942,000	4,384,000	236,000	3,738,000
Stockholders' equity	89,092,000	80,214,000	65,278,000	18,354,000	5,024,000

a. *53-week fiscal year; all others were 52-week fiscal years.*

h

2-17

MANAGEMENT'S DISCUSSION AND ANALYSIS OF RESULTS OF OPERATIONS AND FINANCIAL CONDITION

The data below reflect the percentage relationship between sales and major categories in the Consolidated Statements of Earnings and selected sales data of the percentage change in the dollar amounts of each of the items.

	Fiscal Year[a]			Percentage Increase (Decrease) of Dollar Amounts	
	1985	1984	1983	**1985 v. 1984**	1984 v. 1983
Selected Consolidated Statements of Earnings Data:					
Net sales	**100.0%**	100.0%	100.0%	**61.9%**	68.9%
Gross profit	**25.9**	26.4	27.3	**58.7**	63.3
Cost and expenses:					
Selling and store operating	**19.2**	17.2	17.0	**80.5**	71.1
Preopening	**1.1**	.4	.9	**292.3**	(21.9)
General and administrative	**2.9**	3.0	2.9	**60.4**	73.8
Net gain on disposition of property and equipment	**(.2)**	—	—	**—**	—
Interest income	**(.2)**	(1.2)	(.9)	**(71.7)**	116.2
Interest expense	**1.4**	.9	—	**147.6**	3,863.5
	24.2	20.3	19.9	**92.9**	72.6
Earnings before income taxes	**1.7**	6.1	7.4	**(55.7)**	38.3
Income taxes	**.5**	2.8	3.4	**(72.0)**	39.0
Net earnings	**1.2%**	3.3%	4.0%	**(41.8%)**	37.6%
Selected Consolidated Sales Data:					
Number of customer transactions	**23,324,000**	14,256,000	8,479.000	**63.6%**	68.1%
Average amount of sale per transaction	**$30.04**	$30.36	$30.21	**(1.1)**	.5
Weighted average weekly sales per operating store	**$342,500**	$365,500	$360,300	**(6.3)**	1.4

a. Fiscal years 1985, 1984 and 1983 refer to the fiscal years ended February 2, 1986, February 3, 1985 and January 29, 1984, respectively. Fiscal 1984 consisted of 53 weeks while 1985 and 1983 each consisted of 52 weeks.

Results of Operations

For an understanding of the significant factors that influenced the Company's performance during the past three fiscal years, the following discussion should be read in conjunction with the consolidated financial statements appearing elsewhere in this annual report.

Fiscal Year Ended February 2, 1986 Compared to February 3, 1985

Net sales in fiscal year 1985 increased 62% from $432,779,000 to $700,729,000. The growth is attributable to several factors. First, the Company opened 20 new stores during 1985 and closed one store. Second, second-year sales increases were realized from the three new stores opened in 1984 and from the nine former Bowater Home Center stores acquired during 1984. Third, comparable store sales increases of 2.3% were achieved despite comparing the 52-week 1985 fiscal year to the sales of the 53-week 1984 fiscal year, due in part to the number of customer transactions increasing by 64%. Finally, the weighted average weekly sales per operating store declined 6% in 1985 due to the significant increase in the ratio of the number of new stores to total stores in operation—new stores have a lower sales rate than mature stores until they establish market share.

Gross profit in 1985 increased 59% from $114,319,000 to $181,457,000. This increase was due to the increased sales and was partially offset by a reduction in the gross profit margin from 26.4% to 25.9%. The reduction is primarily due to lower margins achieved while establishing market presence in new markets.

Cost and expenses increased 93% during 1985 and, as a percent of sales, increased from 20.3% to 24.2%. The increase in selling and store operating, preopening expenses and net interest expense is due to the opening of 20 new stores, the costs associated with the former Bowater Home Center stores, and the related cost of building market share. The large percentage of new stores which have lower sales but fixed occupancy and certain minimum operating expenses tends to cause the percentage of selling and store operating costs to increase as a percentage of sales. The net gain on disposition of property and equipment is discussed fully in note 7 to the financial statements.

Earnings before income taxes decreased 56% from $26,252,000 to $11,619,000 resulting from the increase in operating expenses to support the Company's expansion program. The Company's effective income tax rate declined from 46.2% to 29.3% resulting from an increase in investment and other tax credits as a percentage of the total tax provision. As a percentage of sales, earnings decreased from 3.3% in 1984 to 1.2% in 1985 due to the increase in operating expenses as discussed above.

Fiscal Year Ended February 3, 1985 Compared to January 29, 1984

Net sales in fiscal 1984 increased 69% from $256,184,000 to $432,779,000. The growth was attributable to several factors. First, the company opened three new stores during fiscal 1984. Second, the Company had sales of $9,755,000 from the nine former Bowater Home Center stores acquired on December 3, 1984. Third, second-year sales increases were realized from the nine stores opened during fiscal 1983. Fourth, comparable store sales increases of 14% were due in part to 53 weeks in fiscal 1984 compared to 52 weeks in fiscal 1983 and in part to the number of customer transactions increasing by 63%. Finally, excluding the sales of the former Bowater Home Center stores, the weighted average weekly sales per operating store increased 6% to $383,500 in fiscal 1984.

Gross profit in fiscal 1984 increased 63% from $70,014,000 to $114,319,000. This net increase was due to the increased sales and was partially offset by a reduction in the gross profit margin from 27.3% to 26.4%. The reduction in the gross profit percentage is largely the result of the purchase of a high proportion of promoted merchandise by customers in the second quarter.

Costs and expenses increased 73% during fiscal 1984. As a percent of sales, costs and expenses increased from 19.9% to 20.3% due to increased selling, store operating, general and administrative expenses. This planned increase was in preparation of the Company's future expansion. Interest expense increased significantly as a result of the issuance of substantial debt during fiscal 1984 to fund the Company's expansion. These increases were partially offset by reduced preopening expenses and increased interest income resulting from temporary investment of the proceeds of the debt financing.

Earnings before income taxes increased 38% from $18,986,000 to $26,252,000 resulting from the factors discussed above. Such pretax earnings, however, were reduced by a loss from the Bowater stores of approximately $1,900,000 from date of acquisition (December 1984) to year end. The Company's effective income tax rate increased slightly from 46.0% to 46.2% resulting principally from less investment and other tax credits as a percentage of the total tax provision. As a percentage of sales, earnings decreased from 4.0% in fiscal 1983 to 3.3% in fiscal 1984. The decline is a result of the company's reduced gross profit percentage and increases in the operating expenses discussed above.

Impact of Inflation and Changing Prices

Although the Company cannot accurately determine the precise effect of inflation on its operations, it does not believe inflation has had a material effect on sales or results of operations. The Company has complied with the reporting requirements of the Financial Accounting Standards Board Statement No. 33 in note 10 to the financial statements. Due to the experimental techniques, subjective estimates and assumptions, and the incomplete presentation required by this accounting pronouncement, the Company questions the value of the required reporting.

Liquidity and Capital Resources

Cash flow generated from existing store operations provided the Company with a significant source of liquidity since sales are on a cash-and-carry basis. In addition, a significant portion of the Company's inventory is financed under vendor credit terms. The Company has supplemented its operating cash flow from time to time with bank credit and equity and debt financing. During fiscal 1985, $88,000,000 of working capital was provided by the revolving bank credit line, $4,400,000 from industrial revenue bonds, and approximately $15,707,000 from operations. In addition, during fiscal 1985, the Company entered into a new credit agreement for a $200,000,000 revolving credit facility with a group of banks.

The Company has announced plans to open nine new stores during fiscal 1986, two in the new market of northern California and the balance in existing markets. The cost of this store expansion program will depend upon, among other factors, the extent to which the Company is able to lease second-use store space as opposed to acquiring leases or sites and having stores constructed to its own specifications. The Company estimates that approximately $6,600,000 per store will be required to acquire sites and construct facilities to the Company's specifications and that approximately $1,700,000 will be required to open a store in leased space plus any additional costs of acquiring the lease. These estimates include costs for site acquisition, construction expenditures, fixtures and equipment, and in-store minicomputers and point-of-sale terminals. In addition, each new store will require approximately $1,800,000 to finance inventories, net of vendor financing. The Company believes it has the ability to finance these expenditures through existing cash resources, current bank lines of credit which include a $200,000,000 eight-year revolving credit agreement, funds generated from operations, and other forms of financing, including but not limited to various forms of real estate financing and unsecured borrowings.

NOTES TO CONSOLiDATED FINANCIAL STATEMENTS

1. Summary of Significant Accounting Policies

Fiscal Year

The Company's fiscal year ends on the Sunday closest to the last day of January and usually consists of 52 weeks. Every five or six years, however, there is a 53-week year. The fiscal year ended February 2, 1986 (1985) consisted of 52 weeks, the year ended February 3, 1985 (1984) consisted of 53 weeks and the year ended January 29, 1984 (1983) consisted of 52 weeks.

Principles of Consolidation

The consolidated financial statements include the accounts of the Company and its wholly owned subsidiary. All significant intercompany transactions have been eliminated in consolidation. Certain reclassifications were made to the 1984 balance sheet to conform to current year presentation.

Merchandise Inventories

Inventories are stated at the lower of cost (first-in, first-out) or market, as determined by the retail inventory method.

Depreciation and Amortization

The Company's buildings, furniture, fixtures, and equipment are depreciated using the straight-line method over the estimated useful lives of the assets. Improvements to leased premises are amortized on the straight-line method over the life of the lease or the useful life of the improvement, whichever is shorter.

Investment Tax Credit

Investment tax credits are recorded as a reduction of Federal income taxes in the year the credits are realized.

Store Preopening Costs

Non-capital expenditures associated with opening new stores are charged to expense as incurred.

Earnings Per Common and Common Equivalent Share

Earnings per common and common equivalent share are based on the weighted average number of shares and equivalents outstanding. Common equivalent shares used in the calculation of earnings per share represent shares granted under the Company's employee stock option plan and employee stock purchase plan.

Shares issuable upon conversion of the 8½% convertible subordinated debentures are also common stock equivalents. Shares issuable upon conversion of the 9% convertible subordinated debentures would only be included in the computation of fully diluted earnings per share. However, neither shares issuable upon conversion of the 8½% nor the 9% convertible debentures were dilutive in any year presented, and thus neither were considered in the earnings per share computations.

h

2-21

2. Acquisition

On December 3, 1984 the Company acquired the outstanding capital stock of Bowater Home Center, Inc. (Bowater) for approximately $38,420,000 including costs incurred in connection with the acquisition. Bowater operated nine retail home center stores primarily in the Dallas, Texas metropolitan area. The acquisition was accounted for by the purchase method and, accordingly, results of operations have been included with those of the Company from the date of acquisition. Cost in excess of the fair value of net assets acquired amounted to approximately $25,291,000, which is being amortized over forty years from date of acquisition using the straight-line method.

The following table summarizes, on a pro forma, unaudited basis, the estimated combined results of operations of the Company and Bowater for the years ended February 3, 1985 and January 29, 1984, as though the acquisition were made at the beginning of fiscal year 1983. This pro forma information does not purport to be indicative of the results of operations which would have actually been obtained if the acquisition had been effective on the dates indicated.

	Fiscal Year Ended	
	February 3, 1985	January 29, 1984*
	(Unaudited)	
Net sales	$482,752,000	$274,660,000
Net earnings	9,009,000	6,913,000
Earnings per common and common equivalent share	.36	.28

*Includes the operations and pro forma adjustments from the date of inception of Bowater's operations in August 1983.

3. Long-Term Debt and Lines of Credit

Long-term debt consists of the following:

	February 2, 1986	February 3, 1985
8½% convertible subordinated debentures, due July 1, 2009, convertible into shares of common stock of the Company at a conversion price of $26.50 per share. The debentures are redeemable by the Company at a premium from July 1, 1986 to July 1, 1995, will retire 70% of the issue prior to maturity. Interest is payable semi-annually.	$86,250,000	$86,250,000
9% convertible subordinated debentures, due December 15, 1999, convertible into shares of common stock of the Company at a conversion price of $16.90 per share. The debentures are redeemable by the Company at a premium from December 15, 1986 to December 15, 1994. An annual mandatory sinking fund of $2,000,000 per year is required from 1994 to 1998. Interest is payable semi-annually.	14,000,000	14,000,000
Total convertible subordinated debentures	**100,250,000**	100,250,000

	February 2, 1986	February 3, 1985
Revolving credit agreement. Interest may be fixed for any portion outstanding for up to 180 days, at the Company's option, based on a CD rate plus ¾%, the LIBOR rate plus ½% or at the prime rate.	88,000,000	—
*Variable Rate Industrial Revenue Bond (see note 7)	10,100,000	10,100,000
*Variable Rate Industrial Revenue Bond, secured by a letter of credit, payable in sinking fund installments from December 1, 1991 through December 1, 2010	4,400,000	—
9⅝% Industrial Revenue Bond, secured by a letter of credit, payable on December 1, 1993, with interest payable semi-annually	4,200,000	4,200,000
*Variable Rate Industrial Revenue Bond, secured by land, payable in annual installments of $233,000 with interest payable semi-annually	3,267,000	3,500,000
Other	108,000	179,000
Total long-term debt	210,325,000	118,229,000
Less current portion	10,382,000	287,000
Long-term debt, excluding current portion	$199,943,000	$117,942,000

*The interest rates on the variable rate industrial revenue bonds are related to various short-term municipal money market composite rates.

h

Maturities of long-term debt are approximately $10,382,000 for fiscal 1986 and $234,000 for each of the next four subsequent years.

During the fiscal year ended February 2, 1986, the Company entered into a new unsecured revolving line of credit for a maximum of $200,000,000, subject to certain limitations, of which $88,000,000 is outstanding at year-end. Commitment amounts under the agreement decrease by $15,000,000 on July 31, 1990, by $20,000,000 each six months from that date through January 31, 1993, by $35,000,000 on July 31, 1993, and with the remaining $50,000,000 commitment expiring on January 31, 1994. Maximum borrowings outstanding within the commitment limits may not exceed specified percentages of inventories, land and buildings, and fixtures and equipment, all as defined in the Agreement. Under certain conditions, the commitments may be extended and/or increased. An annual commitment fee of ¼% to ⅜% is required to be paid on the unused portion of the revolving line of credit. Interest rates specified may be increased by a maximum of ⅜ of 1% based on specified ratios of interest rate coverage and debt to equity.

Under the revolving credit agreement, the Company is required, among other things, to maintain during fiscal year 1985 a minimum tangible net worth (defined to include the convertible subordinated debentures) of $150,000,000 (increasing annually to $213,165,000 by January 3, 1989), a debt to tangible net worth ratio of no more than 2 to 1, a current ratio of not less than 1.5 to 1, and a ratio of earnings before interest expense and income taxes to interest expense, net, of not less than 2 to 1. The Company was in compliance with all restrictive covenants as of February 2, 1986. The restrictive covenants related to the letter of credit agreements securing the industrial revenue bonds and the convertible subordinated debentures are no more restrictive than those under the revolving line of credit agreement.

Interest expense in the accompanying consolidated statements of earnings is net of interest capitalized of $3,429,000 in fiscal 1985 and $1,462,000 in fiscal 1984.

4. Income Taxes

The provision for income taxes consists of the following:

| | Fiscal Year Ended | | |
	February 1, 1986	February 3, 1985	January 29, 1984
Current:			
Federal	$(578,000)	$9,083,000	$6,916,000
State	366,000	1,539,000	1,096,000
	(212,000)	10,622,000	8,012,000
Deferred:			
Federal	3,306,000	1,464,000	713,000
State	306,000	44,000	—
	3,612,000	1,508,000	713,000
Total	$3,400,000	$12,130,000	$8,725,000

The effective tax rates for fiscal 1985, 1984, and 1983 were 29.3%, 46.2%, and 46.0%, respectively. A reconciliation of income tax expense at Federal statutory rates to actual tax expense for the applicable fiscal years follows:

| | Fiscal Year Ended | | |
	February 2, 1986	February 3, 1985	January 29, 1984
Income taxes at Federal statutory rate, net of surtax exemption	$5,345,000	$12,076,000	$8,734,000
State income taxes, net of Federal income tax benefit	363,000	855,000	592,000
Investment and targeted jobs tax credits	(2,308,000)	(800,000)	(747,000)
Other, net	—	(1,000)	146,000
	$3,400,000	$12,130,000	$8,725,000

Deferred income taxes arise from differences in the timing of reporting income for financial statement and income tax purposes. The sources of these differences and the tax effect of each are as follows:

	Fiscal Year Ended		
	February 2, 1986	February 3, 1985	January 29, 1984
Accelerated depreciation	$2,526,000	$1,159,000	$713,000
Interest capitalization	855,000	349,000	—
Other, net	231,000	—	—
	$3,612,000	$1,508,000	$713,000

5. Leases

The Company leases certain retail locations, office, and warehouse and distribution space, equipment, and vehicles under operating leases. All leases will expire within the next 25 years; however, it can be expected that in the normal course of business, leases will be renewed or replaced. Total rent expense, net of minor sublease income for the fiscal years ended February 2, 1986, February 3, 1985 and January 29, 1984 amounted to approximately $12,737,000, $6,718,000 and $4,233,000, respectively. Under the building leases, real estate taxes, insurance, maintenance, and operating expenses applicable to the leased property are obligations of the Company. Certain of the store leases provide for contingent rentals based on percentages of sales in excess of specified minimums. Contingent rentals for fiscal years ended February 2, 1986, February 3, 1985 and January 29, 1984 were approximately $650,000, $545,000 and $111,000.

The approximate future minimum lease payments under operating leases at February 2, 1986 are as follows:

Fiscal Year	
1986	$ 16,093,000
1987	16,668,000
1988	16,345,000
1989	16,086,000
1990	16,129,000
Thereafter	171,455,000
	$252,776,000

7. Disposition of Property and Equipment

During the fourth quarter of fiscal year 1985, the Company disposed of certain properties and equipment at a net gain of $1,317,000. The properties represented real estate located in Detroit, Houston and Tucson, and the equipment represented the trade-in of cash registers of current generation point of sale equipment. Under the terms of the Detroit real estate sale, the purchaser will either assume the bond obligations of the Company of $10,100,000 after February 2, 1986 or pay the Company the funds disbursed under the bonds in order for the Company to prepay the total amount outstanding. Included in accounts receivable at February 2, 1986 is $13,800,000 related to these transactions.

8. Commitments and Contingencies

At February 2, 1986, the Company was contingently liable for approximately $5,300,000 under outstanding letters of credit issued in connection with purchase commitments.

The Company has litigation arising from the normal course of business. In management's opinion, this litigation will not materially affect the Company's financial condition.

h

2-26

9. Quarterly Financial Data (Unaudited)

The following is a summary of the unaudited quarterly results of operations for fiscal years ended February 2, 1986 and February 3, 1985:

	Net Sales	Gross Profit	Net Earnings	Net Earnings per Common and Common Equivalent Share
Fiscal year ended February 2, 1986:				
First Quarter	$145,048,000	$ 36,380,000	$ 1,945,000	$ .08
Second Quarter	174,239,000	45,572,000	2,499,000	.10
Third Quarter	177,718,000	46,764,000	1,188,000	.05
Fourth Quarter	203,724,000	52,741,000	2,587,000	.10
	$700,729,000	$181,457,000	$ 8,219,000	$ .33
Fiscal year ended February 3, 1985:				
First Quarter	$ 95,872,000	$ 25,026,000	$ 3,437,000	$ .14
Second Quarter	119,068,000	29,185,000	3,808,000	.15
Third Quarter	100,459,000	27,658,000	3,280,000	.13
Fourth Quarter	117,380,000	32,450,000	3,597,000	.14
	$432,779,000	$114,319,000	$14,122,000	$ .56

AUDITORS' REPORT

The Board of Directors and Stockholders,
The Home Depot, Inc.:

We have examined the consolidated balance sheets of The Home Depot, Inc. and subsidiary as of February 2, 1986 and February 3, 1985 and the related consolidated statements of earnings, stockholders' equity, and changes in financial position for each of the years in the three-year period ended February 2, 1986. Our examinations were made in accordance with generally accepted auditing standards, and, accordingly, included such tests of the accounting records and such other auditing procedures as we considered necessary in the circumstances.

In our opinion, the aforementioned consolidated financial statements present fairly the financial position of The Home Depot, Inc. and subsidiary at February 2, 1986 and February 3, 1985, and the results of their operations and the changes in their financial position for each of the years in the three-year period ended February 2, 1986, in conformity with generally accepted accounting principles applied on a consistent basis.

PEAT, MARWICK, MITCHELL & CO.
Atlanta, Georgia
March 24, 1986

h

k

On April 17, 1985, Bill Ahern sat in his office and contemplated a difficult judgment he had to make in the next two days. Two weeks before, Bill had been asked to be an arbitrator in a dispute between the Owner-Player Committee (OPC, the representatives of the owners of the 26 major league baseball teams in collective bargaining negotiations) and the Professional Baseball Players Association (PBPA, the players' union).

The issue Ahern had to resolve was the profitability of the major league baseball teams. The players felt they should share in the teams' profits; the owners maintained, however, that most of the teams were actually losing money each year, and they produced financial statements to support that position. The players, who had examined the owners' statements, countered that the owners were hiding profits through a number of accounting tricks and that the statements did not accurately reflect the economic reality. Ahern's decision on the profitability issue was important because it would affect the ongoing contract negotiations, particularly in the areas of minimum salaries and team contributions to the players' pension fund.

On April 9, Ahern met with the OPC and the representatives of the PBPA. They explained they wanted him to focus on the finances of the Kansas City Zephyrs Baseball Club, Inc. This club was selected for review because both sides agreed its operations were representative, yet it was a relatively clean and simple example to study: the baseball club entity was not owned by another corporation, and it did not own the stadium the team played in. Furthermore, no private financial data would have to be revealed because the corporation was publicly owned. Ahern's task was to review the Zephyrs' financial statements, hear the owners' and players' arguments, and then reach a decision as to the profitability of the team by Friday, April 19.

MAJOR LEAGUE BASEBALL

Major league baseball in the United States was comprised of a number of components bound together by sets of agreements and contractual relationships. At the heart of major

Research Assistant Joseph P. Mulloy prepared this case under the supervision of Professors Kenneth A. Merchant and Krishna G. Palepu as the basis for class discussion rather than to illustrate either effective or ineffective handling of an administrative situation. The case is based on publicly available information. Copyright © 1987 by the President and Fellows of Harvard College. Harvard Business School case 9-187-088.

league baseball were the 26 major league teams. Each team operated as an independent economic unit in such matters as contracting for players, promoting games and selling tickets, arranging for the use of a stadium and other needed facilities and services, and negotiating local broadcasting of games. The teams joined together to establish common rules and playing schedules, and to stage championship games.

The business of most teams was limited exclusively to their major league activities. Very few integrated vertically by owning their own stadium or minor league teams. Most teams were organized as partnerships or privately held corporations, although a few were subunits of larger corporations. While baseball was often thought of as a big business, the individual teams were relatively small. For most of them, annual revenues were between $20 million and $30 million.

Each team maintained an active roster of 24 players during the playing season, plus 16 minor league players "on option," who might see major league action during the season. This made a total of 40 players on major league contracts for each team at any one time. Each team played a schedule of 162 games during the season, 81 at home and 81 away.

Collectively, the team owners established most of the regulations that governed the industry. The covenant that bound them was the Major League Agreement (MLA), to which was attached the Major League Rules. The rules detailed all the procedures the clubs agreed on, including the rules for signing, trading, and dealing with players.

Under the MLA, the owners elected a commissioner of baseball for a seven-year term. The commissioner acted as a spokesperson for the industry, resolved disputes among the clubs and the other baseball entities, policed the industry, and enforced the rules. The commissioner had broad powers to protect the best interests of the game. The commissioner also administered the Major Leagues Central Fund, under which he negotiated and received the revenues from national broadcast contracts for major league games. About one-half of the fund's revenues were passed on directly to the teams in approximately equal shares.

Within the overall structure of major league baseball, the 26 teams were organized into two leagues each with its own president and administration. The American League had 14 teams and the National League had 12 teams, of which one was the Kansas City Zephyrs. Each league controlled the allocation and movement of its respective franchises. In addition to authorizing franchises, the leagues developed the schedule of games, contracted for umpires, and performed other administrative tasks. The leagues were financed through a small percentage share of club ticket revenues and receipts from the World Series and pennant championship games.

In addition to the major league teams, U.S. baseball included about 150 minor league teams located throughout the United States, Canada, and Mexico. Minor league teams served a dual function: they were entertainment entities in their own right, and they were training grounds for major league players. Through Player Development Contracts, the major league teams agreed to pay a certain portion of their affiliated minor league teams' operating expenses and player salaries.

MEETING WITH THE ZEPHYRS' OWNERS

Bill Ahern spent Tuesday reviewing the history of major league baseball and the relationships among the various entities that make up the major leagues. Then he met with the Zephyrs owners' representatives on Wednesday.

The owners' representatives gave Ahern a short history of the team and presented him with the team's financial statements for the years 1983 and 1984 (shown in Exhibits 1 and 2). The current owner was a corporation with five major shareholders, which bought the team on November 1, 1982, for $24 million. The Zephyrs did not own any of their minor league teams or their stadium, but two of the Zephyrs' owners were part owners of the private corporation that owned the baseball stadium.

Ahern studied the financial statements for a short time, and then he met with Keith Strong, the owners' lawyer. The conversation can be summarized by the following exchange:

Bill: I would like to know more about the controversial items in your financial statements. First, could you please explain your players' salaries expense entries?

Keith: Sure. Here is a list of our roster players and what we paid them last year [see Exhibit 3]. The number we show on our 1984 income statement is the total expense of $10,097,000. Most of the expense represents cash outflows in 1984. The only exception is shown in the last column of this exhibit. For our highest paid players, we have agreed to defer a portion of their salary for 10 years. That helps save them taxes and provides them with some income after their playing days are over.

Bill: What is the nonroster guaranteed contract expense?

Keith: That is also player salary expense, but we break it out separately because the salaries are paid to players who are no longer on our active roster. The salaries are amounts we owe to players whom we released who had long-term guaranteed contracts. The amount of $750,000 represents the amount we still owe at the end of 1984 to two players [shown in Figure A on the next page]. Joe Portocararo, one of our veteran pitchers, signed a four-year guaranteed contract last year, but before the season started he suffered a serious injury, and Joe and the team jointly decided it was best he retire. We released U. R. Wilson in spring training, hoping that another team would pick him up and pay his salary, but none did.

We still owe these players the amounts in their contracts. We decided to expense the whole amount in 1984 because they are not active players; they are not serving to bring in our current revenues. We felt it was more meaningful and conservative to recognize these losses now, as they result from the effects of past decisions that did not turn out well.

Bill: Okay. Let's move on to roster depreciation expense.

Keith: When the team was bought in 1982, $12 million—50 percent of the purchase price—was designated as the value of the player roster at that time. This amount was capitalized and is being amortized over six years.

k

1-3

Figure A Calculation of Nonroster Guaranteed Contract Expense ($000)

| Player | Amounts Owed | | | |
	1984	1985	1986	Total
Joe Portocararo	$300.0	$350.0	$400.0	$1,050.0
U. R. Wilson	200.0			200.0
				$1,250.0

Bill: Why 50 percent?

Keith: That is the maximum percentage that the Internal Revenue Code will allow when purchasing a sports team.

Bill: I see. Is there anything else in the statements that the players dispute?

Keith: No, I don't think so. The rest of our accounting is very straightforward. Most of our revenues and expenses result directly from a cash inflow or outflow.

Bill: Well, that answers all my questions. Thank you.

Keith: I have just one more thing to say concerning baseball finances in general. People seem to think that we generate huge profits since we have a relative monopoly, but it should be obvious that the professional baseball leagues do not exist in order to carry out traditional cartel functions. The rules and regulations governing the clubs comprising the league are essential to the creation of the league as an entity and have virtually nothing to do with pricing policies of the individual clubs. The objective of the cooperative agreements is not to constrain the economic competition among them, but rather to create the league as a joint venture that produces baseball during a season of play. Without such rules of conduct, leagues would not exist.

When this meeting was completed, Bill Ahern felt he understood the owners' accounting methods well enough.

MEETING WITH THE PLAYERS

The following Monday, Ahern met with the PBPA representatives and their lawyer, Paul Hanrahan. They presented Ahern with income statements for the years 1983 and 1984 as they thought they should be drawn up (Exhibit 4). As Ahern studied them, he found the players' version of the financial statements showed profits before tax of $2.9 million for 1983 and $3.0 million for 1984 as compared to the losses of $2.4 million and $2.6 million on the owners' statements.

Ahern's conversation with Paul Hanrahan went approximately as follows:

Bill: The income statements you have given me are very similar to those of the owners except for a few items.

Paul: That's true—most of the expenses are straightforward. There are only a few areas we dispute, but these areas can have a significant impact on the overall profitability of the team. We feel that the owners have used three techniques to "hide" profits: (1) roster depreciation, (2) overstated player salary expense, and (3) related-party transactions.

Bill: Let's start with roster depreciation. Why have you deleted it?

Paul: We feel it gives numbers that aren't meaningful. The depreciation expense arises only when a team is sold, so you can have two identical teams that will show dramatically different results if one had been sold and the other had not. We also don't think the depreciation is real because most of the players actually improve their skills with experience, so if anything, there should be an increase in roster value over time, not a reduction as the depreciation would lead you to believe.

Bill: Okay. I understand your reasoning. I'll have to think about that. Let's move on to the next issue.

Paul: That's player salary expense. We think the owners overstate player expense in several ways. One is that they expense the signing bonuses in the year they're paid. We feel the bonuses are just a part of the compensation package, and that for accounting purposes, the bonuses should be spread over the term of the player's contract.

We gathered information on the bonuses paid in the last four years and the contract terms [Exhibit 5]. Then we adjusted the owners' income statements by removing the bonuses from the current roster salary expense and by adding an "amortization of bonuses" line. The net effect of this one adjustment on 1984, for example, was an increase in income of $373,000.[1]

Bill: But the owners have really paid out all the bonuses in cash, and there is no guarantee that the players will complete their contracts.

Paul: That's partly true. Some players get hurt and are unable to compete effectively. But the number of players who do not complete their contracts is very small, and we think it is more meaningful to assume that they will continue to play over the term of their contract.

Bill: Okay. What's next?

Paul: A second adjustment we made to the players' salary line was to back out the deferred portion of the total compensation. Many of the players, particularly those who are higher paid, receive only about 80 percent of their salaries in any given year. They receive the rest ten years later [see Exhibit 3]. We feel that since the team is paying this money over a long period of time, it is misleading to include the whole amount as a current expense. This adjustment increased 1984 income for the Zephyrs by $1,521,000. No salary expense deferred from prior years was added back in because that form of contract is a relatively recent phenomenon.

1. *$1,320,000 less $947,000.*

Bill: I've looked at some of the contracts, and it says very clearly that the player is to receive, say, $500,000, of which $100,000 is deferred to the year 1984. Doesn't that indicate that the salary expense is $500,000?

Paul: No. The team has paid only $400,000 in cash.

Bill: Doesn't the team actually set money aside to cover the future obligation?

Paul: Some teams do, and in such cases, I think we would agree that it is appropriate to recognize that amount as a current expense. But the Zephyrs don't set any money aside.

Bill: Okay. You made a third adjustment to the players' salaries.

Paul: Yes, we think the salaries due to players who are no longer on the roster should be recognized when the cash is paid out, not when the players leave the roster. Unless that is done, the income numbers will vary wildly depending on when these players are released and how large their contracts are. Furthermore, it is quite possible that these players' contracts will be picked up by another team, and the Zephyrs would then have to turn around and recognize a large gain because the liability it has set up would no longer be payable.

Bill: Okay. Let's go to the last area: related-party transactions. You have listed Stadium Operations at about 80 percent of what the owners charged. Why is that?

Paul: You probably know that two of the Zephyrs' owners are also involved with the stadium corporation. But what you probably don't know is that they are the sole owners of that stadium company. We think that the stadium rent is set to overcharge the team and help show a loss for the baseball operations.

Bill: How did you get your numbers?

Paul: This wasn't easy, but we looked at what other teams pay for their stadiums. Every contract is slightly different, but we are sure that two of the five shareholders in the team are earning a nice gain on the stadium-pricing agreement.

Just for your own edification, this is not the only type of related-party transaction where the owners can move profits around. A few of the teams are owned by broadcasting organizations, and as a result, they report no local broadcasting revenues. Their individual losses are consolidated into the overall major league position, thus the overall loss is overstated. I know it's hard to do, but an objective look must be taken at all these related-party transactions if baseball's true position is to be fairly stated.

The overall effect of all these adjustments we have made to the Zephyrs' income statements changes losses to profits. In 1984, the change is from a loss of $1.7 million to a profit of $1.4 million. In the labor negotiations, the owners keep claiming that they're losing money and can't afford the contract terms we feel are fair. We just don't think that's true. They are "losing money" only because they have selected accounting methods to hide their profits.

Bill: Well, you've given me a lot to think about. There are a lot of good arguments on both sides. Thank you for your time. I'll have my answer for you soon.

BILL'S DECISION

By Wednesday, April 17, Bill was quite confused. To clarify the areas of disagreement, he prepared the summaries shown in Exhibit 6; but whereas the sets of numbers were clear, the answers to the conflicts were not. Bill had expected this arbitration to be rather straightforward, but instead he was mired in difficult issues involving the accounting unit, depreciation, amortization of intangibles, and related-party transactions. Now he was faced with a tight deadline, and it was not at all obvious to him how to define "good accounting methods" for the Zephyrs Baseball Club.

k

EXHIBIT 1
Kansas City Zephyrs Baseball Club, Inc.—Income Statements, Owners' Figures (000s omitted)

	Year Ending October 31	
	1983	1984
Operating Revenues:		
Game Receipts	$16,526.0	$18,620.0
National Television	2,360.8	2,730.8
Local Broadcasting	3,147.9	3,575.1
Concessions	2,886.3	3,294.3
Parking	525.1	562.0
Other	786.9	843.9
Total Revenues	$26,233.0	$29,626.1
Operating Expenses:		
Spring Training	$ 545.0	$ 594.0
Team Operating Expenses:		
Players' Salaries:		
Current Roster	9,111.0	10,097.0
Nonroster Guaranteed Contract Expense	0.0	1,250.0
Coaches' Salaries	756.9	825.7
Other Salaries	239.0	260.8
Miscellaneous	2,655.9	2,897.3
Player Development	2,996.0	3,269.0
Team Replacement:		
Roster Depreciation	2,000.0	2,000.0
Scouting	672.8	734.0
Stadium Operations	4,086.0	4,457.0
Ticketing and Marketing	1,907.0	2,080.0
General and Administrative	3,541.0	3,663.0
Total Operating Expense	$28,510.6	$32,127.8
Income from Operations	(2,277.6)	(2,501.7)
Other Income (Expense)	(96.0)	(101.0)
Income Before Taxes	(2,373.6)	(2,602.7)
Federal Income Tax Benefit	855.9	944.2
Net Income (Loss)	$(1,517.7)	$(1,658.5)

EXHIBIT 2
Kansas City Zephyrs Baseball Club, Inc.—Balance Sheets, Owners' Figures (000s omitted)

	Year Ending October 31	
	1983	1984
ASSETS		
Current Assets:		
Cash	$ 488.0	$ 561.0
Marketable Securities	6,738.0	7,786.1
Accounts Receivable	598.0	681.2
Notes Receivable	256.0	234.0
Total Current Assets	8,080.0	9,262.3
Property, Plant & Equipment	1,601.0	1,892.0
Less Accumulated Depreciation	(359.0)	(511.0)
Net PP&E	1,242.0	1,381.0
Initial Roster	12,000.0	12,000.0
Less Accumulated Depreciation	(4,000.0)	(6,000.0)
Net Initial Roster	8,000.0	6,000.0
Other Assets	2,143.0	4,123.2
Franchise	6,500.0	6,500.0
Total Assets	$25,965.0	$27,266.5
LIABILITIES AND SHAREHOLDERS' EQUITY		
Current Liabilities:		
Accounts Payable	$ 909.2	$ 1,020.2
Accrued Expenses	1,207.5	1,461.8
Total Current Liabilities	2,116.7	2,482.0
Long-Term Debt	7,000.0	8,073.7
Other Long-Term Liabilities	2,443.3	3,964.3
Shareholders' Equity:		
Common Stock, par value $1 per share, 500,000 shares issued	500.0	500.0
Additional Paid-In Capital	10,000.0	10,000.0
Retained Earnings	3,905.0	2,246.5
Total Liabilities and Shareholders' Equity	$25,965.0	$27,266.5

Exhibit 3   Detailed Players' Salary Summary—1984

EXHIBIT 3
Detailed Players' Salary Summary—1984 (000s omitted)

Roster Player	Signing Bonus	Base Salary	Performance and Attendance Bonuses	Total Compensation	Portion of 1984 Salary Deferred Until 1994
Bill Hogan	$ 500.0	$ 850.0	$ 250.0	$ 1,600.0	$ 250.0
Corby Megorden	300.0	600.0	225.0	1,125.0	200.0
Manuel Vasquez	200.0	500.0	100.0	800.0	150.0
Jim Showalter		600.0	100.0	700.0	200.0
Scott Van Buskirk	150.0	400.0	100.0	650.0	150.0
Jerry Hyde	150.0	400.0	50.0	600.0	150.0
Dave Schafer		355.0	50.0	405.0	130.0
Leslie Yamshita		300.0	37.5	337.5	100.0
Earl McLain		220.0	37.5	257.5	50.0
Shannon Saunders		210.0	37.5	247.5	50.0
Gary Blazin		190.0	37.5	227.5	40.0
Rich Hayes		160.0	25.0	185.0	30.0
Sam Willett		140.0	17.5	157.5	21.0
Chuck Wright	20.0	115.0	12.5	147.5	
Jim Urquart		115.0	12.5	127.5	
Bill Schutt		115.0	12.5	127.5	
Mike Hegarty		115.0	12.5	127.5	
Bruce Selby		110.0	12.5	122.5	
Dave Kolk		110.0	12.5	122.5	
Bill Kelly		110.0	12.5	122.5	
Dave Carr		110.0	12.0	122.0	
Tom O'Conner		110.0	5.0	115.0	
Jake Luhan		110.0		110.0	
Ray Woolrich		100.0		100.0	
John Porter		100.0		100.0	
Dusty Rhodes		100.0		100.0	
Lynn Novinger		100.0		100.0	
Bill Williams		95.0		95.0	
Jim Sedor		95.0		95.0	
Ralph Young		95.0		95.0	
Ed Marino		95.0		95.0	
Ray Spicer		90.0		90.0	
Eric Womble		90.0		90.0	
Ron Gorena		90.0		90.0	
Gene Johnston		90.0		90.0	
Jack Zollinger		90.0		90.0	
Ken Karr		90.0		90.0	
Tom Crowley		80.0		80.0	
Joe Matt		80.0		80.0	
Bill Brunelle		80.0		80.0	
Roster Player Salary	$1,320.0	$7,605.0	$1,172.0	$10,097.0	$1,521.0

EXHIBIT 4

Kansas City Zephyrs Baseball Club, Inc.—Income Statements, Players' Figures (000s omitted)

	Year Ending October 31	
	1983	1984
Operating Revenues:		
Game Receipts	$16,526.0	$18,620.0
National Television	2,360.8	2,830.8
Local Broadcasting	3,147.9	3,475.1
Concessions	2,886.3	3,294.3
Parking	525.1	562.0
Other	786.9	843.9
Total Revenues	$26,233.0	$29,626.1
Operating Expenses:		
Spring Training	$545.0	$594.0
Team Operating Expenses:		
Players' Salaries:		
Current Roster	5,897.4	7,256.5
Nonroster Guaranteed Contract Expense	0.0	500.0
Amortization of Bonuses	716.0	947.0
Coaches' Salaries	756.9	825.7
Other Salaries	239.0	260.8
Miscellaneous	2,655.9	2,897.3
Player Development	2,996.0	3,269.0
Team Replacement: Scouting	672.8	734.0
Stadium Operations	3,300.0	3,500.0
Ticketing and Marketing	1,907.0	2,080.0
General and Administrative	3,541.0	3,663.0
Total Operating Expenses	$23,227.0	$26,527.3
Income from Operations	3,006.0	3,098.8
Other Income (Expense)	(96.0)	(101.0)
Income Before Taxes	2,910.0	2,997.8
Provision for Federal Income Taxes[a]	1,338.6	1,379.0
City and State Taxes	236.0	253.0
Net Income	$ 1,335.4	$ 1,365.8

a. Tax rate assumed to be 46%.

Exhibit 5 Summary of Signing Bonuses

EXHIBIT 5
Summary of Signing Bonuses ($000)

Contract Length (Years)	Bonuses for Contracts Starting in			
	1981	1982	1983	1984
4	$240	$550	$350	$800
3	210	200	250	200
2	360	250	170	320

EXHIBIT 6

Summary of Items of Disagreement Between Owners and Players ($000)

Items of Dispute	1983			1984		
	Owners	Players	Difference	Owners	Players	Difference
Roster depreciation	2,000.0	0.0	2,000.0	2,000.0	0.0	2,000.0
Current roster salary	$9,111.0	$5,897.4	$3,213.6	$10,097.0	$7,256.5	$2,840.5
Amortization of signing bonuses	0.0	716.0	(716.0)	0.0	947.0	(947.0)
Nonroster guaranteed contract expense	0.0	0.0	—	1,250.0	500.0	750.0
Stadium operations	4,086.0	3,300.0	786.0	4,457.0	3,500.0	957.0
Total effect on net income			$5,283.6			$5,600.5

Effect on Net Income (before tax)	1983	1984
Income before tax per Owners' Financial Statements (Exhibit 1)	($2,373.6)	($2,602.7)
Total items of disagreement	5,283.6	5,600.5
Income before tax per Players' Financial Statements (Exhibit 4)	$2,910.0	$2,997.8

Exhibit 6   Summary of Items of Disagreement Between Owners and Players

I n March 1985, Dianne Simmons, director of research for the Common- wealth Investment Group, called David McIntosh, a newly joined analyst, into her office and presented a request:

> *David, I just received the 1984 annual report and proxy statement of The Murray Ohio Manufacturing Company. A few years ago we bought Murray's stock for our equity income fund. As you know, that fund is marketed to dividend-oriented in- vestors. It's been a good investment so far, thanks to Murray's excellent dividend payment record. I think, though, that it's time for us to take a fresh look at Murray's recent performance and future prospects.*
>
> *I want you to analyze the company's 1984 annual report [Exhibit 3] and make a recommendation. You may find the information on the company's board report- ed in the proxy statement useful [Exhibit 1]. I've also collected some information for you on Murray's stock price in recent months [Exhibit 2]. And here's some background information on the company's business.*

BUSINESS

Murray Ohio Company was based in Brentwood, a suburb of Nashville, Tennessee. The company's stock was listed on the New York Stock Exchange.

Murray Ohio manufactured and sold power mowers and bicycles. During the 1982– 1984 period the shares of these two product lines in the company's sales and operating profits were as follows:

	Sales			Profits		
	1982	1983	1984	1982	1983	1984
Power Mowers	54%	53%	62%	73%	68%	88%
Bicycles	46%	47%	38%	27%	32%	12%

Source: Murray Ohio's 1984 annual report

Murray produced all its products in a 57-acre manufacturing facility located in Lawrenceburg, Tennessee.

Professor Krishna Palepu prepared this case as the basis for class discussion rather than to illustrate either effective or ineffective handling of an administrative situation. Copyright © 1987 by the President and Fellows of Harvard College. Harvard Business School case 9-187-178.

Bicycles

Murray began as a bicycle manufacturer in 1936. The company produced a complete line of bicycles ranging from sidewalk bicycles for small children to lightweight racing bicycles. The bicycles were sold under both the Murray brand name and the private labels of major retailers. Substantially all of the company's bicycles were distributed through department stores, discount stores, toy stores, and other mass merchandise outlets.

In 1984 Murray manufactured approximately one-third of the bicycles made in the United States. The company competed with several domestic bicycle manufacturers including Huffy, Roadmaster, Columbia, and Ross.

INDUSTRY TRENDS.   The demand for bicycles was largely dependent on discretionary income. Thus, higher income consumers comprised a major portion of the market. The maturation of the baby boom generation into their peak earning years and the growing incidence of two-income households as a result of more women in the work force had increased this pool of "upscale"consumers in recent years. Another factor that positively affected the demand was migration of the population to the West and the South, where the weather and access to recreational areas are favorable for outdoor activities.

The bicycle industry grew at a compound annual growth rate of 7.8 percent during the ten-year period 1972–1982 and 0.6 percent during the five years 1977–1982. Domestic shipments of bicycles and parts rebounded strongly in 1983 from one of the industry's worst years in more than a decade. Constant dollar shipments increased an estimated 15 percent in 1983, then slowed to a 4 percent increase in 1984. Much of the slowdown in 1984 domestic shipments was attributable to competition from low-priced imports from the Far East. Even though demand remained strong in 1984, a 50 percent rise of imports in 1984 adversely affected the domestic producers of bicycles.

The following table summarizes the total shipment data for the bicycle industry:

	Bicycle and Parts Shipments				
(in millions of dollars)	1980	1981	1982	1983	1984
Domestic	649	733	565	644	683
Imports	281	327	208	329	494

Source: U.S. Department of Commerce, Bureau of the Census

The long-term demand for bicycles was expected to remain strong. Domestic producers' share of the market would depend on their ability to be cost competitive with foreign producers, particularly those in Taiwan. Import growth would also be influenced by the value of the dollar. In addition, pressure on Taiwanese exporters in the form of proposed tariff legislation and other trade remedies could result in voluntary cutbacks by the exporters. Based on these factors, domestic bicycle shipments were expected to grow at a rate of 3 percent in 1985 and 3.5 percent annually for the five years thereafter.

Power Mowers

Murray entered the power mower market in 1968 and by 1984 had become one of the largest U.S. manufacturers of power mowers. The company had a full line of walk-behind and riding mowers. Some of these models also accepted attachments such as snow blowers, plows, and tillers. Murray also offered a line of tillers to complement its power mower products.

Through 1984 Murray's power mowers were marketed through major national and regional chains, primarily under the Murray label. In early 1985 the company formed a new marketing subsidiary, Sabre Corporation, to sell mowers to outdoor power equipment dealers. These dealers participated in a large share of the higher priced mower market in which Murray was not previously represented.

INDUSTRY TRENDS.   According to the 1982 Census of Manufacturers, 152 firms produced lawn and garden equipment in the United States. However, many of these producers were small and had fewer than 20 employees. In addition to Murray, the major domestic manufacturers included Western International, Roper, MTD, and Aircap. Lawn mower producers tended to specialize in one of two distribution markets: the high-volume, low-to-medium price mass merchandisers, which accounted for about two-thirds of industry sales, or the higher priced independent retailers, who serviced equipment in addition to selling it. Sales through national department stores had been declining since 1978 as specialty retailers and hardware stores were handling a greater share of the market.

Demand for lawn and garden equipment, like demand for other household durables, was closely related to the level of real disposable income and to the health of the housing market. Between 1972 and 1979, constant dollar shipments of lawn and garden equipment increased at a compound annual rate of 5.5 percent. Record high interest rates from 1979 through 1982 severely depressed the housing market, and constant dollar shipments of lawn and garden equipment declined 31 percent to their lowest level since 1972. The recovery began in 1983 as real disposable income and housing starts rebounded. The expansion continued in 1984 with an estimated 12 percent increase in lawn and garden equipment shipments.

The balance of trade in lawn and garden equipment was historically very favorable for U.S. producers. In recent years, however, imports began to make inroads into the U.S. market. In 1984, estimated U.S. imports of lawn and garden equipment increased 178 percent, continuing a trend begun in 1979 when a Japanese producer, Honda, entered the market for lawn mowers.

The following table summarizes recent trends in the lawn and garden equipment industry:

(in millions of dollars)	Lawn and Garden Equipment Shipments				
	1980	1981	1982	1983	1984
Domestic	2419	2270	2387	2536	2956
Imports	26	30	40	66	184

Source: U.S. Department of Commerce, Bureau of the Census

Constant dollar shipments of lawn and garden equipment were expected to increase at a compound annual growth rate of 4 percent between 1984 and 1989. Growth in housing starts, an increase in real disposable income, and an increase in replacement demand were expected to contribute to this growth. Due to its leading position in the world markets, the U.S. industry was expected to expand exports as world economies recovered and as the value of the dollar dropped. U.S. imports of lawn and garden equipment were also expected to continue to increase, especially in the lower priced models.

FINANCIAL PERFORMANCE

Between 1975 and 1979 Murray's sales grew 158 percent, from $126.6 million to $327.1 million; the company's reported profits grew by 125 percent, from $4.7 million to $10.6 million. During this period, the company had relatively stable profitability, with an average return on sales (ROS) of 3.5 percent, and an average return on equity (ROE) of 13.5 percent.

In contrast to the steady growth during the last half of the 1970s, Murray's performance became erratic beginning in 1980 as foreign competition in its product markets increased significantly. Between 1979 and 1983, the company's sales and profits grew by only 31 percent and 16 percent, respectively. Further, the company's average profitability showed a significant decline. The average ROS and ROE from 1980 to 1983 were 2.6 percent and 10.8 percent, respectively. (See Exhibit 3 for more data on the performance from 1975 to 1983.)

1984 was a challenging year for Murray Ohio. The company's management explained:

> The past year, 1984, was a difficult one for our company. While total sales were basically flat with 1983, earnings were down considerably. Two factors primarily accounted for this earnings decline.
>
> First, bicycle imports were up over 55 percent in 1984. This increase, which has been sold almost totally to the mass market merchants, adversely affected our bicycle pricing, production levels, and sales.

Secondly, stronger domestic competition in both our product lines, bicycles and power mowers, increased pressures on our pricing and resulted in a tightening of our profit margins.

The mower segment of Murray's business performed significantly better than the bicycle segment. Following a record sales performance in 1983, Murray's mower sales increased to a new high in 1984, up 15 percent. In contrast, bicycle sales decreased 19 percent in 1984, and operating profits for the year declined by 72 percent.

Murray Ohio's management announced that it would take several steps to improve its future performance: (1) adopting an aggressive bicycle pricing structure to regain market share; (2) improving manufacturing productivity through process modernization, manufacturing resources planning, and better manpower utilization; (3) introducing new and innovative products, including the new Sabre mower line aimed at the power equipment dealers; and (4) working with other domestic producers to lobby the U.S. Congress to increase import tariffs on bicycles.

While these steps were viewed as necessary to prevent further erosion in the company's market share, management realized that profit margin pressure was likely to continue, at least in the short term. Further, the productivity improvement program was expected to require significant capital expenditure outlays. The company increased its capital expenditures in 1984 by 86 percent to $10.9 million, and expected to invest comparable amounts in 1985 as well. Management summed up their view of the future:

We recognize the difficult journey before us. Our past record, however, shows one of success and profitability. With a solid balance sheet and the full commitment of our resources and people, we look forward to the challenges that lie ahead. Our people continue to be our greatest strength. Their innovativeness, team-work, and support provide the company with the impetus it needs. In these times of change, their support and assistance are immeasurable.

DIVIDEND POLICY

David McIntosh knew that the Commonwealth Investment Group had found Murray Ohio's stock attractive for Commonwealth's equity income fund because of its reliable dividend policy. Murray's dividend per share grew steadily from $0.67 in 1975 to $1.20 in 1980. Despite the company's mixed performance between 1980 and 1984, dividends remained constant. As the company's annual report stated, Murray's management was proud of the company's dividend history—it had paid them quarterly without a reduction for the past 49 consecutive years. McIntosh wondered whether Murray Ohio would be able to maintain this record given the company's changed business circumstances. Has the nature of Murray's business changed enough to warrant a reevaluation of its dividend policy? If the company decided to change its longstanding policy, how would investors react?

EXHIBIT 1

The Murray Ohio Manufacturing Company—Board of Directors, 1984

Name	Principal Occupation, Business Experience, and Other Directorships in Public Companies (1)	Age on April 2, 1985	Beginning Year, Period of Service
John N. Anderson (2)	President and Chief Executive Officer of the Company. Director of Third National Bank, Nashville, Tennessee.	60	1979
Lovic A. Brooks, Jr.	Senior Partner in the firm of Constangy, Brooks & Smith, Atlanta, Georgia (attorneys). Constangy, Brooks & Smith has performed legal services for the Company for many years and is expected to continue to do so.	57	1972
Sam M. Fleming (2)	Retired. Former Chairman of the Board, Third National Bank, Nashville, Tennessee. Director of Hillsboro Enterprises, Inc., Nashville, Tennessee.	76	1965
Robert A. Flesher	Retired. Former Vice Chairman of the Board of the Company.	66	1966
Charles W. Geny (2)	Vice President, Alexander & Alexander, Incorporated, Nashville, Tennessee (insurance and bonds).	71	1972
William M. Hannon (2)	Chairman of the Board and retired Chief Executive Officer of the Company. Director of Third National Bank, Nashville, Tennessee.	65	1955
Thomas M. Hudson	Investments. Retired Senior Vice President of the The Robinson-Humphrey Company, Inc. (an investment banking firm). The Robinson-Humphrey Company, Inc. has performed investment banking services for the Company for many years and is expected to continue to do so. Director of the United Cities Gas Company, Nashville, Tennessee.	63	1980
William C. Keyes	Retired. Former Senior Executive Vice President of the Company. Director of Commerce Union Bank, Nashville, Tennessee.	65	1966
H. Theodore Meyer (3)	Partner in the firm of Jones, Day, Reavis & Pogue, which has performed legal services for the Company for many years and is expected to continue to do so.	49	1985
Gerald E. Sheridan	President, Sheridan Construction Co., Nashville, Tennessee.	60	1983
G. Cromer Smotherman (2)	Executive Vice President and Chief Operating Officer of the Company. Director of First National Bank of Lawrenceburg, Lawrenceburg, Tennessee.	59	1971
David K. Wilson	President, Cherokee Equity Corporation, Nashville, Tennessee (holding company). Director of First American National Bank, Winners Corporation, and Genesco, Inc., all located in Nashville, Tennessee, and Torchmark Corporation, Birmingham, Alabama.	65	1983

All directors and officers of the company as a group (26 persons, including those named above) own 10.4 percent of the company's common stock.

EXHIBIT 2

The Murray Ohio Manufacturing Company—Stock Prices, January 1984–March 1985

Month	Murray Ohio's Stock Price at Month End	Standard and Poor's 400 Industrial Index at Month End
1984		
January	21 6/8	184
February	21 4/8	177
March	22 4/8	180
April	22 5/8	182
May	21 5/8	171
June	23 2/8	175
July	20 2/8	171
August	20 7/8	189
September	21 2/8	187
October	20 2/8	187
November	19 2/8	183
December	19 4/8	186
1985		
January	20 5/8	201
February	20 5/8	203
March	20 3/8	202

Murray Ohio's Common Stock β = 0.8 (Value Line estimate).

Interest rates at the beginning of 1985:
3-month Treasury bills: 8.8%
20-year Treasury bonds: 11.7%

m

1-7

EXHIBIT 3

The Murray Ohio Manufacturing Company—1984 Annual Report (Abridged)

LETTER TO SHAREHOLDERS

March 4, 1985

The past year, 1984, was a difficult one for our Company. While total sales were basically flat with 1983, earnings were down considerably. Two factors primarily accounted for this earnings decline.

First, bicycle imports were up over 55% in 1984. This increase, which has been sold almost totally to the mass market merchants, adversely affected our bicycle pricing, production levels, and sales.

Secondly, stronger domestic competition in both our product lines, bicycles and power mowers, increased pressures on our pricing and resulted in a tightening of our profit margins.

Net sales for the year were $383,589,000, a 1% decrease from 1983. Power mower sales, however, were up 15%, with bicycle sales down 19%.

Earnings, after nonrecurring adjustments for 1984, were $7,826,000, a 37% decrease from 1983. The majority of this decrease, as stated above, was due to the bicycle segment of our business. Earnings per share, after nonrecurring adjustments, decreased 43% to $2.01 from $3.53 in 1983. The difference between the percent change in earnings and earnings per share is a result of the June, 1983 equity offering of 770,000 shares of common stock.

The 1984 nonrecurring adjustments are benefits arising from the elimination of a provision for deferred taxes of our international sales operations (DISC) and an accounting change in the method for recognizing investment tax credits. These benefits resulted in earnings of $920,000 and $1,404,000, respectively, or $.24 and $.36 per share.

The declining profitability experienced in 1984 presented Murray with a difficult challenge that we are determined to face. In the third quarter report, we announced the first step in our program to improve profitability. This step involves an aggressive bicycle pricing structure aimed at maintaining our necessary production levels and at regaining market share lost to imports. Our pricing stance has shown success and will help Murray regain lost market share in 1985.

Productivity and Marketing—Steps for the Future

While putting a pricing structure in place to regain bicycle market share, we began major programs in two areas—productivity and marketing—to improve our profitability in both of our product lines. Neither program will create overnight success, but both will help keep Murray on solid ground and a strong course for the future.

Murray's productivity program involves several facets—process modernization, Manufacturing Resources Planning (MRP), and improved manpower productivity.

Our 1984 capital expenditures amounted to $10,878,000, an 86% increase over 1983. This increase strengthened our continuing program of process modernization. Major investments included the installation of modern tube cutting equipment, robot welders, a computer aided design system, and the initial phase of a state of the art press room. The commitment to the modernization of our facilities is one that will continue, and we are projecting comparable expenditures in 1985.

In 1984, we also began installation of a Manufacturing Resources Planning (MRP) System. The MRP System will lead to reduced inventory levels and better control and utilization of our manufacturing facility and processes. Such efficiency will improve our cost of operations.

With regards to marketing, Murray has always been innovative in product introductions. We have been successful in introducing BMX, mountain bikes, and freestyle bicycles into the mass market. Murray revolutionized the riding mower market when we entered this industry in 1968 in both performance and design, and we have continued as an innovator in this industry. In 1984, we reaffirmed our commitment to this type of innovation.

Bicycles and power mowers continue to be viable products for the consumer. We recognize the need to intensify our efforts to compete in these markets. At the same time, we are analyzing our present and related markets for expansion opportunities. This effort is continuing, and its benefits are beginning to show in our marketing plans.

One result of this market analysis was the introduction of our Sabre mower line for the spring of 1985. The Sabre line will target the outdoor power equipment dealer who participates in a large share of the mower market in which Murray is not currently represented. This new line, which will be sold directly to the dealer, offers him high quality merchandise with the ability to improve profit margins. Murray will continue such expansion or diversification moves as prove correct for our business future.

Our power mower products continue to meet with great success. The 1985 Murray line has been well received by our customers, and we expect the momentum created by our steady mower sales rise over the past 15 years to be maintained.

This year again, we were pleased to be selected to receive the Sears "Partners in Progress Award." We were one of only 23 suppliers to receive this award for the third consecutive year. The award is presented for overall excellence as a manufacturer of products for Sears. Sears has a total of over 12,000 suppliers.

We and our industry continue to make every effort in Washington to draw attention to the unfair competition we face from imported bicycles. The industry was successful in May with having H.R. 5754 introduced in the House of Representatives. This Bill provides for a 24% duty on imported bicycles and bicycle parts, a duty comparable to that in foreign markets. No action was taken on this Bill, and it will be reintroduced in the new session of Congress. It is the aim of the domestic industry to have our Government recognize and control the flood of unfairly traded import bicycles coming into this country.

If the economy continues on its present course, our sales for 1985 should improve. While our plans for 1985 and the future will help offset our 1985

pricing structure, we expect continued profit margin pressure.

Board of Director Changes

At the February 1985 Board Meeting, we regretfully accepted the resignation of Eugene T. Kinder, a recently retired partner in the law firm of Jones, Day, Reavis & Pogue. Though leaving our Board, Mr. Kinder will continue to be available as requested to render the excellent counsel that he has given Murray in his 12 years on the Board.

H. Theodore Meyer, also a partner of Jones, Day, Reavis & Pogue and currently Secretary of Murray Ohio, was elected to fill the vacant position. His election continues the tradition since 1925 of having a member of this firm on our Board.

Solid Record for the Future

We recognize the difficulty of the journey before us. Our past record, however, shows one of success and profitability. With a solid balance sheet and the full commitment of our resources and people we look forward to the challenges that lie ahead.

Our people continue to be our greatest source of strength. Their innovativeness, team-work, and support provide the Company with the impetus that it needs. In these times of change, their support and assistance are unmeasurable.

Very truly yours,

W. M. Hannon
Chairman of the Board

John N. Anderson
President and Chief Executive Officer

G. Cromer Smotherman
Executive Vice President and
Chief Operating Officer

FINANCIAL REVIEW

Sales in 1984 were $384 million, which was within 1% of the company's all-time record sales year of 1983. This included an increase of over 15% from the company's previous record for its power mower line, while bicycle sales were adversely impacted by import competition to record a 19% decrease from 1983.

Net income and earnings per common share were $7.8 million and $2.01, respectively, each after non-recurring adjustments. This resulted in profit margins of 2.04% and return on average shareholders' equity of 7.05%.

Murray Ohio has spent approximately $59 million during the past ten years to modernize and automate its facilities, to increase the productive efficiency and to expand the plant capacity. This included a significant increase in 1984 to further pursue the goals stated above.

During this ten-year period, the company has significantly expanded both its power mower and bicycle production capacities at Lawrenceburg, including additions of 600,000 square feet. Other expenditures were for research and development facilities, and an expansion to the corporate office. Another $9.7 million is budgeted for capital expenditures in 1985.

Total long-term debt at the end of 1984 was $23.0 million or 16.9% of total capitalization. This compares to $26.0 million and 19.2% for 1983. Working capital stands at $86.5 million at December 31, 1984, resulting in a current ratio of 2.2 to 1.

Shareholders' equity per share has increased every year for the last ten years to $28.93 at December 31, 1984, an increase of 91% for the ten-year period.

Murray Ohio paid cash dividends of $1.20 per common share in 1984. Murray is proud of its history of paying regular quarterly dividends without a reduction for the past 49 consecutive years. During this period Murray's stock became listed on the New York Stock Exchange and the Midwest Stock Exchange in 1969 and 1971, respectively, and continues to be so listed. Prior to 1969 Murray was listed on the American Stock Exchange.

Murray Ohio's cash payout over the past ten-year period has averaged 43% of net income. At year end, 3,896,670 shares of the company's common stock were outstanding. Of this total, 1,113,041 shares (29%), were owned by directors, officers, and current employees.

QUARTERLY RESULTS OF OPERATIONS

In Thousands of Dollars (except for per share data)

Comparison of Quarterly Results for Years Ended December 31, 1984, and December 31, 1983

	Net Sales							
	Power Mowers and Accessories		Bicycles and Accessories		Other Products		Total	
Quarter	1984	1983	1984	1983	1984	1983	1984	1983
1st	$114,820	$104,446	$ 40,664	$33,918	$22	$ 6	$155,506	$138,370
2nd	94,213	70,445	39,775	48,387	50	16	134,038	118,848
3rd	12,641	11,561	32,908	48,759	11	46	45,560	60,366
4th	14,747	18,584	33,732	50,314	6	12	48,485	68,910
Total	$236,421	$205,036	$147,079	$181,378	$89	$80	$383,589	$386,494

	Income									
	Gross Profit[1]		Income (Loss) Before Cumulative Effect of Accounting Change		Net Income (Loss)		Earnings (Loss) per Common Share Before Cumulative Effect of Accounting Change		Earnings (Loss) per Common Share	
Quarter	1984	1983	1984[3]	1983	1984[3]	1983	1984[3]	1983[2,3]	1984[3]	1983[2,3]
1st	$18,688	$17,625	$4,340	$4,953	$5,744	$4,953	$1.12	$1.58	$1.48	$1.58
2nd	15,147	16,943	2,460	4,296	2,460	4,296	.63	1.37	.63	1.37
3rd	4,782	10,146	285	1,693	285	1,693	.07	.44	.07	.44
4th	6,300	11,570	(663)	1,433	(663)	1,433	(.17)	.37	(.17)	.37
Total	$44,917	$56,284	$6,422	$12,375	$7,826	$12,375	$1.65	$3.53	$2.01	$3.53

(1) Gross Profit represents net sales less those costs directly related to the manufacturing process (i.e. labor, and overhead costs consumed within the factory).

(2) Due to the sale of the Common Shares (See Note J), average common shares outstanding for the year differed from the average common shares outstanding for each quarterly period. Earnings per common share for each period is computed by dividing total net income by the period's average common shares outstanding. As a result, the sum of earnings per common share for the individual quarters will not equal the per share amount for the year. The additional shares caused earnings per share to increase by a smaller percentage than total net income.

(3) Net income for the third quarter ended September 30, 1984 and for the year ended December 31, 1984 reflects the reversal of $920,000, or $.24 per common share, (after deductions of expenses relating to employee fringe benefits) of deferred taxes provided in prior years for the company's export sales through its Domestic International Sales Corporation (DISC).

The company changed its method of accounting for investment tax credit effective January 1, 1984. The cumulative effect of the accounting change increased 1984 first quarter earnings per common share by $.36. Other than the cumulative effect, there was no material impact on net income and earnings per common share in any quarter of 1984.

Refer to the Financial Statements and Management's Discussion and Analysis for further explanation.

Common Stock: Market and Dividend Information

Quarter	1984 Price Range		1984 Dividends Paid	1983 Price Range		1983 Dividends Paid
	High	Low		High	Low	
1st	24 5/8	20 3/8	$ .30	$23 3/4	$20	$ .30
2nd	23 3/8	21 1/8	.30	30 1/2	23 1/4	.30
3rd	23 3/4	20	.30	31 1/4	26 1/8	.30
4th	21 5/8	18 3/8	.30	29 3/8	22	.30
Total	24 5/8	18 3/8	$1.20	$31 1/4	$20	$1.20

The most restrictive provisions of the company's long-term debt agreements place certain restrictions (which do not currently limit any existing or presently contemplated company policies) on the payment of dividends and the purchase or redemption of the company's Common Shares.

STATEMENT OF FINANCIAL POSITION

	December 31	
	1984	1983
ASSETS		
Current Assets		
Cash	$ 1,424,761	$ 1,318,101
Trade accounts receivable, less allowance of $300,000	28,339,695	41,974,966
Other accounts receivable	501,387	764,285
Inventories	123,360,661	95,673,256
Company Common Shares acquired for employees' stock plans, at cost	767,737	777,518
Prepaid expenses	796,138	1,142,561
Deferred federal income tax benefits	1,163,467	1,132,287
Refundable federal income taxes	1,584,413	—
Total Current Assets	157,938,259	142,782,974
Property, Plant and Equipment		
Land	758,122	708,121
Buildings	31,054,300	27,619,109
Machinery and equipment	53,154,907	47,477,011
Allowances for depreciation and amortization (deduction)	(34,172,400)	(31,025,526)
	50,794,929	44,778,715
Deferred Charges, Investments and Other Assets	1,044,177	1,283,642
	$209,777,365	$188,845,331

(continued)

STATEMENT OF FINANCIAL POSITION (continued)

	December 31	
	1984	1983
LIABILITIES AND SHAREHOLDERS' EQUITY		
Current Liabilities		
Notes payable to banks	$ **32,348,675**	$1,190,454
Accounts payable and other liabilities	**24,015,784**	25,459,837
Reserves for product warranty and product liability	**1,400,000**	1,300,000
Accrued payroll, commissions, and other compensation	**8,722,810**	12,803,699
Accrued interest, payroll taxes and other taxes	**1,387,602**	1,494,495
Federal and state income taxes	**444,231**	2,831,203
Portion of long-term debt due within one year	**3,076,075**	3,061,075
Total Current Liabilities	**71,395,177**	48,140,763
Long-Term Debt—less portion shown as current liability		
Notes payable to insurance companies:		
10 1/4% notes	**2,075,000**	2,400,000
9 1/4% notes	**16,000,000**	18,000,000
8% notes	**1,750,000**	2,000,000
6 1/4% notes	**750,000**	1,125,000
Other notes payable	**93,225**	84,300
Lease obligations	**2,310,000**	2,405,000
	22,978,225	26,014,300
Deferred Credits		
Investment tax credit	**—**	2,121,877
Obligations under deferred compensation plans and other deferred credits	**705,685**	747,427
Deferred federal income taxes	**1,977,055**	2,452,554
	2,682,740	5,321,858
Shareholders' Equity		
Serial Preferred Shares, no par value: Authorized 500,000 shares; issued— none		
Common Shares, par value $2.50 a share: Authorized 8,000,000 shares; Issued—3,904,565 shares in 1984 and 1983	**9,761,413**	9,761,413
Additional paid-in capital	**42,292,504**	42,804,155
Retained earnings	**60,848,757**	57,672,939
	112,902,674	110,238,507
Less cost of Common Shares held in treasury (7,895 shares in 1984 and 30,817 shares in 1983)	**(181,451)**	(870,097)
	112,721,223	109,368,410
	$209,777,365	$188,845,331

See notes to financial statements.

m

STATEMENT OF INCOME

	Year Ended December 31		
	1984	1983	1982
Net sales	**$383,589,105**	$386,493,993	$288,642,358
Deductions from (additions to) income			
Cost of product sold (exclusive of depreciation and amortization)	335,374,269	327,134,491	245,394,295
Provision for depreciation and amortization	3,635,096	3,361,666	3,253,897
Selling, general and administrative expenses	30,941,548	30,070,404	23,729,181
Interest on long-term debt	2,438,759	2,627,100	2,711,077
Interest on short-term borrowings	2,250,717	1,709,123	4,136,422
Interest income	(180,842)	(936,412)	(12,165)
	374,459,547	363,966,372	279,212,707
Income before income taxes	**9,129,558**	22,527,621	9,429,651
Federal and state income taxes	**3,628,000**	10,153,000	4,337,000
Reversal of deferred taxes	**(920,000)**	—	—
Net income taxes	**2,708,000**	10,153,000	4,337,000
Income before cumulative effect of change in accounting principle	6,421,558	12,374,621	5,092,651
Cumulative effect of change in accounting principle for investment tax credit	1,404,000	—	—
Net income	**7,825,558**	12,374,621	5,092,651
Earnings per common share:			
Before cumulative effect of change in accounting principle	**$1.65**	$3.53	$1.63
Cumulative effect of change in accounting principle for investment tax credit	**.36**	—	—
Earnings per common share	**$2.01**	$3.53	$1.63
Pro forma based on revised method of accounting for investment tax credit, applied respectively:			
Net income	$ **6,421,558**	$12,520,798	$5,184,024
Earnings per common share	**$1.65**	$3.57	$1.66
Average common shares outstanding	**3,889,345**	3,505,567	3,115,750
Retained earnings at beginning of year	**$57,672,939**	$49,417,310	$48,026,124
Add:			
Net income	7,825,558	12,374,621	5,092,651
Deduct:			
Cash dividends paid, $1.20 per common share each year	4,649,740	4,118,992	3,701,465
Retained earnings at end of year	**$60,848,757**	$57,672,939	$49,417,310

See notes to financial statements.

STATEMENT OF CHANGES IN WORKING CAPITAL

	Year Ended December 31		
	1984	1983	1982
Source of working capital			
From operations:			
Net income	$ 7,825,558	$ 12,374,621	$ 5,092,651
Non-cash charges (credits):			
Cumulative effect of change in accounting principle for investment tax credit	(1,404,000)	—	—
Provision for depreciation and amortization	3,635,096	3,361,666	3,253,897
Deferred income taxes, non-current	(118,474)	1,364,331	1,782,871
Other	88,084	243,269	97,787
Total from operations	10,026,264	17,343,887	10,227,206
Net book value of property, plant and equipment disposals	1,226,924	351,550	115,337
Decrease (increase) in investments	239,735	(15,711)	51,496
Increase in long-term debt	40,000	—	—
Issuance of common stock	—	21,270,179	603,205
Tax benefits for non-qualified stock options exercised	308,105	—	—
Treasury shares reissued under stock option plans	688,646	—	—
Other	37,675	15,907	—
	12,567,349	38,965,812	10,997,244
Application of working capital			
Additions to property, plant and equipment	10,878,234	5,862,985	6,277,156
Decrease in long-term debt	3,076,075	3,061,075	1,056,075
Cash dividends	4,649,740	4,118,992	3,701,465
Stock options exercised from repurchased stock	181,202	71,445	—
Stock options exercised from treasury shares	668,407	—	—
Treasury shares acquired	—	870,097	—
Reclassification of deferred investment tax credit	717,877	—	—
Reclassification of deferred taxes	357,025	—	—
Other	137,918	123,698	123,351
	20,666,478	14,108,292	11,158,047
Increase (decrease) in working capital	(8,099,129)	24,857,520	(160,803)
Working capital at beginning of year	94,642,211	69,784,691	69,945,494
Working capital at end of year	**$86,543,082**	**$94,642,211**	**$69,784,691**

(continued)

m
1-15

STATEMENT OF CHANGES IN WORKING CAPITAL (continued)

	Year Ended December 31		
	1984	1983	1982
Changes in components of working capital			
Increase (decrease) in working capital assets:			
Cash	$ 106,660	$ (134,612)	$ (148,491)
Accounts receivable	(13,898,169)	16,175,577	3,312,330
Inventories	27,687,405	(723,170)	(8,896,653)
Refundable federal income taxes	1,584,413	—	—
Other	(325,024)	(357,151)	1,257,160
	15,155,285	14,960,644	(4,475,654)
Increase (decrease) in working capital liabilities:			
Notes payable to banks	31,158,221	(27,104,946)	1,748,236
Accounts payable and other liabilities	(1,444,053)	6,708,503	(1,366,321)
Reserves for product warranty and product liability	100,000	200,000	—
Accrued payroll, commissions, and other compensation	(4,080,889)	6,239,607	(3,481,353)
Accrued interest, payroll taxes, and other taxes	(106,893)	126,068	(500,166)
Federal and state income taxes	(2,386,972)	1,928,892	(725,247)
Portion of long-term debt due within one year	15,000	2,005,000	10,000
	23,254,414	(9,896,876)	(4,314,851)
Increase (decrease) in working capital	$(8,099,129)	$24,857,520	$(160,803)

See notes to financial statements.

NOTES TO FINANCIAL STATEMENTS

Note A—Accounting Policies

The accounting policies that affect the more significant elements of the company's financial statements are summarized below. Certain reclassifications have been made in the financial statements to conform to the 1984 presentation.

Inventories—Inventories are stated at the lower of cost (last-in, first-out method) or market. The company adjusts the carrying value on a current basis for potential losses from obsolete or slow-moving inventories.

Property, Plant and Equipment—Property, plant and equipment are carried at cost. The company provides for depreciation of property, plant and equipment on annual rates, applied generally by the straight-line method, designed to amortize the cost of the respective assets over the period of their esti-

mated useful lives (buildings—20 to 40 years; machinery and equipment—15 years). Structural die costs are capitalized and amortized up to 3 years. When properties are disposed of, the related costs and accumulated depreciation are removed from the accounts at the time of disposal, and the resulting gain or loss is reflected in income.

Product Warranty and Product Liability—These costs are expensed in the year in which they are incurred. The related reserves are reviewed at each year end for reasonableness of possible future costs applicable to the current year's products.

Federal Income Taxes—Deferred taxes are provided with respect to timing differences resulting from those items for which the period of reporting for income tax purposes is different from the period of reporting for financial statement purposes. Effective for 1984, the company adopted the flow-through method of accounting for investment tax credits. In prior years investment credit had been amortized over a ten-year period for financial reporting, but taken for the full amount of the credit in the year in which the credits were available for tax purposes.

Earnings per Common Share—Earnings per Common Share is calculated by dividing net income by the weighted average number of Common Shares outstanding during the year. The only Common Share equivalents are stock options which have no material dilutive effect on earnings per common share.

Note B—Federal and State Income Taxes

Federal income tax returns filed by the company have been examined and approved by the Internal Revenue Service through the year ended December 31, 1979.

The provision for federal and state income taxes is composed of the following:

	1984	1983	1982
Federal income tax currently payable:			
Gross	$3,405,740	$ 8,866,388	$2,409,611
Investment and other credits	(976,220)	(847,365)	(451,788)
Net	2,429,520	8,019,023	1,957,823
Reversal of DISC deferred taxes	(920,000)	—	—
State income tax currently payable	502,150	1,002,000	325,000
Deferred federal income tax	696,330*	1,131,977*	2,054,177*
	$2,708,000	$10,153,000	$4,337,000

*Accelerated depreciation methods resulted in $1,027,943, $976,510 and $820,609 of deferred tax for the years 1984, 1983 and 1982, respectively. Tool and die amortization methods resulted in deferred tax of $365,811 for 1984. The DISC resulted in $406,275 of deferred tax in 1982.

Reconciliation of U.S. statutory tax rate to effective rate:

	1984
Statutory tax rate	46.0%
Investment tax credits (net of recapture)	(6.0)
PAYSOP tax credit	(4.1)
State income taxes (net of federal tax benefit)	3.0
Other (net)	.8
Subtotal	39.7
Reversal of DISC deferred taxes	(10.0)
Effective tax rate	29.7)

The effective tax rate for 1983 and 1982 was not significantly different from the statutory rate.

Net income for the third quarter ended September 30, 1984 and for the year ended December 31, 1984 reflects the reversal of $920,000, or $.24 per common share, (after deductions of expenses relating to employee fringe benefits and related tax effects) of deferred taxes provided in prior years for the company's export sales through its Domestic International Sales Corporation (DISC). As a result of tax legislation enacted in 1984, the potential payment of these taxes has been eliminated. In accordance with a pronouncement of the Financial Accounting Standards Board, the entire reversal is reflected in the third quarter results.

Note C—Accounting Change (Investment Tax Credit)

Effective January 1, 1984, the company changed to the flow-through method of accounting for investment tax credits. The deferred method had been used in prior years. The change was made to conform to predominant U.S. industry practice. The flow-through method includes these credits in income in the year earned, while the deferred method amortized the credits over a ten-year period. This change in accounting method (after deductions of expenses relating to fringe benefits and related tax effects) increased 1984 net income by approximately $103,000 for credits earned during the year, and by $1,404,000 for the cumulative effect of the change; earnings per common share was increased by $.03 and $.36, respectively. Pro forma net income and earnings per common share amounts reflecting retroactive application of this change are shown on the Statement of Income.

Note D—Long-Term Debt

The company negotiated long-term loans of $6,000,000 at 6¼% annual interest during 1967, $5,000,000 at 8% during 1972, $5,000,000 at 10¼% during 1975, and $20,000,000 at 9¼% during 1978, with groups of insurance companies. Under the provisions of the loan agreements, the company is required to maintain current assets of not less than 150% of current liabilities.

The 6¼% notes mature in equal annual installments from September 1972 to September 1987. The 8% notes mature in equal annual installments from December 1973 to December 1992. The 10¼% notes mature in equal annual installments from April 1977 to April 1991. The 9¼% notes mature in equal annual installments from June 1984 to June 1993.

Capitalized Lease Agreements—During 1971 and 1978, the company entered into lease obligations with the Industrial Development Board of the Town of Franklin, Tennessee, for the lease of its office building and an addition thereto. The lease obligation, in an original amount of $1,600,000, will be repaid over a twenty-year term ending in 1991. The second lease obligation, also in the amount of $1,600,000, will be repaid in total in 1998. The company will own the buildings at the expiration of the lease, and has the option to purchase the underlying land at its market value after July 31, 1992.

Future maturities of long-term debt are as follows:

	Notes	Lease Obligations	Total
1985	$2,981,075	$95,000	$3,076,075
1986	2,981,075	100,000	3,081,075
1987	2,981,075	105,000	3,086,075
1988	2,606,075	115,000	2,721,075
1989	2,575,000	120,000	2,695,000
1990 and later	9,525,000	1,870,000	11,395,000

Rental expense and other future lease commitments are not considered to be material.

In early 1985, the company entered into a lease obligation with the Industrial Development Board of the City of Lawrenceburg, Tennessee, for the lease of environmental control facilities at its factory.

This lease obligation, in an original amount of $2,500,000, will be repaid over a fifteen-year term ending in 2000. The bondholder has the option to redeem the bonds after the tenth year. The company will own the facility upon the redemption of the bonds. This lease obligation is not included in the above maturity schedule.

Note E—Company Stock Plans

Eligible employees may contribute up to 5% of their base compensation to the company's stock purchase plan. The company may contribute an additional 50% of the employees' contributions. The company made such contributions for portions of 1982 and 1983, and for all of 1984. At December 31, 1984, 1,092 of the 2,220 employees eligible to participate in this plan were participants. There were 35,669 and 37,357 Common Shares held for this purpose at December 31, 1984 and 1983, respectively.

Unissued Common Shares of the company are reserved for issuance under stock option plans authorized by the shareholders during 1969, 1973, 1979 and 1984. The terms of the plans provide that qualified or non-qualified options may be issued to key employees, including officers, of the company at a price not less than the market value of the shares at the date of grant. The options generally become exercisable one year from the date of grant ratably over the succeeding four years and expire not later than ten years from the date of grant. The qualified options must be exercised in order of grant dates. The company makes no charges to income in connection with these options.

A summary of option activity follows.

Options	Shares	Option Prices
Outstanding January 1, 1984	283,982	$9.33 – 28.00
Exercised during 1984	(65,237)	$9.33 – 12.25
Expired during 1984	(9,422)	$11.50 – 28.00
Outstanding December 31, 1984	209,323	$9.33 – 28.00

Options	Shares	Option Prices
Exercisable:		
December 31, 1984	167,193	
December 31, 1983	204,107	
December 31, 1982	190,731	
Exercised during 1983	8,374	$9.33 –
		20.88
Exercised during 1982	-0-	

There were 513,369 and 203,947 unoptioned shares at December 31, 1984 and 1983, respectively.

Stock appreciation rights may be granted in tandem with options granted under the company's stock option plans. The amounts recorded each year by the company as income or expense attributable to these stock appreciation rights are insignificant.

The company has maintained since 1970 a Contingent Supplemental Retirement Benefit Plan pursuant to which additional retirement benefits may be awarded on an annual basis in amounts and to key employees of the company as designated by the Compensation Committee of the Board of Directors. Payment of such benefits is contingent upon certain employment conditions.

Note F—Pension Plans

The company has noncontributory pension plans which cover substantially all of its employees. The company makes annual contributions to the plans equal to the amounts accrued for pension expense in the prior year.

The total pension expense was $1,654,100, $2,417,400 and $2,552,900 for 1984, 1983 and 1982, respectively. The decreases in pension expense have resulted principally from the increased assumed rate of return and changes in the employment levels. The company's consulting actuary has estimated certain information for the 1984 and 1983 plan years as follows:

	1984	1983
Date of actuarial valuation:		
Hourly Plan	January 1, 1984	January 1, 1983
Salary Plan	December 1, 1983	December 1, 1982
Net assets available for plan benefits	$47,151,444	$41,586,931
Actuarial present value of plan benefits:		
Vested	27,463,800	27,411,600
Non-Vested	4,496,200	4,362,600
Assumed rate of return*:		
Hourly Plan	8.0%	7.0%
Salary Plan	8.5%	7.0%

*Used in determining the actuarial present value of plan benefits, which would have been approximately $5,900,000 higher had the rate remained at 7%. Actual plan benefits were not affected.

In addition to providing pension benefits, the company provided certain health care and life insurance benefits for retired employees and their dependents. Substantially all of the company's employees who retire under the company's retirement plans may become eligible for these benefits. The cost of retiree health care and life insurance benefits is recognized as an expense as incurred. For 1984, these costs totaled approximately $261,000.

Note G—Short-Term Credit Arrangements

Under lines of credit arrangements for short-term debt with eleven financial institutions, the company may borrow up to $111,100,000 on such terms as may be mutually agreeable. These arrangements do not have termination dates but are reviewed annually for renewal. At December 31, 1984, the unused portion of the credit lines was $78,751,325.

Under various informal and unrestricted arrangements with the financial institutions, compensating balances are maintained at varying terms against credit lines and related borrowings. During 1984, such compensating balances averaged approximately $2,830,000 and were satisfied substantially by float.

m

1-19

Note I—Business Segment Information

The components of revenue, operating profit and other data by business segments are set forth within the following table for the years ended:

December 31, 1984	Power Mowers and Accessories	Bicycles and Accessories	Other Products	Total
Net Sales	$236,421,047	$147,079,185	$88,873	$383,589,105
Operating Profit (loss)	24,533,300	3,352,581	(27,349)	27,858,532
General and Administrative Expense (1)	8,721,454	5,316,076	1,968	14,039,498
Interest (2)	3,222,125	1,467,173	178	4,689,476
Income (Loss) Before Taxes	$12,589,721	$(3,430,668)	$(29,495)	$9,129,558
Identifiable Assets (3)	$119,534,386	$49,353,639	$54,766	$168,942,791
General Corporate Assets				40,834,574
				$209,777,365
Depreciation and Amortization Expense	$1,797,348	$1,613,597	$-0-	$3,410,945
General Depreciation Expense				224,151
				$3,635,096
Identifiable Capital Expenditures	$5,792,543	$4,246,449	$-0-	$10,038,992
General Capital Expenditures				839,242
				$10,878,234
December 31, 1983				
Net Sales	$205,036,387	$181,377,604	$80,002	$386,493,993
Operating Profit (Loss)	25,057,921	12,000,318	(4,639)	37,053,600
General and Administrative Expense (1)	6,505,761	3,682,691	1,304	10,189,756
Interest (2)	2,595,403	1,740,577	243	4,336,223
Income (Loss) Before Taxes	$15,956,757	$6,577,050	$(6,186)	$22,527,621
Identifiable Assets (3)	$84,424,799	$51,061,136	$305,592	$135,791,527
General Corporate Assets				53,053,804
				$188,845,331
Depreciation and Amortization Expense	$1,632,805	$1,537,759	$4,027	$3,174,591
General Depreciation Expense				187,075
				$3,361,666
Identifiable Capital Expenditures	$2,682,958	$2,954,450	$-0-	$5,637,408
General Capital Expenditures				225,577
				$5,862,985
December 31, 1982				
Net Sales	$155,415,363	$133,138,347	$88,648	$288,642,358
Operating Profit (Loss)	18,603,595	7,086,836	(230,795)	25,459,636
General and Administrative Expense (1)	5,815,558	3,365,070	1,858	9,182,486
Interest (2)	4,577,197	2,269,850	452	6,847,499
Income (Loss) Before Taxes	$8,210,840	$1,451,916	$(233,105)	$9,429,651
Identifiable Assets (3)	$94,912,121	$39,142,707	$348,421	$134,403,249
General Corporate Assets				37,329,209
				$171,732,458

(continued)

December 31, 1982	Power Mowers and Accessories	Bicycles and Accessories	Other Products	Total
Depreciation and Amortization Expense	$1,643,064	$1,426,993	$3,811	$3,073,868
General Depreciation Expense				180,029
				$3,253,897
Identifiable Capital Expenditures	$2,099,488	$4,115,209	$-0-	$6,214,697
General Capital Expenditures				62,459
				$6,277,156

(1) General and administrative expenses were directly allocated by segment where reasonable bases existed with the remainder of these expenses allocated based upon the ration of the segment's net sales to total net sales. Interest income, receipts from an antitrust settlement and losses on capital disposals are included in general and administrative expenses. The combination of these items increased general and administrative expenses by $806,000 in 1984, while the same items decreased this category by $1,466,000 in 1983, resulting in $2,272,000 of the total change in general and administrative expenses between the two years. The balance of the increase was composed of a number of different items. The above mentioned items were insignificant in 1982.

(2) Interest expense was partially allocated using the ratio of the segment's identifiable assets to total assets with the portion of interest related to general assets allocated based upon the ratio of the segment's net sales to total net sales.

(3) Identifiable assets by segment includes both assets directly identified with those operations including finished and in-process inventories and an allocable share of jointly used assets. General assets consist of cash, receivables and other unallocable assets.

Of the company's total revenue, its three largest customers provided $69 million, $43 million and $43 million, respectively in 1984, while one customer provided $79 million and $68 million in 1983 and 1982, respectively, from purchases of both power mowers and bicycles.

Note J—Change in Capital Accounts

A summary of changes in capital accounts for 1984, 1983 and 1982 follows.

	Common Shares Outstanding		Additional Paid-In Capital	Treasury Shares
	Number	Amount		
Balance at January 1, 1982	3,099,527	$7,748,818	$22,938,871	—
Stock issued to Stock Purchase Plan	35,038	87,595	515,610	
Credit attributable to deferred compensation			33,132	
Balance at December 31, 1982	3,134,565	7,836,413	23,487,613	—
Stock options exercised from repurchased stock			(71,445)	
Additional common stock issued less cost of issue	770,000	1,925,000	19,345,179	
Treasury shares acquired	(30,817)			(870,097)
Credit attributable to deferred compensation			42,808	
Balance at December 31, 1983	3,873,748	9,761,413	42,804,155	(870,097)
Stock options exercised from repurchased stock			(181,202)	
Treasury shares reissued under stock options plans	22,922		(668,407)	688,646
Tax benefits of non-qualified stock options exercised			308,105	
Credit attributable to deferred compensation			29,853	
Balance at December 31, 1984	3,896,670	$9,761,413	$42,292,504	(181,451)

The company sold 770,000 Common Shares in a public offering during June 1983. The company's net proceeds from this sale totaled $21,270,179. Had these shares been issued at the beginning of 1983 and the proceeds applied to short-term debt at that time, earnings per common share for 1983 would have been $3.31 as compared to the reported amount of $3.53.

Note K—Inventories and Cost of Sales

The inventory components are as follows:

	1984	1983
Finished and in-process products	$121,931,069	$90,822,673
Raw materials	6,695,859	8,859,494
Manufacturing supplies	1,582,733	1,392,089
	130,209,661	101,074,256
Less allowance to reduce carrying value to LIFO basis	(6,849,000)	(5,401,000)
Inventory at LIFO	$123,360,661	$95,673,256

During 1982, certain inventory quantities were reduced, resulting in a liquidation of LIFO quantities carried at the cost prevailing in the prior year. The effect was to increase 1982 net profit by approximately $130,000.

Note L—Non-Monetary Transactions

During 1983 and 1982 the company exchanged certain inventory for advertising services to be received. These transactions resulted in no significant gain or loss. At December 31, 1984, 1983 and 1982, the unused amounts of $577,000, $935,000 and $1,321,000, respectively, were classified as prepaid expenses.

Note M—Miscellaneous Receipts and Charges

Selling, general and administrative expenses include miscellaneous receipts and charges which normally are insignificant. However, in the second quarter of 1984 and the first quarter of 1983 the company received approximately $85,000 and $628,000, respectively, for distributions from a class action antitrust settlement involving certain members of the corrugated container industry. In the fourth quarter of 1984, the company recorded an expense of $998,000 due to the write-off of an inoperative machine.

REPORTS OF INDEPENDENT ACCOUNTANTS AND MANAGEMENT

Report of Independent Accountants

Board of Directors and Shareholders
The Murray Ohio Manufacturing Company
Brentwood, Tennessee

We have examined the statement of financial position of The Murray Ohio Manufacturing Company as of December 31, 1984 and 1983, and the related statement of income, retained earnings and changes in working capital for each of the three years in the period ended December 31, 1984. Our examinations were made in accordance with generally accepted auditing standards and, accordingly, included such tests of the accounting records and such other auditing procedures as we considered necessary in the circumstances.

In our opinion, the financial statements referred to above present fairly the financial position of The Murray Ohio Manufacturing Company at December 31, 1984 and 1983, and the results of its operations and changes in working capital for each of the three years in the period ended December 31, 1984, in conformity with generally accepted accounting principles applied on a consistent basis, except for the change, with which we concur, in the method of accounting for investment tax credits as described in Note C of Notes to Financial Statements.

Ernst and Whinney
Nashville, Tennessee
January 28, 1985

Report of Management

The management of The Murray Ohio Manufacturing Company is responsible for the integrity of all information and representation contained in the financial statements and other sections of this Annual Report. The Company's financial statements are based on generally accepted accounting principles and as such include amounts based on management's judgment and estimates.

The company has a system of internal accounting controls which is designed to provide reasonable assurance that assets are safeguarded, transactions are executed in accordance with management's authorization and financial records are reliable as a basis for preparation of financial statements. The system includes the selection and training of qualified personnel, an organizational structure which permits the delegation of authority and responsibility, the establishing and disseminating of accounting and business policies and procedures and an extensive internal audit program. There are limits inherent in all systems of internal control and a recognition that the cost of such systems should not exceed the benefits to be derived. We believe the company's systems provide this appropriate balance.

The company's independent accountants, Ernst & Whinney, have examined the financial statements. As independent accountants, they also provide an objective review of management's discharge of its responsibility to report operating results and financial condition. They obtain and maintain an understanding of the company's systems and procedures and perform such tests and other procedures, including tests of the internal accounting controls, as they deem necessary to enable them to express an opinion on the fairness of the financial statements.

The Board of Directors pursues its oversight role for the financial statements through its Audit Committee composed of three outside directors. The Audit Committee meets as necessary with management, the internal auditors and the independent accountants. The independent accountants and internal auditors have free access to the Audit Committee without the presence of management representatives to discuss internal accounting controls, auditing and financial reporting matters.

MANAGEMENT'S DISCUSSION AND ANALYSIS OF THE SUMMARY OF OPERATIONS

Sales for 1984 remained basically constant with 1983 as a result of a 15% increase in power mower sales which represented 62% of total sales and a 19% decrease in bicycle sales which represented the remaining 38% of total sales. In 1983 power mower sales represented 53% and bicycle sales represented 47% of total sales. The increase in 1984 power mower sales was attributable to increased volume. The company's bicycle pricing, production levels and sales have been adversely affected by increased bicycle imports and heightened domestic bicycle competition. Net income as a percentage of sales decreased to 2.0% in 1984 from 3.2% in 1983.

Net income for 1984 was down 37% reflecting narrower operating margins than were experienced in 1983 and 1982 for power mowers and especially bicycles. Operating profit as a percentage of sales for power mowers was 10.4%, 12.2% and 12.0% for 1984, 1983 and 1982, respectively. Bicycle operating profit as a percentage of sales was 2.3%, 6.6% and 5.3% for 1984, 1983 and 1982, respectively. Increased domestic competition in both product lines contributed to the narrower operating margins. However, the increasing volume of imports, principally from Taiwan, had an added impact upon the bicycle operating profit for 1984. The decrease in earnings per common share was greater than the corresponding decrease in net income for 1983 to 1984 due to the increase in the average number of common shares outstanding resulting from the sale of additional common shares in June 1983.

Net income for 1984 reflects the reversal of $920,000, or $.24 per common share (after deductions of expenses relating to employee fringe benefits and related tax effects), of deferred taxes provided in prior years for the company's export sales through its Domestic International Sales Corporation (DISC). As a result of tax legislation enacted in 1984, the liability for potential payment of these taxes has been eliminated. For further explanation refer to Note B of Notes to Financial Statements.

m

Effective January 1, 1984, the company changed to the flow-through method of accounting for investment tax credits. The deferred method had been used in prior years. This change in accounting method (after deductions of expenses relating to employee fringe benefits and related tax effects) increased 1984 net income by approximately $103,000 ($.03 per common share) for credits earned during the year, and by approximately $1,404,000 ($.36 per common share) for the cumulative effect of the change. For further information refer to the Statement of Income and Note C of Notes to Financial Statements.

The company experienced an exceptional year in both sales and net income for 1983. The sales and net income increases in 1983 from 1982 were attributable primarily to increased sales volume resulting from the general improvement in the economy. Both the bicycle and power mower product lines contributed to the increased sales and net income in 1983. Net income as a percentage of sales increased to 3.2% in 1983 from 1.8% in 1982.

Selling, general and administrative expenses for 1984 remained relatively constant compared to 1983. Selling, general and administrative expenses for 1984 and 1983 were reduced by approximately $85,000 and $628,000, respectively, for distributions received from a class action antitrust settlement involving certain members of the corrugated container industry. In 1984 an expense of $998,000 was recorded due to the write-off of an inoperative machine. Increased advertising expenditures along with increased costs associated with increased sales caused the company's 1983 selling, general and administrative expenses to increase $6.3 million (26.7%) from 1982.

Interest expense on short-term borrowings reflects an increase for 1984 as compared to 1983 as a result of higher levels of average borrowing at higher interest rates. Short-term borrowings increased in 1984 from 1983 due to higher average inventory levels experienced during 1984 and the use of the proceeds from the common stock offering to repay short-term borrowings in 1983 as later discussed.

Inventories at December 31, 1984 are considerably higher than at December 31, 1983, primarily due to power mower inventory levels reflecting an expectation of increased orders for the 1985 riding mower lines. Notes payable have correspondingly increased due to the increased inventory levels.

Accounts receivable outstanding at year-end decreased in 1984 compared to 1983 primarily due to decreased sales experienced in the fourth quarter in 1984. Traditionally, sales in the last 45 days of the year cause receivables to be correspondingly higher.

Accrued payroll, commissions and other compensation decreased from $12.8 million in 1983 to $8.7 million in 1984. This decrease principally resulted from decreased net income, year-end employment levels and related employee fringe benefits.

The effective income tax rate of 29.7% was significantly lower that the effective rates of 45.1% for 1983 and 46% for 1982. The effective tax rate for 1984 differs from the statutory rate principally because of tax credits and the impact of the reversal of DISC taxes. The company continues to review, and adopt where appropriate, methods of tax accounting, all within tax regulations, which allow the company to defer payment of tax and thus increase its cash flow.

The company's business cycle imposes fluctuating demands on its cash flow, due to the temporary buildup of inventory in anticipation of, and receivables subsequent to, shipping during the peak seasonal periods. The company has in the past used lines of credit arrangements for short-term debt to meet its cash flow demands. These arrangements, the details of which are further discussed in Note G of Notes to Financial Statements, provide the company with immediate and continued sources of liquidity.

During June 1983, the company sold an additional 770,000 shares of Common Stock in a public offering at $29.25 per share. The net proceeds to the company, totaling approximately $21 million were used to repay outstanding short-term instruments pending application to the company's working capital requirements. Decreased interest expense on short-term borrowings and increased interest income for 1983 reflect the use of the proceeds from the sale of Common Stock.

In addition to cash flow and existing lines of credit, management believes that alternatives are available

m

to the company to meet future cash needs. These may include additional short-term debt, commercial paper, or equity securities. The company's strong debt to equity ratio should place it in a favorable position to issue new debt or equity securities. The company reviews these alternatives relative to current market and economic conditions on a continuing basis.

Capital expenditures for 1984 amounted to $10.9 million as compared to $5.9 million in 1983. Major expenditures included modern tube cutting equipment, robot welders, a computer aided design system and the initial phase of a state of the art press room. The company has budgeted $9.7 million for its 1985 capital expenditures. This budget is based on current economic conditions, and is subject to change in the event of significant changes in the

general economy and/or the company's performance. This budget includes projects for further modernization and automation of production processes, and for continued vertical integration. These projects are anticipated to be financed principally from working capital sources. In early 1985, the company entered into a 2.5 million Industrial Development Revenue Bond financing for environmental control facilities at its factory. Refer to Note D of Notes to Financial Statements for further information.

Virtually all costs and expenses are subject to normal inflationary pressures and the company is continually seeking ways to cope with its impact. The effects of inflation on the company's operations are summarized and discussed in Note H of Notes to Financial Statements.

m

TEN YEARS OF GROWTH

Summary of Operations	1984	1983	1982	1981
Net Sales	$383,589,105	$386,493,993	$288,642,358	$332,278,451
Power Mowers and Accessories	236,421,047	205,036,387	155,415,363	161,076,211
Bicycles and Accessories	147,079,185	181,377,604	133,138,347	170,619,908
Other Products	88,873	80,002	88,648	582,332
Cost of Products Sold	335,374,269	327,134,491	245,394,295	283,353,873
Depreciation and Amortization	3,635,096	3,361,666	3,253,897	2,876,664
Interest Expense	4,689,476	4,336,223	6,847,499	7,217,509
Income Before Income Taxes	9,129,558	22,527,621	9,429,651	17,180,728
Federal and State Income Taxes	2,708,000(b)	10,153,000	4,337,000	8,090,000
Income Before Cumulative Effect of Change in Accounting Principle	6,421,558	12,374,621	5,092,651	9,090,728(d)
Cumulative Effect of Change in Accounting Principle for Investment Tax Credit	1,404,000	—	—	—
Net Income (a)	7,825,558(b)	12,374,621	5,092,651	9,090,728(d)
Percent of Net Income to Net Sales	2.04%	3.20%	1.76%	2.74%
Return on Average Shareholder's Equity	7.05%	13.02%	6.39%	11.96%
Earnings per Common Share Before Cumulative Effect of Change in Accounting Principle	1.65	3.53	1.63	2.93(d)
Cumulative Effect of Change in Accounting Principle for Investment Tax Credit	.36	—	—	—
Earnings per Common Share (a, c, e)	2.01(b)	3.53	1.63	2.93(d)
Cash Dividends Paid	4,649,740	4,118,992	3,701,465	3,674,103
Cash Dividends Declared and Paid per Common Share (e)	1.20	1.20	1.20	1.20
Common Shares Outstanding at Year End (net of Treasury Shares) (c, e)	3,896,670	3,873,748	3,134,565	3,099,527
Number of Shareholders (h)	4,813	4,802	5,203	4,711
Average Number of Employees	3,500	3,403	2,868	3,534

Financial Condition at Year End				
Total Assets	$209,777,365	$188,845,331	$171,732,458	$173,521,388
Current Assets	157,938,259	142,782,974	127,822,330	132,297,984
Current Liabilities	71,395,177	48,140,763	58,037,639	62,352,490
Current Ratio	2.2 to 1	3.0 to 1	2.2 to 1	2.1 to 1
Working Capital	86,543,082	94,642,211	69,784,691	69,945,494
Shareholders' Equity	112,721,223	109,368,410	80,741,336	78,713,813
Shareholders' Equity per Common Share (e)	28.93	28.23	25.76	25.40
Property, Plant and Equipment (net)	50,794,929	44,778,715	42,628,946	39,721,024
Capital Expenditures	10,878,234	5,862,985	6,277,156	6,104,077
Total Amount of Long-Term Debt	22,978,225	26,014,300	29,075,375	30,131,450
Long-Term Debt as a Percentage of Total Capitalization	16.9%	19.2%	26.5%	27.7%

(a) Pro forma based on revised method of accounting for investment tax credit, applied retroactively:

	1984	1983	1982	1981	1980	1979	1978	1977	1976	1975
Net Income (000's)	6,422	12,521	5,184	9,242	8,566	10,704	7,936	8,435	5,768	4,850
Earning per Common Share	1.65	3.57	1.66	2.98	2.76	3.46	2.56	2.73	1.86	1.57

b) Income taxes, net income, and earnings per common share for 1984 include the nonrecurring effect of the reversal of certain deferred taxes. Refer to the financial statements and management's discussion and analysis for further explanation.

(c) Earnings per common share are computed based on the average common shares outstanding each year. The average common shares for 1983 (3,505,567) were significantly different from the common shares outstanding at year end due to the issuance in June 1983 of 770,000 common shares.

1980	1979	1978	1977	1976	1975
$294,745,956	$327,137,268	$254,113,710	$212,773,180	$150,815,365	$126,655,353
153,706,766	165,313,297	136,748,819	100,660,828	63,342,453	46,862,481
139,178,541	161,823,971	117,364,891	112,112,352	87,472,912	79,792,872
1,860,649	—	—	—	—	—
251,746,135	283,699,952	220,067,742	181,971,227	127,930,166	106,560,985
2,742,559	2,668,797	2,453,631	1,643,479	1,577,229	1,440,611
7,534,174	4,979,286	3,875,387	1,787,587	1,549,272	1,878,782
15,878,660	20,108,133	15,264,403	16,155,618	11,164,297	9,272,287
7,405,000	9,480,000	7,464,000	7,916,000	5,425,000	4,544,000
8,473,660	10,628,133	7,800,403	8,239,618	5,739,297	4,728,287
—	—	—	—	—	—
8,473,660	10,628,133	7,800,403	8,239,618	5,739,297	4,728,287
2.87%	3.25%	3.07%	3.87%	3.81%	3.73%
11.95%	16.42%	13.33%	15.46%	11.79%	10.41%
2.73	3.43	2.52	2.66	1.85	1.53
—	—	—	—	—	—
2.73	3.43	2.52	2.66	1.85	1.53
3,643,351	3,185,688	3,071,258	2,777,681	2,252,703	2,041,374
1.20	1.05	1.00	.90	.73	.67
3,099,527	3,099,527	3,094,563	3,094,563	3,093,154	3,093,079
5,002	4,874	4,872	4,728	4,663	4,713
3,106	3,676	3,350	3,050	2,423	2,212
$162,593,699	$165,676,630	$137,954,695(f)	$118,184,974	$96,521,505	$77,703,626(g)
123,774,401	128,536,269	104,553,999(f)	92,158,408	74,098,444	56,496,582(g)
56,045,182	62,951,762	41,929,128	47,978,918	31,202,317	15,060,145
2.2 to 1	2.0 to 1	2.5 to 1	1.9 to 1	2.4 to 1	3.8 to 1
67,729,219	65,584,507	62,624,871(f)	44,179,490	42,896,127	41,436,437(g)
73,271,961	68,498,679	60,922,713	56,087,652	50,497,987	46,894,095
23.64	22.10	19.69	18.12	16.32	15.16
36,563,771	34,071,357	30,560,878	24,692,169	20,408,767	19,747,300
5,322,612	6,891,287	7,648,408	5,962,610	2,335,131	1,600,299
31,177,525	32,213,600	33,249,675(f)	12,470,000	13,480,000	14,485,000(g)
29.9%	32.0%	35.3%	18.2%	21.1%	23.6%

(d) Net income in 1981 was reduced by $3,047,000 ($.98 per common share) due to the change to the LIFO, from the FIFO, method of accounting for inventories.

(e) Adjusted for the 3-for-2 stock split distributed August 31, 1977.

(f) Includes a long-term loan of $20,000,000 at 9¼% annual interest.

(g) Includes a long-term loan of $5,000,000 at 10¼% annual interest.

(h) Represents the number of shareholders of record as of the approximate December 15, dividend record date of each respective year.

Marsha Henderson is a loan officer at a large regional bank. She is approached in November 1988 by Lewis Poole, the Vice President of Finance for Pageturner Bookstores, Inc., a franchiser of retail bookstores. Poole is interested in obtaining a $300,000 loan, preferably unsecured. Henderson's bank has had no prior dealings with this company. However, she is favorably impressed by Poole. Moreover, based on his description, Pageturner Bookstores appears to be a quickly growing business.

Given the small size of the possible loan involved, Henderson cannot afford to devote much time to the lending decision. Nevertheless, given that Pageturner appears to hold the potential for substantial growth, it appears that serious consideration of the case is merited.

Poole has furnished to Henderson a document entitled "Pageturner Bookstores Business and Financing Plan." From that document and Henderson's conversation with Poole, she garners the information on the following pages. As she does so, she wonders how difficult the decisions will be. Will Pageturner easily qualify or not qualify for a loan? Or will it be a tough call? If a loan were offered, what kind of loan might be appropriate and how should it be structured? Would collateral be required? What covenants would be required?

CORPORATE STRUCTURE

Pageturner Bookstores is a bookstore franchiser formed in the late 1960s by entrepreneurs in Collegetown, a small city in New England. Pageturner's purpose is to help retail booksellers, through franchising, operate profitable community bookstores. Its franchise network now includes more than 120 stores, with average annual per-store sales in the range of $250,000 to $300,000.

Since 1981, the majority of the outstanding shares of Pageturner Bookstores have been held by PBI, a holding company owned by founders and managers of Pageturner. The remaining shares (14 percent in 1988) are held by franchisees. Beyond Pageturner Bookstores, PBI's only asset is 100 percent ownership of Pageturner-Collegetown, the

This case was prepared by Professor Victor L. Bernard as a basis for class discussion and is not intended to illustrate either an effective or ineffective management of a business situation. The name of the company on which the case is based has been disguised. Assistance of company personnel is gratefully acknowledged.

only company-owned retail bookstore in the network. In addition to acting as the parent organization for Pageturner Bookstores and Pageturner-Collegetown, PBI seeks to develop experience and expertise in the area of retail franchise management in order to apply these assets in the future to ventures other than bookstores.

Pageturner-Collegetown, formed in the early 1970s, is located in Collegetown. It has generated very strong sales volume—around $1 million annually—even though its asset base is not much larger than that of the typical store. However, it has not been profitable. In terms of operations, it is viewed as a "model" store, and serves as a training center for both new and existing owners of franchises.

CORPORATE OPERATIONS AND GOALS

Pageturner Bookstores, Inc. sells business format franchises to establish new retail bookstores and provides management, operational, technical, and promotional support to existing franchised stores. Pageturner's network ranks among the largest retail bookstore chains in the United States, and is the largest franchise chain.

Pageturner Bookstores are general, community-oriented retail bookstores featuring complete selection and a full range of services. They are located primarily in neighborhood shopping centers and outdoor malls in 33 states throughout the United States.

Pageturner franchises are sold for an initial fee of $21,000. After opening, franchisees remit royalties (based on a percentage of franchisee sales) to Pageturner Bookstores, Inc. Franchisees choose to operate within the Pageturner network rather than "go it alone" for at least four reasons. First, Pageturner offers the use of its name. Second, it offers expertise and service in a variety of areas: site evaluation and selection; lease negotiations; store set-up and design; store operating systems (including software); initial training and continuing education programs for both franchise owners and staff; financial planning and management; and ongoing operational assistance. Third, it offers economies of scale in purchasing. Fourth, it offers the benefits of some regional and national advertising programs and marketing materials. To support the franchisees, Pageturner Bookstores' regional managers are in frequent phone and face-to-face contact with the franchisees.

The company's broad goal is to be *the* "independent" bookseller of the 1990s. The company expects that competitive pressures will increasingly encourage a market for conversion franchising whereby existing bookstores will seek the advantages of a national organization. Although this is as yet an unproved opportunity for Pageturner Bookstores, the company believes that its programs and services will secure its position as the organization most poised to capitalize on the conversion market.

The company's specific goal is to accomplish at least $100 million in retail sales during 1992. To achieve this, a total of 200 franchised locations need to be in place by 1992, requiring approximately 20 new stores to be opened each year.

NATURE OF FRANCHISE AGREEMENTS

A Pageturner franchise can be established with a franchisee investment of approximately $100,000—including the initial franchise fee of $21,000, fixtures of $20,000 to $25,000, and inventory of $40,000 to $60,000. The inventory is purchased through Pageturner at cost; fixtures are purchased through Pageturner at a modest markup. Of the $21,000 (nonrefundable) franchise fee, $7,500 is received prior to site development, and $13,500 is due within six weeks of opening. Amounts billed for inventory and fixtures are due eight weeks prior to opening (typically prior to the time Pageturner actually pays for those costs). In 1987, Pageturner recorded revenues from initial franchise fees of $264,000, revenues from sales of inventory to new stores of $582,000, and revenues from sales of fixtures (primarily to new stores) of $325,000. The initial franchise fees are separately identified in Pageturner's income statement; the remaining sales to new stores are included in "Franchise revenue and sales to franchisees." The combined revenues related to new store openings ($264,000 of initial franchise fees and $907,000 of sales to new franchisees) accounted for more than half of total 1987 revenues of $2,155,000. (See Exhibit 1)

After opening, Pageturner receives royalties (typically as a percentage of sales), which are determined in accordance with a 15-year renewable franchise contract. The royalty percentage varies across franchisees, largely as a result of rate increases that have occurred over time. However, typical percentages range from 1.5 to 2.5 percent. Royalty income in 1987 was $457,000. In that year, "Franchise revenue and sales to franchisees" also included revenues from advertising fees of $155,000, and revenues from various other goods and services totaling $245,000.

Pageturner Bookstores' final source of income is generated by retaining a portion of amounts paid by magazine publishers for display space. Publishers typically pay approximately $.05 per magazine (labeled a "Retail Display Allowance," or RDA) for such space. As franchiser, Pageturner Bookstores tracks activity and bills the magazine publishers on a quarterly basis. Pageturner Bookstores retains approximately one-third of the amounts received from publishers, and transfers the remainder to the franchisees (typically after receipt from the publishers). The amount retained is labeled "Retail service income" in Pageturner's financial statements; such income totaled $127,000 in 1987.

COMPETITION

Pageturner's major competitors are Waldenbooks (owned by Kmart) and B. Dalton Bookseller (owned by Barnes and Noble Bookstores). They operate company-owned stores in large regional malls.

Pageturner's competitive strategy could be viewed as combining the economies of a large bookstore chain with the benefits of local ownership. Pageturner franchisees,

opportunity

opportunity

which tend to be located in <u>neighborhood shopping centers</u>, attempt to maintain an advantage by offering a well-trained, professional, knowledgeable staff and wider selection than the chains. Turnover among Pageturner franchisee employees is much lower than that experienced by competitors.

Useful data on the performance of competitors is difficult to obtain. Waldenbooks' financial data are consolidated within Kmart's much larger organization, and B. Dalton Bookseller is owned by a privately-held firm. Similar circumstances describe others in the industry: Crown Books is consolidated within Dart Group; Doubleday Book Shops are consolidated within Bertelsmann, AG; Encore Books is consolidated within Rite Aid. Some bookstore chains, such as Anderson Brothers, are privately held rather than consolidated within larger organizations. Data on some privately-held bookstores are available in aggregated form from Dun and Bradstreet. However, neither these nor any of the above-mentioned groups are directly comparable to a pure franchiser.

Risk - other bookstores are consolidated w/in a larger organization. They have funds available to them.

FINANCIAL PERFORMANCE AND GOALS

Pageturner Bookstores, Inc. has experienced dramatic increases in revenues for several years. However, after producing profits of $35,000 and $45,000 in 1985 and 1986, respectively, the company experienced a loss of $71,000 in 1987. In its Business and Financing Plan, Pageturner explains the loss as follows:

> *The operating loss experienced by the company in 1987 primarily resulted from two factors. These were a temporary hesitation by prospective new franchise owners because of the unsettled economic circumstances of last fall and increased expenses associated with the addition of franchiser staff during the summer of 1987. During 1987 sixteen new franchises were sold when at least twenty-two were budgeted, and new positions were created for a Vice President of Franchise Operations, three regional managers, a Franchise Development Manager and a secretary.*

Pageturner's (unaudited) interim reports for 1988 indicate a pretax profit through September of $27,000. CFO Poole is projecting a pretax profit for the year as a whole of $132,000. Pretax earnings are forecast at $227,000 for 1989, and $336,000 in 1990. (Detailed projections appear in Exhibit 2.)

The projected increases in future earnings are based on expectations that the franchisee network will soon reach the point where ongoing franchise operating revenues can cover the company's expenses without requiring a contribution from the sales of new franchises. In its Business and Financing Plan, Pageturner depicts the path of "operating margin" and "operating expense" as follows:

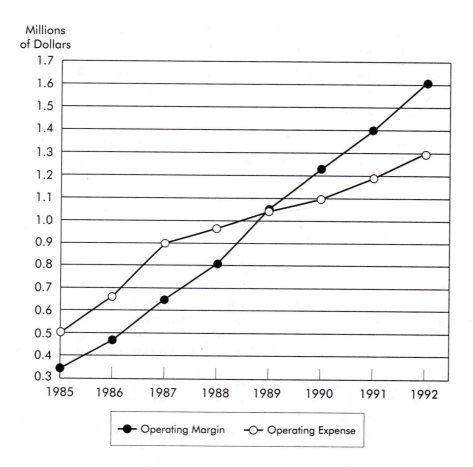

Millions of Dollars

●— Operating Margin —○— Operating Expense

The Business and Financing Plan noted progress towards Pageturner's financial goals in 1988, as indicated below. Note that sales and income figures are based on projections for the calendar year, given information available as of October 1988.

- *Retail sales is expected to surpass $40 million.*
- *Income from operating stores is projected to reach a level sufficient to cover the costs attributable to providing supporting services to franchised stores.*
- *The organizational infrastructure of the company was completed with the hiring of Lewis Poole as Vice President of Finance. In the future, new staff will be required only as franchised locations and retail sales increase.*
- *Minimum inventory investment for new stores was increased by 50 percent to $60,000 to encourage higher sales from new, larger stores.*
- *A computerized retail operating system was installed in ten franchised stores serving as test locations for the entire organization.*

- *A pilot program for collecting co-operative advertising monies from publishers on behalf of individual stores began in September.*

The Business and Financing Plan also stated that the company had adopted five short-term goals for 1988-1989:

- *Earn a 100 percent pre-tax return on equity.*
- *Accentuate responsive service to franchise owners.*
- *Emphasize training and support programs for mature stores.*
- *Make the trademark more visible in the industry as well as in the retail marketplace.*
- *Institute a computerized retail management system for franchised stores.*

REQUEST FOR FINANCING

Pageturner's Business and Financing Plan includes the following request for financing:

During the past five years the company has increased its revenues fivefold while following a course of investing profits in its own growth and development. Currently the infrastructure of franchising staff and store support programs has been established, and beginning in 1989 the revenue stream from opening stores will pay for the company's expenses without requiring a contribution from the sale of new franchises.

Although the company has had some borrowing experience, the growth of the company has primarily been funded internally. The purchase and expansion of the company owned store and the increase of accounts receivable that naturally occurs with growth have all been funded in this manner. The distinct seasonality of the business, with the bulk of earnings being generated in the fourth quarter, exacerbates the difficulties created by short-term financing.

Now that the company's revenue stream and earnings can justify and support the repayment of long-term debt, financing in the amount of $300,000 is sought. Procurement of this financing on a long-term basis will benefit the company in a number of ways. It will be used to:

- *Capture cash discounts from suppliers of over $20,000 annually*
- *Reduce accounts payable and strengthen the company's working capital position*
- *Enhance supplier relationships and increase operating efficiencies in purchasing and payables management*

The company intends to satisfy its capital needs of $300,000 by structuring this financing in either of two ways:

- *Debentures of a ten to fifteen year period, the exact terms of which would be negotiated with the lender. Our preference is for the security to be callable*

after a five year period with the usual call premium. A sinking fund for the security could be established if deemed necessary.
- *Installment note for a five to ten year period. The next five years are expected to be ones of rapid earnings growth for the company and will require a continuing strong working capital position. During that period the company will establish a strong financial position through its earnings stream.*

The request for financing indicates that Pageturner anticipates a borrowing rate of approximately 12 percent. As of October 1988, the yield on 3-month T-bills is 7.8 percent; the yield on 10-year T-bonds is 9.0 percent. The prime rate is 10.1 percent.

The Business and Financing Plan also furnishes a detailed history of prior borrowings. It indicates that in 1984, 1985, and 1986, Pageturner Bookstores or the affiliated Collegetown bookstore had borrowed from another large regional bank four times, in amounts ranging from $25,000 to $100,000, for periods ranging from two months to four years. Each loan had been repaid on or before its due date. The most recent financing occurred in December 1987; at that time Pageturner Bookstores issued a $150,000 note to its primary supplier, to be repaid within 12 months. Pageturner prefers to avoid dependence on its supplier for financing because it could potentially affect flexibility in purchasing. The loan from the supplier had largely been repaid as of September 1988.

[handwritten margin notes:]
Prime + 2½
3 paid ranging 25,000 to 100,000
1 outstanding?

P
1-7

GENERAL PROJECTIONS

Current expectations about earnings growth for the economy as a whole, the retail sector, and retail bookstores are reflected in the following P/E ratios and earnings forecasts:

	P/E ratio	Forecast change in earnings for 1989
S&P 500 composite	12.0	+12.0%
Retail stores composite	14.7	+22.2%
Retail stores: specialty	17.1	+20.7%
Publishing	24.9	+25.6%

HISTORICAL AND PRO FORMA FINANCIAL STATEMENTS

Included in the Business and Financing Plan are Pageturner's financial statements for 1987 (audited by a Big Eight public accounting firm and given a "clean opinion") and projected partial financial statements for 1988 and 1989. Excerpts appear in Exhibits 1 and 2. In discussions with CFO Poole, loan officer Henderson has acquired the following additional knowledge about the financial statements:

Accounting change. Starting in 1988, Poole excludes from the income statement the revenues and costs of inventory delivered to new stores, since those amounts are always offsetting, and to maintain consistency with the handling of inventory for existing franchisees. Note that after franchises are established, they acquire inventory directly from the supplier. Thus, there are and never have been any purchases of inventory and sales to ongoing franchisees recorded by Pageturner.

Cost allocations. In its internal records, Pageturner tracks some costs according to whether they are more closely related to new store development or support of existing stores. In 1987, cost of goods sold includes the cost of inventory sold to new stores ($582,000), the cost of fixtures sold primarily to new stores ($280,000), advertising costs ($164,000), and other costs for existing stores ($190,000) and new stores ($5,000). Selling and administrative expenses of approximately $57,000 were deemed allocable to new store openings; the remainder of the costs were incurred in the process of servicing existing stores ($216,000) and general administration ($312,000). Management fees are billed to Pageturner Bookstores, Inc. by its parent, PBI, primarily for salaries of PBI owner/managers and employees. In 1987, $67,000 of these costs were deemed allocable to new store development, $247,000 to ongoing store operations, and $106,000 to general administration.

Accounts receivable consist primarily of two components. The first (and largest) component includes amounts due from Pageturner stores primarily for royalties. The second component includes gross amounts due from magazine publishers for Retail Display Allowances ("RDA receivables").

Receivables from affiliates include amounts due primarily from Pageturner-Collegetown, but also from PBI. The receivables from Pageturner-Collegetown represent advances used to help cover operating expenses.

Notes receivable are amounts due from franchisees.

Accounts payable consist of amounts due to various suppliers for items purchased by Pageturner on behalf of the franchisees. Also included are "Payables-RDA," representing amounts due to franchisees under the Retail Display Allowance program.

Franchise deposits includes amounts received from franchisees prior to store opening but not yet recognized as Franchise Fee Income.

Exhibit 1 Pageturner Bookstores, Inc.—Financial Statements

EXHIBIT 1
Pageturner Bookstores, Inc.—Financial Statements

BALANCE SHEETS

	December 31	
	1987	1986
ASSETS		
Current assets		
Cash	$ 23,308	$ 44,006
Accounts receivable, less allowance for doubtful accounts of $6,000 in 1987 and 1988	648,463	453,133
Accounts receivable from affiliate	152,319	122,344
Common stock subscriptions receivable	—	9,510
Notes receivable	17,970	21,484
Inventories	29,083	9,928
Prepaid expense	13,329	18,498
Total current assets	884,472	678,903
Notes receivable, interest at 10% to 16%, due in varying amounts through 1997	29,241	20,914
Property and equipment		
Furniture and fixtures	88,578	82,277
Leasehold improvements	1,275	1,275
	89,853	83,552
Accumulated depreciation and amortization	–23,761	–23,276
Net property and equipment	66,092	60,276
	$979,805	$760,093
LIABILITIES AND EQUITY		
Current liabilities		
Accounts payable	$688,788	$538,536
Notes payable (Note 2)	12,350	2,500
Deferred revenue—franchise deposits	95,418	80,903
Long term debt due within one year (Note 3)	62,500	0
	859,056	621,939
Long-term debt (Note 3)	18,254	16,506

(*continued*)

p
1-9

Exhibit 1 Pageturner Bookstores, Inc.—Financial Statements

	December 31	
	1987	1986
Total liabilities	877,310	638,445
Commitments and contingencies (Note 4)		
Stockholders' equity		
Common stock, no par value125,000 shares authorized; 114,149 and 108,017 shares issued in 1987 and 1986, respectively	142,990	81,170
Common stock subscribed:		
4,669 and 951 shares in 1987 and 1986, respectively	46,690	9,510
Less subscriptions receivable	(46,690)	0
Retained Earnings	(40,495)	30,968
Total shareholders' equity	102,495	121,648
	$979,805	$760,093

STATEMENT OF OPERATIONS

	Year ended December 31		
	1987	1986	1985
Revenues			
Franchise revenue and sales to franchisees	$1,764,662	$1,541,146	$1,370,977
Initial franchise fees	264,000	257,000	185,000
Retail service income	126,291	72,951	75,415
	2,154,953	1,871,097	1,631,392
Expenses[a]			
Cost of goods sold	1,221,150	1,083,314	1,010,695
Selling and administrative	584,710	425,761	357,589
Mgmt. fee charged by affiliate (Note 5)	420,556	317,509	227,657
	2,226,416	1,826,584	1,595,941
Income (loss) before charge in lieu of income taxes and extraordinary item	(71,463)	44,513	35,451
Charge in lieu of income taxes (Note 6)	0	2,000	6,000
Income (loss) before extraordinary item	(71,463)	42,513	29,451
Extraordinary item: Tax effect of utilization of net operating loss carryforward	0	2,000	6,000
Net income (loss)	$ (71,463)	$ 44,513	$ 35,451

a. Expenses include depreciation of $6300, $6000, and $6988 in 1987, 1986, and 1985, respectively.

NOTES TO FINANCIAL STATEMENTS

1. Basis of presentation and summary of significant accounting policies

Basis of presentation—PBI owns 90% of Pageturner Bookstores, Inc. (Company). The operations of the Company are comprised of bookstore franchising.

Significant accounting policies

Inventories—Inventories are stated at the lower of cost (first-in, first-out method) or market.

Property and equipment—Property and equipment are stated at cost and are depreciated over the estimated useful lives of the assets on the straight-line method.

Investment tax credits—Investment tax credits are accounted for using the flow-through method.

Sale of franchises—The Company records initial franchise fees after the franchise agreement has been signed and all services or conditions relating to the sale have been substantially performed. Until these services have been substantially performed, receipts from franchisees are recorded as deferred revenue-franchise deposits.

2. Notes payable

Notes payable at December 31, 1987 and 1986 consist of the following:

	1987	1986
Note payable to a stockholder of PBI, due in monthly installments of $2,067 through March, 1988, including interest at 10.5%	$12,350	$ —
Demand note payable, due in monthly installments of $2,500 through January, 1987, plus interest at a bank's prime rate (7.5% at December 31, 1986) plus 2%, secured by substantially all assets of the Company	—	2,500
	$12,350	$2,500

3. Long-term debt

Long-term debt at December 31, 1987 and 1986 consists of the following:

	1987	1986
Note payable to a stockholder of PBI, with interest at the prime rate (7.5% at December 31, 1986)	$ —	$16,506
Note payable due in monthly installments of $6,250 through January, 1989, plus interest at the prime rate (8.75% at December 31, 1987) plus 2.5%, secured by substantially all assets of the Company	68,750	—
Other long term debt	12,004	—
Less: Long-term debt within one year	(62,500)	—
	$18,254	$16,506

Exhibit 1   Pageturner Bookstores, Inc.—Financial Statements

4. Lease commitments and contingent liabilities

Rent expense was $59,000, $33,000 and $38,000 in 1987, 1986, and 1985, respectively.

The Company leases its administrative facilities under a lease that expires in May, 1991. Minimum annual rentals are as follows:

Years ending December 31

1988	$ 62,000
1989	66,000
1990	71,000
1991	24,000
	$223,000

At December 31, 1987, the Company was contingently liable as primary lessee (in event of default by the assignee) for rentals of franchisee locations in the amounts of $39,000 and $5,000 for 1988 and 1989, respectively.

5. Affiliated company transactions

Included in the expenses of the Company are management fees of $420,556 by PBI. These fees are an allocation of salaries and wages to the Company.

During 1987, the Company issued 6,182 shares of common stock, of which 2,500 shares were issued to PBI.

Franchise revenue of $7,000 in 1987, $6,000 in 1986, and $5,000 in 1985 has been charged to Pageturner–Collegetown, which is a subsidiary of PBI and a franchisee of the Company.

A stockholder of PBI provided professional services to the Company of $29,321 in 1987 and $39,096 in 1986.

6. Income taxes

The Company's taxable income (loss) is included in the consolidated income tax returns of its parent company, PBI. Income taxes are provided or allocated to the Company by the parent company based on the ratio of the Company's income before income taxes to the consolidated income before income taxes.

At December 31, 1987, the Company has net operating loss carryforwards for financial statement purposes of approximately $40,000. These net operating loss carryforwards are available to offset future income for financial statement purposes. During the years ended December 31, 1986 and 1985, net operating loss carryforwards of $13,545 and $35,451, respectively, were utilized to offset financial statement income. In 1986, the effective tax rate for financial statement purposes varied from statutory rates due to utilization of investment tax credit carryforwards.

Net operating loss carryforwards for income tax purposes at December 31, 1987, amounted to approximately $74,000 and expire in the amounts of $24,000 and $50,000 through December 31, 1997 and 2002, respectively. The difference between the financial reporting and income tax loss carryforwards results from the use of accelerated depreciation for income tax purposes, which resulted in cumulative tax depreciation exceeding cumulative financial statement depreciation by $34,000 at December 31, 1987.

EXHIBIT 2

Pageturner Bookstores, Inc.—1988 Interim Financial Statements and Pro Forma Projections

PRE-AUDIT BALANCE SHEET
September 27, 1988

	September 27, 1988	
ASSETS		
Current Assets		
Cash	$ 73,000	
Notes Receivable	91,000	
Accounts Receivable Trade	281,000	
Accounts Receivable Affiliates	249,000	
Inventory and Prepaid Expenses	147,000	
Total Current Assets		841,000
Fixed Assets		
Office Furniture & Equipment		82,000
Total Assets		$923,000
LIABILITIES & OWNERS EQUITY		
Current Liabilities		
Accounts Payable Trade	252,000	
Accounts Payable RDA	98,000	
Franchise Deposits	379,000	
Notes Payable	18,000	
Total Current Liabilities		747,000
Total Liabilities		747,000
Owners Equity		
Common Stock	190,000	
Retained Earnings	(40,000)	
YTD Income	26,000	
Total Owners Equity		176,000
Total Liabilities & Owners Equity		$923,000

p

1-13

PRO FORMA INCOME STATEMENTS
Three Years Ended December 1988

	1986 Total	Year to Date September 1987	1987 4th Qtr	Year End Total	Year to Date September 1988	1988 4th Qtr Projected	Year End Projected
Revenues (1)	944,000	798,000	494,000	1,292,000	1,169,000	467,000	1,633,000
Cost of Goods (1)	155,000	187,000	160,000	347,000	303,000	82,000	385,000
Expenses	744,000	756,000	260,000	1,016,000	839,000	280,000	1,119,000
Pre-tax Income	45,000	(145,000)	74,000	(71,000)	27,000	105,000	132,000

PRO FORMA BALANCE SHEET

December 31, 1988

Current Assets

Cash	$ 35,680	
Notes Receivable	88,000	
Accounts Receivable Trade	380,000	
Accounts Receivable Affiliates	260,000	
Inventory & Prepaid Expenses	40,000	
Total Current Assets		803,680
Fixed Assets		
Office Furniture & Equipment		95,000
Total Assets		$898,680
Current Liabilities		
Accounts Payable Trade	120,000	
Accounts Payable RDA	90,000	
Franchise Deposits	95,000	
Notes Payable	12,000	
Total Current Liabilities		317,000
Long Term Liabilities		300,000
Total Liabilities		$617,000
Owners Equity		
Common Stock	189,680	
Retained Earnings	92,000	
Total Owners Equity		$281,680
Total Liabilities & Owners Equity		$898,680

PRO FORMA INCOME STATEMENT
Year Ended 1989

	1st Qtr	2nd Qtr	3rd Qtr	4th Qtr	Total
Revenues					
Franchise Operations	300,000	318,000	334,000	343,000	1,295,000
Franchise Development	84,000	126,000	126,000	84,000	420,000
Office and Administrative	6,000	6,000	5,000	5,000	22,000
Total Revenues	390,000	450,000	465,000	432,000	1,737,000
Cost of Goods Sold					
Franchise Operations	68,000	56,000	68,000	56,000	248,000
Franchise Development	10,000	11,000	11,000	10,000	42,000
Total Cost of Goods	78,000	67,000	79,000	66,000	290,000
Operating Expenses					
Franchise Operations	105,000	124,000	115,000	122,000	466,000
Franchise Development	39,000	49,000	42,000	41,000	171,000
Office and Administrative	141,000	146,000	147,000	149,000	583,000
Total Expenses	285,000	319,000	304,000	312,000	1,220,000
Contribution					
Franchise Operations	127,000	138,000	151,000	165,000	581,000
Franchise Development	35,000	66,000	73,000	33,000	207,000
Office and Administrative	(135,000)	(140,000)	(142,000)	(144,000)	(561,000)
Pre-Tax Profit	27,000	64,000	82,000	54,000	227,000

In late January 1991, Didier Pineau-Valencienne, CEO and Chairman of the French firm Groupe Schneider, was frustrated at his lack of success in building a closer working relationship between his company and Square D, Schneider's American counterpart in the electrical equipment industry. Convinced that a global market was developing for electrical equipment, Pineau-Valencienne believed that Schneider needed to become a major player in the U.S. market to maintain its future competitive position. Given the lack of success in partnering with Square D, he was considering the option of acquiring the company.

THE ELECTRICAL EQUIPMENT INDUSTRY

The electrical equipment industry generates revenue from new construction as well as from the maintenance of existing equipment. Demand for both closely follows general economic conditions. The 1990 economic slump hit the electrical manufacturing segment in the United States severely. However, by early 1991 analysts expected prospects for the industry to brighten with the predicted upturn in the economy and the construction market.

Two related trends dominated the industry in 1990: globalization and industry concentration. The first of these has led many U.S. firms to expand internationally to take advantage of market growth in Western Europe and Pacific Rim countries. These international opportunities have been enhanced by the globalization of product standards in the industry. The most widely accepted standards in the U.S. were developed by the National Electrical Manufacturers Association (NEMA). European products conformed to a different set of standards, developed by the International Electrical Commission (IEC) in Geneva. However, many in the industry expected that the move toward a unified Europe, set for 1992, would ultimately lead IEC standards to become dominant in the world.

The second major trend in the industry, concentration of manufacturing and research capabilities, resulted from increasing costs of development and production as well as from globalization. The development of a new product line costs between $46 million

This case was prepared by Edouard De Vitry D'Avaucourt, under the supervision of Professor Paul Healy. Additional comments and information were provided by Professors Paul Asquith from the MIT Sloan School of Management and Anant Sundaram from the Amos Tuck School.

and $74 million (FF 250 million to FF 400 million). Globalization of markets and product standards enabled firms to take advantage of economies of scale, using their expertise and technologies to create common products for domestic and international markets.

SQUARE D COMPANY

Square D is a major supplier of electrical equipment, services, and systems in the U.S. (see Exhibit 1 for Square D's U.S. market shares). The company was incorporated in 1903 and has grown steadily since then. It currently owns and operates 18 manufacturing plants in 11 foreign countries. Operations are concentrated in two segments: electrical distribution and industrial control. The electrical distribution segment manufactures products and systems used to transmit electricity from power lines to outlets for residential, commercial, industrial, or other types of buildings. The industrial control segment manufactures products and provides services to control power used by electrical devices or processes.

One of Square D's strengths is its network of independent electrical distributors, or wholesalers, which market its products. Individual distributors, selected by Square D, provide products and services to all types of clients (contractors, utilities, industrial users, and original equipment manufacturers). This extensive network is the result of many years of relationship building, and is the envy of most of Square D's competitors.

Square D's major competitors include ABB, Westinghouse, Siemens, Allen Bradley, General Electric, and Schneider (through its subsidiaries Télémécanique and Merlin Gerin). These companies compete across a number of segments. In late 1990, *US Industrial Outlook* ranked Square D second in the U.S. industrial control business after Allen Bradley. In electrical distribution, the company ranks third in the U.S. market behind Westinghouse and General Electric.

Square D has had an impressive financial track record—it has been profitable for each of the last 59 years. In the mid-1980s, however, company performance indicators began to deteriorate, prompting the Board to make a change in top management. Jerre Stead joined Square D as president and COO in 1987, was elected CEO in 1988, and was appointed Chairman of the Board in 1989. Stead led a revitalization plan to restore the company's performance and help it face the new industry challenges. Under the plan the following restructuring changes were made:

- Some facilities in the U.S. and Canada were closed, and others were consolidated.
- The firm's businesses were reorganized into three externally focused sectors serving industrial control, electrical distribution, and international markets.
- The resources generated by redeployments and disposal of operations not closely related to the core were used to strengthen core businesses.

Thanks to these efforts, Square D weathered the 1990 recession better than many of its competitors. In 1990, Square D's sales were $1.7 billion (see Exhibit 2 for financial statements), 71 percent in the electrical distribution segment (85 percent of operating earnings) and 29 percent in the industrial control segment (15 percent of operating earnings). By early 1991 analysts were expressing optimism about the industry's prospects for late 1991 and 1992, especially those for Square D. *Value Line* noted that "a stronger economy, a rebound in housing, and positive operating leverage . . . could enable earnings per share to surge to $5.50 or so in 1992 (from $4.73 in 1990)."

GROUPE SCHNEIDER

Schneider was founded in October 1886 as a partnership and was transformed into a corporation (société anonyme) in 1966. It is one of the largest industrial groups in France and is ranked 184 in Fortune's 500 (worldwide ranking).

In 1981, with the arrival of Pineau-Valencienne as chairman and CEO of the group, Schneider embarked on an ambitious restructuring program. The first stage of the program was to divest all loss-making businesses (shipbuilding, railways, and telephone equipment), which had historically generated much of the firm's sales. The sale of these businesses allowed the group to simplify its operational structure and to strengthen its finances. In the second stage of the restructuring Schneider focused on two core businesses:

- Electrical equipment manufacturing for power distribution and automation of industrial complexes (56 percent of sales, 85 percent of operating profits in 1990)
- Electrical building contracting (44 percent of sales, 15 percent of operating profits in 1990)

As a result of the restructuring efforts, Schneider transformed itself from a diversified holding company into an industrial group focused on electrical equipment, engineering, and contracting. The company was organized around four major industrial subsidiaries:

- *Merlin Gerin*—Manufacturer of high-, medium-, and low-voltage equipment, as well as process control systems
- *Télémécanique*—Manufacturer of automation systems and equipment
- *Jeumont Schneider*—Manufacturer of electrical and electronic engineering equipment
- *Spie Batignolles*—Provider of electrical contracting and civil engineering services

With sales of 51 billion francs (financial statements are presented in Exhibit 3) and 85,000 employees throughout the world in 1990, Schneider ranked second or third in most segments of the global electrical equipment industry.

In the late 1980s, Pineau-Valencienne became convinced that the industry was moving more toward a global industry. In his communications with analysts, he emphasized that IEC standards would gain influence in the U.S. and would become the worldwide standard. In addition, he believed that increasing R&D and manufacturing costs would encourage international concentration. Consequently, Schneider began a third restructuring stage—geographical diversification. This move was initiated with two major acquisitions in 1989:

- Spie Batignolles acquired 15 percent of DAVY, the leading British engineering company.
- Schneider acquired a controlling interest in Federal Pioneer, the leading Canadian electrical equipment manufacturer.

The Relationship Between Schneider and Square D

Schneider became interested in Square D in 1988. In September 1988, Pineau-Valencienne arranged a meeting between the top executives of the two companies, during which Schneider presented its vision of a possible joint venture. After this presentation, operational meetings were scheduled from fall 1988 to spring 1989 to determine the product lines most suitable for such a joint venture. To protect the information exchanged, the companies entered into a confidentiality agreement in late October 1988. This restricted the use and public disclosure of confidential information received during the discussions, but it did not contain any "standstill" provisions limiting purchase of securities or business combination proposals.

Very early in the negotiations it became clear that the two CEOs diverged in their understanding of the nature of the relationship. Pineau-Valencienne had hoped that Schneider would acquire an equity position in Square D to cement the relationship. Stead, however, made it very clear that he did not welcome this, and requested that Square D's independence be respected. In correspondence on September 25, 1989, Pineau-Valencienne made his views very clear, connecting the future of the joint venture discussions to Square D's agreeing to Schneider acquiring a 20 percent interest in Square D. As a result, joint venture discussions between the two firms terminated. Frustrated over this standstill, in September 1990 Pineau-Valencienne indicated to Stead that Schneider's interests in Square D had changed from a joint venture to a "friendly cash merger transaction." Square D's Board subsequently became increasingly hostile to Schneider's proposals.

At the same time that Schneider was making overtures to Square D, Square D was organizing legal defenses against hostile takeovers. In 1989 it moved to Delaware, where state laws require hostile bidders to have a minimum of 85 percent of the shares tendered to effect a takeover. In addition, it created poison pill amendments to fight potential unsolicited bids, including a Common Stock Purchase Plan (see Exhibit 4 for details).

During November 1990, unusual activity was noticeable in Square D's stock. Rumors of a takeover led to a jump in volume and increased the share price from $36.50 on October 22 to $49.75 on November 7 (see Exhibit 5). On November 6, 1990, Stead discussed the unusual activity in a phone conversation with Pineau-Valencienne, who expressed an interest in having the opportunity to propose a transaction to Square D if any other parties were given such an opportunity.

On February 1, 1991, *Value Line Investments Survey* made the following comments:

Square D stock is trading on takeover speculation, as it has for the past three months. Square D has several attractions (including positions in selected electrical equipment markets), and could well be a tempting takeover target, especially to a foreign company trying to establish or to enlarge a market presence in the U.S. An acquirer might be willing to pay $70 a share or more for the company. But after three months of unusually heavy trading in the stock, during which time all of its outstanding shares theoretically have changed hands, no evidence of a pending buyout attempt has appeared. If none is eventually forthcoming, we'd expect the stock to gradually drift lower, perhaps to the range of $40–$45 a share. At this juncture, only speculative investors should be holding these shares.

Potential Acquisition of Square D

One option that Pineau-Valencienne was considering was to make a bid for Square D. After two years of contacts with Square D, he had a number of ideas for synergies and sources of value that could result from a full combination of the two companies. These included:

- Rationalizing R&D efforts between the two companies and sharing the benefits of existing technologies;
- Providing access to larger distribution channels for both companies;
- Rationalizing manufacturing capabilities; and
- Expanding Square D's product lines by selling products developed by Télémécanique or Merlin Gerin.

Lazard Frères, the financial advisor of Schneider, was asked to analyze the stand-alone value of Square D as well as its value to Schneider. To determine Square D's stand-alone value, Lazard Frères prepared a set of base assumptions for the firm's future performance as an independent entity. They projected that (a) sales would grow 3.5 percent in 1991 and 7 percent per year thereafter; (b) EBIT would be 15–16 percent of sales; (c) net working capital would continue to be 11–13 percent of sales; (d) projected capital expenditures would be 5 percent of sales; and (e) depreciation expenses would remain at 4 percent of sales between 1991 and 1997, and 4.3 percent thereafter. Based on the synergies between Schneider and Square D, Lazard Frères estimated that Square D could save approximately $60 million per year in expenses (after tax) if it were combined with Schneider. In addition, the disposal of some of Square D's unrelated assets could generate $150 million in cash. Other data relevant to the valuation of Square D is presented in Exhibit 6.

One other issue that Pineau-Valencienne was concerned about in a possible acquisition of Square D was its effect on Schneider's income. Under French accounting, Schneider would have to amortize goodwill, regardless of whether the offer was cash or stock-financed. Lazard Frères estimated that asset and liability revaluations under an acquisition would be minimal, implying that there would be significant goodwill amortization charges, even if the maximum period of 40 years was chosen. Pineau-Valencienne expected that many analysts would react negatively to the resulting dilution of earnings.

Didier Pineau-Valencienne felt he had to make a quick decision. There were rumors that Square D already had been approached by a number of other companies about a business combination. Pineau-Valencienne was very concerned that other competitors could gain control of Square D, leaving Schneider with few opportunities to gain access to the U.S. market.

Exhibit 1   Schneider and Square D Market Shares, U.S. and Europe

EXHIBIT 1

Schneider and Square D Market Shares, U.S. and Europe

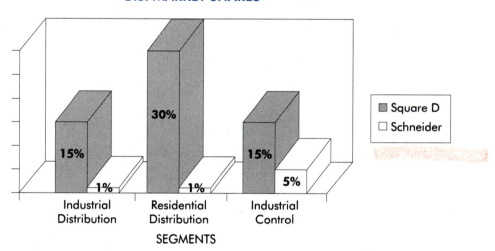

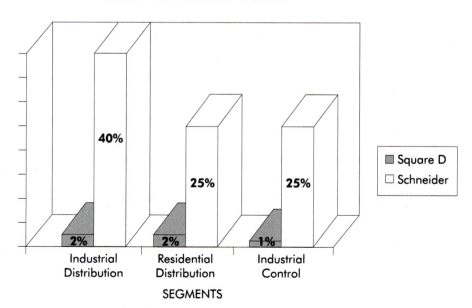

Exhibit 2   Selected Pages from Square D's 1990 Annual Report

EXHIBIT 2
Selected Pages from Square D's 1990 Annual Report

CONSOLIDATED FINANCIAL STATEMENTS

CONSOLIDATED STATEMENTS OF NET EARNINGS

(Amounts in thousands, except per share)	1990	1989	1988
Net Sales	$1,653,319	$1,598,688	$1,497,772
Costs and Expenses:			
Cost of products sold	1,088,977	1,027,348	979,591
Selling, administrative and general	385,903	369,726	338,962
Restructuring charge	—	26,320	—
Operating Earnings	178,439	175,294	179,219
Non-Operating Income	34,740	17,106	17,255
Interest Expense	(28,760)	(31,438)	(22,082)
Earnings from Continuing Operations before Income Taxes	184,419	160,962	174,392
Provision for Income Taxes	67,773	59,856	63,310
Earnings from Continuing Operations	116,646	101,106	111,082
Discontinued Operations:			
(Loss) earnings from operations, net of income tax (benefit) expense: 1990—$(1,188); 1989—$(1,086); 1988—$3,831	(312)	798	7,852
Gain on disposal, net of other provisions; net of income taxes of $1,865	4,391	—	—
Earnings from Discontinued Operations	4,079	798	7,852
Net Earnings	120,725	101,904	118,934
Preferred Dividend, Net of Income Taxes	6,176	3,300	—
Net Earnings Available for Common Shareholders	$ 114,549	$ 98,604	$ 118,934
Earnings per Common Share:			
Primary:			
Continuing operations	$ 4.76	$ 3.95	$ 4.15
Discontinued operations	.18	.03	.29
Net Earnings	$ 4.94	$ 3.98	$ 4.44
Fully Diluted:			
Continuing operations	$ 4.57	$ 3.88	$ 4.13
Discontinued operations	.16	.03	.29
Net Earnings	$ 4.73	$ 3.91	$ 4.42
Weighted Average Number of Common Shares Outstanding:			
Primary	23,181	24,763	26,776
Fully diluted	25,088	25,809	27,016

Year Ended December 31

Exhibit 2   Selected Pages from Square D's 1990 Annual Report

CONSOLIDATED STATEMENTS OF CASH FLOWS

	Year Ended December 31,		
(Dollars in thousands)	1990	1989	1988
Cash and Short-Term Investments at January 1	$ 66,348	$ 65,855	$ 94,488
Cash and Short-Term Investments Were Provided from (Used for):			
Operating Activities:			
Earnings from Continuing Operations	116,646	101,106	111,082
Add (deduct) non-cash items included in earnings from continuing operations:			
Depreciation and amortization	59,300	49,443	45,174
Deferred income taxes	1,707	(25,147)	(8,506)
Deferred income taxes—leveraged leases	15,226	23,445	25,683
(Gain) loss on sale of property, plant and equipment	(1,011)	1,936	657
(Gain) loss on foreign exchange	(2,222)	964	(52)
Minority interest	1,646	985	1,047
Other credits to earnings—net	—	(15)	(63)
Current Items (net of effects of purchase of businesses):			
Receivables	13,501	(58,515)	(20,789)
Inventories	(1,285)	26,568	(52,795)
Prepaid expenses	2,769	12,027	1,635
Accounts payable and accrued expenses	(7,312)	16,736	20,316
Income taxes	(15,253)	(3,319)	8,243
Net cash provided from continuing operations	183,712	146,214	131,632
Net cash (used for) provided from discontinued operations	(484)	2,971	721
Net cash provided from operating activities	183,228	149,185	132,353
Investing Activities:			
Increase in investment in leveraged leases	(3,838)	(2,876)	(4,829)
Purchase of businesses, net of $103 of cash acquired	—	(9,271)	—
Property additions	(83,117)	(80,024)	(70,419)
Proceeds from sale of business	175,476	—	—
Proceeds from sale of property, plant and equipment	21,774	6,186	14,222
Decrease (increase) in other investments	1,281	(12,794)	24,692
Net cash provided from (used for) investing activities	111,576	(98,779)	(36,334)
Financing Activities:			
Net (decrease) increase in short-term debt	(143,983)	142,262	44,430
Increase in long-term debt	27,883	614	11,066
Reductions in long-term debt	(14,412)	(21,580)	(17,910)
Proceeds of note receivable from ESOP trust	125,000	—	—
Loan to ESOP trust	(25,000)	—	—
Cash dividends paid on common stock	(50,128)	(50,590)	(54,601)
Cash dividends paid on preferred stock	(9,956)	(5,000)	—
Common stock issued	6,602	8,929	6,349
Purchase of treasury stock	(34,916)	(126,778)	(111,394)

(continued)

S

1-9

Exhibit 2   Selected Pages from Square D's 1990 Annual Report

CONSOLIDATED STATEMENT OF CASH FLOWS (continued)

	Year Ended December 31,		
(Dollars in thousands)	1990	1989	1988
Redemption of preferred stock	(432)	—	—
Treasury stock issued	54	114	256
Net cash used for financing activities	(119,288)	(52,029)	(121,804)
Effect of Exchange Rate Changes on Cash	3,069	2,116	(2,848)
Net Increase (Decrease) in Cash and Short-Term Investments	178,585	493	(28,633)
Cash and Short-Term Investments at December 31	$244,933	$ 66,348	$ 65,855

See accompanying notes to consolidated financial statements.

CONSOLIDATED BALANCE SHEETS

	December 31,	
(Dollars in thousands, except per share)	1990	1989
ASSETS		
Current Assets:		
Cash and short-term investments	$ 244,933	$ 66,348
Receivables, less allowances (1990—$23,759; 1989—$18,556)	305,241	314,123
Inventories	159,109	151,316
Prepaid expenses	12,664	15,206
Prepaid income taxes	4,714	—
Deferred income tax benefit	34,988	26,459
Net assets of discontinued operation	—	117,116
Total Current Assets	761,649	690,568
Investment in Leveraged Leases	137,182	133,344
Property, Plant and Equipment:		
Land	24,477	22,216
Buildings and improvements	222,105	212,992
Equipment	552,785	501,531
Property, Plant and Equipment—at cost	799,367	736,739
Less accumulated depreciation	349,265	318,261
Property, Plant and Equipment—net	450,102	418,478
Net Assets of Discontinued Operations	36,681	52,949
Excess of Purchase Price Over Net Assets of Businesses Acquired, Less Amortization (1990—$13,769; 1989— $12,978)	51,391	50,528
Other Assets	22,744	26,718
Total Assets	$1,459,749	$1,372,585

Exhibit 2   Selected Pages from Square D's 1990 Annual Report

	December 31,	
(Dollars in thousands, except per share)	1990	1989

LIABILITIES AND COMMON SHAREHOLDERS' EQUITY

Current Liabilities:		
Short-term debt	$ 123,871	$ 263,730
Current maturities of long-term debt	15,067	10,174
Accounts payable and accrued expenses	220,575	200,686
Income taxes	—	10,327
Dividends payable	12,633	11,893
Total Current Liabilities	372,146	496,810
Long-Term Debt	244,820	123,420
Deferred Income Taxes	82,381	74,464
Deferred Income Taxes—Leveraged Leases	127,699	112,473
Other Liabilities	14,000	—
Minority Interest	10,941	9,295
Preferred Stock, No Par Value, Authorized 6,000,000 Shares; Issued 1,709,402 Shares, Outstanding 1,701,822 Shares, Cumulative Series A ESOP Convertible Preferred Stock	$ 124,568	$ 125,000
Note Receivable from ESOP Trust	(25,000)	(125,000)
Unearned ESOP Compensation	(95,400)	—
Common Shareholders' Equity:		
Common stock, par value $1.66⅔, authorized 100,000,000 shares	49,601	49,409
Additional paid-in capital	130,401	120,211
Retained earnings	773,126	713,225
Cumulative translation adjustments	3,262	(8,788)
Treasury stock—at cost	(352,796)	(317,934)
Total Common Shareholders' Equity	603,594	556,123
Total Liabilities and Common Shareholders' Equity	$1,459,749	$1,372,585

S

1-11

Exhibit 2   Selected Pages from Square D's 1990 Annual Report

NOTES TO CONSOLIDATED FINANCIAL STATEMENTS

(Dollars in thousands, except per share)

A. Summary of Significant Accounting Policies

Principles of Consolidation
The financial statements include the accounts of the company and all majority-owned subsidiaries. Investments in unconsolidated affiliates are accounted for by the equity method. All significant intercompany accounts and transactions have been eliminated. The statements are based on years ended December 31, except for substantially all international subsidiaries whose fiscal years end November 30.

Cash and Short-Term Investments
Cash consists of cash in banks and time deposits. Short-term investments consist of a variety of highly liquid short-term instruments with purchased maturities of generally three months or less. Short-term investments are carried at cost, which approximates market.

Inventories
Inventories are stated at the lower of cost or market. Cost of inventories is determined using the last-in, first-out (LIFO) method for substantially all domestic inventories and certain international inventories. The first-in, first-out (FIFO) method is used for substantially all international inventories.

Property, Plant and Equipment
Depreciation of property, plant and equipment is provided on a straight-line basis over the estimated useful lives of the assets. Accelerated methods are used for income tax purposes.

Businesses Acquired
The excess of purchase price over net assets of businesses acquired is amortized on a straight-line basis over not more than forty years.

Income Taxes
Income taxes are accounted for in accordance with APB No. 11. The Financial Accounting Standards Board has issued Statement No. 96, which will change the accounting for income taxes; the company will adopt this statement no later than January 1, 1992.

Off-Balance Sheet Financial Instruments
The company enters into a variety of financial instruments in the management of its exposure to changes in interest rates and foreign currency rates. These instruments include interest rate swap agreements and foreign exchange contracts. These financial instruments do not represent a material off-balance sheet risk in relation to the financial statements.

Earnings per Common Share
Primary earnings per common share are determined by dividing the weighted average number of common shares outstanding during the year into net earnings after deducting

Exhibit 2   Selected Pages from Square D's 1990 Annual Report

after-tax dividends attributable to preferred shares. Common share equivalents in the form of stock options and convertible debt are excluded from the calculation since they do not have a material dilutive effect on per share figures. Fully diluted earnings per share reflect the conversion of all convertible preferred stock and common stock equivalents into common stock.

Reclassifications
Certain amounts in the 1989 and 1988 financial statements have been reclassified to conform to the current year's financial statement presentation.

B. Discontinued Operations

As of June 30, 1990, the company reported its General Semiconductor Industries (GSI) business as a discontinued operation, and as of September 30, 1989, the company reported its Yates Industries (Yates) copper foil business as a discontinued operation. Accordingly, the consolidated financial statements of the company have been reclassified to report separately the net assets and operating results of these discontinued operations. Financial results for periods prior to the dates of discontinuance have been restated to reflect continuing operations.

In January 1990, the company concluded the sale of its Yates operations in Europe and its 50 percent joint venture interest in Japan. In April 1990, the company completed the sale of its Yates operation in Bordentown, N.J. Total gross proceeds from the sale of all Yates operations were $175,476. The proceeds from the sale of Yates operations and the associated costs approximated management's original estimates. Management is actively pursuing the sale of the GSI business.

A gain from the sale of Yates, offset by provisions for a loss on the prospective sale of GSI and costs associated with other previously discontinued businesses, resulted in a gain of $4,391, net of income taxes, in the second quarter of 1990 from discontinued operations. The gain on the sale of Yates is net of a $14,000 provision for long-term environmental costs. The gain from the sale of Yates' foreign locations included a gain of $6,895 from the recognition of cumulative translation adjustments.

Net assets of discontinued operations were $36,681 and $170,065 at December 31, 1990 and 1989, respectively. These amounts consist of current assets; property, plant and equipment; other noncurrent assets; and current and concurrent liabilities.

Sales applicable to the discontinued operations prior to the dates of discontinuance were $16,158, $124,121 and $159,000 in 1990, 1989 and 1988, respectively. Interest expense of $249, $2,730 and $2,246, net of income taxes, was allocated to the discontinued operations prior to dates of discontinuance based on net assets for 1990, 1989 and 1988, respectively. The operating results of GSI from the date of discontinuance to December 31, 1990 were immaterial.

C. Restructuring Charge

In 1989, a restructuring charge of $17,511 net of taxes, or $.71 per share, was incurred by the company as a part of a plan to rationalize and improve profitability of several

Exhibit 2   Selected Pages from Square D's 1990 Annual Report

businesses and product lines both in the United States and abroad. The charge is principally comprised of costs associated with product, facility and organizational rationalization of the electrical distribution segment; product rationalization of the industrial control segment; plant consolidation and organizational restructuring in Canada; reorganization in Europe; and marketing restructuring.

D. Acquisitions

In 1989, the company acquired Crisp Automation, Inc. of Dublin, Ohio. Crisp Automation is a designer of process controls and factory automation systems and operates as part of the Square D Automation Products business. Also in 1989, the company acquired Electrical Specialty Products (ESP) of Montevallo, Alabama. ESP is a manufacturer of electrical connectors and operates as part of the Square D Connectors business. These acquisitions were accounted for as purchases; their sales and net earnings for the periods prior to the dates of acquisition were not material.

G. Inventories

Inventories valued by the last-in, first-out (LIFO) method aggregated $83,941 and $65,017 at December 31, 1990 and 1989, respectively. If the first-in, first-out (FIFO) method had been used, inventories would have been $138,120 and $140,076 higher than reported in the accompanying consolidated balance sheets at December 31, 1990 and 1989, respectively.

Inventories are maintained by element of cost; therefore, it is not practical to determine major classes such as finished goods, work in process and raw materials.

H. Lease Commitments

The company rents various warehouse and office facilities and certain equipment, principally computers and vehicles, under lease arrangements classified as operating leases.

Future minimum rental payments under noncancelable operating leases with initial terms of one year or more as of December 31, 1990 are:

1991	$10,160
1992	7,266
1993	5,520
1994	4,473
1995	975
Remainder	1,224
Total	$29,618

Exhibit 2   Selected Pages from Square D's 1990 Annual Report

J. Debt

Long-term debt consists of:

	1990	1989
ESOP Notes, 7.7%, due on various dates to 2004	$120,400	$ —
Senior Notes, 10.0%, due 1995	75,000	75,000
Industrial Revenue Bonds, 5.6% to 8.8%, due on various dates to 2004	25,715	26,610
First Mortgage Notes, 9.0% to 9.2%, due on various dates to 2009	10,825	11,119
Subordinated Convertible Notes, 9.0%, due 1992 (net of unamortized discount at 13.0%: 1990—$220, 1989—$376)	2,787	4,096
Payable to banks; average rate 1990—13.8%, 1989—10.3%; due on various dates to 1996	1,114	2,423
Other debt: average rate 1990—14.4%, 1989—12.7%; due on various dates to 2000	24,046	14,346
Subtotal	259,887	133,594
Less current maturities	15,067	10,174
Total	$244,820	$123,420

The aggregate annual maturities of long-term debt for the years 1991 through 1995 are $15,067, $14,642, $14,968, $13,877 and $82,187, respectively.

The Employee Stock Ownership Plan (ESOP) Notes include $25,000 of direct borrowings by the company, the proceeds from which have been advanced in the form of a loan to the company's ESOP. Direct borrowings of the ESOP, aggregating $95,400 as of December 31, 1990, have been guaranteed by the company and accordingly, are reported as long-term debt of the company. See Note Q for further discussion.

Industrial Revenue Bonds of $9,115 and the First Mortgage Notes are secured by the property and equipment acquired with the proceeds of the financings.

The Subordinated Convertible Notes are convertible at a rate of 28.57 shares for each one thousand dollars of principal. The company has reserved 85,934 shares of common stock for the conversion.

The company has entered into revolving credit agreements in which twelve of its principal banks participate. The agreements provide for up to $180,000 of revolving credit through 1994. The credit is available in both the domestic and euro markets.

Short-term debt includes bank borrowings of $33,611 and $19,438 and commercial paper of $70,260 and $214,292 at December 31, 1990 and 1989, respectively. Additionally, short-term debt includes a master note agreement of $20,000 and $30,000 at December 31, 1990 and 1989, respectively.

The company has additional unused short-term lines of credit which aggregated $69,501 at December 31, 1990.

Exhibit 2   Selected Pages from Square D's 1990 Annual Report

K. Income Taxes

Pre-tax income from continuing operations is as follows:

	1990	1989	1988
United States	$163,674	$142,855	$155,453
International	20,745	18,107	18,939
Total	$184,419	$160,962	$174.392

Income tax provisions for continuing operations are as follows:

	1990	1989	1988
Current:			
U.S. Federal	$ 33,452	$ 46,784	$ 35,261
International	7,999	4,752	3,989
State	9,037	9,902	6,625
	50,488	61,438	45,875
Deferred:			
U.S. Federal	17,189	(1,375)	17,475
International	(869)	1,479	228
State	965	(1,686)	(268)
	17,285	(1,582)	17,435
Total	$ 67,773	$ 59,856	$ 63,310

The components of the deferred income tax provision are as follows:

	1990	1989	1988
Leasing subsidiary income	$ 17,077	$ 22,502	$ 25,256
401(k) contributions	4,383	—	—
State tax	965	(1,686)	(268)
Tax over book depreciation	2,535	1,301	751
Deferred taxable income on installment sales	—	(13,006)	(5,615)
Alternative minimum tax	—	8,484	1,634
Funding of group health insurance trust	—	(6,863)	(11,634)
Restructuring charge	—	(4,510)	—
Other	(7,675)	(7,804)	7,311
Deferred Income Tax Expense (Benefit)	$ 17,285	$ (1,582)	$ 17,435

Exhibit 2   Selected Pages from Square D's 1990 Annual Report

A reconciliation between the statutory and effective tax rates for continuing operations is as follows:

	1990	1989	1988
U.S. Federal statutory rate	34.0%	34.0%	34.0%
State income taxes, net of Federal benefit	3.6	3.4	2.4
Rate reduction	—	—	(2.5)
U.S. tax on international dividend	0.4	0.3	4.2
International rate differential	0.1	(0.9)	(2.6)
Leasing subsidiary	(0.1)	(0.2)	(0.8)
Restructuring charge	—	0.6	—
Other	(1.3)	—	1.6
Effective tax rate	36.7%	37.2%	36.3%

No provisions have been made for possible international withholding and U.S. income taxes payable on the distribution of approximately $120,009 of undistributed earnings which have been or will be reinvested abroad or are expected to be returned to the United States in tax-free distributions. Provisions for taxes have been made for all earnings which the company presently plans to repatriate.

L. Supplementary Earnings Statement Information

	1990	1989	1988
Non-Operating Income:			
Interest income	$25,501	$14,497	$9,666
Settlement of lawsuit	5,695	—	—
Income from leveraged leases	5,273	6,694	8,219
Gain (loss) on sale of property, plant and equipment	1,005	(1,933)	(673)
Other non-operating (expense) income	(2,734)	(2,152)	43
Total	$34,740	$17,106	$17,255
Research and Development	$55,384	$44,720	$46,533
Maintenance and Repairs	47,328	49,572	47,131
Advertising	26,584	25,933	19,586
Rents	22,857	23,238	19,958
Foreign Currency Transaction (Loss) Gain	(1,423)	292	2,343

O. Pension Plans

The company's domestic operations maintain several pension plans, primarily defined benefit pension plans covering substantially all employees for normal retirement benefits at age 65. Defined benefits for salaried employees are based on a final average com-

Exhibit 2   Selected Pages from Square D's 1990 Annual Report

pensation formula and hourly plans are based on an amount per year of service formula. The company makes annual contributions to the plans in accordance with ERISA and IRS regulations, including amortization of past service cost over the average remaining service life of active employees.

In 1989 the company adopted SFAS No. 87 for its significant international pension plans. For the company's international pension plans that have not adopted SFAS No. 87, the excess of vested benefits over fund assets is insignificant. The company makes annual contributions to the plans in accordance with the laws and regulations of the respective international taxing jurisdictions in which the company operates.

Components of net periodic pension cost for the company's domestic and international pension plans consist of the following:

	1990	1989	1988
Service cost—benefits earned during period	$12,409	$11,039	$9,515
Net deferral and amortization	(42,253)	24,976	(11,621)
Interest on projected benefit obligation	28,547	25,796	25,414
Actual return on plan assets	10,809	(55,795)	(14,388)
Net periodic pension cost	$ 9,512	$ 6,016	$ 8,920

The net periodic pension cost attributable to the company's significant international pension plans was $843 and $1,000 in 1990 and 1989, respectively.

The following tables set forth the company's domestic and international pension plans' funded status and amounts recognized in the company's balance sheet at December 31:

	Overfunded Plans		Underfunded Plans	
	1990	1989	1990	1989
Actuarial present value of benefit obligations:				
Vested employees	$(193,615)	$(194,793)	$(96,325)	$(90,466)
Non-vested employees	(12,169)	(6,073)	(15,407)	(3,251)
Total accumulated benefit obligation	(205,784)	(200,866)	(111,732)	(93,717)
Additional amounts related to projected salary increases	(35,705)	(45,637)	(3,949)	(3,095)
Projected benefit obligation	(241,489)	(246,503)	(115,681)	(96,812)
Fair value of plan assets (primarily common equities and fixed income instruments)	245,953	267,184	75,493	68,884
Projected benefit obligation less than (in excess of) plan assets	4,464	20,681	(40,188)	(27,928)
Unrecognized net (gain) loss	(7,583)	(15,018)	9,451	8,442
Unrecognized prior service cost	(6,374)	(6,934)	17,281	4,673
Unrecognized net liability existing at the date of initial adoption of SFAS No. 87	6,604	1,682	1,378	4,569
(Accrued) Prepaid Pension Cost	$ (2,889)	$ 411	$(12,078)	$(10,244)

Exhibit 2   Selected Pages from Square D's 1990 Annual Report

The economic assumptions used in determining the actuarial present value of the projected benefit obligation of the domestic plans were:

	1990	1989
Weighted average discount rate	9.0%	8.3%
Rate of increase in future compensation levels	5.3	5.3
Rate of return on plan assets	10.0	10.0

The assumed rates for the company's international plans, which reflect the economic conditions of each plan, generally varied from U.S. rates by 1.0 percent to 2.0 percent.

Total pension expense for all plans was $10,914, $8,073 and $12,962 for 1990, 1989 and 1988, respectively. Actuarial assumptions were revised in 1990, 1989 and 1988 principally to update the investment return and rates of pay increase to levels more reflective of current economic conditions. These and other changes increased pension expense in 1990 by approximately $920 and reduced pension expense in 1989 and 1988 by approximately $5,838 and $1,218, respectively.

P. Post-Retirement Benefits

The company provides health plan coverage and life insurance benefits for retired employees of substantially all of its domestic operations. Substantially all of the company's employees may become eligible for these benefits when they retire from active employment with the company. The cost of retiree health coverage is recognized as an expense when claims are paid. The cost of life insurance benefits is recognized as an expense as premiums are paid. These costs totaled $6,165 in 1990, $5,075 in 1989 and $3,982 in 1988.

The Financial Accounting Standards Board has issued Statement of Financial Accounting Standards No. 106, "Employers' Accounting for Post-Retirement Benefits Other Than Pensions." This Statement will require accrual of post-retirement benefits during the years an employee provides services. While the impact of this new standard has not been fully determined, the change will result in significantly greater expense being recognized for these benefits. The company plans to adopt this Statement in 1993.

T. Segment and Geographic Information

The company is engaged in the manufacture and sale of electrical distribution products, systems and services and industrial control products, systems and services, and operates in virtually every major marketing area in the world. Major manufacturing plants are located throughout the United States and in Europe, Latin America, Canada, Australia and Thailand.

The electrical distribution segment primarily consists of the manufacture and sale of products, systems and services used in the distribution of electricity. Distribution equipment is used principally in distributing electricity from the end of transmission lines to points of utilization within residential, commercial, industrial or other types of buildings. Distribution products include industrial molded case circuit breakers, miniature circuit breakers, load centers, safety switches, metering devices, switchboards, panelboards, motor control centers, low and medium voltage switchgear, busways and raceways, dry type transformers and power and cast resin transformers.

Exhibit 2   Selected Pages from Square D's 1990 Annual Report

The industrial control segment mainly consists of the manufacture and sale of control products, systems and services that control the electricity used in the operation of power utilization devices or processes. Control equipment includes motor starters, contactors, push buttons, adjustable frequency motor controllers and sensors. Other products in this segment include programmable controllers, cell controllers, electronic computerized control and data-gathering systems, uninterruptible power systems, power protection equipment, infrared radiation thermometers and pyrometers and snap dome switches and keyboards.

Substantially all products of the electrical distribution and industrial control segments are marketed through the company's own marketing organization and distributed through a system of strategically located warehouses. The majority of all sales are made directly to authorized electrical distributors who, in turn, market the products to electrical contractors, electrical utilities, large industrial plants and other classes of trade.

Sales between geographic areas and industry segments are based on prices approximating current market values. Net sales to a group of customers under common control, for both industry segments, were $161,015 in 1990, $161,156 in 1989 and $176,700 in 1988.

Financial information by industry segment for the three years ended December 31, 1990 is summarized as follows:

Industry Segments	1990	1989	1988
Sales			
Electrical Distribution:			
Unaffiliated customers	$1,170,420	$1,117,619	$1,057,359
Intercompany	18,203	13,083	10,484
	1,188,623	1,130,702	1,067,843
Industrial Control:			
Unaffiliated customers	482,899	481,069	440,413
Intercompany	63,919	51,923	49,244
	546,818	532,992	489,657
Eliminations	(82,122)	(65,006)	(59,728)
Consolidated	$1,653,319	$1,598,688	$1,497,772
Operating Earnings			
Electrical Distribution	$ 152,280	$ 143,541	$ 138,229
Industrial Control	26,302	31,614	40,046
Eliminations	(143)	139	944
Consolidated	$ 178,439	$ 175,294	$ 179,219
Identifiable Assets			
Electrical Distribution	$ 920,781	$ 755,253	$ 701,973
Industrial Control	503,079	447,913	418,247
Eliminations	(792)	(646)	(835)
Identifiable Assets of Continuing Operations	$1,423,068	$1,202,520	$1,119,385
Net Assets of Discontinued Operations	36,681	170,065	181,338
Consolidated	$1,459,749	$1,372,585	$1,300,723

Exhibit 2   Selected Pages from Square D's 1990 Annual Report

Industry Segments	1990	1989	1988
Depreciation and Amortization Expense			
Electrical Distribution	$ 36,688	$ 29,815	$ 26,345
Industrial Control	22,612	19,628	18,829
Capital Additions			
Electrical Distribution	$ 54,763	$ 50,323	$ 43,980
Industrial Control	39,125	30,125	27,975

Effective September 30, 1989, the company changed its reportable segments from Electrical Equipment and Electronic Products to Electrical Distribution Products, Systems and Services and Industrial Control Products, Systems and Services.

Financial information by geographic area for the three years ended December 31, 1990 is summarized as follows:

Geographic Areas	1990	1989	1988
Sales			
United States:			
Unaffiliated customers	$1,332,390	$1,321,769	$1,256,009
Intercompany	73,646	62,253	47,479
	1,406,036	1,384,022	1,303,488
Europe:			
Unaffiliated customers	138,836	115,678	105,471
Intercompany	22,617	23,691	25,207
	161,453	139,369	130,678
Latin America:			
Unaffiliated customers	78,867	68,178	53,242
Intercompany	1,300	1,217	1,761
	80,167	69,395	55,003
Other International			
Unaffiliated customers	103,226	93,063	83,050
Intercompany	447	256	620
	103,673	93,319	83,670
Eliminations	(98,010)	(87,417)	(75,067)
Consolidated	$1,653,319	$1,598,688	$1,497,772
Operating Earnings			
United States	$ 164,155	$ 163,202	$ 156,791
Europe	3,555	212	4,098
Latin America	10,445	12,547	11,212
Other International	650	(463)	3,942
Eliminations	(366)	(204)	3,176
Consolidated	$ 178,439	$ 175,294	$ 179,219

(continued)

Exhibit 2   Selected Pages from Square D's 1990 Annual Report

Geographic Areas (continued)	1990	1989	1988
Identifiable Assets			
United States	$1,131,085	$ 952,865	$ 883,334
Europe	158,637	120,483	109,297
Latin America	65,847	62,171	62,924
Other International	70,203	69,357	64,886
Eliminations	(2,704)	(2,356)	(1,056)
Identifiable Assets of Continuing Operations	1,423,068	1,202,520	1,119,385
Net Assets of Discontinued Operations	36,681	170,065	181,338
Consolidated	$1,459,749	$1,372,585	$1,300,723

Exhibit 2   Selected Pages from Square D's 1990 Annual Report

SELECTED FINANCIAL DATA

	1990	1989	1988	1987	1986	1985
Summary of Operations						
Net sales	$1,653,319	$1,598,688	$1,497,772	$1,330,784	$1,274,932	$1,223,193
Cost of products sold	1,088,977	1,027,348	979,591	838,749	820,457	787,310
Selling, administrative and general expenses	385,903	369,726	338,962	287,386	267,066	237,790
Restructuring charge	—	26,320	—	11,192	—	—
Non-operating income	34,740	17,106	17,255	17,590	26,670	14,486
Interest expense	28,760	31,438	22,082	19,699	24,977	21,191
Earnings from continuing operations before income taxes	184,419	160,962	174,392	191,348	189,102	191,388
Provision for income taxes	67,773	59,856	63,310	75,736	85,191	89,465
Earnings from continuing operations	116,646	101,106	111,082	115,612	103,911	101,923
Earnings (loss) from discontinued operations, net of income taxes	4,079	798	7,852	(5,611)	(4,983)	(14,735)
Net earnings	120,725	101,904	118,934	110,001	98,928	87,188
Financial Information						
Working capital	$ 389,503	$ 193,758	$ 178,399	$ 192,693	$ 204,083	$ 202,076
Property, plant and equipment—at cost	799,367	736,739	673,946	630,754	606,757	570,538
Total assets	1,459,749	1,372,585	1,300,723	1,252,819	1,178,826	1,118,473
Long-term debt	244,820	123,420	135,467	141,085	166,389	201,028
Common shareholders' equity	603,594	556,123	636,029	679,711	670,789	606,139
Capital additions	93,888	80,448	71,955	35,356	71,617	61,880
Depreciation and amortization	59,300	49,443	45,174	42,277	38,548	32,430
Share Data						
Earnings per common share:						
Primary:						
Continuing operations	$4.76	$3.95	$4.15	$4.01	$3.59	$3.53
Discontinued operations	.18	.03	.29	(.19)	(.17)	(.51)
Net earnings	4.94	3,98	4.44	3.82	3.42	3.02
Fully diluted:						
Continuing operations	4.57	3.88	4.13	3.98	3.56	3.50
Discontinued operations	.16	.03	.29	(.19)	(.17)	(.50)
Net earnings	4.73	3.91	4.42	3.79	3.39	3.00
Cash dividends declared per common share	2.20	2.00	1.94	1.86	1.84	1.84
Common shares outstanding at December 31	22,886	23,489	25,691	27,660	28,966	28,864
Common shareholders' equity per share	$26.37	$23.68	$24.76	$24.57	$23.16	$21.00

S

(continued)

Exhibit 2   Selected Pages from Square D's 1990 Annual Report

SELECTED FINANCIAL DATA (continued)

	1990	1989	1988	1987	1986	1985
Key Financial Relationships						
Gross profit	34.1%	35.7%	34.6%	37.0%	35.6%	35.6%
Current ratio	2.0:1	1.4:1	1.5:1	1.7:1	1.9:1	1.8:1
Average total debt to average total equity	66.2%	55.7%	38.2%	29.0%	39.2%	40.5%
Average long-term debt to average capital	23.3%	13.6%	15.6%	16.7%	22.0%	19.8%

All financial data for the periods prior to 1990 have been restated for discontinued operations.
All financial data for the periods prior to 1988 have been restated for the consolidation of a majority-owned subsidiary.

Exhibit 3   Schneider Financial Statements and Accounting Policies

EXHIBIT 3

Schneider Financial Statements and Accounting Policies

STATEMENT OF INCOME

(in FF million for the year ended December 31)	1990	1989	1988
Net sales	**49,884**	**45,127**	**40,493**
Cost of goods sold, personnel and administrative expenses	(44,978)	(41,008)	(36,766)
Depreciation and amortization	(1,565)	(1,166)	(1,272)
Operating expenses	**(46,543)**	**(42,174)**	**(38,038)**
Operating income	**3,341**	**2,953**	**2,455**
Interest expense – net	(832)	(757)	(182)
Income before non-recurring items, amortization of goodwill, taxes and minority interest	**2,509**	**2,196**	**2,273**
Non-recurring items:			
Gains on disposition of assets – net	419	550	484
Other non-recurring income and expense – net	(367)	(343)	(642)
Income before taxes, employee profit-sharing, amortization of goodwill and minority interests	**2,561**	**2,403**	**2,115**
Employee profit-sharing	(158)	(130)	(126)
Income taxes	(802)	(912)	(701)
Net income of fully consolidated companies before amortization of goodwill	**1,601**	**1,361**	**1,288**
Amortization of goodwill	(236)	(235)	(345)
Net income of fully consolidated companies	**1,365**	**1,126**	**943**
Group's share of income of companies accounted for by the equity method	**4**	**17**	**(53)**
Minority interests	(445)	(266)	(330)
Net income (Schneider SA share)	**924**	**877**	**560**
Net income (Schneider SA share) per share – in FF	62.96	63.06	48.85
Net income (Schneider SA share) per share after dilution – in FF	61.65	60.53	N/A

Exhibit 3   Schneider Financial Statements and Accounting Policies

BALANCE SHEET

(in FF million for the year ended December 31)	1990	1989	1988
ASSETS			
Current Assets			
Cash and equivalents	1,841.3	3,400.3	1,579.6
Marketable securities	3,020.9	1,924.3	1,243.7
Accounts receivable – trade	14,597.4	14,987.3	13,998.5
Other receivables and prepaid expenses	4,738.1	3,876.5	4,054.9
Deferred taxes	407.5	290.2	236.9
Inventories and work in process	7,712.6	7,159.0	29,715.3
Total current assets	**32,317.8**	**31,637.6**	**50,828.9**
Non-Current Assets			
Property, plant and equipment	14,293.9	13,107.5	12,019.7
Accumulated depreciation	(6,691.5)	(6,365.6)	(6,409.5)
Property, plant and equipment – net	7,602.4	6,741.9	5,610.2
Investments accounted for by the equity method	175.9	135.7	244.9
Other equity investments	1,727.9	571.3	684.6
Other investments	573.0	618.3	909.8
Total investments	2,476.8	1,325.3	1,839.3
Intangible assets – net	147.5	153.5	115.0
Goodwill – net	7,032.8	6,087.8	5,596.8
Total non-current assets	**17,259.5**	**14,308.5**	**13,161.3**
Total assets	**49,577.3**	**45,946.1**	**63,990.2**
LIABILITIES AND SHAREHOLDERS' EQUITY			
Current Liabilities			
Accounts payable – trade	9,867.9	9,614.6	8,440.8
Taxes and benefits payable	4,822.5	4,795.8	3,748.4
Other payables and accrued liabilities	5,230.4	4,332.2	3,405.5
Short-term debt	3,120.5	3,165.8	3,081.3
Customer prepayments	2,509.5	3,848.3	27,606.1
Total current liabilities	**25,547.2**	**25,756.7**	**46,282.1**
Long-term debt	9,958.4	7,345.9	7,712.1
of which: convertible bonds	3,950.2	1,108.8	500.5
Provisions for contingencies	3,942.6	3,890.0	3,758.8
Invested Capital	**24,030.1**	**20,189.4**	**17,708.1**
Capital stock	1,414.4	1,397.2	1,146.3
Retained earnings	6,091.1	5,344.6	3,046.6
Shareholders' Equity	**7,505.5**	**6,741.8**	**4,192.9**
Minority interests	2,623.6	2,211.7	2,044.3
Total shareholders' equity and minority interests	**10,129.1**	**8,953.5**	**6,237.2**
Total liabilities and shareholders' equity	**49,577.3**	**45,946.1**	**63,990.2**

Exhibit 3   Schneider Financial Statements and Accounting Policies

STATEMENT OF CASH FLOWS

(in FF million for the year ended December 31)	1990	1989
I. Operating activities		
Net income of fully consolidated companies	1,368.5	1,143.7
Depreciation, amortization and provisions, net of recoveries	2,164.0	2,283.0
(Gains) on disposals of assets	(418.7)	(550.1)
Others	(0.8)	(28.7)
Net cash provided by operating activities before changes in operating assets and liabilities	**3,113.0**	**2,847.9**
Decrease (increase) in accounts receivable	(944.4)	1,170.4
Inventories and work in process	675.4	(1,708.6)
Increase (decrease) in accounts payable	578.7	(16.3)
Other current assets and liabilities	(1,681.4)	736.0
Net change in operating assets and liabilities	**(1,371.7)**	**181.5**
Net cash provided by operating activities	**1,741.3**	**3,029.4**
II. Investing activities		
Disposals of fixed assets	712.9	1,394.8
Purchases of property, plant and equipment and intangible assets	(2,589.5)	(2,154.3)
Financial investments	(2,788.2)	(1,068.8)
Other long-term investments	125.5	13.4
Net cash used in investing activities	**(4,539.3)**	**(1,814.9)**
III. Financing activities		
Reduction in long-term debt	(1,626.4)	(3,045.2)
New borrowings	1,508.7	2,435.1
Convertible bonds issued	2,655.6	634.7
Common stock issued	71.9	1,877.0
Dividends paid:		
Schneider SA shareholders	(174.6)	(126.1)
Minority interests	(116.5)	(69.7)
Net cash provided by financing activities	**2,318.7**	**1,705.8**
IV. Net effect of exchange rate and other changes	**13.8**	**178.5**
Net increase (decrease) in cash and cash equivalents (I + II + III + IV)	**(465.5)**	**3,098.8**
Cash and cash equivalents at beginning of year	**3,424.9**	**326.1**
at end of year	**2,959.4**	**3,424.9**

The following notes are an integral part of these financial statements.

Exhibit 3   Schneider Financial Statements and Accounting Policies

SELECTED NOTES TO FINANCIAL STATEMENTS

1. ACCOUNTING PRINCIPLES

The consolidated financial statements of Schneider SA have been prepared in accordance with French generally accepted accounting principles and with the international accounting principles recommended by the International Accounting Standards Committee (I.A.S.C.). The differences between these principles and U.S. GAAP are explained in Note I.m), below.

The financial statements of consolidated subsidiaries, which are prepared in accordance with accounting principles generally accepted in the countries in which they operate, have been restated in accordance with the principles applied by the Group.

a) Consolidation principles

All significant companies that are controlled directly or indirectly by Schneider SA have been fully consolidated.

Companies over which Schneider SA exercises significant influence have been accounted for by the equity method.

As an exception to the above principles, Banque Morhange, in which the Group holds a majority interest but whose operations are not material in relation to the Group as a whole, has also been consolidated by the equity method.

In accordance with French generally accepted accounting principles, joint ventures in which the Group is the managing partner are fully consolidated by Schneider SA, after deducting the other partners' share in the income or loss of the joint venture. In cases where the Group is not the managing shareholder, only Schneider SA's share of the income or loss is accounted for, except for two contracts which are consolidated by the proportional method.

Goodwill is amortized out of income over a maximum of forty years based on estimated useful life.

b) Translation of the financial statements of foreign subsidiaries

The financial statements of foreign subsidiaries are translated into French francs as follows:
– Assets and liabilities are translated at year-end exchange rates;
– Income statement and cash flow items are translated at average exchange rates.

Differences arising on translation are recorded under shareholders' equity.

c) Translation of foreign currency transactions

With the exception of the transactions described below, foreign currency debts and receivables are translated into French francs at year-end exchange rates. As allowed under French law, translation differences are recorded in the income statement under interest income and expense.

Exchange gains as well as carrybacks and carryforwards related to forward purchases and sales of foreign currency used to hedge the Group's trading commitments are deferred and recognized at the same time as the gain or loss on the underlying transaction.

Gains and losses on unhedged forward currency transactions are credited or charged to income. The gain or loss corresponds to the difference between the forward exchange rate provided for in the contract and the exchange rate prevailing at year end for purchases and sales made in the same currency and according to the same term.

In cases where a speculative currency position is considered to exist due to the future interest on fixed to variable currency swaps, the interest is discounted on the basis of the fixed rate and stated at the exchange rate prevailing at year end for cash transactions. The translation difference is credited or charged to income.

d) Financial instruments based on exchange and interest rates

The Group uses financial instruments based on exchange and interest rates. The methods used to account for these instruments are described above.

Exhibit 3   Schneider Financial Statements and Accounting Policies

e) Long-term contracts

Income from long-term contracts is recognized by the percentage-of-completion method, based on the financial status of the contract. Probable losses upon completion of a given contract are provided for in full as soon as they become known. The cost of work in process includes costs relating directly to the contracts and a percentage of overheads.

The estimated cost of the remaining work on contracts expected to generate a loss does not take account of any income from claims, except where such claims have been accepted by the customer and the latter has no major financing problems. Contracts in progress are therefore stated at the lower of cost or realizable value.

In accordance with the logic underlying the percentage-of-completion method, work in process is matched with customer prepayments received upon presentation of a schedule of work performed to date. However, prepayments in connection with the work in process include:

- Prepayments to finance production;
- Prepayments for work in process on contracts which are still in the early stages and for which it is not possible to make any estimate of probable income or losses; and
- Contracts scheduled to last less than twelve months.

f) Research and development expenditures

Internally-financed research and development expenditures are charged to income for the period.

g) Deferred taxes

Deferred taxes corresponding to timing differences between the recognition of income and expenses in the consolidated financial statements and for tax purposes are accounted for by the liability method.

h) Provisions for retirement bonuses

The Group's liability for retirement bonuses is calculated taking into account projected future compensation levels. The method used is in accordance with the Financial Accounting Standards Board (FASB) Statement of Financial Accounting Standards No. 87.

Part of the Group's liability for retirement bonuses is provided for and part is funded by an insured plan. The provisions are calculated for all eligible employees and the same discount and indexation rates are used for all Group companies that have adopted this method. For the insured plan, the current value of the plan assets has been calculated and provision has been made for any unfunded liability.

i) Marketable securities

Almost all marketable securities represent conventional short-term instruments (commercial paper, mutual funds and related securities). They are stated at cost. In the case of bonds and other debt instruments, cost includes accrued interest.

j) Inventories and work in process

Inventories and work in process are stated at weighted average cost. Any difference between cost and realizable value is provided for.

The cost of work in process, semi-finished and finished products includes direct materials and labor costs, sub-contracting costs incurred up to the balance sheet date and a percentage of production overheads

k) Property, plant and equipment

Land, buildings and equipment are stated at cost. Assets held at the time of a legal revaluation are stated at revalued cost. An equivalent amount is recorded in shareholders' equity, under retained earnings or revaluation reserve, and is written back to income in an amount matching the corresponding depreciation and disposals, so that the revaluation has no impact on income.

In the case of subsidiaries operating in high-inflation countries, the impact of legal revaluations is eliminated on consolidation and the resulting translation differences are recorded in retained earnings.

S

1-29

Exhibit 3   Schneider Financial Statements and Accounting Policies

Property, plant and equipment is depreciated on a straight-line basis over the estimated useful lives of the assets.

Property, plant and equipment acquired under a capital lease is capitalized on the basis of the cost of the asset concerned and depreciated in accordance with the above principles. An obligation in the same amount is recorded on the liabilities side of the balance sheet.

l) Non-consolidated equity investments and other investments

Non-consolidated equity investments and other investments are stated at cost, except for investments held at the time of the 1977 legal revaluation. Each year, the carrying value is compared to fair value and any difference is provided for. Fair value is determined by reference to the Group's share in the underlying net assets, the expected future profitability and business prospects of the investee company, and – in the case of listed securities – the market value of the stock.

m) Differences between Schneider SA accounting principles and U.S. GAAP

The main differences between the accounting principles described above and U.S. GAAP are as follows:

Write-ups

As mentioned in Note l.k. above, the Company has performed certain write-ups which are contrary to U.S. GAAP. The write-ups have no impact on income but do affect shareholders' equity.

Consolidation

As indicated in Note a, Banque Morhange, whose operations are not material in relation to the Group as a whole, has been accounted for by the equity method.

Provisions for contingencies

In U.S. GAAP, the part of these provisions related to operating cycles would be considered as accrued liabilities.

Customer prepayments

In the consolidated financial statements, customer prepayments are recorded as a separate component of current liabilities. Under U.S. GAAP, work in process in an amount equal to the cost of the work performed for which no income or loss has been recognized.

Deferred taxes

In December 1987, the FASB issued a new standard concerning the accounting treatment of deferred taxes. The application of this standard is not compulsory in 1990. The Company has not yet decided the date at which it will start applying this standard and, in view of the complexity of the new rules, has not determined the impact that its application would have had on the 1990 financial statements as presented.

Non-recurring income and expense

Non-recurring income and expense includes items that the Company considers to be non-recurring but that would be treated as operating income and expense under U.S. GAAP. In addition, under U.S. GAAP, the amortization of goodwill would have been accounted for under income from continuing operations.

These reclassifications would have the following impact on income from continuing operations:

(in FF million)	1990	1989
Income from continuing operations, before tax	2,509	2,196
Non-recurring income other than extraordinary items	(237)	85
Amortization of goodwill	(236)	(235)
Income from continuing operations, before tax, according to U.S. GAAP	2,036	2,046

EXHIBIT 4   Square D Common Stock Purchase Plan

EXHIBIT 4
Square D Common Stock Purchase Plan

The firm's Articles of Incorporation were modified in August 1988 as follows:

The Company adopted a new Share Purchase Rights Plan and declared a dividend distribution of one new common purchase right on each outstanding share of Square D common stock. The rights are exercisable only if someone acquires 20 percent or more of the company's common stock or announces a tender offer. At any time a person or group acquires 20 percent or more of the company's outstanding common stock and prior to that person acquiring 50 percent or more of the company's common stock, the company may exchange the rights (other than rights owned by such 20 percent or greater shareholder) in whole or in part for one share of common stock per right. If a person or group acquires 20 percent or more of the common stock, or certain events occur, each right not owned by the 20 percent or greater shareholder becomes exercisable for the number of shares of the company having a market value of twice the exercise price of the right. If the company is acquired in a merger or other business combination transaction or 50 percent or more of its assets or earning power are sold at any time after the rights become exercisable, the rights entitle a holder to buy a number of shares of common stock of the acquiring company having a market value of twice the exercise price of each right.

Exhibit 5   Selected Square D Stock Data for the Fourth Quarter 1990

EXHIBIT 5
Selected Square D Stock Data for the Fourth Quarter 1990[a]

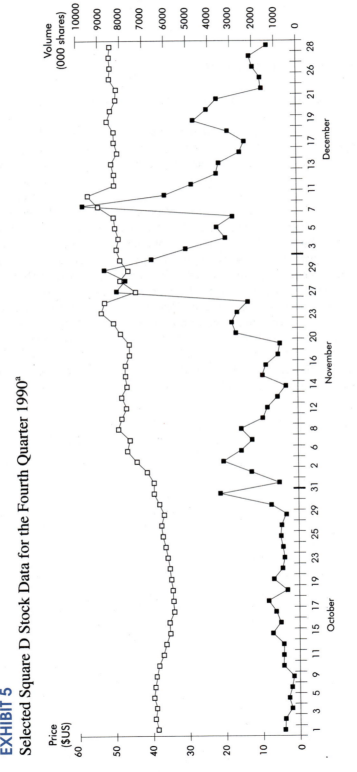

a. In late 1990, approximately 23 million shares were outstanding.

Exhibit 6   Valuation Data for Square D

EXHIBIT 6
Valuation Data for Square D

Square D equity beta	0.95
Moody's corporate bond average yield in February 1991 for major ratings:	
Aaa	8.83%
Aa	9.16%
A	9.38%
Ba	10.07%
Prime rate in February 1991	8.8%
Treasury bills rates in February 1991 (3 months)	6.0%
Government 30-year treasuries rates in February 1991	8.25%
Square D commercial paper rating in February 1991 (on a scale from P3 to P1, P1 being the best rating)	P1
Square D corporate bonds rating in February 1991	Aa3
US federal statutory tax rate in 1990	34.0%
State income tax rate, net of federal benefit in 1990	3.6%

p a r t 5

Compaq Computer Corporation

Compaq Computer Corporation is a world leader in the design, development, manufacturing and marketing of PC servers, desktop, portable and notebook personal computers, and network laser printers. 1992 Annual Report

1992 Annual Report and 10-K Excerpts Financial Highlights Letter to Stockholders Nature of Business Selected Consolidated Financial Data Management's Discussion and Analysis of Financial Condition and Results of Operations Report of Independent Accountants Consolidated Financial Statements Notes to Consolidated Financial Statements

Compaq Computer Corporation
Financial Highlights

	1992	1991	1990
	(in thousands, except per share amounts)		
Sales	$4,099,758	$3,271,367	$3,598,768
Gross margin	1,194,734	1,217,791	1,540,882
Net income	213,152	130,869	454,910
Earnings per common and common equivalent share:			
Primary	2.58	1.49	5.14
Assuming full dilution	2.52	1.49	5.12
Working capital	1,359,091	1,144,634	1,044,899
Total assets	3,142,393	2,826,386	2,717,529
Stockholders' equity	2,006,691	1,930,704	1,859,013

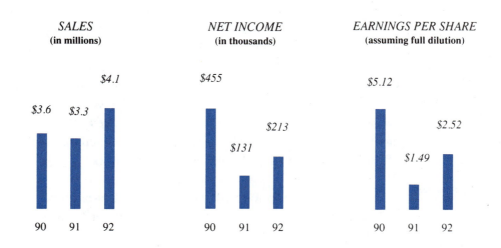

SALES (in millions)	NET INCOME (in thousands)	EARNINGS PER SHARE (assuming full dilution)

To Our Stockholders:

In 1992 Compaq entered a new era as a leader in the personal computer industry. As the year began, we saw an exciting opportunity to gain market share and improve Compaq's financial results by adopting aggressive new strategies. We developed a bold plan to introduce a broad range of high quality products from entry-level to high-end, to price our products competitively, to implement the best customer support program in the industry, and to expand our distribution channels. Then we challenged our worldwide organization to make it happen.

Our people responded. They achieved new economies and efficiencies with fewer resources. They introduced a record number of new Compaq products – more than 80 models from entry-level to high-end performance PCs, servers, and network printers. They built and shipped products in record volumes to meet overwhelming global demand. Their creativity, enthusiasm and hard work helped us maintain our equilibrium and expand our vision of the future. Compaq regained momentum, captured market share, and achieved substantial gains in sales and earnings.

In June Compaq staged one of the most dramatic product rollouts in the history of the industry when it introduced 16 new personal computers – 45 models in all. The introduction included our first low-cost desktop and notebook PCs designed to compete in the large, price-sensitive PC market. These were entirely Compaq-designed, engineered and tested to offer the levels of functionality, compatibility and reliability that users demand. Also included in June's launch were the world's highest performance desktop PC, the world's most advanced color notebook PC and two new families of technologically advanced, upgradable PCs offering impressive graphics and audio technologies.

In August we introduced two new network laser printers, the COMPAQ PAGEMARQ 20 and the COMPAQ PAGEMARQ 15, which offer innovative features and advanced networking functionality. Their output capabilities make them the fastest desktop printers available today. These products incorporate state-of-the-art technology for which Compaq has been granted a number of patents. In the first 30 days following their announcement, Compaq printers received 11 top industry awards.

In October Compaq solidified its leadership in PC servers by introducing the world's fastest PC server, the COMPAQ SYSTEMPRO/XL, which features high speed at an attractive price to make it a leader in its class. It offers exceptional performance and simplified server management for demanding database applications. The COMPAQ ProSignia, also introduced in October, combines high performance and low price for the best value in the market. It is dramatically less expensive than comparable competitive products, yet outperforms them significantly.

Throughout the year we made impressive additions to our distribution channels. Compaq products are now sold in 85 countries through a vast network of marketing partners that includes a variety of dealers, retailers, value-added resellers, distributors and systems integrators. The total number of outlets for Compaq products has more than doubled to 10,600 worldwide.

Each of our employees contributed to the year's many achievements, which also include:
- Strengthening service and support with more than a dozen new programs through CompaqCare, the PC industry's most comprehensive U.S. customer service and support program
- Extending the industry's first three-year warranty on PC products
- Shipping 1.5 million PCs worldwide
- Dramatically reducing costs and cutting overhead per unit by 63 percent
- Winning numerous prestigious product awards worldwide
- Maintaining product quality during rapid growth.

Our winning strategy and employees' hard work paid off. Compaq's market share of PC unit sales worldwide doubled to 7.2 percent. Revenue grew to $4.1 billion, a 25 percent increase from 1991. Net income was $213.2 million, an increase of 63 percent from 1991. Earnings per share grew 69 percent to $2.52 on a fully diluted basis.

Compaq's gains in market share and profitability affirm our plans for the 1990s. The results tell us that the strategy we put in place a year ago – to make Compaq the acknowledged leader in the PC industry and the standard of quality, innovation, performance, value, reliability and support – is succeeding.

1992 SYSTEMS TECHNOLOGY FIRSTS:

-NetFlex Controller

-TriFlex System Architecture

-Automatic Server Recovery

-INSIGHT Manager

1992 DISTRIBUTION % of Outlets

16% Retail *15% Value-Added Resellers/ Systems Integrators*

69% Dealers

COMPAQCARE 1992 ACCOMPLISHMENTS

-3-year warranty/on-site service

-Wide range of support providers

-Free hotline support seven days a week/24 hours a day

-Remote Diagnostic Utility with every PC product

-Wide range of self-help tools

-Self maintenance program

-Customer training

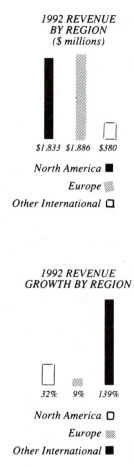

*1992 REVENUE
BY REGION
($ millions)*

$1,833 $1,886 $380

North America ■
Europe ▨
Other International ◻

*1992 REVENUE
GROWTH BY REGION*

32%   9%   139%

North America ◻
Europe ▨
Other International ■

Still, we have hard work ahead. The PC market experienced dramatic price declines in 1992, which are likely to continue in 1993. Additional pricing actions will put further pressure on gross profit margins. In order to maintain or increase profitability, we must control our costs and increase our unit sales substantially.

We are ready for the challenge. Compaq expects the PC market to sustain the enthusiasm that greeted our wave of new products in 1992. Our engineering and design teams plan additional leadership products in 1993, continuing our tradition of technological innovation in exciting new areas like multimedia and personal digital assistant products, as well as PCs using Intel's Pentium microprocessor. We will pursue component sourcing and manufacturing strategies that allow us to remain price competitive and enhance our share of the market. We will bring manufacturing output into line with demand and solve the backlog problems that confronted us in 1992. We know that the growth of our business requires close management of manufacturing utilization, inventory, receivables, and distribution channels.

Our goal is simple: We want to be the leading supplier of PCs and PC servers in all customer segments worldwide. We intend to accomplish that goal by leading the industry in developing new products, pricing competitively, controlling costs, supporting customers and expanding distribution. Compaq understands the dynamics of the industry and is poised to move decisively to exploit new opportunities. In the process, we will continue to raise the standards by which quality, performance, and customer support are measured in the industry.

Eckhard Pfeiffer
President and Chief Executive Officer
March 5, 1993

General

Compaq Computer Corporation, founded in 1982, designs, develops, manufactures, and markets personal computers, PC systems, printers, and related products. The Company operates in one principal industry segment across geographically diverse markets. As used herein, the term "Company" means Compaq Computer Corporation and its consolidated subsidiaries, unless the context indicates otherwise.

Strategy

In 1992 the Company implemented aggressive changes in its business strategy. These changes focused on increasing the Company's market share by expanding sales to new endusers while maintaining its existing customer base. The Company introduced broad-based new programs in pricing, product development, distribution and marketing, and service and support, while continuing to emphasize its traditional areas of strength--product quality and innovation. The Company believes its key to success is leveraging the Company's engineering talent, purchasing power, manufacturing capabilities, and distribution strengths to bring to market high-quality cost-competitive products with different features in different price ranges. This strategy will enable the Company to offer appropriate products to many types of customers.

Compaq Products

The Company's personal computer products consist of desktop personal computers, battery-powered notebook computers, and AC-powered portable computers. The Company also produces tower PC systems that store and manage data in network environments and high performance laser printers designed for network environments. The Company's products are available with a broad variety of functions and features designed to accommodate a wide range of user needs.

In 1992 sales of desktop, notebook, and portable personal computers with accompanying options accounted for almost 90% of the Company's revenue with more than half of its revenue stemming from desktop personal computers and options for desktop computers. In June the Company introduced 16 new personal computers--45 models in all, including the Company's first low-cost desktop and notebook PCs, the world's highest performance desktop PC, and the Company's first color notebook PC as well as two new families of advanced and upgradable PCs offering graphic and audio technologies. The Company's leading unit seller in 1992 was the COMPAQ ProLinea 3/25s Personal Computer, introduced in June. The Company's most popular notebook product in 1992 was the COMPAQ LTE Lite 25 notebook computer, introduced in January 1992.

In its tower PC systems product line, in October 1992 the Company introduced the COMPAQ SYSTEMPRO/XL the world's fastest PC server, as well as the COMPAQ ProSignia, a cost effective tower machine for small business network environments. The Company's leading unit seller in 1992 in its tower PC systems product line was the COMPAQ SYSTEMPRO/LT 486/33 introduced in October 1991.

The Company entered the PC network printer market in August 1992 with the introduction of two new network laser printers--the COMPAQ PAGEMARQ 20 and PAGEMARQ 15 printers, which are the fastest desktop printers available today. These printers incorporate technology for which the Company has been granted a number of patents.

The Company offers a number of related options products for its PC, systems, and printer products, including the COMPAQ ProLiant external disk storage system, which holds up to 7.35 billion bytes of data and allows users to expand the storage capacity of their PC networks to almost 30 billion bytes through the use of multiple ProLiant systems.

Product Development

The Company is actively engaged in the design and development of additional products and enhancements to its existing products. Since personal computer technology develops rapidly, the Company's continued success is dependent on the timely introduction of new products with the right price and features. Its engineering effort focuses on new and emerging technologies as well as design features that will increase efficiency and lower production costs. In 1992 the Company focused on technological developments for PC products related to color and monochrome active matrix flat panels, power conservation, communication devices, and component densification, as well as new technologies applicable to future products in the area of personal computers with full-motion video and stereo sound, pen-based PCs, and other small form-factor devices. In that same period the Company focused on connectivity and compatibility issues, technological developments for systems products related to server systems management from remote locations, and other new technologies applicable to future products in its printer line. During 1992, 1991, and 1990, the Company expended approximately $173 million, $197 million, and $186 million, respectively, on research and development.

Manufacturing and Materials

The Company's manufacturing operations consist of manufacturing finished products and various circuit boards from components and subassemblies that the Company acquires from a wide range of vendors. The Company's principal manufacturing operations are located in Houston, Texas; Erskine, Scotland; and Singapore. Products sold in Europe are manufactured primarily in the Company's facilities in Erskine, Scotland and Singapore. Products sold in the U.S. are primarily manufactured in the Company's facilities in Houston, Texas and Singapore.

The Company believes that there is a sufficient number of competent vendors for most components, parts, and subassemblies. A significant number of components, however, are purchased from single sources due to technology, availability, price, quality, or other considerations. Key components and processes currently obtained from single sources include certain of the Company's displays, microprocessors, mouse devices, keyboards, disk drives, printers and printer components, application specific integrated circuits and other custom chips, and certain processes relating to construction of the plastic housing for the Company's computers. In addition, new products introduced by the Company often initially utilize custom components obtained from only one source until the Company has evaluated whether there is a need for an additional supplier. In the event that a supply of a key single-sourced material, process, or component were delayed or curtailed, the Company's ability to ship the related product in desired quantities and in a timely manner could be adversely affected. The Company believes that the suppliers whose failure to meet the Company's orders could have a material adverse effect on the Company include Intel Corporation and Conner Peripherals, Inc. The Company attempts to mitigate these potential risks by working closely with key suppliers on product plans, strategic inventories, and coordinated product introductions.

Materials and components are normally acquired through purchase orders, as is common in the industry, typically covering the Company's requirements for periods averaging 90 days. From time to time the Company has experienced significant price increases and limited availability of certain components that are available from multiple sources, such as dynamic random-access memory devices. At times the Company has been constrained by parts availability in meeting product orders. Any similar occurrences in the future could have an adverse effect on the Company's operating results.

Marketing and Distribution

The Company distributes its products principally through third-party computer resellers. The Company's products are sold to large and medium-sized business and government customers through dealers, value-added resellers, and systems integrators and to small business and home customers through dealers and consumer channels. In 1992 the Company continued its expansion into new distribution channels, such as consumer electronics outlets and office product superstores, to address the needs of small business and individual consumers. In the first half of 1993 the Company will begin to distribute products directly to customers in the U.S. through a mail order catalogue featuring a variety of personal computers, printers, and software products.

In 1992 European sales constituted 46% of the Company's total revenues with an almost equal amount from sales in North America. The Company's Europe Division, based in Munich, Germany, focuses on opportunities in Europe as well as in parts of Africa and the Middle East.

In March 1992 the Company introduced notebook, desktop, and systems products designed for the Japanese market. The Company continues to expand its international business through entry into new countries, and the Company's highest growth areas are in Asia and Latin America. For further geographic information for 1992, 1991, and 1990, see Note 14 of Notes to Consolidated Financial Statements.

Service and Support

The Company provides support and warranty repair to its customers through full-service computer dealers and independent third-party service companies. In 1992 Compaq announced CompaqCare, a number of customer service and support programs, most notably a three-year warranty on PC products (excluding monitors and batteries) and round-the-clock lifetime telephone technical support at no additional charge to the customer.

Patents, Trademarks and Licenses

The Company held 146 patents (including 18 design patents) and had 125 patent applications (including 10 design patent applications) pending with the United States Patent and Trademark Office at the close of 1992. In addition, the Company has registered certain trademarks in the United States and in a number of foreign countries. While the Company believes that patent and trademark protection plays an important part in its business, the Company relies primarily upon technological expertise, innovative talent, marketing abilities, and management skills of its employees.

The Company has from time to time entered into cross-licensing agreements with other companies holding patents to technology used in the Company's products. The Company holds a license from IBM for all patents issuing on applications filed prior to July 1, 1993. Texas Instruments, Inc. ("TI") has granted the Company an option to acquire a patent license, which would result in an increase in the Company's royalty payments. TI has notified the Company that the option period has begun to run and the Company is evaluating TI's offer. The Company's failure to enter into a license agreement could result in litigation with TI. Because of technological changes in the computer industry, extensive patent coverage, and the rapid rate of issuance of new patents, certain components of the Company's products may unknowingly infringe patents of others. The Company believes, based in part on industry practices, that if any infringements do exist, the Company will be able to modify its products to avoid infringement or obtain licenses or rights under such infringed patents on terms not having a material adverse effect on the Company.

Seasonal Business

Although the Company does not consider its business to be highly seasonal, the Company in general experiences seasonally higher revenues and earnings in the first and fourth quarters of the year. The Company anticipates that the seasonality of its sales may increase as it expands the consumer retail portion of its business.

Working Capital

Information regarding the Company's working capital position and practices is set forth on page 10 of this Form 10-K under the caption "Liquidity and Capital Resources."

Customers

No customer of the Company accounted for 10% or more of sales for 1992. Computerland, Inc. and Intelligent Electronics, Inc. accounted for 9% and 8% of 1992 sales, respectively.

Backlog

The Company's resellers typically purchase products on an as-needed basis. Resellers frequently change delivery schedules and order rates depending on market conditions. Unfilled orders ("backlog") can be, and often are, canceled at will and without penalties. The Company attempts to fill orders on the requested delivery schedules; however, in 1992 the Company experienced significant demand for certain products that it was unable to produce on a timely basis. In the Company's experience, the actual amount of product backlog at any particular time is not a meaningful indication of its future business prospects since backlog rapidly becomes balanced as soon as supply begins meeting demand.

Competition

The computer industry is intensely competitive with many U.S., Japanese, and other international companies vying for market share. The principal elements of competition are price, product performance, product quality and reliability, service and support, marketing and distribution capability, and corporate reputation. While the Company believes that its products compete favorably based on each of these elements, the Company could be adversely affected if its competitors introduce innovative or technologically superior products or offer their products at significantly lower prices than the Company or if the Company is unable to fill orders on a timely basis for an extended period. No assurance can be given that the Company will have the financial resources, marketing and service capability, or technological knowledge to continue to compete successfully.

Environmental Laws and Regulations

Compliance with laws enacted for protection of the environment to date has had no material effect upon the Company's capital expenditures, earnings, or competitive position. Although the Company does not anticipate any material adverse effects in the future based on the nature of its operations and the purpose of such laws and regulations, there can be no assurance that such laws or future laws will not have a material adverse effect on the Company.

Employees

At December 31, 1992, the Company had approximately 9,500 full-time regular employees and 1,800 temporary and contract workers.

Selected Consolidated Financial Data

The following data have been derived from consolidated financial statements that have been audited by Price Waterhouse, independent accountants. The information set forth below is not necessarily indicative of the results of future operations and should be read in conjunction with the consolidated financial statements and notes thereto appearing elsewhere in this Annual Report on Form 10-K.

	Year ended December 31,				
	1992	1991	1990	1989	1988
	(in thousands, except per share amounts)				
Consolidated Statement of Income Data:					
Sales	$4,099,758	$3,271,367	$3,598,768	$2,876,062	$2,065,562
Cost of Sales	2,905,024	2,053,576	2,057,886	1,715,243	1,233,283
	1,194,734	1,217,791	1,540,882	1,160,819	832,279
Research and development costs	172,948	197,277	185,726	132,474	74,859
Selling, general, and administrative expense	698,589	721,622	706,060	538,721	397,363
Unrealized gain on investment in affiliated company			(34,532)	(13,691)	(9,683)
Other income and expenses, net	27,795	144,856	42,195	18,776	2,893
	899,332	1,063,755	899,449	676,280	465,432
Income from consolidated companies before provision for income taxes	295,402	154,036	641,433	484,539	366,847
Provision for income taxes	97,483	42,932	216,205	165,010	119,296
Income from consolidated companies	197,919	111,104	425,228	319,529	247,551
Equity in net income of affiliated company	15,233	19,765	29,682	13,771	7,691
Net income	$ 213,152	$ 130,869	$ 454,910	$ 333,300	$ 255,242
Earnings per common and common equivalent share:-					
Primary	$ 2.58	$ 1.49	$ 5.14	$ 3.89	$ 3.15
Assuming full dilution	2.52	1.49	5.12	3.88	3.13

	1992	1991	December 31, 1990	1989	1988
			(in thousands)		
Consolidated Balance Sheet Data:					
Total assets	$3,142,393	$2,826,386	$2,717,529	$2,090,389	$1,589,997
Long-term debt		73,456	73,996	274,434	274,930
Stockholders' equity	2,006,691	1,930,704	1,859,013	1,171,635	814,554

Management's Discussion and Analysis of Financial Condition and Results of Operations

The following discussion should be read in conjunction with the consolidated financial statements.

Results of Operations

The following table presents, as a percentage of sales, certain selected consolidated financial data for each of the three years in the period ended December 31, 1992.

	Year ended December 31,		
	1992	1991	1990
Sales	100.0%	100.0%	100.0%
Cost of sales	70.9	62.8	57.2
Gross margin	29.1	37.2	42.8
Research and development costs	4.2	6.0	5.2
Selling, general, and administrative expense	17.0	22.1	19.6
Other income and expense, net	.7	4.4	.2
	21.9	32.5	25.0
Income from consolidated companies before provision for income taxes	7.2%	4.7%	17.8%

Sales

Revenue for 1992 increased approximately 25% over the prior year as compared with a decline of 9% in 1991 from 1990. North American revenue, which includes Canada, increased 32% during 1992, compared with a decline of 16% in 1991 from 1990. European revenue increased 9% during 1992 compared to a decline of 5% in 1991 from 1990. Other international revenue, excluding Canada, increased 139% during 1992, compared with an increase of 19% in 1991 from 1990. International revenue, excluding Canada, represented 55% of total revenue in 1992 as compared with 58% in 1991 and 54% in 1990.

The personal computer industry is highly competitive and marked by frequent product introductions, continual improvement in product price/performance characteristics, and a large number of competitors. The

Company significantly altered its product line in 1992 by introducing new notebook, desktop, and server products in June and September 1992 and entering the network printer market with two network printers in August 1992. Additional server products were introduced in October 1992. More than 53% of the Company's unit sales and approximately 50% of the Company's revenue from sales of units in 1992 were derived from products introduced after May 1992. These new products have been designed to allow the Company to lower its product costs while maintaining the quality and reliability for which the Company's products have been known, thereby increasing the Company's ability to compete on price and value.

The lower prices of the Company's new products, as well as price reductions in June and October 1992 on existing products have substantially lowered the Company's average unit sales prices. The Company's increase in revenue in 1992 reflects strong unit sales of the Company's personal computers. In 1992 the Company's worldwide unit sales increased 78% while they held stable in 1991. The Company believes that the personal computer industry as a whole experienced significant increases in unit sales in 1992, with unit growth worldwide increasing approximately 15% in contrast to a 4% increase in 1991. Unit growth did not translate directly into revenue growth because of significantly lower unit prices. Third-party estimates indicate that industry revenue increased by approximately 5% worldwide in 1992.

Gross Margin

Gross margin as a percentage of sales continued to decline in 1992. The gross margin percentage declined to 29.1% in 1992, from 37.2% in 1991, and from 42.8% in 1990, primarily as a result of industrywide competitive pressures and associated pricing and promotional actions outpacing the Company's ability to reduce cost. Although the Company continues to aggressively pursue the reduction of product costs both at the supplier and manufacturing levels, expected pricing actions in 1993 will result in further reductions of gross margin.

The Company's operating strategy and pricing take into account changes in exchange rates over time; however, the Company's results of operations may be significantly affected in the short-term by fluctuations in foreign currency exchange rates. When the value of the dollar strengthens against other currencies, revenues from sales in those currencies translate into fewer dollars. The opposite effect occurs when the dollar weakens.

The Company attempts to reduce the impact of currency movements on net income primarily through the use of forward exchange contracts that are used to hedge a portion of the net monetary assets of its international subsidiaries. The Company also utilizes forward exchange contracts and foreign currency options to hedge certain capital expenditures and inventory purchases. In the third quarter of 1992, the Company began to hedge a portion of the probable anticipated sales of its international marketing subsidiaries through the use of purchased currency options.

The translation gains and losses relating to the financial statements of the Company's international subsidiaries, net of offsetting gains and losses associated with hedging activities related to the net monetary assets of these subsidiaries, are included in other income and expense and were a net loss of $11.2 million in 1992, a net gain of $4.1 million in 1991, and a net loss of $21.4 million in 1990. The gains associated with the hedging of anticipated sales of the Company's international marketing subsidiaries, net of premium costs associated with the related purchased currency options, are included in revenue and were $2.8 million in 1992.

Operating Expenses

Research and development costs declined in absolute dollars (to $173 million from $197 million) in 1992 as compared to 1991 due to a more focused approach to the Company's research and development projects. The

Company's research and development costs had increased in 1991 from 1990 both absolutely and as a percentage of sales. Because the personal computer industry is characterized by rapid product cycles and price cuts on older products, the Company believes that its long-term success is directly related to its ability to bring new products to market on a timely basis and to reduce the costs of new and existing products. Accordingly, it is committed to continuing a significant research and development program and research and development costs are likely to be relatively stable in absolute dollars in 1993.

Selling, general, and administrative expense declined in 1992 due to lower general and administrative expense partially offset by higher selling expense. The decrease in general and administrative expense was primarily the result of cost reductions from the Company's 1991 restructuring. Selling expense increased in connection with the introduction of new products, the entry into new markets (both domestically and internationally), the expansion of distribution channels, a new emphasis on advertising and customer service, and technical support. The Company anticipates that selling expenses will continue to increase in 1993--at least in absolute dollars--as a result of the Company's marketing program and the continuing expansion of its geographic markets.

The Company formally introduced its Japanese marketing subsidiary in March 1992 and has introduced several products tailored to the Japanese market. Due to the size and potential significance of the Japanese market, the introductory costs were and will continue to be significant in comparison to revenue generated. Furthermore, ongoing costs necessary to penetrate successfully new international markets will cause additional selling, general, and administrative expense.

As a result of the changes in the personal computer industry resulting from intense price competition, the Company has taken steps to reduce costs and more efficiently focus its resources. The Company believes its ability to control operating expenses is an important factor in its ability to be price competitive and accordingly continues to pursue cost reduction alternatives throughout the Company. In an environment of increased efforts to penetrate new markets, greater diversity of distribution channels, and increased customer support, the Company may not be successful in identifying areas to cut additional costs.

Other Items

Interest expense, net of interest and dividend income from investment of excess funds, was $11.6 million, $5.4 million, and $19.1 million in 1992, 1991, and 1990, respectively. The fluctuation in net interest expense is due primarily to declines in interest rates earned on investable cash, reduced interest expense associated with lower average borrowings, and changes in interest expense associated with financing resellers' inventories.

In each of the third quarters of 1992 and 1991 the Company recorded restructuring charges associated principally with reducing the number of employees and consolidating and streamlining operations. The charges totaled $73 million in 1992 and $135 million in 1991. In addition, in 1992 and 1991 the Company had charges related to the disposition or write-downs of the carrying value of certain fixed assets.

In the third quarter of 1992 the Company sold its equity interest in Conner Peripherals, Inc. ("Conner") realizing a gain of $85.7 million. The Company's ownership in Conner created an after-tax contribution to the Company's net income of $10.1 million in 1992, $13 million in 1991, and $19.6 million in 1990. In 1990 the Company recorded a pretax gain of $27.1 million on the sale by Conner of new equity securities and an additional pretax gain of $7.5 million on the conversion by Conner of its outstanding debentures into common stock.

The Company's effective tax rate was 33.0% in 1992, 27.9% in 1991, and 33.7% in 1990. The Financial Accounting Standards Board has issued a Statement that will change the method of determining reported income tax expense. The Company will apply the provisions of this Statement in 1993. Application of the provisions of this Statement will have minimal impact on the Company's financial statements.

Liquidity and Capital Resources

At December 31, 1992, the Company had working capital of approximately $1.4 billion, including approximately $357 million of cash and short-term investments. Approximately $834 million consists of inventory, which is not as liquid as other current assets.

On May 16, 1991, the Company's Board of Directors authorized the Company to repurchase up to ten million shares of its common stock on the open market. During 1991 the Company purchased three million shares of its common stock at an aggregate cost of $95.5 million. During the first nine months of 1992 the Company completed the program by purchasing the remaining seven million shares of its common stock at an aggregate cost of $202.2 million.

During 1992 the Company repaid a $73.5 million mortgage loan.

In 1992 the Company discontinued joint technology development with Silicon Graphics, Inc. ("SGI") and entered into a cross-license for technology previously exchanged by the two companies. In addition, SGI paid the Company $150 million and the Company transferred to SGI the 5% convertible preferred stock of SGI that it had acquired in 1991 for $135 million.

The Company estimates that capital expenditures for land, buildings, and equipment during 1993 will be approximately $140 million. Such expenditures are currently expected to be funded from a combination of available cash balances, internally generated funds, and, if necessary, financing arrangements. Although the Company fully expects that such expenditures will be made, it has commitments for only a small portion of such amounts.

During 1992 the Company funded its capital expenditures and other investing activities with cash generated from operations and previously accumulated cash balances as well as the cash generated by the sale of its equity investment in Conner and its transaction with SGI. The Company's ability to fund its activities from operations is directly dependent on its rate of growth, inventory management, the terms and financing arrangements under which it extends credit to its customers, and the manner in which it finances any capital expansion. In December 1992 and January 1993 the Company entered into credit agreements with two banks in which the banks agreed to extend committed lines of credit aggregating $100 million to the Company. At February 24, 1993, the lines of credit were unused and fully available. The Company anticipates entering into additional financing arrangements in the first half of 1993 for utilization if additional operating funds are needed.

Factors that May Affect Future Results

The personal computer industry is characterized by intense price competition. In early 1993 a number of the Company's competitors lowered their prices dramatically, and additional pricing actions likely will occur in the future. In order to maintain or increase its market share, the Company must continue to price its products competitively, which will lower revenue per unit and cause declines in gross margin. To compensate for the impact on its revenue and profitability, the Company must substantially increase unit volumes as well as aggressively reduce its costs. While the Company believes its new pricing and product strategy has created demand for its products and the Company is actively engaged in cost reduction programs, if the Company does not achieve significant volume increases and cost reductions, there will be an adverse impact on revenue and profitability.

To respond to the increase in demand for the Company's products in 1992, the Company increased the utilization of its manufacturing capacity. The Company, however, experienced shortages of certain components that impeded its ability to meet all of its demand. In order to increase its production, the Company has significantly increased its level of inventory. If the Company is unable to manage its inventory position or anticipate demand accurately, maintaining this inventory level may result in increased obsolescence and affect its ability to meet cost reduction goals.

Because of the pace of technological advances in the personal computer industry, the Company must design and develop new and more sophisticated products in relatively short time spans. The Company designs many of its own components for its products. Across the Company's product range, however, certain elements of product strategy are dependent on technological developments by other manufacturers. There can be no assurance that the Company will obtain the delivery of the technology needed to introduce new products in a timely manner or will be able to obtain any competitive advantage in access to such technology. The Company's product strategy focuses in part on marketing products with distinctive features that appeal to a variety of purchasers. If the Company were unable to develop and launch new products in a timely fashion, this failure could have a material adverse effect on the Company's business.

In 1992 the Company broadened its distribution in order to identify and pursue new market opportunities, including the home, education, and small business markets as well as new geographic markets. Certain of the Company's sales in 1992 were to newly appointed distributors and new locations for sale of the Company's products. Offering its products through a variety of distribution channels, including distributors, electronics superstores, and mail order, requires the Company to increase the level of direct sales and support interface with customers. There can be no assurance, however, that this new direction will be effective, or that the requisite service and support to ensure the success of these new channels can be achieved without significantly increasing overall expenses. While the Company anticipates that the number of outlets for its products will continue to increase in 1993, a reduction in the growth of new outlets could affect demand.

The Company's primary means of distribution remains third-party resellers. The Company's business could be adversely affected in the event that the generally weak financial condition of third-party computer resellers worsens. In the event of the financial failure of a major reseller, the Company could experience disruptions in its distribution as well as the loss of the unsecured portion of any outstanding accounts receivable. The Company believes that the expansion of its distribution channels will help mitigate any potential impact on its sales.

General economic conditions have an impact on the Company's business and financial results. Many of the markets in which the Company sells its products are currently experiencing economic recession and the Company cannot predict when these conditions will improve or if conditions in these and other markets will decline. The personal computer market showed unusual robustness despite weak economic conditions in 1992, and there can be no assurance that growth will continue at the same pace in 1993. The value of the U.S. dollar also affects the Company's results. When the U.S. dollar strengthens against other currencies, sales made in those currencies translate into less revenue in U.S. dollars; and when the U.S. dollar weakens, sales made in those currencies translate into more revenue. Correspondingly, costs and expenses incurred in non-U.S. dollar currencies increase when the U.S. dollar weakens and decline when the U.S. dollar strengthens. The Company attempts to reduce the impact of changes in currency exchange rates through forward and option currency contracts. Should the U.S. dollar sustain a strengthening position against currencies in which the Company sells its products or a weakening exchange rate against currencies in which the Company incurs costs, particularly the Japanese yen, the Company's sales or its costs would be adversely affected.

While the effects of the 1992 restructuring will help the Company control its selling, general, and administrative expense in certain areas, several factors, including a new marketing focus directed towards end-user purchasers, are anticipated to cause an increase in such expenses in 1993 in absolute terms although the Company anticipates that these expenses may decline as a percentage of sales during 1993.

Because of the foregoing factors, as well as other factors affecting the Company's operating results, past financial performance should not be considered to be a reliable indicator of future performance, and investors should not use historical trends to anticipate results or trends in future periods.

REPORT OF INDEPENDENT ACCOUNTANTS

To the Stockholders and Board of Directors of
Compaq Computer Corporation

In our opinion, the consolidated financial statements listed in the accompanying index present fairly, in all material respects, the financial position of Compaq Computer Corporation and its subsidiaries at December 31, 1992 and 1991, and the results of their operations and their cash flows for each of the three years in the period ended December 31, 1992, in conformity with generally accepted accounting principles. These financial statements are the responsibility of the Company's management; our responsibility is to express an opinion on these financial statements based on our audits. We conducted our audits of these statements in accordance with generally accepted auditing standards which require that we plan and perform the audit to obtain reasonable assurance about whether the financial statements are free of material misstatement. An audit includes examining, on a test basis, evidence supporting the amounts and disclosures in the financial statements, assessing the accounting principles used and significant estimates made by management, and evaluating the overall financial statement presentation. We believe that our audits provide a reasonable basis for the opinion expressed above.

PRICE WATERHOUSE

Houston, Texas
January 25, 1993

COMPAQ COMPUTER CORPORATION
CONSOLIDATED BALANCE SHEET

ASSETS

	December 31, 1992	December 31, 1991
	(in thousands)	
Current assets:		
Cash and short-term investments	$ 356,747	$ 452,174
Accounts receivable, less allowance of $24,733,000 and $18,265,000	986,735	624,376
Inventories	834,406	436,824
Prepaid expenses and other current assets	141,083	269,203
Total current assets	2,318,971	1,782,577
Investment in affiliated company		142,057
Property, plant, and equipment, less accumulated depreciation	807,653	883,765
Other assets	15,769	17,987
	$3,142,393	$2,826,386

LIABILITIES AND STOCKHOLDERS' EQUITY

	December 31, 1992	December 31, 1991
Current liabilities:		
Accounts payable	$ 516,323	$ 195,582
Income taxes payable	36,073	33,103
Other current liabilities	407,484	409,258
Total current liabilities	959,880	637,943
Long-term debt		73,456
Deferred income taxes	175,822	184,283
Commitments and contingencies		
Stockholders' equity:-		
Preferred stock: $.01 par value; 10,000,000 shares authorized; none outstanding		
Common stock: $.01 par value; 400,000,000 shares authorized; 79,829,488 shares and 84,201,515 shares issued and outstanding	798	842
Capital in excess of par value	399,693	536,814
Retained earnings	1,606,200	1,393,048
Total stockholders' equity	2,006,691	1,930,704
	$3,142,393	$2,826,386

The accompanying notes are an integral part of these financial statements.

COMPAQ COMPUTER CORPORATION
CONSOLIDATED STATEMENT OF INCOME

	Year ended December 31,		
	1992	1991	1990
	(in thousands, except per share amounts)		
Sales	$4,099,758	$3.271,367	$3,598,768
Cost of sales	2,905,024	2,053,576	2,057,886
	1,194,734	1,217,791	1,540,882
Research and development costs	172,948	197,277	185,726
Selling, general, and administrative expense	698,589	721,622	706,060
Unrealized gains on investment in affiliated company			(34,532)
Other income and expense, net	27,795	144,856	42,195
	899,332	1,063,755	899,449
Income from consolidated companies before provision for income taxes	295,402	154,036	641,433
Provision for income taxes	97,483	42,932	216,205
Income from consolidated companies	197,919	111,104	425,228
Equity in net income of affiliated company	15,233	19,765	29,682
Net income	$ 213,152	$ 130,869	$ 454,910
Earnings per common and common equivalent share:			
Primary	$ 2.58	$ 1.49	$ 5.14
Assuming full dilution	$ 2.52	$ 1.49	$ 5.12

The accompanying notes are an integral part of these financial statements.

COMPAQ COMPUTER CORPORATION

CONSOLIDATED STATEMENT OF CASH FLOWS

	Year ended December 31,		
	1992	**1991**	**1990**
		(in thousands)	
Cash flows from operating activities:			
Cash received from customers	$3,594,786	$3,325,465	$3,536,984
Cash paid to suppliers and employees	(3,641,655)	(2,822,648)	(2,721,070)
Interest and dividends received	32,404	32,301	26,889
Interest paid	(42,137)	(36,907)	(46,728)
Income taxes paid	(2,816)	(104,001)	(140,294)
Net cash provided by (used in) operating activities	(59,418)	394,210	655,781
Cash flows from investing activities:			
Purchases of property, plant, and equipment, net	(159,215)	(188,746)	(324,859)
Proceeds from sale of investment in Conner Peripherals, Inc.	241,427		
Investment in Silicon Graphics, Inc.	135,000	(135,000)	
Other, net	13,004	(16,636)	(1,747)
Net cash provided by (used in) investing activities	230,216	(340,382)	(326,606)
Cash flows from financing activities:			
Purchases of treasury shares	(215,505)	(82,275)	
Proceeds from sale of equity securities	56,836	22,637	22,645
Repayment of borrowings	(73,456)	(540)	(30,561)
Net cash used in financing activities	(232,125)	(60,178)	(7,916)
Effect of exchange rate changes on cash	(34,100)	23,824	(47,872)
Net increase (decrease) in cash	(95,427)	17,474	273,387
Cash and short-term investments at beginning of year	452,174	434,700	161,313
Cash and short-term investments at end of year	$ 356,747	$ 452,174	$ 434,700
Reconciliation of net income to net cash provided by operating activities:			
Net income	$ 213,152	$ 130,869	$ 454,910
Depreciation and amortization	159,510	165,824	135,305
Provision for bad debts	13,654	8,542	3,878
Equity in net income of affiliated company	(15,233)	(19,765)	(29,682)
Unrealized gain on investment in affiliated company			(34,532)
Gain on sale of investment in affiliated company	(85,709)		
Deferred income taxes	34,128	(9,639)	40,443
Loss on disposal of assets	14,408	4,200	4,887
Exchange rate effect	11,236	(4,136)	21,422
Income tax refund	51,400		
Other changes in net current assets	(455,964)	118,315	59,150
Net cash provided by (used in) operating activities	($ 59,418)	$ 394,210	$ 655,781

COMPAQ COMPUTER CORPORATION

CONSOLIDATED STATEMENT OF STOCKHOLDERS' EQUITY

	Common stock		Capital in excess of par value	Retained earnings	Total
	Shares	Par value			
			(in thousands, except for shares)		
Balance, December 31, 1989	78,545,808	$ 785	$363,581	$ 807,269	$1,171,635
Issuance pursuant to stock option plans	1,394,413	14	22,631		22,645
Issuance on conversion of convertible subordinated debentures	6,149,426	62	197,461		197,523
Compensation expense associated with grant of nonqualified stock options			200		200
Tax benefit associated with stock options			12,100		12,100
Net income				454,910	454,910
Balance, December 31, 1990	86,089,647	861	595,973	1,262,179	1,859,013
Issuance pursuant to stock option plans	1,111,868	11	22,626		22,637
Purchases of treasury shares	(3,000,000)	(30)	(95,474)		(95,504)
Tax benefit associated with stock options			13,689		13,689
Net income				130,869	130,869
Balance, December 31, 1991	84,201,515	842	536,814	1,393,048	1,930,704
Issuance pursuant to stock option plans	2,627,973	26	56,810		56,836
Purchases of treasury shares	(7,000,000)	(70)	(202,206)		(202,276)
Compensation expense associated with grant of nonqualified stock options			62		62
Tax benefit associated with stock options			8,213		8,213
Net income				213,152	213,152
Balance, December 31, 1992	79,829,488	$ 798	$399,693	$1,606,200	$2,006,691

COMPAQ COMPUTER CORPORATION

NOTES TO CONSOLIDATED FINANCIAL STATEMENTS

Note 1 - Significant Accounting Policies:

The Company has adopted accounting policies which are generally accepted in the industry in which it operates. Set forth below are the Company's more significant accounting policies.

Principles of consolidation -

The consolidated financial statements include the accounts of Compaq Computer Corporation and its wholly owned subsidiaries. The investment in Conner Peripherals, Inc., which represented a less than majority interest, was accounted for under the equity method. All significant intercompany transactions have been eliminated.

Inventories -

Inventories are stated at the lower of cost or market, cost being determined on a first-in, first-out basis.

Property, plant, and equipment -

Property, plant, and equipment are stated at cost. Major renewals and improvements are capitalized; minor replacements, maintenance, and repairs are charged to current operations. Depreciation is computed by applying the straight-line method over the estimated useful lives of the related assets, which are 30 years for buildings and range from three to ten years for equipment. Leasehold improvements are amortized over the shorter of the useful life of the improvement or the life of the related lease.

Intangible assets -

Licenses and trademarks are carried at cost less accumulated amortization, which is being provided on a straight-line basis over the economic lives of the respective assets.

Warranty expense -

The Company provides currently for estimated cost which may be incurred under product warranties.

Revenue recognition -

The Company recognizes revenue at the time products are shipped to its customers. Provision is made currently for estimated product returns which may occur under programs the Company has with its third-party resellers and floor planning arrangements with third-party finance companies.

Foreign currency -

The Company uses the U.S. dollar as its functional currency. Financial statements of the Company's foreign subsidiaries are translated to U.S. dollars for consolidation purposes using current rates of exchange for monetary assets and liabilities and historical rates of exchange for nonmonetary assets and related elements of expense. Revenue and other expense elements are translated at rates which approximate the rates in effect on the transaction dates. Gains and losses from this process are included in results of operations.

The Company hedges certain portions of its foreign currency exposure through the use of forward exchange contracts and option contracts. Generally, gains and losses associated with currency rate changes on forward exchange contracts are recorded currently, while the interest element is recognized over the life of each contract. However, to the extent such contracts hedge a commitment for capital expenditures or inventory purchases, no gains or losses are recognized, and the rate at the time the forward exchange contract is made is, effectively, the rate used to determine the U.S. dollar value of the asset when it is recorded. In addition, during 1992 the Company began to hedge a portion of its probable anticipated sales of its international marketing subsidiaries using purchased foreign currency options. Realized and unrealized gains and the net premiums on these options are deferred and recognized as a component of sales in the period that the related sales occur.

Income taxes -

The provision for income taxes is computed based on the pretax income included in the consolidated statement of income. Deferred taxes result from differences in the timing of recognition of revenue and expenses for tax and financial reporting purposes. Research and development tax credits are recorded to the extent allowable as a reduction of the provision for federal income taxes in the year the qualified research and development expenditures are incurred.

The Financial Accounting Standards Board has issued a Statement which will change the method of determining reported income tax expense. The Company will apply the provisions of this Statement in 1993. Application of the provisions of this Statement will have minimal impact on the Company's financial statements.

Note 2 - Short-term Investments:

The Company held the following short-term investments:

	December 31, 1992	December 31, 1991
	(in thousands)	
Money market instruments	$133,926	$321,527
Commercial paper and other investments	135,324	120,010
	$269,250	$441,537

All such investments are carried at cost plus accrued interest, which approximates market, have maturities of three months or less and are considered cash equivalents for purposes of reporting cash flows.

Note 3 - Inventories:

Inventories consisted of the following components:

	December 31, 1992	December 31, 1991
	(in thousands)	
Raw material	$351,373	$193,843
Work-in-process	124,042	36,450
Finished goods	358,991	206,531
	$834,406	$436,824

Note 4 - Prepaid Expenses and Other Current Assets:

During the early part of 1992, the Company sold its $135 million equity interest in Silicon Graphics, Inc. (SGI) and discontinued the joint technical development agreement with SGI. The transaction resulted in no material gain or loss to the Company. The Company's $135 million equity interest in SGI was included in prepaid expenses and other current assets at December 31, 1991.

Note 5- Investment in Conner Peripherals, Inc.:

In 1992 the Company sold its equity interest in Conner Peripherals, Inc. (Conner) realizing a gain of $85.7 million.

During 1990 Conner issued approximately six million shares of common stock. The per share price of the newly issued shares was higher than the then per share carrying value of the Company's investment in Conner. The increases in the carrying value of the Company's investment in Conner resulting from this stock issuance caused a pretax gain of $27.1 million in 1990. Additionally, in 1990 Conner converted its outstanding debentures into common stock giving rise to a similar pretax gain of $7.5 million.

The Company made disk drive purchases from Conner during 1992 through the date it sold its equity interest and during 1991 and 1990 of approximately $149 million, $197 million, and $255 million, respectively. At December 31, 1991, the Company had balances owing to Conner of $19 million. While the Company controlled approximately 20% of the equity securities of Conner, the Company believes that purchases from Conner were made at market prices.

Note 6 - Property, Plant, and Equipment:

Property, plant, and equipment are summarized below:

	December 31, 1992	December 31, 1991
Land	$ 75,455	$ 70,028
Buildings	531,849	510,049
Machinery and equipment	547,942	615,353
Furniture and fixtures	53,408	54,217
Leasehold improvements	19,768	27,183
Construction-in-progress	55,709	45,652
	1,284,131	1,322,482
Less-accumulated depreciation	476,478	438,717
	$ 807,653	$ 883,765

Depreciation expense totaled approximately $159 million, $164 million, and $134 million in 1992, 1991, and 1990, respectively.

Note 7 - Other Current Liabilities:

The estimated costs which may be incurred under product warranties of approximately $73 million and $39 million were included in other current liabilities at December 31, 1992 and 1991, respectively.

Note 8 - Credit Agreement:

In December 1992 and January 1993 the Company entered into credit agreements with two banks in which the banks agreed to extend short-term committed lines of credit aggregating $100 million to the Company.

Note 9 - Long-term Debt:

On May 4, 1988, the Company issued $200 million of 6 1/2% convertible subordinated debentures due 2013. Approximately $199 million remained outstanding at December 31, 1989. During 1990 substantially all of the outstanding debentures were converted to 6,149,426 shares of the Company's common stock. Deferred debt issuance costs of $3.6 million were charged to capital in excess of par value as a result of the conversion of debentures in 1990.

During 1992 the Company repaid its outstanding mortgage note which had a 9.77% interest rate.

Note 10 - Other Income and Expense:

Other income and expense consisted of the following components:

	Year ended December 31,		
	1992	1991	1990
		(in thousands)	
Restructuring charge	$73,000	$135,000	
Interest and dividend income	(32,404)	(32,301)	($ 26,889)
Interest expense	44,031	37,703	45,986
Realized gain on investment in affiliated company	(85,709)		
Currency exchange (gains) losses, net	11,236	(4,136)	21,422
Loss on disposition of assets, net	14,408	4,200	4,887
Other, net	3,233	4,390	(3,211)
	$27,795	$144,856	$42,195

On October 23, 1991, the Company announced a major restructuring of its operations and a reorganization into distinct product divisions. The restructuring plan included, among other things, a reduction of the Company's worldwide workforce of approximately 14% and provided for the consolidation and streamlining of certain operations. The estimated cost of the restructuring plan, $135 million, was recorded by the Company in the third quarter of 1991 and included approximately $39 million for expenses related to the worldwide reduction in workforce. The restructuring charge also included $63 million for expenses associated with facility rearrangements, consolidations, and writedowns; $20 million for manufacturing equipment disposals and product line consolidations; and $13 million for miscellaneous charges associated with the restructuring. In the third quarter of 1992 the Company recorded $73 million in additional restructuring charges in conjunction with additional plans for consolidating and streamlining operations. The 1992 restructuring charges consisted of approximately $31 million of charges associated with the worldwide reduction of workforce and $42 million related to facility rearrangements, consolidations, and writedowns. Other current liabilities at December 31, 1992 and 1991 included a reserve related to these restructurings of $54 million and $83 million, respectively.

Interest aggregating approximately $3.5 million, $6.2 million, and $8.9 million was capitalized and added to the cost of the Company's property, plant, and equipment in 1992, 1991, and 1990, respectively.

Note 11 - Provision for Income Taxes:

Domestic income (loss) from consolidated companies before provision for income taxes was $99 million, ($33) million, and $332 million in 1992, 1991, and 1990, respectively. The foreign component of income before provision for income taxes was $196 million, $187 million, and $309 million in 1992, 1991, and 1990, respectively. The components of related income taxes were as follows:

	Year ended December 31,		
	1992	**1991**	**1990**
		(in thousands)	
U.S. federal income tax:			
Current	$36,617	$17,478	$ 98,962
Deferred	29,896	(4,487)	38,838
Foreign income taxes:			
Current	26,745	32,798	73,711
Deferred	4,232	(5,152)	1,605
State income taxes	(7)	2,295	3,089
	$97,483	$42,932	$216,205

Total income tax expense for 1992, 1991, and 1990 resulted in effective tax rates of 33%, 27.9%, and 33.7%, respectively. The reasons for the differences between these effective tax rates and the U.S. statutory rate of 34% are as follows:

	Year ended December 31,		
	1992	**1991**	**1990**
Tax expense at U.S. statutory rate	$100,437	$ 52,372	$218,075
Research and development tax credits	(3,048)	(8,826)	(7,893)
Foreign tax effect, net	101	6,076	5,828
Tax exempt Foreign Sales Corporation income	(1,439)	(6,914)	(7,891)
Provision for tax on equity in net income of affiliated company	5,179	6,720	10,092
Other, net	(3,747)	(6,496)	(2,006)
	$ 97,483	$42,932	$216,205

Deferred and prepaid taxes result from differences in the timing of revenue and expenses for tax and financial reporting purposes. The sources and tax effects of these differences are as follows:

	Year ended December 31,		
	1992	**1991**	**1990**
Unremitted earnings of foreign subsidiaries	$35,585	$44,034	$36,057
Intercompany profits not included in net income for financial reporting purposes	(5,329)	31,494	(16,180)
Realized gain on sale of affiliated company	(49,631)		
Unrealized gains on investment in affiliated company			12,069
Equity in net income of affiliated company	5,752	6,720	10,092
Depreciation	2,157	4,895	20
Unrealized currency exchange (gains) losses	9,293	(5,297)	3,978
Restructuring charge	11,359	(35,642)	
Warranty reserve	(6,677)	98	(2,950)
Difference arising from different tax and financial reporting year ends	14,818	(36,915)	(2,185)
Other, net	16,801	(19,026)	(458)
	$34,128	($ 9,639)	$40,443

Deferred tax assets of approximately $77 million and $121 million were included in prepaid expenses and other current assets at December 31, 1992 and 1991, respectively. Accounts receivable at December 31, 1991 included $51 million of refundable U.S. federal income taxes.

Note 12 - Earnings Per Share:

Primary earnings per common and common equivalent share and earnings per common and common equivalent share assuming full dilution were computed using the weighted average number of shares outstanding adjusted for the incremental shares attributed to outstanding options to purchase common stock and assuming the conversion of the outstanding convertible subordinated debentures at the beginning of the period. All share and per-share information has been retroactively restated in the accompanying financial data to reflect the two-for-one stock split effected in the form of a 100% stock dividend declared by the Company in May 1990. Shares used in computing earnings per share were as follows:

	Year ended December 31,		
	1992	1991	1990
		(in thousands)	
Primary	82,641	88,098	89,225
Assuming full dilution	84,726	88,098	89,639

Note 13 - Stockholders' Equity and Employee Benefit Plans:

Equity incentive plans -

At December 31, 1992, there were 23,010,498 shares of common stock reserved by the Board of Directors for issuance under the Company's employee stock option plans. Options are generally granted at the fair market value of the common stock at the date of grant and generally vest over four to five years. In limited circumstances, options may be granted at prices less than fair market value and may vest immediately. Options granted under the plans must be exercised not later than ten years from the date of grant. Options on 6,884,730 shares were exercisable at December 31, 1992. The following table summarizes activity under the plans for each of the three years in the period ended December 31, 1992:

	Shares	Price per share
Options outstanding, December 31, 1989	11,763,844	
Options granted	2,884,626	$37.87- 62.25
Options lapsed or cancelled	(360,731)	
Options exercised	(1,394,413)	.25- 52.75
Options outstanding, December 31, 1990	12,893,326	
Options granted	4,415,600	23.88- 69.75
Options lapsed or cancelled	(1,662,937)	
Options exercised	(1,111,868)	22.25- 73.50
Options outstanding, December 31, 1991	14,534,121	
Options granted	2,745,525	23.63- 42.38
Options lapsed or cancelled	(703,456)	
Options exercised	(2,606,575)	.25- 47.19
Options outstanding, December 31, 1992	13,969,615	

There were 9,040,883; 11,082,952; and 3,847,035 shares available for grants under the plans at December 31, 1992, 1991, and 1990, respectively.

In 1987 the stockholders approved the Stock Option Plan for Non-Employee Directors (the Director Plan). At December 31, 1992, there were 458,602 shares of common stock reserved for issuance under the Director Plan. Pursuant to the terms of the plan, each non-employee director is entitled to receive options to purchase common stock of the Company upon initial appointment to the Board (initial grants) and upon subsequent re-election to the Board (annual grants). Initial grants are exercisable during the period beginning one year after initial appointment to the Board and ending ten years after the date of grant. Annual grants vest over two years and are exercisable thereafter until the tenth anniversary of the date of grant. Both initial grants and annual grants have an exercise price equal to the fair market value of the Company's stock on the date of grant. Additionally, pursuant to the terms of the Director Plan, non-employee directors may elect to receive stock options in lieu of all or a portion of the annual retainer to be earned. Such options are granted at 50% of the price of the Company's common stock at the date of grant and are exercisable during the period beginning one year after the grant date and ending ten years after the date of grant. Options totaling 121,084 were exercisable under the Director Plan at December 31, 1992. Activity under the plan for each of the three years in the period ended December 31, 1992 was as follows:

	Shares	Price per share
Options outstanding, December 31, 1989	40,000	
Options granted	75,690	$30.50-61.00
Options outstanding, December 31, 1990	115,690	
Options granted	37,292	17.88-35.76
Options outstanding, December 31, 1991	152,982	
Options granted	27,895	12.69-25.38
Options exercised	(21,398)	40.25-43.00
Options outstanding, December 31, 1992	159,479	

There were 299,123; 327,018; and 364,310 shares available for grants under the plan at December 31, 1992, 1991, and 1990, respectively.

Pursuant to a plan adopted by the Board of Directors in 1986, the Company granted to selected officers and key employees options on shares of Conner stock owned by the Company. Such options, which were granted at $.09 per share, vested ratably over four years and expire ten years from the date of grant. During 1992 options on 193,499 shares were exercised and no options lapsed or were cancelled. At December 31, 1992, options on 105,178 shares of Conner common stock were exercisable and outstanding.

Compaq Computer Corporation Investment Plan -

The Company has an Investment Plan available to all domestic employees and intended to qualify as a deferred compensation plan under Section 401(k) of the Internal Revenue Code of 1986. Employees may contribute to the plan up to 14% of their salary with a maximum of $8,728 in 1992 ($8,994 in 1993). The Company will match employee contributions for an amount up to 6% of each employee's base salary. Contributions are invested at the direction of the employee in one or more funds or can be directed to purchase common stock of the Company at fair market value. Company contributions generally vest over three years although Company contributions for those employees having five years of service vest immediately. Company contributions are charged to expense in accordance with their vesting. Amounts charged to expense were $13 million, $11.6 million, and $8.3 million in 1992, 1991, and 1990, respectively.

Incentive Compensation Plan -

The Company adopted an incentive compensation plan for the majority of its employees beginning in the second half of 1992. Provision for payments to be made under the plan is based on 6% of net income from operations, as defined, and is payable in August and February. The amount expensed under the plan was $8.3 million in 1992.

Stock Repurchases -

On May 16, 1991, the Company's Board of Directors authorized the Company to repurchase up to ten million shares of its common stock on the open market. During 1992 and 1991 the Company repurchased seven million and three million shares of its common stock, respectively, at an aggregate cost of $202.2 million and $95.5 million, respectively. The shares are held by the Company as treasury stock and accounted for using the par value method.

Post Retirement and Post Employment Benefits -

The Financial Accounting Standards Board has issued Statements requiring accrual basis accounting for post retirement and post employment benefits offered to employees. The Company currently offers very limited post retirement and post employment benefits and accordingly the provisions of the Statements will have minimal impact on the Company's financial statements when applied in 1993.

Stockholder Rights Plan -

The Board of Directors adopted a Stockholder Rights Plan in May 1989 which in certain limited circumstances would permit stockholders to purchase securities at prices which would be substantially below market value.

Note 14 - Certain Market and Geographic Data:

Compaq Computer Corporation designs, develops, manufactures, and markets personal computers. The Company has subsidiaries in various foreign countries which manufacture and sell the Company's products in their respective geographic areas. Summary information with respect to the Company's geographic operations in 1992, 1991, and 1990 follows:

1992	United States and Canada	Europe	Other countries (in thousands)	Eliminations	Consolidated
Sales to customers	$1,833,175	$1,886,109	$380,474		$4,099,758
Intercompany transfers	898,997	49,844	536,695	($1,485,536)	
	$2,732,172	$1,935,953	$917,169	($1,485,536)	$4,099,758
Income from operations	$ 37,415	$ 73,956	$142,531	($ 2,059)	$ 251,843
Corporate income, net					43,559
Pretax income					$ 295,402
Identifiable assets	$2,006,643	$ 961,316	$322,847	($ 505,160)	$2,785,646
General corporate assets					356,747
Total assets					$3,142,393
1991					
Sales to customers	$1,387,758	$1,724,621	$158,988		$3,271,367
Intercompany transfers	838,156	16,490	360,851	($1,215,497)	
	$2,225,914	$1,741,111	$519,839	($1,215,497)	$3,271,367
Income (loss) from operations	($ 29,049)	$ 100,993	$133,163	$ 12,343	$ 217,450
Corporate expenses, net					(63,414)
Pretax income					$ 154,036
Identifiable assets	$1,824,721	$ 695,808	$125,085	($ 271,402)	$2,374,212
General corporate assets					452,174
Total assets					$2,826,386

1990

Sales to customers	$1,657,640	$1,807,499	$133,629		$3,598,768
Intercompany transfers	1,018,981	26,540	329,653	($1,375,174)	
	$2,676,621	$1,834,039	$463,282	($1,375,174)	$3,598,768
Income from operations	$ 414,297	$ 169,280	$121,713	($ 29,327)	$ 675,963
Corporate expenses, net					(34,530)
Pretax income					$ 641,433
Identifiable assets	$1,565,876	$ 662,942	$129,403	($ 75,392)	$2,282,829
General corporate assets					434,700
Total assets					$2,717,529

In each year, the Company's hedging activities are designed to reduce the effects of changes in the value of the U.S. dollar relative to the currencies of those countries in which the Company's international subsidiaries operate.

Cumulative retained earnings of international subsidiaries were $406 million and $345 million at December 31, 1992 and 1991, respectively.

Products are transferred between countries at prices which are intended to approximate those that would be charged to unaffiliated customers in the respective countries. Transactions with one of the Company's resellers accounted for 10% of consolidated sales in 1990.

Note 15 - Commitments and Contingencies:

Litigation -

The Company and certain of its current and former officers and directors are named in a consolidated, alleged class action, lawsuit brought in federal court in Houston on behalf of persons who purchased Compaq stock or held certain types of options during the period December 4, 1990 through May 14, 1991. The complaint alleges, among other things, that the defendants, through certain public statements, misled investors respecting (i) deterioration in the Company's markets and the demand for its products, (ii) the inadequacy of the Company's foreign currency hedging mechanisms to protect it from the rising value of the dollar, (iii) marketing problems such as pricing pressure from competitors and reduced dealer loyalty, and (iv) other industry, competitive and Company conditions. Individual suits making similar allegations have been brought by certain stockholders in Texas state court. The ultimate liability, if any, which may result from these lawsuits cannot be determined at this time. However, management believes that the outcome of this litigation will not have a material adverse effect on the financial condition of the Company.

The Company is also subject to legal proceedings and claims which arise in the ordinary course of its business. Management does not believe that the outcome of any of those matters will have a material adverse effect on the Company's financial condition.

Off-balance sheet risk and concentration of credit risk -

At December 31, 1992 and 1991, respectively, the Company had entered into forward exchange contracts with financial institutions to sell net amounts of $381 million and $325 million of foreign currencies and also had entered into foreign currency option contracts relating to the hedges of certain portions of its foreign currency exposure of the net monetary assets of its international subsidiaries and to hedge purchase commitments. Forward exchange contracts, which are valued in U.S. dollars based on the respective year-end spot rate, had maturity dates ranging from one day to six months. In the event of a failure to honor one of these contracts by one of the banks with which the Company had contracted, management believes any loss would be limited to the exchange rate differential from the time the contract was made until the time it was compensated. At December 31, 1992, the Company had entered into option contracts to sell currency to hedge a portion of its probable anticipated sales over the next nine months of its international marketing subsidiaries. The net unrealized gain deferred on these contracts at December 31, 1992 totaled $25.5 million and if realized will be recognized in the periods that the related sales occur. To the extent the Company has such options outstanding, the amount of any loss resulting from a breach of contract would be limited to the amount of premiums paid for the options and the unrealized gain, if any, related to such contracts.

The Company's cash and short-term investments and accounts receivable are subject to potential credit risk. The Company's cash management and investment policies restrict investments to low risk, highly-liquid securities and the Company performs periodic evaluation of the relative credit standing of the financial institutions with which it deals.

The Company distributes products primarily through third-party resellers and as a result maintains individually significant accounts receivable balances from various major resellers. The Company evaluates the credit worthiness of its resellers on an ongoing basis and may, from time to time, tighten credit terms to particular resellers. Such tightening may take the form of shorter payment terms, requiring security, reduction of credit availability, or the deauthorization of a reseller. In addition the Company uses various risk transfer instruments such as credit insurance, factoring, and flooring planning with third-party finance companies; however, there can be no assurance that these arrangements will be sufficient to avoid significant accounts receivable losses or will continue to be available. While the Company believes that its distribution strategies will serve to minimize the risk associated with the loss of a reseller or the decline in sales to a reseller due to tightened credit terms, there can be no assurance that disruption to the Company's sales and profitability will not occur. If the financial condition and operations of these resellers deteriorate, the Company's operating results could be adversely affected. At December 31, 1992, the receivable balances from the Company's two largest resellers represented approximately 15% of accounts receivable.

The Company's resellers typically purchase products on an as-needed basis through purchase orders. Various of the Company's resellers finance a portion of their inventories through third-party finance companies. Under the terms of the financing arrangements, the Company may be required, in limited circumstances, to purchase certain products from the finance companies. At December 31, 1992 and 1991, amounts owed to third-party finance companies by the Company's resellers under such arrangements aggregated approximately $180 million and $175 million, respectively. Additionally, the Company has on occasion guaranteed a portion of certain resellers' outstanding balances with third-party finance companies. Guarantees aggregating $14.4 million and $18 million were outstanding at December 31, 1992 and 1991, respectively. During the ten years that the Company has supported these financing programs, claims under these arrangements have been negligible. The Company makes provisions for estimated product returns and bad debts which may occur under these programs.

Lease Commitments -

The Company leases certain manufacturing and office facilities and equipment under noncancelable operating leases with terms from one to 30 years. Rent expense for 1992, 1991, and 1990 was $34.8 million, $38.5 million, and $37.3 million, respectively.

The Company's minimum rental commitments under noncancelable operating leases at December 31, 1992 were as follows:

Year	Amount
1993	$ 26,062
1994	19,991
1995	15,379
1996	8,779
1997	7,732
Thereafter	42,493
	$120,436

Note 16 - Selected Quarterly Financial Data (not covered by report of independent accountants):

The table below sets forth selected financial information for each quarter of the last two years.

	1st quarter	2nd quarter	3rd quarter	4th quarter
1992				
Sales	$783,048	$826,976	$1,067,105	$1,422,629
Gross margin	262,343	249,933	299,737	382,721
Net income	45,326	28,996	49,365	89,465
Earnings per common and common equivalent share:				
Primary	.53	.35	.61	1.11
Assuming full dilution	.53	.35	.61	1.10
1991				
Sales	$970,751	$717,845	$ 709,370	$ 873,401
Gross margin	401,653	247,660	243,458	325,020
Net income	114,278	20,285	(70,256)	66,562
Earnings per common and common equivalent share:				
Primary	1.26	.23	(.82)	.77
Assuming full dilution	1.26	.23	(.82)	.77

During the first six months of 1991 the Company estimated that its effective tax rate would be 34%. During the third quarter of 1991, the Company incurred a $135 million restructuring charge which substantially reduced the forecast of 1991 pretax earnings. Consequently, the Company revised its estimated effective tax rate downward to 28%. The actual effective tax rate for 1991 was 27.9%. The full benefit of the lower rate was recorded in the third quarter of 1991 and had the effect of reducing the loss per share for the quarter by approximately $.13. The 1992 third quarter restructuring and other special charges were offset by the gain on the sale of the equity interest in Conner; accordingly, there was no similar effect in 1992.

There were no other unusual or infrequently occurring items or adjustments, other than normal recurring adjustments, in any of the quarters presented.

index